S0-AHE-229

GREAT LIVES FROM HISTORY

GREAT LIVES FROM HISTORY

Ancient and Medieval Series

Volume 2
Chr-Her

Edited by

FRANK N. MAGILL

SALEM PRESS

Pasadena, California Englewood Cliffs, New Jersey

For information address the publisher, Salem Press, Inc., P.O. Box 50062, Pasadena, California 91105.

Library of Congress Cataloging-in-Publication Data
Great lives from history. Ancient and medieval series / edited by Frank N. Magill.
p. cm.
Includes bibliographies and index.
Summary: A five-volume set of biographical sketches, arranged alphabetically, of 459 individuals whose contributions influenced world culture and the social development of societies flourishing in earlier centuries.
Biography—To 500. 2. Biography—Middle Ages, 500-1500. [1. Biography—To 500. 2. Biography—Middle Ages, 500-1500. 3. World history.]
I. Magill, Frank Northen, 1907-
CT113.G74 1988 920'.009'01—dc19 88-18514
[B]
[920]
ISBN 0-89356-545-8 (set)
ISBN 0-89356-547-4 (volume 2)

PRINTED IN THE UNITED STATES OF AMERICA

LIST OF BIOGRAPHIES IN VOLUME TWO

LIST OF BIOGRAPHIES IN VOLUME TWO

GREAT LIVES
FROM
HISTORY

CHRÉTIEN DE TROYES

Born: c. 1140; possibly Troyes, France
Died: c. 1190; probably Troyes, France, or Flanders
Area of Achievement: Literature
Contribution: Chrétien is one of the great names in early French literature and is known as the principal articulator of many significant medieval Arthurian legends.

Early Life

Information about Chrétien de Troyes comes almost solely from indirect evidence in his works, and scholarly speculation has led to much controversy on this subject. A dedication in *Lancelot: Ou, Le Chevalier de la charrette* (c. 1177; *Lancelot*, 1914) to Marie de Champagne and another in *Perceval: Ou, Le Conte du Graai* (before 1191; *Perceval: Or, The Story of the Grail*, 1914) to Count Phillipe of Flanders, suggest that the poet was connected with the courts of Champagne in Troyes and in Flanders. Like most courtly clerks in this period, Chrétien was doubtless well educated in the Latin tradition of the seven liberal arts. Under the influence of the mid-twelfth century romances and tales of antiquity and working in the vernacular with a style forged by contemporary rhetoric, he describes himself in the prologue to his second romance, *Cligés* (c. 1170; *Cligés: A Romance*, 1912), as having already completed certain works in Old French: *Erec et Enide* (c. 1170; *Erec and Enide*, 1913), adaptations of several Ovidian poems, and a version of the Tristan legend (a story which nearly became his shirt of Nessus). It also appears likely, based on several precise topographical references in *Cligés*, that Chrétien visited England at some point in his career.

Life's Work

Most scholars agree that Chrétien's canon embraces five romances. These include *Erec and Enide*, *Cligés*, *Yvain: Ou, Le Chevalier au lion* (*Yvain: Or, The Knight with the Lion*, 1914), and *Lancelot*; the latter two seem to have been composed simultaneously between 1177 and 1181. Chrétien's last work, *Perceval*, dates from before 1191 (when his patron, Phillipe of Flanders, died). Besides these, there are two poems in the Provençal troubadour style and an attributed romance, *Guillaume d'Angleterre* (c. 1170; *King William the Wanderer: An Old British Saga from Old French Versions*, 1904), that draws on the Saint Eustace legend, a non-Arthurian story with obvious hagiographic themes.

The texts of Chrétien's main works are preserved in a fairly large number of manuscripts, the oldest of which dates from the early thirteenth century. He composed the romances in octosyllabic rhyming couplets—averaging seven thousand lines in length—in a language that philologists consider to be standard Old French, although some Champenois or Picard dialectal traits persist, possibly because of his scribes or copyists.

Under Chrétien's powerful influence, courtly literature took on new meaning in the midst of the twelfth century renaissance. The reciprocity of love and friendship, the stress on the values of psychological metamorphosis and self-discovery, and the humanistic rejection of the enthralling obsession and selfish adultery of the Tristan legend all make the romances enduring monuments to his innovative artistry, purity of style, and rich imagination. His ethos embraces a personal freedom actively pursued by his characters (especially the heroines) and an insistence, particularly for his heroes, on a superhuman quest for happiness purified by knightly trials of valor. All of this he presents as an intellectual pastime for a polite, courtly society; it is accomplished with humorous detachment as well.

Chrétien saw himself and is seen still as a synthesizer of several traditions: the Greco-Roman heritage (Vergil, Ovid, Statius), the rich storehouse of Celtic folklore, and occasional scriptural allusions. Chrétien's skillful combination of separate adventures into a unified, well-knit story led Dante to praise him for having made France a leader in narrative poetry. The complicated question of the Welsh traditional tales that form doublets with several of his romances raises the kind of critical issues scholars continue to debate.

Chrétien's first major work is also considered the first Arthurian romance on the Continent. (This general observation must exclude the early Welsh traditional tale *Culhwch ac Olwen*, c. 1100—literally, "how Culhwch won Olwen.") *Erec and Enide*, a brilliant bipartite study in human psychology, poses a timely dilemma: In what manner, after marriage, must a knight maintain that prowess and glory with which he won his beloved in the first place? Can honor and arms and love all be served at the same time? Numbed by marital bliss with his young, submissive bride, Erec neglects his own fame until reminded by Enide that she has heard malicious gossip about him. The hero brusquely undertakes a series of extraordinary adventures, in the company of his bride, and both are put to the test. Enide in fact proves her love by disobeying Erec's commands. Their paired quest leads ultimately to a glorious conclusion.

Arms versus love is a question to which Chrétien adverts again in *Yvain*. It is with his second major work, *Cligés*, however, that he departs from the Arthurian mold by basing his story on popular Greco-Byzantine materials. With great literary virtuosity, dazzling metaphors, and dramatic analyses, he exalts the reciprocal love of Fenice and Cligés. His heroine is a victim of a forced marriage. Many interpretations of the text stress its ironic and mirrored echoing of Iseult's adulterous passion for Tristan. The evidence for profound intertextuality of this romance with classical, especially Ovidian, sources has yet to be fully appreciated.

Interrelationship between texts is quite obvious when discussing *Yvain* and

Lancelot. Chrétien's third and fourth romances were most likely composed more or less simultaneously, as certain events dealing with the location of the characters suggest. The incomplete *Lancelot* recounts another famous story of adultery, that of the hero with his overlord's wife, Guinevere (Arthur's queen). The theme—apparently representing a "case" for debate—was possibly suggested by Marie de Champagne, a confusing but necessary conclusion because of the striking contrast with Chrétien's otherwise frequent praise for fidelity in marriage. That may explain the text's excessive irony and humor, often noted by critics. Lancelot the servile lover of the imperious Guinevere is treated with ridicule. With both *Yvain* and *Lancelot*, however, what becomes truly significant for the author is less the vindicated couple predestined to rule than the individual hero's destiny and place in society.

Yvain is considered by many Chrétien's consummate masterpiece, a sophisticated, witty, and finally wise extravaganza in which the romantic situation of *Erec and Enide* is reversed. Yet the conflicting obligations of marriage and chivalry are treated again. Chrétien's trademark—a deep understanding of human nature and the creation of extraordinary adventures—is clearly embedded in this seductive, persuasive, and humorous treatment of the widow's too hasty marriage to her husband's slayer. Yvain decides, in order to avenge his cousin's honor, to take action before the other knights of the Round Table do so. The failed adventure leads the hero to try to compensate for it. He voyages to the magical storm-provoking fountain in Brocéliande Forest and, as his cousin had done before him, pours water on the stone—which provokes an immediate challenge and attack by the lord of the castle, Esclados, whom Yvain defeats and mortally wounds. In fact, Yvain chases Esclados back to his nearby castle. Lunete, the wily servant of Esclados' widow, Laudine, proceeds to hide Yvain; the knight is smitten with the grieving widow, marries her, and thereby becomes the fountain's new champion.

At the fountain, Yvain must now challenge the visiting retainers of King Arthur, whom he bests, but Gauwain, Arthur's nephew and the model of chivalry, encourages the knightly hero to depart from this land and his marriage and go a-tourneying. Laudine grants the wish, with the condition that he must return within one year. Absorbed by his feats of arms, Yvain forgets to return, is denounced by Laudine, and falls from grace: In shame and grief, he goes stark mad. Magically cured, he rescues a lion, who expresses his gratitude by becoming Yvain's companion. Penitent and valorous after a complex series of liberating adventures, Yvain wins Laudine's pardon, and their happiness in the end restores favor and fulfillment.

Chrétien's last and most curious romance was, like *Lancelot*, left unfinished. Interpreted as a story of initiation, *Perceval* does relate the psychological and spiritual development of the story's protagonist. Arms, love, and religion all figure in the narrative—viewed by some as allegorical. Perceval's naïveté leads to amusing social blunders, but the humiliating intrigue of the whole episode at the Grail Castle, including the mysterious procession, leaves both the young hero and the reader unsatisfied. After numerous fantastic adventures, all becomes clear on a certain Good Friday: Perceval is touched by grace and true charity is revealed to him. He learns that his lack of charity in hastening toward his own self-fulfillment—instead of rushing to his mother's side as she fell in a swoon from grief—prevented him from asking his host (in fact, his uncle) the crucial questions about the Grail and the Bleeding Lance. The quest for the latter, a restorative-destructive instrument, is undertaken by Gauwain in a mysterious series of interrelated yet self-indulgent adventures.

Summary

Chrétien de Troyes's lasting influence extends well beyond twelfth century France. An obvious debt is owed to him by the many compilers of later prose romances, beginning with the Vulgate cycle. Middle High German writers, such as Hartmann von Aue and Wolfram von Eschenbach, and others who composed Dutch, Scandinavian, and Provençal works, adapted his romances freely for their special audiences. From "The Franklin's Tale" in Geoffrey Chaucer's *The Canterbury Tales* (1387-1400) to the heroic and fairy tale-like elements in Edmund Spenser's *The Faerie Queene* (1590, 1596), the French-derived Arthurian legends even found their way into the Wakefield and York mystery-play cycles and, more important, into Sir Thomas Malory's *Le Morte d'Arthur* (1485), which itself has inspired modern adaptations, from Alfred, Lord Tennyson's *Idylls of the King* (1859-1885) to John Boorman's adventure-fantasy film *Excalibur* (1981).

Chrétien's genius conferred upon the Matter of Britain new prestige; his talent exploited the resources of a fledgling vernacular so that aesthetic awareness, logic, and harmony began to emerge in this period. Purity in vocabulary and clarity in syntax are also part of his legacy to the French language, as is the supple rhyme of his narrative poetry. Medieval romance took a giant step with Chrétien de Troyes, a leap into fantasy, legend, adventure, self-discovery, and especially self-actualization, through a tradition of values—marital, erotic, poetic, and literary.

Bibliography

Chrétien de Troyes. *Chrétien de Troyes: The Knight with the Lion, or Yvain*. Edited and translated by William W. Kibler. New York: Garland Publishers, 1986. This fine edition complements Kibler's translation of *Lancelot* (1981) and other volumes in the Garland Library of Medieval Literature series. The series provides excellent introductions, modern English translations facing the Old French texts, and detailed bibliographies.

Frappier, Jean. *Chrétien de Troyes: The Man and His Work*. Translated by

Raymond J. Cormier. Athens: Ohio University Press, 1982. This illustrated critical work includes extensive notes and an index. The considerable bibliography was last revised in 1981.

Kelly, Douglas. *Chrétien de Troyes: An Analytic Bibliography*. London: Grant and Cutler, 1976. Part of the Research Bibliographies and Checklists series, this volume is an indispensable reference tool. Includes index.

Loomis, Roger Sherman, ed. *Arthurian Literature in the Middle Ages*. 2d ed. Oxford: Clarendon Press, 1961. A comprehensive collection of articles on a wide array of Arthurian topics. Illustrated.

Topsfield, L. T. *Chrétien de Troyes: A Study of the Arthurian Romances*. Cambridge: Cambridge University Press, 1981. A useful survey by a specialist in troubadour poetics.

Raymond Cormier

CHRISTINE DE PISAN

Born: c. 1365; Venice, Italy
Died: c. 1430; probably at the Convent of Poissy, near Versailles, France
Area of Achievement: Literature
Contribution: The first woman of letters in France and the first known woman in Europe to earn her living by writing, Christine was a prolific, versatile, and acclaimed lyric poet, didactic writer, and Humanist scholar; she was a precursor to the *femmes savantes* of the Renaissance and to nineteenth and twentieth century feminists.

Early Life

Shortly after Christine was born in Venice in 1364, her father, Tommaso di Benvenuto da Pizzano, who held a chair in astrology at the University of Bologna (where he had also studied medicine and astrology), was offered two attractive invitations—to go to Hungary to the court of Louis I or to Paris to the court of Charles V. Although he was reluctant to leave his family (the invitations were for him alone), Tommaso found the offer to go to the city of the celebrated University of Paris particularly attractive, and he agreed to go to the French court for one year. The king, pleased with the counsels of Thomas de Pisan (as his name was gallicized) in medical, scientific, and political matters, persuaded him to stay as the royal astrologer, alchemist, and physician; in 1368, Thomas sent for his wife and four-year-old daughter.

Thus Christine was reared in the stimulating environment of the court of Charles V, known as "the Wise," an intellectual and progressive monarch. Under his patronage, Thomas prospered and acquired property—the feudal estate of Orsonville—and Christine was reared in a literate and cultured home frequented by leading intellectuals. She studied the liberal arts under the tutelage of her father, whose intelligence and knowledge she admired—despite the fact that her mother disapproved of academic learning for girls. Later, Christine would complain that her education had been restricted on account of her gender, but she was able to learn to read and write, opportunities usually reserved for very high-ranking women.

At fifteen, around 1379, Christine married Étienne du Castel, a twenty-four-year-old graduate scholar born of a noble, though not wealthy, family in Picardy, who became a court notary and secretary. Christine had known Étienne since infancy, and he was well regarded by her father. Étienne promised that they would be "true friends" when they married, and he seems to have kept his promise: The period of her marriage was a very happy one. The two had three children: a daughter, born in 1381, who later became a nun at the Poissy convent; a son who died in infancy; and a second son, Jean, born in 1385, who as a youth was reared in England by Christine's patron, the Earl of

Salisbury, and later joined the household of the dukes of Burgundy.

After 1380, when Charles V died, Christine's father began to lose his prestige and was eventually dismissed from his court appointment. Within a few years, he became ill and died, disillusioned and poor. A greater sorrow followed: In 1389, while accompanying Charles VI to Beauvais on matters of state, Étienne fell victim to the plague and died, at the age of thirty-four. Within two years, Christine had lost both father and husband, the two people to whom she was closest and who had also been her mentors.

Life's Work

Her husband's unexpected and premature death precipitated an abrupt turning point in Christine's life, which she later, referred to as her "mutacion de fortune," in a book of that name. At twenty-five she was forced into "the role of a man," responsible for providing for her children and herself. She had no income or means of support and, in order to recover a small inheritance from her husband, had to engage in protracted and frustrating legal proceedings for the next ten years. Yet she determined to support herself rather than remarry; in a famous ballade written shortly after her husband's death, she declared, "Seulete suy et seulete vueil estre" (I am alone and I want to be alone).

Christine's initial lyrics, considered to be some of her finest work, focus on her love for her husband and her grief over his death. Nevertheless, she soon turned to themes of chivalry and courtly love, more suited to the nobles who became her patrons. Immediately successful, she wrote prolifically on these topics for the next decade in lyric poems, short narratives, and didactic works. There is some evidence to suggest that she also worked as a manuscript copyist during these years to supplement her income from writing.

In 1398, Christine embarked on a rigorous, interdisciplinary program of study (including history, science, religion, philosophy, and literature, both classical and contemporary) and soon began to write her first mature works, *Le Livre de la mutacion de fortune* (1400-1403; the book of changes in fortune) and *Le Livre du chemin de long éstude* (1402-1403; the book of the road of long study). By this point, she had stopped writing about chivalry and courtly love, whose antimarriage and pro-infidelity themes she in fact rejected, suggesting in subsequent writings that the courtly love ethic was devised by men for men and had no redeeming value for women. In *Le Livre de la mutacion de fortune*, a scholarly, allegorical, seven-part poem, she initially recounts her own encounter with the Roman goddess of fortune, whose capriciousness Christine blames for the death of her husband and for transforming her into a man—though at the same time she acknowledges that without the necessity of having to support herself, she would never have become a scholar and writer. The remainder of the encyclopedic, philosophical work presents an account of Fortune's influence in specific moments in world history. (The Wheel of Fortune was a common motif in medieval culture and was used to explain apparently arbitrary vicissitudes of human experience.) *Le Livre du chemin de long éstude*, an allegorical voyage analogous to Dante's *Le divina commedia* (c. 1320; *The Divine Comedy*, 1802), concerns the evils of the world and how to remedy them; Christine dedicated the work to the young Charles VI. On the basis of the renown she achieved from these two works, Christine was commissioned to write a biography of the late Charles V, *Le Livre des fais et bonnes moeurs du sage roi Charles V* (1404; the book of the deeds and virtues of the wise King Charles V), a monarch whose reign she considered exemplary.

During the years Christine was writing *Le Livre de la mutacion de fortune*, *Le Livre du chemin de long éstude*, and *Le Livre des fais et bonnes mœurs du sage roi Charles V*, she concurrently became an important spokesperson in *la querelle des femmes* (the woman question), a debate among intellectuals in response to Guillaume de Lorris and Jean de Meung's *Le Roman de la rose* (thirteenth century; *The Romance of the Rose*, 1900). Proponents of *The Romance of the Rose*'s broad social satire saw its authors, especially Meung, as advocates of progress; its opponents censured the work for subverting public morality. Christine, whose reputation as a scholar was being established, was moved to attack the cynical satire against women in *The Romance of the Rose* and also the tradition of misogynist literature. She presented her arguments in four works: *L'Épistre du dieu d'amours* (1399; the epistle to the god of love), her first feminist work, in which Cupid, who has received complaints from women about deceitful and disloyal men, issues a decree ousting slanderers of women from his court; *Le Dit de la rose* (1401; the tale of the rose), a poem in which the goddess Loyalty founds an order of the Rose, inducting chivalrous knights who promise to uphold the honor of women and speak no ill of them; *Les Épistres sur "Le Roman de la rose"* (1401-1402; epistles on *The Romance of the Rose*), the collected correspondence which came out of the debate; and *Le Livre de la cité des dames* (1404-1405; *The Boke of the Cyte of Ladyes*, 1521, better known as *The Book of the City of Ladies*, 1982), her most famous feminist work.

As *The Book of the City of Ladies* begins, Christine, in her study, ponders the work of Matheolus, a malicious thirteenth century misogynist. Her reading leads her to wonder why, historically, so many philosophers, clerics, poets, and rhetoricians have slandered women: Misogyny has a long and authoritative tradition. Although her own experiences with women cause her to conclude that these authorities are wrong, she nevertheless becomes discouraged and begins to doubt her own judgment. Then, in a dream vision, three crowned ladies, Reason, Righteousness, and Justice, appear to help Christine in her philosophical quest. Lady Reason carries a mirror that shows everything in its true proportions and qualities; she asserts the superiority of experience over authority. The three crowned ladies then announce to Christine that she has been given the prerogative among women to establish and build a city of ladies.

Before Christine's work, written between December, 1404, and April, 1405, the only literary work treating famous women was Giovanni Boccaccio's quasi-satirical *De mulieribus claris* (c. 1361-1375; *Concerning Famous Women*, 1943). Boccaccio wrote about famous women, both illustrious and notorious, regardless of their moral stature. He excluded Christian women, except Eve, saying that in following religious precepts, the actions of Christian women are in fact contrary to human nature—thus, they do not really qualify as exempla of woman. In addition, he wrote about only the women mentioned by the Latin *auctores*, thereby excluding contemporary women, saying that illustrious contemporary women were too few to mention.

Christine used Boccaccio's work as a major source for *The Book of the City of Ladies*; literary critics who compared the two works as recently as 1974 (such as Gianni Mombello) cited Christine's work as derivative and lacking in originality, saying that she was primarily a compiler of received ideas. Since then, literary critics (for example, Marina Warner) have noted that *The Book of the City of Ladies* is a universal history of women, much broader in scope than Boccaccio's work, since it includes both pagan and Christian women up to the time of Christine. Furthermore, in reorganizing and reconstructing the material of her sources, Christine develops original perspectives and new ideas. In *The Book of the City of Ladies*, Lady Reason suggests that "historical tradition" has in fact been shaped by the motives and biases of its writers and that Christine's interpretation of historical reality has equal epistemological validity with any other. Thus Christine takes it upon herself to rewrite history, restoring the lives of virtuous women neglected by history and vindicating the reputations of women maligned.

Throughout the work Christine intersperses observations on her own society's attitudes toward women. Controlled indignation underlies a courteous manner as she discusses such topics as the disappointment women feel at the birth of a daughter; the double standard by which men rape women, then blame women for allowing them to do so; and the lack of access women have to education despite their natural affinity for learning.

Nevertheless, while Christine spent her entire career defending women's causes, her position as a feminist always remained moderate. Coming from a medieval, orthodox Catholic vantage, her concerns were with improving the conditions of women within the existing social order. She sought more equitable treatment for women but never expected total equality with men. A humanist committed to the common good, she encouraged women to seek fulfillment within the few roles open to them—marriage, family, and service to the community; she also urged society to acknowledge women's labor and to recognize their contributions.

Yet while basically accepting the hierarchical gender status quo based on the Christian tradition of the Fall, Christine also invokes Christian tradition in support of her arguments for educational and social advances for women. Referring to Genesis 1:27, she argues that woman, like man, was made in God's image and consequently was endowed by the Creator with the same moral, intellectual, and spiritual aptitude; hence, men and women are equally educable. Suggesting that Christian marriage is based on the model of Christ's caring for His Church, the Bride of Christ, Christine argues that Christian marriage calls for the highest degree of moral commitment between a man and woman, and she does not condone or permit institutionalized domination. Finally, although Christine accepts medieval class/gender hierarchy, she argues that every woman has the potential for true nobility; according to Christine, the term "lady" refers to nobility of the soul rather than nobility of blood. "City of ladies" is a direct allusion to Saint Augustine's *De civitate Dei* (413-427; *The City of God*), suggesting that Christine saw her vision as part of the Christian tradition of political philosophy.

Christine's second major feminist work, *Le Livre des trois vertus* (1405; the book of the three virtues), a companion volume to *The Book of the City of Ladies*, is a didactic work providing guidelines for women aspiring to achieve the "nobility" of the city; it is one of the first didactic works in European literature written by a woman for women. Dedicated to Marguerite of Burgundy on the occasion of her marriage to the French dauphin, Louis of Guienne, the work is nevertheless intended for women of all ages, circumstances, and social classes. The reader encounters Reason, Righteousness, and Justice again, together with Wisdom; the four provide women with instruction in moral precepts as well as in practical matters—with specific counsels according to their social class, marital status, and role in life. The work provides an interesting view of a cross section of fifteenth century medieval society—the royalty, nobility, bourgeoisie, and poor.

Christine's interests in women's issues never diminished, but in the later years of her writing career, in such works as *Lavision-Christine* (1405; the vision of Christine), *Épistre à Isabeau de Bavière* (1405; epistle to Isabelle of Bavaria), *Le Livre du corps de policie* (1406-1407; the book of the body politic), *Lamentation sur les maux de la guerre civile* (1410; lament on the evils of civil war), and *Le Livre de la paix* (1412-1413; the book of peace), she focused her attention on political problems in France—in the tradition made popular by the Italian Humanists. In her lifetime, Christine saw France suffer humiliating defeats in the Hundred Years' War with England, three popular uprisings culminating in the Cabochien revolt in 1413, the Great Schism within the Church, and the bitter Burgundian-Orléanist (later Armagnac) rivalry over the domination of the French regency. The latter began after the death of Charles V in 1380 and led to the murder of Louis d'Orléans in 1407; civil war followed, culminating in the slaying of Jean sans Peur, Duke of Burgundy, in 1419. Meanwhile, widespread anarchy in France (and superior military tactics) permitted Henry V of England to defeat the French at Agincourt in 1415. In 1418, the Burgundians massacred a number of Parisians and many, including Christine, fled the city and went into exile.

Christine, an ardent French patriot who believed in a divine-right, hereditary monarchy, wrote passionately about the necessity of restoring peace and stability in the kingdom. She appealed to rulers, political leaders, and the common people to stop the violence of civil war. As early as 1405, she accurately predicted the events at Agincourt when she warned about the dangers of foreign invaders attacking a weakened country. Undoubtedly Christine was able through her writings to impress influential figures, yet it is not clear that as an individual author she was able to influence in any immediate way the seemingly unstoppable course of events to which she was a witness.

Christine's last known work, "Le Dittié sur Jeanne d'Arc" (1429), a patriotic, narrative account of Joan of Arc, celebrates Joan of Arc's role in liberating Orléans and in leading the dauphin, Charles VII, to his coronation at Reims. News of the occasion reached Christine at the Poissy convent (where her daughter was a nun), to which she had retreated a decade earlier to escape the bloody civil war in Paris. In "Le Dittié sur Jeanne d'Arc," she rejoices both at the event itself, the reinstatement of the legitimate monarchy, and at the fact that it had been brought about by a woman. It seemed as if, in these related events, the Wheel of Fortune were turning favorably, as the principal political and social themes of Christine's writings were realized. While the exact date of her death is not known, it is believed that Christine died soon afterward, in 1430 at age sixty-five, at the Convent of Poissy.

Summary

Gifted, intelligent, and strong-willed, Christine de Pisan overcame personal loss and social prejudice to become the first known woman in Europe to earn her living as a professional writer. She gained the esteem of the aristocracy, many of whom became her patrons, and of the intellectuals of her day, with whom she engaged in philosophical debate. She was recognized as an accomplished lyric poet, and she became a highly respected and widely influential advocate of women's rights and of political theory.

At the time of her death, after a thirty-five-year career, Christine was well-known in France; her fame had also spread to Portugal, Spain, Italy, Flanders, and England, where, with the advent of printing, some of her works—under the titles *The Boke of the Fayt of Armes and of Chivalrye* (1489), *The Epistle of Othea to Hector: Or, The Boke of Knyghthode* (c. 1470), and *The Boke of the Cyte of Ladyes* (1521)—were translated and published. Her renown continued into the fifteenth and sixteenth centuries, as evidenced by the number of authors who cite her—Matthieu Thomassin, Jean Marot, Clément Marot, Jean Bouchet, and Pierre de Lesnauderie—or are influenced by her—Alain Chartier, Charles d'Orléans, Olivier de La Marche, Jean Molinet, Jean Meschinot, François Habert, Georges Chastellain, Pierre Gringore, and Christoval Acosta.

As a literary figure, Christine did not receive notice again until the nineteenth and twentieth centuries. Critical response to her works has been divided: Her detractors argue that she is derivative, pedantic, and arduous to read; her admirers counter than she is versatile and original, intelligent and learned, and stylistically sophisticated. As more and more of her works are coming to print, Christine de Pisan continues to be reevaluated. She is an important interpreter of her times, and her comments on many issues—good and bad rulers, human vice and frailty, women's status in society, and the battle of the sexes—seem as relevant in the twentieth century as they were in the fifteenth.

Bibliography

Chicago, Judy. *The Dinner Party: A Symbol of Our Heritage*. Garden City, N.Y.: Doubleday and Co., 1979. This work describes the creation of a monumental work of art celebrating the contributions of thirty-nine significant female figures in Western civilization. *The Dinner Party* includes Christine for overcoming social barriers placed before women in the Middle Ages and becoming the first female professional writer in France.

Delaney, Sheila. *Writing Woman: Women Writers and Women in Literature Medieval to Modern*. New York: Schocken Books, 1983. This study contains an insightful comparison of Christine and Virginia Woolf, showing similarities in their family backgrounds and education and in the motifs and themes of their works.

McLeod, Enid. *The Order of the Rose: The Life and Ideas of Christine de Pizan*. Totowa, N.J.: Rowman and Littlefield, 1976. A lively, engaging, and comprehensive biography.

Pisan, Christine de. *The Book of the City of Ladies*. Translated by Earl Jeffrey Richards. New York: Persea Books, 1982. This volume includes a translation of Christine de Pisan's major feminist work and an excellent commentary by Marina Warner on the principal themes and stylistic characteristics of Christine's work.

Tuchman, Barbara W. *A Distant Mirror: The Calamitous Fourteenth Century*. New York: Alfred A. Knopf, 1978. A comprehensive history of fourteenth century Europe, Tuchman's work discusses Christine as the one explicit female exponent of women's status in her time.

Welch, Alice Kemp. *Of Six Mediæval Women*. London: Macmillan, 1913. Reprint. Winston, Mass.: Corner House Publications, 1972. Welch's work includes a survey of Christine's life and works which views Christine as a Janus-headed figure in a time of transition.

Willard, Charity Cannon. *Christine de Pizan: Her Life and Works*. New

York: Persea Books, 1984. This is a thorough and scholarly biography, with in-depth analyses of Christine's works and an extensive bibliography.
———. "The Franco-Italian Professional Writer: Christine de Pizan." In *Medieval Women Writers*, edited by Katharina M. Wilson. Athens: University of Georgia Press, 1984. Willard provides a brief, yet thorough, review of Christine's life and works.
Yenal, Edith. *Christine de Pisan: A Bibliography of Writings by Her and About Her*. Metuchen, N.J.: Scarecrow Press, 1982. This is an excellent resource, containing an overview of Christine's background, writings, and ideas; summaries of all of her published and unpublished works; and an annotated bibliography of books and articles dealing with Christine and her works.

Jean T. Strandness

SAINT JOHN CHRYSOSTOM

Born: c. A.D. 354; Antioch, Syria
Died: September 14, A.D. 407; Comana, Pontus
Areas of Achievement: Religion and oratory
Contribution: Chrysostom, the greatest homiletic preacher of the Greek church, later became the patron saint of preachers.

Early Life

John Chrysostom (which means golden mouth) was born around A.D. 354 in Antioch and was reared by a devout mother, Anthousa, who had been widowed at the age of twenty. He received a first-rate education, especially in rhetoric, and his teachers are supposed to have included the renowned orator Libanius and the philosopher Andragathius. Libanius, when asked on his deathbed who should succeed him as head of his school of rhetoric, is said to have replied: "John, if the Christians had not stolen him from us." John's theological studies were undertaken at the renowned exegetical school of Antioch under one of the most illustrious scholars of the period, Diodore of Tarsus. The school favored literal rather than allegorical interpretation of the Bible.

Life's Work

According to Palladius' *Dialogus de vita S. Joannis Chrysostomi* (c. 408; *Dialogue on the Life of St. John Chrysostom*, 1921), "when [John] was eighteen, a mere boy in years, he revolted against the sophists of word-mongering, for he had arrived at man's estate and thirsted for living knowledge." Like many early Christians Chrysostom did not receive baptism until he was about twenty years old. He became a deacon in 381 under Bishop Meletius, a native of Armenia, whose protégé Chrysostom quickly became. To this period of deaconship (381-386) probably belongs his six-book *De sacerdotio* (*On the Priesthood*, 1728), a classic on the subject and one of the jewels of patristic literature. Book 5 is of particular interest because, like book 4 of Saint Augustine's *De doctrina Christiana* (426; *On Christian Instruction*), it constitutes a veritable monograph on the art and science of preaching. Book 6 is also of interest in that it contrasts the active with the contemplative life. Chrysostom had already been attracted to the rigors of the latter; he had spent four years in the mountains sharing ascetic life with an old hermit. This ascetic interlude is reflected in several treatises he wrote on monastic life, including two exhortations to his friend Theodore, later Bishop of Mopsuestia, who was growing tired of the monastic way of life, and the three-book *Adversus subintroductas*, which defended monasticism. In the sixth book of *On the Priesthood*, however, Chrysostom spoke out in favor of the active life, arguing that saving the souls of others demands more effort and generosity than merely saving one's own. He was ordained to the priesthood in 386 and remained in Antioch until 398; most of his great homilies belong to this period. They include more than seventy homilies on Genesis, six on Isaiah, and a particularly fine commentary on fifty-eight selected psalms. Also surviving are ninety homilies on the Gospel of Matthew, eighty-eight on the Gospel of John, fifty-five on the Acts of the Apostles, and thirty-two on Romans, this latter the finest of all his works. Almost half his surviving homilies are expositions of the Epistles of Saint Paul, his lifelong model. A series of seven homilies in praise of Paul survive among his many panegyrics on the saints of the Old and New Testaments.

Chrysostom's reputation as a pulpit orator became so widespread during his Antioch years that he was chosen to succeed Nectarius, Archbishop of Constantinople, upon the latter's death; he was consecrated on February 26, 398, by Theophilus, Bishop of Alexandria. According to Palladius, Theophilus disliked John, "for his custom all along was not to ordain good and shrewd men lest he make a mistake. He wished to have them all weak-willed men whom he could influence."

Despite this ominous installation, Chrysostom entered on a comprehensive program of reform of church officials and church revenues; he even criticized abuses in the imperial court. He used church revenues to set up hospitals and to aid the poor, leading a life of great simplicity himself. He was particularly critical of the luxury and wealth of the upper classes. His outspokenness soon incurred the wrath of the Empress Eudoxia, to whom Chrysostom's enemies suggested that she was the real target of his strictures.

After a synod in Ephesus in 401, when Chrysostom had six simoniac bishops deposed, some neighboring bishops made an alliance with Theophilus in a bid to unseat the archbishop. At the Oak Synod in 403, attended by thirty-six bishops, Chrysostom was deposed and sentenced to exile by order of the emperor. He was recalled the following day because of riots in his support in Constantinople, but after an uneasy peace of a few months, the emperor banished him to Cucusus in Lesser Armenia. To his three-year period there belong more than two hundred extant letters, which testify to his continuing pastoral zeal and interest in reform. This continued "meddling" proved unacceptable to his enemies, who had him transferred to the more distant Pityus, a city on the eastern shore of the Black Sea. Worn out, John Chrysostom died on his way there, at Comana in Pontus, on September 14, 407.

Summary

John Chrysostom is considered one of the four great fathers of the Eastern church and one of the three ecumenical doctors of the church. He has always been regarded as the most outstanding preacher of the Greek church and one of its greatest exegetes; his eloquence had already earned for him the title "Golden Mouth" in the sixth century. He shares with Origen the reputation of being the most prolific writer of the East. His surviving works extend through eighteen volumes of J.-P. Migne's great *Patrologia Graeca* (1842-1853), and there are still others, notably a work translated as *On Vainglory and the Right Way for Parents to Bring up Children* (1951). Chrysostom's recently discovered baptismal homilies add to church historians' knowledge of practices surrounding Christian rites of initiation in the end of the fourth century. His homilies are interesting more for their rhetorical brilliance than for any philosophical or theological profundity; they reflect the simple faith of his audience more than the contemporary struggles with Arianism and Apollinarianism. *On the Priesthood* is deservedly a classic, setting forth the most exacting standards for the clerical life. John Chrysostom's own life is eloquent proof that he practiced what he preached.

Bibliography

Attwater, Donald. *St. John Chrysostom: The Voice of Gold*. Milwaukee, Wis.: Bruce Publishing Co., 1939. A short, accessible account of the great preacher's life, illustrating both the genius and the humility of Chrysostom. Designed for the general reader.

Baur, Chrysostomus. *John Chrysostom and His Times*. Translated by M. Gonzaga. 2 vols. Westminster, Md.: Newman Press, 1959-1960. This work by a German priest is still the most detailed biography, but its style and content are both somewhat antiquated. In need of updating or replacement. Includes a bibliography.

Chrysostom, John. *Apologist*. Translated by Margaret A. Schatkin and Paul W. Harkins. Washington, D.C.: Catholic University of America Press, 1983. Contains first translations of two works, one extolling the martyred Babylas and one upholding the divinity of Christ. These renderings by two seasoned Chrysostom scholars are generally reliable. Succinct notes and helpful bibliographies.

__________. *Homilies on Genesis*. Translated by Robert C. Hill. Washington, D.C.: Catholic University of America Press, 1986. Contains the first seventeen of the homilies that together make up a complete commentary on Genesis. The introduction deals with Chrysostom's exegetical works, the homilist and his congregation in Antioch, the structure of the homilies, and the use of Scripture in them. Select bibliography.

__________. *On Marriage and Family Life*. Translated by Catharine P. Roth and David Anderson. Crestwood, N.Y.: St. Vladimir's Seminary Press, 1986. Includes two hitherto untranslated homilies, with a good introduction showing that Chrysostom, who has often been accused of misogyny, had a better theology of marriage than has been commonly thought.

Palladius. *Dialogue on the Life of St. John Chrysostom*. Translated and edited by Robert T. Meyer. New York: Paulist Press, 1985. Though clearly partial to Chrysostom, this work has value for having been written by a contemporary who was actually present at the Synod of the Oak. Vivid descriptions of the intrigues and violence of Constantinople that led to Chrysostom's downfall and exile.

Wilken, Robert. *John Chrysostom and the Jews: Rhetoric and Reality in the Late Fourth Century*. Berkeley: University of California Press, 1983. Particularly useful in its attempt to separate rhetoric from reality in Chrysostom's *Adversus Iudaeos* (c. 386; *Homilies Against the Jews*, 1889). These were aimed at Judaizing Christians in his congregation who were still attracted to meetings in the synagogue. Chrysostom is seen as a master of invective, and Judaism emerges as a continuing social and religious force in Antioch.

Thomas Halton

CHU HSI

Born: October 18, 1130; Yu-ch'i, Fukien, China
Died: April 23, 1200; Chien-yang County, Fukien, China
Areas of Achievement: Philosophy, education, and government
Contribution: Through writings and educational activities, Chu Hsi reformulated Confucianism. His work helped Confucianism regain intellectual ascendancy from Buddhism and Taoism, establishing basic Confucian orientations for centuries and influencing East Asian culture.

Early Life

Chu Hsi's early years were dominated by the uncertainty in the wake of the loss of northern China to Jurchen conquerors and the reestablishment of the Sung Dynasty in the south in 1128. His father, Chu Sung (1097-1143), after protesting against peace talks, was sent to a local post in Fukien; his fortunes continued to decline to the point that he even lost his position as sheriff of Yu-ch'i shortly before Chu Hsi's birth there in 1130. In the traditional pattern of accounts of great scholars, biographers have presented Chu Hsi as a precocious child, with exceptional interest in metaphysics, filial piety, and classical scholarship; Chu Hsi claimed that by the time he was nine, he was determined to become a Confucian sage.

In 1140, his father's second term of governmental service ended because of his continued opposition to the peace party. Having studied with disciples of the brothers Ch'eng Hao (1032-1085) and Ch'eng I (1033-1107), Chu Hsi's father devoted three years to teaching his son; on his deathbed, he entrusted Chu Hsi to three neighboring scholars. Five years after his father's death, Chu Hsi passed the national civil service examinations at the age of eighteen, which was about half the average age of successful candidates that year. During these early years, Chu Hsi suffered much grief; in addition to his father, two brothers and two of the three neighboring scholars who taught him died. These deaths may have contributed to Chu Hsi's fascination with Buddhism and Taoism during his teens as well as his sense of mission as a survivor. He was apparently of good health, in spite of complaints beginning in his mid-fifties about unspecified illnesses and foot ailments.

Beginning in 1153 and lasting for five years, Chu Hsi held his first government position as a registrar in T'ung-an County in Fukien, where he concentrated on reforming the management of local taxation and police, upgrading educational standards, and drafting codes for decorum and ritual. After leaving that post, he enjoyed his first sinecure appointment as overseer of a mountain temple; such honorary positions provided him with the leisure to study and write.

An invasion by the Jurchen, which renewed debate about foreign policy, provoked Chu Hsi into submitting memorials to the emperor in 1162 and

1163. In those memorials and the resulting audience with the emperor, he followed his father's lead in criticizing peace advocates. To Chu Hsi, war to liberate northern China was the only moral course of action. Although appointed a professor at the military academy, he resigned upon hearing that the government was making peace. Returning home to Fukien, he repeatedly declined office until 1178. Yet he remained active in local affairs, such as emergency famine relief.

During the 1150's and 1160's, Chu Hsi continued to evolve intellectually. His teacher Li T'ung convinced him to abandon Buddhism and Taoism and led him to a definitive embrace of Confucianism by the time he was twenty-eight. During the 1160's he accepted as standard the teachings of the Ch'eng brothers; moreover, his exchange of letters with Chang Shih about the cultivation of the mind in action and tranquillity demonstrated that by 1169, nearing forty, Chu Hsi had attained intellectual maturity in his interpretation of Confucianism.

Life's Work

Although he repeatedly declined many offices during his remaining thirty years, Chu Hsi's political career was eventful. In 1178, he was appointed a prefect in Nan-k'ang, Kiangsi, where he concentrated on preventing famine and improving education. In addition to lecturing advanced students at least once every five days, he reestablished the once-flourishing White Deer Grotto Academy. Under Chu Hsi's leadership, the academy became an educational model which endured for almost seven centuries. The next post he assumed was as a regional superintendent in Chekiang, where he was in charge of famine relief. In addition to establishing community granaries and other relief measures, he toured the countryside to ferret out corrupt and incompetent officials. Impeaching several county and prefectural heads—including T'ang Chung-yu, who was a relative of the prime minister—Chu Hsi aroused such controversy that he resigned from office after serving for roughly a year.

The indictment of a noted scholar whose Confucianism differed from Chu Hsi's added to the controversy about the *Tao hsüeh* (learning of the true way) tradition, which was rooted in the teachings of the Ch'eng brothers. In his memorials to the emperor, Chu expounded upon the need for government officials to follow the ethical principles of this tradition if they were to reform themselves and provide for the welfare of the people. Resentment at court toward such advice hindered his career, but he did serve as prefect of Chang-chou, Fukien (from 1190 to 1191), and of T'an-chou, Hunan (1194), where he continued his educational and community service reforms.

In 1194, Chu Hsi was summoned to court to be a lecturer to the emperor but was so outspoken that he was dismissed and returned to Fukien after only some forty days as a member of the emperor's court. Soon the officials whom he had criticized launched a purge of political opponents and an attack upon *Tao hsüeh* for being "false learning." Although every major intellectual of the day was implicated in this attack, Chu Hsi was the leading figure whose teachings were proscribed. Chu Hsi died in 1200, still in official disfavor, but several thousand people dared to attend his funeral; indeed, he was regarded by many of the literati of the era as a martyr and a symbol of the Confucian scholar defending ethical principles against arbitrary exercise of governmental power. Soon the political climate improved, and he was exonerated. Later, in 1241, the government honored him with a place in Confucian temples.

Although he held office for only nine years, Chu Hsi contributed significantly to reform of educational and community institutions and family rituals. Nevertheless, his reputation rests primarily on his scholarship. Over the course of forty years, he wrote a series of commentaries on the "Four Books," and these commentaries best demonstrate his agenda. The Four Books are ancient classics, available in English translation since 1861: Confucius' *Lun-yü* (late sixth or early fifth century B.C.; *Analects*), Mencius' *Meng-tzu* (wr. 311-289 B.C.), the *Ta hsüeh* (*Great Learning*), and the *Chung yung* (*Doctrine of the Mean*). Although some earlier *Tao hsüeh* masters had focused on these four works, Chu Hsi was the first to make them explicitly the pedagogical foundation of all Confucian studies. In his series of commentaries on these books, he corrected the mistakes of earlier Confucians and established what he considered to be the true interpretation of these most crucial texts. Chu Hsi reinterpreted other classics as well and directed a rewriting of the standard history of China in order to subject historical issues to ethical judgments.

Chu Hsi's writings and activities aimed at building a community among Confucian scholars. Joining with Lü Tsu-ch'ien (1137-1181), he compiled the *Chin ssu-lü* (1175; *Reflections on Things at Hand*, 1967) as a primer to direct Confucian learning based on statements by earlier *Tao hsüeh* masters. In 1175, he began having disagreements with Lu Chiu-yüan about the relative priority of erudition and intuition of essential virtues as a basis for the Confucian way of life. In the 1180's, Chu Hsi was challenged by Ch'en Liang's utilitarian idea of using results to define virtues and his historicist penchant for regarding the Tao as having evolved with temporal and spatial changes. To Chu Hsi, Lu Chiu-yüan followed the mistakes of Ch'an Buddhists in concentrating too exclusively on personal enlightenment and reducing normative patterns to aspects of the mind. Ch'en Liang pursued social and political achievement at the expense of ethical training; moreover, historicism devalued the constancy of ethical norms, according to Chu Hsi.

These Confucians did agree on a wide range of political and philosophical issues; moreover, they shared a sense that scholars needed to be part of a community with a sharper awareness of Confucian traditions. Although Lu

Chiu-yüan more often reached beyond scholars directly to the masses and Ch'en Liang directed his comments mostly to scholar-officials, Chu Hsi had a clearer educational pedagogy; hence, although he concentrated more on the literati and sought to reach the masses through them, his educational work and his work for the community reached the largest audience.

Chu Hsi was arguably the most systematic philosopher, with the broadest scope of interests in traditional China; moreover, he sought to apply his philosophical understanding to all areas of inquiry: Each thing had an inherent pattern (order or principle) that should be investigated and placed in the context of its relation to the universal order. Although he made careful observations of diverse things, the subject of Chu Hsi's inquiry was essentially Confucian ethical thought and action.

Summary

The scope of Chu Hsi's scholarship and the power of his intellect joined with his contributions to education, community oneness, and ritual bonding within the family to make him the most influential scholar after Confucius in China. Even if they disagreed with his restructuring of the tradition, Chinese scholars have been unable to ignore his writings and terms of discourse. From 1313 to 1905, his commentaries on the Four Books were decreed to be the standard interpretation and the authority of the civil service examinations.

Later emperors, far more autocratic than the ones he personally admonished, observed the popularity of Chu Hsi among the literati and discovered that aspects of his philosophy of inherent pattern and his effort to build a Confucian community could be appropriated to enhance intellectual orthodoxy as well as hierarchical social and political order. Appealing to both literati and rulers in traditional Korea and Japan, Chu Hsi has also had more influence than any other Chinese thinker since the third century B.C. on various areas of culture in those countries. Although he has been blamed by intellectuals and political reformers during the twentieth century for much of the oppressiveness in East Asian cultures, some since the 1960's have increasingly emphasized positive impacts of his legacy on philosophy, education, and ethics.

Bibliography

Bruce, J. Percy. *Chu Hsi and His Masters: An Introduction to Chu Hsi and the Sung School of Chinese Philosophy*. London: Probsthain and Co., 1923. The first major study in English of Chu Hsi's life and his principal mentors. Although dated, it is useful, because English-language accounts are still limited. Includes an index.

Chan, Wing-tsit. *Chu Hsi: Life and Thought*. Hong Kong: Chinese University Press, 1987. Essays survey the history of Chu Hsi's impact on China,

Korea, Japan, Europe, and the United States. Special attention is given to changing attitudes toward Chu Hsi in the twentieth century. Chan has done more than anyone else to introduce Chu Hsi's philosophy in the English language. Includes bibliography and index.

__________, ed. *Chu Hsi and Neo-Confucianism*. Honolulu: University of Hawaii Press, 1986. An international collection of essays by thirty-one senior scholars covers diverse areas of Chu Hsi's philosophy but emphasizes his metaphysics. The volume is especially noteworthy for including most of the major twentieth century Chinese and Japanese historians of Chinese thought. One essay relates Chu Hsi's life to his philosophy, and several evaluate his influence upon later generations in East Asia. Includes an index.

Gardner, Daniel K. *Chu Shi and the "Ta-hsüeh": Neo-Confucian Reflection on the Confucian Canon*. Cambridge, Mass.: Harvard University Press, 1986. In addition to an original annotated translation based on Chu Hsi's writings, Gardner provides a study of the *Ta hsüeh* text, its history through the Sung, and the reasons Chu Hsi found the text so philosophically compelling. Includes annotations, bibliography, index, and the Chinese text.

Tillman, Hoyt Cleveland. *Utilitarian Confucianism: Ch'en Liang's Challenge to Chu Hsi*. Cambridge, Mass.: Harvard University Press, 1982. In addition to analyzing the issues between Ch'en Liang and Chu Hsi, this study also surveys the evolving intellectual and political environment during the eleventh and twelfth centuries. The lives and personal relations of the two principals are also discussed. Includes bibliography and index.

Hoyt Cleveland Tillman

CH'Ü YÜAN

Born: c. 343 B.C.; Ch'u, China
Died: 278 B.C.; in the Mi-lo River, China
Areas of Achievement: Government and literature
Contribution: A skilled statesman who always tried to speak the truth no matter what the cost, Ch'ü Yüan exemplified the Confucian ideal of the virtuous official; his country's first widely known poet, he became one of the founding fathers of Chinese literature.

Early Life

Ch'ü Yüan was born about 343 B.C. in the southern Chinese state of Ch'u, which was centered in what is the modern province of Hubei. The Warring States period (which extended from 481 to 221 B.C.) was characterized by China's fragmentation into a multitude of rival kingdoms, of which Ch'u was one of the major powers. Although little is known of Ch'ü Yüan's childhood, tradition holds that his father's name was Po-yung and that he was related to Ch'u's royal family. Ch'ü Yüan is also reputed to have achieved great distinction as a student and to have been marked for high government service from an early age.

In his late twenties, Ch'ü Yüan was appointed to the important post of *tso-tu*, or "left counselor," in his country's bureaucracy. He became the most influential confidant of the reigning King Huai Wang, and his advice was sought on all significant matters of both foreign and domestic policy. As a young man who believed in the ethical ideals inculcated by Confucianism, Ch'ü Yüan tried to convince the king that he should look for these qualities in his new officials and cease the automatic preferment of the nobly born which had been the traditional way of doing things.

The king's son, Tse Lan, successfully argued that to do so was obviously not in the interest of the aristocracy; Ch'ü Yüan fell out of favor, his counsels were disregarded, and eventually, he was banished to a remote area in Ch'u's northern hinterlands. In the years to come, Ch'ü Yüan's star would rise and fall several times as his country changed rulers and policies, but he never again would wield the kind of influence he had with Huai Wang. It was the disappointment of these youthful hopes for thorough reform that turned Ch'ü Yüan toward literature, in which he was destined for far greater fame than he could ever have achieved in his homeland's civil service.

Life's Work

Ch'ü Yüan's political aspirations had received a crushing blow, but his profoundly idealistic nature was not much affected by his being sent away from court. His poem "In Praise of the Orange Tree," which was written about this time, articulated his confidence in what the future would have to say about his unwillingness to play partisan politics with his country's future:

> Oh, your young resolution has something different from the rest.
> Alone and unmoving you stand. How can one not admire you!
> Deep-rooted, hard to shift: truly you have no peer!

The rural region north of the Han River to which Ch'ü Yüan was banished proved to be a rich source of myths and folktales, many of them related to the shamanistic cults which still flourished in the area. A set of poems known as *Chiu ko* (third century B.C.; *The Nine Songs*, 1955), thought to be among his earliest literary works, includes many references to such deities as the River God and the Mountain Spirit, and it is possible that the songs were originally sacred hymns that Ch'ü Yüan used as a basis for poetic composition.

Whatever their origin, *The Nine Songs* combined religious and romantic impulses in a manner completely new to Chinese poetry. Just as Homer described a world in which gods and men were akin in terms of psychology if not in their respective powers, so Ch'ü Yüan envisaged crossing the barriers that divided humanity from the deities it worshipped. This excerpt from "The Princess of the Hsiang" depicts a god waiting for his human lover:

> I look for my queen, but she comes not yet:
> Of Whom do I think as I play my reed-pipes?
> North I go, drawn by flying dragons . . .
> And over the great River waft my spirit:
> Waft, but my spirit does not reach her;
> And the maiden many a sigh heaves for me.

The Nine Songs immediately established Ch'ü Yüan as the foremost literary figure of his time.

During the first of what would prove to be several periods of banishment for Ch'ü Yüan, Huai Wang was murdered in 297 while participating in a supposed peace conference—which Ch'ü Yüan had warned him against attending—in the neighboring state of Ch'in. This shocking event sparked one of Ch'ü Yüan's most fervently emotional poems, "Great Summons"; the refrain "O soul, come back!" expresses both general fear of death and specific anxiety as to what would now become of the poet. For the moment, however, his fortunes took a turn for the better: The new King of Ch'u, Ching Hsiang, remembering that Ch'ü Yüan had argued against the visit to Ch'in, recalled him to the court and at first followed his adviser's policy of breaking off relations with those who had executed his father. For the next two or three years, Ch'ü Yüan was once again his country's most respected political adviser.

Despite this esteem, Chiang Hsiang's younger brother Tse Lan, who had engineered Ch'ü Yüan's first downfall, worked unremittingly to bring about his second. The crisis came when Ch'in attacked and subdued one of Ch'u's neighbors in 293 and threatened to invade Ch'u unless normal relations were restored. Ch'ü Yüan counseled against this, but Tse Lan's opposing faction won the day: Chiang Hsiang married a Ch'in princess, Ch'u and Ch'in reestablished diplomatic contact, and Ch'ü Yüan was once more banished, this time to another remote province south of the Yangtze River.

In the remaining fifteen years of his life, Ch'ü Yüan was several times recalled to court when Ch'in aggression seemed imminent, but his refusal to compromise with Tse Lan's pro-Ch'in faction led to his swift dismissal each time. After one of these disappointments, he considered emigrating to some other country but finally decided that it was his destiny to set an example for those who would come after him. He now wrote the autobiographical poem that is considered his finest achievement: *Li Sao* (c. 293-278 B.C.; *The Li Sao*, 1895), literally "encountering sorrow," offers a moving account of the agonies and ecstasies of his turbulent career as poet and politician.

The Li Sao opens with the birth of Ch'ü Yüan, who is given the names "True Exemplar" and "Divine Balance" by his father. His youthful enthusiasm is soon quenched by a sobering dash of political reality: He learns that "All others press forward in greed and gluttony" while he alone seems to care about leaving behind "an enduring name." His greatest disappointment comes when he learns that even the king is subject to an all-too-human inconstancy of mind, but Ch'ü Yüan is nevertheless determined to continue campaigning for what he believes is right:

> But I would rather quickly die and meet dissolution
> Before I ever would consent to ape their behaviour.

Ch'ü Yüan presents his love of beauty and poetry as a kind of contrapuntal relief from his political misfortunes, and it is these passages which make *The Li Sao* such a landmark in Chinese verse. Just as he had combined religion and romanticism in his early poetry, so this later work merges the conduct of contemporary affairs with the more permanent consolations offered by aesthetic accomplishment and appreciation. In a world where most people are too busy seeking power to care about either art or morality, Ch'ü Yüan argues that a sensitive soul must protect its natural heritage of grace and good conduct against the constant temptation to conform.

The implications of the conclusion of *The Li Sao*, which announces that the author intends to "go and join P'eng Hsien in the place where he abides," are still a matter of some disagreement among students of Chinese literature. The statement has been interpreted as a decision to become a hermit as well as a desire to commit suicide; since nothing is known about P'eng Hsien, it seems unlikely that the issue will ever be resolved. This ongoing debate demonstrates how timelessly relevant *The Li Sao* is to questions of individual and social morality and of the artist's role in the world, and it helps to explain why Ch'ü Yüan is so important a figure in Chinese literature.

After years of gradual encroachment, the Ch'in armies sacked Ch'u's capital in 278 and threw the country into turmoil. This final disaster was too much for Ch'ü Yüan to bear: He drowned himself in the Mi-lo River, a tributary of the Yangtze, shortly thereafter. Nevertheless, his name lived on as a symbol of selfless dedication to both the highest standards of morality and the good of his country; in addition, he was commemorated by a national holiday. On the day of the annual Dragon Boat Festival, small boats are raced as an expression of the desire to rescue him from drowning, while specially prepared rice balls are thrown into the water so that his spirit will not go hungry.

Summary

Very few people have been accorded the degree of respect given to Ch'ü Yüan in traditional Chinese culture. He exemplified the ideal Confucian official, so loyal to the state that he would not compromise his opinions even when aware that they would be negatively received; his development of his literary talents exemplified the Renaissance-man wholeness that Confucius had advocated but which was often neglected by bureaucrats who found it easier to conform to tradition than attempt to expand it.

Even the People's Republic of China, which has discouraged the respect paid to many traditional historical figures on the grounds that they were reactionary influences, considers Ch'ü Yüan's exemplary loyalty to the state a model of correct social behavior. This esteem has had the important incidental effect of maintaining his status as one of the founding fathers of Chinese literature, and his work has thus been preserved as an important element of his country's cultural heritage. Many poets of subsequent generations, among them Sung Yü, T'ao Ch'ien, and Li Po, were deeply affected by Ch'ü Yüan's energetic defense of the highest ethical and aesthetic standards. Even today he is often acknowledged as an influence by writers striving for a balance between imaginative idealism and moral realism. Wherever Chinese is spoken, his name remains synonymous with personal integrity above and beyond worldly success.

Bibliography

Hawkes, David, trans. *Ch'u tz'u: The Songs of the South, an Ancient Chinese Anthology*. Oxford: Clarendon Press, 1959. The only complete English translation of Ch'ü Yüan's poetry (which was first collected with that of other writers in an anthology entitled *Ch'u tz'u*). Hawkes's versions of the poems, which are accompanied by excellent notes, are somewhat different from those of earlier translators and are generally considered more accurate by his fellow scholars.

__________. "The Quest of the Goddess." In *Studies in Chinese Literary*

Genres, edited by Cyril Birch. Berkeley: University of California Press, 1974. This article places Ch'ü Yüan's work in its cultural perspective, compares it with that of his predecessors and successors, and argues that he represents the victory of a written, secular approach to literature over earlier oral and religious modes of expression. A seminal discussion by Ch'ü Yüan's foremost modern interpreter.

Schneider, Laurence A. *A Madman of Ch'u: The Chinese Myth of Loyalty and Dissent*. Berkeley: University of California Press, 1980. A well-researched account of the development of Ch'ü Yüan's reputation into a synonym for political rectitude. The treatment is basically historical and culminates in a convincing demonstration of how he became the patron saint of modern Chinese intellectuals. The poetry is used merely as thematic evidence, but even those more interested in Ch'ü Yüan as a poet will find the book a useful source for social and cultural insights.

Waley, Arthur. *The Nine Songs: A Study of Shamanism in Ancient China*. London: Allen and Unwin, 1955. Waley stresses the religious origins of Ch'ü Yüan's verse, suggesting that its depth of feeling may be an indication of the author's madness. Although his grasp of the historical context is second to none and makes the book still worth consulting, Waley was not a very sophisticated literary critic; his diagnosis has been disregarded by most subsequent commentators.

Watson, Burton. *Early Chinese Literature*. New York: Columbia University Press, 1962. Includes a detailed discussion of Ch'ü Yüan's work in its historical and textual aspects. A descriptive rather than interpretive approach that occasionally ventures opinions regarding symbolic or thematic significances; a good introduction for the general reader.

__________, trans. *Records of the Grand Historians of China: Translated from the Shih Chi of Ssu-ma Ch'ien*. 2 vols. New York: Columbia University Press, 1961. Includes the original historical evidence upon which all subsequent research about Ch'ü Yüan is based. Its biographies of his era's political contemporaries provide a vivid sense of what life was like during the Warring States period.

Paul Stuewe

CHUANG-TZU

Born: c. 365 B.C.; Mêng, Kingdom of Sung, China
Died: c. 290 B.C.; Nan-hua Hill, Ts'ao-chou, Kingdom of Ch'i, China
Areas of Achievement: Philosophy, monasticism, and literature
Contribution: Chuang-tzu was the greatest thinker of the Chinese Taoist school of philosophy. He went much beyond its founder, Lao-tzu, in constructing an apolitical, transcendental philosophy designed to promote an individual's spiritual freedom.

Early Life

Chuang-tzu was born sometime around 365 B.C.; according to his biographer, Ssu-ma Ch'ien, the philosopher was a native of the town of Mêng in the Kingdom of Sung. His personal name was Chou. Beyond this, little is known regarding Chuang-tzu's life and career. He was born into a time known as the Warring States period, during which China had become divided into many small, fiercely competitive states as a result of the collapse of the Chou Dynasty. Thus, Chuang-tzu was a contemporary of the famous Confucian philosopher Mencius.

For a brief time, Chuang-tzu served as a government official in Ch'i-yuan, not far from his birthplace. He soon tired of public life, however, and resolved to pursue philosophical meditation and writing. Thereupon, he retired to the state of Ch'i, where he took up residence on Nan-hua Hill, in the prefecture of Ts'ao-chou. Here he spent the remainder of his life.

Chuang-tzu's disillusionment with law and politics is apparent in an anecdote recorded in chapter 17 of the *Chuang-tzu*:

> Once, when Chuang Tzu was fishing in the P'u River, the king of Ch'u sent two officials to go and announce to him: "I would like to trouble you with the administration of my realm."
>
> Chuang Tzu held on to the fishing pole and, without turning his head, said, "I have heard that there is a sacred tortoise in Ch'u that has been dead for three thousand years. The king keeps it wrapped in cloth and boxed, and stores it in the ancestral temple. Now would this tortoise rather be dead and have its bones left behind and honored? Or would it rather be alive and dragging its tail in the mud?"
>
> "It would rather be alive and dragging its tail in the mud," said the two officials.
>
> Chuang Tzu said, "Go away! I'll drag my tail in the mud!"

A portrait of this stubbornly independent thinker has been preserved in Taipei's National Palace Museum. It shows a rather short, slightly built man with sparse hair and penetrating eyes. He stands with his hands clasped over his chest, a pose that conveys dignity and serenity.

Life's Work

The Taoism of Chuang-tzu's time derived from the *I Ching* (*Book of Changes*), the ancient manual of divination based on the concept that the world and the laws of change are an ordered, interdependent unit, and from Lao-tzu's *Tao-te Ching*, which described the workings of the Tao (the Way), the primordial generative principle that is the mother of all things. Tao was interpreted as "the Way of Heaven," or natural law, and the Taoists explained natural phenomena and the social order in reference to this principle. Proper human behavior consisted of not interfering with the Tao but living in harmony with it. Thus, the Taoists taught the doctrine of *wu-wei* (not doing), or, more explicitly, *wei-wu-wei* (doing by not doing). This standard did not imply absolute quietism but rather acting intuitively, spontaneously, and effortlessly in imitation of the Tao, which manages to accomplish everything naturally. Although some Taoists retired entirely from the world and lived as hermits, Taoism was not designed for the hermit but for the Sage king, who, though not withdrawing from the world, seeks to avoid interfering with it.

For the Taoists, then, the best government was the least government. Indeed, they reasoned, if all men acted in harmony with the Tao, government as an institution would be unnecessary. Government by law and even the notions of good and evil were regarded by the Taoists as deviations from the Tao and unwarranted interference with it. Such an attitude gave Taoists considerable independence in regard to politics and worldly affairs generally.

It is evident that Chuang-tzu's decision to withdraw from political entanglements was amply supported by Taoist teachings. His interpretations of this and other doctrines have been passed down in the *Chuang-tzu*, an imaginative compilation of anecdote and dialogue. In the words of a modern scholar, in the *Chuang-tzu* "animals speak, natural forces are personified, and dialogues which begin in soberness unexpectedly veer into humor, fantasy, and absurdity."

Where the *Tao-te Ching* of Lao-tzu sets forth the universal Tao as a political and social ideal, the *Chuang-tzu* is mostly concerned with the individual and his or her intellectual and spiritual freedom. Unlike Lao-tzu's work, which is addressed to rulers, the *Chuang-tzu* addresses anyone, ruler or private person, who wishes to become a member of the spiritual elite. To achieve this goal, the seeker must begin by achieving an awareness of the existence and workings of the universal Tao and of his or her own relation to the scheme of things.

The Tao is nameless; the name assigned to it is merely a convenient label. Though it is preexistent, formless, and imperceptible, it latently contains all forms, entities, and forces; it permeates all things. All Being issues from it and returns to it. The life and death of human beings take part in this transformation from Non-being into Being and back again to Non-being.

After accepting this metaphysical scheme, the seeker faces the second step on the ladder of knowledge: the realization of the importance of making full and free use of his natural ability. Whatever ability he possesses stems from his *tê*, the power within him that comes directly from the Tao. The individuated forms of things come from their *tê*, which confers on them their natural properties and abilities. Things differ both in their nature and in their natural abilities. One kind of bird can fly a thousand miles; another kind has difficulty flying from one tree to another. It is no use for a man to discuss the ocean with a frog that has lived its whole life in a well.

It is important for the seeker to distinguish between what is heavenly—that is, of nature—and what is entirely human. What is heavenly is internal; what is human is external. The human is all that is artificial: the artifacts of man; his institutions of government, education, and religion; his cultural codes of etiquette, law, and morals. All these artificialities involve restrictions on man's independence and freedom. To the extent that a person can exercise his natural abilities independently of or in spite of the restrictions imposed on him, he ought to do so. In so doing, he will achieve a measure of happiness, although it will be a relative, not an absolute, happiness. Interference with nature should be avoided, according to Chuang-tzu's teachings. Government that seeks to rule people by strict laws and strong institutions is pictured as putting a halter around a horse's neck or a cord through an ox's nose. The use of violence by governments is like trying to lengthen the short legs of a duck or to shorten the long legs of a crane.

Relative happiness, then, can be attained by making good use of one's natural ability; yet, other factors such as avoiding injury and disease and overcoming fear of death are also necessary to happiness. If the seeker gains a proper understanding of the nature of things, he can greatly mitigate his anxiety regarding death as well as the grief he may feel when a loved one dies. Chapter 18 of the *Chuang-tzu*, "Perfect Happiness," records an anecdote that illustrates this notion. Chuang-tzu's wife had died, and Hui-tzu had gone to pay his condolences to the philosopher. Upon entering his house, Hui-tzu was amazed to find the master "sitting with his legs sprawled, pounding on a tub and singing." Scandalized, Hui-tzu hastened to remind Chuang-tzu that he had lived with his wife a long time, that she had borne and reared his children, and that she had grown old along with him. Hui-tzu reproached his friend: "It should be enough simply not to weep at her death. But pounding on a tub and singing—this is going too far, isn't it?" Chuang-tzu replied:

> "You're wrong. When she first died, do you think I didn't grieve like anyone else? But I looked back to her beginning and the time before she was born. Not only the time before she was born, but the time before she had a body. Not only the time before she had a body, but the time before she had a spirit. In the midst of the jumble of wonder and mystery a change took place and she had a

> spirit. Another change and she had a body. Another change and she was born. Now there's been another change and she's dead. It's just like the progression of the four seasons, spring, summer, fall, winter.
>
> "Now she's going to lie down peacefully in a vast room. If I were to follow after her bawling and sobbing, it would show that I don't understand anything about fate. So I stopped."

Thus, death is simply a phase in the turning of the wheel of fortune that is the Tao. The turning of the wheel voids the identity and disintegrates the material body of the dead person. From the standpoint of the Tao, however, no state of being is more desirable than another. As a natural event in the cycle of human life, death is neither to be feared nor to be sorrowed over.

How does the seeker reach the third and last rung of his upward way? To answer this question, Chuang-tzu proposed an epistemology, a theory of knowledge. Knowledge, he said, is of two kinds: lower and higher. The lower involves sense perception, reason, and language; it depends on relativity, finitude, and memory. Higher knowledge involves suprasensible perception, intuition, and silence; it depends on the unity of opposites, infinitude, and forgetfulness. Lower knowledge lacks understanding. Higher knowledge is filled with understanding, a condition in which everything is illuminated by "the light of Heaven."

To achieve higher knowledge, the seeker must forget the knowledge that he has acquired. He must transcend all relativity, finitude, and apparent contradictions implied in conventional opposites such as right and wrong, great and small, life and death. The seeker can transcend such distinctions when he realizes that the Tao makes them all one. Once he has attained this realization, he has no use for categories. Where "ordinary men discriminate and parade their discriminations before others," the enlightened man "embraces things." Thus, forgetfulness and "no-knowledge" constitute the highest wisdom.

The lower level of knowledge permits the use of speech. Good language is dispassionate and calm; bad language is "shrill and quarrelsome." At the higher level of knowledge, however, language is inadequate: "The Great Way is not named; Great Discriminations are not spoken. . . . If discriminations are put into words, they do not suffice." The holy man does not speak, for him silence reigns supreme. Content within himself because he has forgotten self and the world, he may be said to have entered Heaven. He has achieved absolute happiness.

Summary

If the real Chuang-tzu is a barely perceptible shadow cast by the dim light of history, he is brightly visible in the pages of the *Chuang-tzu*. Here he emerges as a living, breathing, dynamic human being, radiant of mind, wide-ranging in imagination, full of wit and humor. The *Chuang-tzu* is a monumental book and a great classic of Chinese literature. Its style is brilliant, full of clever rhetorical devices, satire, fantasy, metaphor, jokes, dreams, and parody. Although it is a work of philosophy, it may also be termed "protofictional." It not only uses historical characters, such as Confucius, fictionally, but also creates fictional characters as foils for its protagonist. In this way, the *Chuang-tzu* contributed to the development of later Chinese fictional genres such as *hsiao-shuo* and *chih-kuai*.

Philosophically, Chuang-tzu went beyond Lao-tzu in offering a clear alternative to the philosophies of his age. He emphasized the personal ideal of the emancipation of the individual for his own sake in place of the social ideal of the harmonious society ruled by the Sage king. Although the *Chuang-tzu* never gained the popularity and influence of the *Tao-te Ching*, it continued to command the interest and admiration of Chinese rulers and philosophers. The Neo-Taoist philosophers Hsiang Hsiu (c. A.D. 221-c. 300) and Kuo Hsiang (who died around A.D. 312) both wrote commentaries on the *Chuang-tzu*, seeking to reconcile the social ideal of Confucius with the private ideal of Chuang-tzu. Despite their criticism of Chuang-tzu, they performed the important service of transmitting his work and preserving it for posterity.

In the West, the *Chuang-tzu* has made a decided impression on numerous prominent thinkers, beginning perhaps with the great German philosopher G. W. F. Hegel, who in 1816 lectured at the University of Heidelberg on Taoism and Confucianism, based on the *Book of Changes* and the *Chuang-tzu*. His concept of the Absolute as a process rather than a source and his description of the dialectical process (thesis and antithesis merging into a synthesis) are reminiscent of Chuang-tzu's concept of the Tao and the underlying unity of opposites. Later thinkers such as Pierre Teilhard de Chardin, Carl Jung, Jacques Maritain, Jacques Lacan, and Thomas Merton all show evidence in their writing of an intimate acquaintance with Taoism and the thought of Chuang-tzu.

Bibliography

Chan, Wing-tsit, trans. and comp. *A Source Book in Chinese Philosophy*. Princeton, N.J.: Princeton University Press, 1963. Readable translations of the basic texts of Chinese philosophy, including the *Chuang-tzu*. The early texts, however, follow Neo-Confucian interpretations. Some dubious translations of important terms: *ch'êng* is translated "sincerity" in places where it means something else; *tê* is translated "character" rather than "virtue" or "power."

Chang, Chung-yuan. *Creativity and Taoism: A Study of Chinese Philosophy, Art, and Poetry*. New York: Julian Press, 1963. Shows the important part Taoism has played in Chinese artistic and intellectual activity.

Chuang-tzu. *Chuang-tzŭ: The Seven Inner Chapters and Other Writings from the Book of Chuang-tzŭ*. Translated by A. C. Graham. Boston: Allen and Unwin, 1981. This volume offers more than a new translation. Graham attempts to resolve major textual problems and edits the texts in terms of new categories. Lucid and interesting. Highly recommended.

———. *The Complete Works of Chuang-Tzŭ*. Translated by Burton Watson. New York: Columbia University Press, 1968. The translation of the extant thirty-three-chapter version of the *Chuang-tzu*. It incorporates the modern research of Japanese scholars. It is perhaps the best translation available.

Creel, H. G. *Chinese Thought from Confucius to Mao Tsê-tung*. Chicago: University of Chicago Press, 1953. Good general survey of Chinese thought except that the philosophies most prominent from the fourth century through the seventeenth century—Buddhism, Neo-Taoism, and Neo-Confucianism—are not given adequate coverage.

———. *What Is Taoism? And Other Studies in Chinese Cultural History*. Chicago: University of Chicago Press, 1970, reprint 1982. A collection of essays well worth reading. Includes Creel's notable essay "The Great Clod: A Taoist Conception of the Universe."

Durrant, Stephen. "*Chu-tzŭ pai-chia* (The Various Masters and the Hundred Schools)." In *The Indiana Companion to Traditional Chinese Literature*, edited by William H. Nienhauser, Jr. Bloomington: Indiana University Press, 1986. A relatively brief but nevertheless excellent survey of its topic.

Merton, Thomas. *The Way of Chuang Tzŭ*. New York: New Directions, 1965. The author was a poet, prose writer, mystic, and Trappist monk. Knowing no Chinese, he made an effort here to capture his intuitive sense of Chuang-tzu's spirit on the basis of translations in Western languages. He succeeds as well as the translators.

Watson, Burton. *Early Chinese Literature*. New York: Columbia University Press, 1964. A history of Chinese literature—"literature" meaning history, philosophy, and poetry—from the Chou Dynasty to the middle of the Later Han Dynasty. An informative and enjoyable volume. The translations are readable and generally accurate, with only a few minor errors.

Richard P. Benton

CICERO

Born: January 3, 106 B.C.; Arpinum, Latium
Died: December 7, 43 B.C.; Formiae, Latium
Areas of Achievement: Government, law, oratory, philosophy, and literature
Contribution: With courageous and principled statesmanship, Cicero guided Rome through a series of severe crises. While he was not able to save the Republic, he transmitted its political and cultural values in speeches and treatises that became models of style for posterity.

Early Life

Marcus Tullius Cicero, the elder son of Marcus Tullius Cicero and Helvia, was born a few miles from Arpinum, a small town in Latium, southeast of Rome. Long established in the district, his family had, like many other Roman families, a rather undignified source for its name: *Cicer* is Latin for chick-pea, or garbanzo. According to one story, "Cicero" originated as the nickname of a wart-nosed ancestor. The Tullius clan was of equestrian, or knightly, rank—that is, they were well-to-do but their members had never served in the senate. Cicero was to be the first in the family to attain nobility as a magistrate.

Centuries earlier, Arpinum had been a stronghold of the Volscians in their unsuccessful struggle to avoid subjugation by Rome. For nearly one hundred years before Cicero's birth, however, the people of Arpinum had enjoyed full Roman citizenship. Cicero took pride in his local origins as well as in his Roman citizenship, and he sometimes referred to his "two fatherlands." His description in *Cato Maior de Senectute* (44 B.C.; *On Old Age*, 1481) of the slow, well-regulated growth of Arpinum's figs and grapes suggests the influence of his birthplace on his politics at Rome: He was a lifelong defender of order and gradual change, an enemy of both mob violence and aristocratic privilege.

Cicero's first exposure to learning came through the papyrus scrolls in his father's library at Arpinum. While still very young, both Cicero and his brother, Quintus, showed such zeal to study philosophy and oratory that their father took them to Rome to seek the best instruction available. This move to Carinae Street in the capital, coinciding with his father's retirement from active life, presented young Cicero with an opportunity to excel academically and advance socially.

Latin literature had yet to come into its own. Early Roman poets such as Livius Andronicus and Quintus Ennius simply did not compare well with Homer, and the educators of the day made heavy use of Greek poetic works to teach elocution and rhetoric. One of Cicero's teachers was the Greek poet Aulus Licinius Archias, who himself had come to Rome in 102 B.C. and whom Cicero afterwards credited with having sparked his interest in literature. Cicero adapted the cadences of Greek and Latin poetry to his original orations, developing a complex but supple rhetorical and literary style that became a standard for his own time and for the Renaissance, fifteen hundred years later. In retrospect, however, Cicero faulted the education of his youth for not teaching how to obtain practical results through rhetoric—a problem he set himself to solve through legal studies.

In 89 B.C., at age seventeen, he interrupted these studies to serve on Rome's side in the Social War, a rebellion by Rome's Italian allies. His brief role in this disastrous ten-year conflict aroused in him a lifelong hatred of military service. He became more convinced than ever that his success would lie in progressing through the prescribed sequence of public offices, as it had for his models at the time, the orators Lucius Licinius Crassus and Marcus Antonius Creticus (grandfather of Marc Antony). He continued to study rhetoric and also resumed his legal studies under Quintus Mucius Scaevola, the augur (priest of the state religion), who had been consul some twenty-eight years previously.

Life's Work

Among Cicero's important achievements was a series of celebrated orations in connection with legal cases. His oratorical skills aided him in the pursuit of public office and helped secure his place in history as the savior of Rome.

Cicero launched his career as an orator and advocate in 81 B.C., during the dictatorship of Lucius Cornelius Sulla. Under that regime no one's life was safe; to become conspicuous through forensics was especially dangerous. Not only did Cicero confront this risk, but from his earliest cases onward he also often bravely opposed the established leaders. *Pro Quinctio* (81 B.C.), his first speech in a court of law, had little importance in itself; in taking on this case, however, Cicero pitted himself against the leading advocate of the day, Quintus Hortensius Hortalus.

The following year, in *Pro Roscio Amerino*, Cicero defended a young man accused of parricide by Chrysogonus, a favorite of Sulla's. After the father of Roscius was murdered, Chrysogonus had fabricated a charge to get the dead man's name on Sulla's list of proscribed citizens—those banished from Rome for certain offenses. By law the property of a proscribed person, dead or alive, was put up at auction; Chrysogonus wanted to buy the dead father's property cheaply. He later conspired to make Roscius appear responsible for the murder. It was a bold and dangerous step to reveal in a public speech this evil scheme of Sulla's favorite. Yet Cicero resolutely undertook the defense of Roscius and carried it off so effectively that his reputation was immediately established. Suddenly his services as advocate were in great demand, and Cicero sought to capitalize on this trend by publishing some of his forensic speeches.

Apparently Sulla bore Cicero no ill will; in any case, the dictator abdicated in 79 B.C. The next two years, however, Cicero spent away from Rome, studying philosophy and oratory in Greece and Rhodes under Molo, who had also taught Julius Caesar. During this period, Cicero regained his health; it was also during this time that he formed the great friendship of his life, with Titus Pomponius Atticus, to whom he would address some of his best known letters.

In 77 B.C., Cicero returned to Rome and married Terentia, the daughter of a well-to-do and socially prominent family. He was old enough to campaign for quaestor (financial officer), the first rung of the public-office ladder. Elected at the minimum age of thirty in 76 B.C., Cicero served in Sicily and distinguished himself in office by sending large supplies of grain to the capital in a time of near famine. In gratitude, the senate admitted him to membership.

Meanwhile, Cicero continued to offer his services as orator and advocate, since Roman law prescribed an interim between terms of service as a magistrate. In 70 came another noteworthy event in his career: his impeachment of Gaius Verres, Governor of Sicily from 73 to 71. Most provincial governors pursued a policy of extortion to enrich themselves, but Verres had been uncommonly greedy and cruel. Having spent two months preparing a painstakingly well-documented case, Cicero prosecuted Verres so vigorously that the defendant's legal adviser—the same Hortensius whose primacy Cicero had challenged ten years earlier—gave up the defense, and Verres went into voluntary exile.

Cicero's skill as a speaker in public trials was an important factor in his election to public office, especially since he was not from one of Rome's leading aristocratic families. He won by a landslide the office of aedile (roughly, superintendent of public works) in 69 B.C. Two years later, he was chosen praetor, or judicial officer, and in 63 came the supreme honor: election as consul, Rome's chief executive. Two consuls were elected each year, and Cicero's colleague in office, Gaius Antonius Hybrida, was politically insignificant. Essentially, he allowed Cicero complete control during what became a year of crisis.

First, Cicero felt compelled to oppose a bill that ordered the distribution of state-owned land to the poor. The real significance of this particular bill lay in the powers it accorded to a commission that would be appointed to implement it. Sponsoring the bill were two wealthy aristocrats, Crassus and Caesar. Cicero, a professed "man of the people," soundly defeated the measure, but at the cost of appearing to be an ally of the moneyed, landowning classes, while Caesar seemed a champion of the masses.

An aristocrat was similarly responsible for the next crisis, the Catilinarian conspiracy. After losing several bids for high office, Lucius Sergius Catilina (Catiline), in desperation, began plotting a coup. He recruited popular support by promising to cancel all debts and proscribe the wealthy if he came to power. When Catiline tried to enlist a group of tribal delegates from Roman Gaul, however, they informed Cicero, who arranged that they should be arrested while carrying incriminating letters from the plotters. The evidence was incontrovertible, and Cicero called for summary execution.

This bold move proved a serious mistake that almost destroyed Cicero's political career. Roman law provided that no citizen should be put to death without the privilege of final appeal to the people. Cicero, in his fourth Catilinarian oration, held that those who had plotted against their country were no longer citizens and thus had lost the right of final appeal. Despite the danger to the Republic—Catiline's supporters outside Rome were virtually in a state of rebellion—Cicero pressed for an arbitrary interpretation of the law. He had the power to do so, for in October, because of the crisis, the senate had practically given him dictatorial power. Catiline himself escaped but was soon killed in the battle that finally ended the conspiracy. Cicero prevailed upon the senate to pass the death sentence on the other ringleaders. Thereafter, he was hailed as a "savior" and "father of the fatherland." Nevertheless, there were to be reprisals.

Publius Clodius Pulcher, a favorite of Caesar's and a private enemy of Cicero's, introduced a bill to exile anyone who had put Roman citizens to death without the right of public appeal. Cicero was not named, but the measure was clearly aimed at him. His attempts to block it failed, and in 58 B.C., stricken with grief, he was forced to leave Rome. Clodius and his followers tore down Cicero's house in Rome and persecuted Terentia.

Cicero was recalled to the capital, however, after eighteen months. Perhaps as a reaction to Clodius' excesses, the people gave Cicero a hero's welcome. His house and wealth were restored, and Julius Caesar courted him as a potential ally. Cicero's dream at this time, however, was to save the Republic by detaching Pompey the Great from the Triumvirate. Caesar and Pompey did indeed fall out, but the breakup of the Triumvirate did not save the Republic. During the years between 57 and 51 B.C., Cicero lived in retirement and concentrated on philosophical and rhetorical studies and the writing of treatises in these fields, works in which he articulated the political and moral philosophy he had tried to exemplify in his life. In 51, sick of living in ignominious luxury, he leaped at the opportunity to govern the province of Cilicia as proconsul. Unlike most provincial governors, he was a just, sympathetic administrator, sincerely desirous of improving the lot of the Cilicians, who had been severely exploited by his predecessors.

Cicero never forgave Caesar for putting an end to the Republic, though he took no part in Caesar's assassination in 44 B.C. Afterward, he expected to see the Republic restored, but he soon came to fear Antony as a second Caesar. When the Second Triumvirate was formed by Antony, Octavian (later Augustus), and Marcus Aemilius Lepidus, Cicero and other defenders of the old Republic were proscribed. Antony's supporters hunted Cicero down and killed him in Formiae, Latium, on December 7, 43 B.C. To disgrace him, Antony had his head and hands mounted on the Rostra at Rome.

Summary

It was for his political acts than Marcus Tullius Cicero most wanted to be remembered, and, having acted courageously and decisively at certain critical moments—notably during the Catilinarian conspiracy—he was viewed in his own time as the savior of Rome. Nevertheless, Rome as Cicero knew it—the Republic—could not be saved. Though Cicero did often set an example of personal courage for his contemporaries, his more lasting value is in having articulated the political and moral ideals of the Roman Republic at the very moment when their realization was no longer possible. Through his writings, Cicero also helped to shape the form and style of a literature that was just coming into its own. In his orations and philosophical essays, he showed that the Latin language could be employed with the same grace and elegance as Greek. Though his philosophical reasoning was seldom profound, it adequately served his avowed practical purpose—in literature as in life—of helping humanity find a way of life and a consistent purpose. By recording the ideals of Republican Rome, Cicero may have ensured their availability in other times when their realization may be more feasible.

Bibliography

Bailey, D. R. Shackleton. *Cicero*. New York: Charles Scribner's Sons, 1971. Provides a detailed biography of Cicero and discusses his writings in the context of his life. Part of the Classical Life and Letters series.

Balsdon, J. V. P. D., ed. *Roman Civilization*. Harmondsworth, England: Penguin Books, 1969. Includes chapters by various specialists on early Roman history, law, architecture, and engineering. The chapter on education and oratory focuses on Cicero.

Cicero. *Letters of Cicero: A Selection in Translation*. Compiled and translated by L. P. Wilkinson. New York: W. W. Norton and Co., 1966. Provides translations of Cicero's important letters from the year after his consulship to the end of his life, with an informative introduction.

Cowell, F. R. *Cicero and the Roman Republic*. Harmondsworth, England: Penguin Books, 1964. Contains detailed chapters on Roman history, culture, and commerce, as well as discussions of Cicero's political relationships.

Mackail, J. W. *Latin Literature*. Edited with an introduction by Harry C. Schnur. New York: Collier Books, 1962. Contains a chapter with literary evaluations of Cicero's forensic oratory, political philosophy, philosophy, and epistolary prose. Includes a bibliography.

Sihler, Ernest G. *Cicero of Arpinum: A Political and Literary Biography*.

New York: Cooper Square Publishers, 1914. A classicist's approach to the study of Cicero's life and character. Special emphasis is placed on Cicero's writings.

Thomas Rankin

EL CID
Rodrigo Díaz de Vivar

Born: c. 1043; Vivar, Spain
Died: July 10, 1099; Valencia, Spain
Area of Achievement: Warfare
Contribution: El Cid, through military skill and leadership, halted the Almoravide advance on the peninsula, and by exemplifying his times' ideals of courage, loyalty, and force of will became the national hero of his people.

Early Life

Rodrigo (Ruy) Díaz was born in Vivar, a small village to the north of Burgos in old Castile. Although not of the higher nobility, his family had long held a respected position in the history of the province and at the Castilian-Leonese court. Rodrigo himself was educated in the household of Prince Sancho, heir to the throne. In spite of the many legends and ballads dealing with his early life, little can be proven historically.

Eleventh century Spain was a swirling of shifting frontiers, an armed camp, divided into numerous Moorish and Christian kingdoms whose allegiances were constantly changing. Castile, because of its pivotal geographical position, had long been in a state of warfare. Its final independence from Navarre had been achieved only five years before Rodrigo's birth, but its King Ferdinand I quickly proceeded to unite all northwestern Spain under his rule. He then turned his attention to the Muslim principalities, the taifas, conquering several and subjecting many others to the payment of tribute.

Rodrigo, in such an atmosphere, quickly rose to prominence by his military prowess and strategic skills. His first military action was probably at Graus, where in 1063 the Castilians with Moorish help defeated the Aragonese. After this, Rodrigo's life seems to have been one long continuous battle. At the death of Ferdinand in 1065 and Sancho's accession to the throne, Rodrigo became commander in chief of the Castilian forces. Single combat was still the principal method of settling border disputes between rival states, and the obligation to defend Castile's honor was Rodrigo's. His victories in these duels and in battle made him famous throughout Christian Spain, earning for him the title "Campeador" (great warrior).

In 1072, however, Rodrigo's friend and patron Sancho was assassinated before the walls of Zamora, the last act in the bloody civil wars which had erupted immediately after the death of Ferdinand. Ignoring the lessons of his own struggle for power, Ferdinand had divided his kingdom among his five children, Sancho receiving Castile, Alfonso receiving León, García receiving Galicia, and Urraca and Elvira inheriting the livings of various monasteries. After a brief alliance with Alfonso in order to depose García, Sancho turned upon the others. Legend states that it was at the incitement of Urraca, perhaps abetted by Alfonso, that Vellído Dolfos traitorously stabbed and killed Sancho at the siege of Zamora, Urraca's last stronghold. Rodrigo de Vivar had grown up with the royal family, and, in spite of his position as the military leader of Sancho's forces, he had tried to mediate between the warring parties. At Sancho's death, however, Rodrigo became the spokesman for the Castilian cause. Without a viable candidate for the throne, the Castilian nobles agreed to accept Alfonso as king if he would swear under oath three times in public assembly that he had played no part in his brother's death. This famous oath was administered by Rodrigo in the Church of Santa Gadea in Burgos. Satisfied (at least officially) of Alfonso's innocence, Rodrigo, as a loyal vassal, kissed Alfonso's ring after the oath. His king, in return, angered at this insult to his dignity and jealous of Rodrigo's reputation as the outstanding Christian military figure, stripped Rodrigo of all the offices and honors he had enjoyed under the patronage of Ferdinand and Sancho. In fact, the Castilian was never again to hold a central place at the court, which was now dominated by the powerful Leonese Vani-Gómez family, the counts of Carrión, whose hostility toward the "Castilian upstart" was to become famous in history and legend. During these years of obscurity, after Sancho's death, the only favor granted to Rodrigo was his arranged marriage in 1074 to Jimena Díaz, cousin to the king, daughter of the Count of Oviedo and granddaughter of Alfonso V of León.

Life's Work

Paradoxically, the essence of Rodrigo Díaz de Vivar's greatness lies not in the concrete details or consequences of what he did, but the manner in which he achieved it, in the journey he took to become El Cid. It is a journey which started at the lowest ebb of his fortunes. In 1079, sent to collect the tribute due from the Moorish king of Seville, al-Mu'tamid, his forces were attacked by those of Granada assisted by García Ordóñez, the favorite of King Alfonso. Ordóñez was defeated and taken prisoner. After his release, humiliated, he spread the rumor that Rodrigo had kept part of the Sevillian tribute for himself. Gladly taking advantage of this and other pretexts, the king gave Rodrigo nine days to leave the kingdom. Shorn of all his property and rents, accompanied by vassals, relatives, and servants, but without his wife and young children, Rodrigo embarked on a life of exile. This bitter abandonment by his king is vividly portrayed in the opening of the famous epic poem *Cantar de mio Cid* (c. 1140; also known as *Poema de mio Cid*; *The Poem of the Cid*). Forbidden to give him aid, the citizens of Burgos hid behind closed doors and shuttered windows as their hero departed, never to return.

His efforts to obtain the patronage of Christian princes proving unsuccessful, Rodrigo became the commander of the Moorish army at Saragossa. There was nothing unusual in this. Although supposedly sworn religious enemies, Christians and Moors often formed alliances according to the political necessities of the moment. Saragossa at that time was one of the most brilliant courts on the peninsula, for its leaders, al-Muqtadir and (later) al-Mu'tamin, had surrounded themselves with Jewish and Arabic scholars. They were happy to accept not only the Castilian's military services but also his renowned skill as a diplomat and legal expert. It was perhaps in Saragossa, where he remained from 1082 to 1089, that Rodrigo acquired the title "Mio Cid" or "El Cid," which comes from the Arabic *sayyid* (lord) and was a common title of respect throughout the Muslim world. During his own lifetime, however, the title came to be specific to Rodrigo, superseding his given name.

Although El Cid led his forces against many Christian armies and had ample reason to defy Alfonso, he never abandoned his loyalty to the man he considered to be his sovereign lord, and he refused to do anything detrimental to Castile's interests. In fact, El Cid's only son, Diego, was to die tragically at Consuegra in 1097, fighting at Alfonso's side in the terrible defeat. Relations between Alfonso and El Cid were always uneasy, but, faced with the greatest threat to the peninsula since the first Moorish invasion in 711, El Cid and the king met in Toledo in December, 1086, or January, 1087, to discuss the growing Almoravid problem. Headed by Yusuf ibn Tashufin and centered in Morocco, the Almoravids were religious zealots who by 1086 ruled a vast empire. The established taifas of Moorish Spain considered the Almoravids little better than barbarians. Alfonso, needing a buffer between his kingdom and the fanatical newcomers, pardoned El Cid and granted him possession of all the lands which he might gain by force of arms in the Levant.

The great prize was Valencia, the rich Moorish city coveted by everyone. Al-Qadir, its weak leader, was under Alfonso's protection. Therefore, when threatened by an internal revolt, he appealed to El Cid and his ally al-Musta'in for aid. Once in command of Valencia, however, al-Musta'in himself decided to claim the city, and El Cid was forced to fight against his former employer. Meanwhile, threatened Moorish emirs in other cities had persuaded Yusuf to intervene personally. Yusuf complied but soon left in disgust at the infighting between the Moorish factions. He returned in 1090 determined not only to humble the Christians but to scourge the taifas themselves of their decadence and godlessness. The Spanish Moors then realized too late that their only hope lay in cooperation and partnership with the Christian states. One by one the taifas fell; in Valencia, Almoravid rebels, encouraged by the news of the advancing army, murdered al-Qadir and took control of the city. After months of fruitless negotiations, El Cid placed his army between Yusuf's and the city walls and opened up the irrigation canals to flood the fields. The Almoravids, afraid to fight their formidable opponent under these conditions, retreated. Weakened by twenty months of siege, Valencia finally surrendered, and on June 15, 1094, El Cid took possession of the city. El Cid tried to govern the Moorish inhabitants fairly, but immediately set about the task of converting Valencia into a Christian outpost, even inviting the Cluniac bishop Jerome to establish a Catholic see. Installed in his fortified city, El Cid finally felt secure enough to send for his wife and children.

This newfound sense of security was brief: Yusuf attacked again. El Cid, seeing his forces badly outnumbered, decided to take the enemy by surprise. On October 25, 1094, he led his men out of the city in darkness; attacking at dawn, El Cid became the first military leader, Christian or Moor, to defeat the Almoravid army in the field. Though he had achieved a stunning victory, during the last years of his life challenges continued to arise. His most incredible victory may have been the battle at Játiva in 1097. Trapped between towering cliffs and the Moorish army on one side and the sea and the Moorish fleet on another, with part of his army fleeing in panic, El Cid managed to rally the rest by the sheer force of his will and routed the enemy. The coast was awash with the Moorish dead who had drowned trying to reach the safety of their ships.

In 1099, Rodrigo de Vivar died unexpectedly. A French chronicle comments: "His death caused the most profound sorrow in Christendom and great joy among the pagan enemies." He died in the knowledge that by his own strength and skill he had risen from obscurity to power. Shortly before his death, he had seen his daughters, María and Cristina, married into the royal families of Navarre and Catalonia.

Without El Cid, Valencia could not hold out for long. In 1101, the Almoravids laid siege to the city for seven months. Alfonso, in response to Jimena's cry for help, lifted the siege, but, realizing that it would be impossible to defend the city, ordered its destruction and abandonment. The Christians returned to Castile, bringing El Cid's body to be buried in the Monastery of San Pedro de Cardeña. It would take them 130 years to regain Valencia.

Summary

El Cid, even during his lifetime, personified the hopes and aspirations of his people. Neither a powerful Moorish army nor an unjust Christian king could stop him in his path to glory. Personifying the ideal of the lone individual who conquers by force of will and persistence, his life became a symbol, the fit subject for an epic poem. Unlike the typical legendary hero, however, he was a man of flesh and blood, and even *The Poem of the Cid* never treats him as other than that. The poem celebrates the virtues and qualities of a very human man.

El Cid's life was a harsh one. He had had to earn his bread by luck and the strength of his sword. His faults are well documented. He was ambitious and could be cruel and ruthless, but he was also capable of great loyalty. In concrete military terms, he saved the peninsula from being overrun by the Almoravids and gave the Christian forces time to regroup. He also seems to have been one of the few who, rising above the multitudinous petty dissensions and political divisions, saw Spain, both Muslim and Christian, as a single entity worthy to defend. He used all of his skill as diplomat and legal expert to further that end. This rare concept of national unity and loyalty can be seen in his unwavering allegiance to Alfonso.

The aptest compliment paid to him may be found in the words of an enemy. Ibn Bassam, an Arab chronicler, rejoiced at the news of El Cid's death and cited examples of his cruelty and ambition, yet added, "Although this man was the scourge of his times, yet he must also be accounted, by virtue of his restless and clear-sighted energy, his manly strength of character, and his heroic courage, one of God's great miracles."

Bibliography

Crow, John A. *Spain, the Root and the Flower: A History of the Civilization of Spain and the Spanish People*. New York: Harper and Row, Publishers, 1963. An impressionistic history of Spain which contains a discussion of the values underlying El Cid's elevation to national hero.

MacKay, Angus. *Spain in the Middle Ages: From Frontier to Empire, 1000-1500*. New York: St. Martin's Press, 1977. Contains good background information on the civil wars that preceded El Cid's exile.

O'Callaghan, Joseph F. *A History of Medieval Spain*. Ithaca, N.Y.: Cornell University Press, 1975. Interesting in its use of contemporary chronicles, not only peninsular, as source material.

Read, Jan. *The Moors in Spain and Portugal*. London: Faber and Faber, 1974. Told from the Moorish point of view, Read's history makes use of many Arabic sources and includes a fine chapter on El Cid.

Smith, Colin. Introduction and notes in *Poema de mio Cid*. Oxford: Clarendon Press, 1972. Contains perhaps the definitive edition of the epic poem as well as an exhaustive introduction, a bibliography, and historical footnotes.

Charlene E. Suscavage

CIMABUE
Bencivieni di Pepo

Born: c. 1240; Florence
Died: c. 1302; Florence
Area of Achievement: Art
Contribution: Cimabue introduced a more naturalistic depiction of the human body in medieval painting and is commonly regarded as a transition figure between the relatively stiff Byzantine mode and the freer style that evolved in Italy during the fourteenth century.

Early Life

Almost nothing is known of the early life of Cimabue, whose real name was apparently Bencivieni di Pepo. Cimabue, or "Oxhead," is a nickname of unknown significance. The meager facts of Cimabue's life and career are recorded in various documents and narratives, mostly in Italian, dating back as far as Cimabue's lifetime. Ernst Benkard's *Das literarische Porträt des Giovanni Cimabue* (1917; the literary portrait of Giovanni Cimabue) and the research of Karl Frey form the basis for examination of Cimabue's life, and a synopsis of this work is given in the first two appendixes of Alfred Nicholson's *Cimabue: A Critical Study* (1932).

A few years after Cimabue's death, the poet Dante wrote:

> In painting Cimabue thought to hold
> The field; now hath Giotto all the cry,
> So that the other's fame is less extolled.

Several later commentators also mention Cimabue in connection with Giotto. Lorenzo Ghiberti's *Commentarii* (c. 1447; commentaries) tells of how Cimabue came upon the youthful shepherd boy Giotto as he was drawing sheep on a rock, inviting Giotto to become his student. Sixteenth century writers, especially Antonio Billi, continued to associate Cimabue with Giotto. Giovanni Battista Gelli referred to Cimabue's "Greek" style and called him Italy's first indigenous painter.

Although later scholars have rejected many of Giorgio Vasari's attributions of paintings to Cimabue, his famous study, *Le vite de' più eccellenti architetti, pittori, et scultori italiani* (1549-1550; *Lives of the Most Eminent Painters, Sculptors, and Architects*, 1850-1907), gives the fullest account of Cimabue's accomplishments. Vasari relates that the young Cimabue was sent to the convent of Santa Maria Novella in Florence to study literature, but the boy spent all of his time sketching men, horses, and houses. The city fathers at that time had hired numerous Greek painters to renew the art of painting, and as they worked on the chapel near Santa Maria Novella, Cimabue would escape from school and watch the painting. His passion for painting—and obvious aptitude—led his father to withdraw him from school and put him in the service of the Greek painters. Vasari's comment sums up the basis for Cimabue's enduring reputation in art history:

> From this time he labored incessantly, and was so far aided by his natural powers, that he soon greatly surpassed his teachers both in design and coloring. For these masters, caring little for the progress of art, had executed their works as we now see them, not in the excellent manner of the ancient Greeks, but in the rude modern style of their own day. Wherefore, though Cimabue imitated his Greek instructors, he very much improved the art, relieving it greatly from their uncouth manner, and doing honour to his country by the name he acquired, and by the works which he performed.

Life's Work

According to Vasari's account, Cimabue's career began with several much-appreciated paintings in Florence, including the altar of Santa Cecilia, a Virgin Mary on one of the pilasters at Santa Croce, a panel depicting Saint Francis surrounded by twenty small pictures on a gold background, and a large Madonna with angels for the abbey of Santa Trinita. For the front of the hospital of the Porcellana he did a fresco with life-size figures of the Virgin, Jesus Christ, and Luke. Vasari praises the innovative realism of this fresco and Cimabue's imaginative advance beyond the rules of the Greek painters.

Vasari then cites a colossal crucifix painted by Cimabue for the church of Santa Croce, an execution so praised that Cimabue was requested to complete some works in Pisa. His Pisan works brought him such renown that he was invited to Assisi to paint the roof and walls of the church of Saint Francis. Vasari lauds the work at Assisi as "truly great and rich, and most admirably executed," adding that private affairs called Cimabue back to Florence before the work was finished and that Giotto completed it many years later.

After his return to Florence, Cimabue worked on the cloister of Santo Spirito and then is said to have painted a picture of the Virgin for the church of Santa Maria Novella, a work known as the Rucellai *Madonna*, because it was suspended next to the Rucellai family chapel. Modern scholars, however, attribute this work to the Sienese painter Duccio di Buoninsegna, not Cimabue. Yet, according to Vasari, "it was carried in solemn procession, with the sound of trumpets and other festal demonstrations, from the house of Cimabue to the church, he himself being highly rewarded and honoured for it."

As a result of the fame he had acquired, Cimabue was appointed, along with the artist Arnolfo Lapi, to direct the construction of Santa Maria del Fiore in Florence. Without further narration, Vasari relates that "at length" Cimabue died in Florence, leaving behind many disciples, most notably Giotto.

Summary

The life recounted by Vasari is brief, and, in addition to the Rucellai *Madonna*, many other works he ascribes to Cimabue have been challenged by more recent scholars. Of the very few works attributed with confidence to Cimabue, the *Madonna Enthroned* that he painted for the Church of San Francesco in Pisa is judged one of his greatest. Napoleon Bonaparte appropriated it from Pisa as a prize of war, and it now hangs in the Louvre in Paris. It was painted at about the same time as the similar Rucellai *Madonna*, circa 1285, and its merits and its relationship to the Rucellai *Madonna* are still debated by scholars. The principles involved in these debates are of such intimidating nicety as to discourage participation by all but the boldest and most self-confident critics.

Nicholson provides an authoritative summation of Cimabue's genius and influence:

> He developed his peculiar idiom to its logical conclusion, and few could have approached the height of his argument. Moreover, the time was ripe for a closer observation and portrayal of man's common inheritance—the earthly and obvious. Thus the change for which the Romanized Giotto was so greatly responsible was both fortunate and inevitable. And though this by no means adequately explains the aesthetic greatness of Giotto's art, it does much to explain its immediate popularity. But it was the overwhelmingly stimulating influence of Cimabue's accomplishment which must have incited his late contemporaries, especially Giotto, to excel in other ways.

Bibliography

Battisti, Eugenio. *Cimabue*. University Park: Pennsylvania State University Press, 1967. Translated from the Italian, this work provides an overview of Cimabue's life and work.

Berenson, Bernhard. "A Newly Discovered Cimabue." In *Studies in Medieval Painting*. New Haven, Conn.: Yale University Press, 1930. A rather breathless account of a triptych that Berenson—the doyen of art history and criticism at the time—ascribed to Cimabue.

Canaday, John. *The Lives of the Painters*. 4 vols. London: Thames and Hudson, 1969. A popular account of its topic. The first volume discusses Cimabue briefly and places him in the context of medieval art.

Crowe, J. A., and G. B. Cavalcaselle. *A History of Painting in Italy, Umbria, Florence, and Sienna from the Second to the Sixteenth Century*. 2d ed. 6 vols. London: John Murray, 1903-1914. A reliable history of the Italian tradition in painting.

Nicholson, Alfred. *Cimabue: A Critical Study*. Princeton, N.J.: Princeton University Press, 1932. Reprint. New York: Kennikat Press, 1972. An excellent, thorough study, replete with illustrations.

Previtali, Giovanni. *Early Italian Painting*. New York: McGraw-Hill Book

Co., 1964. A slender volume in McGraw-Hill's Color Slide Program of the World's Art. The discussions are brief but informative, and there are twenty-four accompanying slides—one of Cimabue—to put the whole topic into its proper visual context.

Van Marle, Raimond. *The Development of the Italian Schools of Painting*. 19 vols. The Hague: Martinus Nijhoff, 1923-1938. A scholarly and reliable history.

Vasari, Giorgio. *Lives of the Most Eminent Painters, Sculptors, and Architects*. Translated by Mrs. Jonathan Foster. London: George Bell, 1878. The famous history that was originally published in the mid-sixteenth century.

Frank Day

CIMON

Born: c. 510 B.C.; place unknown
Died: c. 451 B.C.; near Citium (modern Larnaca), Cyprus
Areas of Achievement: Politics and warfare
Contribution: Through skillful military leadership and diplomacy, Cimon became an important force behind the establishment of the Delian League—a Greek alliance against the Persians—and its later transformation into the Athenian Empire. Domestically, he struggled unsuccessfully against the further extension of democracy in ancient Athens.

Early Life

As the oldest child of Miltiades the Younger, the victor of the Battle of Marathon, and Hegesipyle, the daughter of King Olorus of Thrace, Cimon inherited the political leadership and influence of one of the most ancient and respected aristocratic families in Athens, the Philaidae clan. He received a traditional Athenian education, emphasizing simple literacy skills and athletic prowess, as opposed to the stress upon rhetoric and speculative philosophy which would prevail in later generations. As a youth, however, Cimon disappointed his fellow clan members and other Philaidae supporters by his dissolute behavior. His riotous living and heavy drinking recalled to Athenian minds the infamous conduct of his grandfather and namesake, Cimon, nicknamed *koalemos* (the "nincompoop"). The younger Cimon's irresponsible attitudes threatened to cast the Philaidae clan into obscurity in an Athenian political arena where familial relationships and alliances counted for much in the competition for power.

Although Cimon possessed the personal assets essential to successful political leadership—high intelligence and an impressive physical appearance—he also entered manhood in the 480's with crippling liabilities. His father's conviction in 489 for "deceiving the people" had cast disrepute upon the Philaidae, while responsibility for the enormous fine imposed at the trial impoverished Cimon for several years after Miltiades' death. Inability to provide a dowry for his beautiful sister, Elpinice, forced him to support her in his own household under circumstances which incited rumors of incestuous relations. (Ancient and modern historians have debated the nature of Cimon's relationship with Elpinice. Many believe that she was his half-sister, and thereby, appropriately married to Cimon under Athenian law and custom, which allowed such unions.) Cimon's hopes for a successful political career appeared dim.

Persia's invasion of Greece in 480 thrust Cimon into the limelight and decidedly reversed his political fortunes. When the Persian King Xerxes I invaded Attica and threatened Athens, the city's leaders had difficulty persuading the populace to adhere to the previously agreed-upon strategy: evacuation of noncombatants and concentration of military resources and personnel with the fleet in the Bay of Salamis. Cimon resolved to set an example for the young aristocrats who traditionally formed the small, Athenian cavalry contingent. He led his comrades up to the Acropolis, where he was the first to dedicate his horse's bridle on the altar of Athena. Seizing a shield from the wall of the sanctuary, he then joined the fleet at Salamis as a simple hoplite. His actions inspired his fellow Athenians. After fighting courageously at the subsequent Battle of Salamis, Cimon emerged a hero from the Great Persian War. He was not slow to utilize his refurbished reputation.

Life's Work

About 480, Cimon was married to Isodice, an Athenian woman from the Alcmaeonidae clan. This marriage produced at least three sons: twins, Lakedaimonios and Oulios, and Thettalos. According to some ancient sources, Cimon also had three other sons—Cimon, Miltiades, and Peisianax—although most modern historians are skeptical of the existence of these children. Marriage to Isodice promised important political advantages, yet Cimon also loved her passionately, and the depth of his devotion to her was unusual enough to induce comment from contemporary observers and ancient historians.

Shortly after his own marriage, Cimon was able to find a husband for Elpinice. She was betrothed to Callias of Alopeke, a member of the Hipponikos clan and the richest man in Athens. This new brother-in-law assisted Cimon in paying his father's fine and recouping the Philaidae clan's finances. More important, the marriages of Cimon and Elpinice forged an alliance between three of the most politically important clan-factions in Athens: the Philaidae, Alcmaeonidae, and Hipponikos. This coalition may have been directed against Themistocles, who had emerged from the Great Persian War as the leading Athenian politician; his skilled courting of the populace engendered defensive reactions from fellow aristocrats.

Although Cleisthenes of Athens had instituted democratic reforms to the Athenian constitution, aristocratic clan-factions, especially those based in Athens itself, still exerted considerable influence over the city's political life. Because payment for public officials was as yet unknown in Athens, only men of independent financial means could spare the time and energy necessary to state service. Ordinary Athenian voters tended to coalesce around aristocratic leaders, who could assist them with financial and judicial problems. In the 470's and 460's, Cimon was especially renowned for his skillful use of this "politics of largesse," that is, the disbursement of monetary and commodity gratuities in the hope of securing votes.

Changes in Athenian constitutional practices during the 480's strengthened aristocratic influences on government. The prestige of the Areopagus—a judicial-administrative body composed of former archons drawn from the upper classes—increased during the Persian War because of its skilled handling of the crisis. Moreover, the decision in 488/487 to select archons by lot actually enhanced the ability of the aristocracy to direct Athenian politics, because consequently the *strategoi* (board of generals) increasingly assumed leadership of the Assembly and the Council of Five Hundred. Unlike the archons, the *strategoi* could be elected to office consecutively and as many times as possible. During the 470's and 460's, aristocratic defenders of the status quo, such as Cimon and Aristides, served as *strategoi* for years, dominating Athenian foreign policy and influencing domestic developments.

These years also witnessed the establishment of the Delian League, an alliance between Athens and numerous Ionian and Aegean city-states, by which continuous war was vigorously pursued against the Persian Empire. In the 470's, Cimon's fair treatment of Athens' allies in the League spread his fame over the Greek world and ensured for him perennial command of major military expeditions. Between 476 and 469, he expelled the renegade Spartan commander Pausanias from Byzantium, seized Eion on the Strymon River from the Persians, and conquered Scyros from Dolopian pirates and colonized it with Athenians. During the latter expedition, Cimon discovered and transported to Athens the supposed bones of Theseus, the mythical founder of the Athenian state, an act which fulfilled an ancient oracle and won for him great applause.

Cimon's finest military achievement, however, took place at the mouth of the Eurymedon River around 468. There, utilizing a self-designed trireme which accommodated a greater number of hoplites, Cimon destroyed a large Persian fleet and defeated an accompanying army on land. A Phoenician fleet sailing to reinforce the Persians was similarly devastated by the new triremes. Cimon had brought Athens and the League to the pinnacle of success. Persian presence in the Aegean, in Ionia, and on the shores of southern Asia Minor had been obliterated. Cimon's foreign policy—peace with Sparta and other Greeks and concentration on the traditional Persian enemy—had proved its value.

The leader of the Philaidae, nevertheless, teetered dangerously on the brink of political disaster, as his tremendous success had aroused the jealousies of aristocratic rivals. Following Cimon's successful siege of Thasos—a city-state which had attempted to secede from the Delian League—and his conquest of the Persian-occupied Chersonese, he was brought to trail for allegedly accepting a bribe from Alexander I of Macedon not to attack his territory. Although Cimon was acquitted, the charge was an ominous portent of difficulties to come: The accusation had been brought by a young Pericles and other aristocrats, intent upon further democratizing the Athenian state to their own political advantage.

During the trial, Cimon had convincingly pleaded his incorruptibility by citing his long tenure as *proxenos* (a Greek who officially represented the interests of another city-state to his fellow citizens) for Sparta, whose citizens were known for their self-imposed poverty and inability to provide large monetary rewards for services rendered. Cimon's admiration for Spartan culture and military institutions was well-known to his fellow Athenians, but previously his loyalty to his own city-state had gone unquestioned. Worsening relations between Athens and Sparta would soon cast suspicion upon Cimon and his pro-Spartan foreign policy and thereby wreck his political career.

By the late 460's, an earlier spirit of cooperation and friendship between Athens and Sparta, proceeding from the Persian War, had been replaced by fear and hostility. The tremendous growth of Athens' power—realized through the gradual conversion of the Delian League into an Athenian Empire—was largely responsible for this change. The Spartans so greatly resented Athenian usurpation of their traditional leadership role in Greece that they promised Thasos an invasion of Attica to support the Thasian secession attempt. Before the Spartans were able to execute their plan, however, Laconia was struck by a severe earthquake and a widespread helot (serf) rebellion. Sparta was forced to call upon other Greek cities, including Athens, for aid.

Among the Athenians, the debate over aid to Sparta grew acrimonious. The so-called democratic party, led by Ephialtes, strongly opposed assisting the Spartans, regarding them as dangerous rivals. Cimon, on the other hand, argued that abandoning the Spartans would weaken all Greece, while he referred to Sparta as Athens' "yoke-fellow." In the end, his position prevailed, because the Athenians had not yet learned of Spartan complicity in the Thasian revolt. In 462, Cimon led a large Athenian army into Laconia to assist in the suppression of the helots.

With Cimon away on this expedition, Ephialtes and Pericles moved to weaken the foundations of conservative rule in Athens. They began by bringing forth accusations of malfeasance against prominent members of the Areopagus. Meanwhile, in Laconia, Cimon and his army suffered the ignominy of a curt dismissal by the Spartans, who probably feared that progressive Athenian political ideas would exacerbate Sparta's current problems with subject peoples. When Cimon returned to Athens, he faced the wrath of prideful Athenians, distrustful of Sparta and humiliated by the recent events in Laconia. With emotions running high against the Spartans, Cimon's admiration for them appeared treasonous to many Athenians. In 461, he was ostracized, a formal, political procedure by which leaders considered dangerous to Athens were exiled for ten years. In Cimon's absence, Ephialtes and Pericles stripped the Areopagus of nearly all of its judicial and administrative powers and strengthened those of the Assembly, the Council of Five Hundred, and the law courts. Athens had entered the final, radical phase of democratization.

With Cimon in exile and his pro-Spartan policies thoroughly discredited, relations between Athens and Sparta deteriorated. In 459, war broke out between the two cities and their allies. This conflict, known as the First Peloponnesian War, lasted until 445. Initially, the Athenians enjoyed success, despite the fact that the war with Persia continued in Cyprus and Egypt, and necessitated the dispersal of Athens' resources over several theaters of action. In 457, however, the Spartans and their allies counterattacked by invading central Greece and directly threatening to invade Attica.

The Athenians, Spartans, and their respective allies met at Tanagra, a small city in southern Boeotia. Athenian morale was low because of pervasive rumors of a pro-Spartan conspiracy by Cimon's supporters and other clan-factions against the new democratic state. Nevertheless, before the battle began, Cimon appeared fully armed and offered his services to the Athenian generals. Although suspicion of Cimon's motives caused his offer to be spurned, the leader of the Philaidae exhorted his friends and relatives along the Athenian battleline to give their greatest efforts to demonstrate their loyalty to Athens. In the subsequent battle, the Philaidae faction fought courageously, making up a disproportionate number of the Athenian dead. Sympathy for Cimon revived in Athens.

While Cimon's gift for political theatrics rejuvenated his public image, events elsewhere set the stage for his return to Athens. In 454, the large Athenian expeditionary force in Egypt was annihilated by the Persians. This reversal of fortunes incited several revolts against Athenian rule in Ionia and the Aegean. Cimon was recalled from exile as the statesman who could best attenuate Athens' overextended military commitments by making peace with Sparta. In 451, he returned to Athens and negotiated a five-year truce with the Spartans. In the next year, serving again as *strategos*, Cimon led an expedition to Cyprus, where he died while besieging Citium, fighting once again the Persians.

Summary

Although as fiercely competitive as any Greek aristocrat, Cimon was extraordinary in his dedication to principle and a loyalty to his city-state. By adhering to three policies—aristocratic predominance in Athenian democracy, peace and fair-dealing with fellow Greeks, and war against the Persians—he remained unusually consistent over a long career. His political style transcended the personal and clan rivalries which had structured Athenian politics for centuries and presaged a reshaping of political competition along ideological lines in the latter fifth and fourth centuries.

Bibliography

Burn, A. R. *Pericles and Athens*. London: English Universities Press, 1948. Contains useful material on the relationship between Cimon and Pericles.

Burn's depiction of Cimon as a myopic, obtuse conservative is overdrawn. It was Cimon, after all, not Pericles, who stressed Greek unity against the Persians, in anticipation of similar fourth century visions.

Kagan, Donald. *The Outbreak of the Peloponnesian War*. Ithaca, N.Y.: Cornell University Press, 1969. Serves well as an introduction to interstate relations in the Aegean and eastern Mediterranean worlds during the period of Cimon's career. Important chapters on Spartan and Athenian internal politics show the relationships between domestic developments in these city-states and the growth of hostility between them. May also be used as a guide to the ancient sources on Cimon and his times.

Laistner, M. L. W. *A History of the Greek World from 479 to 323 B.C.* 3d ed. London: Methuen, 1957. This introductory book should be consulted first by those unfamiliar with Cimon's era. It is also useful as a broad outline of ideological interpretations of Athenian politics after the Great Persian War.

McGregor, Malcolm F. *The Athenians and Their Empire*. Vancouver: University of British Columbia Press, 1987. Written especially for students and nonprofessional historians, this is a very useful introduction to its subject. Although lacking footnotes, the information is highly reliable. Numerous maps, appendices, charts, and a glossary of Greek political terminology make this volume required reading for beginners.

Meiggs, Russell. *The Athenian Empire*. Oxford: Clarendon Press, 1972. This is the standard, scholarly work on its subject, replete with footnotes which can be used to guide the reader to ancient sources. Also contains detailed discussions of the controversial issues surrounding the Athenian Empire.

Plutarch. *The Rise and Fall of Athens: Nine Greek Lives*. Translated by Ian Scott-Kilvert. Harmondsworth, England: Penguin Books, 1960. An adaptation of Plutarch's famous *Bioi parallēloi* (c. A.D. 105-115; *Parallel Lives*), this volume contains the biographies of nine important Athenians. Plutarch's "Life of Cimon," contained herein, is the most significant source of information on him and the place to start serious research. Use Plutarch only in conjunction with modern histories, however, because his love of a good story often led him to errors, which later historians have corrected.

Sealey, Raphael. *A History of the Greek City-States, c. 700-338 B.C.* Berkeley: University of California Press, 1976. Written by a prominent proponent of the prosopographical approach to Greek politics, that is, the concept that personal and familial relations overrode ideological issues in shaping events. Includes discussion of major aspects of Cimon's life and times, with ancient sources referenced. Most historians have not found Sealey's interpretation of Athenian politics in the era 480 to 450 to be persuasive, because ideology does seem to have structured political behavior much more clearly after the Great Persian War than before.

Thucydides. *The Peloponnesian War*. Translated and edited by Rex Warner.

Rev. ed. Harmondsworth, England: Penguin Books, 1972. Book 1 contains Thucydides' famous account of the period between the Great Persian War and the outbreak of the Second Peloponnesian War. While recounting the development of hostility between Athens and Sparta, Thucydides reveals much about the Athenian Empire and Cimon's role in its establishment and expansion.

Michael S. Fitzgerald

CLAUDIUS I

Born: August 1, 10 B.C.; Lugdunum, Gaul
Died: October 13, A.D. 54; Rome, Italy
Area of Achievement: Government
Contribution: Coming to power after the politically and financially devastating reign of Caligula, Claudius I completed the centralizing tendencies of Roman imperial government by creating a bureaucracy that was totally professional in training and totally loyal in its devotion to the imperial concept of government.

Early Life

Tiberius Claudius Drusus Nero Germanicus was born in Lugdunum, Gaul (modern Lyons, France), the youngest son of the Elder Drusus and Antonia Minor. Claudius' father was the stepson of the emperor Augustus and his mother was Augustus' niece. Despite such illustrious parentage, Claudius was never expected to hold any important government office or military post. Although his elder brother Germanicus was adopted into the imperial family by his uncle, the future emperor Tiberius, Claudius was not considered to be in line for the throne because he was physically handicapped. In an age when physical beauty and perfection were admired, he was an embarrassment to the imperial family.

Claudius' multiple handicaps and infirmities were readily apparent. He had weak knees, trembling hands, and a wobbly head; he dragged his right foot, walked with a limp, stuttered when he spoke, and drooled uncontrollably. Desiring to preserve an image of power and authority in the eyes of the Roman people, the imperial family kept Claudius' public appearances to a minimum. Although not permitted a career in government service, Claudius received an excellent education. As he grew older, he became more and more interested in historical studies and wrote numerous scholarly works on Roman, Etruscan, and Carthaginian history. In addition, he wrote an apology for Cicero and composed an autobiography. Not content to limit himself to historical work, Claudius studied philological problems of Latin and introduced three new letters into the Latin alphabet.

During the reigns of Augustus and Tiberius, Claudius continued to have little role in affairs of state. When his nephew Caligula ascended the throne, however, Claudius' life changed dramatically. In July, A.D. 37, Claudius became consul along with Caligula. Although consuls lacked any real power, they enjoyed considerable prestige. Still, such public recognition only made life more difficult for Claudius. Even though he was related to the reigning emperor, Claudius was the frequent butt of cruel jokes and insults, the ever-present, easy target for court jesters and practical jokers. Indeed, this was probably the most difficult and dangerous time of his life. To protect himself from the murderous whims of his mad nephew, Claudius endured the insults and played the fool. People were all too ready to believe him mentally as well as physically handicapped. The role of the simpleton was a convenient ruse which saved Claudius' life on more than one occasion.

Life's Work

When Caligula became so autocratic as to attempt the establishment of a Hellenistic-style monarchy, assassins killed him along with his wife and daughter. While searching the imperial palace, a soldier of the Praetorian Guard discovered Claudius hiding behind a curtain. After dragging Claudius to the Praetorian camp, the soldiers quickly realized the advantage to them of perpetuating the imperial system. Thus, the Praetorian Guard hailed Claudius emperor on January 25, A.D. 41, while the senate was still trying to decide what to do.

Despite the unusual circumstances of his coming to the throne, Claudius was not a revolutionary. He wasted no time in capturing and punishing the assassins of Caligula while simultaneously distancing himself from his predecessor's policies. As emperor, Claudius looked upon Augustus as his role model, following his lead in attempting to revive the traditional religious practices and political institutions of the Roman Republic. Despite his amicable overtures toward the senate, Claudius learned what Augustus had learned: The senate, never having renounced its claim to state leadership, was resentful of being dominated by an emperor. Claudius tried to show respect for the senate by giving back provinces that Tiberius had made imperial (Achaea and Macedonia), appointing imperial legates of senatorial rank, allowing the senate to issue copper coinage in the provinces, and enforcing senatorial resolutions. Despite all of his efforts at cooperation, the senate was not very receptive. Eventually, this lack of response led Claudius to work against the senate and to concentrate all the power of the government in his own hands.

After a lapse of sixty-eight years during which the office of censor had gone unoccupied, Claudius temporarily restored and held it for eighteen months in 47-48. As a result of his censorship, numerous old senatorial families were discredited and expelled from the senate, while many new provincial families were admitted. Imperial oversight of the senate also extended to those aspects of government which had been traditionally controlled by the senate. The *aerarium Saturni* and the *fiscus* were both brought under close imperial supervision through the imperial appointment or nomination of the officials who ran these treasuries.

Not able to rely upon the old senatorial aristocracy for administrative support, Claudius set himself the task of creating an executive staff manned by freedmen who were to be obedient only to the emperor. While freedmen had been used in government since the reign of Augustus, Claudius made more extensive use of them by placing them in charge of government departments and entrusting them with confidential tasks. This practice guaranteed the emperor's independence from the senate and antagonized the aristocratic elite of Rome. The freedmen Narcissus and Pallas became rich and powerful as Claudius' closest and most trusted advisers. With the establishment of a centralized administration directly under the emperor's control, Claudius was able to extend his jurisdiction into senatorial provinces.

At the same time, Claudius sought uniformity of administration and equal status for the provinces. Historically, Rome and Italy had enjoyed privileged positions within the empire, while the provinces' status had been inferior. Claudius tried to eliminate this inequality by extending citizenship rights to various provincial communities and by establishing Roman colonies, particularly in the newer imperial provinces such as Britain and Mauretania. This policy, while politically and militarily motivated, had the effect of quickening the pace of provincial Romanization.

Claudius was as aware as Augustus had been that the army was the real power base of the Roman government. Although he lacked military experience, Claudius needed to assume the image of a military leader and so was hailed *imperator* twenty-seven times. While not known in history for his military exploits, Claudius did expand the empire. Under Claudius, Rome conquered Mauretania in 41, Britain in 43, and Thrace in 46. In addition, Claudius established the province of Lycia in 43 and the province of Judaea in 44.

In an effort to improve communications and the movement of troops, Claudius instituted a great road-building program. Not only did these roads tie the provinces closer to Rome, but they also stimulated trade between and among the provinces. Whenever Claudius saw an opportunity to expand trade and commerce, he immediately improved area roads and port facilities and built warehouses. The level of trade within the empire and with foreign lands increased dramatically under Claudius.

Despite his emphasis on improving the economic condition of the provinces, Claudius did not neglect Italy, in general, or Rome, in particular. In central Italy, Claudius employed thirty thousand men for eleven years to drain the Fucine Marsh and reclaim much-needed arable land. What Julius Caesar and Augustus had only planned, Claudius accomplished. To increase the water supply of the capital, Claudius completed an aqueduct, begun by Caligula, which brought water to Rome from a distance of sixty-two miles; he also built the Aqua Claudia, which brought water from forty-five miles away. To guarantee Rome a secure supply of grain all year round, Claudius insured grain shippers against any loss so that they would continue to sail in the winter months. If a ship owner put his ships in the service of the grain trade for six years, he was granted full Roman citizenship. In order to handle the increased volume of trade, Claudius rebuilt the port of Ostia and built the new port of Portus, outfitting both ports with appropriate warehouses.

Keeping true to his Augustan ideals, Claudius tried to rekindle the old republican virtues through a religious restoration. By reviving ancient religious rites and linking them to Rome's glorious past, he tried to instill in the Romans of the empire both the patriotism and the religious belief of an earlier generation. Claudius founded a College of Haruspices and held the Secular Games for Rome's eight hundredth birthday. To keep the religion of Rome focused on the traditional gods, Claudius extended the *pomerium* (religious boundary) and expelled Jews from the city. Religion as practiced outside Rome, however, was a different matter. With the exception of Druidism (because of its practice of human sacrifice), religious practices indigenous to the provinces were allowed to flourish.

If Claudius had a failing, it was in his relationships with his wives. Despite marrying four times, Claudius was unable to achieve happiness with his wives. His first two marriages, to Plautia Urgulanilla and Aelia Paetina, ended in divorce. His marriage to Valeria Messalina produced two children, Octavia (who later married Nero) and Britannicus. Messalina was executed in 48 as a result of the intrigues of Narcissus. Claudius' fourth marriage was to his niece Agrippina, whose cause was championed by Pallas. Agrippina succeeded, in 50, in getting Claudius to adopt her son Nero (from an earlier marriage) as his heir and the guardian of his own son, Britannicus.

Having lived his early life as a scholarly historian, Claudius ended his days as a very involved ruler of one of the greatest empires in history. A dish of poisoned mushrooms offered to him by Agrippina was the cause of his death. Although Claudius had pulled Rome from the brink of chaos after the disastrous reign of Caligula, he did not show the same acumen in leaving Rome in the hands of Nero. While Nero was not as outrageous as Caligula, he proved to be such a major disappointment to the Romans that he was the last of the Julio-Claudians to rule.

Summary

Claudius, a man never intended to assume control of Rome, a man having symptoms of what may have been cerebral palsy, a man more comfortable in a scholar's library than in an emperor's palace, ruled and profoundly changed the Roman Empire. While trying to maintain an empire-wide approach to the administration of the empire, Claudius was, nevertheless, a major contributor to the evolution of a highly centralized and autocratic governmental administration.

Claudius' reforming tendencies and his emphasis on equality and justice show a basic contradiction in thinking. In trying to bring about equality by admitting provincials to the senate, Claudius was perpetuating the inequality of the old republican class structure. While honoring the senate in various ways, he actively worked to undermine it by creating an executive staff that guaranteed that all would be under the emperor's control. Thus, even though

Claudius was attempting new approaches to old problems, he was bound too closely to Augustan tradition to be a strong champion of the new ideals of his age.

Bibliography

Levick, B. M. "Antiquarian or Revolutionary? Claudius Caesar's Conception of his Principate." *American Journal of Philology* 99 (1978): 79-105. The author maintains that Claudius was not a disinterested observer of contemporary events before his accession to the throne. As a historian, Claudius developed his own ideas on how the imperial government should be organized. Levick believes that Claudius used Julius Caesar as his role model rather than Augustus.

Momigliano, Arnaldo D. *Claudius: The Emperor and His Achievement.* Cambridge: W. Heffer and Sons, 1934, rev. ed. 1961. Momigliano believes that Claudius modeled himself on Augustus and tried to find some common ground with the senate. The centralization of the imperial administration was the direct result of the senate's rejection of Claudius' offer of cooperation. Despite its brevity, this book is one of the seminal works on Claudius.

Scramuzza, Vincent M. *The Emperor Claudius*. Cambridge, Mass.: Harvard University Press, 1940. The first and only full-scale biography of Claudius to appear in English. The author has gathered and analyzed all the available archaeological, epigraphic, and literary evidence on the life of Claudius and has presented it in a most readable form. The coverage is comprehensive, thorough, and sound.

Scullard, H. H. *From the Gracchi to Nero: A History of Rome from 133 B.C. to A.D. 68*. New York: Frederick A. Praeger, 1959, 2d ed. 1963. Gives a straightforward account of Roman history during the last century of the Roman Republic and the first century of the Roman Empire. Scullard shows the financial and administrative problems caused by Gaius (Caligula) and the important changes that occurred under Claudius.

Suetonius. *The Twelve Caesars*. Revised and translated by Robert Graves. Harmondsworth, England: Penguin Books, 1957, rev. ed. 1979. Contains a chapter on Claudius, together with other chapters on his predecessors and successors. While Suetonius is one of the most important sources of information on Claudius, he is not always reliable. Still, he is useful because he preserves much contemporary detail which otherwise would be lost.

Peter L. Viscusi

CLEISTHENES OF ATHENS

Born: c. 570 B.C.; place unknown
Died: After 510 B.C.; place unknown
Areas of Achievement: Government and law
Contribution: The famous lawgiver and reformer Cleisthenes was the real architect of Athenian democracy. His statesmanship created radical innovations in the constitution: the representative principle and the idea of political equality.

Early Life

Cleisthenes was a son of the Athenian Megacles, a member of the illustrious Alcmaeonid family, and a non-Athenian, Agariste, daughter of Cleisthenes of Sicyon. Little is known of his personal life.

The Alcmaeonidae had been in exile during the tyranny of Peisistratus but regained favor by their generosity in the rebuilding of the temples, and the oracle of Delphi pressed upon the Spartan king, Cleomenes I, for their reinstatement. Hippias, the tyrant leader of Athens, was overthrown by the Spartans in 510 B.C., leaving Athens at the mercy of the powerful families.

Cleisthenes returned to Athens and realized that he would not be accepted as a leader of another oligarchy, nor would the people tolerate another tyranny. Cleisthenes did not covet personal power but wanted to benefit the city. Although the way seemed open for Athenian self-government, the problem of competing families or clans would have to be overcome. His initial attempt at reform met with aristocratic resistance. Cleisthenes had to retreat but returned after the opposition, Cleomenes and Isagoras, were forced out by the *demos*, that is, "the people."

Life's Work

Unlike Solon and Peisistratus, Cleisthenes did not work within the existing system but introduced a completely new scheme which he thought out in detail. He did not abolish or destroy existing institutions; instead, he insisted that the government function within the new plan. He systematically introduced into the constitution a well-coordinated and harmonic operation of government founded upon political equality of all the citizens and the representation and participation of all.

The age-old division of Attica into four tribes, each with three brotherhoods and ninety clans, based on blood, led to many conflicts of loyalties. Cleisthenes' objective was to direct Athenian loyalty to the community. A long period of time would seem necessary for this transfer of loyalty, but Cleisthenes brought the transfer very quickly. He developed an artificial plan for public loyalty.

Cleisthenes' basic plan abolished the four ancient tribes and created ten new ones in their place. He also persuaded the god Apollo to tell him after what legendary heroes he was to name them. The new tribes represented national, not local, interests and unity. The marketplace of Athens had a statue of each tribal hero. Each tribe also had its own shrine and its own hero cult but was not controlled by a particular family or local group.

Cleisthenes was able to destroy the old territorial loyalties of the Coast, the Plain, and the Hill. Before Cleisthenes' reform, the adult citizen population was 10,800. After the changes introduced by Cleisthenes, fifth century Athens numbered between twenty thousand and thirty thousand citizens.

To take the place of the old ship districts, Cleisthenes created a new unit of local government called the *deme*, or village. More than one hundred such villages were established, divided into ten groups to correspond with the ten tribes. Membership in the *deme* was made hereditary, and a family maintained its name wherever it moved. Blood ties were weakened, because one was now recognized as "Cleisthenes of Athens," for example, rather than as "son of Megacles." This artificial arrangement separated and weakened the authority of strong families and encouraged the enrollment of new citizens. The old, established aristocracy, with its agricultural concerns, would gradually have to share its influence with the seafaring commercial population of the coast.

Each of the ten tribes was made up of three *trittyes* (thirds), and the *trittyes* of *demes*. The *deme* corresponded geographically to a district of the city and was the local administrative unit. Membership in the *deme* guaranteed citizenship. The *trittyes* were divided into three geographical groups—coastal, inland, and city—and each tribe contained one from each group. The city itself had six *demes* in five different tribes, and the other five tribes were in the suburbs and the coast.

The Athenians were mistrustful of entrenched representatives or experts; they preferred that the government be run by intelligent amateurs. According to Athenians, the person of ordinary intelligence was capable of political responsibility. Thus, the people were the supreme authority and gave in the Assembly their vote to all acts. All business was discussed prior to the assembly in the Boule, or Council, and passed on to the Assembly for ratification. The Council was composed of five hundred members elected annually, fifty from each tribe. Each *deme*, according to the number of citizens on its rolls, elected candidates for the Council, and from these candidates, Council members were elected by lot, fifty being selected from each tribe. The Council was divided into ten committees, one of which was on duty for the tenth part of each year. This committee of fifty members, called a *prytany*, held office for a tenth of the year under a chairman who sat for one day and was chosen by lot. He was acting head of the government and had the keys to the Acropolis, the state seal, and the archives. He could not be reelected. Part of the prytany remained on duty day and night, eating and sleeping in the Tholos, a round building provided for this purpose. The Council prepared matters for the Assembly and was also responsible for fiscal policy, receiving an account from all civil officials leaving office.

Cleisthenes established ostracism in a systematic manner as a safeguard against conflict. The Assembly voted once a year whether to have an ostracism. An affirmative vote meant that each member would write on a piece of pottery, *ostrakon*, the member he would like to see exiled. The person who received the most votes, six thousand or more, went into honorable exile for a period of ten years without loss of property. This measure may well have been a deterrent in neutralizing opposition; there is no record of its being used until 487 B.C., after Cleisthenes' time.

Legislative powers were in the *ecclesia*, or assembly that discussed and passed laws. Judicial authority was with the *heliaea*, the court of popular representatives, elected by the tribes in the same manner as the council. Judicial functions were controlled by people's juries, selected from an annual panel of six thousand citizens chosen by lot from the same units.

The magistrates, the nine archons, and the *colacietae* and *strategoi* were elected from among the wealthier citizens. The former were concerned with finance; the latter commanded ten companies of militia. This organization may have been reasonable, since the state did not pay citizens in discharging their public duties.

Each tribe supported a regiment of infantry and a squadron of cavalry who were commanded by elective officers, called *taxiarchi* and *hipparchi*. Each of the ten *strategoi* commanded the army in turn. The army was similar to a national militia. Cleisthenes, however, did not reform the navy.

Summary

The constitution of Cleisthenes of Athens was put into effect in 502 B.C. While it did not end the conflict between parties or the unequal distribution of wealth, it did mitigate many of the problems. The government was no longer something external or alien but identified with the life and goals of each citizen. At the time of Cleisthenes' death, the *demes* were the real rulers of Athens, although they were led by the aristocracy. Cleisthenes created a strong and well-organized state and constitution. At the end of the Peloponnesian War there was a brief oligarchic reaction, but Cleisthenes' reforms were restored in 403 B.C.

Cleisthenes is credited with the complete breakdown of the patriarchal idea of the state as a corporation. It was never restored in Athens. He established new tribes, enrolled aliens as new citizens, and contributed to the idea of free communication and interchange between different peoples. This idea, together with the principles of representation and of political equality, strengthened democracy.

Bibliography

Aristotle. *The Athenian Constitution*. Translated by P. J. Rhodes. New York: Penguin Books, 1984. Contains the great philosopher's brief history and description of the Athenian state with a helpful commentary. This 208-page work is an essential source for the workings of Cleisthenes' constitution. Aristotle provides a good introduction to study of Cleisthenes.

Davis, J. K. *Democracy and Classical Greece*. Stanford, Calif.: Stanford University Press, 1978. This study is the clearest reexamination of the present state of knowledge about democratic ideas in Athens. It emphasizes archaeological evidence in social and political history.

Ehrenberg, Victor. *From Solon to Socrates: Greek History and Civilization During the Sixth and Fifth Centuries B.C.* New York: Methuen, 1973. An excellent illustrated political textbook on the central period of Greek history during the sixth and fifth centuries B.C. Contains good references to primary and secondary sources.

Forrest, William G. *The Emergence of Greek Democracy, 800-400 B.C.* New York: McGraw-Hill Book Co., 1966. This work is a clear, lively interpretation of the reforms of Cleisthenes and provides a general account of his time. It is written in an interesting style and describes the social and political developments and the transition from aristocracy to democracy in Athens. The notes are especially good.

Highnett, Charles. *A History of the Athenian Constitution to the End of the Fifth Century B.C.* Oxford: Clarendon Press, 1967. Scholarly treatment of the development of the Athenian constitution, discussing its successive phases of growth from the early monarchy and aristocracy to the decline of the Athenian empire. An important and thought-provoking analysis of the beginnings of Athenian democracy.

Larsen, Jakob A. O. "Cleisthenes and the Development of the Theory of Democracy at Athens." In *Essays in Political Theory Presented to George H. Sabine*, edited by Milton R. Konvitz and Arthur E. Murphy. Ithaca, N.Y.: Cornell University Press, 1948. A discussion of the early characteristics of Athenian democracy. Particularly good for insights into the Greek political mind.

Staveley, E. S. *Greek and Roman Voting and Elections*. Ithaca, N.Y.: Cornell University Press, 1972. This study illuminates many practices in the Athenian government and the spirit of public service over several centuries.

Zimmern, Alfred. *The Greek Commonwealth: Politics and Economics in Fifth Century Athens*. 5th ed. New York: Oxford University Press, 1961. This classic work presents an interesting analysis of fifth century Athens but lacks an adequate bibliography. Important aspects of Cleisthenes' career and the cultural background of this period are discussed.

Peter F. Macaluso

CLEMENT I

Born: Date unknown; perhaps Rome
Died: c. 99; perhaps in the Crimea
Area of Achievement: Religion
Contribution: Clement was the first of the Apostolic Fathers about whom anything is known and, according to tradition, was the third successor to Peter as Bishop of Rome. Clement was also the author of the earliest and most valuable surviving example of Christian literature not included in the New Testament.

Early Life

Of the life of Clement very little is known with absolute certainty. He is called Clement of Rome (Clemens Romanus) to distinguish him from the later Clement of Alexandria (Clemens Alexandrinus). No reliable source gives even the approximate date or place of his birth. An early Christian work attributed to him entitled *Recognitions* (third century) states that he was born in the city of Rome and that he was from his early youth given to meditating and sober reflection on such serious subjects as the nature of life, whether there was a preexistence, and the possibility of immortality. According to that work, he was converted to Christianity by the disciple Barnabas, who came to Rome to preach and thereafter introduced him to Peter, who received him with great joy.

Such a story is not inconsistent with other information now known about Clement. Nevertheless, true authorship of *Recognitions* cannot be ascribed to Clement himself, since most scholars believe that it was penned more than a century after his time. Despite this doubt, however, the work is not completely without value; indeed, it seems to preserve traditions which contain some kernels of truth.

Undoubtedly, Clement was a younger contemporary of Peter and Paul. The early church scholars and theologians Origen (c. 185-254), Eusebius of Caesarea (c. 260-339), Epiphanius (c. 315-403), and Jerome (331-420) all identify Clement of Rome as the Clement spoken of in Philippians 4:3. This Scripture calls him Paul's fellow laborer. Similarly, Irenaeus (c. 120-202) states that Clement saw the Apostles and talked with them, that their preaching was so fresh in his mind at the time he rose to prominence that it still rang in his ears, and that many of Clement's generation had been taught personally by the Apostles. Clement himself intimates that he was closely associated with Peter and Paul.

Clement was probably of Jewish descent. His close association with the Apostles, who were all Jewish, and his wide use of and familiarity with the Old Testament, as demonstrated in the one surviving authentic Clementine work, lend support to this inference. Clement's style of writing is colored with Hebraisms but he probably possessed no real understanding of Hebrew, knowing only the Septuagint (Greek) translation of the Old Testament as many Jews of the day did.

An ancient tradition identifies Clement with a certain Flavius Clemens, a distinguished Roman nobleman who held the office of consul in 95 and was the nephew of the emperor Vespasian. It is difficult to believe that the same man held both the consulship and the bishopric, since these times were difficult ones for the Church because of Roman antagonism.

It is also unlikely that the Hellenistic Jewish style of Clement's epistle would be as prominent if Clement came from the Roman classical culture of a court circle. It is more likely, then, that the future church leader was a freedman or former slave belonging to the house of Clemens and that in accordance with custom he assumed the name of his patron when fully liberated.

Life's Work

At some point in his life, Clement became a leader in the Roman church and was ultimately ordained bishop of that Christian community about the year 90. While Tertullian, writing about 199, says that Clement was ordained by Peter before the Apostle's death (c. 64), other ancient, reliable authorities state that Clement was preceded by two other successors to Peter (Linus and Anacletus) and thus was the fourth Bishop of Rome. Clement's fame rests on both his designation as the first known Apostolic Father and his authorship of the epistle to the Corinthian church.

The expression "Apostolic Fathers" seems to have been used first by Severus of Antioch, Patriarch of Alexandria in the sixth century and scholar of early Christian literature. The phrase referred to those who were not Apostles but disciples of the Apostles and who authored writings contemporaneous with or prior to those of Irenaeus in the second century. The Apostolic Fathers, then, were the earliest orthodox writers outside the New Testament. Clement was the first, chronologically, of this group, which includes Ignatius of Antioch, Polycarp, Barnabas, and Hermas. *Klementos pros Korinthious epistola prōtē* (first century A.D.; *The First Epistle of Clement to the Corinthians*, also known as *First Clement*) is the earliest extant Christian document outside the New Testament.

The epistle to the Corinthians was Clement's most important achievement. Although Clement's name is not mentioned in the letter, he seems to have been from the first recognized as its author. About 170, Dionysius, Bishop of Corinth, while acknowledging another letter written from the church of Rome to the church of Corinth, mentions that the letter written by Clement was still read from time to time in their Sunday assemblies. Eusebius also speaks of the epistle to the Corinthians as being Clement's, as do Irenaeus, Origen, and Clement of Alexandria.

Clement wrote his epistle sometime after he became Bishop of Rome, though the exact date of its composition is not known. The second century Christian historian Hegesippus, who visited the Corinthian church on a trip to Rome, learned that the letter was written during the reign of Domitian (81-96). If one considers an allusion which Clement makes in the epistle to the persecutions of Christians which took place at Rome under Domitian in 93, the date of the epistle can be narrowed down to between the years 93 and 96.

Clement's main objective in writing *The First Epistle of Clement to the Corinthians* was to restore peace and unity to that Greek branch of the Church. The Corinthians had been led by some young, rebellious individuals to rise up against their lawfully appointed presbyters. The significance of Clement's epistle is twofold. First, it outlines the organization or structure of the apostolic church. Second, it seems to have helped lay the foundation for the birth of the Roman Catholic Papacy and papal theory.

Clement states that the action taken by the seditious persons at Corinth was inexcusable. He declares that Christ was sent forth by God, the Apostles were sent by Christ, and the Apostles, preaching throughout the known world, appointed the first fruits of their proselytizing activity to be bishops after having proved them by the Spirit. Clement also says that the Apostles gave instructions that when these bishops appointed by them should die, other approved men should succeed them in their ministry by appointment from the Apostles or other eminent men with the consent of the whole church. He urges the schismatics at Corinth to return to the true order of the church, to put away strife, disorder, jealousy, and pride.

While no claim is made by the Roman church leader to interfere with another on any grounds of superior rank, the unmistakably authoritative tone of the letter gives its author more than merely a peacemaker's role. Using Clement's epistle as a precedent, Roman bishops of the second century began to assume preeminent authority to resolve general Christian disputes. By the mid-third century, the practice had arisen of reckoning Peter not only as chief Apostle but also as first Bishop of Rome. Gradually, the term "pope" or "father" (Latin *papa*), which had been used for any bishop in Western Europe, began to be directed toward the Bishop of Rome exclusively.

Clement served as Bishop of Rome about nine years. Besides writing his epistle, Clement's time as head of one of Christianity's most important communities was taken up with duties centering on proselytism, exhortation, keeping the Church unified, and helping it to survive attacks and persecutions such as the one promoted by Domitian.

Concerning the death of Clement there are conflicting tales. According to Eusebius and Jerome, he died a natural death in the third year of the reign of the emperor Trajan. Other traditions, however, reckon him among the martyrs.

The apocryphal *Acts of the Martyrs* relates how, toward the end of his life and tenure of office, Clement converted more than four hundred Romans of rank; as a result, Trajan banished the bishop to the Chersonese Peninsula in the Black Sea area. There Clement set to work converting the people of the country (two thousand in number), who built seventy-five churches. Trajan then had Clement thrown into the sea with an iron anchor around his neck. This story circulated for many years until around 868 when Saint Cyril, Apostle to the Slavs, dug up some bones and an anchor in the Crimea. Hailed as the relics of Clement, these remains were carried back to Rome and deposited by Pope Adrian II with the relics of Ignatius of Antioch in the Basilica of Saint Clement in Rome.

Summary

Next to the Apostles themselves, Clement was for many generations the most esteemed figure in the Church. Clement of Alexandria called him an Apostle. Jerome referred to him as an apostolic man, and Rufinus said that he was almost an Apostle.

Clement's letter to the church at Corinth was for centuries considered canonical by many and on a par with the epistles of Paul. Eusebius speaks of the public reading of Clement's letter as the ancient custom of many churches down to his own time. The list of ancient Christian authorities and leaders who quoted *The First Epistle of Clement to the Corinthians* includes Polycarp and Ignatius, themselves Apostolic Fathers.

Numerous spurious writings have been attributed to Clement. The most celebrated among these was probably the second century *The Second Epistle of Clement to the Corinthians*, purporting to supplement the first. This second letter was also held in great respect by early Christians. It is interesting to note that the two epistles disappeared from the Western Church in the sixth century. They were rediscovered in the year 1628, when an ancient manuscript of the Greek Bible was presented to King Charles I of England by the Patriarch Cyril Lukaris.

Much is not known about Clement. What is known, however, sheds a glimmer of light on a very poorly illumined but critical period in the history of one of Western civilization's most significant institutions—the Church.

Bibliography

Clemens Romanus. *The First Epistle of Clement to the Corinthians*. Edited by W. K. Lowther Clarke. London: Society for the Promotion of Christian Knowledge, 1963. Prepared by a British scholar, this concise volume contains introductory notes and a translation of Clement's authentic epistle. The translation is rendered in the style of the Revised Standard Version of the Bible. The explanations of the text illuminate Clement's life and the historical context of the letter.

Grant, Robert M. *The Apostolic Fathers*. Vol. 1, *An Introduction*. New York: Thomas Nelson and Sons, 1964. This is, perhaps, the best and most accessible single volume on the Apostolic Fathers and their world. It discusses who the Apostolic Fathers were and their historical circumstances, theological outlook, and writings. It also presents the place and significance of Clement and his epistle within the context of early Christianity and Hellenistic Judaism. The relationship between Clement and the other Apostolic Fathers is also discussed. Though the volume contains no index or bibliography, a detailed and well-organized table of contents greatly aids the reader.

Grant, Robert M., and Holt H. Graham. *The Apostolic Fathers*. Vol. 2, *First and Second Clement*. New York: Thomas Nelson and Sons, 1965. A companion volume to the introductory volume above, this work includes a translation (in idiomatic English) of, and commentary on, the two epistles ascribed to Clement. Its value lies in the numerous and detailed annotations and cross-references for virtually every verse of the two epistles. Though not a long book, its detail reflects a depth of scholarship on the part of the translators which may, at first, overwhelm the newcomer. Its strength is its correlation and analysis of literature and motifs similar to the two letters.

Lightfoot, J. B. *The Apostolic Fathers, Part I: S. Clement of Rome*. 2 vols. London: Macmillan, 1890. This is the most extensive and most authoritative work ever done on Clement and his writing. It presents a facsimile of the actual Greek texts of the two epistles along with translations, notes, and commentaries on the texts. Lightfoot synthesizes and distills all the references to Clement in ancient literature and history to attempt to fill in the gaps concerning his life.

Richardson, Cyril C., ed. *The Library of Christian Classics*. Vol. 1, *Early Christian Fathers*. Philadelphia: Westminster Press, 1953. This first volume in a series on the classic documents of Christianity contains a fine translation of both epistles, as well as a brief but thorough introduction to Clement and his writing. Its greatest value is the extensive bibliography on Clement and his work.

Staniforth, Maxwell. *Early Christian Writings*. New York: Penguin Books, 1981. Available in paperback, this work is a very readable introduction to the Apostolic Fathers and their writings. The section on Clement contains an introduction to the man and his work and a translation of the two epistles. It is valuable because of the informative footnotes it presents and the way the introduction discusses the significance of Clement's bishopric for the Church.

Andrew C. Skinner

CLEOPATRA VII

Born: 69 B.C.; Alexandria, Egypt
Died: 30 B.C.; Alexandria, Egypt
Area of Achievement: Government
Contribution: Cleopatra VII, as the last of the Ptolemaic Greek rulers of an independent Egypt, tried to come to terms with the ceaseless expansion of the Roman Empire throughout the Mediterranean and at her death left behind a rich, imperial province which continued to flourish as a center of commerce, science, and learning under Roman rule.

Early Life

Cleopatra VII was the daughter of Ptolemy XII Auletes and (possibly) of his sister and wife, Cleopatra Tryphaena. Such brother-sister marriages were common among the members of the Egyptian ruling house. It is believed that Cleopatra had three sisters, two older and one younger, and two younger brothers. Her representation with Negroid features by Michelangelo and her depiction as an Egyptian in cult paintings conceal her Macedonian ancestry; her family traced its lineage back to the Macedonian house of the Lagid Ptolemies, which had succeeded to the Egyptian throne after the untimely death of Alexander the Great in the early fourth century B.C. The Ptolemaic rule of Egypt was centered in Alexandria, the beautiful and populous city Alexander had founded to the west of the delta of the Nile when he invaded Egypt in 332.

Cleopatra was reared in a court beset by violence, murder, and corruption and dominated by the reality of Roman military might—all of which had played an important role in her father's accession to the throne. In 80, upon the death of Ptolemy Soter II, the only legitimate male Ptolemaic heir came to the throne as Ptolemy Alexander II. He was confirmed in power by the Romans but after murdering his wife, Berenice III, was himself murdered. Two illegitimate sons of Ptolemy Soter II were now claimants to the kingship.

The Romans put one brother in control of Cyprus. The other, Cleopatra's father, Ptolemy Theos Philopator Philadelphos Neos Dionysos or, as he was known to the Alexandrians, Ptolemy XII Auletes (the Flute Player), succeeded to the throne of Egypt. His relations with his subjects were difficult, in part because he recognized, unlike them, the growing power of Rome throughout the Mediterranean and realized that the only way to secure his position was to maintain close contact with the rulers of the world. During a visit to Rome, when he was hoping by means of massive bribes to secure the aid of the Roman army, his daughter, Berenice, in alliance with Archilaus, son of Mithridates, seized the throne, only to be put to death by her father upon his return.

When Ptolemy XII Auletes died in 51, after nearly thirty stormy years in office, he willed the kingdom of Egypt to his seventeen-year-old daughter and his ten-year-old son, who ruled jointly as Cleopatra VII and Ptolemy XIII Philopator. The young Ptolemy, however, soon fell under the influence of his advisers—Pothinus, a eunuch; Theodotus, a rhetorician; and Achillas the army commander—who must have found the boy king far more manipulable than his older sister, the intelligent, headstrong, energetic Cleopatra. As a result, Cleopatra was driven from Alexandria. When Julius Caesar arrived in Egypt, in pursuit of Pompey, after the Battle of Pharsalus in 48, Cleopatra was in Pelusium, on the eastern frontier of Egypt, with her newly acquired army preparing to attack her brother and his associates.

Caesar, as Rome's official representative, was in a position to arbitrate between the siblings, and his plan to reconcile Cleopatra and Ptolemy might have worked had not Ptolemy's advisers decided that power should remain in their own grasp. In the resulting showdown, known as the Alexandrian War, Caesar was victorious—but not without a struggle. Pothinus, Achillas, and Ptolemy were all killed, and Cleopatra was restored by Caesar to the throne, this time with Ptolemy XIV, her younger brother, as consort. By 48, Cleopatra was in control of Egypt.

Life's Work

From this point onward, Cleopatra's future is inexorably intertwined with that of Rome and her leaders. In their writings, Plutarch and Suetonius dwell on the love affair that developed between Julius Caesar, then in his fifties, and the twenty-one-year-old Cleopatra. In spite of the arguments to the contrary, the child born to Cleopatra shortly after Caesar left Egypt on his eastern campaign was probably Caesar's son. At any rate, Cleopatra, by naming the child Caesarion, was claiming that her son was indeed the son of the Roman conqueror. Moreover, young Octavian, Caesar's heir, who had most to fear if Julius Caesar had a genuine son, had Caesarion put to death in 30, immediately after the death of Cleopatra.

Little is known about Cleopatra's rule of Egypt, although there is evidence that she tried to win the favor of the farmers by reducing their taxes. From 46, she was living in Rome with Caesarion and Ptolemy XIV. The reason stated for her visit was that she had come to ask the senate for confirmation of her father's treaty of friendship; yet she was lodged by Caesar, along with Caesarion and Ptolemy XIV, in his villa in Trastevere, where she attempted to cultivate good relations with as many influential Romans as possible. Caesar also put a golden statue of Cleopatra in the temple of Venus Genetrix at Rome, thus associating her with the goddess who was in legend the mother of Aeneas and thus of the Julian line. He may have planned to gain special permission from the Roman people to contract a legal marriage with her, since his Roman wife was childless. The plans were frustrated by Caesar's assassination in 44, and Cleopatra probably left Rome shortly afterward.

Egypt's wealth did not pass unnoticed by the Romans, so it is not surprising that during Marc Antony's eastern campaign after the Battle of Philippi in 42 he saw the chance of subsidizing his wars by taxing Cleopatra's subjects. Cleopatra was shrewd enough to realize that her personal charms would be far more effective in preserving her kingdom than would open confrontation. Plutarch's account of the meeting between Antony and Cleopatra brilliantly describes both the fabulous wealth of the monarch and her grace. Just as Cleopatra had captivated Julius Caesar in her "salad days" when she "was green in judgment," she now in her maturity set out to win the heart of Antony.

After the formation of the so-called Second Triumvirate between Antony, Octavian, and Lepidus, which was sealed by Antony's marriage to Octavian's half sister Octavia, Cleopatra was left to rule Egypt. In 37, however, Antony's march eastward led to renewed friendship and an understanding between the two, which made available to Antony the resources of Egypt. From this time onward, Cleopatra's influence over Antony grew. She also now assumed Egyptian dress that represented the goddess Isis and is reported to have adopted the following oath: "As surely as I shall one day dispense judgment in the Roman Capitol." When Antony arranged for Caesarion and his own three children by Cleopatra to share in ruling both Egypt and Roman provinces in Asia Minor and formally divorced Octavia, Octavian declared war not against his fellow Roman Antony but against Cleopatra. He must have realized that Antony could not help but join Cleopatra.

At the Battle of Actium in 31, Cleopatra's Egyptian forces, together with Antony's Roman forces, faced Octavian's fleet, commanded by Marcus Vipsanius Agrippa. When Cleopatra retreated, she was quickly followed by Antony. Cleopatra's suicide in 30 marked the end of Ptolemaic rule and the beginning of direct Roman rule in what was now an imperial province.

Summary

The historical picture of Cleopatra VII is one-sided. Very little is known of her apart from her association with the two Roman generals, Julius Caesar and Marc Antony. As one might expect, the Roman writers do little to enhance her reputation. In the work of Augustan poets, she is never mentioned by name, but merely as "the queen," "the woman," or "that one." She is chiefly seen as a crazy drunkard, surrounded by wrinkled eunuchs. Horace also pays tribute to her courage, but he, Vergil, and Sextus Propertius, whose livelihood depended upon Octavian's bounty, quite clearly toe the party line in suggesting that she received no more than she deserved. William Shakespeare's depiction of her as high-spirited, shrewd, sensuous, and fickle is based on that found in Plutarch, a Greek biographer, who mentions her only in association with his two heroes, Caesar and Antony. Yet Plutarch also depicts her as a highly intelligent woman who, unlike her Ptolemaic predecessors, actually went to the trouble of learning the language of her subjects. He reports, moreover, that she could converse easily with "Ethiopians, Troglodytes, Hebrews, Arabians, Syrians, Medes, or Parthians" in their own languages.

Although Cleopatra is often imagined as a ravishing beauty because of the ease with which she seduced experienced and mature soldiers such as Caesar and Antony, a few coins survive depicting her as large-nosed, sharp-chinned, and determined. She was also ruthless. After the Alexandrian War, Caesar thought it sufficient to expel Cleopatra's sister, Arsinoe, for her part in the uprising; Cleopatra later had her put to death.

Plutarch in fact describes not so much her beauty as her charm, humor, and ability to amuse and delight her company. She probably also made a powerful impression on the Romans by her intelligence and political ambition. The Roman political system was in a period of transition. Republican government had proved inadequate. Egypt in Cleopatra's time and afterward was essential as a source of wheat for the Roman populace, and its master, if properly armed, could dictate his terms to Italy and the Roman senate. As the creation of Alexander the Great and the place where he was buried, Alexandria provided an obvious starting point for the revival of his empire and its extension even as far as India. The capital of the Roman Empire would eventually be shifted to the east anyway, by Diocletian and Constantine the Great. Legend related that the Romans' ancestor Aeneas originated from Troy in Asia Minor. There may well be some truth in the stories that Caesar intended, if he had lived, to remove the capital to the old site of Troy, and Antony may have been captivated by his dead commander's vision. Cleopatra gambled that, with the aid of such Roman generals, she could make her dynasty a partner in a new eastern empire that would reduce Rome to second place. Like Caesar and Antony, she failed because she was ahead of her time. Her failure has fascinated many throughout the centuries—including Shakespeare and George Bernard Shaw—who have felt the romance and energy of her ambitions.

Bibliography

Bevan, Edwyn. *The House of Ptolemy: A History of Egypt Under the Ptolemaic Dynasty*. Chicago: Argonaut, 1927, rev. ed. 1968. In chapter 13, Bevan offers a brief account of the final days of Ptolemaic rule. Includes illustrations of coins depicting Cleopatra.

Fraser, P. M. *Ptolemaic Alexandria*. 3 vols. Oxford: Clarendon Press, 1972. The most comprehensive and scholarly treatment of the entire period of Ptolemaic rule. Especially valuable for the massively detailed citation of primary sources.

Lindsay, Jack. *Cleopatra*. New York: Coward-McCann, 1971. A complete treatment of Cleopatra's achievements, aspirations, and influence. Many details of political events of the period help to place Cleopatra's defeat in a Roman context. Lindsay includes full notes citing ancient sources and provides a bibliography.

Marlowe, John. *The Golden Age of Alexandria*. London: Victor Gollancz, 1971. A popular treatment of one of the most famous cities, from antiquity to its capture in the sixth century A.D. Includes a discussion of Cleopatra.

Plutarch. "Caesar." In *Fall of the Roman Republic*, translated by Rex Warner. Harmondsworth, England: Penguin Books, 1958. The meeting of Caesar and Cleopatra is recounted in chapters 48 and 49. Plutarch accepts Caesar's paternity of Caesarion.

__________. "Mark Antony." In *Makers of Rome*, translated by Ian Scott-Kilvert. Harmondsworth, England: Penguin Books, 1965. Offers by far the best depiction of the intelligence, vivaciousness, shrewdness, cunning, and ruthlessness of Cleopatra. This life of Antony was used to great effect by Shakespeare in his famous play.

Pomeroy, Sarah B. *Women in Hellenistic Egypt: From Alexander to Cleopatra*. New York: Schocken Books, 1984. Chapter 1, which discusses the queens of Ptolemaic Egypt, places Cleopatra in a historical context. Pomeroy's discussion of married women, slaves, and women of the capital city of Alexandria—and the overall role of women in the economy in Cleopatra's time—brilliantly depicts the female subjects of this great queen.

Volkmann, H. *Cleopatra: A Study in Politics and Propaganda*. Translated by T. J. Cadoux. New York: Sagamore Press, 1958. Volkmann's excellent treatment provides a full account of all periods of Cleopatra's life and reign and her influence on world history. His appendix gives a brief survey of modern and ancient literature, and his genealogical tables and maps are helpful.

Weigall, Arthur. *The Life and Times of Cleopatra Queen of Egypt*. New York: G. P. Putnam's Sons, 1924. Although dated, this book gives a shrewd assessment of Cleopatra's relationship with Caesar and Antony. Weigall argues that Caesar was quite clearly intending to move the center of Roman power to the east and that in Cleopatra he had found an ally uniquely qualified to help him realize his plans.

Frances Stickney Newman

CLOVIS

Born: c. 466; probably Tournai
Died: November 27, 511; Paris
Areas of Achievement: Government, warfare, and religion
Contribution: In the early sixth century, Clovis extended his Frankish domain by conquest to form the nucleus of France and, in the process, united his interests with those of the orthodox Church in the West, which he saved from the threat of the Arian heresy.

Early Life

Clovis, or Chlodovech (noble warrior), was born probably in 466 at or near the Frankish stronghold of Tournai, near the present-day Franco-Belgian border; he was the son of the Frankish chieftain Childeric I. The family was descended from a West German barbarian tribe, the Salian (dwellers by the sea) Franks, that had settled two centuries earlier near the North Sea, on the outskirts of Roman Gaul. From there, they had gradually spread in small groups perhaps as far south as the Loire River. Another branch of the Franks, the Ripuarian (dwellers by the riverbank), had settled along the west bank of the Rhine River near the city of Cologne.

Clovis was the grandson of Meroveus, "the sea-fighter," who had conquered Tournai in 446 and installed the Merovingian dynasty, which was to dominate Frankish political history for three centuries. By the time of Meroveus, the Franks, unlike other generally migratory German tribes, appear to have become permanently settled in this region. They had begun to gain the acceptance of native Gallo-Romans, whom they supported against Attila and the Huns in a battle at Châlons (Mauriac Plain), near Troyes. Indeed, a significant determinant of the Franks' success in creating a powerful and long-lasting kingdom in Gaul was that they expanded gradually from a homeland—a settled base of strength in which they gained the allegiance of the native population as Roman imperial control disintegrated in the West.

The acceptance of the Franks by the Gallo-Roman natives is reflected in the work of Gregory of Tours. Gregory, who lived in the second half of the sixth century, was himself a Gallo-Roman aristocrat who succeeded to the bishopric of Tours, an ecclesiastical seat long held by his family. He became a prominent political and religious leader in western Gaul, but his greatest contribution was as a historian. Gregory was the author of the *Historia Francorum* (late sixth century; *The History of the Franks*, 1927), one of the great narratives of the early Middle Ages and the one which provides the only near-contemporary account of Clovis and the early Merovingians. To Gregory, the Franks, and Clovis in particular, were the divinely ordained saviors of the Church from the heresy of Arianism, to which other German tribes had been converted. Indeed, the Clovis of history is Gregory's Clovis, and all subsequent accounts of Clovis' career, with minor modifications of later scholarship, reflect their indebtedness to the Gallo-Roman cleric.

Nothing is known of Clovis' early life, and no contemporary artistic representation of his appearance has survived. The only clues regarding his early life are found in the contents of his father's burial chamber, discovered in Tournai in 1653. Childeric's tomb contained ornaments, weapons, and hoards of coins, demonstrating that he had established important contacts with the Roman Empire as well as with the barbarians. He was, without question, a very rich man. Clovis, therefore, appears to have been groomed to succeed his father as chieftain.

Life's Work

Clovis was only fifteen years of age when he succeeded his father, in 481 or 482, as leader of the Frankish tribes that recognized the supremacy of Tournai. The use of the title "king" at this point seems premature, although it has become traditional. It would appear that Clovis was regarded by his people as nothing more than a chieftain and that the magical element associated with kingship did not come until later, after his identification of himself and his dynasty with Christianity.

Clovis spent most of his reign fulfilling the obligations of a Frankish chieftain: by cunning—and when necessary cruelty and brutality—securing booty and additional land with which to reward himself and his retainers. In the process, he created a kingdom encompassing much of what later became France and West Germany. He first contracted alliances with two relatives, Ragnachair and Chararic, who were Salian Frankish chieftains at Cambrai and Saint-Quentin. Within five years, with their aid, he moved against Syagrius, the last independent Roman ruler in Gaul, who ruled over most of the area around Soissons. Ruthlessly, Clovis put to death Syagrius, his former allies Ragnachair and Chararic, and their brother, Rigomer, who had ruled the region of Le Mans. Having conquered their territories, Clovis was recognized as Syagrius' successor in northern Gaul by certain Gallo-Roman bishops, especially Bishop Rémi of Reims. This recognition by the regional clerical hierarchy of a *fait accompli* was of great significance to Clovis, since he was still a pagan and not yet acknowledged by the emperor in Byzantium.

The fateful bond between the Franks and Catholicism was then strengthened by another event: During the early 490's, the most obscure period of his reign, Clovis married a Burgundian princess, Clotilda, who is credited with converting him to Christianity. Soon after, Clovis succeeded in expanding his Frankish state by bringing the Ripuarian Franks under his protection. Their allegiance to him was necessitated by their fear of the fiercest of the West German tribes, the Alamanni, who, well-armed and on horseback, were moving from Alsace in a northwesterly direction toward the Ripuarian settlements along the banks of the Rhine River. At the famous Battle of

Tolbiacum (now Zülpich), on the borders of Alsace and Lorraine, the combined Frankish forces under Clovis defeated the Alamanni and extended their control as far south as Basel.

Clovis' victory at Tolbiacum was, according to Gregory of Tours, the central event of his reign and indeed of Frankish history, for it is from this battle that Gregory dates Clovis' conversion to Catholicism. All Clovis' subsequent military engagements are portrayed by Gregory as purposeful crusades for the advancement of Christianity. Although it is now generally believed that Clovis' conversion came some seven years later, the precise date of his conversion is irrelevant to its significance. According to Gregory, Clovis invoked the aid of Jesus during the course of the battle and, in the tradition of the Emperor Constantine, promised his belief and baptism in return for victory. Following the victory, Queen Clotilda asked Bishop Rémi to instruct her husband in the Christian religion. There soon followed the baptism of Clovis and three thousand of his soldiers at Reims. The doubtful tradition of Clovis' baptism was important in the history of the French monarchy, for it established the feature of canonical investiture, adding a mystical religious element to the earlier military component. The site of the baptism, Reims, was also to become traditional for the coronation of French monarchs.

Of greatest contemporary significance was that Clovis and the Franks converted to orthodox Christianity and acknowledged the authority of the Pope. The Franks, alone among the German tribes that moved into the western Roman Empire, never subscribed to the heresy of Arianism. This anti-Trinitarian belief had been first propounded by an early fourth century priest from Alexandria, Arius, who held that Christ, the Son, was not the coequal of God the Father. Arius contended that God was self-existent throughout eternity and immutable. Christ, however, had become existent and incarnate; he had been created by God and, in human form, was subject to growth and change. Christ was different from God the Father and, being His creation, by inference, inferior. He did not fully share in divinity. Arius and his teachings had been condemned on the basis of the arguments of Athanasius, the future bishop of Alexandria, at the Council of Nicaea, called by the Emperor Constantine in 325. The Athanasian position, which the Church established as orthodox, held that the Son is "of one substance with the Father," that He had existed throughout eternity, that He was begotten, not created, and that He is God's coequal and completely divine. Christ's total divinity and his coequality with God were central to the legitimacy of the Church and its clergy, to whom Christ had entrusted the dispensation of the Sacraments and the task of mediating between Christ and the believers. As the authority of the Roman Empire declined in the West during the fourth and fifth centuries, the Church, through its clergy, assumed many former imperial functions and sought to solidify its position by enforcing religious orthodoxy. The native Gallo-Roman population submitted to orthodoxy; the German barbarian tribes, however, had converted to Arianism before they entered Western Europe. As a result, they were unacceptable to the Church there and found their beliefs to be an impediment to popular acceptance and assimilation. Clovis' conversion to orthodoxy, eliciting not only the Church's acceptance of the Franks but also its support of Clovis' campaign to conquer Arian German tribes, significantly aided in the establishment of a permanent Frankish successor state in Roman Gaul.

The chronology of the events of Clovis' reign is disputed, probably as a result of the naïve confusion of Gregory, who, obsessed with the consequences of Clovis' conversion, preferred to view additional military campaigns as religious crusades against the Arian Germans. According to tradition, after his conversion, Clovis turned his attention to the Burgundians and the Visigoths, Arian Germans located respectively in southeastern and southwestern Gaul. Having recently allied himself with the Burgundian ruler of Geneva, an orthodox Christian, Clovis defeated the army of Gundobad, the Arian Burgundian chieftain of Lyons, in battle near Dijon. Gundobad was forced to flee to Avignon, which was besieged until he agreed to pay tribute. Clovis' final campaign was against the Visigoths. At Vouillé, near Poitiers, the Visigothic leader, Alaric II, was killed. Visigothic power north of the Pyrenees collapsed to Clovis, who pillaged Alaric's treasury at Toulouse before returning to give thanks at the shrine of the Merovingian patron, Saint Martin, at Tours. During his sojourn at Tours, Clovis received a legate from the Emperor Anastasius in Constantinople. The imperial representative brought with him letters bestowing on Clovis the title of consul. Clovis now had received imperial recognition of his legitimacy and preferment to add to his earlier recognition from the Church. Only Provence in southern France remained free of Frankish control in Gaul. Theodoric, the powerful Ostrogothic ruler of Italy, in alliance with the Burgundians permanently blocked Clovis' advance toward the Mediterranean.

After leaving Tours, Clovis returned to previously conquered Paris, which became the seat of his kingdom for the remainder of his reign. There he constructed his royal palace and, with Clotilda, oversaw the construction of the Church of Saints Peter and Paul (later known as the Church of Sainte-Geneviève), where he was subsequently entombed. In his last years, Clovis became a lawgiver and statesman rather than conqueror. On his orders, the Lex Salica (Salian law), a code of criminal law applied by Clovis to the Franks, was drawn up. Shortly before his death, he convened the first national church council held in Gaul, at Orléans. He died in November 27, 511, at forty-five years of age.

Summary

Clovis' kingdom in France did not long survive him; according to Frankish tradition, it was divided among his four surviving sons. Nevertheless, Clovis left an indelible imprint on the history of early medieval Europe. He brought together all the areas, except for Provence, that would make up the nucleus of the nation of France, which, as the native and Frankish populations were assimilated, began to develop its unique identity. He also, perhaps more by necessity than conviction, saved Christian orthodoxy from the encroachments of Arianism and in so doing played a major role in subverting the Unitarian heresy in the West. In turn, having recognized his military and administrative talents, the clerical leadership in Gaul adopted Clovis and the Franks as the logical successors to secular Roman imperial authority in Gaul. Together, Clovis and the Church restored order, religious orthodoxy, and political legitimacy to a region that had long endured the chaotic political vacuum left by the decline of Roman imperial authority.

Bibliography

Cantor, Norman F. *Medieval History: The Life and Death of a Civilization*. New York: Macmillan, 1963. Although the scope of this work is broad, it is still helpful, given the dearth of material available in English on Clovis. Cantor discusses Clovis at some length and credits him with his proper significance.

Castries, Due de. *The Lives of the Kings and Queens of France*. Translated by Anne Dobell. New York: Alfred A. Knopf, 1979. Although the treatment of Clovis, whom the author portrays as the creator of France and its first king, it is brief, is balanced and contains a surprisingly large amount of information about Clovis' conversion and conquests.

Gregory of Tours. *The History of the Franks*. Translated and edited with an introduction by O. M. Dalton. 2 vols. Oxford: Clarendon Press, 1927. This translation of the only contemporary account of the early Merovingians should be consulted by any serious student of Clovis, for Gregory provided the portrayal of the Frankish chieftain upon which all later historians have been required to base their evaluations of his significance, especially as the savior of Christian orthodoxy.

Wallace-Hadrill, J. M. *The Barbarian West, A.D. 400-1000: The Early Middle Ages*. New York: Harper and Row, Publishers, 1962. Although the scope of this book is broad, the foremost modern historian of the Franks devotes considerable attention to the Franks and to Clovis. This contains the best comprehensive treatment of the Franks and their significance in European history available.

__________. *The Long-Haired Kings and Other Studies in Frankish History*. London: Methuen and Co., 1962. This and the above volume are the two indispensable works in English on Clovis and the Franks.

J. Stewart Alverson

CONFUCIUS
K'ung Ch'iu

Born: 551 B.C.; state of Lu, China
Died: 479 B.C.; Ch'u-fu, state of Lu, China
Areas of Achievement: Philosophy, education, and ethics
Contribution: Confucius' teachings had little impact on his own times, but through his disciples and followers Confucianism became the official state philosophy in the second century B.C., while its texts became the basis of formal education. Confucianism, modified and developed by succeeding centuries of interpreters, remained the dominant philosophy of China until the early twentieth century and still has a major influence on people throughout East Asia.

Early Life

The name Confucius is the latinized version of a formal title, K'ung Fu-tzu, meaning "The Master K'ung." He was born as K'ung Ch'iu somewhere in the state of Lu (in the present-day province of Shantung), into a family that was part of the official class but had fallen on hard times. It is said that his great-grandparents had emigrated from the neighboring state of Sung. Confucius is believed to have lost his father when still a small child and to have been reared in poverty by his mother.

Nevertheless, Confucius learned the arts of a courtier, including archery and charioteering; at age fifteen, he began to study ancient texts. In his mid-twenties, Confucius held minor posts in Lu, first as a bookkeeper and later as a supervisor of royal herds. His approach to the problems of statecraft may have begun in his thirties, but he is best known for the period after the age of fifty when he was an established teacher or philosopher-master to young men. The actual teachings that have been handed down are contained in epigraphic and somewhat disjointed form in the *Lun-yü* (*Analects*). The book is a compilation of moral teachings, usually in the form of brief dialogues between Confucius and a questioner, who might be either a high feudal lord or one of Confucius' own disciples. Tradition holds that Confucius had an ungainly personal appearance, but nothing is actually known about his looks. He was married and had a son.

During Confucius' lifetime, China was divided into contending states under the nominal rule of the Chou Dynasty. By the eighth century B.C., the Chou rulers had lost all effective control over their subordinate lords, who became independent rulers. By Confucius' day, these rulers often were themselves figureheads, controlled by powerful individuals or families close to the throne. Murder, intrigue, and double-dealing had become the common coin of political exchange. Moreover, established authority and traditional social distinctions were violated in daily life. In this atmosphere of treachery and uncertainty, Confucius emerged as a teacher who valued constancy, trustworthiness, and the reestablishment of the rational feudal order contained in the codes of the Chou Dynasty.

Life's Work

Confucius was already known as a teacher, but desired to become an adviser or government minister, when sometime before his fiftieth year he went to live in the powerful neighboring state of Ch'i. The Duke of Ch'i honored Confucius as a moral teacher but did not give him an important position in the government; eventually, Confucius returned to Lu.

When the ruler of Ch'i asked Confucius the best way to govern, he replied, "Let the ruler be a ruler, the subject a subject, the father a father, and the son a son." The ideas contained in this moral maxim are central to Confucius' teaching. He taught that social order and stability could be achieved at a societal and a personal level if individuals studied and followed the proper standards of behavior. Confucius taught that if one acted properly in terms of one's own social role, others would be influenced positively by the good example. That worked for a ruler in state and for an individual in his or her daily life. Thus, Confucianism, from its earliest teachings, contained an approach useful for both practical living and governing.

Virtue (*te*) displayed by living properly brought one into harmony with the correct human order, called "the Way" (*tao*). Confucius acknowledged the existence of an overarching force in life called "Heaven" (*t'ien*) but did not accept any concept of a God or gods. He specifically opposed the belief in spirits and was not interested in the immortality of the soul.

For Confucius, the human order and human character are fundamentally good, but there is a tendency to slip away from proper behavior through laxity and lack of understanding. A primary responsibility of leaders and elders is to uphold the social ideals through positive demonstration in their own lives. In Confucianism, the most complete statement of this approach is called the doctrine of the Rectification of Names (*cheng-ming*). One begins with study to establish the original meaning of the Chou feudal order. Once that understanding is gained, individuals should alter their behavior in order to fulfill completely and sincerely the social roles they are assigned, such as minister, father, or brother. This entire process constitutes the Rectification of Names, which Confucius believed would restore the ideal social order.

Upon his return to Lu around the year 500, Confucius took up an official position under the sponsorship of Chi Huan-tzu, the head of the Chi clan, who were the real power holders. His post was not an important one, and Confucius resigned shortly over a question of improper conduct of ritual sacrifices. Ritual (*li*) plays a central role in Confucius' teachings. He downplayed the supernatural or religious aspects of ritual but taught that meticulous and sincere observance of rituals imparted moral improvement.

The state of Lu where Confucius lived derived from a collateral line of the Chou Dynasty and was known for careful preservation of Chou ritual practices. Confucius used this tradition as a proof of the importance of rituals. In addition to the moral training acquired by the mastery of ritual, Confucius taught ritual as a means to acquire the practical skills needed to carry out the functions of high office.

In 497, after his resignation over the ritual issue, Confucius set out, with a few disciples, as a wandering philosopher-teacher, looking for a ruler who would try his methods of governing. This long trek, which lasted from 497 to 484, led to his enhanced reputation for uprightness and wisdom, but he never obtained a significant office. In his mid-sixties, he was called back to Lu, possibly through the influence of his disciple Jan Ch'iu, who had become the chief steward of the Chi family. Upon his return, however, Confucius denounced Jan Ch'iu's tax policies as exploitative of the common people.

Confucius' approach to government stressed that the ruler should be benevolent and sincerely concerned about the well-being of his subjects. In Confucius' hierarchical conception of the social order, the ruler's concern for his subjects would be repaid by obedience and support. Confucius believed that the same hierarchical yet reciprocal principles applied to all social relationships.

Although later Confucius came to be deified as a sage of infinite powers, in the *Analects* he appears as a dignified, austere, but gentle man who suffered ordinary human disappointments. Significantly, his ideas are colored by a strong humanism. His teachings as recorded in the *Analects* emphasize benevolence (*jen*), meaning a love of one's fellowman, as the key virtue of the ideal man, whom he referred to as a "gentleman" (*chün-tzu*). Benevolence begins with straightforwardness (*chih*) of character and then is trained or modified through practice of the rituals. Ritual and music impart the inner character needed by a gentleman. Confucius taught that a gentleman would have other virtues as well, such as loyalty (*chung*), righteousness (*i*), altruism (*shu*), and filial piety (*hsiao*). This last virtue—the love and concern of a child for his parents which expresses itself in dutiful and sincere concern for their well-being—became particularly important in Chinese and East Asian civilization. All Confucius' teachings about social relationships demand the subordination of the individual; thus, Confucius was neither an egalitarian nor a libertarian.

During his last years, Confucius lived in Lu and was often consulted by the titular ruler, Duke Ai, and the new head of the dominant Chi clan, Chi K'ang-tzu, but still was never an important minister. Many of his statements from this period are preserved in summary form and enhance the elliptical tone of the *Analects*.

Confucius, before his death at the age of seventy-two, completed the editing of several ancient texts. Both tradition and modern scholarship connect him with three classical texts. These are the *Shu-ching* (*Book of Documents*), which contains pronouncements by the founders of the Chou Dynasty, the *Shih Ching* (*Book of Songs*), which preserves 305 songs from the time before 600 B.C., and the *Ch'un-ch'iu* (*Spring and Autumn Annals*). The last is a terse chronicle of events in the state of Lu from 722 to 481 B.C. and has been closely studied through the centuries, for it was believed that Confucius edited it with the intent of transmitting moral messages about good government. Confucius also studied the *I Ching* (*Book of Changes*), but the tradition that he edited that cryptic ancient book of divination is not widely accepted today.

Confucius' concern to compile correct versions of ancient texts fits the image of him that survives in the *Analects*. There Confucius stressed his own role as simply a transmitter of the knowledge and ways from the past. Confucius' model from history was the Duke of Chou, who acted as regent for the infant King Ch'eng, "The Completed King," who reigned from 1104 to 1067. Confucius taught that the Duke of Chou was the perfect minister who served his ruler and carried out his duties in complete accord with the feudal codes of the Chou. The story of the Duke of Chou, as a good regent and loyal minister, emphasizes the exercise of power in accord with the established social codes. Much of the appeal of Confucianism to later dynasties can be found in Confucius' emphasis on loyalty to proper authority.

At the same time, Confucius' teachings have been seen as democratic, in that what he valued in others was their good character, benevolence, humanity, and learning rather than their social position, cunning, or strength of will. His teaching that anyone may become a gentleman, or good person, with proper training and devotion established the important Chinese social ideal of personal cultivation through study.

Summary

Confucius died in 479, disappointed in his own career, upset at some disciples for their inability to follow his own high standards of conduct, and saddened by the deaths of both his own son and his favorite disciple, Yen Hui. Like Socrates, Confucius became known primarily as a teacher through the preservation of his teachings by his disciples. Some of those disciples went on to government service and others took up their master's calling as teachers.

By the second century B.C., the study of Confucian texts had become the norm for those aspiring to official posts. Young men were trained to memorize a set group of Confucian texts. That educational regime remained the heart of learning in China until the early twentieth century. The flourishing of his pedagogical approach is eloquent testimony to Confucius' genius. His concepts of the goodness of man and the importance of benevolence and humanity in political and personal affairs were developed by Mencius and given a more practical and realistic interpretation by the philosopher Hsün-tzu. By the second century B.C., students of Confucian teachings were highly valued for their skills in ritual, knowledge of ancient texts, and mastery of other learning that rulers needed to regulate their courts and administer their states. During the Former Han Dynasty (206 B.C.-A.D. 8), Confucianism became the official court philosophy and then was elevated to a state cult. Confucianism continues to be a powerful philosophy in China, Japan, and other states of East Asia.

Bibliography

Confucius. *The Analects*. Translated by D. C. Lau. New York: Penguin Books, 1979. The best available translation of the *Lun-yü*, with an outstanding introduction to Confucius' ideas and his life.

__________. *The Analects of Confucius*. Translated by Arthur Waley. New York: Vintage Books, 1938. Another version of the *Lun-yü*, rendered into elegant English by a British poet and scholar of Chinese. Contains only limited material to help the reader understand the often elusive context of the *Analects*.

Creel, H. G. *Chinese Thought from Confucius to Mao Tsê-tung*. Chicago: University of Chicago Press, 1953. A readable, nontechnical summary that puts Confucius in the overall context of Chinese philosophy.

Dawson, Raymond. *Confucius*. New York: Oxford University Press, 1982. A short, general introduction and biography of Confucius written for a series on great individuals. Stresses Confucius' ethical and moral influence.

Fingarette, Herbert. *Confucius: The Secular as Sacred*. New York: Harper and Row, Publishers, 1972. An interpretive essay that attempts to explain Confucius' attention to ritual (*li*) and to show how this can be reconciled with his humanism.

Schwartz, Benjamin I. *The World of Thought in Ancient China*. Cambridge, Mass.: Harvard University Press, 1985. Contains a long chapter on Confucius that includes extensive comparisons with ancient Western philosophers. Schwartz emphasizes Confucius' role as a teacher who was both a perpetuator of tradition and an innovator.

Ssu-ma Ch'ien. *Records of the Historian*. Translated by Yang Hsien-yi and Gladys Yang. Hong Kong: Commercial Press, 1974. Contains a translation of the biography of Confucius written c. 90 B.C. for inclusion in the monumental *Shih chi* (*Records of the Historian*). Modern scholars do not accept many of the details about Confucius' life and career recorded by Ssu-ma Ch'ien, but his characterization of Confucius is still important.

David D. Buck

CONSTANTINE THE GREAT

Born: February 17 or 27, c. 272-285; Naissus (in modern Yugoslavia)
Died: May 22, 337; Nicomedia
Areas of Achievement: Warfare, government, and religion
Contribution: As the result of a series of successful wars, Constantine became ruler of Rome and its empire. As the first Christian emperor of Rome, he was primarily responsible for initiating the great changes which in a few decades turned the pagan empire into a Christian one. Finally, Constantine refounded the old Greek city of Byzantium as the New Rome, which, as Constantinople, became Europe's greatest city during the next millennium.

Early Life

Flavius Valerius Constantinus (Constantine) was born at a crucial time in the long history of Rome. According to the eighteenth century English historian, Edward Gibbon, the second century A.D. had been a golden age, but the third century saw economic decline, barbarian invasions, and political instability, the latter often brought about by the ambitions of Rome's many generals and their armies. Constantine's father, Flavius Valerius Constantius, born in the militarily crucial Danubian provinces, was a successful general who rose to high political position. Constantine's mother, Helena, came from a lower-class background and was probably not married to Constantius, who himself later married a daughter of Marcus Aurelius Valerius Maximianus (Maximian), by whom he had several additional children. Little is known of Constantine's early life; even the year of his birth is unknown, but it was probably between A.D. 272 and 285.

In 293, the emperor Gaius Aurelius Valerius Diocletianus (Diocletian), in a continuing attempt to stem the long imperial decline, created a tetrarchy for administrative and defensive reasons. He retained the position of augustus in the east and appointed Maximian as augustus in the west. Constantius became Maximian's caesar, or assistant, and Gaius Galerius Valerius Maximianus (Galerius) was caesar to Diocletian. During the years which followed, young Constantine remained in the east at Diocletian's imperial court, possibly as a guarantee of good behavior by Constantius. What type of formal education Constantine received is unknown, and historians have long argued over his intellectual abilities. There is, however, no question that he successfully learned the military arts.

Diocletian abdicated his throne in 305, forcing Maximian to do the same. Galerius became augustus in the east, as did Constantius in the west. When the latter requested that Constantine be allowed to join him, Galerius was reluctant, but in 306, Constantine was reunited with Constantius in Britain and when Constantius died later that year in York, Constantine was acclaimed the new western augustus by his army. Galerius, however, only reluctantly granted Constantine the lesser rank of caesar, the position of the western augustus going to one of Galerius' own favorites.

Conflict dominated the next several years, as a result of the ambitions of the empire's many leaders. Maximian's son, Marcus Aurelius Valerius Maxentius, seized power in Rome with the help of his father. They joined forces with Constantine and resisted attempts at deposition by Galerius. Maximian, who had earlier given his daughter, Fausta, in marriage to Constantine, then attempted to seize power himself, first from his son and then from his son-in-law, Constantine, but the latter forced him to commit suicide. In the east, Galerius still ruled, joined by Valerius Licinianus (Licinius), who had also become an augustus. In the west, Maxentius and Constantine survived as rivals, each also claiming the rank of augustus. Diocletian's tetrarchy no longer had subordinate caesars, only ambitious and warring augusti.

Life's Work

Despite his important role in furthering Christianity, Constantine's religious beliefs remain uncertain. During the previous century the worship of the sun, Sol Invictus, had spread throughout the empire, and that religion seemed more important to Constantius and Constantine than the traditional pantheon of Roman gods. Christianity had also taken root in parts of the empire, although it was still a movement which lacked general acceptability. After several decades of toleration, Diocletian instituted a period of Christian persecution, but in the west, Constantius apparently refused to pursue that policy. The connection, or the confusion, between the Christian God and Sol Invictus is still unclear as regards Constantine's beliefs.

Whatever his religious convictions were, they soon became inextricably tied to his political ambitions. After Galerius died in 311, Constantine invaded Italy in early 312, hoping to unite the empire under his rule. Constantine and Licinius became allies through Licinius' marriage to Constantine's sister, and Maxentius seemed reluctant to face Constantine on the battlefield. Favorable omens from the gods eventually encouraged Maxentius, and on October 28, 312, he led his army out of the city gates of Rome and across the Tiber River on the Milvian Bridge. Constantine's army fought with the sign of the Christian cross on their shields and banners, and at battle's end, Maxentius lay drowned in the Tiber, leaving Constantine sole ruler in the west. When Constantine and Licinius met at Milan in 313, just prior to Licinius' struggle against the other eastern augustus, Galerius, they granted religious toleration to all sects. This edict especially benefited the Christian minority, the primary victims of persecution during the past decade. In his subsequent victory against Galerius, Licinius upheld the cause of monotheism against the traditional Roman gods. It had become impossible to divide politics and war from religion.

There is considerable difficulty when it comes to determining Constantine's own religious beliefs at the battle of the Milvian Bridge. In the first biography of Constantine, the *Vita Constantini* (339; *Life of Constantine*, 1845) by Bishop Eusebius of Caesarea, written after the emperor's death, Eusebius recalls that Constantine told him of a vision he had on his journey from Gaul to Italy in 312. He saw a cross in the sky, an apparition visible to his entire army. Later he said that he had a dream in which Christ appeared with the cross. Another version, by Lactantius, writing only a few years after 312, tells that Constantine, on the very eve of the battle at Milvian Bridge, had a dream in which he was told to put the sign of the cross on the shields of his soldiers. Some later historians have accepted those stories as sufficient evidence of Constantine's Christian commitment before his conquest of Rome, and they have argued that he was a sincere believer. Others have expressed doubts, contending instead that he was always primarily a hypocritical opportunist. Also, the depth of Constantine's perception of the Christian beliefs is still in question. Did he have a fundamental knowledge of the doctrines of Christianity in 312, or were his actions merely a superstitious adoption of a new god of battle against other, older gods?

What is not in question is that in the years which followed, Constantine favored more and more the Christian religion and its adherents. Property seized during the persecutions was returned, Christian bishops were freed from taxes and certain public obligations in order to pursue their religious calling, and Christian advisers at court became commonplace. Other religions and their followers were not immediately discriminated against or proscribed. In Rome, in particular, where the old religion was so much a part of the political and social fabric of the city, the upper classes remained generally in favor of the traditional gods. Many of the soldiers in Constantine's armies probably remained pagan, and he never dispensed entirely, even among his close advisers, with some who opposed, peacefully, the new religion.

Two continuing disputes between Christian factions, the Donatist and the Arian heresies, posed the greatest problems to Constantine in the years which followed his victory. In North Africa, the Donatists, who believed that the efficacy of Christianity depended on the sanctity of the priest or bishop, argued that those Christian clerics who had surrendered holy writings during the period of persecution were unfit either to consecrate other clergy or to distribute the sacraments to believers. The opposition claimed that the institution of the church itself was sufficient, not the personal holiness of the individual cleric. Constantine sided against the Donatists, for he believed that the church should be inclusive, or catholic, an attitude largely based on his belief that both his well-being and that of the empire depended upon a unified church. The issue remained unresolved.

Meanwhile, in the east, in a dispute over the relationship between Christ and God, the Arians argued that the Son was subordinate to the Father.

Constantine participated at the first general church council in Nicaea in 325, which issued the Nicene Creed and condemned the Arian position as a heresy. Until the end of his reign, however, Constantine was to waver between the two positions, often depending upon which advocate last caught his ear. Constantine was the first Christian emperor of Rome, but it was often easier to win victories on the battlefield than over one's fellow believers.

Licinius, who still ruled the eastern part of the empire, acknowledged Constantine's position as senior Augustus, but Constantine refused to accept permanently such a division, even with his brother-in-law. The friction continued for many years, sometimes resulting in war, usually at Constantine's instigation. When Licinius began to persecute Christians, possibly in reaction to Constantine's active support of Christianity, Constantine found justification for a final confrontation, from which he emerged victorious. In 324, Licinius was allowed to abdicate, but within a short time he was executed. Constantine stood alone as ruler of the empire.

Following Licinius' defeat, Constantine, as befitting a great conqueror, founded a New Rome in the east. For more than a century, Rome had not been the effective capital of the empire; a government positioned closer to the Rhine and Danube rivers was better able to defend against the ever-threatening barbarian tribes. In addition, Rome had proved to be less tractable to Constantine's rule and religion. The site picked for the New Rome was the old Greek city of Byzantium, a natural crossroads between Europe and Asia Minor and between the Mediterranean and the Black Sea, rededicated as Constantinople in 330. Unlike Rome, Constantinople was much more a Christian city, and the emperor spent lavishly on his new creation, as he had in constructing churches throughout the empire, particularly in Jerusalem, where basilicas were erected to commemorate Christian holy places. Constantine's New Rome became in time the greatest city in Europe.

Initially, Constantine intended to be buried in Rome, but after the founding of Constantinople he made the decision to be buried there, and he directed the building of his own tomb in the Church of the Holy Apostles in Constantinople. As was usual in his era, he was only baptized a Christian on the eve of his death. He had hoped to have that ceremony performed in the Jordan River, but in the spring of 337, his health began to fail. He left Constantinople in order to seek a cure at the springs of Helenopolis, named after his mother, who on a pilgrimage to the Holy Land had purportedly discovered the cross on which Christ had been crucified. On his return to Constantinople, Constantine worsened in Nicomedia, was baptized there, and died on May 22.

Summary

The empire under Constantine's rule was prosperous and secure, at least in comparison to the previous century, if not to Gibbon's golden age of the second century A.D. By the time he died, Constantine had eliminated his rivals, so that there were only members of his family, sons and nephews, to inherit the empire; heredity was to determine once again the ruler, or rulers, of Rome. In 326, he had ordered the execution of his eldest son, Crispus, and then his own wife, Fausta, in reaction to an unknown scandal. After Constantine's death, his nephews were summarily executed, leaving the empire divided among his three surviving sons. Constantine II was killed by his brother, Constans, in 340, who in turn was killed in 350. The last brother, Constantius II, died while suppressing a rebellion by Julian, the son of one of Constantine's half-brothers.

At the time of his death, the force of Constantine's influence was yet to be realized. Militarily, he had created a reserve force, more mobile, supposedly better able to respond to the barbarian threat than the less mobile legions. Perhaps more ominously, increasing numbers of German barbarians were enlisted in the empire's armies. This was not new, but it was a portent for the future. Constantinople was still a secondary city, whose ultimate importance would arrive only after the sack of Rome in 410, the fall of the western empire in 476, and the consolidation of the eastern empire under Justinian in the sixth century. Julian, who succeeded Constantius II, followed the old gods of Rome, and the various heretical movements within the Church continued long after 337. Julian, however, was the last of the pagan emperors, and the empire, governed from Constantine's New Rome, survived to protect the west and to preserve the ancient heritage for the next thousand years before falling to Islam in 1453. As the first Christian emperor of the Roman Empire, Constantine became, for better or worse, one of the founders of the medieval world.

Bibliography

Barnes, Timothy D. *Constantine and Eusebius*. Cambridge, Mass.: Harvard University Press, 1981. The author accepts the reality and the sincerity of Constantine's religious commitments and his desire to create a Christian empire. Concentrates particularly upon religious issues, using as a focus Constantine's contemporary biographer, Eusebius of Caesarea, and the various issues, doctrinal and otherwise, which affected the church and empire, especially in the east.

Baynes, Norman H. *Constantine the Great and the Christian Church*. London: Oxford University Press, 1972. This brief essay, first published in 1931, still commands attention. The author argues that Constantine was a sincere Christian who believed that he had a mission to maintain unity in the church and convert the nonbelievers to his new faith, in part because of his belief that his future and that of Rome depended upon the Christian God.

Burckhardt, Jacob. *The Age of Constantine the Great*. Garden City, N.Y.:

Doubleday and Co., 1956. This classic was first published in 1852. Burckhardt portrays Constantine, not as a sincere Christian, but rather as a worldly and accomplished politician who aimed only at success and whose religious beliefs were a combination of superstition and opportunism.

Eadie, John W., ed. *The Conversion of Constantine*. New York: Holt, Rinehart and Winston, 1971. The author has collected and edited a number of historical works, from the fourth century onward, which discuss the question of the meaning and importance of Constantine's religious beliefs. An excellent summary of different viewpoints on one of the central issues of his reign.

Gibbon, Edward. *History of the Decline and Fall of the Roman Empire*. London.: T. Cadell, 1828. Reprint. Vol. 1. New York: Modern Library, 1932. This elegantly written work by the eighteenth century historian is one of the literary classics of Western civilization. Gibbon's writings have posed questions about the fall of empires that historians have been pursuing ever since. Reflecting the Enlightenment era, Gibbon has little empathy with any religious movement, thus Constantine is pictured finally in negative terms.

Grant, Robert M. *Augustus to Constantine: The Thrust of the Christian Movement into the Roman World*. New York: Harper and Row, Publishers, 1970. Traces the development of Christianity from its beginnings to the fourth century, and argues that Constantine was a sincere Christian, in whose era Christianity finally triumphed.

Jones, A. H. M. *Constantine and the Conversion of Europe*. London: Hodder and Stoughton, 1948. This work, by an eminent scholar, was written for the general reader. Jones argues that Constantine was not a great ruler, that he was too emotional and easily distracted. His major abilities were military, but his impact upon religion and politics was profound because of his control over both church and state as the first Christian emperor.

Jordan, David P. *Gibbon and His Roman Empire*. Urbana: University of Illinois Press, 1971. This is a study of Gibbon and his great work. The author, in a chapter on Constantine, notes that Gibbon believed that Constantine was the central figure, and thus the villain, in the decline and fall of the empire, because he turned away from the religion which had created the empire.

MacMullen, Ramsay. *Christianizing the Roman Empire, A.D. 100-400*. New Haven, Conn.: Yale University Press, 1984. This brief volume is a sensitive and complex essay on the appeal, and lack of appeal, of Christianity during its early centuries, what groups were most likely to respond to the Christian message, what approach would succeed, and the major difference that Constantine made as an emperor who was a convert himself.

___________. *Constantine*. New York: Dial Press, 1969. This well-written biography of Constantine by a serious scholar is written for the general reader. An excellent summary of the various aspects of the life of the emperor, including war, politics, and religion. The author sees Constantine in many ways as a traditional Roman emperor, but of great significance because he was the first Christian emperor.

Pelikan, Jaroslav. *The Excellent Empire: The Fall of Rome and the Triumph of the Christian Church*. San Francisco: Harper and Row, Publishers, 1987. In this provocative series of lectures, Constantine's establishment of Christianity is perceived as the key to both fall and triumph. The author particularly focuses upon the ideas and writings of Saint Augustine of Hippo and Edward Gibbon.

Eugene S. Larson

CTESIBIUS OF ALEXANDRIA

Born: fl. c. 270 B.C.; Alexandria, Egypt
Died: Probably after 250 B.C.; Alexandria, Egypt
Areas of Achievement: Invention and technology
Contribution: One of the great mechanical geniuses and inventors of antiquity, Ctesibius was the father of pneumatics, the first to employ compressed air to run his devices. He is credited with a number of inventions, including a water pump, a water organ, a more precise water clock, and bronze spring and pneumatic catapults.

Early Life

Biographical details about Ctesibius are scarce. He was from Alexandria in Egypt and would have grown up during the reign of Ptolemy I, who, following the death of Alexander the Great, founded the Ptolemaic dynasty in Egypt in 322. Ctesibius' father was a barber, a trade he apparently taught his son. Ctesibius is said to have married a woman named Thais.

Vitruvius, the first century B.C. architect and military engineer who utilized Ctesibius' lost treatise on pneumatics, describes him as an industrious youth endowed with great natural ability who occupied much of his time amusing himself with the ingenious devices he routinely fashioned. The most famous anecdote about Ctesibius has him devising a counterweight system to raise and lower a mirror in his father's barbershop. As the counterweight moved rapidly through a narrow channel, it compressed trapped air which escaped with a loud noise. The sounds and tones created supposedly gave Ctesibius the idea for his water organ, for which he used pipes of different lengths to vary pitch and water to pressurize the air.

The same barbershop experiment apparently also inspired Ctesibius' water pump, which consisted of two vertical cylinders, each with a plunger worked reciprocally by a rocker arm. Water was drawn into a cylinder chamber through a valve connected to a water source when its plunger was raised and then was forced out in the direction desired through another valve when its plunger was lowered. Continuous pumping on the rocker arm handle guaranteed a steady flow of water.

Life's Work

Much of Ctesibius' adult life was spent during the reign of Ptolemy II, for whom he fashioned a singing cornucopia for a statue of Arsinoe, the king's deified wife, about 270. Because of his mechanical skills, it can be safely assumed that he was often employed by Ptolemy to produce other machines, both serious and amusing (for example, singing birds to grace water clocks and call out the hour).

Alexandria at that time had become the cultural center of the Hellenistic world. The Ptolemaic court was never more brilliant than under Ptolemy II, who, while expanding Egyptian power overseas, was responsible for the Great Library and Museum and one of the Seven Wonders of the Ancient World, the lighthouse on the island of Pharos at the entrance to Alexandria's harbor. This was almost certainly the period of Ctesibius' greatest achievements, which, because his own work is lost, are known primarily through three later technical writers—Vitruvius (*De architectura*, c. 25 B.C.; *The Ten Books on Architecture*, 1914), Philon of Byzantium (*Mechanikē syntaxis*, third century B.C.), and Hero of Alexandria (*Pneumatica*, c. A.D. 62).

In addition to inventing the water organ and pump, Ctesibius also perfected the first accurate water clock. Previous water clocks did not keep precise time because the flow of water to the clock could not be correctly regulated. Ctesibius first fashioned orifices of gold or other substances which would not be worn by the action of water and did not collect dirt. Having guaranteed an uninterrupted water flow into the first chamber of the clock, Ctesibius then devised a way to keep the water level in that chamber constant. An automatic valve, worked by a float, shut off the supply when the water in the chamber rose too high and opened it again as soon as enough water had drained into the clock's second chamber. The flow of water from the first chamber to the second, consequently, was always the same, and the passage of a certain amount of water represented the passage of so much time. On the simplest of water clocks, elapsed time could be determined by noting the markings on the side of the second chamber. More elaborate water clocks had complex and imaginative ways of denoting the time.

Summary

While perhaps not as familiar today as some of his famous scientific and technological contemporaries, Ctesibius of Alexandria was one of the greatest Hellenistic inventors and the founder of pneumatics. Primarily a craftsman, Ctesibius had little interest in theoretical issues, but was a mechanical genius of the first rank. He was influenced by and contributed to the cultural and intellectual atmosphere characterizing the reigns of Ptolemy I and especially Ptolemy II, by whom he was employed. Over his lifetime, he produced several important devices which would have lasting value, among them a water pump, a water organ, the first accurate water clocks, and improvements to artillery.

Bibliography

Cohen, M. R., and I. E. Drabkin. *A Source Book in Greek Science*. New York: McGraw-Hill Book Co., 1948. A compilation of passages from ancient writers about science and technology, including references to Ctesibius.

Drachmann, A. G. *The Mechanical Technology of Greek and Roman Antiquity*. Copenhagen: Munksgaard, 1963. The standard study of the literary sources for Greek and Roman technology, particularly Hero of Alexandria's *Mechanica* (c. A.D. 62; *Mechanics*).

Landels, J. G. *Engineering in the Ancient World*. Berkeley: University of California Press, 1978. The best recent survey of ancient engineering. Includes discussion of Ctesibius' contributions, some illustrated.

Lloyd, G. E. R. *Greek Science After Aristotle*. New York: W. W. Norton and Co., 1973. A good brief survey of ancient science, beginning with the Hellenistic period. Discusses Ctesibius' work, with some illustrations.

Sarton, George. *A History of Science*. Vol. 2. New York: W. W. Norton and Co., 1959. A standard survey of the history of Hellenistic science and culture. Ctesibius' achievements are considered.

Vitruvius. *The Ten Books on Architecture*. Translated by Morris Hicky Morgan. Cambridge, Mass.: Harvard University Press, 1914. In books 9 and 10, Vitruvius provides more details about Ctesibius and his work than any other ancient writer.

Robert B. Kebric

SAINT CYRIL and SAINT METHODIUS

Saint Cyril

Born: c. 827; Thessalonica, Greece
Died: February 14, 869; Rome

Saint Methodius

Born: c. 825; Thessalonica, Greece
Died: April 6, 884; probably near Velehrad in Great Moravia
Areas of Achievement: Religion and linguistics
Contribution: Through their spiritual commitment, Cyril and Methodius expanded Christianity in central and eastern Europe and established the foundations of Slavic culture and literature with the development of the Glagolitic alphabet.

Early Lives

The brothers Constantine (Cyril was a religious name taken just before his death) and Methodius were born in the Greek city of Thessalonica (modern Salonika). At the time, Thessalonica was the second most important city of the Byzantine Empire and the provincial capital of the region to the west of Constantinople. Their father Lev (Leo) was a high-ranking military officer in the province and a man of some importance; he was known at the imperial court in Constantinople. Of the two brothers, Constantine, the younger, was the more gifted intellectually and socially. Certainly, he was better known. Methodius, by contrast, functioned in Constantine's shadow until after the latter's death in 869, despite his own considerable talents and intelligence. This lesser position is suggested by the facts that much more has been written about the early life of Constantine than has been about that of Methodius and that whenever their activities are discussed, Constantine is always cited first.

Following the death of his father in 841, Constantine was sent to Constantinople, where he became the protégé of Theoctistus, the legothete or imperial chancellor to the Byzantine empress Theodora. Impressed with Constantine's intellectual and linguistic capabilities, Theoctistus arranged for him to study at the imperial court academy. There Constantine studied philosophy and theology under the tutelage of Photius, the most important Byzantine philosopher and theologian of his time and a future patriarch of Constantinople. By 849, Constantine had acquired not only a reputation as an outstanding scholar of philosophical and theological matters but also the exalted title "Philosopher."

Cognizant of Constantine's extraordinary skills, Theoctistus sought to utilize those talents for the empire by offering him a place at the imperial court and marriage to his adopted daughter. Constantine, however, spurned these worldly opportunities and opted instead for a life of spiritual piety. Undaunted, Theoctistus proposed to ordain Constantine as a deacon in the Church and to appoint him to the office of chartophylax (librarian) or secretary to Ignatius, the last of the Byzantine iconoclastic patriarchs. Although initially accepting this offer, because of his disagreement with Ignatius' iconoclast policies, Constantine mysteriously disappeared. Finally, in 850, he was named professor of philosophy at the imperial academy where he had previously studied. He was only twenty-three years of age. Constantine remained at the academy until 855, when he retired to join Methodius in a monastery on Mount Olympus, near the Sea of Marmora in northwestern Turkey, which was the center of monastic life in the ninth century.

As to Methodius, very little is known of his early life. There are only brief references to his activities prior to 863; nothing exists to illuminate his formative years or his education. It is recorded, however, that he did serve as a provincial governor in the region where he was born. Despite this eminent position, however, Methodius tired of the vicissitudes of worldly life. He became a monk and entered a monastery on Mount Olympus, where he would be joined by Constantine.

Life's Work

Constantine and Methodius' main achievement centers on their activities among the Great Moravians of central Europe between 863 and 885. The focus of this effort was primarily religious and linguistic in that they sought to develop a Slavonic liturgy and to train an ecclesiastical hierarchy to support the emerging Christian church in Moravia. From the outset, their work was enmeshed in the religious and political rivalries involving the Byzantines, the German Franks, and the Papacy during the ninth century. Despite these difficulties, the brothers achieved their goals; their success gave rise to the later appellation "Apostles to the Slavs."

In 862, Rostislav, the King of Great Moravia, appealed to the Byzantine Emperor Michael III for a group of missionaries to develop a liturgy and to train an ecclesiastical hierarchy for Moravia. In making this petition, Rostislav specifically requested the inclusion of Constantine and Methodius, since their reputations as scholars and linguists had spread well beyond Byzantium. Although Rostislav couched his plea to Michael in religious terms, he was motivated by his own political interests. At issue was his desire to reduce or even eliminate the influence of the Bavarian Franks in his kingdom, since their presence threatened Moravian independence. To achieve this goal, however, Rostislav needed to reduce Moravian dependence upon the Franks' ecclesiastical leadership. For their part, the Byzantines were not oblivious to the political and religious advantages of Rostislav's overture. It offered the prospect for expansion of the Byzantine rite into central Europe, where Rome and Constantinople were rivals for religious authority. At the same time, it presented an opportunity to forge an alliance with Moravia against Bulgaria, whose activities threatened Byzantium. Such were the circumstances confronting Constantine and Methodius as they began their Moravian mission.

Upon arriving in Moravia in 863, the apostles were warmly received by Rostislav. Before they could begin their work, however, it was necessary to overcome the absence of a written Moravian language. To resolve this difficulty, Constantine turned his attention to the development of a Slavonic alphabet that would correspond to the spoken Slavonic language used by the Moravians. Constantine was well suited for this task; he was fluent in Slavonic since the language was common to Thessalonica.

To derive a Slavonic alphabet, Constantine used the letters of the Greek alphabet as a foundation. Spoken Slavonic, however, had numerous inflected sounds and diphthongs for which there was no Greek equivalent. Therefore Constantine was forced to create additional letters to represent the unique Slavonic sounds. The result was the Glagolitic alphabet, which became the basis for Old Slavonic or Church Slavonic and the precursor to the later Cyrillic alphabet. Constantine's accomplishment meant that the Moravians now possessed the means to acquire their own liturgy and to educate an independent ecclesiastical hierarchy. The next four years saw the brothers translating critical elements of the Byzantine liturgy into the new Glagolitic script for this purpose. By the autumn of 867, their mission seemingly completed, the apostles departed from Moravia, returning to Constantinople with the new liturgy and a group of disciples who were candidates for ordination. Once ordained, these disciples were to return to Moravia and continue the work begun by Constantine and Methodius.

Unfortunately, the apostles never completed their journey to Constantinople; fate intervened in the form of an invitation from Pope Nicholas I to visit Rome. Turning toward Rome, the brothers intended to remain there briefly and then continue their journey to Constantinople. Instead, the Roman sojourn lasted more than two years and had a major impact on their work in Moravia. As in 863, the primary cause of this situation was the continuing rivalries in central Europe. Although Constantine and Methodius attempted to remain above these conflicts and intrigues, they could not escape the impact of events.

By the time the apostles arrived in Rome in late December, 867, or early January, 868, Nicholas was dead and Adrian II was the new pope. The brothers had accepted Nicholas' invitation in part because they wished an opportunity to ordain the Moravian disciples. By doing that in Rome, the new clerics could return to Moravia and begin their work much sooner than had they proceeded to Constantinople. These hopes were quickly realized since

Adrian approved not only the ordination but also Constantine's Slavonic liturgy. Certainly the reputation of Constantine and Methodius contributed to Adrian's decision. It is also possible, however, that Adrian sensed an additional political advantage for Rome. Granting a Slavonic liturgy and an ecclesiastical hierarchy for Moravia would neutralize Frankish influence there. Moreover, it afforded an opening for the extension of Roman ecclesiastical authority into the region by reversing the earlier rejection of Moravian requests for a religious mission from Rome, a rejection which had originally prompted the Byzantine mission.

Adrian's actions marked the high point of the brothers' stay in Rome as summer, 868, brought distressing news from Constantinople. Reports told of the overthrow and assassination of Michael III by his coruler, Basil I, in the previous September. No less disturbing was the deposing of Patriarch Photius and his replacement by the iconoclast Ignatius. The cause of these events was the conflict between Constantinople and the Papacy over Roman religious penetration of Bulgaria, a circumstance both Photius and Michael adamantly opposed. By removing the two men, the new leadership in Constantinople hoped to improve relations with Rome and to eliminate Roman influence in Bulgaria. The effect of the developments was to leave Constantine and Methodius in limbo. They were uncertain of their status in Constantinople and of the future of their work. Meanwhile, Constantine, already ill, continued to decline. He died in Rome on February 14, 869. Before he died, however, he became a monk and received the name Cyril in recognition of his new spiritual standing.

The burden of their work fell to Methodius. By now it was certain that he could not return to Constantinople, but he did not wish to see the work in Moravia disrupted. It was important, he believed, for the Slavs to have their own liturgy and ecclesiastical leadership. With this in mind, he accepted the appointment by Adrian to return to Moravia as papal legate. Methodius remained there until his death on April 6, 885. It was this final demonstration of spiritual concern that ensured the preservation of the Slavonic liturgy among the Slavic peoples.

Summary

In retrospect, the significance of the work of Cyril and Methodius was not confined to their activities in central Europe. Although their mission was a major factor in the development and expansion of Christianity among the Moravians and the other Slavic peoples that inhabited the region, the broader impact of the brothers was to the east in Bulgaria and Russia. The reason for this observation can be found in the historical events which transpired after the ninth century. First, Rome was able to assert its religious and ecclesiastical influence in central Europe. The effect was the latinization of these peoples culturally, linguistically, and liturgically. Byzantine influence, never really strong there, declined. Second, the disciples of Methodius, driven eastward in the late ninth and early tenth centuries, found refuge in Bulgaria, where their Glagolitic alphabet and Slavonic liturgy took root and flourished. During the next two centuries, these elements gave rise to a distinctive Slavic culture. For the first time in their history, the Slavs had a written language. In turn this language led to the evolution of a national literature in the form of hagiography and historical chronicles. The result was the emergence in Bulgaria of a Slavic unity where none had previously existed. In the twelfth century, the expansion of the Slavonic language and culture fostered a similar cultural and linguistic unity in Kievan Russia. Subsequently, this Slavic unity was transmitted to medieval Russia though the Russian Orthodox church and become one of the significant unifying forces of early Muscovite development. Thus, Cyril and Methodius richly deserve the appellation "Apostles to the Slavs."

Bibliography

Alexander, Paul J. "The Papacy, the Bavarian Clergy, and the Slavonic Apostles." *The American Slavic and East European Review* 1 (1941): 266-293. Alexander provides a concise analysis of the political and religious rivalries, conflicts, and intrigues surrounding the mission of Constantine and Methodius in Moravia.

Duichev, Ivan, ed. *Kiril and Methodius, Founders of Slavic Writing: A Collection of Sources and Critical Studies*. Translated by Spass Nikolev. New York: Columbia University Press, 1985. Contains a tenth century hagiography on the life and acts of Cyril by a probable disciple of Methodius. Also includes an encomium or eulogy by the same author on the death of Methodius.

Dvornik, Francis. *Byzantine Missions Among the Slavs: SS. Constantine-Cyril and Methodius*. New Brunswick, N.J.: Rutgers University Press, 1970. The standard work on the activities of Constantine and Methodius among the Slavs by the leading scholar of Slavonic and Byzantine church history. It represents a major reinterpretation of earlier scholarship, including that of the author, and is coupled with supporting appendices, an exhaustive bibliography, and an index.

__________. "Sts. Cyril and Methodius in Rome." *St. Vladimir's Seminary Quarterly* 7 (1963): 20-30. A detailed discussion of the events and circumstances surrounding the stay of Cyril and Methodius in Rome. Also discussed is the impact of these events and circumstances on the Moravians after 868.

__________. "The Significance of the Missions of Cyril and Methodius." *Slavic Review* 23 (1964): 195-211. A carefully developed discussion of the religious and cultural impact of the Byzantine mission on Moravia and Bulgaria.

____________. *The Slavs: Their Early History and Civilization*. Boston: American Academy of Arts and Sciences, 1956. A broad general history of the Slavic people, from their origins to the mid-thirteenth century, which focuses on all aspects of their development. Also included are maps, an extensive bibliography organized by chapters, and an index.

Kantor, Marvin, and Richard S. White, trans. *The Vita of Constantine and the Vita of Methodius*. Ann Arbor: University of Michigan Press, 1976. A complete and authenticated primary source on the lives of Cyril and Methodius which has been translated from the earliest extant and verified manuscripts. The introduction and commentaries are most helpful for an understanding of the actual textual material, which is presented in hagiographical form.

David K. McQuilkin

CYRUS THE GREAT

Born: c. 601-590 B.C.; Media (modern northern Iran)
Died: c. 530 B.C.; Scythia (southern Russia)
Areas of Achievement: Warfare and government
Contribution: Cyrus conquered Media and brought Persia into the arena of world leadership by defeating the Neo-Babylonians (Chaldeans) in Babylon (c. 539 B.C.). He created a Persian Empire—the Achaemenian dynastic empire—stretching from Turkey to India. His unusually beneficent treatment of conquered peoples was widely praised throughout the Ancient Near East as well as the later Greco-Roman world.

Early Life

The most lengthy accounts of Cyrus' early life are found in the Greek historians Xenophon and Herodotus. Xenophon's *Cyropaedia* (fourth century B.C.), however, is not so much a biography of Cyrus as a "historical romance," that is, largely fiction, with only a few bits of factual information. Most of the valuable information in Xenophon is that dealing with Cyrus' conquest of Babylon. Information dealing with Cyrus' early life is of little value or interest. In like manner, the information in Herodotus' *Historiai Herodotou* (c. 425 B.C.; *The History of Herodotus*, 1709) contains very speculative legends dealing with the birth and youth of Cyrus that were most likely borrowed from earlier legends, such as those surrounding the birth of Sargon of Akkad from the twenty-fourth century B.C., and there is even some similarity with the legends dealing with Romulus, the founder of Rome in the eighth century B.C. Therefore, little confidence can be placed in the information dealing with Cyrus' early life. That Cyrus was half Median and half Persian, however, seems to be quite likely, and he probably spent part of his youth in Media with his grandfather, Astyages. Cyrus' father was a Persian named Cambyses, and his mother, Mandane, was a Median.

Life's Work

Most of Herodotus and Xenophon's accounts of Cyrus deal with his military campaigns, which were widespread throughout Media, Lydia (western Turkey), former provinces of the Neo-Assyrian and Neo-Babylonian empires, including Babylon itself, and later the unsuccessful campaign against the Massagetae, a nomadic tribe in Scythia.

Cyrus began his military rule over the Persians about 559, and by 550, he had taken over neighboring Media and added it to his kingdom. The decisive battle over the Medes was probably at Pasargadae, the city that was to become Cyrus' own capital. He also conquered the capital city of Media, Ecbatana.

Of considerable interest to Herodotus was Cyrus' first contact with the Greek world when he defeated Croesus, King of Sardis, in Lydia in 546. Shortly afterward the Greeks of the regions of Aeolia and Ionia (also in western Turkey) submitted to the rule of Cyrus. A revolt in the city of Miletus in 499 was to bring on the famous conflict between the Greeks of the mainland and the Persian Empire.

Between 546 and 540, Cyrus campaigned primarily in the Near East. The famous Behistun Inscription of the Persian Darius the Great mentions that by 520 several areas were already under Persian rule, many of which were probably added while Cyrus was still alive, including Parthia, Bactria, and Sogdiana.

The most famous conquest of Cyrus was that of Babylon in 539. Considerable information dealing with this battle is known from the Bible, Babylonian cuneiform, and the writings of Xenophon and Herodotus.

Isaiah 45:13 records the prediction that Cyrus would set the Jews free from their slavery in Babylon. The same theme of Jewish return was mentioned by other biblical prophets, including Jeremiah (16:14-15; 23:7-8; 25:12-14; 50:8-10), Ezekiel (11:14-21; 28:24-26; 34:11-16; 37:1-39:29), Daniel (6:28; 10:1), and the apocryphal work Bel and the Dragon (1-2).

The Judeo-Roman historian Flavius Josephus of the first century A.D. said that Cyrus was so impressed with these predictions that he decided to free the Jews on the basis of them (*Antiquitates Judaicae*, c. A.D. 93; *The Antiquities of the Jews*). For whatever reason Cyrus made his decision, one should not assume that the treatment of the Jews was unique. One of the most notable features of Cyrus' reign was his benevolent treatment of former captive peoples who had served as provincial servants of the Neo-Assyrians and later of the Neo-Babylonians. Their former plight was in marked contrast under Cyrus' rule. Little wonder, then, that Cyrus was admired by many of his new subjects as being a benevolent ruler.

The benevolent rule of Cyrus in the biblical texts is correlated in the cuneiform sources called the "Nabonidus Chronicle," the "Cyrus Cylinder," and the "Verse Account." These sources mention that Nabonidus, the last of the Neo-Babylonian rulers, was so preoccupied with the worship of the moon god Sin that he neglected the worship and state-cult of Marduk. This infuriated the priests of Marduk and much of the population of Babylon. Therefore, when Cyrus and his generals attacked that great city, they probably had assistance from defectors of the city of Babylon. In fact, the "Cyrus Cylinder" mentions that Marduk specifically chose Cyrus as a champion of the rights of the Babylonian people.

In the classical Greek sources, Herodotus and Xenophon, Cyrus was described as an ideal general, politician, and diplomat. In later times, Cicero and Scipio Africanus expressed admiration for the military exploits of Cyrus.

In spite of all the great military victories of Cyrus, his death was at the hands of a nomadic tribe, the Massagetae of Scythia. To make matters more embarrassing for the great king of Persia, the Massagetae were led in battle by a woman, Queen Tomyris. According to Herodotus, Tomyris decapitated Cyrus, dipped his head in a skin full of human blood and gore, and said that Cyrus could now have his fill of blood.

Summary

The remarkable interest in the life and influence of Cyrus the Great exhibited by the Hebrews, Babylonians, and later the Greek historians can be explained most easily by understanding the harshness of earlier rule by the Assyrians and Babylonians. Both the Assyrians and the Babylonians were oppressive in their collection of tribute, taxes, and gifts in honor of state events, and, on occasion, quotas of military men were required of conquered provinces. In addition to these humiliating aspects of their rule, they sometimes destroyed temples and shrines of the subjected provinces and forced the people to make an oath of allegiance, under "divine" penalty if the oath was broken.

Therefore, Cyrus' popularity arose from his restoration of native religious observances; his tolerance of their cults was a welcome relief from earlier oppression. The famous biblical example of such tolerance found in the "Cyrus Decree" in Ezra 1:1-4, which mentions that the Jews (former captives of the Babylonians) could return home to Jerusalem in Judah and rebuild their temple, is typical of Cyrus' policies.

Cyrus' burial monument in Pasargadae was humble by ancient standards. It was inscribed with words to the effect that he wanted to be remembered as founder of the Persian Empire and master of Asia.

Bibliography

Bickermann, Elias J. "The Edict of Cyrus in Ezra 1." *Journal of Biblical Literature* 65 (September, 1946): 249-275. Provides an able defense of the probable historicity of the decree of Cyrus authorizing the Jews to return to their homeland and rebuild their temple.

Dougherty, Raymond Philip. *Nabonidus and Belshazzar: A Study of the Closing Events of the Neo-Babylonian Empire*. New Haven, Conn.: Yale University Press, 1929. In volume 15 of the Yale Oriental Studies series, Dougherty arranges the cuneiform evidence in probable chronological order, showing the sequence of events leading to Cyrus' capture of Babylon.

Drews, Robert. "Sargon, Cyrus, and Mesopotamian Folk History." *Journal of Near Eastern Studies* 33 (October, 1974): 387-393. Compares the legendary birth accounts of Sargon and Cyrus, and concludes that the Greek historians borrowed oral legends about Cyrus' birth and early life.

Harmatta, J. "The Rise of the Old Persian Empire: Cyrus the Great." *Acta Antiqua* 19 (1971): 3-15. Tries to make sense of the early birth legends, and also describes Cyrus' military conquest over Media and consolidation of rule in Persia.

Lawrence, John M. "Cyrus: Messiah, Politician, and General." *Near East Archaeological Society Bulletin*, n.s. 25 (1985): 5-28. An attempted comparison and harmonization of the accounts of Cyrus from the biblical, cuneiform, and classical sources.

___________. "Neo-Assyrian and Neo-Babylonian Attitudes Towards Foreigners and Their Religion." *Near East Archaeological Society Bulletin*, n.s. 19 (1982): 27-40. Describes the cruelty and oppression of the Assyrians and Babylonians prior to Cyrus' freeing of countless provinces of their former captives and the stark contrast of Cyrus' benevolent rule.

Mallowan, Max. "Cyrus the Great (558-529 B.C.)." *Iran* 10 (1972): 1-17. Provides a chronology of the conquests of Cyrus and a linguistic-historical analysis of some of the cuneiform inscriptions that mention Cyrus.

Wiseman, Donald J. *The Chronicles of the Chaldaean Kings (626-556 B.C.) in the British Museum*. London: Trustees of the British Museum, 1956. Includes historical background for the struggle between the Assyrian and Babylonian empires shortly before Cyrus conquered Babylon.

John M. Lawrence

ENRICO DANDOLO

Born: 1108?; Venice
Died: 1205; Constantinople
Area of Achievement: Government
Contribution: As Doge of Venice from 1193 to 1205, Enrico Dandolo presided over the Republic of Venice and founded its commercial, colonial, and maritime empire in the eastern Mediterranean Sea. He was the outstanding leader of the Fourth Crusade, 1201-1204, and played the key role in its diversion from the Holy Land to Constantinople.

Early Life

Enrico Dandolo was born about 1108 into the Venetian merchant aristocracy. This birth date, which the best and earliest sources provide, has been called into question by some modern historians, who doubt that a nonagenarian who was blind and a businessman to boot could have led chivalric Crusaders into battle. The primary sources from the Fourth Crusade agree that Dandolo was blind and very aged, and modern doubts would seem to involve latent prejudices about old age and physical handicaps rather than any real evidence. The birth date in 1108 would have Dandolo eighty-five years old in 1193 when he was elected Doge (or Duke) of Venice, which agrees well with the earliest sources.

During the early twelfth century, Dandolo made no special mark, so his early life has left little record. It may be presumed that he had the characteristic career of scions of the Venetian merchant aristocracy and served in the navy and marines, on a succession of government boards, assemblies, and councils, and in diplomatic posts overseas. In Venetian diplomatic service Dandolo rose to the top by 1170 to become ambassador of Venice to the Byzantine Empire at Constantinople. He also worked in his family's business, married, and had children, including a son who acted as his deputy in Venice when Dandolo was overseas on crusade.

During the twelfth century, Venice, Genoa, and Pisa were commercial rivals in the Mediterranean, but Venice was almost a satellite of the Byzantine Empire, culturally in its shadow, politically often under its thumb, and economically beholden to it for trade concessions and favors. Venice's territorial ambitions along the Adriatic Balkan coast and in the islands of the Ionian and Aegean seas brought the republic into collision with the Byzantine Empire and the rising Balkan power of Hungary, which became a vassal kingdom of the Papacy. At the head of the Adriatic Sea, Venice was also placed in an exposed position between the Papacy and its allies and the Holy Roman Empire. Venice's geographic and economic situation required inspired diplomacy in order to maintain the republic's freedom and to increase its power.

Life's Work

While Dandolo was the Venetian ambassador at Constantinople in 1170, his life suddenly and terribly changed. In the anti-Latin rioting that year in Constantinople, the Byzantines arrested and blinded Dandolo. There survive several accounts of his blinding, the most credible being the obscure *Novgorodskaia letopis* (*The Chronicle of Novgorod, 1016-1471*, 1914), which is also the one most consistent with the other evidence.

Byzantine agents had identified Dandolo as the ablest of the Latins and a statesman very likely to rise to power in the Republic of Venice. The Byzantine emperor therefore ordered him seized and blinded by a fiendish apparatus of glass which used concentrated reflected sunlight to destroy his retinas without changing the appearance of his eyes or leaving any apparent injury. The intent was to disable Dandolo, demoralize and depress him, disqualify him from future leadership positions, and, in a devious manner, discredit him should he try to explain his blindness.

The disability would have crushed most men, but Dandolo persevered in his quest for the dogeship. He was not only undeterred by his disability but also strengthened in his resolve and purpose of liberating Venice from Byzantine influences. The blind Dandolo saw more perceptively than his contemporaries and even later historians the strategic geopolitical realities around 1200, when the traditional Crusade aimed at Jerusalem had become obsolescent, peripheral, and largely irrelevant.

Dandolo's notion of crusading combined diplomacy, mastery of the seas, and a plan to attack directly at centers of power in Egypt and Asia Minor, not at symbols such as Jerusalem. In this he anticipated the later development of crusading. More controversially, Dandolo regarded the Byzantine Empire not as a necessary buffer state between Western Christendom and Islam but as a degenerate, wicked, and treacherous ally which really was an obstacle to the attainment of the goals of crusading. Dandolo's familiarity with the East and his cosmopolitan sophistication were very different from the naïve chivalry and piety of the French Crusaders, for whom crusading meant armed pilgrimage to Jerusalem, not mastery of complex power politics.

In order to achieve his ends, Dandolo capitalized on a series of opportunities which chance provided. First, in 1201, he negotiated the Treaty of Venice with the French Crusaders contracting for transportation across the sea to Egypt. By 1202, however, too few Crusaders had assembled at Venice to pay their part of the contract. Venice faced financial catastrophe because the republic had overextended itself on shipbuilding and provisioning the Fourth Crusade on Crusader credit.

Dandolo renegotiated the treaty and drove a hard bargain. It was argued that the Fourth Crusade would not proceed directly to Egypt but instead divert to besiege Zadar, a Christian port on the Adriatic Sea which had rebelled against the Venetian empire. Late in 1202, Christian Zadar fell to the Fourth Crusade, much to the shock of Christendom.

At Zadar, Dandolo and the Crusaders renegotiated their agreement, and taking advantage of dynastic turmoil in the Byzantine Empire and the private ambitions of some great Western noblemen, Dandolo secured another diversion of the Fourth Crusade. The Crusaders were to move from Zadar in 1203 to Constantinople, the capital of the Byzantine Empire, ostensibly to place an exiled pretender on the throne where he would further the Crusade.

In July of 1203, the Fourth Crusade stormed the fortifications of Constantinople. The Venetians breached the seaward walls, led by Dandolo in front with the Venetian banner, setting the example of bravery. He was at this time about ninety-five years old and blind. After this first conquest of the capital, new dynastic turmoil soon led to the expulsion of the Crusaders. In April of 1204, the Crusaders took Constantinople a second time and sacked the city, plundering it for three days.

The Fourth Crusade ended here and never reached the Holy Land. The Crusaders chose Baldwin of Flanders as the new emperor of what would prove to be the ill-fated Latin Empire of Constantinople (1204-1261) and divided the city and Byzantine territories. Venice received three-eighths of the city; trade concessions; the lion's share of the booty in religious relics, works of art, and precious commodities; and a network of island and peninsular territories in the Aegean and Ionian seas, the foundations of Venice's vast maritime empire. His work done, Dandolo died in Constantinople in 1205.

Summary

The long life span of Dandolo saw the transformation of the crusading ideal from the religious fervor and idealism which had marked the First Crusade to the political realism and secularism which marked the Fourth Crusade. Dandolo had been trained in the hard school of power politics and could capitalize on this transformation in the interest of the Republic of Venice, which he probably regarded as in line with the interest of all Christendom. Some romantic medievalists may criticize this crusty old bourgeois businessman for lacking the visionary idealism of a naïve French knight, but in the new age Dandolo's commercial bourgeois values certainly were more realistic and successful. Perhaps more important, Dandolo overcame serious physical disabilities and achieved resounding victory for his Republic of Venice. This blind nonagenarian businessman of unexampled bravery, vigor, and imperial vision was medieval Venice's greatest doge, diplomat, naval commander, and statesman.

Bibliography

Brand, Charles M. *Byzantium Confronts the West, 1180-1204*. Cambridge,

Mass.: Harvard University Press, 1968. The Fourth Crusade and its background from the perspective of its Byzantine victim. Predictably hostile to Dandolo and skeptical about his blindness and old age, though grudgingly appreciative of his great abilities.

Godfrey, John. *1204: The Unholy Crusade*. Oxford: Oxford University Press, 1980. A work for the general reader, stressing "the medieval mind" and condemning the Fourth Crusade.

McNeill, William H. *Venice: The Hinge of Europe, 1081-1797*. Chicago: University of Chicago Press, 1974. Fascinating study which interprets the greatness of medieval and early modern Venice in terms of geopolitics, history of technology, economic history, and cultural diffusion. Lucidly explains the pivotal position and power of Venice.

Queller, Donald E. *The Fourth Crusade: The Conquest of Constantinople 1202-1204*. Philadelphia: University of Pennsylvania Press, 1977. A scholarly and detailed study, sympathetic to the Venetians and by far the best secondary source on the Crusade.

Queller, Donald E., and Susan J. Stratton. "A Century of Controversy on the Fourth Crusade." *Studies in Medieval and Renaissance History* 6 (1969): 235-277. Extremely important analysis of the modern historical writing about the Fourth Crusade. Especially incisive and informative on the controversial "diversion question" and equitable in judgment.

Robert de Clari. *The Conquest of Constantinople*. Translated and edited by Edgar Holmes McNeal. New York: W. W. Norton and Co., 1969. Primary account of the Fourth Crusade by a French knight from the Crusader rank and file. Robert de Clari certainly admired Dandolo, though it was difficult for the knight to appreciate the doge's bourgeois values.

Setton, Kenneth M., ed. *A History of the Crusades*. 2d ed. 5 vols. Madison: University of Wisconsin Press, 1969-1985. This massive and standard collaborative scholarly work contains important chapters on the Fourth Crusade and Venice.

Villehardouin, Geoffrey de. "The Conquest of Constantinople." In *Chronicles of the Crusades*, edited and translated by M. R. B. Shaw. Baltimore: Penguin Books, 1963. The key primary source by a great French nobleman and leader of the Fourth Crusade.

Terence R. Murphy

DANTE

Born: May, 1265; Florence, Italy
Died: September 13 or 14, 1321; Ravenna, Italy
Area of Achievement: Literature
Contribution: Dante's *The Divine Comedy*, written in vernacular Italian *terza rima*, synthesizes classical and medieval thought in a confessional format which is at once universal and intensely personal.

Early Life

A welter of legend surrounds the life of Dante, author of the tripartite masterpiece *La divina commedia* (c. 1320; *The Divine Comedy*). Still, certain facts are clear. His neighbor Giovanni Villani wrote a brief sketch, and Giovanni Boccaccio wrote a eulogy which appeared sometime after Dante's death. These accounts agree on a birth date in May of 1265. His family had had noble origins at least several generations before Dante's birth, and their surname was originally Alagherius or Alaghieri. Dante's own name is a shortened form of Durante. His mother died during his childhood, and his father, who remarried, died in 1283. Dante had two sisters (one a half sister named Tana from his father's second marriage) and a half brother named Francesco. Although his family was nominally ennobled, it was neither rich nor especially prominent.

By all accounts, Dante's early life was a happy one. His family recognized the value of education and sent him to an elementary school run by the Dominicans and subsequently to the school of Santa Croce. He read both Provençal and Italian poets during these early years and acquired a knowledge of metrics entirely on his own. His readings gave him vivid impressions of country as well as city life; he also enjoyed art and practiced drawing.

Florence was the center of the literary and artistic world in the late Middle Ages, and the city continued to flourish during the Renaissance. It was during these transitional years that the young Dante and those with whom he associated lived there. The poet Guido Cavalcanti, although Dante's senior, became "the first among [his] friends," as Dante records in *La vita nuova* (c. 1292; *Vita nuova*, 1861; better known as *The New Life*), and his literary adviser. In the *Inferno*'s circle of Epicureans, Guido's father Cavalcante de' Cavalcanti learns of his son's death in one of the canticle's most poignant scenes. Guido was a man of his times in every sense; he disliked classical verse in general and Vergil's poetry in particular, primarily because of its imperialism and religious piety.

Brunetto Latini, a scholar and author of a French prose encyclopedia called *Li Livres dou tresor* (1266; the books of treasure), was another important influence on Dante. Much conjecture surrounds Dante's placing his mentor among the Sodomites of the *Inferno*. The best explanation, cogently argued by John Freccero, is that Dante came to recognize the pridefulness a comprehensive encyclopedia of knowledge implies and realized, as had Saint Augustine, that one could be seduced by glib language.

Practically nothing is known about the musician Mario Casella aside from Dante's affection for him—and that he serenades the Pilgrim Dante and the penitents in the *Purgatorio* and shaped Dante's love of music. Casella died sometime before 1300, the year in which *The Divine Comedy* is set. Not much more can be said of Dante's contemporaries the poets Lapo Gianni and Cino da Pistoia, except that they saw themselves as the vanguard of new poets who would change the character of Italian verse.

Life's Work

The literary ferment of Dante's time was matched and exceeded by political instability and violence, and Dante found himself thrust into this atmosphere. Florence was an essentially independent municipality controlled by its trade unions and intense partisan interests. In 1289, Dante, a young poet married for several years to Gemma Donati, participated in the Battle of Campaldino, fighting against the rival town of Arezzo. His wife was a fourth cousin of Corso and Forese Donati, perhaps of the same family as the Buoso degli Abati of the *Inferno*; certainly, however, Corso Donati was an infamous leader of the Florentine political faction known as the "Blacks." Dante and his wife had at least three, possibly four, children during the period they lived together: two sons, named Pietro and Jacopo, and one or two daughters, Antonia and, less certainly, Beatrice. Dante's was an arranged marriage (with the dowry set in 1277), but it was not necessarily an unhappy one, as some contend. His wife did not follow Dante into exile in 1302, probably because her family ties to Florence were so strong.

The political conflict between "Blacks" and "Whites" had its origins in a continued class struggle between Guelfs and Ghibellines. The emerging middle class (essentially Ghibelline) was despised by the old military aristocracy (primarily Guelf), which built fortifications throughout and surrounding Florence, and although a battle fought at Benevento in 1266 brought a seemingly decisive defeat of the Ghibellines, the two factions reorganized around the Black Guelfs of the Donati family and the White Ghibellines of the Cerchi family. To assert aristocratic prerogative, the Blacks enlisted the aid of Pope Boniface VIII, who hoped to make Tuscany part of the Papal States. In 1302, Boniface sent an army into Tuscany under Charles de Valois (supposedly to establish order); the Whites, Dante among them, were driven from Florence. Dante would never return to his beloved city; he would also never forgive Boniface for what he saw as a perversion of papal authority. He alludes to Boniface with relentless bitterness in the *Inferno*.

Dante's Ghibelline sympathies and his having held municipal office in the years following 1295 had made him a conspicuous figure embarrassing to his

Guelf in-laws. His publication of *The New Life* had, by this time, attracted the attention of literary Florence as well. The work was noticed first as an anthology of sonnets in Italian rather than Latin. The influence of the young Cavalcanti is clear in Dante's decision to break with tradition here. Curiosity surrounded (and continues to surround) the identity of Beatrice, a woman the poet had loved since their childhood. *The New Life* records Beatrice's death, and, although Dante does not divulge her surname, she is generally considered to have been Beatrice dei Portinari, daughter of the prominent Florentine Folco dei Portinari and wife of the banker Simone dei Bardi. Her tragic early death and innocence make her a recurring figure of saintliness in Dante's verse, and it is Beatrice who leads the Pilgrim Dante through Heaven in the *Paradiso*, the last canticle of *The Divine Comedy*.

By 1302, then, Dante was considered a brash young poet and a political troublemaker. He was separated from his wife and family, dispossessed of his property, and (cruelest of all for him) banished formally from his city under the threat of death by fire. The charges against him are vague, obliquely involving misappropriation of municipal funds left in his charge. The real reason for his expulsion involves his White sympathies. He could have purchased a pardon in 1315 by submitting to Guelf authority, but he refused to do so.

For several years after the sentence of exile was imposed, Dante wandered from town to town, first consorting with exiles who appeared to have like political sympathies but ultimately, disgusted with their grandiose plans and incipient violence, going his own way and depending on his writing for his living. These were essentially rootless and wandering years. Around 1307, he wrote *Il convivio* (*The Banquet*, 1903), a popular exposition of philosophy which contains a commentary of fourteen of his own poems. Dante sought peace in its writing and probably adapted that volume from sets of lectures given in various university cities, Bologna and Paris possibly among them. He completed only four of the work's projected fifteen treatises. Also incomplete and written during these years is a formal treatise in Latin, *De vulgari eloquentia* (c. 1306; English translation, 1890).

One can only guess how Dante lived during this period. The Scala family of Verona housed and supported him for a time, generously as it appears, until the death of his patron Bartolommeo (Alboino) della Scala in 1304. In 1306, Dante acted for the Malaspina family of Lunigiana in negotiating a peace with the Bishop of Luni. By 1310, he was actively involved in supporting the Holy Roman Emperor Henry VII of Luxembourg, in an attempt to reunite church and state in Northern Italy. The emperor's invasion attempt was foiled from the beginning and faced the united opposition of nearly all Tuscany. Dante's outspoken encouragement of Henry VII in the form of three letters, probably written at Pisa from 1310 to 1311, did little to endear him to his fellow Florentines, and Henry VII's inglorious death at Siena in 1313 ended Dante's hope for return to his native city.

Fortunately, Dante was able to turn again to the Scala family of Verona, and Can Grande della Scala became his new champion. By the time of his return to Verona, in 1314 or 1315, Dante had completed the *Inferno* and probably a large part of the *Purgatorio*. It was relatively soon after this, possibly as early as 1316, that Guido da Polenta, a nephew of Francesca da Rimini whom Dante had immortalized in the *Inferno*, offered Dante permanent sanctuary at Ravenna. Dante accepted the offer, probably in part because two of his children, Pietro and Antonia (who had become a nun and taken "Beatrice" as her religious name) resided there.

It appears that these final years at Ravenna were happy. Dante found respect and peace there and took some sort of diplomatic mission to Venice during this period. He continued to enjoy the friendship and patronage of Can Grande and to work on the *Paradiso*, which would ultimately be published as the final canticle of *The Divine Comedy*. He died peacefully at Ravenna, never again seeing his beloved Florence, on September 13 or 14, 1321.

Contemporary engravings of Dante, almost always idealized, portray him as a professorial-looking man of about fifty, his face unlined and seemingly untroubled by the political and personal turmoil of what would have been essentially homeless years of exile. He, like the Pilgrim Dante of *Purgatorio* and *Paradiso*, has eyes upraised toward a more sublime existence, found in some measure in the friendship of his Verona and Ravenna patrons.

Summary

Perhaps Dante always knew that his real contribution would be to pioneer the *dolce stil nuovo* (sweet new style) of vernacular Italian verse. Indeed, each canto of *The Divine Comedy* presents a technical challenge to the poet which matches the physical obstacles facing the Pilgrim. It is no accident, therefore, that Dante's predecessor in poetry, Vergil, whom he calls *Maestro* (master), is left behind once the Pilgrim enters Paradiso. Vergil cannot guide the Pilgrim through Heaven because no poet has ever sought to describe the infinite nature of God in finite human language. Dante, who brought allegory from its classical associations with a sacred text to a secular poem paradoxically filled with the universal and individual search for a Divine Unity, clearly saw the struggles of his life against the difficulties of writing this sublime poem.

That is not to imply that Dante was so idealistic as to believe the wretchedness of Tuscan politics could be altered by a philosophy of poetry. Change needed an agent, and Dante looked hopefully to one earthly savior after the next. One always senses, however, despite his letters of encouragement to Henry VII, despite his prophecy of a Hound (Can Grande?) in the *Inferno* who will subdue the rapacious Wolf, that Dante knew the wait would be a long one.

Bibliography

Auerbach, Erich. *Dante: Poet of the Secular World*. Translated by Ralph Manheim. Chicago: University of Chicago Press, 1961. Auerbach applies his mimetic theory to *The Divine Comedy* to illustrate how the poet used the circumstances of his own life to shape a poetic fiction which holds universal reality for its readers. Auerbach's work continues to have a profound influence on contemporary Dante studies.

Barbi, Michele. *Life of Dante*. Edited and translated by Paul G. Ruggiers. Berkeley: University of California Press, 1954. Remains the best scholarly biography, with full notes, general analyses of Dante's works, and a useful, if somewhat dated, bibliography.

Cosmo, Umberto. *A Handbook to Dante Studies*. Translated by David Moore. Oxford: Basil Blackwell, 1950. This volume, available in most libraries, lists periodicals, major critical works, and sources for further reading. It can be used effectively by students as well as Dante specialists.

Freccero, John. *Dante: The Poetics of Confession*. Cambridge, Mass.: Harvard University Press, 1986. This is a collection of Freccero's major articles on Dante, a poet he sees as heir to the Augustinian tradition of confessional literature. Freccero concentrates on Dante's ability to make his poem move beyond finite language at the same time as it reveals Dante both as Pilgrim and Poet.

__________, ed. *Dante: A Collection of Critical Essays*. Englewood Cliffs, N.J.: Prentice-Hall, 1965. A collection of classic essays by Auerbach, Luigi Pirandello, T. S. Eliot, Bruno Nardi, Leo Spitzer, Charles S. Singleton, and others. Contains an introduction by the editor, a chronology of Dante's life, and a short bibliography.

Holmes, George. *Dante*. New York: Oxford University Press, 1983. This volume in the Past Masters series provides a good introduction for the student and general reader. Contains a selected bibliography.

Singleton, Charles S., ed. and trans. *Dante: The Divine Comedy*. 6 vols. Princeton, N.J.: Princeton University Press, 1973-1975. This work is the classic translation and commentary on Dante's magnum opus. It contains full Italian text and apparatus for the scholar and a readable translation on facing pages. The separate commentary volumes allow for easy reference, and the commentary itself, though scholarly, is never esoteric.

Robert J. Forman

DARIUS THE GREAT

Born: 550 B.C.; place unknown
Died: 486 B.C.; Persepolis, Persia
Areas of Achievement: Government and law
Contribution: Darius consolidated and expanded the Persian Empire through humane, wise, and judicious administration. He respected the languages, religions, and cultures of his subject nations, and in return they fought his battles, built lavish palaces for him, and brought him precious gifts.

Early Life

According to his own account in the Behistun friezes, somewhat different from that of Herodotus in *Historiai Herodotou* (c. 425; *The History*, 1709), Darius was the son of Hystaspes, grandson of Arsames, and great-grandson of Ariaramnes. This genealogy is important: Ariaramnes and Cyrus I were grandsons of Achaemenes, the eponymous ancestor of the Achaemenian dynasty.

Upon the death of their father, Teispes, Cyrus I became the ruler of Anshan; Ariaramnes inherited the principality of Parsua. By the time of Cyrus the Great, Ariaramnes' son, Arsames, ruled Parsua. Cyrus the Great deposed Arsames and annexed Parsua to his own share of the inheritance, calling himself the King of Anshan and Parsua. A charismatic leader, Cyrus expanded his small kingdom to imperial heights within a short time by defeating Media (which included Assyria) and capturing Sardis in Asia Minor. Babylonia, his neighbor and ally, capitulated to his rule soon after. Cyrus' star rose in power and prestige, while that of Ariaramnes fell.

Before his death, Cyrus made plans to capture Egypt and Ethiopia. Grain from Egypt and ivory from Ethiopia were necessary commodities for the upkeep of the empire that Cyrus envisaged. After Cyrus' death, Cambyses II continued his father's plans for expansion. He captured Egypt and remained there in the hope of adding Ethiopia, the oasis of Ammon, and Carthage to the empire. He succeeded, however, only in subjugating the Greeks of Libya.

The king's long absence prompted a severe sociopolitical upheaval in Persia and Media. A usurper—either the king's brother Smerdis (also called Bardiya) or a pretender—assumed rulership and gained public sanction. When Cambyses, returning hastily to Persia, died in Syria from a self-inflicted wound, Darius appeared in Media to claim his own Achaemenian divine right. With the help of six Persian noblemen, his father-in-law Gobryas among them, he invaded the palace of the pretender and ended his rule after seven months. It is not clear who the pretender was; according to Darius, he was Gaumata, a Magian. Smerdis, Darius explained, had already been slain by Cambyses in secret.

Thus, ten years after the death of Cyrus, the twenty-eight-year-old son of

Hystespes returned the Achaemenian throne to the house of Ariaramnes. There is no information on Darius' childhood and early youth. It is assumed that, as the son of a satrap, he was educated in the basic disciplines and in the martial arts. As a youth, he was ambitious; Cyrus suspected him of treason. After Cyrus' death, Darius commanded the prestigious ten thousand Immortals and served as the new king's spear bearer and bodyguard in Egypt. Tall, with long, curly hair and a long beard, he cut an impressive figure.

Darius' claim to legitimacy was slender. As descendants of Achaemenes, his immediate ancestors had lost the *farr* (divine sanction), and both Arsames and Hystespes were still living. During the reign of Cambyses II, Darius' father, Hystespes, had been the satrap of Parthia and Hyrcania. Darius had to create legitimacy; he had to provide visible proof that the god Ahura Mazda favored him and his family. During the first year of his rule, he married Atossa, the daughter of Cyrus the Great, and he fought nineteen battles and captured nine rebel leaders. A gigantic bas-relief commemorating the end of his ordeal depicts the nine rulers standing crestfallen before the king. The king has his foot on the slain Gaumata. Ahura Mazda, the king's helper and embodiment of legitimacy, hovers above the assembly. Columns of cuneiform writing inform the spectator that the rebellious provinces included Persia, Elam, Media, Assyria, Egypt, Parthia, Margiana, and Scythia, and that the strategically important provinces were brought within the fold quickly, while the subjugation of Scythia and Egypt took a while longer. Some provinces did not give up after the first defeat. Susa, for example, rose up three times before it was completely crushed. When the resistance finally ran its course and tranquillity returned to the land, Darius became convinced that his rulership was undisputed and set his sights on expansion of his empire.

Life's Work

Subjugation of the unruly elements in the empire had taken about three years. After tranquillity had returned, the only threat Darius could envisage was an external threat: an invasion of the northern provinces of the empire by the Scythian tribes who had fought and killed Cyrus II. To prevent this, Darius attacked the Scythians to the east of the Caspian Sea and pushed them far back into Soghdia. He also captured the fertile Indus Valley, adding this region to the empire for the first time.

By 518, the empire was tranquil enough for Darius to visit Egypt as king. The visit to this ancient and important land fulfilled two objectives: adding to the king's prestige at home and consolidating Persian rule in Egypt, the empire's southwestern flank, which had been neglected since the death of Cambyses.

Darius lived at a time when men thought it possible to unify the world and to rule it with justice. Darius, duty-bound to expand Zoroastrianism, also considered himself obliged to subjugate the Greeks and to put an end to their intrigue in lands under Persian domination in Asia Minor. In 513, therefore, he crossed the Bosporus and the Danube and pushed the Scythians so far into Europe that he eventually had to abandon the campaign for lack of provisions. Thrace and Macedonia were subjugated by Persian satraps.

With the lifeline of the Greek islands in his hands, Darius decided to postpone any further campaigns in Europe and return to Persia. His return, however, did not preclude a systematic invasion of Attica at a later date. While he knew that he had shown enough might to intimidate Greece for the present, he also knew that the Greeks would continue to incite riots in Persia's Greek settlements in Asia Minor and force him to return to the battlefield.

Darius' decision to return to Persia, rather than engage his troops in a new European theater, was wise. He lacked sufficient information to formulate a coherent strategy. Intelligence on the naval capability of Greece was especially crucial, because without it, Darius could not address the question of logistics or establish a stable supply line between his land army and his navy. Furthermore, to take on Greece and her neighbors, he needed a better equipped and stronger military and naval force than Persia could afford at the time. In addition, he was not sure that his subjects would be able to withstand the trauma of a prolonged war. After all, the young empire comprised diverse religious and cultural entities, some of which, such as Egypt and Babylonia, had enjoyed a glorious past.

Darius' forte was administration. He now brought this strength to bear on the problem of bringing Europe under Persian rule. Following Cyrus' lead, he had allowed his subjects to retain their languages, religions, and cultures. He now instituted the rule of justice under the divine right of kings throughout the empire. This rule of justice would require numerous changes in the makeup of the empire. These changes were implemented with a reform of the tax system—the amount of tax was measured by ability and by the yield of the land—and the introduction of a monetary system based on the darik to replace payment in kind.

The introduction of currency led not only to further utilization of the mineral wealth of Persia but also to the institution of a simple system of banking. The guardianship of wealth, hitherto the sole privilege of the royal court and of the priests, was gradually turned over to the people. More money in the hands of the populace meant better *qanats* (subterranean water conduits) and canals for agriculture, better roads for trade, and overall a more unified kingdom. To free the weak from the bondage of the strong further, Darius instituted a fixed system of wages. Tablets discovered at Persepolis indicate the rates at which men, women, and children were paid for their labor.

The vast empire of Darius stretched from Macedonia and Egypt to the Jaxartes River and the Indus Valley. It could not be managed by one man. His three long years of struggle to establish his credibility had proved to Darius that he needed trustworthy men to help him rule. Toward this end, he revamped the satrap system introduced by Cyrus, increasing the number of satraps to twenty. The satraps were chosen from among the Persians of royal blood and appointed to the provinces. Each satrapy had a governor (the satrap) and a secretary to organize the affairs of the state. The secretary had a small army attached to his office. When necessary, the secretary could mobilize this army to unseat an ambitious satrap. The satrapy was also assigned a tax collector and a military general, both of whom reported to the king.

In order to safeguard his position further, Darius appointed a fifth person, an individual referred to as the "eyes and ears" of the king, to each satrapy. This officer kept the king abreast of events in his part of the empire and reported on abuses of power and activities that bordered on treason. An inspector would arrive unannounced to examine the satrapy's books and file a report at court.

Such an elaborate administrative machine could not function without a similarly elaborate communications system. Darius therefore built a royal road, 1,677 miles in length, to connect Sardis to Susa. A similar road connected Babylon to the Indus Valley. Royal *chapars* (messengers) carried the king's messages on fresh horses provided at 111 stations. In addition, Darius completed the construction of the 125-mile canal in the Nile Delta, a project that had been abandoned by the pharaoh Necos.

In 499, incited by Greece and Eretria, the Ionians of Asia Minor revolted against Darius and set the city of Sardis on fire. The insurrection was quickly suppressed. Seven years later, Darius' son-in-law, Mardonius, was sent on an expedition to subjugate Eretria and Athens. When Mardonius' fleet was destroyed in a storm near Mount Athos, Darius sent another expedition under Datis, a Mede. Datis conquered Eretria but failed to impress its population. His maltreatment of the Eretrians convinced the Greeks that they should prevent any further Persian advance in Europe. Datis' actions thus roused the Greek states to join forces and defeat the Persians.

After a defeat at Marathon, Darius could no longer focus his efforts on a final assault on Europe. Internal problems plagued the empire. Chief among them were two: the question of succession and a revolt in Egypt. The competition regarding succession had pitted Xerxes, Darius' son by Atossa, against Artabazanes, his eldest son by the daughter of Gobryas. Darius chose Xerxes to succeed him. Yet the more pressing problem of Greek infiltration in the uppermost stratum of Persian administration, infiltration that had resulted in revolt in Egypt, remained unresolved. Darius died, after thirty-six years as the King of Kings of Persia, in 486.

Darius had worn the Achaemenian crown and the royal robes very well. As a king, he was wise, determined, and a good judge of human character. More than anything, he was a builder in both the physical and the abstract senses of the word. The foundation of his empire survived not only Alexander's invasion but also the Arab invasion of Iran.

Summary

Because of the dubious validity of his claim to the throne, Darius had to impose his rule by force. Once his credibility was established and order was restored, he launched a series of reforms that improved agriculture and trade. These reforms provided a solid foundation for notable military triumphs and expansion of the Persian Empire.

Darius had a deep concern for the welfare of the individual. He studied the most reliable literature available at his time, the civil law code of Hammurabi, and devised his own set of rules for the Persian Empire. In the satrapies, such as Egypt, he provided guidance for the priests who wrote the local codes.

Though according to some sources Darius was the ruler who imposed the Zoroastrian religion on the Persians, he did not force his subject nations to follow the dictates of Ahura Mazda. On the contrary, in Egypt he built a temple to Ammon and endowed another. In 519, following Cyrus' long-neglected decree, he ordered that work be resumed on rebuilding the temple at Jerusalem.

Darius was fond of massive building projects. Indeed, he used these projects as a means to unify the country. For example, in building Persepolis, the palace wherein he received foreign dignitaries on the occasion of the Now Ruz (Persian new year), he employed the full spectrum of human and mineral resources of the empire so that everyone could have a share in the product. Babylonian bricklayers, Median and Egyptian goldsmiths and designers, Ionian and Carian carpenters, and others cooperated. They gathered a wealth of material—ivory from Ethiopia, cedar from Lebanon, turquoise from Khorazmia, and gold from Lydia—and constructed Persepolis as a genuinely cosmopolitan landmark.

Darius, however, failed to do for his nation-states what he did for his individual subjects. He did not allow subject nations such as Egypt and Babylonia to participate in the administration of the empire. In time, this policy drove the frustrated elites of those societies to conspiracy and revolt. Furthermore, Darius underestimated Greece, which, making capital use of the king's vulnerability, had sown discord in Asia Minor and Egypt before the burning of Sardis, which incited Darius to march on its territories. Greek policy, therefore, should be credited for both the defeat of Darius' military might at Marathon and the establishment of Western superiority over the empire of the East.

Bibliography

Burn, A. R. *Persia and the Greeks: The Defense of the West c. 546-478 B.C.*

London: Arnold, 1962. Contains detailed discussion of the campaigns of Darius in Europe. The book includes maps, charts illustrating battle formations, and genealogies for the major figures.

Cook, J. M. "The Rise of the Achaemenids and Establishment of Their Empire." In *The Cambridge History of Iran*, vol. 2, edited by Ilya Gershevitch. Cambridge: Cambridge University Press, 1985. This article examines the principal sources on ancient Iran and the extent and composition of the empire. Toward the end, an assessment is made of the leadership that raised Persia to the head of the world's first empire.

Frye, Richard N. *The Heritage of Persia*. London: Weidenfeld and Nicolson, 1962. Frye's account of ancient Iran is unique. It focuses on the eastern provinces of the ancient kingdom but, unlike other accounts, it draws on cultural, religious, and literary sources. The book is illustrated; it includes an index, maps, genealogies, and an informative bibliography.

Ghirshman, Roman. *The Arts of Ancient Iran from Its Origins to the Time of Alexander the Great*. New York: Golden Press, 1964. This massive volume, with incomparable illustrations in color and black and white, deals with Iranian art, especially Achaemenian art, and its influence on the art of the Western world and of India. The book also includes a comprehensive list of illustrations, a glossary, and good maps.

__________. *Iran from the Earliest Times to the Islamic Conquest*. Harmondsworth, England: Penguin Books, 1954. In this account of prehistory to Islamic times in Iran, Ghirshman juxtaposes textual information and archaeological data to place ancient Iran in proper perspective. The book is illustrated with text figures as well as with plates. It includes an index and a selected bibliography.

Herodotus. *The Histories*. Translated by Aubrey de Sélincourt; revised with an introduction and notes by A. R. Burn. Baltimore: Penguin Books, 1972. This, the most comprehensive classical account of the rise of Darius to kingship, also includes information on his administrative reforms, campaigns in Europe, and defeat at Marathon. This book should be read alongside other authoritative sources. The Penguin edition features poor maps but a good index.

Kent, Roland G. *Old Persian: Grammar, Texts, Lexicon*. New Haven, Conn.: American Oriental Society, 1950. Although set forth as a textbook, this volume provides an English translation of the most important Old Persian texts left for posterity by the Achaemenian kings, especially by King Darius.

Olmstead, Albert T. *History of the Persian Empire, Achaemenid Period*. Chicago: University of Chicago Press, 1948, 3d ed. 1966. This detailed history of the Achaemenid period remains the chief secondary source for the study of ancient Iran. The book includes a topographical index, maps, and many carefully selected illustrations.

Warner, Arthur G., et al. *The Shahnama of Firdausi*. London: Kegan Paul, Trench, Trübner and Co., 1905-1915. This nine-volume versified translation of Iran's major epic provides a wealth of information on ancient Iranian religion, social hierarchy, and military organization. It especially underscores the role of the king—an absolute ruler carrying out a divine decree.

Wilber, Donald N. *Persepolis: The Archaeology of Parsa, Seat of the Persian Kings*. New York: Thomas Y. Crowell, 1969. Wilber provides an account of Achaemenian history and of the monuments at Persepolis built by Darius and his successors. He discusses the layout of the palaces and their division into the *apadana*, harem, and throne hall.

Iraj Bashiri

DAVID

Born: c. 1030 B.C.; Bethlehem, Judah
Died: c. 962 B.C.; Jerusalem, Israel
Area of Achievement: Religion
Contribution: According to Hebrew tradition and the biblical record, David was the greatest king of Israel. It was prophesied of him that through his lineage the promise of a latter-day Messiah and other spiritual blessings would be fulfilled, making him a key monarch in the history of Israel and of importance to the development of both Christianity and later Judaism.

Early Life

The record of the life of David is found in the Bible in the historical writings of 1 Samuel 16 through 1 Kings 2, with some material repeated in 1 Chronicles 2-29 and in selected psalms attributed to him in the Old Testament. The early story of David's life is contained in 1 Samuel 18-19, though there are references to his life scattered throughout the rest of the Old Testament and in the New Testament. In the latter book, the birth of Jesus of Nazareth is specifically linked with the line of David and serves as one of the criteria Jesus and his later followers used to proclaim him the Messiah and King of the Jews. Most modern scholars accept the substantial historicity of these narratives.

The dating of David's birth and early life is primarily informed guesswork, but archaeological consensus is that David was born sometime around the second half of the eleventh century B.C. The great-grandson of Ruth and Boaz, David was the youngest of eight sons of Jesse, evidently a wealthy man who owned property and livestock and faithfully worshipped Yahweh, the God of Abraham, Isaac, and Jacob. As part of the lineage of Judah, David was qualified by Jewish tribal tradition for rulership in Israel. In the Bible, he alone is named David, symbolic of his prominence and importance in sacred history to both Jews and Christians.

David's early fame and preparation for kingship arose from his humble shepherding and his affinity for music; he was said to be a boy who could tame both beasts and the belligerent with his sweet tones. When Saul, the King of Israel, was to be deposed as a result of his lack of obedience to God, the prophet Samuel was commissioned by God to anoint the young David, much to the jealous chagrin of his elder brothers. There ensued from this set of events much intrigue between David and Saul, as the rejected king's fall from the throne was accompanied by an apparent madness or manic-depressive state that affected his ability to govern even himself, a malady which the young shepherd-musician was called upon to soothe with his music.

After David was put to the test in his legendary confrontation with the giant Philistine, Goliath, his stature as a leader began to overshadow that of Saul. In this familiar tale, David kills the taunting adversary with his slingshot and then beheads him, giving the glory of the victory to God. As the reputation of David spread from this heroic exploit, Saul became less enamored of the young shepherd boy who had befriended his son Jonathan, and he began to see David as a bitter rival, ignorant of the fact that God had already chosen David to be his successor. Soon David was under siege, as attempts were made upon his life. He was saved from one plot against him by the ingenuity of his wife Michal, one of Saul's daughters. (An irony of these court intrigues was the support David received from Saul's household through Jonathan and Michal.) The next stages in the life of David were marked by finding refuge from Saul, awaiting the former king's demise and his own coronation as king. During this time, David wrote many of the psalms attributed to him in the Book of Psalms, autobiographical poems and songs that reveal the inner conflict he experienced while trying to evade the plots on his life that were initiated by Saul and his followers.

Life's Work

As the reign of Saul came to an end, David had two opportunities to assassinate Saul and assume the throne immediately, but he chose to spare the king's life. In battle against the Philistines, Jonathan and Saul's other two sons were killed. Himself mortally wounded, Saul committed suicide rather than fall into the hands of the enemy. When David learned of their deaths, he tore his clothes and wept. David was eventually anointed by his own tribesmen and established his reign in Hebron at the age of thirty. He remained in Hebron for seven and a half years; eventually after a fierce but brief civil war between supporters of David and the remaining followers of Saul, he moved the capital to Jerusalem. David's reign in Jerusalem lasted more than thirty-three years, and the early decades of it were quite successful and blessed by God. With David's skillful military leadership, Israel conquered many of its enemies, including the ever-threatening Philistines and neighboring rivals Moab, Ammon, and Edom. During David's reign, Israel's dominance grew from the Egyptian boundaries to the upper Euphrates River. Major highways were built for travel and trade, and the kingdom prospered mightily. David was motivated, however, by more than a desire for military conquest and social prosperity for his people. At the center of his commitment was a religious devotion to God, Who he believed had brought him to power.

In response to his devotional impulses, David won back from the Philistines the ark of the covenant, a sacred vessel that housed the tablets for the Ten Commandments and other sacred relics of Israel's history. It was then returned to a special tabernacle prepared for it in Jerusalem. This acquisition gave Jerusalem even more prominence in a time when Israel was just coming to maturity as a nation-state and looking for a center of influence. The irony of David's laudable motivations to restore these important religious artifacts to Israel, and thus to inspire Israel to greater faith and devotion, is that his adultery with Bathsheba and the arranged murder of her husband occurred in this time period. The biblical record suggests that while gazing from his palace, David saw below the figure of Bathsheba, who bathed seductively in open view. Acting upon his lust, David committed adultery, and a child was conceived. David then ordered her soldier-husband, Uriah, to the front lines, where he was killed. The prophet Nathan, commissioned by God to confront David with his sins, told the king a parable of a rich man who stole a lamb from a poor man. David was crushed by the weight of his sin and the subsequent death of the child born to Bathsheba. Bathsheba gave birth to another child of David's, Solomon, who later succeeded his father upon the throne. David's reign, however, never quite recovered from this defiant act, and it symbolized the turning point in his kingship. Absalom, David's son by his wife Maacah, began to plot against his father to take over the throne but was defeated by David's loyal commander, Joab. David's last days as king were marred by the internecine warfare between Adonijah and Solomon for his throne.

The one triumph of his career that would have meant most to David was the construction of a temple of worship to Yahweh in Jerusalem. This privilege, however, was ironically denied to David, the master of ode, music, and song, "the sweet psalmist of Israel" (2 Sam. 23:1), and left for his son Solomon. David was denied this honor because he had been a man of war. David died, however, with the reassuring words of the prophet Nathan on his heart: "When your days are fulfilled and you lie down with your fathers, I will raise up your offspring after you, who shall come forth from your body, and I will establish his kingdom. He shall build a house for my name, and I will establish the throne of his kingdom for ever" (2 Sam. 7:12-13). Many later Christian writers interpret this prophecy as messianic, as pointing to the coming of Jesus. In the Book of Acts, the Apostle Peter, in his first message after the ascension of Christ, refers to many of David's deeds and words as being fulfilled in the life of Jesus.

Summary

David is clearly a pivotal figure in the history of ancient Israel and in the development of Christianity. In regard to the latter, he is mentioned fifty-eight times as an ancestor, forerunner, and foreshadower of Jesus Christ. David's impact and influence can be directly related to his personality, at once winsome and capable. His understanding of military strategy and administrative decision making allowed him to achieve innumerable successes. He was also clearly a flawed character, however, one given to momentary flights of wild misjudgment, including lust, that magnified the instability of his family life. In a time of polygamy, David fared no better than most men in maintaining multiple households, often engendering much strife among his sets of children and in his notorious relationship with Bathsheba.

Nevertheless, it was to David and the city he built, Jerusalem, to which Israel's people repeatedly turned for inspiration. When later generations sought relief from foreign domination or unwise kings, they longed for a king like David and looked forward to a time when the Messiah, promised to David himself, would sit upon his throne and reign over Israel.

No summary of David's life would be complete without a discussion of the many psalms that are attributed to him in the Old Testament's Book of Psalms. While it is difficult to determine how many of the psalms were actually composed by him, a number of them can be seen as true reflections of a man of many triumphs and sorrows. Perhaps the two most famous psalms attributed to David are Psalm 23 and Psalm 51. The former is the famous "shepherd psalm," in which David compares his relationship to God with that of a sheep to a shepherd. The latter psalm is an intensely autobiographical poem that details David's adultery with Bathsheba and his confession of that sin. In this most personal, psychologically complex psalm, the writer calls out desperately for mercy, recognizing that what is needed is not another animal sacrifice but a "broken spirit." Many generations of Jewish and Christian believers have been enriched by the psalmic literature attributed to David. The psalms have formed the basis for many Christian hymnals and prayer books since their compilation in the late centuries B.C. The confessional nature of many of these psalms also has inspired religious writers from Saint Augustine to Anne Bradstreet to John Bunyan to create autobiographical narratives detailing their estrangement from and reconciliation with God.

Bibliography

Albright, William Foxwell. *The Archaeology of Palestine*. New York: Penguin Books, 1963. This standard work on the archaeology of the ancient world remains the most comprehensive and informed overview of the historical data gleaned from that time. Overall, it provides the reader with an authentic sense of the civilization from which David originated and the one in which he became a prominent ruler.

Alexander, David, and Pat Alexander, eds. *Eerdmans' Handbook to the Bible*. Grand Rapids, Mich.: Wm. B. Eerdmans, 1973. A comprehensive handbook to biblical history and geography with helpful historical interpretations that trace David's rise to power in the Kingdom of Israel and illuminate for the lay reader the specific episodes in his life drawn from the biblical text.

Bright, John. *A History of Israel*. Philadelphia: Westminster Press, 1975. Probably the most thorough and compelling nontheological treatment available of the history of Israel. Sections on the world of the kingdoms and civilizations contemporary with the rule of David shed light on the story of his life and sustain the interest of both the common reader and the scholar with helpful anecdotal commentary on life in ancient times.

Bruce, F. F. *Israel and the Nations*. Grand Rapids, Mich.: Wm. B. Eerdmans, 1963. A comprehensive historical analysis of the kings of Israel beginning with Saul and David and continuing through the Davidic line. Provides a clear and succinct overview of the reign of David and the impact of David's rule throughout Israeli history.

Finegan, Jack. *Light from the Ancient Past: The Archeological Background of the Hebrew-Christian Religion*. Princeton, N.J.: Princeton University Press, 1959. A serious historical and archaeological work that concentrates primarily on corroborating the historicity and historical accuracy of the Old Testament accounts of the exploits, wars, and founding of nations that occurred during the rise and reign of David.

Harrison, R. K. *An Introduction to the Old Testament*. Grand Rapids, Mich.: Wm. B. Eerdmans, 1972. A complete overview of the origin, message, and impact of each book of the Old Testament, speaking directly to the issues of the chronology and authenticity of the biblical narrative of David's life and discussing his influence both in ancient Israel and in the present. A massive, comprehensive scholarly work with extensive documentation.

Kidner, Derek. *The Psalms*. 2 vols. Downers Grove, Ill.: Inter-Varsity Press, 1976. Comprehensive overview and interpretation of the psalms written by David. Illuminates and authenticates much of the life of David by revealing the private thoughts of the greatest king of Israel in ancient times.

Kitchen, K. A. *The Bible in Its World*. Downers Grove, Ill.: Inter-Varsity Press, 1977. An insider's look at the world of archaeology and how it functions in validating ancient records and narratives. It is particularly helpful in its extensive examination of antiquity's cultural artifacts and social conditions against the backdrop of the age of Saul, David, and Solomon, and the remainder of David's lineage.

Schultz, Samuel J. *The Old Testament Speaks*. New York: Harper and Row, Publishers, 1970. Written for the lay reader, this cogent and lucidly written volume presents an objective, historical analysis of the lives of the patriarchs, including a major section on David and the kings of Israel and their role in the evolution of ancient Israel.

Thompson, J. A. *Handbook to Life in Bible Times*. Downers Grove, Ill.: Inter-Varsity Press, 1986. A colorful, lavishly illustrated reference tool with key sections on the domestic life, travel, family customs, and cultural preoccupations of the biblical world. Illuminates the life and times of Israel and its kings in the period between 1400 and 1000 B.C., and thus is a helpful contextualizing volume for a study of David.

Bruce L. Edwards

DEMOCRITUS

Born: c. 460 B.C.; Abdera, Thrace
Died: c. 370 B.C.; Abdera, Thrace
Area of Achievement: Philosophy
Contribution: Democritus worked out a far-reaching atomism, which he applied to science, metaphysics, and ethics. His view that the world is made up of changing combinations of unchanging atoms was addressed to one of the central questions of his age—"How is change possible?"—and provided a model of reasoning that was mechanistic, materialist, and non-supernatural.

Early Life

Democritus was born, probably to wealthy parents, in the city of Abdera, Thrace. Although Leucippus, the philosopher who became his teacher, can properly be regarded as the founder of Greek atomism, Leucippus himself wrote very little, and very little is known about him. Democritus, however, was a prolific writer who developed a well-reasoned atomistic view and applied it to a wide variety of fields, including science, metaphysics, and ethics.

As a young man, Democritus traveled to Egypt, Persia, and Babylonia. Some ancient sources hold that he went as far south as Ethiopia and as far east as India, but modern scholars consider this doubtful. It is reported that Democritus boasted that he had visited more foreign lands and carried out more extensive inquiries and investigations than anyone else of his time. He traveled both for the "broadening" experience that falls to any inquisitive traveler and in order to receive instruction from those who were considered wise in many lands. When he returned to Greek soil, he himself earned a reputation for wisdom. He carried with him an aura of the exotic, having delved into cultures that the Greeks thought of as exotic and foreign: the cultures of Egypt, Persia, and Babylonia.

In character, Democritus is reported to have been a man of serenity, strength, and cheerfulness. The ancient Romans referred to him as "the laughing philosopher," alluding, perhaps, to his attitude toward the typically human fault of taking oneself too seriously.

As a thinker and writer, he addressed the most pressing philosophical and intellectual issues of the age in his works, which numbered at least fifty. Unfortunately, his texts have survived only in fragmentary form.

Life's Work

During the years following his travels, when Democritus began to develop his philosophical system, the Greek intellectual world was occupied with grave difficulties arising from the philosophy of Parmenides of Elea and his followers, the Eleatics. Parmenides was a practitioner of strict deductive logic. Taking premises that he thought would be generally acceptable, he argued logically to necessary conclusions. Many people admired his strong reliance on reason and thought; nevertheless, Parmenides arrived at conclusions that were deeply problematic. He concluded that there is no such thing as change and that no more than one thing exists. This clearly conflicts with common experience, which seems to show constant change and plurality. Still, Parmenides held fast to logic and reasoning as sources of knowledge that are more reliable than sense experience. If reason rules out change and plurality, he thought, then change and plurality do not exist.

The basis of his argument—an argument that Democritus and Leucippus had no choice but to grapple with—is the idea that reason either apprehends something or it apprehends nothing. If it apprehends nothing, then it is not reason (that is, not an apprehending) after all. Thus, reason apprehends what exists, not nothing. Now if things came into existence or passed out of existence, or if things changed their qualities over time, then reason would have to think of the things or qualities as not existing at some time (that is, before coming into existence or after passing out of existence). Reason would then, however, be apprehending nothing—and this, it was said, cannot occur. Similarly, if more than one thing existed, and there was empty space between the things, reason would again have to apprehend nothing. The conclusion is that only one thing exists, and this one thing is eternal, never coming into existence, never passing out of existence, and never changing. This one thing Parmenides called "the One."

One of the great achievements of Democritus and the atomists lies in overcoming this argument—an argument that probably seemed much more convincing to the ancient Greeks than to modern thinkers—while retaining some of its logical points and, at the same time, acknowledging the reality of change, plurality, and other commonsense ideas that Parmenides apparently denied.

It is a fundamental principle of Democritean atomism that "nothing exists but the atoms and the void." The atoms (literally, in Greek, "the indivisibles" or "the uncuttables") are the smallest units of matter, the smallest pieces of "being," and cannot be further divided. The void, considered "non-being," is thought to be just as real as the atoms. It was very important for Democritus that both exist: being and non-being, the atoms and the void. In a sense, the atoms are individually much like the One of Parmenides. They do not come into existence or pass out of existence, and they do not change (internally). Nevertheless, the void—a necessary feature of atomism—makes it possible for the atoms to combine and separate and recombine in changing arrangements.

As Democritus envisioned them, atoms differ from one another only in shape, size, and position. Qualities such as color and flavor were said to arise from the particular arrangements of (inherently colorless and flavorless) atoms and their interaction with the senses of the observer.

Atoms are constantly in motion, according to Democritus' theory. They do not require any force or intelligence to put them into motion. Surrounded by the void, they are not held in any one position but move quite freely. Atoms crash into one another, become entangled with one another, and sometimes establish regular motions or streams of motion. There is no limit to the void or to the number of atoms, and Democritus thought that the universe visible to human beings was only one among countless worlds, many of which must also contain stars, planets, and living things.

The atomism of Democritus was a reaffirmation of the reality of change as experienced in everyday life, yet it agreed with Parmenides concerning the unchanging reality that lies behind observed phenomena. The theory attempted to do justice to both experience and reason, change and permanence. Democritus envisioned a world in which combinations and configurations of atoms change within the void, but the atoms themselves never undergo internal change. Thus it is the void that makes change possible. Ironically, it could be said that in the theory of Greek atomism it is really the void (and not the atoms) that is innovative and enables the theory to escape from the unpalatable conclusions of Parmenides and the Eleatics.

Democritus also addressed questions raised by an entirely new movement in Greek thought. Previous to the time of Democritus, Greek philosophers had been almost exclusively concerned with physical and metaphysical questions—for example, questions about being and change. Around the time of Democritus, however, a revolution in philosophy was brought about by the Sophists and Socrates, who raised questions about human nature, society, and morality, rather than questions that focused on the physical world.

Democritus approached all these questions through his atomism. The soul, he surmised, is made up of highly mobile spherical atoms, which disperse at death. He hypothesized that people who seem to die but who "come back to life" have actually retained their atomic integrity all the while; they did not really die and come back to life. Eventually, in a real death, the atoms in the body begin to lose their connections with one another. This process is gradual, however, so that hair and fingernails might grow for a while even after the life-breath (and the necessary spherical atoms) was gone. Then, as the atoms lose their connections, the entire body decays.

Democritus taught that people should have no fear or apprehension concerning supernatural matters or an afterlife. Since the totality of reality consists of the atoms and the void, when the atoms of a person disperse and the person dies, the person no longer exists. Therefore, according to Democritus, there is nothing to fear in death. The corollary conclusion is that people should not delay pleasures in anticipation of an afterlife. It is in this life—this arrangement of atoms—that human beings can find their only fulfillment and happiness.

The best life is one that is characterized by contentedness and cheerfulness. Democritus believed that passions are powerful, disturbing factors that tend to upset the natural harmony and balance in the arrangement of atoms in human beings. Democritus used his atomism to support traditional Greek views that strong passions can cause much trouble and that moderation is best. The key to moderation and to the achievement of happiness in life is knowledge. Knowledge determines one's proper goals and activities, while passion is a threat.

It is important, however, to distinguish Democritus' knowledge-passion polarity from that of many later Platonic thinkers. Platonic thinkers (and some Christian Neoplatonists) are dualists. They distinguish between one's spiritual or intellectual part—the seat of reason, which is divine and immortal—and one's physical or irrational part—the seat of passion, which is animal and mortal. The first is the spiritual soul and lives forever; the second is the body, which suffers death and decay. In contrast, Democritus was a thoroughgoing naturalist and materialist; he believed that all the atoms disperse at death and nothing survives. Knowledge was seen as important and passion was seen as a threat, not for religious or supernatural reasons but because of their import for human contentedness and cheerfulness.

Ancient sources agree that Democritus lived to a remarkably advanced age. Few details of his later life, however, are known. The legend that he blinded himself (in order to root out lustful desires, according to Tertullian) is denied by Plutarch. Democritus is thought to have died in Thrace around the year 370 B.C.

Summary

The theory of atomism was not favored by Plato (c. 427-347 B.C.) and Aristotle (384-322 B.C.), the two major Greek philosophers who followed Democritus, but it was adopted by the Greek Epicurus (341-270 B.C.) and the Roman Lucretius (c. 98-55 B.C.). Epicurus was attracted to the moral teaching of Democritus and held that human well-being is best achieved by eliminating pain and the painful desire for things that people cannot (or cannot easily) obtain. Consequently, he aimed to live a life of utmost simplicity. Both Epicurus and Lucretius followed Democritus in denying supernatural influences on human life and rejecting the idea of an afterlife. Moreover, all these thinkers believed that their position on these points was not only true but also useful in freeing people from superstitions that lead to pain and suffering.

Atomism, as an essentially physical and mechanical account of the world that leaves no place for "higher purposes" or "meanings," was particularly unacceptable to religious and theological writers of the Christian tradition, which dominated Western philosophy from about the fourth to the fourteenth century. In the wake of the Renaissance and the scientific revolution (that is, since about the fifteenth and sixteenth centuries), however, the influence of Democritus has again become apparent in philosophy and science. Modern science, like ancient Democritean atomism, deals with the world purely in terms of physical objects operating according to natural laws; the question of higher purposes or meanings is considered to lie beyond the scope of science. In some points of detail there is significant agreement between ancient atomism and the modern scientific view. On both accounts, for example, qualities such as the color of a book or the taste of a cup of coffee are thought to be attached not to individual atoms—there are no red atoms or coffee-flavored atoms—but to combinations of atoms in interaction with a perceiver. One obvious difference between the two forms of atomism, however, is that in the Democritean view atoms cannot be split, while the modern scientific view upholds the existence of many kinds of subatomic particles and has even led to the development of atom-splitting technology that can unleash great power.

It must be remembered, however, that the atomism of Democritus is not a scientific theory and does not pretend to be based on experiment, experience, and observation. It is basically a philosophical theory, based on argument, which was designed to refute the theory and the arguments of Parmenides and the Eleatics. Thus, interesting as it is to compare ancient and modern atomism, it is not really fair to think of the two views as competing in the same arena. Democritus and the Greek atomists succeeded in developing an attitude toward the world that enabled them to look upon it as thoroughly physical and mechanical, and it is this attitude, or significant aspects of it, that many modern scientists have shared. According to this view, observable phenomena are explainable in terms of unseen movements which occur according to natural (not supernatural) law.

Bibliography

Bailey, Cyril. *The Greek Atomists and Epicurus*. Oxford: Oxford University Press, 1928. Reprint. New York: Russell and Russell, 1964. Contains a thorough historical account of the origins of Greek atomism, the contributions and elaborations that derive specifically from Democritus, and the further adaptation of the view at the hands of Epicurus. Bailey stresses the differences between Leucippus, Democritus, and Epicurus.

Brumbaugh, Robert S. *The Philosophers of Greece*. Albany: State University of New York Press, 1981. Chapter 11 covers Democritus, atomism, and the development of materialism. Brumbaugh compares Greek, Roman, and modern atomisms. The chapter is brief, but Brumbaugh shows the place of Democritus and the atomists within Greek philosophical history.

Burnet, John. *Greek Philosophy: Thales to Plato*. London: Macmillan, 1914. A classic work that has been reprinted many times. Burnet's chapter 11 is entitled "Demokritos," but refers to the philosopher generally known as Democritus. Burnet's strictly Greek spelling here is evidence of his overall carefulness. This is a scholarly work, with indexes of both English and Greek terms.

Freeman, Kathleen. *Ancilla to the Pre-Socratic Philosophers*. Cambridge, Mass.: Harvard University Press, 1948. A complete translation of all the Greek philosophical fragments that were first collected and translated (into German) by the German scholar Hermann Diels. About thirty pages are given to fragments of works and titles of works by Democritus. Most of the fragments relate to the ethics of atomism rather than to its physics.

Guthrie, W. K. C. *A History of Greek Philosophy*. Vol. 2. Cambridge: Cambridge University Press, 1965. A very useful volume that contains more than one hundred pages on Democritus, an appendix on atomism, a long bibliography, and three indexes. Democritus has been called an encyclopedic thinker, and Guthrie shows the truth of this remark by exploring a great number of areas with which Democritus was concerned.

Kirk, G. S., and J. E. Raven. *The Presocratic Philosophers*. Cambridge: Cambridge University Press, 1960. Chapter 17 covers Leucippus, Democritus, and the theory of atomism. This book contains the actual Greek texts of the philosophers, always accompanied by English translations and explanations. Kirk and Raven concentrate on the physics of atomism; the ethics of atomism is treated very briefly.

Vlastos, Gregory. "Ethics and Physics in Democritus," *Philosophical Review* 54/55 (1945/1946): 578-592, 53-64. This long article, printed in two parts in two volumes of the same journal, argues, against Cyril Bailey (cited above), that the ethics and the physics of Democritus are indeed linked. Vlastos stresses the relationship between the naturalism (nonsupernaturalism) of the physical worldview of atomism and the naturalism of the ethics of atomism.

Stephen Satris

DEMOSTHENES

Born: 384 B.C.; Athens, Greece
Died: 322 B.C.; Calauria, Greee
Areas of Achievement: Law and politics
Contribution: Demosthenes' life and career as an orator were consumed by his titanic struggle with Philip II of Macedonia and by his efforts to recall Athenian spirit and vigor to its former greatness. The single-mindedness, sincerity, and intense patriotism of Demosthenes—combined with his consummate genius and mastery of oratorical technique—make him one of the most notable personalities of antiquity.

Early Life

Demosthenes was born in Athens in 384 B.C., the son of Demosthenes, an Athenian citizen of the deme of Paeania, and Cleobule, the daughter of Gylon. The elder Demosthenes, the owner of a lucrative weapons workshop, died when his son was only seven, bequeathing him a substantial fortune. Most of this patrimony, however, was embezzled by the child's three guardians, Aphobus, Demophon, and Theryppides, who handed over to the young Demosthenes, when he came of age, only a fraction of his inheritance. As a boy, Demosthenes had witnessed the orator Callistratus win a stunning victory in the courtroom and had thereupon vowed to become an orator himself. He had turned his attention to the art of oratory and studied with Isaeus, an orator known for his acumen in cases involving questions of inheritance. This early training was now to bear fruit: Demosthenes, at only eighteen years of age, brought a series of actions against his guardians and secured a decisive victory; it is unlikely, however, that he recovered more than a little of what was owed him.

Employing his knowledge of the law and oratory, Demosthenes turned to professional speech writing (logography) and enjoyed success as a composer of orations for others. His own speaking debut before the Assembly, however, met with little approval from the people, for he was short of breath, weak in voice, and hampered by some sort of speech impediment. Chagrined, Demosthenes then began the legendary regimen of oratorical training that has become for subsequent generations a paradigm of the efficacy of hard work and perseverance in overcoming the defects or shortcomings of nature: He pronounced periods with pebbles in his mouth, declaimed to the waves over the roar of the sea, spoke while running up hill, and shaved one side of his head so that his humiliating appearance would confine him to his underground practice studio for several months at a time.

By the age of thirty, with physical impediments overcome and oratorical skills honed to near perfection, Demosthenes found himself increasingly involved in legal cases whose character was essentially political in nature.

In 354, he delivered his first major speech before the Assembly, wherein he countered the rumored threat of war against Athens by the King of Persia, cautioned against rash action, and proposed an elaborate revision of the method for outfitting the navy. In this speech, as well as others written and delivered during this period, Demosthenes tended to support the conservative program of Eubulus, leader of the dominant party in Athens at the time, who advocated peace abroad and financial security at home. The impact of these orations thrust Demosthenes dramatically into the arena of politics and statesmanship, from which he retired only at his death.

Life's Work

It was to the north that Demosthenes now directed his attention, troubled, like many of the Greeks, by the startling and unexpected ascendancy of Philip II of Macedonia in Thrace and Thessaly. Henceforth the story of Demosthenes' life was to be the drama of his all-consuming struggle to persuade the Athenians and the rest of the Greeks to oppose the Macedonian threat to their freedom. Encroaching southward, Philip had run roughshod over Athenian interests and sources of supply in Amphipolis and the Thermaicus Sinus. Alarmed by these acts of aggression, Demosthenes delivered the impassioned "First Philippic" in 351, rousing his fellow citizens to take notice of the threat posed by Philip and calling them to military preparedness. This speech, injected with a newfound vigor and intensity, made clear his volte-face from the policy of Eubulus and established the orator as leader of the opposition to Macedonia's infringement upon Athenian and Greek liberty.

Philip's subsequent advance on Olynthus spurred the orator to respond with three stirring speeches, known as the "Olynthiacs," in 349, aimed at securing aid for Olynthus. Demosthenes urged the Athenians to resist the onslaught of Philip with all of their physical and financial resources, going so far as to propose that the Theoric Fund (the public dole that paid for the poor's admission to the theater) be made available for the necessities of war. The Athenians did respond—but too late and with too little assistance: Olynthus and several of the confederate towns were razed by Philip in 348.

Seeing that Athens was weak, vulnerable, and in need of time to collect its resources and strength, Demosthenes acceded to peace talks with Philip. In February of 346, he, along with several other ambassadors, including Aeschines and Philocrates, was sent to negotiate a treaty. Demosthenes' rhetorical collapse before Philip proved to be one of the most embarrassing ordeals in the orator's life and marked the beginning of enmity between him and Aeschines, to whom Philip apparently directed his reply. Nevertheless, it was Demosthenes who had been able to detect Philip's real intentions; thus, he condemned the terms of the treaty to his fellow citizens. Aeschines, on the other hand, rashly assured the Athenians of Philip's goodwill. Demosthenes' worst fears were realized when Philip, dallying before taking the final oath of ratification, secured more territory, crushed Phocis, assumed a place on the Amphictionic Council, and took from Athens the right of precedence in consulting the oracle at Delphi.

In response to the growing bitterness of the Athenians over Philip's continued successes and perhaps to deflect criticism aimed at his conduct during the peace negotiations, Demosthenes impeached his rival Aeschines in 343. Charged with having caused grave injury to Athens by delaying the embassy, rendering false reports, giving bad advice, disobeying orders, and opening himself to bribery, Aeschines counterattacked with a speech and, with the support of Eubulus and other pro-Macedonians in Athens, was narrowly acquitted. Yet it was clear that the pro-Macedonian party had lost ground and that Demosthenes' hard-line anti-Macedonian stance was finally beginning to win support among the Athenians.

By 342, Philip had firmly incorporated Thrace in his kingdom and was now turning his eye toward the Chersonese, an area vital to Athens because of its geographically strategic location on the supply route from the Black Sea. In his speech "On the Chersonese" (341), Demosthenes countered Philip's complaints about Athenian supported activity in this area. Shortly thereafter he reiterated his plea for support of the Chersonese; in the "Third Philippic" Demosthenes was at his oratorical best, arguing that Philip's actions had already amounted to a violation of the peace and a declaration of war and passionately insisting on a union of all Greeks under the leadership of Athens.

The years immediately following were certainly Demosthenes' "finest hour" and represent the high point in his career. The naval reforms that he had earlier proposed were effected, and his eloquence and indefatigable energy finally prevailed to secure an alliance of almost all Greek states with Athens at its head. After Philip's declaration of war in 340, Demosthenes moved to suspend the allocation of surplus funds to the Theoric Fund and managed at length to secure an alliance between Athens and her traditional enemy, Thebes. For his actions during this time, the Athenians honored him, now their recognized leader, with two golden crowns, one in 340 and another in 339.

Demosthenes' dream of a unified Greek front, temporarily realized, was short-lived. In 338, Philip crushed the Greek allied forces on the battlefield of Chaeronea. Demosthenes, who took part in the battle, was said by his enemies to have fled disgracefully, but back in Athens it was Demosthenes who organized the city's defenses and who, in fact, was called upon by the citizens to deliver the funeral oration over those who had fallen in the fray.

To the surprise of some, Philip treated his enemies graciously in victory and refrained from occupying Athens. Nevertheless, such clemency failed to secure the goodwill or cooperation of Demosthenes. On the contrary, after

Philip's assassination in 336, Demosthenes once again urged his countrymen to rally their support against Macedonia, reassured by rumors about the demise of Alexander (known later as Alexander the Great), Philip's son and successor. When Alexander's quick and decisive action against a rebellious Thebes (335) proved him to be as formidable a foe as his father, it was only through the agency of a special embassy that Demosthenes and other anti-Macedonian statesmen were spared.

In 336, a man named Ctesiphon proposed that Demosthenes should be awarded a crown at the festival of the Greater Dionysia because, in service to the state, "he continually speaks and does what is best for the people." Aeschines, bent on prolonging his feud with the orator, immediately charged Ctesiphon with an illegal action, thereby preventing the award of the crown. After several delays the case finally came to trial in 330 in what was, perhaps, the most celebrated oratorical contest of all time. Demosthenes' defense of Ctesiphon ("On the Crown"), in reality an apologia for himself and his entire political career, is not only the orator's masterpiece but also, in the judgment of many scholars throughout the centuries, the most sublime oratorical work of antiquity. To Demosthenes' repeated question, "What else could I have done?" the Athenian jury answered resoundingly with an overwhelming verdict in his favor; Aeschines, who received less than one-fifth of the votes, was forced into exile.

Some six years later, in 324, Demosthenes' shining victory was tarnished by charges of having accepted a bribe from Alexander's fugitive treasurer, Harpalus. Although the precise details of the case are obscure, Demosthenes was convicted of the charge and fined fifty talents. Unable to pay, he escaped from prison and fled into exile. In the following year, however, Alexander's death occasioned a dramatic reversal for the orator: He was recalled to Athens in triumph, and his fine was paid by the citizens who offered him fifty talents for preparing and adorning the altar for the sacrifice to Zeus the Savior. Macedonian power seemed broken once again, but once again Demosthenes and the Athenians were deluded: Antipater, Alexander's successor, defeated the Greeks in the Lamian War and demanded that Demosthenes be handed over to him. The orator fled to the island of Calauria off the coast of Argolis and there, on the approach of Antipater's minions in 322, committed suicide by drinking poison concealed in his stylus.

Summary

To the ancients, Demosthenes was simply "the orator," in much the same way Homer had always been "the poet." His singleness of purpose, the compelling vehemence and force of his argumentation, his sincerity and intensity, and the lucidity, rapidity, flexibility, and variety of his style established him as the model for subsequent speakers, including the great Roman orator Cicero. For many he has symbolized the patriot par excellence, the champion of a lost cause, fighting to preserve the Athenian democracy in its death throes, a tragic hero and an eloquent spokesman battling for political freedom against the tyrannical threats and designs of the Macedonian aggressor. Others have had little sympathy for his policies, sharing Aeschines' view of him as a humorless "water-bibber" among wine drinkers, a stiff-necked politician whose stubbornness in the face of a new order and a powerful, inevitable force brought destruction upon himself and his homeland.

In the final analysis, no matter what judgment is rendered regarding his policies as a statesman, Demosthenes' ability to persuade is unquestionable. In his life and career he accomplished what few orators have ever been able to approach. Although a consummate master of every rule and artifice of rhetoric, Demosthenes rejected their use as ends in themselves in a mere show of rhetorical relativism; rather, the entire force of his oratorical talent was directed as a means to greater ends, namely the recovery of the public spirit, the restoration of public vigor, the preservation of the Athenian democracy and its institutions, and the reestablishment of Athens' preeminent influence and reputation among the Greek cities. In pursuit of that goal, Demosthenes lived, spoke, and died.

Bibliography

Adams, Charles Darwin. *Demosthenes and His Influence*. New York: Cooper Square Publishers, 1963. In addition to chapters on the life and oratory of Demosthenes, Adams includes important chapters on the influence of Demosthenes in antiquity, modern Europe, and on English and American oratory. Adams' apologia on behalf of Demosthenes is slightly overstated, but in general the volume is an excellent introduction.

Jaeger, Werner W. *Demosthenes: The Origin and Growth of His Policy*. New York: Octagon Books, 1963. Systematic attempt to reconstruct the origin and growth of Demosthenes' policy, considering his youth, education, early career, turn to politics, and the development of his political thought. A balanced presentation that offers a corrective to the nineteenth century notion that Demosthenes stood only as an obstacle to the inevitable progress of Panhellenism.

Kennedy, George A. *Art of Persuasion in Greece*. Princeton, N.J.: Princeton University Press, 1963. Standard handbook on Greek rhetorical theory and practice that offers perceptive analyses of Demosthenes' major orations and places them in their proper historical and rhetorical context.

Murphy, James J., ed. *Demosthenes' "On the Crown": A Critical Case Study of a Masterpiece of Ancient Oratory*. New York: Random House, 1967. Includes Plutarch's biography of Demosthenes, an analysis of Demosthenes' oratorical career by George Kennedy, John J. Keaney's excellent translation of "On the Crown," and an examination of the background, style, and argument of the speech.

Pearson, Lionel. *The Art of Demosthenes*. Decatur, Ga.: Scholars Press, 1981. Concerned with Demosthenes the orator, Pearson attempts to provide analysis and exposition of the speaker's technique, including his command of argumentation and his skill in narrative. Both forensic and deliberative speeches are examined.

Pickard-Cambridge, A. W. *Demosthenes and the Last Days of Greek Freedom*. New York: G. P. Putnam's Sons, 1914. Reprint. New York: Arno Press, 1979. A sympathetic but balanced and reliable view of Demosthenes' life and career set in its historical and political context. Contains a chronological table (404-322 B.C.), several illustrations, maps, and diagrams of battles. An authoritative, sound introduction to Demosthenes.

James M. May

DIOCLES OF CARYSTUS

Born: c. 375 B.C.; Carystus, Greece
Died: c. 295 B.C.; Athens?, Greece
Area of Achievement: Medicine
Contribution: Diocles was a fourth century B.C. Greek physician who was regarded in antiquity as second only to Hippocrates. He wrote several medical works, including the first separate treatise on anatomy and the first herbal. His best-known contributions to medicine are in the area of hygiene.

Early Life

Not much is known of Diocles' early life. His father's name was Archidamos and he was a native of Carystus, a small town on the southern tip of the island of Euboea, off the eastern coast of mainland Greece. According to the Roman writer Pliny, Diocles was second in age and fame to the famous physician Hippocrates (probably 460-377 B.C.). He has traditionally been placed in the first half of the fourth century B.C. It has been observed, however, that the language of his extant writings points to the latter rather than to the earlier half of the fourth century B.C. It is likely that he was a younger contemporary of Aristotle (384-322 B.C.) and thus was active until 300 or perhaps later. Diocles is the only physician between Hippocrates and the Hellenistic period about whom very much is known.

Diocles probably learned his trade from his father, who was a physician, for medicine in the ancient world was a craft that was often passed from father to son. The ordinary physician acquired his skill and knowledge through an apprenticeship where he learned the elements of traditional practice. Diocles wrote a work entitled *Arkhidamos* (date unknown), dedicated to his father's memory, in which he argued against his father's condemnation of the practice of rubbing the body down with oil because he believed that it overheated the body. Diocles suggested instead that in the summer a mixture of oil and water be employed, while in the winter only oil be used. There is good evidence, on the basis of Diocles' language and thought, that he was a pupil of the philosopher Aristotle, who founded his philosophical school, the Lyceum, in Athens in 335. Whether Diocles came to Athens specifically to study at the Lyceum or had earlier established residence there is not known. He was the first Greek to write medical treatises in Attic Greek rather than in Ionic, which was the dialect normally employed by medical writers. He seems to have belonged to the same generation of Aristotle's pupils as Theophrastus and Strato, who provide the earliest evidence for Diocles' work.

Diocles employs Aristotelian terminology and shows the influence of Aristotle's ethics, for example, in his use of the ideas of proportion and suitability in his theory of diet. On the other hand, it is quite possible that Diocles in turn influenced his master, perhaps as a source for Aristotle's zoological works. Although Diocles was apparently closely associated with the Peripatetic school, which was the chief center of scientific research in the Greek world until the founding of the Museum at Alexandria, Aristotle was not the only source of his ideas. He apparently had access to a collection of Hippocratic treatises and may, in fact, have been the first medical writer to assemble such a collection. His indebtedness to Hippocratic medicine is indicated by his treatises, some of which resemble Hippocratic works in title and subject matter. Diocles' thought also shows a debt to the Sicilian school of medicine, which was dominated by the philosopher and physician Empedocles (c. 490-430 B.C.). A later member of the school, Philistion of Locri (427-347 B.C.), who was a contemporary of Plato, also influenced him. Nevertheless, Diocles was no slavish follower of Aristotle or of any medical or philosophical system. He borrowed elements from Hippocratic medicine, from the Sicilian school, and from Aristotle, all the while maintaining his own independence and making original contributions.

Life's Work

Diocles was a prolific writer. The titles of seventeen of his medical treatises are known, including *Peri puros kai aeros* (on fire and air), *Anatomē* (anatomy), *Hugieina pros Pleistarkhon* (directions on health for Plistarchus), *Peri pepeseōs* (on digestion), *Peri puretōn* (on fevers), *Peri gunaikeiōn* (on women's diseases), *Peri epideomōn* (on bandages), *Peri tōn kat iētreion* (on the equipment of a surgery), *Prognōstikon* (prognostic), *Peri therapeiōn* (on treatment), *Pathos aitia therapeia* (sickness, causes, and treatment), *Rhizotomika*, *Peri lakhanōn* (on vegetables), *Peri thanasimōn pharmakōn* (on lethal drugs), *Arkhidamos*, and *Dioklēs epistolē prophulaktikē* (a letter to King Antigonus on preserving health). Of these works, more than 190 fragments have been preserved by later medical writers. Diocles' style is polished, with some literary pretensions, and shows the influence of rhetorical devices (for example, the avoidance of hiatus), while maintaining a deliberately simple style that reflects the influence of Aristotle.

According to the physician Galen (A.D. 129-199), Diocles' *Anatomy* was the first book written on that subject. In it he described the heart, lungs, gall bladder, ureters, ovaries, fallopian tubes, and ileocecal valve. Diocles' *Anatomy* was based on the observation of animals and not human beings (he is said to have dissected animals). Nevertheless, his work marked a significant turning point in the study of human anatomy, and other writers after him began to produce treatises on the subject. Diocles was indebted to Empedocles for his views on embryology. He believed that both the male and the female contributed seed, which originated in the brain and spinal marrow, to the embryo. The embryo, he believed, required forty days to develop fully;

boys, who developed on the warmer, right side of the uterus, grew more quickly than girls. Diocles was interested in the problem of sterility and dissected mules to determine the causes of infertility. He also wrote on gynecology. From Empedocles he adopted the view that menstruation began at fourteen and lasted until sixty in all women. He also described signs of expected miscarriage and suggested causes of difficult birth.

In physiology, Diocles was also indebted to Empedocles, perhaps by way of Philistion. Like Empedocles, he believed that there were four elements (fire, air, water, and earth), which he equated with the four qualities (heat, cold, moisture, and dryness) that were responsible for the processes of the body. The body, possessing an innate heat, altered food that was consumed, producing the four humors (blood, phlegm, yellow bile, and black bile). Health was the result of an equilibrium of the four qualities, while disease was the result of an excess or deficiency of one of them. Diocles wrote that health and disease also depended on external factors (for example, wounds, nourishment, or sores) and on pneuma (air), inhaled or absorbed into the body through the pores in the skin. Pneuma then went to the heart, the central organ, from which it was distributed throughout the body by means of veins. Pneuma was essential to life, and if its passage was blocked, a humor disease or death would result. The heart was believed to be the chief organ of sensation and thought and the source of blood in the body. Diocles' theory of pneuma was also taken over from Empedocles and came to exercise much influence in Greek medical thought. Diocles recognized that fever was not itself a disease but rather the symptom of a disease. He also distinguished between pneumonia, which is a disease of the lungs, and pleurisy, which is an inflammation of the pleura (the lining over the lung).

Diocles wrote as well on botany and pharmacology. He compiled the first Greek herbal, *Rhizotomika*, which described the nutritional and medical value of plants. This treatise was widely used by later writers on the subject until replaced in the first century A.D. by the definitive work of Pedanius Dioscorides. While herbal drugs had been mentioned in the Hippocratic treatises, before Diocles no descriptions had been given of the plants themselves. Diocles' work on botany was no doubt influenced by his teacher's interest in the subject, and his work was apparently known to Theophrastus, a fellow student at the Lyceum and Aristotle's successor, who founded scientific botany.

It was in dietetics and hygiene that Diocles made his greatest contribution to Greek medicine. In the late fifth century, dietetic medicine had become a means of maintaining health rather than (as it had been earlier) a method of treating disease by restoring the proper balance to the body. Treatises appeared on hygiene containing detailed instructions for a daily regimen that regulated food and drink, rest and sleep, swimming, massage, gymnastic exercise, physical cleanliness, and sexual activity. Diocles treated the subject of hygiene in several partially extant works. In *Directions on Health for Pleistarchos* (written after 300), addressed to a Macedonian prince who was the son of Antipater, a general of Alexander the Great, Diocles reproduced (with some variations) the recommendations of earlier Hippocratic works on the subject of regimen. In an earlier work, *Dioklēs epistolē prophulaktikē* (c. 305-301), addressed to King Antigonus, another of Alexander's generals (which is quoted by the Byzantine writer Paul of Aegina), Diocles discussed, among other subjects, the matter of diet, advising that food and drink be adjusted to the seasons in order to counteract the effects of seasonal variation.

Diocles also wrote a treatise on diet that is preserved in fragments quoted by Oribasius, who was the physician to the Roman Emperor Julian from A.D. 361 to 363. The treatise describes a complete routine, from rising to bedtime, for one typical day of each of the four seasons of the year. Gymnastic exercise in both morning and evening plays an important part in Diocles' regimen. This work reveals the influence of Aristotle's concepts of the mean and suitability to the individual and his circumstances. Although Diocles prescribes an ideal regimen, chiefly intended for a man of means and leisure, it is one that can be adapted to the needs of those who have less time as well as to those of different ages.

Summary

Diocles was an important medical figure in his own day, as his reputation as a "second Hippocrates" indicates, and he forms a significant link between Hippocratic and Hellenistic medicine. He was indebted to the Sicilian school, particularly in his pneumatic pathology, but his work also shows the influence of Hippocratic medicine in hygiene and therapeutics. No mere compiler, he synthesized and improved upon the work of his predecessors. Like the Hippocratics, he realized the importance of prognosis. Some later writers considered Diocles to have been a leading member of the dogmatic sect, which sought "hidden causes" in medicine and supplemented experience with reason and speculation. He lived too early to be labeled a dogmatic, however, and his independent and synthetic approach to medicine would in any event seem to rule out this possibility.

Diocles wrote on a number of medical subjects: dietetics, embryology, anatomy, botany, pharmacology, and gynecology. He also invented a device, called the "spoon of Diocles," for extracting barbed arrows. He influenced subsequent medical writers, beginning with his own pupil, Praxagoras of Cos, who became head of the Hippocratic school, and he is quoted by Galen, Oribasius, Caelius Aurelianus, and Paul of Aegina. Galen praises him as a "physician and rhetorician" and credits him with having arranged Hippocratic medicine in a more logical form. Diocles appears as well to have been, like many of the early Peripatetics, something of a Renaissance man, whose interests extended beyond medicine to botany, meteorology, zoology, and even mineralogy.

Bibliography

Edelstein, Ludwig. *Ancient Medicine: Selected Papers of Ludwig Edelstein*. Edited by Owsei Temkin and C. Lilian Temkin. Translated by C. Lilian Temkin. Baltimore: Johns Hopkins University Press, 1967. This work includes discussions of the dates of Diocles and the importance of dietetics to Greek ideas of health and medicine.

Jaeger, Werner. *Aristotle: Fundamentals of the History of His Development*. 2d ed. Oxford: Oxford University Press, 1948. A detailed argument for dating Diocles in the late fourth and early third centuries and a discussion of Aristotle's influence on Diocles.

———. *Paideia: The Ideals of Greek Culture*. Vol. 3, *The Conflict of Cultural Ideals in the Age of Plato*. Translated by Gilbert Highet. New York: Oxford University Press, 1944. A fine discussion of the Greek ideal of health and the place of Diocles and his views on dietetic medicine in the context of the Greek emphasis on health.

Phillips, E. D. *Aspects of Greek Medicine*. New York: St. Martin's Press, 1973. A summary of Diocles' medical doctrines that includes a list of the titles of his known works.

Sigerist, Henry. *A History of Medicine*. Vol. 2, *Early Greek, Hindu, and Persian Medicine*. New York: Oxford University Press, 1961. A summary of Diocles' views on diet and hygiene against the background of Greek views of hygiene.

Gary B. Ferngren

DIOCLETIAN

Born: c. 245; possibly Salona
Died: December 3, 316; Salona
Area of Achievement: Government
Contribution: Diocletian put an end to the disastrous phase of Roman history known as the Military Anarchy or the Imperial Crisis and laid the foundation for the later Roman Empire known as the Byzantine Empire. His reforms ensured the continuity of the Roman Empire in the East for more than a thousand years.

Early Life

Little is known for certain about Diocletian's early life. He was a native of the Dalmatian coast and was of very humble birth, and was originally named Diocles. He was either the son of a freedman or a slave by birth who was later set free. His father may have been a scribe. He grew up in the household of the senator Anullinus, and it is unlikely that he received much education beyond the elementary literacy he may have learned from his father. The scanty evidence suggests that he was deeply imbued with religious piety. Later coin portraits give an impression of his appearance: They show a close-cropped beard in the current Illyrian style, a wide forehead, and eyes spaced far apart. He had a wife, Prisca, and a daughter, Valeria, both of whom reputedly were Christians.

During Diocletian's early life, the Roman Empire was in the midst of turmoil. In the early years of the third century, emperors increasingly insecure on their thrones had granted inflationary pay raises to the soldiers. The additional costs could be met only by debasing the silver coinage, which soon became worthless, causing the ruin of the Roman economy. The only meaningful income the soldiers now received was in the form of gold donatives granted by other leaders. This practice served to encourage emperor-making. Beginning in 235, armies throughout the empire began to set up their generals as rival emperors.

The resultant civil wars opened up the empire to invasion in both the north, by the Franks, Alemanni, and Goths, and the east, by the Sassanid Persians. Another reason for the unrest in the army was the great gap between the social background of the common soldiers, who were recruited from the more backward provinces of the empire, such as Illyria, and the officer corps, made up largely of cultured senators. As of the 250's, however, this situation began to change. Many legionaries made their way to high rank. Beginning in 268, some even were acclaimed emperors themselves. These individuals, the so-called Illyrian or soldier emperors, gradually were able to bring the army back under control, even though their newfound status aroused enmity against them from the senators.

Like many of his countrymen, Diocletian sought his fortune in the army. He showed himself to be a shrewd, able, and ambitious individual. He soon rose to high rank. He is first attested as Duke of Moesia (an area on the banks of the lower Danube River), with responsibility for border defense. He was a prudent and methodical officer, a seeker of victory rather than glory. In 282, the legions of the upper Danube proclaimed the praetorian prefect Carus emperor. Diocletian found favor under the new emperor and was promoted to Count of the Domestics, the commander of the cavalry arm of the imperial bodyguard. In 283 he was granted the honor of a consulate.

In 284, in the midst of a campaign against the Persians, Carus was killed, struck by a bolt of lightning which one writer noted might have been forged in a legionary armory. That left the empire in the hands of his two young sons, Numerian in the east and Carinus in the west. Soon thereafter, Numerian died under mysterious circumstances near Nicomedia, and Diocletian—he had, by this time changed his name from Diocles to Diocletian—was acclaimed emperor in his place. In 285, Carinus was killed in a battle near Belgrade, and Diocletian gained control of the entire empire.

Life's Work

As emperor, Diocletian was faced with many problems. His most immediate concerns were to bring the mutinous and increasingly barbarized Roman armies back under control and to make the frontiers once again secure from invasion. His long-term goals were to restore effective government and economic prosperity to the empire. Diocletian concluded that stern measures were necessary if these problems were to be solved. More than earlier emperors, he believed that it was the responsibility of the imperial government to take whatever steps were necessary, no matter how harsh or unorthodox, to bring the empire back under control. Earlier emperors, with typical Roman conservatism, by and large had attempted to apply the methods instituted by the first emperor, Augustus (who reigned from 27 B.C. to A.D. 14), even if they no longer were appropriate for the times. Diocletian believed that contemporary needs required him to abandon the Augustan "Principate" and to strike out on his own.

Diocletian was able to bring the army back under control by making several changes. He subdivided the roughly fifty existing provinces into approximately one hundred. That would put less authority into the hands of each governor. The provinces also were apportioned among twelve "dioceses," each under a "vicar," and later also among four "prefectures," each under a "praetorian prefect." As a result, the imperial bureaucracy became increasingly bloated. He institutionalized the policy of separating civil and military careers, so that provincial governors would not also be the commanders of armies. He divided the army itself into so-called border troops, actually an ineffective citizen militia, and palace troops, the real field army, which often were led by the emperor in person.

Following the precedent of Aurelian (reigned 270 to 275), Diocletian transformed the emperorship into an out-and-out oriental monarchy. The emperor now became a truly august, godlike figure, removed from the rest of society. He wore gold and purple robes and a pearl diadem. Access to him became restricted; he now was addressed not as "princeps" (first citizen) or the soldierly "imperator" (general), but as "dominus noster" (lord and master). Those in audience were required to prostrate themselves on the ground before him.

Diocletian also concluded that the empire was too large and complex to be ruled by only a single emperor. Therefore, in order to provide an imperial presence throughout the empire, he introduced the Tetrarchy, or Rule by Four. In 285, he named his lieutenant Maximianus "caesar," or "junior emperor," and assigned him the western half of the empire. This practice began the process which would culminate with the de facto split of the empire in 395. Both Diocletian and Maximianus adopted divine attributes. Diocletian was identified with Jupiter and Maximianus with Hercules. In 286, Diocletian promoted Maximianus to the rank of augustus, "senior emperor," and in 293 he appointed two new caesars, Constantius (the father of Constantine I), who was given Gaul and Britain in the west, and Galerius, who was assigned the Balkans in the east.

By instituting his Tetrarchy, Diocletian also hoped to solve another problem. In the Augustan Principate, there had been no constitutional method for choosing new emperors. The result of this, especially in the third century, had been civil wars when different armies named their own generals as the next emperor. According to Diocletian's plan, the successor of each Augustus would be the respective caesar, who then would name a new caesar. Initially, the Tetrarchy operated smoothly and effectively. Even though Diocletian and Maximianus technically were of equal rank, it always was clear that Diocletian really was in charge.

Once the army was under control, Diocletian could turn his attention to other problems. The borders were restored and strengthened. In the early years of his reign, Diocletian and his subordinates were able to defeat foreign enemies such as Alamanni, Sarmatians, Saracens, Franks, and Persians, and to put down rebellions in Britain and Egypt. The eastern frontier was actually expanded.

Another problem was the economy, which was in an especially sorry state. The coinage had become so debased as to be virtually worthless. Diocletian's attempt to reissue good gold and silver coins failed because there simply was not enough gold and silver available to restore confidence in the currency. A Maximum Price Edict issued in 301, intended to curb inflation, served only to drive goods onto the black market. Diocletian finally accepted the ruin of the money economy and revised the tax system so that it was based on payments in kind (the "annona") rather than in the now-worthless money. The annona came to be recalculated in periodic reassessments (indictions) every fifteen years. The soldiers, too, came to be paid in kind. Their only salary of value eventually became donatives issued at five-year intervals in gold and silver.

In order to assure the long-term survival of the empire, Diocletian identified certain occupations which he believed would have to be performed. These were known as the "compulsory services." They included such occupations as soldiers, bakers, members of town councils (the "decurions"), and tenant farmers (the "coloni," who evolved into the serfs of the Middle Ages). These functions became hereditary, and those engaging in them were inhibited from changing their careers. The repetitious nature of these laws, however, suggests that they were not widely obeyed. Diocletian also expanded the policy of third century emperors of restricting the entry of senators into high-ranking governmental posts, especially military ones.

Like Augustus and Decius (249-251), Diocletian attempted to use the state religion as a unifying element. Encouraged by the caesar Galerius, Diocletian in 303 issued a series of four increasingly harsh decrees designed to compel the Christians to take part in the imperial cult, the traditional means by which allegiance was pledged to the empire. This began the so-called Great Persecution.

On May 1, 305, wearied by his twenty years in office and determined to implement his method for the imperial succession, Diocletian abdicated. He compelled his co-regent, Maximianus, to do the same. Constantius and Galerius then became the new augusti, and two new caesars were selected, Maximinus (305-313) in the east and Severus (305-307) in the west. Diocletian then retired to his palace at Split on the Yugoslavian coast. In 308 he declined an offer to resume the purple, and the aged former emperor died in 316.

Summary

Diocletian recognized that the empire as it had been established by Augustus simply did not meet the needs of his own time. He therefore instituted many administrative reforms. Not all of them, however, were completely successful. His Tetrarchy, for example, in the choice of new emperors, bypassed obvious dynastic choices. As a result, another round of civil wars swept the empire. Constantine, the son of Constantius, emerged as the victor. Diocletian's retention of the ineffective border troops created a great drain on the treasury, and his abandonment of the money economy meant the ruin of much of the private business in the empire. The Great Persecution ended in failure in 311, and soon after Constantine identified Christianity itself as a more viable unifying factor.

Diocletian's successes, however, greatly outweighed his failures. He was much more skilled as an administrator than as a general, but an administrator was just what the empire needed at that time. The pattern he established was maintained, and expanded, after his death. Emperors continued to claim absolute authority in all matters, and to try to solve problems by legislative decree. Diocletian's reforms brought the empire back from the brink of extinction and laid the foundation for the Byzantine Empire.

Bibliography

Arnheim, M. T. W. *The Senatorial Aristocracy in the Later Roman Empire*. Oxford: Clarendon Press, 1972. A detailed discussion of the evolution of the ruling class of the empire under Diocletian and his successors. Uses the methodology known as "prosopography," or "collective biography."

Barnes, Timothy D. *The New Empire of Diocletian and Constantine*. Cambridge, Mass.: Harvard University Press, 1982. An investigation of the administrative restructuring of the empire which occurred under Diocletian.

Brauer, George C. *The Age of the Soldier Emperors: Imperial Rome, A.D. 244-284*. Park Ridge, N.J.: Noyes Press, 1975. A clear discussion of the Illyrian emperors of the third century, culminating in the reign of Diocletian. Particular use is made of the numismatic evidence.

Brown, Peter. *The World of Late Antiquity: From Marcus Aurelius to Mohammed*. London: Thames and Hudson, 1971. A very broad and well-illustrated discussion of the social and cultural background of the new age which began in the later part of the third century.

Jones, Arnold H. M. *The Later Roman Empire, 284-602: A Social, Economic, and Administrative Survey*. Norman: University of Oklahoma Press, 1964. The standard scholarly discussion of the Roman world beginning with the restructuring which occurred during the time of Diocletian. Places Diocletian's reforms in their broader context. Very fully annotated, with many citations from original sources.

Sutherland, C. H. V. "The State of the Imperial Treasury at the Death of Diocletian," in *Journal of Roman Studies* 25 (1935).

__________. "Diocletian's Reform of the Coinage," in *Journal of Roman Studies* 45 (1955).

__________. "The Denarius and Sestertius in Diocletian's Coinage Reform," in *Journal of Roman Studies* 51 (1961). In this series of articles Sutherland discusses the Roman economy and attempts at economic reform under Diocletian, paying particular attention to the coinage.

Williams, Stephen. *Diocletian and the Roman Recovery*. New York: Methuen, 1985. A detailed, chronological biography of Diocletian. Includes an extensive bibliography of other scholarship on Diocletian, as well as some illustrations.

Ralph W. Mathisen

DIOPHANTUS

Born: fl. c. A.D. 250; place unknown
Died: Date unknown; place unknown
Area of Achievement: Mathematics
Contribution: Diophantus wrote a treatise on arithmetic which represents the most complete collection of problems dating from Greek times involving solutions of determinate and indeterminate equations. This work was the basis of much medieval Arabic and European Renaissance algebra.

Early Life

Almost nothing is known about Diophantus' life, and there is no mention of him by any of his contemporaries. A reference to the mathematician Hypsicles (active around 170 B.C.) in his tract on polygonal numbers and a mention of him by Theon of Alexandria (fl. A.D. 365-390) give respectively a lower and an upper bound for the period in which Diophantus lived. There is also evidence that points to the middle of the third century A.D. as the flourishing period of Diophantus. Indeed, the Byzantine Michael Psellus (latter part of the eleventh century) asserts in a letter that Anatolius, Bishop of Laodicea around 280, wrote a brief work on the Diophantine art of reckoning. Psellus' remark seems to fit well with the dedication of Diophantus' masterpiece *Arithmētika* (*Arithmetica*) to a certain Dionysius, who might possibly be identified with Saint Dionysius, Bishop of Alexandria after 247. The only dates known about Diophantus' life are obtained as a solution to an arithmetical riddle contained in the *Greek Anthology*, which gives thirty-three for his wedding age, thirty-eight for when he became a father, and eighty-four for the age of his death. The trustworthiness of the riddle is hard to determine. During his life, Diophantus wrote the *Arithmetica*, the *Porismata*, the *Moriastica*, and the tract on polygonal numbers.

Life's Work

Diophantus' main achievement was the *Arithmetica*, a collection of arithmetical problems involving the solution of determinate and indeterminate equations. A determinate equation is an equation with a fixed number of solutions, such as the equation $x^2 - 2x + 1 = 0$, which admits only 1 as a solution. An indeterminate equation usually contains more than one variable, as for example the equation $x + 2y = 8$. The name indeterminate is motivated by the fact that such equations often admit an infinite number of solutions. The degree of an equation is the degree of its highest degree term; a term in several variables has degree equal to the sum of the exponents of its variables. For example, $x^2 + x = 0$ is of degree two, and $x^3 + x^2y^4 + 3 = 0$ is of degree six but of degree three in x and degree four in y.

Although Diophantus presents solutions to arithmetic problems employing methods of varying degrees of generality, his work cannot be fairly described as a systematic exposition of the theory of solution of determinate and indeterminate equations. The *Arithmetica* is in fact merely a collection of problems and lacks any deductive structure whatsoever. Moreover, it is extremely hard to pinpoint exactly which general methods may constitute a key for reading the *Arithmetica*. This observation, however, by no means diminishes Diophantus' achievements. The *Arithmetica* represents the first systematic collection of such problems in Greek mathematics and thus by itself must be considered a major step toward recognizing the unity of the field of mathematics dealing with determinate and indeterminate equations and their solutions, in short, the field of Diophantine problems.

The *Arithmetica* was originally divided into thirteen books. Only six of them were known until 1971, when the discovery of four lost books in Arabic translation greatly increased knowledge of the work. The six books which were known before the recent discovery were transmitted to the West through Greek manuscripts dating from the thirteenth century (these will be referred to as books IG-VIG). The four books in Arabic translation (henceforth IVA-VIIA) represent a translation from the Greek attributed to Qusta ibn Luqa (fl. mid-ninth century). The Arabic books present themselves as books 4 through 7 of the *Arithmetica*. Since none of the Greek books overlaps with the Arabic books, a reorganization of the Diophantine corpus is necessary.

Scholars agree that the four Arabic books should probably be spliced between IIIG and IVG on grounds of internal coherence: The techniques used to solve the problems in IVA-VIIA presuppose only the knowledge of IG-IIIG, whereas the techniques used in IVG through VIG are radically different and more complicated than those found in IVA-VIIA. There is also compelling external evidence that this is the right order. The organization of problems in al-Karaji's *Fakhri* (c. 1010), an Islamic textbook of algebra heavily dependent on Diophantus, shows that the problems taken from IG-IIIG are immediately followed by problems found in IVA. The most interesting difference between IG-VIG and IVA-VIIA consists in the fact that in the Greek books, after having found the sought solutions (analysis), Diophantus never checks the correctness of the results obtained; in the Arabic books, the analysis is always followed by a computation establishing the correctness of the solution obtained (synthesis).

Before delving into some of the contents of the *Arithmetica*, the reader must remember that in Diophantus' work the term "arithmetic" takes a whole new meaning. The Greek tradition sharply distinguished between arithmetic and logistics. Arithmetic dealt with abstract properties of numbers, whereas logistics meant the computational techniques of reckoning. Diophantus dropped this distinction since he realized that although he was working with numerical examples, the techniques he used were quite general. Diophantus has often been called "the father of algebra," but this is inaccurate: Diophantus merely uses definitional abbreviations and not a system of notation which is completely symbolic. At the outset of the *Arithmetica*, Diophantus gives his notation for powers of the unknown x, called *arithmoi* (and indicated by the symbol σ), and for their reciprocals. (For example, x^2 is denoted by Δ^{ν} and x^3 by K^{ν}). Diophantus has no signs for addition and multiplication although he has a special sign for minus and a special word for "divided by."

It is impossible to summarize here the rich content of the 290 problems of the *Arithmetica* (189 in the Greek and 101 in the Arabic books), but from the technical point of view a very rough description of the books can be given as follows: IG deals mainly with determinate equations of the first and second degree; IIG and IIIG address many problems which involve determinate and indeterminate equations of degree no higher than two; IVA to VIIA are mainly devoted to consolidating the knowledge acquired in IG-IIIG; and IVG to VIG address problems involving the use of indeterminate equations of degree higher than two.

Throughout the *Arithmetica*, Diophantus admits only positive rational solutions (that is, solutions of the form p/q where p and q are natural numbers). Although negative numbers are used in his work, he seems to make sense of them only with respect to some positive quantity and not as having a meaning on their own. For example, in VG.2 (where 2 refers to problem 2 of VG), the equation $4 = 4x + 20$ is considered absurd since the only solution is -4.

In IG are found many problems involving pure determinate equations, such as equations in which the unknown is present only in one power. The solution to IG.30, for example, requires solution of the equation $100 - x^2 = 96$, which gives $x = 2$. Note that Diophantus is not interested in the solution $x = -2$. Diophantus gives a general rule for solving pure equations:

> Next, if there results from a problem an equation in which certain terms are equal to terms of the same species, but with different coefficients, it will be necessary to subtract like from like on both sides until one term is found equal to one term. If perchance there be on either side or on both sides any negative terms, it will be necessary to add the negative terms on both sides, until the terms on both sides become positive, and again to subtract like from like until on each side only one term is left.

In other words, Diophantus reduces the equation to the normal form $ax^m = c$. If the result were a mixed quadratic, however, such as $ax^2 + bx + c = 0$, Diophantus might have solved it by using a general method of solution similar to the one commonly learned in high school. As an example, problem VIG.9 can be reduced to finding the solution of $630x^2 - 73x = 6$, for which Diophantus merely states the solution to be $x = 6/35$. Although the possibility that Diophantus might have solved these problems by trial and error is open, internal evidence strongly suggests that he knew more than is relayed in the *Arithmetica*. In fact, the passage immediately following the above quoted reads, "we will show you afterwards how, in the case also when two terms are left equal to a single term, such an equation can be solved." The promised solution may be in the lost three books.

Diophantus also solves problems involving equations (or systems of equations) of the form

(a) $a_n x^n + a_{n-1} x^{n-1} + \ldots + a_1 x - a_0 = y^2$ (where n is at most 6)
(b) $a_n x^n + a_{n-1} x^{n-1} + \ldots + a_1 x - a_0 = y^2$ (where n is at most 3)

The methods are seldom general, however, and rely on special cases of the above equations as found in VIG.19, where one finds the system given by the two equations $4x + 2 = y^3$ and $2x + 1 = z^2$. (The reader is reminded that Diophantus always works with numerical cases and so equations in abstract form are not to be found in his work.)

In many problems, Diophantus needs to find solutions which are subject to certain limits imposed by a condition of the problem at hand. He often uses some very interesting techniques to deal with such situations (so-called methods of limits and approximation to limits).

The tract on polygonal numbers has been transmitted in incomplete form. Whereas the *Arithmetica* used methods which could be called algebraic, the treatise on polygonal numbers follows the geometrical method, in which numbers are represented by geometrical objects.

Of the other two works, *Porismata* and *Moriastica*, virtually nothing is known. The *Moriastica* was mentioned by Iamblichus (fourth century A.D.) and seems to have been merely a compendium of rules for computing with fractions similar (or identical) to the one found in IG. The *Porismata* is referred to often by Diophantus himself. In the *Arithmetica*, he often appeals to some results of number theoretic nature and refers to the *Porismata* for their proofs. It is unclear, as in the case of the *Moriastica*, whether the *Porismata* was part of the *Arithmetica* or a different work. There are other number theoretic statements which are used by Diophantus in the *Arithmetica* and which might have been part of the *Porismata*. They concern the expressibility of numbers as sums of two, three, or four squares. For example, Diophantus certainly knew that numbers of the form $4n + 3$ cannot be odd and that numbers of the form $8n + 7$ cannot be written as sums of three squares. It was in commenting on these insights of Diophantus that the distinguished mathematician Pierre de Fermat (1601-1665) gave some of his most famous number theoretic statements.

Summary

Diophantus' *Arithmetica* represents the most extensive treatment of arithmetic problems involving determinate and indeterminate equations from Greek times. It is clear from the sources that Diophantus did not create the field anew but was heavily dependent on the older Greek tradition. Although it is difficult to assess how much he improved on his predecessors' results, his creativeness in solving so many problems by exploiting new stratagems to supplement the few general techniques at his disposal was impressive.

The *Arithmetica* was instrumental in the development of algebra in the medieval Islamic world and Renaissance Europe. The Arabic writers al-Khazin (c. 940), Abul Wefa (940-998), and al-Karaji (c. 1010), among others, were deeply influenced by Diophantus' work and incorporated many of his problems in their algebra textbooks. The Greek books have come to the West through Byzantium. The Byzantine monk Maximus Planudes (c. 1260-c. 1310) wrote a commentary on the first two Greek books and collected several extant manuscripts of Diophantus which where brought to Italy by Cardinal Bessarion. Apart from a few sporadic quotations, there was no extensive work on the *Arithmetica* until the Italian algebraist Rafael Bombelli ventured into a translation (with Antonio Maria Pazzi), which was never published, and used most of the problems found in IG-VIG in his *Algebra*, published in 1572. François Viète, the famous French algebraist, also made use of several problems from Diophantus in his *Zetetica* (1593). In 1575, the first Latin translation, by Wilhelm Holtzmann (who Grecized his name as Xylander), appeared with a commentary. In 1621, the Greek text was published with a Latin translation by Claude-Gaspar Bachet. This volume became the standard edition until the end of the nineteenth century, when Paul Tannery's edition became available. A new French-Greek edition of the Greek books is planned since the Tannery edition is long outdated.

Bibliography

Heath, Thomas L. *Diophantos of Alexandria: A Study in the History of Greek Algebra*. Cambridge: Cambridge University Press, 1885, 2d ed. 1910. This volume is still the major reference work on Diophantus in English. It gives an extensive treatment of the sources, the works, and the influence of Diophantus. The appendix contains translations and a good sample of problems from IG-VIG of the *Arithmetica* and translations from the tract on polygonal numbers. The second edition also contains a supplement dealing with some of Pierre de Fermat's and Leonhard Euler's work on Diophantine analysis.

___________. *A History of Greek Mathematics*. 2 vols. Oxford: Clarendon Press, 1921. Reprint. New York: Dover Press, 1981. The second volume of this classic study contains a very thorough exposition of Diophantus' work with a rich analysis of types of problems from the *Arithmetica*. It is probably the best secondary source for the reader who wants to know more about Diophantus.

Rashed, Roshdi. *Les Arithmétiques*. Vols. 2/3. Paris: Société d'Édition "Les belles lettres," 1984. An edition with French translation of the Arabic books IV to VII with a mathematical commentary and a discussion of the Arabic tradition of Diophantus. (These are part of a projected four-volume series which will include a new edition with translation of the Greek books.) The same author prepared an edition of the Arabic text in 1975 in Arabic.

Sesiano, Jacques. *Books IV to VII of Diophantus' Arithmetica: In the Arabic Translation Attributed to Qusta Ibn Luqa*. New York: Springer-Verlag, 1982. A detailed analysis of the Arabic books with a translation and a commentary on the text. The introduction presents a summary of the textual history of arithmetic theory in Greek and Arabic. The English translation and the commentary are followed by an edition of the Arabic text. Other features include an Arabic index, an appendix which gives a conspectus of the problems in the *Arithmetica*, and an extensive bibliography. (The same author offers a brief overview of the contents of the Arabic books in "Diophantus of Alexandria," *Dictionary of Scientific Biography*, volume 15, supplement 1, 1981.)

Thomas, Ivor, ed. *Greek Mathematical Works*. 2 vols. Cambridge, Mass.: Harvard University Press, 1939-1941. Volume 2 of this work contains selections from the *Arithmetica* and the quotations from the *Greek Anthology*, Psellus, and Theon of Alexandria which are relevant for Diophantus' dates. Greek texts with English translation.

Vogel, Kurt. "Diophantus of Alexandria." In *Dictionary of Scientific Biography*, vol. 4. New York: Charles Scribner's Sons, 1981. A survey of Diophantus' life and works with an extensive selection of types of problems and solutions found in the *Arithmetica*.

Wilbur R. Knorr
Paolo Mancuso

PEDANIUS DIOSCORIDES

Born: c. A.D. 40; Anazarbus, Roman Cilicia (modern Turkey)
Died: c. A.D. 90; place unknown
Area of Achievement: Medicine
Contribution: Through wide travel and much observation, Dioscorides compiled, organized, and published the most comprehensive pharmacological text produced in the ancient world. The work, *De materia medica*, remained a standard reference work for herbalists and physicians for some sixteen hundred years.

Early Life

Pedanius Dioscorides came from the city of Anazarbus, located along the banks of the Pyramus River in Roman Cilicia, in the far southeastern corner of Asia Minor. In his day, Anazarbus considered itself a worthy rival to its more famous neighbor Tarsus for preeminence in this province. Other than for Dioscorides, Anazarbus is most famous for its red stone buildings and for having produced the poet Oppian in the second century A.D.

Dioscorides probably received his early education and medical training in Tarsus, a city famous for its pharmacologists (experts in the preparation, administration, and effects of drugs). Scholars have inferred that Dioscorides was schooled in Tarsus, not only because of Tarsus' reputation but also because Dioscorides dedicated his *De materia medica* (c. 78; *The Greek Herbal of Dioscorides*, 1934, best known as *De materia medica*) to the physician Arius of Tarsus, from whom he seems to have received his medical training. It is also worth noting that Galen, the most famous of all Greek medical writers, referred to Dioscorides as Dioscorides of Tarsus, rather than of Anazarbus, indicating that Dioscorides was closely associated with the medical traditions of Tarsus in the minds of later scholars.

It may also have been in Tarsus that Dioscorides acquired his Roman name, or nomen, Pedanius. Even after the Romans had made the entire Mediterranean area part of their vast empire, it remained common for Greeks to have only one name. Yet it was also common for provincials who were granted Roman citizenship to recognize their Roman patrons by adopting their names. Most likely, Dioscorides took his name from a connection with a member of the gens, or family, of the Pedanii (one of whom, Pedanius Secundus, had served as governor in the neighboring Roman province of Asia in the 50's).

There is some debate over whether—and in what capacity and for what duration—Dioscorides served in the Roman military. It is quite possible that Dioscorides did serve in the military; if he did, it would account for some of his wide travels and would likely have brought him into contact with people from distant parts of the Roman world. Yet his military experience does not account for his genius, and his later work does not greatly reflect the most pressing concerns of a field surgeon: treating wounds. It will suffice to say that his military experience was not an obstacle to his later career.

Life's Work

Virtually all that is known about Dioscorides comes from the single source of his lasting fame, his great book on the medical properties of plants and other natural agents, *De materia medica*, which he wrote in Greek. In this book, a pharmacological text which describes hundreds of plants—as well as animals and minerals—and their properties when employed as drugs, Dioscorides reveals himself to be high-minded and genuinely concerned with the physician's essential task of healing his fellowman. Although Dioscorides may have been associated with the empirical school of medicine, his writing shows no trace of the contentious spirit or rancor so prevalent elsewhere in the ancient medical corpus. He was, almost without question, a physician himself rather than, as has sometimes been suggested, a traveling drug dealer. Selling drugs was a highly lucrative profession during Dioscorides' time and quackery was a serious problem, as pharmacists and so-called root-cutters competed for business with physicians. There were no licensing boards to protect patients from malpractice or fraud in the ancient world, and the motto of the day was *caveat emptor*, "let the buyer beware." Dioscorides, by producing his encyclopedic reference book on pharmacy, did much to alleviate this problem.

Dioscorides' system of classifying plants based on their pharmaceutical properties is an original one. He divided his study into five books, each concerned with a different broad group of medicinal agents. Within these books, he then discussed each plant, animal, or mineral in its own chapter. He methodically lists the plant's name (including common variants or synonyms), presents a drawing of it, gives its habitat and a botanical description, and then discusses its properties as a drug. He not only discusses positive qualities of these drugs but also warns of dangerous side effects. He instructs his readers on how and when to harvest, prepare, and store each plant or compound. He hastens to add in most cases that he has traveled extensively through the eastern Mediterranean and as far afield as India, Arabia, North Africa, Spain, and Gaul to examine these plants personally.

Book 1 of *De materia medica* deals with aromatics, oils, salves, trees, and shrubs. Book 2 covers animals, their parts and products, cereals, pot herbs, and sharp herbs. Book 3 is devoted to roots, juices, herbs, and seeds, while book 4 continues with more roots and herbs. Finally, in book 5, Dioscorides deals with wines and minerals. Throughout his work, Dioscorides stresses the importance of observation. Plants are living organisms, and they have different properties in youth and decay, when flowering and in seed, and they are affected by both the changing weather of the seasons and the local environment. A physician cannot expect plants gathered at different stages of growth and in different seasons to have the same effect on patients. Naturally, he also stresses the importance of observing the action of these medicaments on each and every patient. The body of medical knowledge must constantly be updated.

Dioscorides is notable for two characteristics. One is simply his excellence. Because he was a gifted empirical observer, his work was particularly valuable. Beyond that, he was moving toward a systematic classification of drugs based on their actions. If Dioscorides is compared, for example, to his near contemporary Scribonius Largus, the difference in outlook is immediately evident. Scribonius organized his book of drugs, called the *Compositiones* (c. A.D. 43-50), based on ailments. He begins with compounds useful for headaches and proceeds downward to the patient's feet. Dioscorides, on the other hand, is concerned with what effect a particular drug has. Much as a modern physician's reference book classifies drugs into categories such as analgesics, anesthetics, antibiotics, decongestants, and so on, Dioscorides was concerned with whether a particular drug had a warming effect, was an astringent, was a laxative, and so on. Once its properties were established, its medical applications could be discussed. Thus, plants are organized not so much by botanical similarity—as many later writers supposed—as by similar pharmacological properties.

Unfortunately, although the usefulness of Dioscorides' *De materia medica* was recognized at once, the potential medical and scientific implications of his attempt at classification were not. By the end of the Roman Empire, his work had been reissued in new editions in which the plants had been arranged alphabetically, undermining the basic principles that Dioscorides had laid out. Thus, while his work continued to receive study, it came to be seen as the culmination of a process rather than the beginning that its author intended. Had this not been the case, the progress of medical science in the next thousand years might well have been drastically different.

Summary

The medical arts in the ancient world had progressed fitfully at best. Despite the genius of individual physicians such as Hippocrates and Galen, the medical profession was often disrupted by internal disputes between rival schools. Pedanius Dioscorides is one of the few writers of his day to rise above such personal concerns and produce a reference work of use to members of all medical schools. His great herbal was a landmark achievement and an instant success.

In terms of his influence, Dioscorides can rightly be placed amid the greatest of ancient medical writers. If he is not to be classed with Hippocrates and Galen, he certainly belongs in the distinguished company of such authorities as Aulus Cornelius Celsus and Pliny the Elder. Until his classification was supplanted by that of Carolus Linnaeus in the eighteenth century, he stood as the foremost authority on pharmacy for more than sixteen hundred years. He was recognized not only by later Roman and Byzantine writers but also by Islamic scholars. Throughout the Middle Ages, his writings were a veritable goldmine of information for herbalists, who often copied his work—in true medieval fashion—without citing their debt to him. Nevertheless, *De materia medica* was first published as a printed book in 1478, barely twenty years after Johann Gutenberg perfected the use of movable type, and by the sixteenth century, Dioscorides' writings had found a central position in the curriculum of virtually every university in Europe.

If Dioscorides' reputation was tarnished by Linnaeus and subsequent followers of "scientific medicine," it was at least in part because they did not genuinely understand his system. Moreover, it is likely that in years to come Dioscorides will once again be studied and his fame will once again be widespread. In the modern age, many doctors and scientists have become increasingly aware that traditional remedies do in fact possess medicinal properties. The plant kingdom, as Dioscorides well knew in the first century, is a giant pharmacopoeia, waiting to be used for the benefit of humankind.

Bibliography

Allbutt, T. Clifford. *Greek Medicine in Rome*. Reprint. New York: Benjamin Blom, 1970. Part of the FitzPatrick Lectures on the History of Medicine delivered at the Royal College of Physicians of London (1909-1910), this volume is a very readable, standard survey of Roman medicine by a pioneer in the field. Particularly valuable for an appreciation of Dioscorides is chapter 17, "Pharmacy and Toxicology."

DeFelice, Stephen. *From Oysters to Insulin: Nature and Medicine at Odds*. Secaucus, N.J.: Citadel Press, 1986. This book by one of the champions of research into natural substances by the pharmaceutical industry, advocates a return to the perspective and lessons of Dioscorides.

Gunther, Robert T., ed. *The Greek Herbal of Dioscorides*. Oxford: Oxford University Press, 1934. Based on the translation made by John Goodyer in 1655, this work is the only complete translation of Dioscorides' *De materia medica*. This edition is enhanced by the inclusion of some 396 illustrations taken from a sixth century A.D. Byzantine manuscript.

Hamilton, J. S. "Scribonius Largus on the Medical Profession." *Bulletin of the History of Medicine* 60 (1986): 209-216. This article is a translation of and commentary on the preface to the *Compositiones* of Scribonius Largus, a contemporary of Dioscorides, who addressed many of the same concerns as Dioscorides. He was particularly concerned with the ethical and practical issues relating to the administration of drugs by physicians and with the many internal divisions by which the medical profession of his day was riven.

Riddle, John M. "Dioscorides." In *Catalogus Tranlationum et Commentariorum: Medieval and Renaissance Latin Translations and Commentaries, Annotated Lists, and Guides*, edited by F. Edward Crane and Paul Oskar Kristeller, vol. 4. Washington, D.C.: Catholic University Press, 1980. The first dozen pages of this article provide a clear and concise synopsis of Dioscorides' life, career, and influence. The following 130 pages trace his great work, *De materia medica*, through its tortuous history of subsequent editions and commentaries. This is meant for specialist scholars but will provide students of all levels with insight into the remarkable—and tenuous—process by which knowledge of the ancient world has been preserved.

__________. *Dioscorides on Pharmacy and Medicine*. Austin: University of Texas Press, 1985. This book not only contains the best analysis of the work of Dioscorides available in English but also evaluates the sources of information available for the life of the distinguished pharmacologist. The book is made even more valuable by its extensive bibliography. Contains a number of instructive diagrams and illustrations.

Sadek, M. M. *The Arabic "Materia medica" of Dioscorides*. Quebec: Éditions du Sphinx, 1983. This book provides a brief illustration of the extent to which Dioscorides' writings had an impact on Arab medicine in the Middle Ages, a period in which Arab physicians equaled or excelled their Western counterparts.

Scarborough, John. *Roman Medicine*. Ithaca, N.Y.: Cornell University Press, 1969. An excellent brief overview of the development and status of the medical profession in the Roman world. The book is extensively illustrated and contains a useful appendix of very brief biographical sketches of Greek and Roman medical writers and practitioners.

Scarborough, John, and Vivian Nutton. "The Preface of Dioscorides' *De materia medica*: Introduction, Translation, Commentary." *Transactions and Studies of the College of Physicians of Philadelphia* 4 (September, 1982): 187-227. This article provides the most accurate English translation of Dioscorides' own preface to *De materia medica*, along with an extensive commentary. The preface is particularly important because, in it, Dioscorides explains his system of classifying plants and drugs and also reveals virtually all that is known of his own life and medical education.

J. S. Hamilton

SAINT DOMINIC

Born: c. 1170; Calaruega, Old Castile, Spain
Died: August 6, 1221; Bologna, Italy
Areas of Achievement: Religion and monasticism
Contribution: Through faith, courage, and practicality, Dominic established the Dominican Order in 1215, which revolutionized the monastic movement of the Middle Ages and filled a vital need for apostolic preaching in the Church.

Early Life

Dominic was born in Calaruega, Old Castile, Spain, the third son of Jane of Aza and Felix de Guzman, both of noble blood. Little is known about his father, and it appears that he died when Dominic was young. Dominic inherited his exceptional sensitivity to the suffering of others from his mother. When he was six or seven years old, old enough to learn how to read, Dominic was handed over to an uncle, an archpriest, to begin his education. At fourteen, Dominic went to Palencia, where he received a thorough grounding in theology and the Scriptures. As a student, Dominic was something of a loner with a reputation for being mature beyond his years. He did not, however, isolate himself from current events. In the mid-1190's, Spain was in great misery. War had broken out against the Muslims, and with war came famine. In the course of a terrible famine that occurred while Dominic was at Palencia, few of the rich or the authorities did anything to help the starving masses. Repulsed by their indifference and inspired by Scripture (Luke 18: 18-26), Dominic sold all that he had, including his books with his personal glosses, saying that he would not study on dead skins while people were dying of hunger.

Life's Work

In 1196, Dominic became a canon and then a priest of the cathedral chapter of Osma. There he met Diego of Acebo, Bishop of Osma, a man of intense zeal who would change the course of Dominic's life. Diego returned the chapter to the apostolic life as described in the Acts of the Apostles 4:32-33. He also had a gift for evangelism, and Diego quickly recognized Dominic as a gifted, deeply spiritual priest. The two became inseparable.

In 1203, Diego was sent to Rome with Dominic by King Alfonso VIII to secure a marriage contract for the king's son. Their route took them through Languedoc in southern France, and they discovered that what had been rumored in Spain was true: Languedoc was infested by the rapidly growing Waldensian and Catharist (Albigensian) heresies. The primary reason for the success of these heresies was the state of the clergy. Most of the parish priests were illiterate and lived lives hardly different from the poor people of their flock. Ignorant and worldly, they were unable to command respect and, more significant, they were unable to teach and defend the faith. The ostentation and worldly life-style of many, though certainly not all, of the higher clergy stood in stark contrast to the moral and humble lives of the majority of the heretics.

The contrast with the Church's position in Spain must have shocked both men. In Spain, the Church, under constant pressure from its enemy, Islam, was united and strong. In southern France, with its rich, productive land, numerous towns, and more sophisticated economy, the Church had become complacent, corrupt, unable to inspire and win souls. This was the decisive moment in Dominic's life. The recognition of the Church's need burdened his soul and charted his life's work. Unknowingly, Diego and Dominic spent their first night in Languedoc in the home of a Catharist. They would not have known their host was a heretic by outward statement or appearance. Possibly he made some spiritual comment about the Church or expressed anticlerical feelings. In any event, Dominic passed the night in conversation with his host. After a night of honest debate, in which Dominic first tried to understand his host's position and then countered with his own beliefs, the heretic was converted back to the faith.

Their experience in southern France convinced Diego and Dominic to become missionaries. When they reached Rome, Diego asked Pope Innocent III to permit him to resign as Bishop of Osma so that he, with Dominic, could be a full-time missionary. It is a measure of Diego's reputation as a bishop that Innocent III refused Diego's request, and both men returned to Languedoc.

Dominic began to perfect his approach to the heretics. Since the night he converted his host, Dominic had been convinced that genuine discussion was the only effective way to confront heresy. He went to great lengths to comprehend fully the heretics' arguments before contradicting them. He debated them without scorn or condescension, and he was not afraid to appoint a heretic to officiate at a debate and to determine the victor. Dominic saw the heretics in a humane light. He knew that they were in error, but he also realized that they had some justifiable positions and that many of them lived virtuous lives. For example, upon close examination, the Waldensians were seen as Christians who took the Bible seriously and who had been pushed into heresy by not being allowed to preach. In fact, Dominic adopted some of the Waldensians' orthodox views into his own movement. It is an indication of his greatness that in trying to understand the Waldensians, Dominic was able to take what was good and incorporate it into the Church. If priests and churchmen lived simple and virtuous lives, the great anticlerical impetus for heresy would be stopped. This approach was something new; the accepted response to heresy then in vogue was force and oppression. It is interesting to speculate how church history would have changed had Dominic been able to elaborate his plan. Two events, however, prevented this from happening: the death of Diego and the Albigensian Crusade.

On December 30, 1207, Diego, Bishop of Osma, died. Dominic's sense of loss must have been enormous. For ten years, they had shared everything together, complementing each other perfectly. Diego had played an important part in developing Dominic's innovative approach to heresy. Dominic now faced the daunting apostolic task of evangelizing southern France alone. In the coming months, the situation would only continue to deteriorate. In January, 1208, Peter of Castelnau, Cistercian legate to Languedoc, was assassinated by a member of the household of Raymond, Count of Toulouse, who if not a Catharist himself, resisted any firm actions against that sect. This set in motion a chain of events that culminated in the savage Albigensian Crusade, which soon deteriorated into a war of conquest by the northern French nobility. Any plan to combat heresy via religious debate was quickly halted; the ravages of warfare made calm discussion impossible.

With the situation in southern France so poisoned by the Albigensian war, Dominic retreated into his religious house at Prouille. The bloodshed and savagery of the war repelled him. Dominic understood that force never truly converted anyone, and he wanted nothing to do with the violence. Dominic had attracted a small band of preachers around him and now realized that a new religious order was necessary to carry out effectively the missionary work. The members of this order would be priests, who would not withdraw from the world. Rather, their designated duty would be to preach the word of God to regain for the Church those who had lost their way. They were to persuade others to Christ, and this would require that they be educated men themselves. Therefore, study was to be as important as prayer. Dominic, however, would also demand that these men live a life worthy of the Gospels, and so poverty was mandatory. Dominic's insistence on poverty, unlike that of Saint Francis of Assisi, was totally practical. It would allow the members of the order to concentrate on preaching without being distracted by material goods and would also add moral force to their mission.

An important element of Dominic's vision was the inclusion of women. His followers at Prouille included a number of female converts, apparently of noble birth. From the outset of his development of the new order, he established what was called a double monastery, with a convent for the nuns and a priory for the friars. The nuns were trained to teach the local children and to instruct converts to the faith. Dominic considered their example an essential part of the work of the order.

Placed in the context of the thirteenth century, this was a revolutionary monastic movement. In October of 1215, after having been granted a religious house by Bishop Fulk of Toulouse in that city, Dominic requested that Innocent III formally confirm his new order. Innocent III refused. The Church was deeply concerned about the development and control of new religious orders and movements and had forbidden the creation of new orders. Innocent III understood the worsening condition of the Church and the clear need for effective preaching, but Dominic's proposed order broke too much with the past and seemed to have unreachable goals. Innocent III did concede that if Dominic would incorporate his order into an established monastic rule, it would be approved. Dominic agreed and chose the Augustinian rule, with which he had been familiar as a canon of Osma.

Dominic viewed the Pope's approval of the order in 1216 only as a beginning, and he moved rapidly to expand. By 1217, he had friars in Toulouse, Paris, Bologna, Madrid, and Rome. By the time the order had its first general chapter (essentially a congress of the whole order), at Bologna on May 17, 1220, six houses had been established in Lombardy, four in Provence, four in France, three in Tuscany and Rome, two in Spain, and groups of preachers had traveled to England, Germany, Hungary, and Scandinavia.

Dominic not only organized the order and traveled extensively but also devoted himself personally to the grueling ministry of preaching. In 1220-1221, Dominic started on an enormous mission of evangelizing in northern Italy, but the effort proved to be too much. All the deprivation and exertions of the past caught up with him, and he fell ill at Bologna.

Dominic called together his closest brothers in the order to give them his final instructions. Throughout his career, Dominic the man was hard to discern. He was a person of true humility, who chose to remain in the background of events and avoided self-promotion. In his last words, some of the man is seen. Dominic told his brethren never to accept any kind of property and then confessed that, while he had remained a virgin all of his life, he had taken more pleasure in conversation with young women than with old. As his friars prayed, Dominic died, on August 6, 1221.

Summary

Dominic's emphasis on education and intellectual excellence quickly placed the order into the heart of the medieval universities. By 1245, general houses of the order had been opened at Paris, Oxford, Cologne, Montpellier, and Bologna—all centers of important universities. The order produced some of the greatest scholars of the period, such as Saint Albertus Magnus and his pupil, Saint Thomas Aquinas. Aquinas would lead a successful defense of Christian doctrine against the skeptical philosophy of Averroës, and Aquinas' *Summa Theologica* (c. 1265-1274), which, in essence, reconciled faith and reason, would be the apex of medieval scholarship. Thomistic philosophy would become a foundation of church doctrine.

The Dominicans were also leaders in the expansion and defense of the faith. Bartolomé de las Casas, author of *Historia de las Indias* (written 1520-1561), protested the horrible exploitation of the Indians by the Spaniards. By 1600, Dominicans had gone into the Philippines, China, Taiwan, and Japan.

Dominicans were in the forefront in the struggle against Protestantism; 130 Dominican bishops and theologians were present at the Council of Trent, and their Thomistic positions had a major influence on the council's decrees. Indeed, prior to the inception of the Jesuit Order, the Dominicans were the chief champions of the Church. They were also the order most involved with the Inquisition. Dominic deserves no blame for this identification. The Inquisition operated in complete opposition to his beliefs, and there is no doubt that Dominic would have condemned the Inquisition in the strongest possible terms.

Possibly the Dominicans' greatest impact was on the everyday operations of the Church. In the period from 1221 to the twentieth century, there were two Dominican popes, Saint Pius V (1566-1572) and Benedict XIII (1724-1730), forty-one cardinals, and more than one thousand archbishops and bishops.

Bibliography

Hinnebusch, William A. *The History of the Dominican Order*. Vol. 2, *Intellectual and Cultural Life to 1500*. New York: Alba House, 1973. This book, the second volume of a four-volume set, discusses such topics as the importance of study to the order, the order's impact on doctrine, the development of libraries, and the writings of various Dominican authors in biblical, pastoral, and spiritual theology as well as history. This is an excellent, scholarly work best appreciated if one has a basic understanding of the order's history. Detailed notes, extensive bibliography, and index.

Jarrett, Bede. *Life of Saint Dominic (1170-1221)*. London: Burns, Oates, and Washburn, 1924, 2d ed. 1934. This is a standard biography of Dominic which, while not as detailed as Vicaire's, is still considered one of the better works on the life of the saint. Includes an index.

Ladurie, Emmanuel L. *Montaillou: The Promised Land of Error*. Translated by Barbara Bray. New York: G. Braziller, 1978. Based on a Dominican inquisition, this exceptional book re-creates the small village of Montaillou and most of its inhabitants from 1294 to 1324. While it does not discuss Dominic, this book covers the history, social life and customs, and religious life of a town that was deeply infected with the Catharist heresy. Thus Ladurie's account reveals what Dominic had to confront on a daily basis. Includes maps, index, and bibliography.

Lehner, F. C., ed. *Saint Dominic: Biographical Documents*. Washington, D.C.: Thomist Press, 1964. This is an excellent source for English translations of the principal primary sources on the life of Dominic. With a bibliography.

Nigg, Walter. *Warriors of God: The Great Religious Orders and Their Founders*. Translated by Mary Ilford. London: Secker and Warburg, 1959. Includes a succinct account of Dominic's life and work. There is little material on his early life, but the description of his work in Languedoc, the evolution of the order, and its impact on the development of the Church is excellent.

Vicaire, M.-H. *Saint Dominic and His Times*. Translated by Kathleen Pond. New York: McGraw-Hill, 1964. This is considered by most historians to be the definitive study of Dominic. The first section covers his early childhood, education, spiritual growth, encounters with heretics, and events surrounding the establishment of the order in 1215. Part 2 details Dominic's life in Rome and his successful efforts to organize and expand the order. Extensive bibliography, notes, appendices, and index.

Ronald F. Smith

DUCCIO DI BUONINSEGNA

Born: c. 1255; possibly Siena
Died: August 3, 1319; Siena
Area of Achievement: Art
Contribution: By blending techniques borrowed from French Gothic, Florentine, and Byzantine art, Duccio created a distinct Sienese style of painting. His attempts at three-dimensionality and his inventive use of architectural structures in his painting influenced future generations of Italian and French artists.

Early Life

The importance of Duccio di Buoninsegna's work is often overshadowed in art criticism by the exuberant praise of the work of his contemporary, Giotto, even though many of the works attributed to the latter may not have actually been done by him. Another handicap in the assessment of Duccio's work stems from the fact that he was born in Siena and not Florence, the center of Italian art in the late thirteenth and early fourteenth centuries. According to the art historian John White:

> It is hard to think of any major painter who, when it comes to generalizations about his art, is less appreciated for himself, and on his own terms, and who is more consistently considered in a framework of relative and qualitative comparisons than Duccio.

Of his personal life, little of substance is known. He was married to a woman named Taviana, with whom he had six sons and one daughter. Three of his sons later became painters themselves, yet nothing is known of their lives or work. Duccio's everyday life was apparently filled with numerous confrontations with the rigid stratification of Sienese society. A large number of recorded fines against the young artist have suggested a bohemian lifestyle to some; yet most of the infractions were petty in nature, such as breaking of curfew, failing to attend a public meeting to which he was summoned, and refusing to swear allegiance to a superior. Perhaps Duccio was as independently oriented toward his civic duties as he was toward his art.

Between 1295 and 1302, the artist undertook a series of trips, first to Paris and then to Rome. In Paris, he worked as a miniaturist, or manuscript illuminator. Upon seeing Chartres Cathedral, located a short distance from the capital city, Duccio succumbed to the spell of French Gothic art. His visit to Chartres profoundly affected his later work, particularly the Rucellai *Madonna*, the only true Gothic painting of the thirteenth century in Italy, which borrows directly from the famous cathedral window "La Belle Verrière." Most experts agree that the artist also traveled to Constantinople about this same time, for few can believe that the Byzantine influences so visible in Duccio's major work could have been acquired at second hand.

By the beginning of the fourteenth century, Duccio had become the head of his own large workshop, which may have included as many as twelve assistants. Although his later life would be spent in constant and profitable work which ultimately permitted him to purchase a small vineyard, not far from Siena, his children renounced his will, for it contained nothing but debts.

Life's Work

Perhaps as many as nine or ten of Duccio's paintings survive; nevertheless, his reputation hinges on three principal works: the Crevole *Madonna* (1280), the Rucellai *Madonna* (1285), and his masterwork, the climax of his career, the *Maestà* (1308-1311), a representation of the lives of the Madonna and Christ child, created for the Duomo of Siena.

The Crevole *Madonna* clearly shows its Byzantine origins, most notably, in the subtle color alterations of the Madonna's drapery, which range from a gentle pink to dark vermilion, the flowing golden hemline, the soft cream-white tunic of the Christ child, and the crystal blues of the cloaked angels in the corners. The figures themselves reflect the artist's concern for a new humanization of the Holy Mother and Child. The babe is gently extending his right hand to touch the headdress of the Madonna, yet he does not actually touch her face, suggesting both closeness and separation, reminding the viewer of both Christ's Passion and the Holy Mother's intuition of its nature. Despite the charming proportions of Christ's figure, to the modern eye, the infant resembles more a miniature of the adult Christ than an infant.

Even though the work lacks a true three-dimensional character, the chubby, cherublike representation of the child represents one of the earliest attempts at three-dimensionality in painting. Many of the innovations which characterize Duccio's mature work and set him apart from his contemporaries are in evidence here: the close attention to detail, the transparency of the draperies which distinctly reveal the figure of the child, and the precision of the facial tones and lines.

Duccio's second extant masterpiece is the Rucellai *Madonna*, commissioned in Florence on April 15, 1285, for the Chapel of the Laudesi. Signed "Duccio di Buoninsegna, the painter, of Siena," it is a majestic work, measuring fifteen feet high by ten feet wide. For several centuries the work was attributed to the Florentine painter Cimabue, but most twentieth century critics agree that it was done entirely by the hand of Duccio. The work presents the immaculate Virgin Mary and the Christ child surrounded by six angels. An exquisitely feminine Mary, seated on a massive, ornately carved throne done in Byzantine fashion, cradles the child on her left arm. Of particular interest, both historical and aesthetic, is the complex pose of the child, his right arm extending across and away from the Madonna, his legs slightly crooked to convey a comfortable, childlike position of safety on his mother's knees. Of further importance is the absence of eye contact between mother and child, a symbolic foreshadowing of the tragic separation of Christ from the world after the Passion.

Duccio's Gothic heritage is again much apparent in this work. The soft, undulating folds of the Madonna's drapery model the angle of the legs beneath, so that, despite the relative absence of three-dimensional perspective, the position of the limbs beneath the garments is clearly indicated. A gilded hem serpentines across the front of her garment, accentuating the Gothic curves and cascades of material. The six angels, three on either side of the principal figures, seem to be floating in golden air, accentuating their celestial mission; Mary is obviously enthroned in Heaven, not on Earth.

The depiction of the heavenly throne on which Mary is seated reveals the innovation that Duccio was attempting. With consummate finesse, Duccio emphasizes the structural supports of the throne to create a feeling of its massive weight and stability. Upon observing the celestial throne, one critic noted that Duccio's technique lay "far outside the imaginative range or the executive ability of any of his contemporaries."

Despite the genius of these two early works, it is the *Maestà*, created for the high altar of the chapel of the Duomo of Siena, which has assured Duccio his place among the ranks of such masters as Giotto and Cimabue. The work has an interesting history. On the day that it was carried to the cathedral, June 9, 1311, there was a spectacular procession, as reported by one anonymous chronicler of the time:

> On the day on which it was carried to the Duomo, the shops were locked up and the Bishop ordered a great and devout company of priests and brothers with a solemn procession accompanied by the Signori of the Nine and all the officials of the Commune, and all the populace, and all the most worthy were in order next to the said panel with lights lit in their hands; and then behind were the women and children with much devotion; and they accompanied it right to the Duomo. . . .

The work had taken two years and eight months to complete. The prestigious nature of this commission for Duccio is revealed by the fact that the *Maestà* was to replace a revered Sienese icon.

In 1771, the *Maestà* was sawed into seven pieces and disassembled to make room for a new altarpiece. Although much of the work was returned to the cathedral in 1776, many of the panels have since been scattered to various museums. In the late nineteenth century the major parts of the work were moved from the cathedral to the Museo dell'Opera del Duomo in Siena, where they have remained since.

In its original state the *Maestà* consisted of one large, two-sided altarpiece.

Duccio himself painted only the front panels; the back panels were executed by the numerous apprentices in his workshop. Forty-six panels from the original fifty-four or fifty-eight are extant. Majestic and complex, the work originally stood on a base with seven scenes from the early life of Christ, beginning with the "Annunciation" and ending with the "Teaching in the Temple." The main frontal panel, an expansive paean to the Virgin, centers on the scene of "Virgin Enthroned with Angels and Saints." Above the principal panels are half portraits of those ten apostles not represented in the central panels. Two central panels are missing from the original but were probably the "Assumption" and the "Coronation of the Virgin." These *predella*, independent yet thematically related panels arranged in chronological order, are the earliest extant examples of this technique in Italian art.

On the back are twenty-six scenes from the Passion. The series follows an imaginative order unique to Duccio's work, beginning from the bottom left with the "Entry into Jerusalem" and ending at the top right with the "Apparition on the Road to Emmaus." Six panels at the top complete the sequence. The central panels of the work represent the "Agony in the Garden," "The Betrayal," and "The Crucifixion." Two panels from the main central column are missing but were probably "The Ascension" and "Christ in Majesty."

A masterpiece of painting, architectural construction, and engineering, the *Maestà* required a precision of measurement and awareness of perspective generally unheard of at the time. The overall compositional effectiveness of the work eschews monumentality in favor of an elegant grandeur and scrupulously sustains the symbolic relationships of the various parts to the whole. The entire effect dramatically testifies to the genius of the artist.

Duccio's attention to iconographic and realistic detail, his flawless sense of harmony and unity within complexity, and his surety of line and color combine in the *Maestà* to produce a work of incomparable proportion and beauty. The narrative character of the work is typical of the period in which Duccio was working, yet here again he left his particular imprint. Rather than having the panels relate the story of Christ's life in the traditional, linear fashion, Duccio selected a sort of zigzag pattern to suggest the simultaneity of actions and events in time, as they might actually have occurred.

Summary

Duccio di Buoninsegna's recognizable Tuscan style emerged out of subtle blending of the Byzantine mosaic style with French Gothic, Roman, and Florentine influences. In addition to his experimentations with proportion and perspective, and with color, shadings, and line, Duccio introduced several startling compositional innovations into his work. In one of the most famous panels of the *Maestà*, "The Healing of the Man Born Blind," Duccio produced the first surviving example of a cityscape which actually encloses the figures in the foreground. The buildings on the right side of the work, encircling the blind man, seem to lunge forward to frame the work. Although by modern standards these structures still appear flat and disproportionate, and the figures still appear to be pasted over the background, a sense of an enclosed space is dramatically present.

Duccio's attempts to represent coherently the perspective of background structures can also be seen in the panel "Annunciation of the Death of the Virgin," in which the two figures are completely enclosed by an architectural space. Never before had an artist so clearly suggested the three-dimensionality of space on a flat canvas. Always in the past, architectural space had appeared behind the figures. Such experimental techniques greatly hastened the movement of Italian art toward the new kind of realism of the Renaissance.

Although Duccio's direct influence on later generations of Italian artists pales in comparison to that of Giotto, his influence on artists outside Italy, and particularly in France, was significant. In the work of Jean Pucelle, for example, whose Parisian illumination workshop was the most famous in Europe between 1320 and 1350, Duccio's influence is explicitly present. In a well-known Book of Hours, a sort of private prayer book, for Jeanne, Queen of France, the "Annunciation" illumination borrows both its composition and its general conception of interior space from the panel of the same name in the *Maestà*. Among the later Italian artists who continued to model on Duccio's work, only one disciple, Simone Martini, achieved any distinction. While he abandoned Duccio's lyrical style, Martini continued to develop many of the master's techniques.

Bibliography

Focillon, Henri. "Gothic Painting of the XIII and XIV Centuries." In *The Art of the West in the Middle Ages*. Vol. 2, *Gothic Art*. New York: Phaidon Publications, 1963. Focillon has chosen to sacrifice depth of treatment of specific painters for a panoramic view of the general character of artistic production of the thirteenth and fourteenth centuries in Italy. The work is thus most useful for the generalist as an overview, for Focillon provides sensitive judgments on the influences of earlier periods on Duccio's work and of the artist's impact on later painters.

Janson, H. W. *History of Art: A Survey of the Major Visual Arts from the Dawn of History to the Present Day*. Englewood Cliffs, N.J.: Prentice-Hall, 1962, rev. ed. 1969. Janson's renowned work has deservedly become the standard of art history classroom texts. As the subtitle indicates, the text provides a sweeping view of art from cave painting to postmodernism. Illustrated with more than eight hundred black-and-white reproductions and eighty-seven color plates, the prose vibrates with clarity, precision, and sensitivity. The substantive, if brief, treatment of Duccio includes reproductions of his works and a lucid analysis of his position among the Italian masters of the fourteenth century.

Morey, Charles Rufus. "Late Gothic: The Realistic Movement." In *Medieval Art*. New York: W. W. Norton and Co., 1942. The majority of the material in Morey's well-known work reflects the standard assessment of Duccio's work prior to the current general agreement about the attribution of several major pieces to the artist. Line drawings rather than photographic reproductions of the artist's principal works illustrate the text. The work does provide a clear context for situating Duccio among the other great Late Gothic painters in Italy.

Stubblebine, James H. *Duccio di Buoninsegna and His School*. 2 vols. Princeton, N.J.: Princeton University Press, 1979. This two-volume work provides a complete and reasoned analysis of Duccio's work, major and minor. After a detailed study of the author's life, Stubblebine meticulously documents the location, size, attribution, condition, and provenance of each of the artist's works, providing a critical evaluation of each. In all cases, the author presents a balanced view of the problems of influences on Duccio's work and on the debates concerning attribution. The text of volume 1 refers to the plates of volume 2, black-and-white photographic reproductions of all the master's work and of many of his disciples'.

White, John. *Duccio: Tuscan Art and the Medieval Workshop*. London: Thames and Hudson, 1979. White's study of Duccio's life and work is the standard scholarly work on the subject. Beginning with a general introduction to life of the artist in late thirteenth century Italy and moving into a detailed study of Duccio's life and work, this highly readable text, complemented by numerous black-and-white reproductions, explores the painter's origins and influences from the historical to the aesthetic. Two long chapters on the *Maestà* and on Duccio's influence and achievement are particularly informative. A "portfolio" of Duccio's work completes the work.

William C. Griffin

SAINT ELIZABETH OF HUNGARY

Born: 1207; Sárospatak, Hungary
Died: November 17, 1231; near Wittenberg, Thuringia
Areas of Achievement: Religion and social reform
Contribution: Elizabeth, seeking to live according to the Christian ideal, established the first orphanage for homeless children in Central Europe and actively cared for the poor and the unemployed.

Early Life

Elizabeth of Hungary was born in Sárospatak in 1207 to King Andrew II of Hungary and Gertrud of Andechs-Meran. Her mother met a tragic death in 1213, when Hungarian conspirators had her murdered. Elizabeth's two maternal uncles, Berthold, titular Patriarch of Aquileia, and Bishop Eckbert of Bamberg, who had played a role in the assassination of Philip of Swabia and sought refuge at the Hungarian court, were high ecclesiastics. In 1211, Hermann I, Landgrave of Thuringia, sent a delegation led by Knight Walter of Vargila to Pozsony to request the hand of Elizabeth in marriage for his son, Hermann. The landgrave probably wanted to restore his weakened social and financial resources through this marriage with the Hungarian royal family. He may also have hoped to rely on the support of the Eastern monarch in the deadly struggle between Otto of Brunswick and Frederick, the new papal protégé for the German throne. Bishop Eckbert may have suggested the plan, though it is possible that Otakar of Bohemia may have also tried to establish a triple alliance by including the King of Hungary. From another point of view, family ties between one of the leading noble families in the empire and the Hungarian court might have enhanced the diplomatic position of Andrew II against some German princes, who still looked upon Hungary as a country to be invaded and plundered. Knight Vargila successfully concluded a marriage agreement, and the four-year-old bride, richly endowed, was dispatched to the Thuringian court at the castle of the Wartburg, near Eisenach. A bathtub of pure silver and a thousand pieces of gold formed only a portion of her dowry. It is known from her second husband, Louis, that the Thuringian court had never before seen such riches. They also expressed surprise at Elizabeth's large personal entourage of servants and nurses.

Hermann I maintained an elaborate court and provided for poets and artists of the age. It may be that Walther von der Vogelweide or Wolfram von Eschenbach (while working on his *Parzival*, c. 1200-1210; English translation, 1894) spent some time at the castle at Wartburg. Hermann I and his wife, Sophia, met the young Elizabeth at Eisenach, and the official engagement celebration was held soon after at Wartburg. Elizabeth was educated at the Thuringian court; the curriculum included the study of contemporary poetry and writers, the history of leading families in the empire, art appreciation, Latin, and religion. As a child, Elizabeth liked to play, ride horses, and participate in games as well as pray in the chapel. Even as a child she displayed empathy and compassion toward the poor. Concerned with Elizabeth's appearance as a lady of society, however, her mother-in-law cautioned her about being too loud and exuberant.

In 1213, when her mother was murdered, the six-year-old Elizabeth saw her bloody, mutilated body in a dream. After that, she spent more time in prayer before the crucifix and began to dress more simply. She began to pray for the murderers of her mother. Elizabeth was nine when she lost her fiancé, Hermann, and one year later her father-in-law died. It was at this time that Louis, her fiancé's younger brother, became Elizabeth's protector and good friend. After discussing Elizabeth's uncertain future, Louis decided that she would be his wife. They were married in 1221 in the presence of the nobles of Thuringia and of other German regions. Knight Vargila led Elizabeth to the altar, and her father sent additional gifts. At the end of September, 1222, the young couple visited King Andrew at Pozsony. Traveling by horse, they were horrified at the destruction and decline of the country. It was the year of the Hungarian Golden Bull, by which the Hungarian nobles, discouraged by the nearly total disintegration of law and order in the realm, had forced the king to share his government with them.

Life's Work

Under the guidance of her confessor, Father Rodinger, a Franciscan friar, Elizabeth began to lead a deeper spiritual life, carried out charity work, and established an orphanage (the first in Central Europe). She cared for lepers, of whom she was not afraid, and constructed a twenty-eight-bed hospital for them. She then came under the spiritual directorship of Master Conrad of Marburg, the noted mystic, Franciscan preacher, and ascetic.

In 1225, Louis embarked on a military campaign summoned by the emperor, and in his absence, Elizabeth governed Thuringia. She healed the wounds caused by natural disasters and was concerned about social discrimination among the disadvantaged; she fed nine hundred poor people daily, provided tools and obtained work for the able-bodied unemployed men, and taught the women to spin. At the same time, she represented her husband in high society, received distinguished guests at the court, and participated in hunting parties.

In 1227, Louis was again summoned by the emperor and joined a Crusade; Elizabeth was expecting their third child. By the time Gertrud was born, Louis was already dead, having fallen ill at Otranto. Elizabeth's brothers-in-law, uneasy about her spending habits, forbade her to handle her own fiscal affairs, prompting her to leave Wartburg in October, 1227, with her three small children. Nobody in Eisenach, however, would accommodate them.

After placing the children in foster homes, Elizabeth, accompanied by two of her royal servants, Guda and Isentrud, finally found shelter in an innkeeper's stable. She spun cloth for a living until Mechtild, Abbess of Kitzingen, provided for her in the abbey. Her uncle, the Bishop of Bamberg, placed his castle at Pottstein at her disposal. The bishop tried to persuade her to marry Emperor Frederick II, but Elizabeth firmly declined the proposal. Only the future of her children concerned her; for herself, she desired to live in poverty. She had her husband's remains buried in the monastery which he had founded at Reinhardsbrunn. After the burial, and with Knight Vargila's support, she regained her right to manage the estates she had inherited as a widow. Making a vow in the Franciscan church in Eisenach to renounce all earthly love and free will, she retained her property for the sake of her children, Hermann, Sophia, and Gertrud, and for making provision for the poor. She did not live in the castle at Wartburg but in nearby Wehrda, in a primitive house built of blocks of dirt. She spun to earn her living and assisted in the hospital she had founded.

In order to deepen Elizabeth's humility, Conrad used crude methods such as flagellation and beatings, the dismissal of her two servants, forbidding her to distribute large sums of money to the poor, and allowing her to give only one slice of bread each to the hungry. Elizabeth used her own bed to care for a young boy sick with dysentery; when he died, she put a girl with leprosy in her bed. Augmenting the abuse and humiliation suffered at the hand of Conrad, gossip now began to undermine Elizabeth's reputation. She was ridiculed for her loud laughter, her refusal to dress in black, and the apparent ease with which she forgot her deceased husband. There were even rumors that she was happily engaged in an affair with the friar, about which she was confronted by Knight Vargila. In response, Elizabeth showed the marks of the flagellations and beatings received from Conrad.

Knowing that she was weak and would die soon, Elizabeth stayed in bed for the last two weeks of her life, finalizing the arrangements for the distribution of her wealth and her children's future. Three days before she died, she sent everyone away from her except Conrad, who remained at her bedside. She died in the early hours of November 17, 1231. Her body lay in state for four days in the Franciscan church at Eisenach, dressed in clothing of the poor. During this time, the inhabitants of Thuringia came to her coffin not to pray for her but to ask for her intercession on their behalf. It is reported that during the following days and weeks, numerous miracles occurred at her grave.

Conrad informed Pope Gregory IX of the death of Elizabeth, and the pontiff authorized the friar to make preparations for her canonization. When Conrad was murdered in July, 1233, the Bishop of Hildesheim carried on with the canonization process. It was then that the *Libellus de dictis IV ancillarum* (depositions of Saint Elizabeth's four handmaidens—Isentrud,

Guda, Iremngard, and Elisabeth) was recorded in writing, followed by a strict ecclesiastical investigation. On May 26, 1235, in Perugia on the Feast of Pentecost, Pope Gregory IX entered Elizabeth's name in the canon of saints (papal bull *Gloriosus in maiestate*). The first church erected in her honor was built by her brother-in-law Conrad, who was grand master of the German Order, at Marburg. On May 1, 1236, her coffin was elevated upon the altar in the presence of her children, brothers-in-law, four archbishops, eight bishops, and a multitude of German, Hungarian, Czech, and French pilgrims.

Summary

Saint Elizabeth of Hungary lived according to the Christian ideal, fusing it with the pastoral concept of the mendicant orders in teaching and practicing humility and social equality. She did not believe that social stabilization could occur by suddenly elevating the lower strata; rather, she believed that the upper classes should willingly descend to the aid of the poor. In addition to building a hospital and establishing an asylum for homeless children, Elizabeth demonstrated an attitude toward the poor that was realistic as well as humane. Thus, although she developed a plan for feeding the poor, she abhorred idleness, quoting from Saint Paul that one who did not work would not eat.

Bibliography

Bihl, Michael. "Elizabeth of Hungary." *Catholic Encyclopaedia* 5 (1909): 389-391. A thorough report on Saint Elizabeth and her time in accordance with early biographies and sermons, such as those preached by the late fifteenth century Franciscan friar Pelbart of Temesvár. The work colorfully depicts the Hungarian royal court, life in Thuringia, and the background of the Crusades in the early thirteenth century.

Butler, Alban. "St. Elizabeth of Hungary, Widow." In *Lives of the Saints*, edited by Herbert Thurston and Donald Attwater, vol. 4. New York: P. J. Kennedy and Sons, 1956. A readable and informative account which includes quotes from the depositions of Elizabeth's loyal servants. Reveals the remarkable depth of Elizabeth and Louis' relationship; treats Conrad's spiritual directorship dispassionately.

De Robeck, Nesta. *Saint Elizabeth of Hungary: A Story of Twenty-four Years*. Milwaukee, Wis.: Bruce Publishing Co., 1954. This volume is well written and clever but does not provide much new information about Saint Elizabeth.

Huyskens, Albert. *Quellenstudien zur Geschichte der hl. Elisabeth, Landgräfin von Thüringen*. Marburg, Germany: N. G. Elwert, 1908. This volume provides German interpretations of the life of Saint Elizabeth, based upon available source material. In other parts of the work, Huyskens discusses and analyzes the political and economic background of the age and the role assumed by religion.

Kranz, Gisbert. *Elisabeth von Thüringien*. Augsburg, West Germany: Verlag Winfried-Werk, 1957. Relying primarily on translations of the sources and secondary literature, Kranz brings Saint Elizabeth's life closer to the reader in this very readable book.

Nigg, Walter, and Helmuth Nils Loose. *Die hl. Elisabeth: Das Leben der Landgräfin von Thüringien*. Freiburg, Switzerland: Christophorus Verlag, 1979. A thorough background study of the social and economic conditions of the age in Hungary and the German empire. The authors narrate the life of Saint Elizabeth while attempting to present her as a real, earthly person.

Z. J. Kosztolnyik

EMPEDOCLES

Born: c. 490 B.C.; Acragas, Sicily
Died: c. 430 B.C.; in the Peloponnese, Greece
Areas of Achievement: Philosophy, science, and natural history
Contribution: Empedocles was one of the earliest of the Greek philosophers to provide a unified theory of the nature of the world and the cosmos.

Early Life

Born c. 490 in Acragas, Empedocles was a member of the aristocracy. Much of his life has become shrouded in legend; fact is more difficult to discover. It is known that he spent some time with Zeno and Parmenides in the city of Elea; some time after that, he studied with the school of Pythagoras. Later, he left the Pythagoreans for reasons that are not completely clear and returned to Acragas.

In Acragas, he became a political figure, eventually participating in a movement to depose a tyrant, despite his aristocratic background. He made enemies, however, and they used their influence, while he was absent from Acragas, to banish him from his home. He would spend much of his life in exile.

Life's Work

Empedocles' two main works, *Peri Physeōs* (fifth century B.C.; *On Nature*) and *Katharmoi* (fifth century B.C.; *Purifications*), exist only in fragments. *On Nature* is an expression of Empedocles as a cosmic philosopher and as one of the earliest natural scientists. An essay on the ability of humans to experience the world, in general *On Nature* describes Empedocles' theory of the cosmology of the world. Parmenides believed that the world can be apprehended through the use of reason; Empedocles, however, believed that neither reason nor the senses can provide a clear picture of reality: Reason is a better instrument for dealing with abstraction, and the physical senses are best suited for the phenomenological world.

Unlike Parmenides, Empedocles assumed that the universe is in motion and that it is composed of a multitude of separate parts, but that their nature is such that the senses can perceive neither the motion nor the great plurality of living and spiritual forms that inhabit the natural world. In his conception, the basic building blocks of true reality lie in the four archaic "roots": earth, air, fire, and water. In the abstract, these four elements are also represented by spiritual beings: Aidoneus is associated with earth, Hera with air, Zeus with fire, and Nestis with water. The elements can neither be added to the natural world nor deleted from it: The universe is a closed system. The elements can be mixed with one another, however, and the mixture of these elements in various proportions constitutes the stuff of the perceived world.

Every physical entity is a composite of the four elements, in varying forms and degrees of mixture. Empedocles' own analogy was that the blending of the elements could be likened to the creation of a painting: A few basic colors on the palette could be blended in such a manner that all the colors of the rainbow could be achieved.

He saw living things as only a matter of appearance: While they live, they have control over their corporeal forms and assume that the forms of life are as they perceive them. At the time of their death, when the bonds that hold together the elements of which they are composed are loosened, they die.

Empedocles believed that two opposing principles, Love and Strife (also variously called Love and Hate, Harmony and Disharmony, Attraction and Repulsion), are engaged in a constant struggle in the universe, a process that gives rise to a continual mixing and shifting of the basic particles of earth, air, fire, and water. The two powers alternate in their dominance in a great cosmic cycle that involves the whole universe. When Love dominates, the particles of matter are brought into a homogeneous mass. When Strife is in the ascendant, the effect is to separate the mixed elements into four separate and discrete masses. These alternating states form the poles of existence; the periods when neither dominated were times of flux during which the power of one gradually increased as the power of the other waned. The human world is one where Strife is in the process of slowly overcoming Love: a place of relative disintegration.

In the beginning of the cycle, the elements are separated, under the control of Strife. As the powers of Love manifest themselves, the integrative process creates from the earth random or unattached portions of animals. These combine in various haphazard ways, creating monsters. A similar integrative process creates unattached human parts: disembodied heads, shoulderless arms, unattached eyes. Through chance wanderings, the parts begin to join, creating human monsters, such as many-handed creatures with double faces, cattle with human faces, and people with the faces of oxen.

Nevertheless, some join in a manner which allows them to survive. As time and chance do their work, more and more improvements allow certain forms to prosper; eventually, human form, because of its relatively high survival value, becomes established and flourishes. The same process brings about the various orders of beasts.

After a relatively short period, the flux begins again. Strife becomes gradually more powerful, and the cycle is eventually completed. Empedocles may have meant his theory of Love and Strife to apply to human experience as well: These two forces, acting in the world of men, are the causes of the harmony of friendship and the disharmony of hatred.

Empedocles thought that every entity in the universe was endowed with particular consciousness. In addition to being conscious of each other, Love and Strife are aware of their effect on the elements. The elements in turn are conscious of the workings of Love and Strife. Finally, the four elements—fire, air, earth, and water—are aware of one another, both pure and in their various mixtures, and thus humans have consciousness, if only on a lower level, as well. Everything in the world constantly gives off emanations into the atmosphere, consisting of the particles of which they are made. As these particles pass through the air, humans absorb them (through their pores), transmitting them through the body by the blood.

In addition, the four elements and their combinations are aware of themselves; for example, the water in the air is conscious of the water in a human body. A particle that enters the human body is eventually be transported to the heart, which is a particularly sensitive organ: It is closely associated with the creation and perception of human thought. The blood is the prime medium for this transfer, because it contains equal proportions of the four elements. The operation of the senses also is based on the awareness of the elements: The particles in the air are perceived differentially by the particles in the sense organs.

After Empedocles had completed *On Nature*, he apparently changed many of his beliefs—probably after he had studied among the Pythagoreans. Especially attractive was the Pythagorean doctrine concerning the transmigration of the soul. Earlier, Empedocles seems to have thought that the human, having been formed from the four elements, died, both body and soul. In *Purifications*, however, Empedocles seems to have adopted the Pythagorean idea that an individual's soul survives physically, going through a series of incarnations. Each soul has to pass through a cycle somewhat like the cosmic cycle of Love and Strife.

Sinfulness, as conceived in Christian thought, was not a factor in the Greek world. Nevertheless, *Purifications* reflects a concept of sin and atonement. The most likely source for such an abstraction would be the Buddhist Middle East, and Empedocles was probably aware of certain Buddhist doctrines.

Empedocles linked his cycle of incarnations with the concept of sin. The soul is initially in a state of sinlessness when it enters the world. In this stage, it is pure mind—a beatific state. As it resides in the world, the soul becomes tainted, especially by the sin of shedding the blood of humans or animals. The sinful soul is condemned to undergo a series of physical incarnations for thirty thousand years (an indeterminate period of time; Empedocles never defined the length of a season). The soul is incarnated in bodily forms that are in turn derived from air (such as a cloud), water, earth, and fire. Empedocles recounted some of his own incarnations: He was a boy; in another life he was a girl; he was also a bird, a bush, and a fish at various times. Each successive incarnation allows the sincere soul an opportunity to better itself. Declaring that he had progressed to the company of such people as doctors, prophets, and princes, Empedocles hoped to be reborn among the gods.

One interesting facet of Empedocles' greatness is his pioneering work in the field of biology. Implicit in his observations on anatomy is the assumption that he conducted experiments on the bodies of animals and humans. He conjectured that blood circulates throughout the body in a system powered by the heart, that respiration occurs through the pores of the skin, and that some of the organs of the human body are similar in function to the organs of animals. He also observed that the embryo is clearly human in form in the seventh week of pregnancy.

Most interesting of Empedocles' theories is his concept of evolution. In *On Nature*, he assumed that the first creatures were monstrosities, crudely formed; some of these were, by chance, better adapted to survive than others. As the millennia passed, certain mutations (Empedocles did not use the word) made some forms more efficient in basic matters, such as eating and digesting and adapting their anatomy to catch and kill prey. In the passage of time, the successful body forms became nearly perfectly adapted to living in a particular environment.

Despite the great differences in the forms of various animals, Empedocles still saw unity in the whole of life. All organisms adapted safeguards against predation; all reproduced, breathed air, and drank water; and all had a particular consciousness—they rejoiced in the act of living and grieved at physical death.

Empedocles seems to have been many-faceted. According to contemporary accounts, his wardrobe was idiosyncratic, and some of his actions were bizarre. In his own works, and according to other testimony, he claimed to be a god. This claim seems to have gained credence: He boasted that crowds of people followed him, entreating him to use his magical healing powers. He claimed to be able to resurrect the dead as well as to have some control over the weather.

Several versions of Empedocles' death have survived: He hanged himself; he fell and broke his thigh; he fell from a ship and was drowned. From the second century B.C., one version superseded all others: He disappeared in a brilliant light when a voice called his name. The best-known version, however, is that made famous by Matthew Arnold in his poem *Empedocles on Etna* (1852), in which Empedocles jumped into the crater of the volcano, apparently to prove that he was immortal.

Summary

In many ways, Empedocles influenced medieval and Renaissance conceptions of science and anticipated modern theories. For example, despite some criticism, Plato and Aristotle adopted his biological theories; his conception of the four elements, probably derived from the work of Hippocrates, thus had influence until the scientific revolution in the seventeenth century. Finally, his ideas on human and animal evolution foreshadow modern theories, and his conception of a universe in which elements maintained a constant though ever-changing presence presages the law of the conservation of energy.

His accomplishments were honored by his contemporaries, and his memory was revered. Aristotle called him the father of rhetoric, and Galen considered him the founder of the medical arts. According to Lucretius, Empedocles was a master poet, and the extant fragments of his works support this claim. His main contribution was philosophical, however, and his two works were an important influence on early Greek philosophy.

Bibliography

Kirk, Geoffrey S., and John E. Raven. *The Presocratic Philosophers*. Cambridge: Cambridge University Press, 1957. Much of the material on pre-Socratic philosophers is subject to interpretation; this book presents both sides of dozens of equivocal topics. It has a useful chapter on Empedocles.

Lambridis, Helle. *Empedocles: A Philosophic Investigation*. University: University of Alabama Press, 1976. This book begins with a preface by Marshall McLuhan, entitled "Empedocles and T. S. Eliot." The book itself serves two useful purposes: It is a good and comprehensive survey, and it is the best analysis of the poetry of Empedocles. Both modern and ancient Greek criteria are brought to bear on the poetry.

Millerd, Clara E. *On the Interpretation of Empedocles*. Chicago: University of Chicago Press, 1908. Reprint. New York: Garland Publishing, 1980. This important study discusses a number of topics concerning the intellectual background and development of Empedocles' ideas. The discussions are well written and knowledgeable. Though by no means obsolete, the book is somewhat dated.

O'Brien, D. *Empedocles' Cosmic Cycle*. Cambridge: University of Cambridge Press, 1969. The most comprehensive and scholarly discussion of Empedocles' *On Nature*. Contains a useful section of notes, following the text, in which relatively minor but interesting topics are discussed. Its exhaustive annotated bibliography is as valuable in itself as is the text.

Wright, M. R. *Empedocles: The Extant Fragments*. New Haven, Conn.: Yale University Press, 1981. This modern critical work includes the Greek text of Empedocles' works, a translation, and a closely written and copious set of notes.

Richard Badessa

QUINTUS ENNIUS

Born: 239 B.C.; Rudiae, Calabria
Died: c. 169 B.C.; Rome?
Area of Achievement: Literature
Contribution: Known as the father of Latin poetry, Ennius extended the Latin language into areas previously reserved for Greek, offering explanations for Roman origins. He thus paved the way for the Golden Age of Latin poetry and influenced poets as different as Lucretius and Vergil.

Early Life

Not much is known concerning Quintus Ennius' early life aside from the material he included in his own works. Because of the popularity of his writings, it is likely that this information is accurate: His contemporaries could easily have contradicted him, and that would have been, at the least, embarrassing, given the important circles in which Ennius moved after his arrival at Rome. It is clear that Ennius was born in Calabria and that his circumstances were humble. His origins were a point of personal pride which he would conscientiously maintain throughout his life. Even when established at Rome as a teacher and recognized poet, Ennius lived with somewhat awkward simplicity in the wealthy surroundings of the Aventine and employed but a single servant.

Ennius began his career as a soldier rather than as a poet and served with distinction during the Second Punic War. It was, paradoxically, his military talent rather than his skill in writing verse which first brought him to the attention of Cato the Censor, whose surname and hatred for Carthage made him a symbol of stern discipline and morality, even in his own time. It was during these years, while stationed in Sardinia, that Cato, then serving as military quaestor (a post with many of the same duties as quartermaster), tutored Ennius, his centurion, in Greek. Cato introduced Ennius to Scipio Africanus and Fulvius Nobilior; these men would further Ennius' interests after he came to Rome. Ennius subsequently served on Fulvius' staff during the Anatolian campaign, and in 184 B.C. Fulvius' son, with the approval of the Roman people, awarded Ennius a lot among the *triumviri coloniae deducendae*. This award constituted a grant of citizenship, though it brought him no personal wealth. Scipio, too, remained friends with his junior officer, and (at least according to tradition) asked that a bust of Ennius be placed next to his tomb.

Copies of this bust from the tomb of the Scipios may surprise the person who imagines Ennius as an old Roman ascetic. If this bust is, indeed, of Ennius (and some would disagree), he was full-faced, with an aquiline nose, thick lips, and generally provincial features. His hair is close-cropped in the republican mode but with straight locks rather than the "crab-claw," curled ones found in imperial sculpture. He wears the expected laurel wreath, but, again unlike imperial sculpture, the artist has made no attempt to idealize his subject. One should contrast this frank rendering of Ennius with the sensitive, idealized (also suspect) sculptures of his successor Vergil. These are products of Augustan Rome and present Vergil as an idealized poet of an idealized city.

Life's Work

At first, Ennius supported himself in Rome after his military service by teaching, armed with impressive recommendations from Cato, Scipio, and Fulvius; these were essential to attract good students, and Ennius, no doubt, attracted the best. Even so, Ennius must always have had intentions of making his mark in literature, and he wrote from his first arrival in the city.

Circumstances favored his efforts. The dramatist Livius Andronicus died in 204, and his colleague Gnaeus Naevius retired soon after, thus leaving a place to be filled. Ennius began writing dramas, primarily on mythic themes related to the Trojan War: *Achilles*, *Aiax* (*Ajax*), *Andromacha* (*Andromache*), *Hectoris lytra* (*The Ransom of Hector*), and *Hecuba*. He seems also to have chosen mythic subjects which would allow one to draw moral lessons on the folly of excess and pride: *Alexander*, *Andromeda*, *Athamas*, *Erechtheus*, *Eumenides*, *Iphigenia*, *Medea*, and *Thyestes*. Clearly, the Trojan War plays would have been very popular among republican audiences. Rome wistfully traced its uncertain origins to an amalgam of Trojan, Latin, and native Italic stock and consequently saw its history in its myth. Similarly, moralizing was popular in republican Rome; at least, high moral standards were officially privileged. The second group of subjects provided fertile ground for this. Unfortunately, these works (indeed all Ennius' writings) survive only as fragments quoted by subsequent authors. Even order of composition and dates of first performances are uncertain.

What is clear is that Ennius became popular quickly after 204 and that he was versatile. Though he continued to write drama throughout his life, he is best known as an analyst historian, that is, one who chronicled Roman history by using the *Annales Maximi*, official lists of significant events recorded year by year from the traditional date of Rome's founding, 753. His own now-fragmentary *Annales* (*Annals*, 1935) was originally written in eighteen books of verse and spanned Roman history from the legendary period of Aeneas' arrival in Italy to his own day. This work was begun sometime after his success as a playwright and occupied him throughout his middle years until his death.

Its eighteen books were originally circulated in groups of three and almost immediately became a part of the school curriculum. In part, they satisfied a need for material on Rome's past; they also were elegantly written style models and were patriotic in tone. If the content of the lost sections can be judged from extant passages such as the "Dream of Ilia" (the daughter of Aeneas) and the "Auspices of Romulus and Remus," each about ten lines, the *Annals* must have struck a responsive note in the hearts of patriotic Romans. In fact, Ennius' patriotic themes, combined with his sophisticated use of the Latin language, not only made his works subject matter studied by Roman youth but also won for him the title "father of Latin poetry." His simple manner of living, even amid the luxury of the Aventine, served to support the popularly held notion of his personal ethos and integrity.

Widespread early acceptance of his works likely encouraged Ennius to write at least one *praetexta* (a historical drama played in Roman dress), known as *Sabinae*, on the rape of the Sabine women, and perhaps another, the *Ambracia*, in praise of Fulvius, though the authorship of these works is open to question. If Ennius did indeed write *praetextae*, he would then have been trying his hand at a form to that time associated with Andronicus and Naevius. Only a few lines of these *praetextae* remain, not enough to establish his certain authorship.

Ennius' prolific writing, accomplished in his comfortable but simple quarters in Rome, kept him for the most part out of the public arena even as it made him a popular literary figure. He never possessed great wealth, though his old Roman simplicity did not prevent his living well. Personal references in his works note his longtime suffering with gout. Unfortunately for those interested in his private life during these middle years, such mundane asides in his works are rare. It is clear, however, that he was struggling at this time, with varying degrees of success, to fashion Latin epic and dramatic meters which could worthily mirror their Greek antecedents. This struggle to make the Latin tongue literary sums up the contradictory impulses of Ennius himself: distrustful of Greeks and all non-Romans, yet an admirer of Greek literature and art, in this sense a grecophile; an innovator in his use of the Latin language, yet one who consistently portrayed himself as an upholder of Roman tradition.

Despite his incontestable patriotism, Ennius was fond of saying that he "possessed three hearts" (that he could speak three languages—Greek, Latin, and Oscan—and was at home in each culture). He saw no particular difficulty in maintaining both his cosmopolitanism and his staunch Roman loyalties. Indeed, Roman audiences took pleasure in his Latin adaptations of the Greek dramatists, and his *Annals* made him the "Roman Homer."

Recognition and success in drama and historical epic allowed Ennius to devote considerable energy in the last third of his life to his *Saturae* (*Miscellanies*, 1935). This work is a collection of miscellaneous poems in various meters on everything from Pythagorean philosophy (specifically that of Epicharmus) and the Pythagorean mythology of Euhemerus to gastronomy and assorted personal reflections. It is in this work and in Ennius' epigrams that personal content is greatest, though both *Miscellanies* and the epigrams are fragmentary. What personal information survives concerns Ennius' early life.

Summary

One of the best known of Quintus Ennius' epigrams is a panegyric to the Roman military hero Scipio Africanus. Scipio is precisely the kind of personality Ennius would favor, and in a sense he sums up Ennius' ideas of well-lived Roman life. Ennius too made his mark in military affairs, but he made an easy transition to the literary world and used his considerable skills to write sophisticated Latin verse. Though he used Greek models, particularly for his plays, and prided himself on his sophistication, he nevertheless fashioned poetry appropriate to the high morality and ethical standards of the Roman Republic.

Ennius is most associated with Roman history, though *Annals* is actually a historical epic which inspired subsequent Roman poets as diverse as Lucretius (author of the philosophical epic *De Rerum Natura*, c. 69 B.C., *On the Nature of Things*) and Vergil, whose *Aeneid* (c. 29-19 B.C.) often quotes, modifies, and improves upon Ennian verse.

In the second century B.C., the critic Volcacius Sedigitus drew up a list of the ten best poets up to that time. He includes Ennius and supposedly does so only because of his early date. This action indicates that Ennius was not considered the equal of his predecessors in drama. His greatest contribution to Latin literature, recognized in his own times as well, is his historicizing of Roman myth in the *Annals*. The Roman historian Suetonius called Ennius "semi-Graecus," since origins and long residence in southern Italy had culturally made Ennius a Hellenized Roman. In spirit, however, as well as in his verse, Ennius could not have been more Roman, even if he had been born within the walls of the city.

Bibliography

Beare, W. *The Roman Stage: A Short History of Latin Drama in the Time of the Republic*. London: Methuen and Co., 1950, 3d ed. 1964. This is a scholarly history of the development of Roman drama with chapters on playwrights and the various genres of dramatic poetry. It discusses Ennius as successor of Livius Andronicus and Naevius and considers the mechanics of drama production as well.

Duff, J. Wight, and A. M. Duff. *A Literary History of Rome in the Silver Age: From Tiberius to Hadrian*. 3d ed. New York: Barnes and Noble Books, 1963. Chapter 3 discusses at some length Livius Andronicus, Naevius, and Ennius, and chapter 5 considers Roman tragedy after Ennius, with emphasis on Pacuvius, Accius, and the *praetextae*. Analysis of the fragments appears as well as what is known about the lives of the playwrights.

Jocelyn, H. D., ed. *The Tragedies of Ennius*. Cambridge: Cambridge Univer sity Press, 1967. Though primarily a Latin text of the fragments, the general reader will find Jocelyn's introduction both to Ennius and to his era interesting and meaningful. Those who cannot read Latin can still use Jocelyn's English commentary against the translation of the fragments in the Loeb edition, noted below.

Skutsch, Otto. *Studia Enniana*. London: Athlone Press, 1968. This is a collection, in quite readable English, of previously published articles on all areas of Ennian studies. All were written by Skutsch, and those on the *Annals* are excellent. Included as well are articles on Ennius' *Iphigenia*, *Medea*, and Ennian tragedy.

Warmington, E. H., trans. *Remains of Old Latin*. Vol. 1. Cambridge, Mass.: Harvard University Press, 1935. This volume, one of four on the earliest Latin writers, contains all the extant Ennian fragments in its first half with English and Latin texts on facing pages. It is kept in print as part of the Loeb Classical Library, separate volumes with original texts and English translations of all the major Greek and Latin authors.

Robert J. Forman

EPAMINONDAS

Born: c. 410 B.C.; Thebes
Died: 362 B.C.; Mantinea, Greece
Areas of Achievement: Government and warfare
Contribution: The greatest military tactician of the classical Greek period, Epaminondas broke the hegemony of Sparta and made Thebes the most powerful state in Greece.

Early Life

Little is known of Epaminondas' early life. His father, Polymnis, was from a distinguished yet impoverished Theban family, and the relative poverty of his youth may explain the simple life-style for which Epaminondas was later famous. The young man displayed an intellectual bent and formed a close attachment to the Pythagorean philosopher Lysis of Tarentum, who served as his primary tutor. Another close friend was Pelopidas, with whom he would eventually share the leadership of Thebes. While the ancient writers' contrast between the rich, athletic, daring family man—Pelopidas—and the reflective, frugal bachelor—Epaminondas—is no doubt overdrawn, it may reflect something of their characters and relationship. If the story is true that the young Epaminondas saved the life of his wounded friend during battle in 385, then he was probably born about 410.

Epaminondas' city-state, the home of the legendary Cadmus and Oedipus, was the largest of the dozen or so towns in Boeotia, a district in central Greece whose inhabitants shared a distinct dialect and ethnic identity. Because its central location so often made Boeotia the arena for battles between the major Greek city-states, Epaminondas referred to his land as "the dancing floor of Ares." Although in the fifth century Thebes rose to considerable influence as head of a federation of Boeotian towns, the city remained a secondary power behind Athens and Sparta. The Thebans sided with Sparta in the Peloponnesian War (431-404 B.C.), which destroyed the Athenian empire and made Sparta supreme in Greece, but they were quickly disillusioned by Sparta's selfish settlement of the war. As Sparta aggressively exercised its hegemony and extended its area of control, Thebes led Athens and other resentful city-states against Sparta in the Corinthian War (395-386 B.C.). Sparta's superior military capabilities gave it the upper hand in the war, however, and an accommodation with the Great King of Persia allowed Sparta to force its opponents to accept the "King's Peace" on terms favorable to Sparta.

Thebes was the worst victim of this settlement, which did not recognize the Boeotian confederacy. Thebans, among them the maturing Epaminondas, then had to watch as Sparta dismembered the federation and installed pro-Spartan oligarchies in the newly autonomous towns of Boeotia. The nadir of Theban fortunes came in 382, when a faction headed by Leontiades betrayed the city to a Spartan force. Backed by a Spartan garrison, Leontiades' pro-Spartan oligarchy ruled the city for three years, and many anti-Spartan Thebans, including Pelopidas, went into exile. Perhaps because he was not yet politically active, Epaminondas remained in Thebes without suffering harm.

Life's Work

When Pelopidas returned with other exiles in 379 to liberate the city, Epaminondas made his political debut in a decisive fashion. As the exiles entered the city at night to begin their revolt, Epaminondas came to their aid with a group of armed men whom he had recruited. The next day, he presented the exiles to the Theban assembly and rallied citizens to support the revolution. Following the liberation, the Thebans formed an alliance with Athens and, despite repeated Spartan invasions of Boeotia, gradually reconstituted the Boeotian federation on a democratic basis. By 373, citizens from practically all the Boeotian towns voted at Thebes in a common assembly and annually elected seven Boeotarchs, who had wide powers as the primary administrative, diplomatic, and military officials of the confederacy. Epaminondas' role in these developments is not clear, but it is likely that he honed his military skills in various operations with the federal army. By 371, his reputation was such that he was elected Boeotarch, a position he subsequently would hold almost every year.

As a member of the Boeotian delegation to the peace conference at Sparta in 371, Epaminondas faced a dilemma. If he acquiesced in the Spartan refusal to recognize the Boeotian Confederacy and signed the treaty for Thebes alone, the newly reconstructed federation would crumble and Sparta would again be able to dominate the individual towns of Boeotia. If, on the other hand, he refused to sign except as representing all Boeotia, he would place Thebes in a precarious position: A Spartan army was already poised on the frontier of Boeotia, and Athens had deserted Thebes in favor of reconciliation with Sparta. Apparently Epaminondas wavered and at first signed the peace treaty for Thebes alone. Before the conference ended, however, he spoke out strongly against Spartan arrogance and infuriated Agesilaus, the Spartan king, by asserting that Thebes would dissolve its confederacy when Agesilaus made independent the many Laconian towns dominated by Sparta. Agesilaus immediately excluded Thebes from the peace agreement, and Epaminondas hastened home to prepare for the impending Spartan attack.

At Leuctra in July, 371, Epaminondas stunned the Greek world when he led a smaller Boeotian force to victory over the heretofore invincible Spartan army. By his innovative use of an unequally weighted battle line in an oblique attack, Epaminondas overwhelmed the strongest part of the enemy formation, and his troops killed four hundred Spartans, among them the junior king Cleombrotus. This victory made Epaminondas famous throughout Greece and encouraged a number of Sparta's southern allies to defect.

While some Boeotians were now content to consolidate the confederacy's position in central Greece, others, including Epaminondas, successfully argued for a more aggressive policy toward Sparta. Consequently, Boeotia joined in alliance with those southern city-states that had defected from the Spartan alliance after Leuctra, and in the winter of 370 Epaminondas took the federal army south to aid these states against Spartan retaliation. This campaign was to be a short one in defense of allies, but, upon discovering the extent of Sparta's weakness, Epaminondas seized the opportunity to strike at Sparta herself.

When his fellow Boeotarchs objected that extending the campaign would be illegal, Epaminondas promised to take full responsibility and led the army in a daring invasion of Sparta's home district of Laconia. Although he did not dare assault the city itself, he secured the defection of many Laconian towns around Sparta and ravaged a rich land that had not seen an invader in centuries. Worst of all for the future of Sparta, Epaminondas liberated Messenia, the rich agricultural district west of Sparta where the bulk of Sparta's huge slave population resided. He then organized the freed Messenians into an autonomous city-state and oversaw the construction of a marvelously fortified capital city. The freeing of Messenia impoverished Sparta and presented it with a hostile new neighbor.

By his victory at Leuctra and the invasion of Laconia Epaminondas had broken Sparta's hold over Greece, and he now undertook to establish the hegemony of Thebes in its place. Some Thebans opposed this effort, but his enormous prestige usually allowed Epaminondas to pursue his goals as he saw fit. When a political rival brought him to trial for his illegal extension of the campaign against Sparta, Epaminondas made no defense and agreed to accept the death penalty—provided his tombstone bear a list of his accomplishments, which he proudly enumerated. Upon hearing this, the judges laughed the case out of court, and Pelopidas soon obtained the banishment of Epaminondas' accuser.

The two friends shared the conduct of Boeotian foreign policy. While Pelopidas secured the northern frontier with his operations in Thessaly, Epaminondas devoted his attentions to the southern alliance. Twice he led invasions designed to force further defections from the Spartan league and strengthen the band of allies that hemmed in Sparta. One notable success of the second invasion was the founding of Megalópolis, a great fortified city in Arcadia that permanently blocked Spartan access to Messenia.

Epaminondas' efforts reached their peak of success in 365, when Sparta's most powerful traditional ally, Corinth, along with several of its neighbors, made peace with Thebes on terms that recognized the autonomy of Messenia. Athens and Sparta refused to accept Theban ascendancy, but the Persian king looked upon Thebes as the preeminent state of Greece and subsidized the construction of a Boeotian fleet with which Epaminondas hoped to disrupt Athens' revived naval league.

Within a year, however, the Theban position began to deteriorate. To be sure, Epaminondas was given warm receptions by three of Athens' most important naval allies when he sailed with the new Boeotian fleet in 364. His expedition failed to defeat the Athenian naval league, however, and the Persians suspended their subsidy of the Boeotian fleet, which never sailed again. Upon returning home, Epaminondas learned that Pelopidas had met his death in battle in Thessaly. He also discovered that in his absence the Thebans had destroyed the Boeotian town of Orchomenus. Provoked by an oligarchic conspiracy and fed by an ancient rivalry, this act of vengeance engendered suspicion and criticism from abroad. Worst of all, Epaminondas had to reckon with serious dissension among his southern allies. Resentful of Theban preeminence, the Arcadians had formed an alliance with Athens and now waged a territorial war that led Elis, the westernmost member of the anti-Spartan alliance, to renew its tie to Sparta. Complicating matters further, Arcadian democrats struggled against the resurgent Arcadian oligarchs of Mantinea, who also reestablished links with Sparta.

To prevent the complete collapse of his anti-Spartan coalition, in June of 362, Epaminondas undertook his fourth invasion of southern Greece. Aware that the combined might of his opponents would be formidable, he sought to confront and destroy them one by one before they could unite. Unfortunately, misinformation led him to abandon the ambush he had set for the Athenians near Corinth, and the treachery of a deserter barely prevented him from taking Sparta unguarded. Consequently, near Mantinea Epaminondas drew up his force for a conflict that would involve contingents from every major Greek city-state. Against the combined forces of Sparta, Athens, Mantinea, and their allies, he employed the same tactics that had brought him victory at Leuctra but on a far grander scale in this battle, which involved nearly fifty thousand men. Catching his enemy off guard, Epaminondas opened the battle with an effective attack of his excellent cavalry and then crushed the Spartan formation with an oblique strike by his massively overbalanced left wing.

Tragically, as his troops stood poised to pursue the broken enemy and complete a brilliant victory, Epaminondas himself fell, mortally wounded. At the news of their leader's fall, the stunned Boeotians immediately abandoned the fight and allowed the beaten enemy to escape. When he was informed of the seriousness of his wound, Epaminondas reportedly advised the Thebans to make a speedy peace. The loss of Epaminondas completely nullified any gains that this well-fought battle brought and marked the end of the Theban ascendancy.

Summary

A brave and resourceful general, Epaminondas was without question the outstanding tactician of the Greek classical period. His masterful use of cavalry and his oblique, unbalanced battle formation won for him two great victories and transformed the Greek art of war. He successfully employed his military skills to break the oppressive hegemony of Sparta and to make Thebes the most powerful state in Greece. The victory at Leuctra, the liberation of Messenia, and the foundation of Megalópolis ensured that Sparta would never again dominate Greece. To his credit, Epaminondas did not imitate the earlier imperial practices of Athens and Sparta: He respected the autonomy of his allies and refused to impose garrisons or levy tribute. Unfortunately, his attempt to rule Greece could not succeed without some institutional means of expressing consensus and resolving disputes among the many autonomous Greek city-states. A formal league headed by Thebes could have been a viable vehicle, but Epaminondas' simple anti-Spartan alliance inevitably required repeated armed interventions of the kind that led to the conflict at Mantinea. If he failed to envision a new political order for Greece, his achievements were nevertheless substantial. They are well expressed in the funeral verses that the Thebans inscribed on his statue:

> This came from my counsel:
> Sparta has cut the hair of her glory:
> Messene takes her children in:
> a wreath of the spears of Thebe
> has crowned Megalopolis:
> Greece is free.

Bibliography

Adcock, Frank E. *The Greek and Macedonian Art of War*. Berkeley: University of California Press, 1957. This short volume provides the best brief introduction to Greek warfare, with appropriate references to Epaminondas.

Anderson, John K. *Military Theory and Practice in the Age of Xenophon*. Berkeley: University of California Press, 1970. This work provides a thorough analysis of military developments during Epaminondas' time. It includes plates and battle diagrams. See especially chapter 10 on the Battle of Leuctra, with a diagram and discussion of the sources.

Buck, R. J. *A History of Boeotia*. Edmonton: University of Alberta Press. 1979. Although this study stops short of Epaminondas' time, it provides good historical and geographical background material on Boeotia.

Buckler, John. *The Theban Hegemony, 371-362 B.C.* Cambridge, Mass.: Harvard University Press, 1980. This thorough work is the starting point for serious study of Epaminondas' career. It provides excellent analysis of the political and constitutional questions and full treatment of the diplomatic and military developments. Includes an evaluation of the sources for Boeotian history in this period and a full bibliography of modern works.

Bury, J. B., S. A. Cook, and F. E. Adcock, eds. *The Cambridge Ancient History*. Vol. 6, *Macedon, 401-301 B.C.* Cambridge: Cambridge University Press, 1923-1939. Chapters 2 through 4 of volume 6 provide a detailed treatment of Spartan, Athenian, and Theban developments during Epaminondas' time.

Pausanias. *Guide to Greece*. Translated by Peter Levi. 2 vols. Harmondsworth, England: Penguin Books, 1971. In book 9 this first century traveler preserves valuable details of Epaminondas' life, probably largely derived from Plutarch's lost biography.

Plutarch. "Pelopidas." In *Plutarch's Lives*, translated by Bernadotte Perrin, vol. 5. Cambridge, Mass.: Harvard University Press, 1968. This brief (fifty-page) biography describes the friendship of Pelopidas and Epaminondas and provides important details of Epaminondas' early life and his role in the liberation of Thebes, as well as a description of the Battle of Leuctra.

Xenophon. *A History of My Times*. Translated by Rex Warner. New York: Penguin Books, 1979. In this work, the Athenian soldier-historian provides a contemporary narrative of the entire period of Epaminondas' life, the only such account to survive complete. Xenophon participated in many of the events he describes and provides many revealing details. Unfortunately, he is biased in favor of Sparta and suppresses many of Epaminondas' accomplishments. Note especially the descriptions of the Battles of Leuctra and Mantinea.

James T. Chambers

EPICURUS

Born: 341 B.C.; Greek island of Samos
Died: 270 B.C.; Athens, Greece
Area of Achievement: Philosophy
Contribution: Epicurus founded the Garden School of Greek philosophy, which has had a significant influence on philosophers, statesmen, and literary figures throughout the history of Western culture.

Early Life

Epicurus was born on the Greek island of Samos, about two miles off the coast of Turkey. His father, Neocles, was an immigrant from an old Athenian family who had moved to the distant island for economic reasons and who made his living as an elementary school teacher. Epicurus was forever disadvantaged in the eyes of the men of Athens because of his rustic birth and the low social status of his father's occupation. To make matters worse, his mother was reputedly a fortune-teller. His experiences as her apprentice might well account for Epicurus' later criticism of all kinds of superstitions, and even for his controversial renunciation of the ancient Greek myths and stories.

Epicurus shared a happy family life with his parents and three brothers, Neocles, Chaeredemus, and Aristobulus, who would eventually become his disciples. It is recorded by Diogenes Laertius that he began to study philosophy at the age of fourteen, because he was unsatisfied with his schoolmasters' explanations of the meaning of "chaos" in Hesiod. Others contend that he was drawn to philosophy by the works of Democritus, echoes of which can be seen in Epicurus' later writings.

At eighteen, Epicurus served his two years of compulsory military duty in Athens, at an exciting time when both Xenocrates and Aristotle were lecturing. He clearly familiarized himself with the works of Aristippus, Socrates, and Pyrrhon of Elis. He served in the garrison with the future playwright Menander, with whom he established a close friendship. Many critics believe that they see the impress of Epicurus' ideas on Menander's later plays.

After his military service, Epicurus rejoined his family, who, with other Athenian colonists, had been expelled from Samos by a dictator and had subsequently moved to Colophon. Not much is known of the ten years that Epicurus spent at Colophon, but it might be surmised that he spent much of his time in study and contemplation, perhaps even visiting the intellectual center of Rhodes. At around the age of thirty he moved to Mytilene, on the island of Lesbos, to become a teacher. As he developed his own philosophy, he came into conflict with the numerous followers of Plato and Aristotle on that island, and after only a short stay, he left. He took with him, however, Hermarchus, a man who would become a lifetime friend and perhaps more important, after Epicurus' death, the head of his Athenian school.

Hermarchus and Epicurus moved to Lampsacus on the Hellespont for the fertile years between 310 and 306 B.C. At Lampsacus, Epicurus gathered around him the devoted disciples and the influential patrons who would make it possible for him, at the age of thirty-five, to move to Athens and begin the major stage of his career. They presented to him the house and the garden in the outskirts of Athens which would be both his school and his home for the rest of his life.

Life's Work

Once established in Athens, Epicurus founded his Garden School, whose name came from the practice of the resident members, who in almost monastic fashion provided for their own food by gardening. The many statues, statuettes, and engraved gems which bear the image of Epicurus' long, narrow, intelligent face, with its furrowed brows and full beard, attest the devotion of his followers and the unusually enduring influence of his ideas.

Epicurus organized his Garden School in a strict hierarchical system, at the apex of which stood only himself: The Master. One of the common slogans of the school was: "Do all things as if Epicurus were looking at you." While this motto may sound dictatorial, it represented a benevolent tyranny to which all the disciples and students of Epicurus happily adhered, and it no doubt accounts for the consistently accurate promotion of his philosophical ideas, even after his death. Three men—Metrodorus, Hermarchus, and Plyaenus—reached the rank of associate leaders in the Garden School and were understood to follow in their master's footsteps so closely that they might teach the Epicurean doctrine in its purest form. Beneath them were the many assistant leaders, unfortunately unknown to modern scholars by name, and the numerous students. It is important to mention that among Epicurus' students were women (for example, the distinguished Leontion) and slaves (Epicurus' own slave Mys was one of his favorite students). The accessibility of the Epicurean philosophy, which eschewed most classical learning, ensured a remarkably heterogeneous following.

Despite many later slanders against him, by writers who misconstrued his emphasis on pleasure as a license for sensory excess, the overwhelming evidence supports the idea that Epicurus lived in his Garden School simply and privately, following his own dictate to "live unobtrusively." His health, which was delicate and complicated by a bladder or kidney stone, would certainly not have survived the riotous living ascribed to him by his detractors.

Fortunately, both Epicurus and his closest disciples were prolific writers, and in some ways the home of Epicurus was a kind of publishing house for their works. Still, only a small portion of that original writing is extant, and an even smaller part is translated into English. Of Epicurus' three hundred or more books (it is best to think of them as scrolls), all that remains are some fragments of his central work *De natura* (c. 296 B.C.; *On Nature*), three important letters recorded by Diogenes Laertius in the early third century B.C., and some miscellaneous correspondence, which shows Epicurus' affectionate relationship with his friends. Yet, as Plato had his Socrates, Epicurus had the Roman poet Lucretius, from whose book *De rerum natura* (c. 60 B.C.; *On the Nature of Things*) most of our understanding of Epicurus' ideas comes.

Through Lucretius' works one is introduced to Epicurus' theories on matter and space, the movements and the shapes of atoms, life and the mind, sensation and sex, cosmology and sociology, and meteorology and geology. In addition to Epicurus' atomic theory, which in some interesting respects presages modern physics, the parts of Epicurus' philosophy that still have the power to move people are the simple axioms of behavior around which he organized life at the Garden School.

Rejecting much of traditional education because it did not foster happiness through tranquillity (which was the ultimate goal of life), Epicurus had a more profound respect for common sense than for classical learning. Prudence was an important virtue, and the senses were the ultimate sources of all knowledge. The highest good in life was attaining a secure and lasting pleasure. To Epicurus, pleasure was not unbridled sensuality but freedom from pain, and peace of mind. These two goods could easily be obtained by simple living, curbing one's unnecessary desires, and avoiding the stresses and compromises of a public life. It might even be profitable to avoid love, marriage, and parenting, since they usually bring more pain than pleasure. Friendship, on the other hand, was regarded as one of the highest and most secure forms of pleasure.

Epicurus thought that the great aim of philosophy was to free men of their fears. Epicurus was not an atheist, but he considered the gods to be very remote—living in Epicurean serenity—and not likely to be tampering viciously with the lives of men. For Epicureans, the soul dies with the body and, therefore, not even death was to be feared.

Perhaps the most salient criticisms of Epicurus' ethics of self-reliance and free will are that they are very negative (viewing wisdom as an escape from an active, hazardous, but possibly full life) and very selfish (placing the good of the individual above the needs of society or the state). While these criticisms may be valid, the life of Epicurus showed that there was much everyday merit in his philosophy. He was blessed with many lifelong friendships which became legendary throughout Greece. His enthusiastic followers kept his ideas alive long into the fourth century. Even on his deathbed, he exhibited that almost Eastern detachment and calm which was the major goal of his philosophy. In a letter that he wrote to friends at his last hour, he commented that the extreme pain of his abdomen was considerably relieved by the happy thoughts he had of his talks with them.

Summary

Epicurus' thought outlived most other important Greek philosophical systems, but it too was finally overwhelmed in the fourth century by Christianity, which considered it just another pagan creed. Some critics believe, however, that the writer of Ecclesiastes in the Old Testament was likely a member of the Garden School and that the Epistles of Saint Paul in the New Testament were strongly influenced by Epicurean thought.

Ironically, it was a French priest, Pierre Gassendi, who revived interest in Epicurus in the seventeenth century with his short treatise *De vita et moribus Epicuri libri octo* (1647; eight books on the life and manners of Epicurus). This interest was manifested in English by Walter Charleton and further fueled by Sir William Temple, a renowned seventeenth century English essayist. In the early nineteenth century, the United States had an avowed Epicurean as its president: Thomas Jefferson.

Discoveries of inscriptions and manuscripts in Asia Minor and Herculaneum have kept scholars debating the issues raised in the works of Epicurus up to the present day. Richard W. Hibler, for example, has studied Epicurus, focusing on what he has to teach about pedagogy. There is no question that as long as humans worry about ethics, strive after the good life, or try to make sense of the universe, the voice of Epicurus will continue to be heard.

Bibliography

Durant, Will. *The Life of Greece*. New York: Simon and Schuster, 1939. Contains an excellent chapter, "The Epicurean Escape," which places Epicurus in the context of his times and also evaluates the tenets of his philosophy.

Edwards, Paul. *The Encyclopedia of Philosophy*. 4 vols. New York: Macmillan, 1967. Contains the most lucid short explanation of Epicurus' complex theory and a definitive scholarly bibliography.

Frischer, Bernard. *The Sculpted Word: Epicureanism and Philosophical Recruitment in Ancient Greece*. Berkeley: University of California Press, 1982. A somewhat eccentric work whose premise is that the sculptures and other images of Epicurus, which were so common in the ancient world, were used by the Epicureans as charismatic recruitment devices. The book contains an important set of plates showing many of the images of Epicurus in statues and in print.

Hibler, Richard W. *Happiness Through Tranquillity: The School of Epicurus*. New York: University Press of America, 1984. Hibler's interest in Epicurus is primarily as a great teacher; consequently, he follows his discussion of the philosopher's life and works with a summary of twenty points which are especially relevant to readers who wish to know more about Epicurus' educational methodology.

Hicks, R. D. *Stoic and Epicurean*. New York: Russell and Russell, 1961.

Hicks compares the Stoics with the Epicureans. He gives an excellent, extended account of Epicurus' theory. This book contains a useful chronological table and is well indexed.

Laertius, Diogenes. *Lives of the Philosophers*. Edited by A. Robert Caponigri. Chicago: Henry Regnery Co., 1969. The most valuable parts of this early third century work are the many quoted extracts directly from the writings of Epicurus. Laertius' unusual focus on the ancient philosophers as living men gives an interesting view of Epicurus, who is, surprisingly, treated more extensively in this work than Socrates.

Lucretius. *On the Nature of the Universe*. Translated by Ronald Latham. Baltimore: Penguin Books, 1964. This philosophical poem forms the basis of the modern reading of Epicurus. Lucretius, in true Epicurean fashion, avoided the usual occupations of his times—war and politics—to devote himself to an extensive exposition of Epicurus' teachings.

Rist, J. M. *Epicurus: An Introduction*. New York: Cambridge University Press, 1972. Rist describes his book as an unambitious and elementary account of the philosophy of Epicurus. It is, in fact, a fine introduction to the thought of Epicurus and takes full advantage of the most important developments in Epicurean scholarship.

Cynthia Lee Katona

ERASISTRATUS

Born: c. 325 B.C.; Iulis, Island of Ceos
Died: c. 250 B.C.; possibly Mycales, Ionia, Asia Minor
Area of Achievement: Medicine
Contribution: Erasistratus made numerous physiological and anatomical discoveries, perhaps using—like his contemporary Herophilus—an exceptional combination of human and animal dissection (and possibly vivisection) to explore the structure and workings of the human body. By creating illuminating alternatives to Hippocratic and Aristotelian models of physiopathological explanation, he also paved the way for the influential Asclepiades of Bithynia.

Early Life

Already during his childhood on the rocky, forested Aegean island Ceos, Erasistratus was no stranger to medicine. His father, Cleombrotus, was a physician, as was his mother's brother Medius (or Medias). His brother, Cleophantus, joined this family tradition as well. Erasistratus apparently left Iulis for apprenticeships, perhaps with the doctor Metrodorus (whom one ancient source identifies as the third husband of Aristotle's daughter Pythias) and Metrodorus' teacher Chrysippus of Cnidus, whom Erasistratus regarded as his main mentor. He may also have attended lectures by Theophrastus, Aristotle's successor as leader of the Peripatetic school of philosophy in Athens, and come under the philosophical influence of Theophrastus' successor, Strato of Lampsacus, but this remains a matter of dispute.

Where Erasistratus subsequently practiced and conducted his research has become a controversial question, but the ancient evidence suggests that he was at the court of the Seleucid rulers in Syrian Antioch (founded on the Orontes River in 300 B.C.) for at least some time in the late 290's. Several ancient sources report that Erasistratus cured a mysteriously ill, suicidal Antiochus (the future King Antiochus I Soter) in Antioch. Through imaginative observation of the patient's face, demeanor, heart, and pulse, it is said, the physician correctly diagnosed that young Antiochus was in love with his stepmother Stratonice. Erasistratus subtly persuaded Antiochus' father, King Seleucus I Nicator, to give up Stratonice in order to save his son; the king promptly arranged the marriage of his wife and son.

Whether Erasistratus also practiced in Alexandria, as many modern historians have assumed, is less certain. No ancient evidence explicitly confirms his presence in Alexandria, but there is suggestive indirect evidence that he may have worked in Alexandria for at least some time during the lifetime of Herophilus.

Life's Work

Erasistratus' ingenuity as a physiologist overshadows his anatomical discoveries, but the two are closely linked. By dissecting animals—and possibly, like his brilliant contemporary Herophilus, by dissecting and vivisecting humans, as one ancient source claims—Erasistratus made major anatomical and physiological discoveries. Among his achievements, two, in particular, won high praise from later authors. First, he described the heart valves (more accurately than did Herophilus), noting the irreversibility of the flow through the valves and detailing the heart's pumping action. Second, his account of the brain includes descriptions of its four ventricles, the convolutions of the cerebrum and the cerebellum (which he linked to humans' superior intelligence), and the origin of the nervous system in the brain (or, as Erasistratus originally believed, in the dura mater, the outermost, toughest of the three membranes covering the brain and the spinal cord).

Three strikingly consistent features of Erasistratus' physiology are his use of mechanical principles rather than Aristotelian innate powers or invisible "faculties" to explain processes in the body, his willingness to verify hypotheses by means of experiments, and a teleological perspective (which he shares with Aristotle and others). In his version of the vascular system, the veins contain only blood, whereas the arteries transport only pneuma, a warm, moist, airlike substance ultimately derived from the atmosphere by respiration. From the lungs the "vein-like artery"—that is, the pulmonary vein—carries pneuma to the left ventricle of the heart, where it is refined into "vital" (life-giving) pneuma before being pumped into the arteries. If, however, the arteries contain only an airlike substance, how does Erasistratus account for the fact that blood flows from a punctured artery? Resorting to one of his favorite mechanical principles, he argues that when the artery is cut its pneuma escapes, creating an empty space into which blood instantly rushes from the adjacent veins (veins being connected to the arteries throughout by means of *synanastomōseis*, or capillarylike communications). The underlying mechanical principle—"following toward what is being emptied," later called *horror vacui*—is that if matter is removed from a contained space, other matter will inevitably enter to take its place, since a natural massed void or vacuum is impossible. It is therefore blood from the veins, not from the artery, that escapes when a lesion of an artery occurs.

Erasistratus' similarly mechanical explanation of the pulse is closer to the truth than his view of the content of the arteries. Whereas Herophilus believed that a "faculty," flowing from the heart to the arterial coats, draws or pulls a mixture of blood and pneuma from the heart into the arteries when they dilate, Erasistratus recognized that the heart functions as a pump: Every time the heart contracts, according to his account, its left ventricle pushes pneuma through a one-way valve into the aorta and the whole arterial network, causing the arteries to dilate. Since the left cardiac ventricle is empty after contraction, pneuma from the lung rushes into it again as it dilates, in accordance with the *horror vacui* principle, and thus the cycle continues, the systole of the heart always being simultaneous with the diastole of the arteries. Once in the arteries, the pneuma cannot return to or through the heart because of the one-way valves. After circulating through the arteries and providing the body with air, the pneuma apparently passes out of the body through the pores, making room for the fresh pneuma constantly being pumped into the arteries.

Erasistratus tried to prove experimentally that it is the heart, functioning as a pump, that causes pulsation, rather than some invisible "pulling" faculty in the arterial coat. After exposing an artery in a living subject, he tied a ligature around the artery. Below the ligature he made a lengthwise incision in the artery, into which he inserted a tube or hollow reed. The incised section of the artery was then ligated, with linen thread wound all around the tube and the surrounding tissue. When the ligature above the tube was undone, Erasistratus claimed, the pulse could be observed below the tube as well as above it, proving that the content of the arteries, pumped in by the heart, causes the pulse. The pulse could not, then, be attributed to a faculty in the incised, ligated, and hence "interrupted" coats of the arteries. (Galen, who reports this experiment, claims that he repeated it with opposite results.)

The central blood-making organ of the body, according to Erasistratus, is not the heart but the liver, where digested food finally is converted into blood. From the liver blood is carried as nourishment for the entire body through the veins. The largest vein in the body, the vena cava, carries blood into the right side of the heart through the tricuspid valve to nourish the heart. From the heart blood flows to the lungs through the pulmonary valve and pulmonary artery, or, as Erasistratus called it, the "arterial vein." The liver, however, cannot in and of itself account for the flow of the blood, since it has no pushing or pulling motion of its own. It is possibly for this reason that Erasistratus described the heart as the *archē* (origin, principle, or rule) not only of the arteries but also of the veins, despite his regarding the liver as the central blood factory. "The heart itself," Galen reports Erasistratus saying, after each contraction "expands like a blacksmith's bellows and draws in matter, filling itself up by its dilation." The *horror vacui* principle thus renders the heart responsible for the movement of blood into and from the heart and consequently, it would seem, for the motion of all blood through the veins, just as it is for the movement of pneuma through all the arteries (although blood is also absorbed into tissues throughout the body, thus creating space for fresh blood in the veins).

The nervous system, muscular activity, respiration, appetite, digestion, and vascular system are all united by Erasistratus in a brilliantly coherent and comprehensive physiological model. External air moves into the lungs through the windpipe and bronchial ducts when the thorax expands. While the air (pneuma) is in the lungs, the left ventricle of the heart draws some pneuma into itself by its own expansion or diastole, contributing to the cycle described above. Excess air, having absorbed some of the superfluous body heat produced by the heart, is then exhaled by the lungs as the thorax contracts, after which the thorax expands once again, drawing in fresh air. The breathing cycle of the lungs thus both cools the body and provides the arteries with the pneuma they need for the body's life and health, whereas appetite and digestion—both of which are similarly explained in terms of the *horror vacui* principle—along with the liver, provide the veins with the food-derived nourishment that the body needs.

The nerves, like the arteries, carry pneuma that is ultimately derived from respiration, but it is a more highly refined version of air. Some of the vital pneuma produced in the left ventricle of the heart is carried by the arterial system to the brain, where it is refined into "psychic" pneuma, which in turn is distributed to the body through the nerves emanating from the brain. Not unlike Herophilus, Erasistratus distinguished between sensory and motor nerves; in his system, it is presumably by means of psychic pneuma that data and impulses are transmitted through the nerves to and from the brain.

Voluntary motion takes place through the muscles, which—like the nerves and perhaps all organic structures in the body—consist of triple-braided strands of veins, arteries, and nerves. Pneuma carried to the muscles by the arteries or nerves endows them with the ability to contract or relax—that is, to increase their width while simultaneously reducing their length, or vice versa, the speed of the muscular motions standing in direct relation to the amount of pneuma in the muscle at a given time.

Erasistratus' efforts in pathology were marked by some innovation as well. He emphasized three related causes of disease which, though not entirely inconsistent with humoral and other earlier theories, introduce some new perspectives. Plethora or hyperemia is a condition marked by excessive blood-nutriment in the veins, which can cause swollen limbs, diseases of the liver and stomach, epilepsy, spleen and kidney ailments, fever, inflammation, blockage of the arteries, and mental disorders (in part because excessive blood in the veins can spill over into the arteries through the *synanastomōseis* between veins and arteries, thus impeding the flow of vital pneuma). Second, disease can result from other disturbances of the arterial flow of pneuma, such as when blood enters a punctured artery (*horror vacui*) and some of it remains trapped in the artery after the wound has healed. Third, digestive dysfunctions cause the presence of sticky, bad moistures in the body that give rise to ailments such as apoplexy and paralysis. In Erasistratus' system, all bodily malfunctions, like all functions, must be understood in terms of the actions and interactions of matter, whose ultimate constituents are solid, possibly atomlike particles.

Numerous diseases, their symptoms, and their causes were described by Erasistratus; his works, which are all lost, addressed subjects such as dropsy, diseases of the abdominal cavity, and fevers.

Summary

In his *Hoi katholou logoi* (general principles) and other lost works, Erasistratus succeeded in accounting for practically all bodily functions within a single explanatory model whose economy, coherence, and scope is unmatched in antiquity except perhaps by Aristotle and Galen. Especially striking is his amalgam of mechanical principles and teleology. The latter is expressed in his Platonic-Aristotelian view of Nature as a supreme artisan, whose providential care for living beings is revealed in the perfection and beautiful purposiveness of every part of the human body. Erasistratus' anatomical discoveries were, however, not as numerous as those of Herophilus, and there are some weak links in his system, such as his reproductive theory.

Bold in his theories, Erasistratus advocated restraint in practice. He assigned higher priority to preventive hygiene, on which he wrote a treatise, than to therapeutics, which, along with the study of symptoms, he regarded as a merely "stochastic," or conjectural, venture (in contrast to etiology and physiology). Proper treatment of patients requires the clear identification of the causes, both proximate and ultimate, of their diseases, as well as an individualized, mild therapy. Opposed to drastic cures, he also rejected the tradition of therapeutic bloodletting in all but a few cases, thereby provoking the notorious ire of Galen, who wrote an entire treatise against Erasistratus' views on bloodletting (and another against the Erasistrateans of Galen's own time, who were defending their Cean patriarch). Instead of bloodletting, Erasistratus advocated drawing off morbid substances through fasting, vomiting, inducing perspiration, urine, plasters, poultices, steam baths, fomentations, fairly conventional dietary prescriptions, and exercise.

For all of their theoretical differences, Erasistratus and Herophilus shared this combination of theoretical audacity and clinical restraint, exceptional scientific originality and pragmatic conservatism. To a greater degree than in the case of Herophilus, Erasistratus' views—as transmitted through fragments and secondhand reports, since none of his works is extant—were met with the polemics of Galen. Yet even a hostile Galen could not refrain from repeatedly acknowledging Erasistratus' significant stature in the history of medicine. Galen also recognized his enemy's scientific honesty: Even in old age, he reports, Erasistratus stood ready to correct his errors in the light of fresh observations. In his search for a better understanding of the human body, the great theorist did not allow the systematic coherence of his theories to stand in the way of his own scientific progress.

Bibliography

Brain, Peter. *Galen on Bloodletting*. Cambridge: Cambridge University Press, 1986. Includes translations of Galen's works against Erasistratus and the Erasistrateans, with extensive annotations.

Fraser, P. M. "The Career of Erasistratus of Ceos." *Istituto Lombardo,*

Rendiconti 103 (1969): 518-537. Argues that Antioch on Orontes (Syria), not Alexandria, was the center of Erasistratus' activity, and that he did not perform extensive dissections.

Galen. *On Respiration and the Arteries*. Edited by David J. Furley and J. S. Wilkie. Princeton, N.J.: Princeton University Press, 1984. Pages 26 to 37 offer an excellent introduction to Erasistratus' views on respiration, the heart, and the arteries. The volume also includes an annotated translation of three Galenic works that are important sources for Erasistratus' physiology.

__________. *On the Doctrines of Hippocrates and Plato*. Edited and translated with commentary by Phillip De Lacy. 3 vols. Berlin: Akademie-Verlag, 1978-1984. Excellent translation of, and commentary on, an important source for Erasistratus' views on the brain, nerves, and heart.

__________. *On the Natural Faculties*. Translated by Arthur John Brock. New York: Heinemann, 1916. Translation of a polemical but vitally informative introduction to Galenic and Erasistratean physiology. Part of the Loeb Classical Library.

__________. *Three Treatises on the Nature of Science*. Translated by Michael Frede and Richard Walzer. Indianapolis, Ind.: Hackett Publishing Co., 1985. A useful source for aspects of Erasistratus' theory of scientific method and his epistemology.

Harris, C. R. S. *The Heart and the Vascular System in Ancient Greek Medicine*. Oxford: Clarendon Press, 1973. Chapter 4 presents the most extensive analysis available of Erasistratus' description of the vascular system, with some attention to his theories of respiration and the nerves.

Lloyd, G. E. R. "A Note on Erasistratus of Ceos." *Journal of Hellenic Studies* 95 (1975): 172-175. Argues against Fraser (see above) that Erasistratus performed human dissection, was an outstanding anatomist, and worked for at least some time in Alexandria.

Lonie, I. M. "Erasistratus, the Erasistrateans, and Aristotle." *Bulletin of the History of Medicine* 38 (1964): 426-443. A thoughtful analysis of Erasistratus' theory of the vascular system and of the expropriation of Aristotle by later Erasistrateans to justify aspects of Erasistratus' views.

Pope, Maurice. "Shakespeare's Medical Imagination." *Shakespeare Survey* 38 (1985): 175-186. Traces the influence of Erasistratus' physiology on Renaissance poetry.

Smith, W. D. "Erasistratus' Dietetic Medicine." *Bulletin of the History of Medicine* 56 (1982): 398-409. Argues that attention to Erasistratus' own words, in the literal fragments preserved by Galen and others, reveals a less revolutionary, less contentious, and more conventional Erasistratus than the one suggested by Galen's polemics. Shows that his dietetics was a conservative development of an earlier tradition.

von Staden, Heinrich. "Experiment and Experience in Hellenistic Medicine."

Bulletin of the Institute of Classical Studies 22 (1975): 178-199. Relates the growth and decline of experimentation in Erasistratus' century to changing theories of scientific method; includes a close analysis of some of Erasistratus' experiments.

Heinrich von Staden

ERATOSTHENES OF CYRENE

Born: c. 285 B.C.; Cyrene
Died: c. 205 B.C.; Alexandria
Areas of Achievement: Literature, geography, and mathematics
Contribution: Through his energetic directorship, Eratosthenes helped make the Library of Alexandria the greatest repository of learning in the Mediterranean world, and his varied contributions made him the most versatile scholar and scientist of the third century B.C.

Early Life

Eratosthenes was born in the Greek North African city of Cyrene about 285 B.C. The only surviving ancient biographical reference places his birth in the 126th Olympiad (276-273 B.C.), but this is too late to allow his reported meeting in Athens with Zeno of Citium, founder of Stoicism, who died around 261. His subsequent career suggests, moreover, that he was about forty years of age when he was called to Alexandria in 245; a birth date in the mid-280's therefore seems accurate. Because neither his name nor that of his father, Aglaus, is otherwise mentioned in Cyrenaean records, it seems that Eratosthenes was not of an especially prominent family.

While his family was not illustrious, his mother city had achieved considerable renown. Founded by Greeks from Thera before 600, Cyrene had prospered as an independent city-state. Following the death of Alexander in 323, however, the Hellenistic Age brought a new political order in which large, bureaucratic monarchies dominated and absorbed the formerly autonomous city-states. Cyrene grudgingly accepted incorporation into the neighboring Ptolemaic kingdom of Egypt, which was ruled from Alexandria.

Founded by Alexander the Great in 331, by Eratosthenes' time this harbor city was well on the way to becoming the commercial and cultural center of the Mediterranean world. Thanks to the generous subsidies of the Ptolemies, the city boasted the great Library and its adjunct Museum, a school of advanced studies that attracted scholars in literary and scientific studies, including Callimachus of Cyrene.

The most famous poet of the early third century and compiler of the Library's first catalog, Callimachus was the latest in a long line of Cyrenaean intellectual figures. Eratosthenes thus followed in a well-established tradition of Cyrenaean learning and scholarship when he undertook his early training at home with the renowned grammarian Lysanias. One might have expected him to pursue advanced studies in nearby Alexandria in the company of his countryman Callimachus, but the young man was primarily interested in philosophy, and for philosophy one went to the city of Socrates and Plato. Therefore, at age fifteen, Eratosthenes sailed to Athens, where he would remain for twenty-five years.

Life's Work

Eratosthenes later recalled that in Athens he found more philosophers than had ever been known to exist within the walls of one city. The eager student sampled all of their offerings and came away disappointed. He studied Stoicism with the aged Zeno, founder of the school, but he spent more time with Zeno's revisionist pupil, Ariston of Chios, who became the subject of one of Eratosthenes' earliest works, a biographical sketch entitled *Ariston*. He also witnessed the flamboyant diatribes of Bion of Borysthenes, the son of a former slave and a prostitute, who preached the doctrines of Cynicism on street corners and dockside. Eratosthenes accused Ariston of not living true to his Stoic principles and Bion of adorning his philosophy to attract more attention, much like a tart in gaudy clothes.

Eratosthenes seems to have been more receptive to the Platonism that he learned from Arcesilaus, head of the Academy in this, its "middle" period. His first seriously intellectual work, the *Platōnikos* (*Platonicus*), followed the dialogue format pioneered by Plato and explored traditional Platonic cosmological and mathematical themes. He also wrote another philosophical study entitled *Peri agathōn kai kakōn* (*On Good and Evil Qualities*), which has been lost. Eratosthenes' eclectic approach to his philosophical studies together with his criticisms of established philosophers provoked some later scholars to accuse him of dilettantism.

Less than satisfied with his experiences in philosophy, Eratosthenes fared somewhat better with poetry, the field in which he first achieved a degree of recognition. Although none of his early poetic pieces survives, two poems are known by name. The hexameter *Hermes* (c. 250) recalled the birth and career of that god, while the *Erigone* employed elegiac verse to portray the legendary suicide of an Athenian maiden. Both displayed the highly polished style of Callimachus, and the latter poem was later described as completely faultless. Without a doubt it was his early reputation as a poet, not his work in philosophy, that brought Eratosthenes' name to the attention of the royal patrons in Alexandria, when the poet Apollonius of Rhodes retired from his position as librarian in 245.

Ptolemy III Euergetes must have considered other, equally famous poets for the position, but personal and political factors led him to invite Eratosthenes to Alexandria. While Eratosthenes had pursued his studies in Athens, his homeland had enjoyed a period of independence under the rule of Magas, a renegade Ptolemaic governor who had broken with the government in Alexandria and for several decades styled himself King of Cyrene. In 245, Cyrene had only recently returned to Ptolemaic rule, largely as a result of the conciliatory marriage of Ptolemy III to Berenice, the daughter of Magas. Less than a year on the throne, the young king sought a further gesture of reconciliation to Cyrenaean opinion. Many Cyrenaeans enjoyed Ptolemaic patronage in Alexandria, but none of them, not even the great Callimachus, had been offered the prestigious post of librarian. In addition, the aging Callimachus no doubt lobbied the king on behalf of his countryman Eratosthenes. Consequently, the invitation arrived in Athens, probably in 245, and Eratosthenes sailed for Alexandria to begin the greatest phase of his life.

In assuming the title Director of the Library, Eratosthenes accepted a post of huge prestige, one which brought great responsibilities as well as opportunity. In addition to serving as tutor to the royal children, he admirably fulfilled his primary obligation to maintain and develop the largest repository of learning in the world.

During his tenure, the Library acquired authentic texts of the great tragic dramas of Aeschylus, Sophocles, and Euripides and opened an entire section dedicated solely to the study of Homer. As competition for manuscripts developed with the founding of a rival institution at Pergamum, it may have been at Eratosthenes' behest that the Alexandrian harbor authorities began requiring all ships to surrender their books for inspection and possible duplication.

Despite his archival and tutorial duties, Eratosthenes found time to take advantage of the scholarly opportunities offered by his position—full access to the immense holdings of the Library and to the circle of resident scholars at the nearby Museum. Because he refused to specialize and instead explored almost every area of learning, his admirers gave him the nickname "Pentathlos," for the all-around athletes of the Olympic pentathlon. His critics preferred to call him "Beta," that is, second-best in many endeavors but never first. That he abandoned his original interest in philosophy in favor of other fields is understandable, for the intrigue-ridden court of an authoritarian monarch was not the place to pursue moral and constitutional questions. Although none of his works survives intact, it is possible to reconstruct the main lines of his achievement.

Eratosthenes' three-volume *Geōgraphika* (*Geographica*) drew upon the work of earlier geographers, but in two ways it represented a more scientific and systematic approach to the subject. He completely rejected the commonly accepted notion that writings such as Homer's *Odyssey* (c. 800 B.C.) contained reliable geographic information. He angered many established geographical authorities when he declared: "You will find the scene of the wanderings of Odysseus when you find the cobbler who sewed up the bag of the winds." Nor was Eratosthenes content merely to describe geographical phenomena and assign them to the various continents. Instead, by establishing distances and positions in relation to two primary axes intersecting at Rhodes, he created the first reasonably accurate map of the world. Admittedly crude, Eratosthenes' map anticipated the modern system of longitude and latitude, and it was the first to incorporate the knowledge of Eastern regions derived from Alexander the Great's expedition.

Eratosthenes' *Peri tēs avametrēoeōs tēs gēs* (*On the Measurement of the Earth*) presented his most famous geographical achievement—a calculation of Earth's circumference. By means of a novel and elegantly simple application of two of Euclid's geometric propositions, Eratosthenes reasoned that the distance from Alexandria to Syene in Upper Egypt represented one-fiftieth of Earth's circumference. Coupling this figure with the known distance between the two cities, a measurement perhaps obtained at his request by Ptolemy's royal surveyors, Eratosthenes arrived at his figure of 252,000 stades (24,662 miles). Far more accurate than the then generally accepted estimate of 300,000 stades, Eratosthenes' result falls within 1 percent of the best modern measurements.

As he attempted to systematize geography, Eratosthenes also sought to replace the myriad local chronographical schemes with a universal chronology for all Greek history. A preliminary study, the *Olympionikai*, prepared an authoritative list of Olympic victors that could serve as a chronological yardstick. In his *Chronographiai* (*Chronological Tables*), which covered the period from the Trojan War to the death of Alexander, Eratosthenes placed events from various local and regional traditions in one coherent chronological system based on Olympiads.

In the field of mathematics, Eratosthenes is best known for his "sieve"—a method for discovering prime numbers—and for his solution to the "Delian Problem," the long-standing problem of doubling a cube. For the latter, Eratosthenes composed a proof and designed a mechanical instrument, his "mesolabe," to demonstrate it. In Alexandria he dedicated a monument bearing a model of the instrument, the proof, and his poem in praise of his patron, Ptolemy III. His longest mathematical treatise, *On Means*, of undetermined content, formed part of the Royal Mathematical Collection. Although Eratosthenes' mathematical work did not match his outstanding achievements in geography and chronography, it is worth noting that the greatest mathematician of his day, Archimedes, valued his opinion and corresponded with him on mathematical issues.

The most important of his works on literary subjects was the *Peri archaias kōmōidias* (*Ancient Comedy*), in at least twelve books, which dealt with the foremost authors of that genre—Aristophanes, Cratinus, Eupolis, and Pherecrates. The few surviving fragments indicate that Eratosthenes was concerned with variations in the dialect and vocabulary of the plays, as well as the history of their revisions and stagings.

A fragment of Eratosthenes' last work, the *Arsinoē* (*Biography of Arsinoe III*), reveals the aging scholar's sympathy for the wife and sister of Ptolemy IV. Eratosthenes recalls that while walking with him at the palace during the rowdy "Feast of the Beakers," the queen shared with him her disgust over her husband's drunken celebrations. Shortly after the murder of this hapless queen in 205, Eratosthenes, at age eighty, met his own death, reportedly by voluntary starvation after he had gone blind. He was buried at Alexandria within sight of the Library.

Summary

In his career, Eratosthenes perfectly exemplifies the apolitical cosmopolitan culture of the Hellenistic period. Uninterested in the political affairs of his city-state, he abandoned Cyrene for the cultural attractions of Athens, just as he later accepted the patronage of the Ptolemies. His work as librarian helped make Alexandria the outstanding center of learning in the Mediterranean world. Sadly, his remarkable scholarship had limited influence on later generations, and his reputation faltered. This circumstance is explained by his failure to produce students and by the envy that his exceptional versatility engendered. The outstanding geographer and chronographer of his day, Eratosthenes also applied his powerful and independent intellect to important questions of mathematics and to literary studies. A polymath of extraordinary abilities, he definitely was no dilettante. Perhaps Eratosthenes is best recalled by the name that he coined to describe himself—*philologos*, a lover of human reason in all its various forms.

Bibliography

Fraser, P. M. "Eratosthenes of Cyrene." *Proceedings of the British Academy* 56 (1970): 175-207. This fairly technical article attempts to resolve the considerable chronological and source problems associated with Eratosthenes' life. It is the best single work on Eratosthenes' career.

___________. *Ptolemaic Alexandria*. 3 vols. Oxford: Clarendon Press, 1972. This monumental work provides a detailed view of Alexandrian society, politics, and intellectual life. It is especially good on the history of the Library and the Museum. Most valuable are its sensible reconstructions based on the fragments of Eratosthenes' lost works.

Freeman, Kathleen. *Greek City-States*. New York: W. W. Norton and Co., 1963. Chapter 6 provides a brief history of Eratosthenes' city-state of Cyrene.

Heath, Thomas L. *A Manual of Greek Mathematics*. Oxford: Clarendon Press, 1931. This volume places Eratosthenes in the context of the overall development of Greek mathematics, especially chapters 7 and 11.

Lloyd, G. E. R. *Greek Science After Aristotle*. New York: W. W. Norton and Co., 1973. Provides an excellent overview of Greek science in Eratosthenes' time but has only a brief reference to him in chapter 4. Includes a diagram of his measurement of the Earth.

Pfeiffer, Rudolf. *History of Classical Scholarship: From the Beginnings to the End of the Hellenistic Age*. Oxford: Clarendon Press, 1968. This standard study of Greek scholarship in the classical and Hellenistic periods has an excellent chapter that briefly discusses the chronological problems associated with Eratosthenes' life and provides a complete catalog of the works attributed to him.

Strabo. *The Geography of Strabo*. Translated by Horace Leonard Jones. 8 vols. London: Heinemann, 1917-1933. The first century historian and geographer Strabo provides important information for the reconstruction of Eratosthenes' early career and his geographical theories in books 1 and 2 of his *Geography*. He must, however, be studied with the understanding that he is hostile to Eratosthenes' rejection of Homer and presents him as a dilettante.

Tarn, W. W., and G. T. Griffith. *Hellenistic Civilisation*. 3d rev. ed. London: E. Arnold and Co., 1959. This classic study provides an overview of Eratosthenes' world, most notably in the chapters on Ptolemaic Egypt and Hellenistic intellectual life.

Thomas, Ivor. *Greek Mathematical Writings*. 2 vols. London: Heinemann, 1949. Includes all the important sources pertaining to Eratosthenes' mathematical achievements, with notes and commentary. See chapter 3 for Eratosthenes' "sieve," chapter 9 for the duplication of the cube, and chapter 18 for the measurement of Earth.

Thomson, James Oliver. *History of Ancient Geography*. Cambridge: Cambridge University Press, 1948. This study provides an overview of the evolution of geographical knowledge and theory from early Babylonia to the later Roman period. See chapter 4 for a discussion of Eratosthenes; includes two excellent maps based on his theories.

James T. Chambers

EUCLID

Born: 335 B.C.; probably Greece
Died: 270 B.C.; Alexandria, Egypt
Area of Achievement: Mathematics
Contribution: Euclid took the geometry known in his day and presented it in a logical system. His work, the *Elements*, became the standard textbook on the subject down to modern times.

Early Life

Little is known about Euclid himself, and even the city of his birth is a mystery. Medieval authors often called him Euclid of Megara, but they were confusing him with an earlier philosopher, Eucleides of Megara, who was an associate of Socrates and Plato. It is virtually certain that Euclid came from Greece proper, and probable that he received advanced education in the Academy, the school founded by Plato in Athens. By the time Euclid arrived there, Plato and the first generation of his students had already died, but the Academy was the outstanding mathematical school of the time. The followers of Aristotle in the Lyceum included no great mathematicians. The majority of the geometers who instructed Euclid were adherents of the Academy.

Euclid traveled to Alexandria and was appointed to the faculty of the Museum, the great research institution that was being organized under the patronage of Ptolemy Soter, who ruled Egypt from 323 to 283. Ptolemy, a boyhood friend of Euclid and then lieutenant of Alexander the Great, had seized Egypt soon after the conqueror's death, became the successor of the pharaohs, and managed to make his capital, Alexandria, an intellectual center of the Hellenistic Age that outshone the waning light of Athens. Euclid presumably became the librarian, or head, of the Museum at some point in his life. He had many students, and although their names are not specifically recorded, they carried on the tradition of his approach to mathematics, and his influence can still be identified among those who followed in the closing years of the third century B.C. He was thus a member of the first generation of Alexandrian scholars, along with Demetrius of Phalerum and Strato of Lampsacus.

Two famous remarks are attributed to Euclid by ancient authors. On being asked by Ptolemy if there was any easier way to learn the subject than by struggling through the proofs in the *Stoicheia* (*Elements*), Euclid replied that there is no "royal road" to geometry. Then when a student asked him if geometry would help him get a job, he ordered his slave to give the student a coin, "since he has to make a profit from what he learns." In spite of this rejoinder, his usual temperament is described as gentle and benign, open, and attentive to his students.

Life's Work

Euclid's reputation rests on his greatest work, the *Elements*, consisting of thirteen books of his own and two spurious books added later by Hypsicles of Alexandria and others. This work is a systematic explication of geometry in which each brief and elegant demonstration rests upon the axioms and postulates given previously. It embraces and systematizes the achievements of earlier mathematicians. Books 1 and 2 discuss the straight line, triangles, and parallelograms; books 3 and 4 examine the circle and the inscription and circumscription of triangles and regular polygons; and books 5 and 6 explain the theory of proportion and areas. Books 7, 8, and 9 introduce the reader to arithmetic and the theory of rational numbers, while book 10 treats the difficult subject of irrational numbers. The remaining three books investigate elementary solid geometry and conclude with the five regular solids (tetrahedron, cube, octahedron, dodecahedron, and icosahedron). It should be noted that the *Elements* discusses several problems which later came to belong to the field of algebra, but Euclid treats them in geometric terms.

The genius of the *Elements* lies in the beauty and compelling logic of its arrangement and presentation, not in its new discoveries. Still, Euclid showed originality in his development of a new proof for the Pythagorean theorem as well as his convincing demonstration of many principles that had been advanced less satisfactorily by others. The postulate that only one parallel to a line can be drawn through any point external to the line is Euclid's own invention. He found this assumption necessary in his system but was unable to develop a formal proof for it. Modern mathematicians have maintained that no such proof is possible, so Euclid may be excused for not providing one.

Other works by Euclid are extant in Greek. *Ta dedomena* (*Data*) is another work of elementary geometry and includes ninety-four propositions. The *Optika* (*Optics*), by treating rays of light as straight lines, makes its subject a branch of geometry. Spherical geometry is represented by the *Phainomena* (*Phaenomena*), which is an astronomical text based in part on a work of Autolycus of Pitane, a slightly older contemporary. Euclid wrote on music, but the extant *Katatomē kanonos* (known by its Latin title, *Sectio canonis*) is at best a reworking by some later, inferior writer of a genuine text by Euclid, containing no more of his actual words than some excerpts. Discovered in Arabic translation was *Peri diaireseon* (*On Division*), for which the proofs of only four of the propositions survive.

Also discovered have been the names of several lost books by Euclid on advanced geometry: The *Pseudaria* exposed fallacies in geometrical reasoning, and *Kōnika* (*Conics*) laid some of the groundwork for the later book of the same title by Apollonius of Perga. There was a discussion of the relationships of points on surfaces entitled *Topoi pros epiphaneia* (*Surface-Loci*), and *Porismata* (*Porisms*), a work of higher geometry, treated a kind of proposition intermediate between a theorem and a problem.

In addition to the last two books of the *Elements*, there are works bearing Euclid's name that are not genuinely his. These include the *Katoptrica* (*Catoptrica*), a later work on optics, and *Eisagōgē armonikē* (*Introduction to Harmony*), which is actually by Cleonides, a student of Aristoxenus. None of Euclid's reputation, however, depends on these writings falsely attributed to him.

Summary

Euclid left as his legacy the standard textbook in geometry. There is no other ancient work of science which needs so little revision to make it current, although many modern mathematicians, beginning with Nikolay Lobachevski and Bernhard Riemann and including Albert Einstein, have developed non-Euclidean systems in reaction to the *Elements*, thus doing it a kind of honor. The influence of Euclid on later scientists such as Archimedes, Apollonius of Perga, Galileo Galilei, Sir Isaac Newton, and Christiaan Huygens was immense. Eratosthenes used his theorems to measure with surprising accuracy the size of the sphere of the Earth, and Aristarchus attempted less successfully, but in fine Euclidean style, to establish the size and distances of the moon and the sun.

Other Hellenistic mathematicians, such as Hero, Pappus, Simplicius, and most important, Proclus, produced commentaries on the *Elements*. Theon of Alexandria, father of the famous woman philosopher and mathematician Hypatia, introduced a new edition of the *Elements* in the fourth century A.D. The sixth century Italian Boethius is said to have translated the *Elements* into Latin, but that version is not extant. Many translations were made by early medieval Arabic scholars, beginning with one made for Harun al-Rashid near A.D. 800 by al-Hajjaj ibn Yusuf ibn Matar. Athelhard of Bath made the first surviving Latin translation from an Arabic text about A.D. 1120. The first printed version, a Latin translation by the thirteenth century scholar Johannes Campanus, appeared in 1482 in Venice. Bartolomeo Zamberti was the first to translate the *Elements* into Latin directly from the Greek, rather than Arabic, in 1505. The first English translation, printed in 1570, was done by Sir Henry Billingsley, later the Lord Mayor of London. The total number of editions of Euclid's *Elements* has been estimated to be more than a thousand, making it one of the most often translated and printed books in history and certainly the most successful textbook ever written.

Bibliography

DeLacy, Estelle Allen. *Euclid and Geometry*. New York: Franklin Watts, 1963. A good introduction for the general reader.

Euclid. *The Thirteen Books of Euclid's "Elements."* Translated by Thomas Little Heath. 3 vols. Cambridge: Cambridge University Press, 1908, 2d ed.

1925. Reprint. New York: Dover Publications, 1956. Translated from the text of Heiberg, with introduction and commentary. This work is the definitive English translation, with extensive commentary, of Euclid's *Elements*. This admirable work supersedes all previous translations and has not been outdated. It contains a full introduction, 151 pages in length, touching on all the major problems.

Fraser, P. M. *Ptolemaic Alexandria*. 3 vols. Oxford: Clarendon Press, 1972. Has a useful section on the intellectual background and influences of Euclid but is primarily valuable in providing a study of the cultural setting of Alexandria in Euclid's day.

Heath, Thomas Little. *A History of Greek Mathematics*. Vol. 1, *From Thales to Euclid*. Oxford: Clarendon Press, 1921. Places Euclid in the context of the development of ancient mathematics and is a thoroughly dependable treatment.

Knorr, W. R. *The Evolution of the Euclidean Elements: A Study of the Theory of Incommensurable Magnitudes and Its Significance for Early Greek Geometry*. Boston: D. Reidel Publishing Co., 1975. An important, very professional and technical treatment.

Mueller, Ian. *Philosophy of Mathematics and Deductive Structure in Euclid's "Elements."* Cambridge, Mass.: MIT Press, 1981. A study of the Greek concepts of mathematics found in the *Elements*, emphasizing philosophical, foundational, and logical rather than historical questions, although the latter are not totally neglected. Attention is directed to Euclid's work, not that of his predecessors. This monograph requires mathematical literacy and the general reader may find it overly technical.

Reid, Constance. *A Long Way from Euclid*. New York: Thomas Y. Crowell, 1963. An explanation of how modern mathematical thought has progressed beyond Euclid, written for those whose introduction to mathematics consisted mainly of studying the *Elements*. Accessible to the general reader, this study takes Euclid as its starting point and shows that he did not provide the reader with all the answers, or even all the questions, with which mathematicians concern themselves.

Szabo, Arpad. *The Beginnings of Greek Mathematics*. Translated by A. M. Ungar. Boston: D. Reidel Publishing Co., 1978. Places Euclid within the context of the development of the Greek mathematical tradition.

J. Donald Hughes

EUDOXUS OF CNIDUS

Born: c. 390 B.C.; Cnidus
Died: c. 335 B.C.; Cnidus
Areas of Achievement: Mathematics and astronomy
Contribution: Eudoxus and his disciples resolved classical difficulties in the fields of geometry and geometric astronomy. Their approach became definitive for later research in these fields.

Early Life

As for so many ancient figures, little is known about the life of Eudoxus of Cnidus. If one follows the account of the ancient biographer Diogenes Laertius (c. A.D. 250), Eudoxus first visited Athens at age twenty-three to study medicine and philosophy. He soon returned home, however, and from there, joining the company of the Cnidian physician Chrysippus, he moved on to Egypt, where for more than a year he studied among the priests and engaged in astronomical investigations. Later, as he traveled and lectured in the wider Aegean area (specifically, Cyzicus and the Propontis), he built up a following and thus returned to Athens a man of considerable distinction. His main subsequent activity seems to have centered on Cnidus, where he was honored as a lawgiver. His renown extended to many areas, including astronomy, geometry, medicine, geography, and philosophy.

There is disagreement over his dates. The ancient chronologist Apollodorus sets Eudoxus' prime activity in 368-365 B.C. In general, the prime means age forty; if that holds here, Eudoxus' birth would be set circa 408. There is reason for doubt, however, since this early a date conflicts with other biographical data. G. L. Huxley favors circa 400; G. de Santillana and others argue for circa 390. Since Eudoxus is reported to have died at the age of fifty-three, the corresponding date would be 355, 347, or 337.

Life's Work

None of Eudoxus' writings survives, but fragments cited by ancient authors offer a reasonable impression of their diversity and significance. His principal efforts were in the areas of mathematics and astronomy, the former best represented in portions of *Stoicheia* (c. fourth century B.C.; *Elements*) of Euclid, the latter in astronomical discussions of the fourth-century cosmology of Aristotle and the ancient commentaries on it.

According to Archimedes (287-212 B.C.), Eudoxus was the first to set out a rigorous proof of the theorems that any pyramid equals one-third of the associated prism (that is, having the same height and base as the pyramid), and that any cone equals one-third of the associated cylinder. Eudoxus also appears to have proved two other theorems, that circles are as the squares of their diameters, and that spheres are as the cubes of their diameters. The proofs of these four theorems constitute the main part of book 17 of *Elements* and the technique used there is likely to derive from Eudoxus.

To take the circle theorem as an example, one could imagine a regular polygon having so many sides that it seems practically indistinguishable from a circle. Since two such polygons (with equally numerous sides) are proportional to the squares of their diameters, the same could be supposed for the corresponding circles. Presumably, an argument of this sort was assumed by geometers who used the circle theorem in the time before Eudoxus. In the strict sense, however, the reasoning would be invalid, for only by an infinite process can rectilinear figures eventuate in the circle.

In the Eudoxean scheme, one assumes the stated proportion to be false: If two circles are not in the ratio of the squares of their diameters, then one can construct two similar regular polygons, one inscribed in each circle, and one can make the difference between the polygon and its circle so small that the polygon is found to be simultaneously greater and less than a specified amount. Since that is clearly impossible, the stated theorem must be true. (This indirect manner for proving theorems on curved figures is often called, if somewhat misleadingly, the "method of exhaustion.")

A key move in this proof is making the polygon sufficiently close to the circle. To this end, one observes that as the number of sides is doubled, the difference between the polygon and the circle is reduced by more than half. The procedure of successively bisecting a given quantity will eventually make it less than any preassigned amount, however, as Euclid proves in *Elements*. According to Archimedes, however, it seems that Eudoxus took this bisection principle as an axiom.

The notion of proportion itself runs into a similar difficulty with the infinite. As long as quantities are related to one another in terms of whole or fractional numbers (for example, if one area is 7⁄5 of another area), their ratios can be specified from these same numbers (that is, the ratio of the one area to the other will be 7 to 5). Yet what if no such numbers exist? For example, it was found, a century or so before Eudoxus, that the diagonal and side of a square cannot equal a ratio of whole numbers. (In modern terms, one calls the associated number $\sqrt{2}$ "irrational"; its decimal equivalent 1.414 . . . will be nonterminating and nonrepeating.) Only by means of some form of infinite sequence can "commensurable" quantities (those whose ratio is expressible by two integers) equal the ratio of incommensurable ones. Geometers in the generation before Eudoxus had pursued the study of incommensurables with considerable interest, but Eudoxus was the first to see how the theorems on ratios could be rigorously proved when their terms were incommensurable.

It is usually supposed that Eudoxus' approach was identical to that given by Euclid in book 5 of *Elements*. Other writers, in particular Archimedes, however, knew of a different technique of proportions that seems more like what Eudoxus would have proposed. By this technique, one first establishes the stated theorem for the case of commensurable quantities. For the incommensurable case, one uses an indirect argument: If the proportionality does not hold, one can find commensurable terms whose ratio differs by less than a specified amount from the ratio of the given incommensurable terms—this is done by successively bisecting one of the givens until it is less than the difference between two others; when the commensurable case of the theorem (already proved) is applied, a certain term will be found to be simultaneously greater and less than another. Since that is impossible, the theorem must be true.

The defining notions of the proportion theory in Euclid's book 5 can be derived as a simple modification of this technique, for the role that the intermediate commensurable terms play in it is assumed by the Euclidean definition of proportion: that A:B = C:D means that for all integers m, n, if $m\text{A} > n\text{B}$, then also $m\text{C} > n\text{D}$; the same holds true if = or < are substituted for >. Proofs in this Euclidean manner do not require a division into commensurable and incommensurable cases, nor do they make use of the bisection principle; in general, they are rather easier to set up than in the alternative technique. It is thus possible to see Euclid's approach as an intended refinement of the Eudoxean.

In either the Eudoxean or Euclidean form, this manner of proportion theory can be made to correspond to the modern definition of real number, as formulated by the German mathematician Julius Wilhelm Richard Dedekind. In each example, the real term (possibly irrational) is considered to separate all the rationals into those greater and those less than it.

It seems likely that Eudoxus also contributed to the study of incommensurable lines. His predecessor Theaetetus (died c. 369) had shown that if the squares of two lines are commensurable with each other but do not have the ratio of square integers, then the lines themselves will be incommensurable with each other; further, if two such lines A, B are taken, the lines A ± B will be incommensurable with them, not only as lines but also in square (lines of this latter type were called *alogoi*, literally, "without ratio"). The further study of the *alogoi* lines, as collected in book 10 of Euclid's *Elements*, divided into twelve classes all the *alogoi* formed as the square roots of R(A ± B), where R is a unit line, and A and B are commensurable with each other in square only. Presumably, Eudoxus and his followers played a part in this investigation.

Eudoxus' efforts are rooted in a concern for logical precision in geometry, and this interest may reflect his close association with the Platonic Academy at Athens. Two anecdotes (of questionable historicity) celebrate this connection. The first explains how Eudoxus came to be involved in seeking the cube duplication, the so-called Delian problem. To allay a plague, the citizens of Delos were commanded by the oracle to double a cube-shaped altar. When their attempts failed, they sent to Plato, who directed his mathematical associates Archytas, Menaechmus, and Eudoxus to solve it. When they did so, however, Plato criticized their efforts for being too mechanical. The solutions of a dozen different ancient geometers are known, but that of Eudoxus has not been preserved. It supposedly employed "curved lines" of some sort, and reconstructions have been proposed.

In a second story, Plato is said to have posed to Eudoxus the problem of "saving the phenomena" of planetary motion on the restriction to uniform circular motion. An account of Eudoxus' scheme is transmitted by Simplicius of Cilicia (sixth century A.D.) in his commentary on Aristotle's *De caelo* (fourth century B.C.; *On the Heavens*). From this account a reconstruction has been worked out by the Italian historian of astronomy Giovanni Virginio Schiaparelli in 1875. The Eudoxean system reproduces the apparent motion of a planet by combining the rotations of a set of homocentric spheres. The planet is set on the equator of a uniformly rotating sphere. If a second sphere is set about the first, rotating with equal speed to the first but in the opposite direction and having its axis inclined, then the planet will trace out an eight-shaped curve (which the ancients called the *hippopede*, or horse fetter), so as to complete the full double loop once for every full revolution of the spheres. One superimposes over this a third spherical rotation, corresponding to the general progress of the planet in the ecliptic, and finally over this a fourth rotation, corresponding to the daily rotation of the whole heaven. In this way, each of the five planets requires four spheres, while the Sun and the Moon each take three.

Schiaparelli's exposition thus revealed the ingenuity of Eudoxus' scheme for reproducing geometrically the seemingly erratic forward and backward (retrograde) motion of the planets. Nevertheless, the model proves unsuccessful in some respects: Since the planets do not vary in distance from the earth (the center of their spheres), Eudoxus cannot account for their variable brightness or for asymmetries in the shape of their retrograde paths. Even worse, the values that Eudoxus had to assign for the rotations of the spheres do not produce retrogrades for Mars or Venus, and the Sun and the Moon are given uniform motions, contrary to observation. Apparently, the latter two defects were recognized, for Eudoxus' follower Callippus introduced seven additional spheres (two each for Sun and Moon, one each for Mercury, Venus, and Mars) to make the needed corrections.

The Eudoxean-Callippean scheme is enshrined in Aristotle's *Metaphysica* (c. 335-323 B.C.; *Metaphysics*), where it serves as the mathematical basis of a comprehensive picture of the entire physical cosmos. Doubtless, Eudoxus proposed his geometric model without specific commitments on physical and cosmological issues. Nevertheless, it suited well the basic Aristotelian principles—for example, that the cosmos separates into two spherical realms, the celestial and, at its center, the terrestrial, and that the natural motions of matter in the central realm (for example, earthy substances moving in straight lines toward the center of the cosmos) differ from those in the outer (where motion is circular, uniform, and eternal). Ironically, these Aristotelian principles persisted in later cosmology, even after astronomers had switched from the homocentric spheres to eccentrics, epicycles, and other geometric devices.

Eudoxus also produced works of a descriptive and empirical sort in astronomy and geography. His *Phainomena* (fourth century B.C.; phenomena) and *Enoptron* (fourth century B.C.; mirror) recorded observations of the stars—the basis, one would suppose, of a systematic almanac of celestial events (for example, solstices and equinoxes, lunar phases, heliacal risings of stars). He adopted, as Diogenes and others report, an *oktaeteris*, or eight-year calendar cycle. As known to later authors, an *oktaeteris* is one of the cycles found to reconcile the solar year of 365.25 days with the period of the moon's phases (somewhat over 29.5), by parsing out the 2,922 days in eight years into ninety-nine lunar periods (fifty-one of thirty days and forty-eight of twenty-nine). Yet it is unclear whether this was the arrangement used by Eudoxus. His geographical treatise, the *Gēs periodos* (fourth century B.C.; circuit of the Earth), systematically described the lands and peoples of the known world, from Asia in the east to the western Mediterranean. A connection with his astronomical studies can be seen in the use of the ratio of longest to shortest periods of daylight for designating the latitudes of places.

Summary

However interesting Eudoxus' contributions to calendarics, geography, and philosophy may be, they are secondary to his achievement in mathematics, for he may justly be viewed as the most significant geometer in the pre-Euclidean period. He advanced the study of incommensurables, introduced a new technique for generalizing the theory of proportion, and made exact the theory of limits with his new method of "exhaustion." Remarkable for the logical precision of his proofs, Eudoxus here set the standard against which even the foremost of the later geometers, such as Euclid and Archimedes, measured their own efforts.

Eudoxus' influence on geometric astronomy is more subtle. Already, early in the third century B.C., astronomers had discarded his system of homocentric spheres in their pursuit of viable geometric models for the planetary motions. If the shortcomings of Eudoxus' model were evident, however, it nevertheless defined for later astronomers the essence of their task: to represent the planetary phenomena by means of uniform circular motion. Eudoxus' success thus remains implicit in the later development of astronomy, from Apollonius and Hipparchus to Ptolemy.

Bibliography

De Santillana, G. "Eudoxus and Plato: A Study in Chronology." In *Reflections on Men and Ideas*. Cambridge, Mass.: MIT Press, 1968. A revised chronology of Eudoxus' life is argued on the basis of a detailed examination of the ancient biographical data and collateral historical evidence.

Huxley, G. L. "Eudoxian Topics." *Greek, Roman, and Byzantine Studies* 4 (1963): 83-96. Huxley provides a survey of Eudoxus' life and work, including a discussion of the problems of dating.

Knorr, W. R. *The Ancient Tradition of Geometric Problems*. Boston: Birkhäuser, 1986. Chapter 3 considers Eudoxus' studies of "exhaustion" and cube duplication, discussed in the wider context of pre-Euclidean geometry.

__________. "Archimedes and the Pre-Euclidean Proportion Theory." *Archives internationales d'histoire des sciences* 28 (1978): 183-244. The Eudoxean theory of proportion is here reconstructed on the basis of materials from Archimedes and others and set in the context of the Euclidean theory (*Elements*, book 5).

Neugebauer, O. *A History of Ancient Mathematical Astronomy*. New York: Springer-Verlag, 1975. All facets of Eudoxus' contributions to astronomy are covered; particularly detailed is the discussion of his planetary models. Includes an index.

Van der Waerden, B. L. *Science Awakening*. New York: Oxford University Press, 1961. The author provides a brief, insightful review of Eudoxus' mathematical work.

Wilbur R. Knorr

EUPALINUS OF MEGARA

Born: c. 575 B.C.; Megara, Greece
Died: c. 500 B.C.; place unknown
Area of Achievement: Engineering
Contribution: Eupalinus was the architect of the tunnel and aqueduct on the island of Samos that bear his name. Probably built for the tyrant Polycrates in the sixth century B.C., they still stand today as monuments to the advanced engineering skills of the Greeks of the archaic period.

Early Life

Eupalinus, the son of Naustrophos, was from the Greek city-state of Megara, in the district of Megaris, located between Athens and Corinth. No details of his life have been preserved, but much can be inferred from what is known about the history of his birthplace in the sixth century B.C. Eupalinus was born into a prosperous land. Megara had experienced much growth in the years before his birth and was the mother city of numerous colonies. The young Eupalinus doubtless heard stories from his father and grandfather about the tyrant Theagenes, who had diverted water from the mountains to the city. The waterworks were still in operation, and the youth must have observed for himself the extensive underground conduit system which the tyrant had built to provide the city with water. The Megaris area was not well endowed with water, and the management of that precious resource was a prime concern. It is possible that a fountain house built in Megara toward the end of the century could have been designed by Eupalinus. In any case, it is likely that he gained some reputation in hydraulic engineering before being called to Samos for the great tunnel project.

Education for boys of Megara in the sixth century was mostly a matter of training for military activities and of learning manners and politics from their elders during banquets and symposia (drinking parties). Eupalinus would also have observed the productions of some of the first comedies, for the Megarians were said to have invented this dramatic form during Eupalinus' youth. As a result of his upbringing, it is likely that he was cultured and comfortable in "polite company."

Eupalinus probably lived most of his life in the democracy that followed the tyranny but would have observed the many struggles between the wealthy conservative oligarchs and the poorer supporters of popular rule. The poetry of Theognis of Megara preserves many of the passions that this strife aroused. The differences between rich and poor were exacerbated by the introduction of coinage, which also took place during Eupalinus' lifetime, as did the *Palintokia*, or debt-relief measures meant to help farmers. Eupalinus had firsthand experience with siege and warfare as well. Throughout the sixth century, Megara fought a series of wars with neighboring Athens. In one incident, the Athenian Peisistratus is said to have besieged and captured the Megarian harbor Nisaea. This background points to Eupalinus' later success in his life's work: He had a worldly background in politics and culture and a good knowledge of warfare and hydraulic engineering. These elements point to his future favor in the court of Polycrates.

Life's Work

Eupalinus is known from statements by Herodotus to have been the architect of the tunnel cut through the mountain bordering the capital city of the island Samos. Herodotus says that on Samos were the three greatest constructions of all the Greeks and lists the tunnel of Eupalinus first, describing its dimensions fairly accurately. The other two marvels of construction were Polycrates' great harbor works and temple of Hera. Today, the tunnel is by far the best preserved of the three. Archaeological evidence points to a date somewhere between 540 and 530 B.C. for the beginning of the work. Scholars have inferred that the tyrant Polycrates called Eupalinus from Megara to direct the project.

The task facing Eupalinus was formidable: In order to keep the Samians supplied with water in time of siege, he was to bring water from a spring on the north side of Mount Ampelus (now called Kastro) into the walled city on the other side. His solution was ingenious, consisting of an 850-meter-long underground conduit (high enough for a man to walk) that led from the spring to the entrance of a straight tunnel cut almost one kilometer through the mountain. The conduit was circuitous, so as to make disposal of the fill easier on the hilly terrain and to make detection more difficult and thus secure the Samians' water supply. The tunnel not only had a channel for the water, but also provided a convenient escape route should the city ever be taken. The system was so efficient that it continued to be used into Byzantine times, after which it fell into disrepair. The system was so well hidden that it lay undiscovered until 1853, when some of the conduit pipes were found, but the tunnel itself was not located by archaeologists until 1882, when a German team began excavations. The results of their work are still being published.

The tunnel itself was cut through solid limestone by workmen using only hammer and chisel. It consists of two levels: an upper level where people could walk—approximately two meters in height and width—and a deeper shaft on the east side up to seven and a half meters deep, where the water flowed in a channel made of ceramic tiles.

Eupalinus instructed his workmen to divide into two teams, each of which began digging at opposite ends of the mountain. The method which he used to ensure that they met in the middle has not yet been discovered. The teams were only two meters apart when they could hear each other's chisels and abruptly turned east. The northern team then broke through into the southern tunnel at a right angle. It has been calculated that had the diggers continued digging in a straight line, they would have met head-on although the northern shaft was a bit higher than the southern one. A conduit within the town led from the south end of the tunnel, not only providing drinking water for the inhabitants, but possibly also a steady stream to operate the town's water clock.

It is not known how long Eupalinus took to complete the tunnel—estimates range from five to fifteen years—nor is it known how many men he employed; certainly the size of the shafts would have permitted only a few workers on each team. It is obvious that Eupalinus took pride in his work and was something of a perfectionist, for the quality of the carving is very high, and there are niches carved in the walls to support lamps. In addition, Eupalinus saw to it that the tunnel was well provided with fresh air, which flowed through a ventilation hole and the conduits themselves.

It is likely that the tyrant Polycrates had ulterior motives when he hired Eupalinus. In addition to wanting the citizens of Samos to have a safe water supply and full employment, the tyrant was concerned that his people be occupied with large projects so as not to have time or desire to revolt against his power. Aristotle compares Polycrates' constructions to those undertaken by tyrants at Athens and Corinth. While the tunnel on Samos is the only undisputed work of Eupalinus, the similarity of the pipes used in its construction to those found in the Peisistratean aqueduct at Athens has led some to think that Eupalinus was the architect of that water system also, but no certain proof has yet been offered.

Summary

Eupalinus was not the first of the ancients—or the last—to engineer an underground tunnel for water transport. His contribution was not one of originality, but of quality: He proved that tunneling through a mountain for an aqueduct could be done efficiently with a simple technology. Although his northern team worked at a higher level than the southern tunnelers, and though the tunnel did not meet in a perfectly straight fashion, the work was nevertheless outstanding for its excellence: No other ancient tunnel matched its standards. Two hundred years earlier, a tunnel was constructed at Jerusalem between the Virgin's Pool and Siloam. Like Eupalinus' aqueduct, this construction was begun at both ends, but it was not as straight as the Samian tunnel. In fact, the Jerusalem tunnel wasted more than 150 meters on its winding way. A Roman tunnel project in northern Africa, at Saldae (modern Bejaïa), that used the two-team technique—more than five hundred years after Eupalinus—is also known. This project failed because the teams were unable to find each other. Their courses were so misdirected, in fact, that they dug a total distance that exceeded the mountain's width.

Eupalinus' engineering methods are not fully understood and probably combined empirical "trial and error" with some surveying techniques which have yet to be discovered. He might have aligned poles carefully up one side of the mountain and down the other or have used a method of triangulation that the engineer Hero of Alexandria described six hundred years later. It is also possible that Eupalinus kept the shafts straight by having his workmen keep their eyes on a light behind them at the end of the tunnel or shining through a hole cut in the roof. Whatever his methods were, they were effective, and the tunnel that bears his name stands as one of the most impressive engineering feats of antiquity.

Bibliography

Burns, Alfred. "The Tunnel of Eupalinus and the Tunnel Problem of Hero of Alexandria." *Isis* 62 (Summer, 1971): 172-185. An excellent analysis of Hero of Alexandria's first century A.D. treatise, *Dioptra*, in relation to the tunnel, with diagrams from Hero's work compared with the Samian topography. Includes a good discussion of Pythagorean mathematics in relation to the surveying problem. This is a well-reasoned approach by a former industrial engineer. Illustrated.

Figueira, Thomas J., and Gregory Nagy, eds. *Theognis of Megara: Poetry and the Polis*. Baltimore: Johns Hopkins University Press, 1985. The best historical background of archaic Megara. Includes a chronological table with extensive annotations, a discussion of Megarian society and education during Eupalinus' lifetime, and a thorough treatment of the Theognidean elegy and the city-state of Megara.

Goodfield, June. "The Tunnel of Eupalinus." *Scientific American* 210 (June, 1964): 104-110. An account of a scientific/photographic expedition to investigate the tunnel. Contains summaries of the German excavators' findings and engineering problems, and excellent diagrams, photographs, and maps.

Goodfield, June, and S. Toulmin. "How Was the Tunnel of Eupalinus Aligned?" *Isis* 56 (Spring, 1965): 45-56. This article argues against the theory that the tunnel was planned by mathematical triangulation like that described later by Hero of Alexandria. Instead, the authors think that Eupalinus used a line of vertical posts over the mountain above the tunnel. This article should be read with Burns's corrective. Illustrated.

Legon, Ronald P. *Megara: The Political History of a Greek City-State to 336 B.C.* Ithaca, N.Y.: Cornell University Press, 1981. A good source for the historical background of Eupalinus, discussing Megarian geography, tyranny, oligarchy, democracy, and commerce. Also treats the fountain house of Theagenes and Eupalinus' possible role in its construction.

Mitchell, B. M. "Herodotus and Samos." *Journal of Hellenic Studies* 95 (1973): 75-91. In the course of discussing Herodotus' relations with Samos and information about the town, Mitchell includes a concise and well-documented discussion of the tunnel, with speculations on date, manpower, rate of work, and use.

Shipley, Graham. *A History of Samos: 800-188 B.C.* Oxford: Clarendon Press, 1987. Contains an account of the tunnel of Eupalinus with a summary of scholarship on it. Since most of the work considering the tunnel is in German, this book is useful for English readers. The author uses the tunnel to date Polycrates' accession to the tyranny.

White, K. D. *Greek and Roman Technology*. Ithaca, N.Y.: Cornell University Press, 1983. This book includes a section on hydraulic engineering with a discussion of the tunnel, comparative material from other ancient waterworks, and an extensive bibliography, as well as an explanation of Eupalinus' use of the channel on the east side of the tunnel. Discusses surveying problems and Hero of Alexandria's solution. Illustrations.

Daniel B. Levine

EURIPIDES

Born: c. 485 B.C.; Phlya, Greece
Died: 406 B.C.; Macedonia, Greece
Areas of Achievement: Theater and drama
Contribution: Ranking with Aeschylus and Sophocles as a master of Attic tragedy, Euripides was the most "modern" of the great Greek tragedians, often criticizing traditional mythology and realistically working out the logical implications of ancient legends.

Early Life

Little is known of Euripides' life, since few records were kept in his time. Philochorus, a careful annalist who lived in the early third century B.C., wrote a biography of Euripides, fragments of which have survived; it is long on anecdotes but short on dates. What is reasonably certain is that Euripides' father, Mnesarchos, was an affluent merchant and that his mother, Cleito, was of aristocratic descent. When he was four years old, the great naval battle of Salamis, in which the Greeks defeated the Persians, caused Euripides' family to flee the small town of Phlya for Athens. When the boy was eight, the ruined walls of Athens were rebuilt, after the Greeks had decisively defeated Persia on land as well as sea. Freedom had triumphed over despotism—only temporarily, as Euripides was to discover.

In 466, Euripides became officially a "youth," whereupon the state conscripted him for garrison duty in the frontier forts of Attica. Full military service ensued when he was twenty. He distinguished himself as an athlete, did some painting and sculpting, and undoubtedly participated in what may have constituted the greatest intellectual awakening in Western history. As the mother-city of the Ionian territories, Athens had become the harbor for a great influx of artists, poets, historians, philosophers, and scientists fleeing Persian repression. Euripides is known to have been involved with the Sophists, particularly Protagoras, author of the doctrine that "Man is the measure of all things" and a skeptic about the universal validity of science or religion. Euripides may also have associated with Anaxagoras, a philosopher concerned with theories of the mind; Archelaus, Anaxagoras' pupil; Diogenes of Apollonia; and Socrates. Sophocles was his contemporary; undoubtedly, the tragedians knew each other's works, but no evidence exists that they socialized with each other.

Euripides had his first play produced in 455, competing at the Great Festival of Dionysus one year after the death of Aeschylus and thirteen years after Sophocles' first victory. Titled *Peliades* (daughters of Pelias), it was a trial run of his later *Mēdeia* (431 B.C.; *Medea*); the manuscript is not extant.

Life's Work

Altogether, Euripides wrote ninety-two plays, of which eighty-eight were entered in the Dionysian contests, although he won on only four occasions. Seventeen of his plays survive, compared to seven out of eighty for Aeschylus and seven out of 123 for Sophocles.

His earliest extant play is a tragicomedy, *Alkēstis* (438 B.C.; *Alcestis*), based on a folktale. It was placed fourth in a set of Euripidean plays, in the position usually accorded a comic satyr play, but its comic elements are minor. In this play, Admetus, a Thessalian king, has his young wife Alcestis agree to die in his place. The visiting Heracles, however, wrestles with Death and forces him to yield his beautiful victim. Euripides exposes the underside of this romantic legend: Admetus behaves as a warmly courteous host to Heracles and weeps over his "dead" wife, but essentially he is a coward. He lacks the courage to die at the time appointed for him, instead complacently allowing his wife to replace him; moreover, he fails to admit his selfishness even to himself.

Euripides' next surviving drama was *Medea*, his most famous work. Athenians watching the first performance would have known the drama's mythic background: Medea, a barbarian princess and sorceress related to the gods, helped Jason the Argonaut to steal the Golden Fleece and even murdered her own brother so that she and Jason could safely escape pursuit. In the play's action, Medea's beloved Jason has tired of his dangerous foreign mistress and agreed to marry the daughter of Creon so that he can succeed to the throne of Corinth. Desolate and maddened, Medea pretends reconciliation with Jason's bride and sends her a poisoned robe which fatally burns both her and Creon. Medea proceeds to kill her two children by Jason and then sails away on a magic dragon-chariot sent by her grandfather Helius, god of the sun. Euripides' treatment of Jason and Medea renders their personalities in a rather modern fashion: He is calm, self-confident, and rational, but cold; she is devoted and kind, but her rage at being rejected transforms her into an elemental incarnation of vengeful hatred. Their arguments constitute brilliant fireworks of articulated feelings and clashing temperaments.

Hippolytos (428 B.C.; *Hippolytus*) is more restrained and economical. It was his second version of the Phaedra-Theseus-Hippolytus plot; the first has been lost. Framing the drama is a prologue spoken by Aphrodite and an epilogue spoken by Artemis. The tragedy consists of the conflict between them, since Phaedra is identified with love and lust, Hippolytus with chastity and a consequent neglect of Aphrodite's charms. The scorned Aphrodite causes Phaedra, Theseus' newest wife, to fall hopelessly in love with her stepson Hippolytus. Refused by him, she writes a letter falsely accusing him of having raped her; then she commits suicide. Upon reading the letter, Theseus curses Hippolytus, and Poseidon fulfills the malediction by having a monster fatally wound the young man. It is Artemis who reveals the truth to Theseus so that father and son can at least be reconciled before Hippolytus' death. Though

Euripides magnificently celebrates the frustrated passion of his heroine, he permits the play to end in rhetorical commonplaces as Hippolytus and Theseus first argue, then forgive each other.

From a structural perspective, the most innovative achievement of *Hippolytus* is the freedom Euripides grants his characters to change their minds: Phaedra first resolves not to reveal her love, then does so; the nurse gives her mistress conflicting advice; and Hippolytus first decides to reveal his stepmother's lust to his father, then chooses not to do so. In his focus on the unpredictability of his characters' wills, Euripides anticipates psychological dramas such as those of Henrik Ibsen and Luigi Pirandello.

Numerous relatively minor works were also first mounted in the 420's and 410's. Many of these reflect events of the Peloponnesian War, the decisive struggle between Athens and Sparta. While Athens had become a model of democracy under the leadership of Pericles, Sparta favored despotic oligarchies. Euripides, still subject to military service, presumably saw combat during the first years of this agonizing conflict, which eventually ended with Athens' capitulation. *Hērakleidai* (c. 430 B.C.; *The Children of Heracles*), a mutilated text, presents a humane Athens as the protector of Heracles' children, standing for fairness, mercy, and right principles. *Hekabē* (425 B.C.; *Hecuba*) is a pacifist tragedy whose heroine, like Medea, is transformed by unbearable wrongs from dignified majesty to vindictive bitterness. *Ēlektra* (413? B.C.; *Electra*) is a melodrama which presents the protagonist as a slave princess in rags, morbidly attached to her dead father and inexorably jealous of her mother. *Andromachē* (c. 426 B.C.; *Andromache*) makes the Spartan king its villain; with its direct denunciations of Sparta, the play is virtually a wartime propaganda polemic. *Hiketides* (c. 423 B.C.; *The Suppliants*) also expresses Athenian wartime feeling, centering on the ceremonial lamentations of bereaved mothers over their sons' corpses.

Trōiades (415 B.C.; *The Trojan Women*) paints an even bleaker portrait of war's havoc. Only a few years earlier, Athens had emerged from an indecisive ten years' struggle with Sparta. In the spring of 415, Athens was but weeks away from launching the Sicilian expedition, which would touch off the last, disastrous phase of the same war. The Sicilian venture had been voted when Euripides presented a trilogy of which only *The Trojan Women*, its concluding tragedy, survives. It shows the conquest of Troy by the Achaeans degenerating into calamity: The ancient Greeks have committed *hybris* by insulting the altars of the gods, killing all Troy's male inhabitants, and defiling virgins in holy places. The Trojan princesses must be the slaves of their Greek captors: Hecuba, Priam's widow, has been allotted to Odysseus; Cassandra, the virgin priestess, will be Agamemnon's concubine; Hector's widow, Andromache, will become slave to Pyrrhus, Achilles' son; and Hector and Andromache's son, the boy Astyanax, is taken from her arms and thrown to his death. Two of the mightiest scenes in Attic drama elevate this play to heart-breaking greatness: first, the parting between Andromache and Astyanax, and second, Hecuba's lament upon receiving the boy's dead body after it has been flung from Troy's battlements. The work justifies Aristotle's designation of Euripides as "the most tragic . . . of the poets"; in this work, he is also the most nihilistic.

Euripides' later plays fall into two main divisions. One category consists of lighter, more romantic works with happy endings. These include *Iphigeneia ē en Taurois* (c. 414 B.C.; *Iphigenia in Tauris*), in which the heroine succeeds in saving her brother Orestes from the murderous Taurians; with this work, Euripides can be said to have written literature's first melodramatic thriller. *Iōn* (c. 411 B.C.; *Ion*) is Euripides' most intricately plotted and irreverent play: Apollo is treated as a selfish, mendacious rapist who is thoroughly discredited amid complex intrigues. *Helenē* (412 B.C.; *Helen*) is another melodrama, loaded with reversals: It was only Helen's ghostly double who went to Troy to start the Ten Years' War, while the substantive Helen takes refuge in Egypt and outwits its barbaric king. Her husband, Menelaus, arrives, and the two are able to escape.

An alternative line of development continues Euripides' ruthlessly probing tragedies. *Orestēs* (408 B.C.; *Orestes*) is a densely textured work focusing on Orestes' fate some days after he murdered his mother. He is intermittently mad and ill, nursed by Electra; both are imprisoned in the royal palace by an angry, rebellious populace and condemned to death for their matricide. A blazing climax—Orestes' party sets the palace on fire—leads to the intervention of Apollo, who orders Orestes to go to Athens, there obtain acquittal for his crime and then marry Menelaus and Helen's daughter, Hermione, in order to restore peace to the House of Atreus. *Iphigeneia ē en Aulidi* (405 B.C.; *Iphigenia in Aulis*) was discovered after Euripides' death in incomplete form and finished by another hand. It shows an irresolute Agamemnon preparing to sacrifice his youngest daughter, Iphigenia, but a messenger's speech predicts the ending Euripides presumably would have written had he lived longer: Artemis' last-minute substitution of a deer as the victim.

Probably Euripides' finest tragedy is a play he did finish, though it, too, was posthumously produced: *Bakchai* (405 B.C.; *The Bacchae*). The work features Dionysus playing a central role as both actor and Fate. He is described in the opening scene as "of soft, even effeminate, appearance. . . . His long blond curls ripple down over his shoulders. Throughout the play he wears a smiling mask." His identity remains elusive as well as demonic as he mingles gentleness with cruelty, flirtation with terror, coldness with passion. He presents himself as universal humanity, protean, both female-in-male and male-in-female, essentially amoral, blessing those who worship him and having no mercy on those who deny him. He personifies the bestial, primitive constituent of the psyche, free from ego constraint, at once superhuman and subhuman.

Dionysus' chief victim is the young ruler Pentheus, intemperate, self-willed, disdainful of tradition, scoffingly arrogant. Pentheus masks his primitive instincts behind authority and orderliness, only to have Dionysus crack his shell of artificial self-control, maddening him into frenzies of voyeurism and sadism. The civilized, rational ruler is transformed into a bisexual Peeping Tom who costumes himself in women's clothes so that he can spy on the Bacchantes' orgies. His frenzied mother Agave takes her son for a wild lion and, in the grip of Dionysian delusion, slaughters him. Thus, Pentheus dies as both a convert to and a victim of the instinctual life. Dionysus has ruthlessly destroyed the self that is ignorant of its nature. Euripides in this way dramatized the pitiless drive of the unconscious and the precariousness of human existence.

Legend has it that Euripides in old age was a sad man who conversed little and sat for long hours in his cave by the sea on Salamis. In 408, he exiled himself to the court of King Archelaus in Macedonia. Details of his subsequent death, in the winter of 406, are unknown. Philochorus claims that when Sophocles introduced his chorus during the 406 Dionysian festival, he brought the men onstage without their customary garlands as a sign of mourning for his great rival.

Summary

Anticipating such later playwrights as Henrik Ibsen and George Bernard Shaw, Bertolt Brecht and Jean-Paul Sartre, Euripides was an innovative, agile thinker who used the stage as a forum for his ideas about the world. The second half of the fifth century B.C. saw immense cultural convulsions involving the destruction of the Hellenic world's religious and political stability. Euripides recognized a world devoid of rational order and hence of Sophoclean notions of human responsibility and divine wisdom. He often highlighted the discrepancy between received traditions and experienced reality of human nature. Thus, his Admetus is shown as a shabby egotist, his Odysseus as a sly demagogue, his Agamemnon as an incompetent general, his Jason as an opportunistic adventurer. In contrast to the pious, conventional plays of Aeschylus and Sophocles, Euripidean drama is skeptical, rational, and diagnostic, stressing an often-difficult encounter between culture and the individual. It was this dramatic confrontation between mythic traditions and the elemental demands of the human psyche that chiefly interested Euripides.

His characters often find themselves captive to myths that strain their personalities: Euripides' Orestes murders his mother in an Argos that provides for judicial fairness; his Odysseus, Medea, Hermione, and Electra are all divorced from a culture in which their conduct was appropriate and are set instead in an alien time which distorts and misunderstands their choices. Euripidean personages tend to behave in self-contradictory and self-destructive ways, anticipating William Shakespeare's problematic Angelos, Claudios, and Lucios, August Strindberg's Miss Julie, and Eugene O'Neill's Cabots and Tyrones. Euripides' theater sabotages the conventions of ancient tragedy, replacing them with a challenging, turbulent, and revolutionary drama that bridges the gap between classical integration and contemporary chaos.

Bibliography

Conacher, D. J. *Euripidean Drama: Myth, Theme, and Structure*. Toronto: University of Toronto Press, 1967. Conacher conducts the reader on an erudite tour of Euripidean treatments of myths, beginning with such conventional texts as *Hippolytus* and ending with romantic melodramas such as *Alcestis*.

Kitto, H. D. F. *Greek Tragedy: A Literary Study*. Garden City, N.Y.: Doubleday and Co., 1954. This is a paperback reprint of a distinguished study first published in 1939. Kitto devotes five of his thirteen chapters to Euripidean tragedy.

Murray, Gilbert. *Euripides and His Age*. Reprint. London: Oxford University Press, 1965. The great British Hellenist's work remains vivid, vigorous, and lucid. His perspective is that of an Enlightenment liberal for whom religion is a form of superstition.

Segal, Erich, ed. *Euripides: A Collection of Critical Essays*. Englewood Cliffs, N.J.: Prentice-Hall, 1968. An anthology of ten essays by distinguished classical scholar/critics. Part of the Twentieth Century Views series. All the essays are worth reading; long studies by Bernard Knox of the *Hippolytus* and Thomas Rosenmeyer of *The Bacchae* are particularly rewarding.

__________. *Greek Tragedy: Modern Essays in Criticism*. New York: Harper and Row, Publishers, 1982. Segal reprints eight of the essays from the above-cited text and includes three additional articles of merit, one of which, by Jacqueline de Romilly, compares Aeschylus' and Euripides' treatments of fear and suffering.

Webster, T. B. L. *The Tragedies of Euripides*. London: Methuen and Co., 1967. Webster's highly detailed study contains a vast amount of information, but his style is pedestrian and his focus on metrics may deter the reader who has not mastered ancient Greek.

Gerhard Brand

EUSEBIUS OF CAESAREA

Born: c. 260; probably Caesarea, Palestine
Died: May 30, 339; Caesarea, Palestine
Areas of Achievement: Historiography and religion
Contribution: Living through both the last major Christian persecutions and the legalization of Christianity under Constantine the Great, Eusebius interpreted human history in terms of an upward process toward a divine purpose. He formulated the political philosophy of unity of church and state under the providence of God that became standard in the East.

Early Life

Relatively little is known of Eusebius' early life. He was likely born near Caesarea to peasant parents. The church historian Socrates, writing in the fifth century, states that Eusebius received Christian teaching and baptism at Caesarea and was later ordained a presbyter there.

Eusebius' mentor, a presbyter from the church at Alexandria named Pamphilus, was one of the leading biblical and theological scholars of the day, a disciple of the Christian philosopher Origen. He founded a school in Caesarea and gathered a large library of both pagan and Christian works there. Eusebius read widely under his teacher's guidance. By 303, Eusebius had completed early versions of at least two of his most important historical works, *Chronicon* (c. 300, 325; *Chronicle*) and *Historia ecclesiastica* (c. 300, 324; *Ecclesiastical History*).

Eusebius grew very close to Pamphilus, eventually adopting the surname Pamphili (son of Pamphilus). During the persecution begun by the emperor Diocletian, Pamphilus was imprisoned for two years, eventually suffering martyrdom in 309 or 310. Before his teacher's death, Eusebius assisted him in completing five volumes of a six-volume defense of Origen.

It is possible that Eusebius was jailed for his faith for a short period in Egypt following Pamphilus' death. At the 335 Synod of Tyre, which dealt with the continuing Arian controversy, Eusebius was accused by Potammon, a rival bishop from Egypt, of having sacrificed to the emperor cult to avoid torture while in prison. The charge was probably false, judging by the harsh stance the Church took toward Christians who lapsed into such actions and by the honors Eusebius received immediately after the persecution. These honors included his consecration as Bishop of Caesarea about 314, shortly after the proclamation of peace by Constantine and Licinius.

Life's Work

Eusebius lived in a period when one of the most dramatic events in the Church's existence occurred: the transformation of the Roman Empire, under Constantine's direction, from persecutor to supporter and protector of

Christianity. Eusebius' work cannot be fully understood without recognizing the importance of this apparent miracle for his thought. The first editions of his works, however, were certainly composed before Constantine's rise, probably during the first years of Diocletian's reign. A cautious optimism pervaded Christian circles at that time as a result of the lack of persecution, and Eusebius seems to have developed his idea of Christianity as the culmination of the course of human history in the first editions of his *Chronicle* and *Ecclesiastical History*.

It was when the Church again came under attack in 303 that Eusebius felt compelled to set forth his views at length, doing so primarily in the works *Praeparatio evangelica* (c. 314-318; *Preparation for the Gospel*) and *Demonstratio evangelica* (after 314; *Proof of the Gospel*). Eusebius' notions of history and its meaning were greatly influenced by his work in and interpretation of the Scriptures. For him, the Bible was the key to a correct understanding of human history. His beliefs were deeply rooted in the study of the Old Testament, where he saw the beginning of Christianity—not in Judaism proper, but rather in the earlier era of the patriarchs.

Christianity from its earliest days had been extremely sensitive to the charge that it was of recent origin. In *Contra Celsum* (248), Origen quoted the pagan writer Aulus Cornelius Celsus as scornfully saying, "A few years ago he [Christ] began to teach." The earliest Christian apologists tied Christianity to its Jewish roots and insisted that the loftiest ideas of paganism had actually been borrowed from the Hebrews. Eusebius did not consider that explanation to be adequate; he reinterpreted the biblical accounts to show that Christianity was, in fact, the most ancient of all the religions of mankind.

Eusebius, like Origen, saw history as having begun with a fall away from God, as illustrated in the Old Testament by the sin of Adam and Eve. Human beings after the Fall were characterized by savagery and superstition. There were some, however, who were able to see that God transcended the created world. These friends of God were the patriarchs, to whom were made known divine truths by the *Logos* (Christ). The patriarchs were the original Christians, knowing both God the Father and His Son, the divine Word. The unenlightened contemporaries of the patriarchs were the original pagans.

Judaism came into Eusebius' scheme as a purely transitional phase, to prepare the way for the new covenant of Jesus which would diffuse the religion of the patriarchs to all mankind. Following the period of the Mosaic Law came the central period of history, which began with the nearly simultaneous appearance of Christ and Caesar Augustus, the foundation of church and empire. He saw the reign of Constantine as the culmination of human history, the last era before the end of the world. The whole story was a "salvation history" which set the Christian experience into a context of historical knowledge that was basically shared by all educated people in the ancient world.

The whole of Eusebius' *Ecclesiastical History* could be interpreted as the account of the Church's continual movement forward in the working out of its victory over the demoniac powers. He viewed Constantine as leading people into the way of truth, as preached by the Church. Under his influence, the Gospel could be preached everywhere, and when that was accomplished, the end of the world and the return of Christ would take place. *Oratio de laudibus Constantini* (335-336; *In Praise of Constantine*, 1976) and *Vita Constantini* (339; *Life of Constantine*, 1845) contain several passages in which Eusebius seems to express hope of seeing the end in his own time.

It is likely that Constantine first took notice of Eusebius at the Council of Nicaea in 325. This council was called by the emperor to put an end to the strife in the Church over the doctrines of Arius, a presbyter of Alexandria, who taught that Christ was a created being and therefore not eternal. Although Eusebius had at first opposed action against Arius and evidently favored his subordinationist position, Eusebius was primarily interested in preserving unity in the Church. He was the leader of a moderate group at Nicaea which attempted to steer a middle course between the position of Arius and that of his chief antagonist, Athanasius.

Eusebius had been provisionally excommunicated by an earlier council in Antioch for his refusal to sign its strongly anti-Arian creed. At Nicaea, Eusebius presented a creed used in Caesarea as proof of his orthodox beliefs and as a possible solution statement to the question of the relationship between the Father and Son in the Godhead. This Caesarean creed, however, was expanded considerably before the bishops arrived at a final form. The most notable addition was of the term *homoousios* (Greek for "of the same substance" as God) to describe Christ. Although Eusebius reluctantly subscribed to the new creed for the sake of unity, during subsequent years he was involved in various actions against Athanasius, including the Synod of Tyre in 335, which formally condemned him.

Eusebius gained the respect of Constantine because of his peacemaking attitude; he enjoyed a rather close relationship with the emperor through the rest of his life. In 336, in celebration of the thirtieth anniversary of Constantine's accession, Eusebius praised the ruler in a lengthy speech which had as its theme the resemblance of Constantine to Christ. When Constantine died in May, 337, Eusebius immediately set about writing his *Life of Constantine*, which was left unfinished at his death in 339. His successor as Bishop of Caesarea, Acacius, finished and published the book later the same year.

Summary

Eusebius' approach to historiography is unique in several ways. He was the first Christian apologist to bring the literary-historical point of view to his works. While all other early opponents of paganism and heresy wished only to enter into polemical discussion, occasionally mentioning chronological facts only when it served their argument, Eusebius fixed the dates of writers and cataloged their works, clearly grasping the concept of a Christian literature.

In the ancient world, Eusebius' *Ecclesiastical History* was so successful that no one tried to supersede it. Instead, 150 years after his death, three writers, Socrates, Sozomen, and Theodoret, continued Eusebius' history down to their own times. The approach of Eusebius was dominant in the writing of church history almost until the time of the Enlightenment in the eighteenth century. The *Ecclesiastical History* is classed as one of the four or five seminal works in Western historiography.

Eusebius' overriding theme was celebration of the success of Christianity in the Roman world. He produced the reformulation of Christian political theory necessitated by the legalization of Christianity under Constantine. In his reinterpretation, the government became a positive institution in which Christians could take a more active part and for which they began to take more responsibility. In the Eastern Empire, his idea of the Church under the jurisdiction of a Christian ruler remained the norm until the fall of Constantinople in the fifteenth century.

Eusebius' optimistic theory of the general advance of human history under God proved to be the only real alternative to the historical views that would be developed in the fifth century by Saint Augustine of Hippo. Augustine was as much influenced in his comparatively pessimistic concept by the sack of Rome in 410 as Eusebius had been by the triumph of Constantine.

Bibliography

Barnes, Timothy D. *Constantine and Eusebius*. Cambridge, Mass.: Harvard University Press, 1981. An extremely well-documented and interesting volume which the author describes as an "interpretive essay" on Eusebius and Constantine as individuals and their relationship to each other. Of the 458 pages, more than 180 contain helpful apparatus, including copious notes to the chapters, a bibliography, a list of editions of Eusebius' works, and a chronology of his life.

Chestnut, Glenn F. *The First Christian Histories*. Paris: Éditions Beauchesne, 1977. Details the historical work of Eusebius and the historians who followed him—Socrates, Sozomen, Theodoret, and Evagrius—placing them in the context of historiography in the pagan world of their times. Shows the importance of Eusebius' work in the development of a Christian historiography. Footnotes but no bibliography.

Drake, H. A. Notes to *In Praise of Constantine: A Historical Study and New Translation of Eusebius' Tricennial Orations*. Berkeley: University of California Press, 1976. Although focusing primarily on Eusebius' laudatory speech of 336, this slender volume of 191 pages is much more than simply a critical edition of the speech. It provides a number of valuable insights into the thought and actions of Eusebius throughout his life. Sixty pages of notes and bibliography make it very valuable for a study of Eusebius.

Eusebius. *The History of the Church from Christ to Constantine*. Translated by G. A. Williamson. Baltimore: Penguin Books, 1965, reprint 1984. A popular and widely available edition of Eusebius' most famous work. An introduction by the translator, a map, and several helpful appendices of names mentioned in the text make this volume of the Penguin Classics series a must for students of Eusebius.

Grant, Michael. "Eusebius." In *The Ancient Historians*. New York: Charles Scribner's Sons, 1970. A chapter in Grant's monumental work, which, though only fifteen pages long, is valuable for its insights into Eusebius' place among historians of the ancient world. The book itself is lengthy and more than most students need for a study of Eusebius alone, but very valuable for a context of ancient historians. The notes and brief bibliography are of limited value.

Grant, Robert M. *Eusebius as Church Historian*. Oxford: Clarendon Press, 1980. An in-depth study of the *Ecclesiastical History* and an evaluation of Eusebius as a historian. Focusing on seven major themes (including apostolic succession, heretics, persecution, martyrdom, and the canon of Scripture), Grant points out both strengths and weaknesses of the first church historian's work. Footnotes and a brief bibliography are included.

Mosshammer, Alden A. *The Chronicle of Eusebius and Greek Chronographic Tradition*. Cranbury, N.J.: Associated University Presses, 1979. A critical study of Eusebius' seminal work of historical chronology which details the possible sources for the work and places it in the context of early Greek chronography. While much of the book is of a technical nature and of little use to the general student, the sections dealing with the *Chronicle* and other writings and with the sources upon which Eusebius based his work are of some value.

Valesius (Valois), Henri de. "Annotations on the Life and Writings of Eusebius Pamphilus." Translated by S. E. Parker. In *The Ecclesiastical History of Eusebius Pamphilus*. London: G. Bell and Sons, 1879. Reprint. Grand Rapids, Mich.: Baker Book House, 1955. An important early study done by the French lawyer and classical scholar Henri de Valois in 1659. Valois was quite familiar with the ancient literature known in his day and took great pains to substantiate and document all citations he made from these sources. While more recent scholarship has gone beyond Valois, his work is a very helpful compilation of information on a figure about whom relatively little is known.

Wallace-Hadrill, D. S. *Eusebius of Caesarea*. London: A. R. Mowbray and

Co., 1960. While not a full-scale "life and works" of Eusebius, this volume comes closer than any other to that description. Wallace-Hadrill gives a chapter on the life of Eusebius, then treats various topics in Eusebius' intellectual life, including his views on Scripture, the work of Christ, the Arian controversy, and the purpose of God in human history. A chronological listing of the works of Eusebius following the chapter on questions of dating is valuable, but the notes and brief bibliography are far less helpful than those of Barnes or Drake.

Douglas A. Foster

EZEKIEL

Born: c. 627 B.C.; Jerusalem
Died: c. 570 B.C.; Babylonia
Area of Achievement: Religion
Contribution: As a visionary and prophetic leader, Ezekiel was one of a number of individuals who held the Jewish community together during the early years of the Babylonian Exile (586-538 B.C.). His visions and consolatory prophecies encouraged those in exile to look toward the day of the restoration of the Temple in Jerusalem.

Early Life

All knowledge about Ezekiel is drawn from direct statements in the Book of Ezekiel or inferences from it. To develop a picture of his life, one must compare this material with that gathered from other books of the Hebrew Bible and additional contemporary texts. The tendency to discount much of the Book of Ezekiel as later editorial writing, prevalent throughout much of the twentieth century, has given way to an acceptance of the bulk of the material as coming from Ezekiel; later revisions are assumed to have originated from Ezekiel himself or those close to him.

Ezekiel was born in Jerusalem around the time of the Josiah reforms (c. 627) to a priestly family of the Zadok line. His father's name is given as Buzi. Ezekiel in his writing shows great familiarity and concern with the temple cult, and it is likely that he was part of the priestly cult and an important member of the hierarchy.

Ezekiel's life and career were played out against the background of ancient Near Eastern world events. By the end of the seventh century B.C., Nebuchadnezzar II had helped his father, Nabopolassar, defeat the Assyrians and take over the southern part of that empire, including the Kingdom of Judah. As long as Judah remained a faithful ally, it was secure, but when Nebuchadnezzar succeeded his father as king, Judah, under King Jehoiakim and with the encouragement of Psammetichus II of Egypt, rebelled against Babylon (2 Kings 24:2). In 598, Nebuchadnezzar marched against Judah. Jehoiakim was assassinated by those hoping for milder treatment, and his eighteen-year-old son, Jehoiachin, also known as Coniah, was placed on the throne. Three months later, defeated, he and his court were taken into exile in Babylon, and his uncle, Zedekiah, was given control of the state.

Ezekiel was one of those taken with King Jehoiachin into exile by Nebuchadnezzar in 597. This event was sufficiently important for Ezekiel to use it as the starting point for calculating the dates of his prophecies. Those prophecies that are dated are based on the number of years from the beginning of Jehoiachin's exile.

It would be expected that Ezekiel was married and had a family. His marriage is attested by a reference to his wife's death in Babylonia. He had a residence which was sufficiently large to hold a gathering of the elders of the Israelites in Babylonia. His prophecies suggest that he was resident at Tel Aviv near Nippur in Babylonia.

Ezekiel's mystic personality and his prophetic role should not be allowed to mask his position as an important member of the priestly establishment who continued to function in a leadership role in exile. While there is no direct proof, the linguistic similarities and priestly concerns exhibited in Ezekiel's own writings are not inconsistent with his inclusion among the "priestly" writers who were responsible for the preservation of many of the Israelite traditions of history and worship, which culminated in the creation of Torah.

Life's Work

Ezekiel's call to prophecy is dramatically described in the opening phrases of his book. He was thirty years old at the time, resident in Tel Aviv and standing on the Chebar canal. Ezekiel, in his prophetic actions and utterances, is revealed to be a dramatic mystic. Some have described his condition as that of a catatonic schizophrenic, and his actions as reported by him are congruent with clinical descriptions of that condition.

After Ezekiel received his call, he apparently abandoned all normal discourse and spoke only to utter the words of the Lord, Yahweh, as revealed to him, accompanied on several occasions by graphic symbolic actions. In this first period, Ezekiel's prophecies centered on the forthcoming destruction of Jerusalem, the impious actions of Zedekiah (the regent in Jerusalem), the futility of depending on Egypt for deliverance, and the false nature of prophets who predicted such deliverance. The prophecies were written in a mixture of poetry and prose notable for their graphic imagery, dramatic vocabulary, and extensive parables. In addition to the prophecies against Jerusalem, the prophecies against foreign nations reserved most of their invective for Tyre and Egypt, the two allies of Zedekiah against Babylon. In all these matters, Ezekiel's prophecies were paralleled by those of Jeremiah writing from Egypt to Babylonia. In both cases, their prophecies stemmed from activities taking place in Jerusalem and the importance of the homeland for the exiles.

After the final fall of Jerusalem to Nebuchadnezzar in 586 and the entrance of the second wave of exiles into Babylonia, the general tenor of Ezekiel's prophecies changed from one of denunciation to one of hope and encouragement. It is assumed that at that time Ezekiel returned to normal, everyday activity. Even in this period, however, he seems periodically to have gone into a catatonic state in which he claimed to have visionary and out-of-body experiences, which he then recorded in detail. Of these, the most famous are the vision of the valley of the dry bones and that of the restored Temple and the city of Jerusalem. This extensive passage shows the idealized

Temple under priestly control.

In the period after 586 B.C., there were several overreaching problems facing the Israelite (or Jewish) community. First, and most important, was gathering the community together and encouraging it to continue the ancestral belief in the Lord and the covenant agreement. To the exile this was no small problem, for the destruction of the Temple by the Babylonians would have universally been regarded as a defeat of Yahweh by the chief Babylonian god, Marduk, through the actions of Nebuchadnezzar. With Marduk having proved himself the stronger god, there would have been no compelling reason to continue the cult of Yahweh, particularly in exile. It was uniquely Ezekiel in Babylonia and Jeremiah in Egypt who interpreted the actions of Nebuchadnezzar as directed by Yahweh against His own people for not upholding the covenant agreement. The emphasis on the position of the deity in Ezekiel is made clear by the constant use in the prophecies of the phrase "Adonai Yahweh," which emphasizes His continuing power. (Since "Adonai" is usually translated as "Lord," most translations use "Lord God," which is the normal translation of the Hebrew "Adonai Elohim." Grammatically, the form in Ezekiel is usually described as an emphatic form.)

Ezekiel's prophecies either ceased or were not recorded after 571. There was a revision to the prophecy of the destruction of Tyre which suggests an unwillingness on the part of Ezekiel or his editor to change the wording of the earlier prophecy, preferring instead to add a corrected version. He may well have continued his nonprophetic activities after that date, including the preparation of the Book of Ezekiel.

Evidence of Ezekiel's death, although recorded late and not from the most secure sources, should not be neglected. Evidence from the third century A.D. Dura Synagogue wall painting and the fourth century Christian work on the lives of the prophets suggests that Ezekiel was arrested by the authorities and executed under the orders of Jehoiachin. What brought this about is unknown, but given Ezekiel's orientation it is not hard to conclude that his words could have aroused official opposition. It has been suggested that Ezekiel had realistic expectations of the restoration of the Temple in his lifetime. Only the death of Nebuchadnezzar and the incompetence of his successors postponed that event until the reign of Cyrus, the Persian liberator of Babylon.

Summary

The personality of Ezekiel as expressed in his book is a forceful and enduring one that has become part of the religious heritage of Judaism and Christianity. He presents himself as a mixture of opposites. There is the mystic visionary and the priest concerned with minutiae of cult and religious law. He is a superb poet but at the same time can write in the most pedestrian prose. His words seem strange, even repulsive, but then reveal a sympathetic and sensitive nature. He revels in symbolic acts and elaborate allegories one moment and speaks with directness and bluntness the next. By uniting these contradictions, he has impressed himself on tradition.

Ezekiel was one of the primary architects of Judaism. Faced with a historical situation in which the abandonment of the covenant was a high probability, not only was Ezekiel one of the few who demanded that the Israelites keep the covenant, but he also outlined the procedures and methods for doing so in the exilic environment, thus laying the foundations for Judaism. In addition to emphasizing the importance of the covenant, Ezekiel was one of the first to stress the importance of individual responsibility over collective or familial responsibility. In the recognition of God working outside Judah and through non-Israelite rulers, Ezekiel developed a concept of a universal deity while still holding to particularistic practices that became basic to all subsequent Judaism.

The influences of Ezekiel on Christianity have been less obvious but are nevertheless significant. His concepts of salvation and divine grace point to the reinterpretations of the concepts by the Apostle Paul. The unique prophetic use of the term "Son of Man" (in Hebrew, *ben-adam*) to indicate Ezekiel's special position as prophet had a strong effect on early Christian writers. His general mysticism found its way into the writings of the Apostle John and the Book of Revelation. This influence is most clear in Ezekiel's prophecies on Gog and Magog as the ultimate foes before the establishment of God's kingdom.

Bibliography

Broome, Edwin C., Jr. "Ezekiel's Abnormal Personality." *Journal of Biblical Literature* 65 (September, 1946): 277-292. A fascinating and convincing account of the mental state of the prophet. Based on modern case studies, it is particularly helpful in suggesting that Ezekiel's visions and descriptions are not incompatible with his being able to remember them in detail and to function normally while not in such a condition.

Eissfeldt, Otto. *The Old Testament: An Introduction*. Translated by Peter Ackroyd. New York: Harper and Row, Publishers, 1965. This volume is still the best of the introductions, of which there are many. Skilled exposition, clear analysis, and extensive bibliographies up to 1965.

Goodenough, Erwin R. *Jewish Symbols in the Greco-Roman Period*. Vols. 9-11, *Symbolism in the Dura Synagogue*. New York: Pantheon Books, 1964. The short section in this rather large work concerned with the late Roman synagogue paintings at Dura is the best available clear exposition of the traditions of the death of Ezekiel.

Gottwald, Norman K. *The Hebrew Bible: A Socio-Literary Introduction*. Philadelphia: Fortress Press, 1985. Well-written and up-to-date analysis of the Hebrew Bible. Gottwald's ideas are not always in the mainstream of critical thinking, but in this work he is more general than usual and is thus easier to read and more useful for information on the background of Ezekiel and on the prophet himself. Excellent bibliography.

Greenberg, Moshe. *Ezekiel, 1-20*. Garden City, N.Y.: Doubleday and Co., 1983. Included in the Anchor Bible series, the most definitive translation available with extensive introduction, translation, notes on the translation and textual problems, commentary, and bibliography. The introduction is rather skimpy here, but a more extensive introduction is promised for the next volume, which will complete Ezekiel. The notes and comments are particularly extensive.

Jewish Publication Society, trans. *The Prophets, Nevi'im*. Philadelphia: Jewish Publication Society, 1978. Readers will differ in their choice of the translations of Ezekiel, Jeremiah, and 2 Kings they will wish to use. This new translation by the Jewish Publication Society follows the traditional text with annotations where readings can be improved from other sources. It is written in clear, modern English with particular attention to translation of poetic passages in poetic form. For more detail consult the Anchor Bible series.

Michael M. Eisman

EZRA

Born: Late sixth or early fifth century B.C.; southern Mesopotamia
Died: Date unknown; probably Jerusalem
Area of Achievement: Religion
Contribution: As a "scribe skilled in the law of Moses," Ezra led a religious reform movement which transformed the identity of the Jewish community which had returned from exile to Jerusalem. This new identity of the Jewish people was premised upon a return to observance of the Law (Torah).

Early Life

Nothing of substance is known about the early years of Ezra, though his genealogy is given in Ezra 7:1-5. There he is called the son of Seraiah, and he is presented in the priestly heritage, with his ancestral line traced all the way back to Aaron, the first high priest and brother of Moses. While in the Bible Ezra is never specifically called the high priest or chief priest, he is so referred to in Flavius Josephus' *Ioudaikē archaiologia* (c. A.D. 93; *The Antiquities of the Jews*).

Ezra was born, like many Jews in the fifth century, in captivity under the yoke of the great Persian Empire. It actually had been about a century earlier, under the imperialistic policies of the Neo-Babylonian Empire in the early sixth century, that the stage had been set for several generations of Jews to be born in exile. Beginning in 597, when Jerusalem fell under the onslaught of Nebuchadnezzar, the Babylonian king, a series of deportations was initiated in which large numbers of people within the Kingdom of Judah were physically transported to Babylon and other tightly controlled sectors in southern Mesopotamia.

For almost six decades after 597, the exiles lived and worked under Babylonian control. Although sources describing the daily life of the exiles are meager, there is evidence that suggests that some were put to forced labor for various building projects; perhaps the greatest numbers were relocated to agricultural communities with a relative amount of freedom. Remarkably, the once-powerful Babylonian Empire was overthrown with ease. To the east of the empire, the Persians had been a growing threat for many years. By 539, the great city of Babylon was taken, virtually without a fight. Cyrus the Great, the Persian king, embarked on a series of military campaigns with the goal of securing the bulk of territory once controlled by the Babylonians. Within a year, much of the Near East was under Persian influence. Cyrus determined to control his new empire via a novel approach: as liberator. Thus, the Assyrians and Babylonians' traditional methods of terror and deportations were cast aside in favor of very tolerant policies. It is within this framework that Ezra 1:1-4 relates how Cyrus, in 538, issued a decree which allowed and even encouraged the exiled Jews to return to their homeland.

Indeed, they did return. Under the leadership of Sheshbazzar, and later his nephew Zerubbabel, those who returned resettled and even commenced rebuilding the Temple, which had been destroyed by the Babylonians. Construction began in 520, and by 515 the work had been completed. Chapter 6 of the Book of Ezra relates the events of completing and dedicating the new Temple and the observance of Passover in the spring of 515. With this accomplishment, the stage was set for the return of even more exiles and the coming of Ezra to Jerusalem. Ultimately, Ezra would provide the leadership and spiritual direction needed by the Jewish community of Jerusalem in order to restore and invigorate its once-rich religious heritage.

Life's Work

Between the close of the biblical narrative in Ezra 6 and the introduction of Ezra himself at the start of chapter 7, a substantial number of years passed. It was probably early during this period, sometime after 515, that Ezra was born. With virtually no information concerning his early years, the real story of Ezra begins with his return to Jerusalem along with groups of other Israelites, as mentioned in Ezra 7:7. It is at this point that one of the more vexing problems in biblical studies arises: the dating of Ezra's return to Jerusalem. Artaxerxes I ruled the Persian Empire from 464 to 423. The text of Ezra 7:8 states that Ezra and his retinue arrived in Jerusalem in the fifth month of the seventh year of Artaxerxes' reign; by this reckoning, Ezra came to Jerusalem in 458. This straightforward calculation would place him in Jerusalem before Nehemiah. There are, however, some murky waters surrounding the chronological relationship between Ezra and Nehemiah. For this reason, two other theories concerning the date of Ezra's return have been articulated. Some believe that a scribal error marred the biblical text and that "the seventh year" should read "the thirty-seventh year" of Artaxerxes. This would place the return of Ezra to Jerusalem in 428. Although supported by some, this position has not met with widespread acceptance. There is a third possibility: "The seventh year of Artaxerxes" does not refer to Artaxerxes I but rather to Artaxerxes II, who ruled from 404 to 359. Accordingly, the seventh year would be 398. The thorny problem of dating Ezra's return has by no means been resolved. To deal pragmatically with the events of Ezra's life, however, the traditional date of 458 for his return to Jerusalem has been adopted here.

As a "scribe skilled in the Law of Moses" (Ezra 7:6), Ezra received a special royal commission from the Persian king Artaxerxes. The document, which was written in Aramaic, is preserved in Ezra 7:12-26. This document presented Ezra with far-reaching powers to teach and enforce measures of the Law among the members of the Jewish community residing in the Persian satraphy of Abar-nahara—thus including not only those in Palestine proper but also the Jews in the Trans-Euphrates area. The idea that the Persian king would so empower a man to impose the Law of Moses upon Jewish subjects within the Persian Empire might seem on the surface to be unreasonable. Yet many attested Persian documents clearly demonstrate that, indeed, most of the kings implemented such policies. There was a longstanding Persian commitment to giving official sanction to the various religious elements within the empire.

Armed with the royal decree, Ezra, upon his return to Jerusalem, initiated a program of religious reform which was designed to renew loyalty to the Law in the hearts and minds of Jews. He had been given explicit authority to appoint magistrates and judges and to teach those who had no knowledge of the laws of God. He was even granted authority to mete out punishment upon those who did not comply with the Law, as Ezra 7:26 states: "Whoever does not obey the law of your God and the law of the king must surely be punished by death, banishment, confiscation of property, or imprisonment."

There is great variance of opinion over the chronological order of the events which followed. What is clear is that Ezra initiated changes which brought about profound religious reforms and the reconstituting of the Jewish community along lines drawn within the Law. Some scholars hold that the narrative of Nehemiah 8 probably reflects the events shortly after Ezra's arrival in Jerusalem. As priest and scribe, Ezra presented the Law publicly to the people in what must have been a very solemn ceremony. Standing on a platform before an assembly of "men and women and all who were able to understand," Ezra read from the Law from dawn until noon. The next day, Ezra, along with the heads of certain families and various priests and Levites, gathered to study the precepts of the Law. They read about the Feast of Tabernacles, proclaimed in Leviticus 23. Realizing that the observance of this festival had long been neglected, Ezra immediately issued a decree throughout the country that the people were to gather materials necessary for the construction of the booths that were requisite for the celebration. The people's response was overwhelming: Nehemiah 8:17 states that "the whole company that had returned from exile built booths and lived in them. From the days of Joshua son of Nun until that day, the Israelites had not celebrated it like this. And their joy was very great." The reforms of Ezra were under way.

The public reading of the Law and the celebration of the Feast of Tabernacles made a powerful spiritual impact upon the people. They began fasting, wearing sackcloth, and confessing their sins as they came to understand the wickedness of their ancestors and their own role in Israel's recent and unfortuitous history. Yet, in this very humbling circumstance, the people were encouraged by the rehearsing of their place as God's chosen and as beneficiaries of redemptive works performed by God on their behalf throughout history. Their repentance and gratitude are articulated in a long penitential prayer recorded in Nehemiah 9. The spiritual underpinnings of the community were being reshaped as the Law began to find a central place within the lives of individuals.

As the spiritual leader of a society which was reaping the consequences of years of abuse and neglect of the Law of God, Ezra exerted remarkable influence in addressing a basic problem within Israelite culture: intermarriage. The Law strictly forbade marriages between Jews and pagans, and clearly intermarriages had created innumerable problems throughout Israelite history. Marriage to foreigners did nothing but water down the worship of Yahweh and the observance of God's ordinances. When a contingent of elders reported that intermarriage was rampant and that certain leaders and officials had, in fact, led the way in this pattern of activity, Ezra reacted with the emotion of one understanding the true nature of God's holiness and His utter hatred of sin: "When I heard this, I tore my tunic and cloak, pulled hair from my head and beard and sat down appalled." The passion of Ezra for the Law and holiness before God was further revealed as he prostrated himself and prayed:

> What has happened to us is a result of our evil deeds and our great guilt, and yet, our God, you have punished us less than our sins have deserved and have given us a remnant like this. Shall we again break your command and intermarry with the people who commit such detestable practices?

Ezra now moved in such a way as to penetrate the conscience of the entire community. Broken before God because of the calamity of intermarriage, Ezra prayed to God near the Temple. As he was praying, weeping, and confessing this great sin, the people were moved. A large crowd gathered around him, spellbound by the realization of their sin. Masses began to weep bitterly and confess their sins. It was one of those few times in history when a solitary individual touches the inner recesses of an entire nation's soul. Ezra, the scribe, by revealing his contrition and weeping in anguish before the Lord and before the people, moved the nation of Israel that day. Leaders from the community issued a declaration that all the exiles must assemble themselves in Jerusalem within three days. Anyone not complying would be removed from the ranks of Jewish community life. In what must have been an incredible scene, all the exiles gathered near the Temple in a driving rainstorm to hear Ezra's public rebuke and plea for change. The result was that the people did acknowledge their sin, and a program was established for separating themselves from the foreigners. Within three months, all mixed marriages had been dissolved. Once again, the Law became foremost in the hearts of the people.

Summary

Ezra did not become a long-standing force in the Jerusalem community. In fact, he was probably an active leader for only about a year after arriving in the city. He does not appear in any biblical narratives of later events. According to Josephus, after the accomplishment of his mission, Ezra died and was buried in the Holy City. How does one accurately judge the impact of Ezra? Certainly, his reputation in the succeeding generation suggests a level of awe and respect comparable to that afforded to Moses, the unquestioned hero of the faith. Yet reputation is not the proper criterion for judging an individual's significance. In this case, Ezra's pragmatic reforms, which reorganized and reenergized the struggling Jewish community, should serve as a measuring rod.

Undoubtedly, the elevation of the Law to a place of centrality in the Jewish community was Ezra's paramount achievement. The primacy of the Law in the lives of the people was a renewed force which enabled the Jews to survive as a separate entity. Although the stringency of the reforms concerning intermarriage may have seemed unreasonable to some, the observance of the Law aided them in realizing anew their stature as a people chosen by God. The acceptance of the Law as presented by the faithful scribe Ezra brought about a reorganization of the people which was desperately needed in the tumultuous years after the return from exile.

Bibliography

Bossman, D. "Ezra's Marriage Reform: Israel Redefined." *Biblical Theology Bulletin* 9 (1979): 32-38. The focus of this article is the intermarriage problem addressed by Ezra and the restructuring of Israel around the Law. Bossman shows that cultic aspects of the Jewish community were purified through the reforms of Ezra.

Bright, John. *A History of Israel*. Philadelphia: Westminster Press, 1959, 3d ed. 1981. Chapter 10 of this work is a very useful overview of the Jewish community in the fifth century. A full discussion of the problems involved in the dating of Ezra's mission to Jerusalem is included in an excursus to the chapter.

Childs, Brevard S. *Introduction to the Old Testament as Scripture*. Philadelphia: Fortress Press, 1979. Chapter 42 presents an in-depth bibliography of resources dealing with the Ezra-Nehemiah era. Although there is no focus upon the life of Ezra specifically, short summaries are presented which address, among other issues, the chronological controversies and the reforms initiated by Ezra.

Fensham, F. Charles. *The Books of Ezra and Nehemiah*. Grand Rapids, Mich.: Wm. B. Eerdmans, 1982. This volume is part of the New International Commentary on the Old Testament. Particularly valuable is the introductory matter, which presents a clear and concise discussion of the major issues, such as sources, historical background, and theology.

LaSor, William, David Allan Hubbard, and Frederic William Bush. *Old Testament Survey: The Message, Form, and Background of the Old Testament*.

Grand Rapids, Mich.: Wm. B. Eerdmans, 1982. Chapter 50 of this book offers an excellent presentation of the crux of the Ezra and Nehemiah narratives. Among the gems to be discovered in this work are potent insights into the achievements and significance of Ezra.

Williamson, H. G. M. *Ezra and Nehemiah*. Waco, Tex.: Word Books, 1985. This commentary, volume 6 in the Word Biblical Commentary series, presents full bibliographies for each literary unit within the books of Ezra and Nehemiah. It includes a fresh translation of the text along with insightful commentary on the historical aspects of the narratives about Ezra.

W. R. Brookman

FAKHR AL-DIN AL-RAZI

Born: 1148 or 1149; Rayy, Iran
Died: 1210; Herat, Khorasan Province, Iran
Area of Achievement: Religion
Contribution: Fakhr al-Din al-Razi was among the last representatives of Islamic theology to espouse the systematic orthodox school founded by al-Ash'ari. An itinerant scholar, al-Razi's personal contributions as a teacher left an indelible mark on the intellectual life of the eastern provinces of the late twelfth and early thirteenth century Islamic Caliphate; his writings were distributed widely, in both the Iranian (eastern) and Arabic (western) provinces of the caliphs' empire.

Early Life

Fakhr al-Din al-Razi, whose full name was Abu 'Abd Allah Muhammad ibn 'Umar ibn al-Husayn ibn 'Ali al-Imam Fakhr al-Din al-Razi, was the son of Shaykh Diya al-Din 'Umar, *khatib* (preacher) of Rayy, a key city in the north-central area of Iran. The family claimed both a long tribal ancestry (associated with the Taimi tribe) and descent from the family of Abu Bakr, the first caliph. Al-Yafi'i, whose biographical sketch of al-Razi survives in manuscript form only, cites a long pedigree of family teachers (originally named by al-Razi himself, in his *Tahsil al-haqq*), going back to Abu al-Hasan al-Ash'ari (c. 873-c. 935), the famed figure of classical Islamic orthodox scholarship. This line of scholars led in a chain to the generation and person of al-Razi's father, who was his first teacher in the fields that would make his fame. Some traditional Islamic biographers claim that the young student was also interested, in the early stages of his education, in alchemy and astrology. Such interests are reflected only very little within his known works as a mature scholar.

Following his father's death, al-Razi received specialized training not only in *fikh* (Islamic law) but in *'ilm al-kalam* (Islamic theology) and philosophy as well. His teacher in the latter field, Majd al-Din al-Jili (from Jilan Province), had clearly been involved in controversial subjects, since at least one of his other students, Shihab al-Din al-Suhrawardi, faced a death sentence for expounding beliefs that bordered on heresy. Al-Razi's exposure to al-Jili, however, did not result in such controversy. What was most significant for this early stage of al-Razi's adult life, perhaps, was the opportunity he received to accompany al-Jili to the region of Maragheh, where the latter was engaged as a preacher. This experience, which brought a widening of both intellectual and geographical horizons for the youth, left a mark of cosmopolitanism which became characteristic of al-Razi's entire career.

Life's Work

At some point after passing his thirtieth year (thus in the 1180's), al-Razi began to travel very widely, not to the central Iraqi and Syrian provinces, but to the eastern reaches of the Islamic Caliphs' domains. He first left his mark as a philosophical itinerant in Khwarizm (the Amu Darya basin, north of Khorasan Province in eastern Iran). There, representatives of the Mu'tazilah (best-known for their contention that the Koran was created scripture, not the timeless word of God) engaged him in debates which, because of their controversial tenor, led to his expulsion by the authorities. Next came a brief sojourn (between 1184 and 1186, when al-Razi would have been thirty-six to thirty-eight years old) in the Iranian/Turkish frontier zone of Transoxiana.

Some traditionalists maintain that the brevity of al-Razi's stay in Transoxiana was connected with his involvement in the philosophical and theological debates that formed the corpus of his edited work *Munazarat jarat fi bilad ma wara'a al-nahr* (*Transoxianian Controversies*, 1966). It is also possible that not only intellectual but also material considerations pushed the itinerant scholar from place to place. It is known that the next stage of his career was played out in the palace at Ghor, part of the Islamic domain of Ghazni (south of Kabul in modern Afghanistan). There, al-Razi obtained formal patronage, with material compensation, from the Ghurid ruler Mu'izz al-Din Muhammad. This privileged status proved to be tenuous, however, when al-Razi's combination of orthodox and philosophical approaches to Islamic doctrine was opposed by representatives of the extremist Karramiyah doctrine, which was championed locally.

A better climate for profitable patronage for al-Razi's modes of philosophical and theological analysis appeared in the eastern Iranian province of Khorasan. There, the ruler 'Ala' al-Din Tukush appointed al-Razi tutor to the crown prince, Muhammad. Service to the eventual successor brought its rewards: first, in the form of high appointed office with privileged material status, and second, through marriage links to the Tukush court (al-Razi's daughter was married to the vizier, or chief minister, 'Ala' al-Mulk).

Whether it was in Khorasan or in another position of patronage (the standard accounts vary on this point), it appears that al-Razi's reputation as a teacher earned for him the honor of having a special *madrasah*, or Islamic seminary, built in his name and for his use. Although it is not known how long al-Razi retained such privileged status, by 1203, when he was in his fifties, he was able to move to Herat, in southeastern Khorasan, where he settled, investing some of his acquired wealth in propertied estates. The seven years he spent in Herat before his death (in 1210) did not shield him from bitterness at having had to defend himself from critics of his thought wherever he went. Some of the scholar's resentment of the unending controversy over his ideas is reflected in his last testament. As recorded in Ibn Abi Usaibi'ah's biographical collection, *'Uyun al-anba fi tabaqat al-atibba*, the testament that al-Razi dictated to his student Ibn 'Ali al-Isfahani read:

> Know I was a lover of knowledge, and . . . wrote about every question that I might know its quantity and quality, irrespective of whether it was true or false. . . . I have examined the methods of theology and philosophy, but I did not find in them the profit I found in the Koran, for the Koran ascribes glory and majesty to God, and forbids preoccupations with obscurities and contradictions. These only teach us that the human intellect disintegrates in these deep narrows and hidden ways.

What was the nature of al-Razi's interpretations of Islamic philosophy and theology that aroused so much controversy? First, one should remember that al-Razi did not distinguish himself only as an author of works that were easily acceptable as reflecting Sunni (orthodox) views. In fact, in stages, and after having been tempted by rationalistic Greek thought, he became associated with the well-established Ash'ari school, which sought to find a synthesis between orthodox religious principles (such as the uncreated nature of the Koran and the absolute power and grace of God) and human efforts to use reason. Among al-Razi's major works which reflected such principles, the famous *Kitab muhassal afkar al-mutaqaddimin wa-al-muta'akhkhirin* (compendium of the ideas of scholars and theologians; best known as *Muhassal*) is worthy of note. The *Muhassal* discusses (among a wide variety of subjects) the general characteristics of being, cause and effect, and prophecy and eschatology. A second landmark work is his *Kitab al-tafsir al-kabir* (great commentary on the Koran). Although both of these works became Islamic classics, modern commentators on al-Razi, including Louis Gardet, make it clear that al-Razi's theology is marked by philosophical and even some scientific references to Greek sources. Gardet provides a key to understanding why those of al-Razi's contemporaries who were bound to strict religious tenets might have opposed the originality of his interpretations. Referring to al-Razi's Koranic commentary, Gardet cites G. C. Anawati, who says, "It . . . is both philosophical and *bi'l-ra'y*, i.e., it does not rely on tradition alone, but on the considered judgment and reflection of the commentator."

Summary

The career of Fakhr al-Din al-Razi is a striking example of the survival, into the thirteenth century, of eclectic intellectual currents which had roots in the classical age of Greece and Rome as well as that of Persia, currents which contributed to the great tradition of Islamic scholarship. Anawati's suggestion that much of al-Razi's analysis of legal and theological questions reflects the use of personal opinion (*bi'l-ra'y*) is significant, especially in the light of what would follow. To be certain, Islamic religious orthodoxy had never been at ease with certain philosophers' tendency to introduce secular rational approaches into religious debates. Nor was mysticism—an element present in Islam from the earliest years following Muhammad's death—fully or openly accepted. It was the task of great thinkers such as al-Ash'ari and al-Ghazzali (1058-1111) to attempt to forge *kalam*, or theology, into a set of systematic principles that could resist the criticism of full rationalists, on the one hand, and satisfy the need which mystics felt for personal religion, on the other.

During this process, which was at its peak in Islam during the eleventh and twelfth centuries, the movement for orthodox systematization, of which al-Razi was a part, still left the *bab al-ijtihad* (door of independent reasoning) open wide enough to allow, not deviation, but at least diversification, in modes of analysis. That al-Razi used diverse approaches to arrive at systematic conclusions is illustrated in several scholars' appraisals of his famous commentary on the Koran as containing elements of Greek thought and even Greek physical science.

The two or three centuries that followed the generation of al-Razi witnessed what would be called the "closing of the door of *ijtihad*." The effects of this narrowing of acceptable principles for individual scholarly analysis of theological and legal questions would be to underline further the uniqueness of al-Razi's latter-day contributions to Ash'arism. Such originality would not be seen again until currents of intellectual rationalization challenged orthodox Islamic values near the end of the nineteenth century. When that happened, there was a call for a "reopening of the door of *ijtihad*," and classical but very individualistic commentaries such as that of al-Razi resurfaced after centuries of near oblivion.

Bibliography

Gardet, Louis. "Religion and Culture." In *The Cambridge History of Islam*, edited by Peter M. Holt, Ann K. S. Lambton, and Bernard Lewis, vol. 2. Cambridge: Cambridge University Press, 1970. This chapter in the well-known Cambridge series is particularly useful for placing the life and work of al-Razi in the wider context of Islamic history. Although there is not great detail here on the specific phases of al-Razi's life, the various schools of thought to which he reacted are identified. The same volume serves the general reader by offering, in addition to Gardet's piece on religion and culture, chapters titled "The Geographical Setting" and "Literature," both of which are helpful discussions of the intellectual milieu within which al-Razi lived.

Kholeif, Fathalla. *A Study on Fakhr al-Din al-Razi and His Controversies in Transoxiana*. Beirut: Dar el-Machreq Press, 1966. This may be the only monographic study of al-Razi in English. It includes a substantial section on his life and works in general, but focuses on the text of the famous *Transoxiana Controversies*, which appears in the Arabic original and in English translation. The work is organized around sixteen questions, some of which deal with philosophy and theology ("The Vision of God," "Is the

World Eternal or Created?"), and others with Islamic law (for example, "Slavery and Kinship," "Prayer on Usurped Land"). A list of all al-Razi's known works, published or in manuscript form (or presumed lost), appears in the index.

Kraus, Paul. "The Controversies of Fakhr al-Din Razi." *Islamic Culture* 12, no. 2 (1938): 131-150. An abbreviated study which focuses on the *Transoxiana Controversies*. Although Kraus's pioneer work on al-Razi was criticized in 1966 by Fathalla Kholeif as incomplete, its attraction for general readers is considerable. Kraus works from the assumption that because the *Transoxiana Controversies* is a synthesis of a number of different subjects, it can provide a better idea of the evolution of al-Razi's thought than that afforded by his major works of theology and Koranic commentary. The second attribute of Kraus's approach is his desire to show reflections of al-Razi's personality and character in the text.

Powers, David S. *Studies in Qur'an and Hadith: The Formation of the Islamic Law of Inheritance*. Berkeley: University of California Press, 1986. This specialized publication is primarily concerned with technical questions of Islamic law. Its value for students interested in al-Razi is that it shows how representatives of the Ash'ari school organized their arguments around specific legal issues that were of particular interest to Koranic commentators. In this book, al-Razi's treatment of the Koranic provisions on bequests and testaments is the focus of analysis.

Rahman, Fazlur. *Islam*. London: Weidenfeld and Nicolson, 1966. Rahman's text on the institutions of Islam is extremely extensive and detailed. The discussion of schools of thought, both within and outside orthodox tradition, includes analysis of the two currents that influenced al-Razi most: Mu'tazilism and Ash'arism. Al-Razi receives a substantial amount of coverage in this respect, both in the chapter titled "Dialectical Theology and the Development of Dogma" and in the concluding chapter, titled "Legacy and Prospects," which deals with the general meaning of orthodox dogma and moral or spiritual principles and ideals.

Byron D. Cannon

FIRDUSI

Born: Between 932 and 941; Tus, Khorasan Province, Iran
Died: Between 1020 and 1025; Tabaran, near Tus, Iran
Area of Achievement: Literature
Contribution: Firdusi's *Shahnamah* is the supreme example of the epic in the Persian language. Through centuries of foreign invasion and conquest, it has served as a major means of preserving Iran's cultural identity.

Early Life

Firdusi, the national poet of Iran, flourished during the tenth and early eleventh centuries. What Homer was to the ancient Greeks and Vergil was to the Romans, Firdusi has been for centuries to all speakers of Persian. He was born in the vicinity of Tus, near modern Mashhad, in the northeastern Iranian province of Khorasan, but nothing is known regarding his parentage or his formative years. Even his personal name is unknown, Firdusi being a pen name, from the word *firdaus*, meaning paradise. What is reasonably certain is that he belonged to the ancient class of hereditary landowners known as *dihqans* and that during the earlier part of his long life he enjoyed a modest financial independence, presumably an income derived from property inherited from his father.

Apart from a visit to Baghdad, Firdusi seems to have spent his entire life in Khorasan or in the adjoining regions of Afghanistan and Mawarannahr (the modern Uzbek, U.S.S.R.). Either in Tus or in the course of his later wanderings, he would have imbibed the cultural traditions and the pride in the values of the pre-Islamic Iranian past which were cultivated among the *dihqan* class and at the courts of local Iranian dynasts such as the Samanids of Bukhara, the Buyids of western Iran, and the Ziyarids of Tabaristan. Among both rulers and landowners there lingered a nostalgic attachment to the memory of the imperial Sassanid dynasty, which had ruled over the Iranian plateau and the surrounding regions from the early third to the mid-seventh century.

In such a milieu, Firdusi began to compose and organize his great epic, the *Shahnamah* (c. 1010; the book of kings), a paean to the glories of ancient Iran and its famous rulers. The actual completion of this enormous undertaking (*Shahnamah* manuscripts can range from forty-eight thousand to more than fifty-five thousand distichs, or two-line units) is said to have taken at least thirty-five years, with perhaps sometime around 975 as its starting point and 1010 as its terminal date. Although the twelfth century belletrist Nezami-ye ʻAruzi states that Firdusi's reason for writing the *Shahnamah* was to earn a reward sufficient to provide a proper dowry for his daughter and sole surviving child, it is difficult not to imagine its composition as a labor of love, a self-appointed mission. Nevertheless, it does appear that at some time in middle life Firdusi's financial resources became depleted, for whatever reason, and that consequently he was compelled to go in search of patrons.

Life's Work

The late tenth century was an inauspicious time for a poet who sang of ancient Iranian greatness to find a patron. The openhanded Iranian rulers of Firdusi's youth had all but disappeared, and the age of the Turkish warlord was dawning. In the north, beyond the Amu Darya, the noble Samanids of Bukhara had been swept away by the seminomadic Qarakhanids. On the Iranian plateau itself, the celebrated Turkish conqueror Sultan Mahmud of Ghazna (reigned 998-1030) held sway from his capital in eastern Afghanistan. To him, perhaps as a last resort, Firdusi made his way. Almost everything which is known of the dealings of Sultan Mahmud with Firdusi originated a century or more after the death of both men and therefore partakes more of literary legend than of historical fact. Supposedly, Mahmud initially encouraged Firdusi to complete his epic and to dedicate it to him (Mahmud was a great "collector" of poets, mainly panegyrists, and men of letters, some of whom he forcibly recruited). On receiving it, however, he declined to pay Firdusi the princely sum originally promised, dismissing him with a payment which the poet regarded as insulting. It is not clear whether Mahmud acted thus out of niggardliness or because, as some scholars have suggested, Firdusi's subject matter, the splendors of ancient Iran, offended the ruler's self-esteem as a Turk and the son of a slave. More likely than either explanation is the possibility that Firdusi's enemies at court whispered in the ear of the Sunni Muslim sultan that the poet was a secret Shi'ite.

According to Nezami-ye 'Aruzi, Firdusi, bitterly disappointed at his paltry reward, went to a bathhouse in Ghazna, where he bathed and ordered a cup of sherbet. He then took the sultan's gift and divided it between the bathhouse keeper and the sherbet seller. To offer so public an insult to a ruler was rash in the extreme, and Firdusi promptly fled from Ghazna to Herāt, and thence to Tus and Tabaristan. His pursuers never caught up with him. Perhaps they lost the trail or—more probably—Mahmud called off the hunt, unwilling to go down in history as the persecutor of the greatest poet of the age. Finally, if Nezami is to be believed, Mahmud relented and belatedly made amends by sending to Firdusi a valuable consignment of indigo loaded on the sultan's own camels. As the caravan entered one of the gates of Tabaran, a town in the Tus district where Firdusi had been living, however, the corpse of the poet was being carried out the opposite gate. Firdusi's daughter, a woman "of very lofty spirit," proudly spurned the sultan's gift.

The Iranians have always ranked Firdusi among their greatest poets, along with Jalal al-Din Rumi (1207-1273), Sa'di (c. 1200-1291), Hafiz (c. 1320-c. 1390), and Jami (1414-1492). Unlike these other poets, however, Firdusi displays virtually no interest in contemporary religious issues or values and no trace whatsoever of a mystical calling. Still, his writing is rooted in a strong tradition of personal ethics, tempered by a strain of unmistakable pessimism, both of which are integral to his thematic concerns. The subject matter of the *Shahnamah*, which is composed in metrical rhymed couplets of ten syllables, is the entire history of Iran down to the Arab-Islamic conquests of the mid-seventh century. For the Sassanid period (A.D. 224-651), the epoch preceding the Arab invasions, Firdusi provides detailed narratives, partly legendary and partly historical, derived from both chronicles and oral traditions. Of the long-lived Parthian regime which the Sassanids overthrew, he has almost nothing to say; the same is true with regard to the prior Seleucids and Achaemenids, except for a fantastic episode in which King Darab (Darius) marries a daughter of King Filicus (Philip) of "Rum" (in this instance, Greece) but then sends her back to her father in disgrace. He does not know, however, that she is already pregnant by him and soon to give birth to a child "splendid as the sun," Iskandar (Alexander). Meanwhile, Darab takes a new wife, who provides him with an heir, Dara (also Darius), who eventually succeeds him. In this way, the stage is set for the great duel between Persia and Greece, the Achaemenids and the Macedonians, and also for the inclusion of much colorful material derived from *Iskandar nama* (an Alexander romance often referred to as the *Pseudo-Callisthenes*).

It serves no purpose to look to Firdusi for the early history of Iran, for he does not provide it. Instead, he offers an epic spanning the life histories of two wholly legendary dynasties, the Pishdadian and the Kayanian, redolent with the splendors of mighty monarchs and the heroic deeds of peerless warriors. Here is a gallery of memorable figures: wise, rash, and foolish kings, and their paladins, among whom the most famous is the Iranian Hercules or Roland, the giant Rustam (sometimes spelled Rostam). Action centers upon the ceaseless conflict between the warriors of Iran and Turan, the latter subjects of the malevolent but ultimately tragic King Afrasiyab. Nor is there any lack of romance, such as in the love story of Zal and Rudaba and that of Bijan and Manija. The obsession of the impetuous Sudaba for her stepson, Siyavush, is resonant of the Koranic version of the story of Joseph and Potiphar's wife, as well as of the myth of Phaedra. Finally, in the mortal conflict of Rustam and Sohrab, father and son, there is tragic denouement of a high order (as the Victorian Matthew Arnold was quick to perceive and adapt in his 1853 poem "Sohrab and Rustum"). It is these legendary scenes in the *Shahnamah* which have so endeared it to generations of Iranian readers and audiences.

It is scarcely possible to overestimate the influence of the *Shahnamah*. Rulers and members of the elite vied among themselves to acquire sumptuous manuscripts, finely bound and illustrated. Familiarity with Firdusi's masterpiece, however, was not restricted to the literate. The epic was conceived as much for recitation as for reading, and there eventually emerged a class of professional reciters of the *Shahnamah* (known as *Shahnamah-Khvand*), who were perhaps heirs to a minstrel tradition of Sassanid or even Parthian times. Bards who memorized the entire epic were particularly revered, and a few such have been heard of even in the twentieth century. Recitations took place on festive occasions such as weddings or at the time of the Nuruz (the pre-Islamic New Year celebrations), but reciters also entertained humbler audiences more informally in village teahouses or in caravansaries, where travelers sheltered for the night. Thus, the *Shahnamah* became better known among the general population than any other book (the Koran excepted), influencing ordinary speech and molding popular attitudes and values, as well as contributing to a literary tradition in which it fathered many imitations.

The *Shahnamah* was no less influential in the development of Persian painting. Islam prohibited representational art, especially religious subject matter, an injunction which only the Shi'ites at times disregarded. The *Shahnamah*, however, contained no material which could in any sense be viewed as Islamic, and it was brimful of graphic and picturesque episodes (battles, hunting scenes, durbars, and banquets) which were natural subjects for illustration. Consequently, both in Iran and in those lands influenced by the Persian iconographic tradition, scenes from the *Shahnamah* became favorite subjects for book illustration and miniature painting. Were an inventory to be taken of all surviving Persian miniatures down to the nineteenth century, it is probable that the great majority would consist of scenes from the *Shahnamah*.

Summary

The *Shahnamah* has always held a special place in Iranian hearts. In the twentieth century, nationalists and modernizers seized upon Firdusi's glorification of the remote Iranian past to belabor the "Islamic centuries" between the seventh century Arab conquests and their own day as the source of the obscurantism and backwardness of Iranian society. For such as these, Firdusi provided the model of a distant Golden Age. During the rule of the Pahlavi dynasty (1925-1979), Firdusi's praise for the monarchical tradition of ancient Iran, associated with the concept of *farr* (in Old Persian, the divine favor reserved for kings) and of *hvarna* (the charisma of kingship), provided the government with ready-made propaganda. Thus, Reza Shah Pahlavi ordered the construction of a conspicuous monument on the alleged site of Firdusi's grave, proclaimed in 1934 the one thousandth anniversary of the poet's birth, and issued commemorative postage stamps. Under Mohammad Reza Pahlavi, dramatic scenes from the *Shahnamah*, especially those emphasizing loyalty or gratitude to the monarch, were regularly performed on state-run television. With the advent of the Islamic Revolution, however, Firdusi, the least Islamic among Persian poets, fell from official favor.

Western students of Persian literature have been almost unanimous in praise of Firdusi's genius, the one obvious exception being the English scholar Edward Glanville Browne, who found the *Shahnamah* monotonous and repetitive. More typical was the Czech Iranologist Jan Rypka. The *Shahnamah*, he wrote,

> has become the common property of all Iranians and has contributed in no small measure to the strengthening and consolidation of the national consciousness. For the rest this was the ultimate aim of the poet himself. . . . In depicting the illustrious past the poet appeals for a rebuilding of erstwhile greatness. . . . This call to action lent strength to the nation whenever it had to raise itself up again after disintegration and subjugation.

Bibliography

Browne, Edward G. *A Literary History of Persia*. 4 vols. Cambridge: Cambridge University Press, 1902-1924. This is still the standard account of classical Persian literature, usefully woven into a historical narrative which places authors' lives and works in their contemporary setting. Volume 2 contains much valuable information relating to Firdusi.

Firdusi. *The Epic of the Kings: Shāh-nāma, The National Epic of Persia by Ferdowsi*. Translated by Reuben Levy. London: Routledge and Kegan Paul, 1967. Few translators have dared to tackle the *Shahnamah*, most of them in the nineteenth century. This volume contains Levy's free-flowing prose translation of some of its most famous episodes.

__________. *The Tragedy of Sohrab and Rostam*. Translated by Jerome W. Clinton. Seattle: University of Washington Press, 1988. A verse translation accompanied on facing pages by a recent edition by Russian scholars of the Persian text. The preface is helpful for putting the work into the context of its time.

Huart, Claude, and Henri Massé. "Firdawsī." In *The Encyclopaedia of Islam*, vol. 2. 2d ed. Leiden, Netherlands: E. J. Brill, 1965. This is the best short account of Firdusi and his work. The encyclopedia contains many other entries of interest regarding Islamic writers and their sociopolitical contexts. Includes bibliographies.

Nizami Aruzi Samarqandi. *Revised Translation of the Chahar Maqala ("The Four Discourses")*. Translated by Edward G. Browne. London: Luzac and Co., 1921. These anecdotal accounts of poets, astrologers, and others by a twelfth century belletrist include the earliest surviving biographical information about Firdusi.

Rypka, Jan, with Otakar Klíma and others. *History of Iranian Literature*. Edited by Karl Jahn. Dordrecht, Netherlands: D. Reidel Publishing Co., 1968. Translated from the Czech. Pages 151-166 offer an exceptionally interesting account of Firdusi within the context of the tradition of epic poetry in Iran. The volume includes a map and an extensive bibliography.

Von Grunebaum, Gustave E. "Firdausi's Concept of History." In *Islam: Essays in the Nature and Growth of a Cultural Tradition*. Menasha, Wis.: American Anthropological Association, 1955. This is a stimulating essay by a distinguished Islamicist on Firdusi's vision of the past. This volume is part of the Comparative Studies of Cultures and Civilizations series. Includes bibliographical footnotes.

Yarshater, Ehsan, ed. *Persian Literature*. Albany, N.Y.: State University of New York Press, 1988. Essays of particular interest in this volume cover such topics as early Persian court poetry, the development of epic Persian verse, and Firdusi and the tragic epic. Includes an index and a bibliography.

Gavin R. G. Hambly

SAINT FRANCIS OF ASSISI
Francesco di Pietro di Bernardone

Born: c. 1181; Assisi, Umbria, Italy
Died: October 3, 1226; Assisi, Umbria, Italy
Areas of Achievement: Religion and monasticism
Contribution: Through the rejection of material values and the establishment of the Franciscan Orders, Francis of Assisi contributed to the reform movement of the medieval Church during the early thirteenth century.

Early Life

Francesco di Pietro di Bernardone, better known as Francis of Assisi, was born around 1181 in Assisi, Umbria, Italy. He was the son of Pietro and Pica di Bernardone. His father was a prosperous merchant, and Francis grew up in a comfortable environment and developed an appreciation of life's pleasures. Francis was provided a Latinist education at the school associated with the Church of Saint Giorgio in Assisi. Based on his later demonstrations of knowledge of contemporary French literature and art, and the works of the famous French troubadours in particular, it has been assumed that he received instruction in French language and literature sometime during his formative period. His family's prosperity and his extroverted personality resulted in Francis being recognized as a promising young leader not only in Assisi but throughout Umbria; he was expected to assume a prominent position in the political and economic life of his society.

In about 1202, Francis participated in a war between Perugia and Assisi and was captured and imprisoned; released by the Perugians in 1203, he returned to Assisi in poor health. After a prolonged period of recuperation, he attempted to renew his military career by involving himself in the war (1205-1206) between several northern Italian states and cities against the Holy Roman Empire. At the Appenine town of Spoleto, however, Francis had a mystical experience in which he was bidden to return to Assisi to await news of what he should undertake as his life's work. This experience redirected Francis from secular interests centered on worldly values to a life of poverty and spirituality.

Life's Work

Based on his own later writings and documented conversations, Francis of Assisi continued to have spiritual experiences which directed him toward a new life. At one time, Christ appeared to him, and on another occasion, a voice emanated from the crucifix in the dilapidated Church of Saint Damiano and directed Francis to undertake the reformation and rebuilding of Christ's church. According to Francis, he then returned to his father's shop and took a quantity of cloth, which he sold in a nearby town. Returning to the Church of Saint Damiano, he tried to give the money to the priest, to be used in renovating the building. Pietro di Bernardone reprimanded his son for this action, and hearings before civil and religious leaders occurred. In the end, Francis repudiated his father's values and his connection with his family; he left for the outskirts of Assisi.

Francis began to renovate churches in need of repair and led a life of poverty. While attending Mass at the Chapel of Saint Mary of the Angels in February, 1208, Francis was moved by a reading from the Gospel of Matthew enjoining the active repudiation of worldliness and the need to lead a spiritually based life. Francis began to preach and to gain disciples. In the following year, a reluctant Pope Innocent III approved of his band's simple rule of life and the establishment of the Franciscan Order. Francis and his followers set out to duplicate the selfless life-style of Christ; at the cornerstone of the Franciscan rule were faith and simplicity. Francis' sermons were free of complicated disputations. He maintained that the Franciscan friars should assist others by working in the world rather than being confined to a monastery, that they should care for the sick and the dying, that they should preach the Gospel, and that they should lead lives of poverty and chastity in order to move closer to a Christlike state.

Francis of Assisi extended his new values to a theology of nature, arguing that all aspects of God's creation were interconnected and that man should exist in a state of respect and harmony with all other manifestations of nature. His work "Il cantico delle creature" ("Canticle of Creatures," which has been also been called "The Canticle of the Sun" and "Laudes creaturatum") was an expression of the comprehensive Franciscan worldview in which the natural elements and inanimate physical objects are recognized as integral parts of God's cosmic design.

The Franciscan Order grew rapidly, extending throughout Italy and beyond. By 1215, there were more than five thousand men in the Franciscan Order. In 1212, Francis had established an order for women, named the Poor Clares after its first member, Clara of Assisi. In 1221, Francis set up the Third Order of Franciscan Brothers and Sisters of Penance. During the period from 1212 to the early 1220's, the Franciscan Order grew so rapidly that it required additional structuring to manage its affairs effectively. The position of Vicar of the Order was established; Peter Catanii was the first vicar, but he died shortly after his appointment. Elias of Cortona, who replaced Catanii, did much of the organizational work and managed the day-to-day operations of the order through the 1220's. A new rule, which provided for a period of orientation, training, and review, was developed; it was approved by Pope Honorius III in 1223.

Francis of Assisi dreamed of visiting the Holy Land and evangelizing the Muslims in Spain, but accidents and poor health prohibited these journeys. In 1219, however, he did go to Egypt during a crusade and had an opportunity to preach to a Muslim sultan. According to some accounts, the sultan was so impressed with Francis that he granted him and his companions the right to visit the Holy Land; there is no documentation to substantiate this tale, and it is known that Francis never did visit the Holy Land.

The last years of Francis' life were spent in Assisi and its environs. He had another mystical experience in 1224 during a prolonged fast. In a vision, an angel appeared to Francis and filled him with the experiences of the crucified Christ; the consequence was the appearance of the stigmata on his body. Francis' health declined steadily after 1224. Encroaching blindness was aggravated by a more serious but unspecified medical problem; apparently, the last two years of his life were painful, and medical remedies were applied to no avail. Francis of Assisi died on October 3, 1226, in Assisi. In 1230, his remains were moved from their temporary depository in the Church of Saint Giorgio to the new basilica which had been constructed under the supervision of Elias of Cortona. On July 16, 1228, Francis of Assisi was canonized a saint by Pope Gregory IX.

Summary

Saint Francis of Assisi's life and work were representative of the conflicting forces of his age. Born to wealth and influence and seemingly destined to exercise power, Francis repudiated this inheritance and emerged as the most earnest and visible advocate of reformed values within and outside the Church during the early thirteenth century. Though an unordained layman, Francis of Assisi became the most prominent spokesman for change in the Church. As a leader, he established religious orders which were committed to simplicity in striving to realize the Christian ideal, to be Christlike. The religious orders which Francis founded were not in the monastic tradition, for they did not seek to isolate their members from the world, but, quite to the contrary, they were committed to a mission of evangelism and charity which demanded active public involvement.

Within the medieval Church, the Franciscans emerged as a new alternative for a new age. The popularity of the orders was demonstrated by their rapid growth and expansion and by the papal recognition which was extended to them. The Franciscan Orders have survived and multiplied through the centuries, becoming one of the largest and most influential religious communities in the world. The basilica at Assisi has been maintained and serves as a popular shrine for Catholics as well as others from throughout the world.

One of the most enduring legacies of Francis of Assisi was his exemplary life of simplicity and piety. His emphasis on active life within society and his views on the interdependence of all created beings have inspired subsequent generations to this day.

Bibliography

Daniel-Rops, Henri. *Cathedral and Crusades: Studies of the Medieval*

Church, 1050-1350. 2 vols. Garden City, N.Y.: Doubleday and Co., 1963. Still one of the finest and most readable studies of the Church during an age of corruption and reform. Daniel-Rops discusses the environment, both spiritual and otherwise, of the medieval Church and is sympathetic to the Franciscans.

Fremantle, Anne. *Age of Faith*. New York: Time, 1965. A fine introduction to the period and to the forces which affected the Church of the Middle Ages. Lavishly illustrated with photographs of architecture and artwork of the era, this brief volume is ideal for the general reader. A select bibliography is included.

Gasnick, Roy M. *The Francis Book: A Celebration of the Universal Saint*. New York: Macmillan, 1980. A sympathetic account of Francis of Assisi and the establishment of the Franciscan Order. An adequate bibliography is provided.

Hollister, C. Warren. *Medieval Europe: A Short History*. 5th ed. New York: John Wiley and Sons, 1982. One of the best one-volume scholarly studies of the era. The roles of the Church and the new religious orders are discussed against the backdrop of the emerging political order. Hollister draws upon a wide range of academic research in forming his conclusions.

Iriarte, Lazaro. *History of the Franciscan Order*. Chicago: Franciscan Herald Press, 1983. A partisan but substantial account of the life of Francis of Assisi, the founding of the order, and its subsequent development. Iriarte's work is documented and should not be discounted for its sympathetic bias.

Knowles, David. *Christian Monasticism*. New York: McGraw-Hill Book Co., 1977. This slender but insightful volume offers an analytical and provocative study of monasticism from the primitive church through the medieval period. In addition to the highly readable narrative, Knowles provides statistical data on the emergence of and shifts in monasticism and an excellent bibliography.

Ross, James Bruce, and Mary Martin McLaughlin, eds. *The Portable Medieval Reader*. New York: Viking Press, 1960. This compendium of contemporary sources provides readers with selections which relate to Francis of Assisi and the Franciscans as well as a broad range of other material. Collectively, the excerpts place specific topics in the perspective of other issues.

Taylor, Henry Osborn. *The Medieval Mind: A History of the Development of Thought and Emotion in the Middle Ages*. 4th ed. 2 vols. Cambridge, Mass.: Harvard University Press, 1959. A standard and authoritative work which advances seminal theses on medieval priorities as identified through the intellectual and cultural history of the period. Excellent documentation.

Thompson, James Westfall, and Edgar Nathaniel Johnson. *An Introduction to Medieval Europe*. New York: W. W. Norton and Co., 1937. While clearly dated as a general survey, this book is still noteworthy in its treatment of reform within the medieval Church in general and the impact of the Franciscans in particular.

Tierney, Brian, ed. *The Crisis of Church and State, 1050-1300*. Englewood Cliffs, N.J.: Prentice-Hall, 1964. A collection of essays and sources which shed light on the manifold aspects of the struggle between the universal Church and the rising nation-states during the High and Late Middle Ages.

Zacour, Norman. *An Introduction to Medieval Institutions*. 2d ed. New York: St. Martin's Press, 1979. An insightful and carefully designed study of the structure of medieval society, with significant comments on the role of the Church and the functioning of religious orders within it.

William T. Walker

FREDERICK I BARBAROSSA

Born: c. 1123; Germany
Died: June 10, 1190; Seleucia, Armenia
Area of Achievement: Government
Contribution: For thirty-eight years Frederick ruled over the chaotic area of the Holy Roman Empire. While he failed to unite effectively his German territories with the city-states of northern Italy, he nevertheless imposed his personality and power on a strong German feudal state.

Early Life

Germany in the twelfth century was undergoing enormous social transformation. An increase in the population, unmatched by a corresponding economic revolution, put great pressure on a political structure based largely on personal loyalties. Simultaneously there was a growing division between the secular power of the Holy Roman Emperor and the ecclesiastical power of the Papacy. The Investiture Controversy (the quarrel over whether the pope or the emperor would invest the bishops with their symbol of authority) led Emperor Henry IV to subordinate himself to the pope and ultimately resulted in a compromise at the Concordat of Worms. Still, a bishop had a dual function as secular and spiritual prince, and his strength diminished the potential power of the emperor.

In these tumultuous times, Frederick Barbarossa (a name derived from his red beard) was chosen King of Germany in 1152; he was elected by the princes and bishops of Germany to succeed his uncle Conrad III. The unanimous election of so young a man—he was not yet thirty years old—reflected not only his personal strength and intellect but also, more important, the fact that he was related by blood to the two major families in Germany whose past quarrels had shaken the security of the Empire. The powerful Welf and Staufen families had long dominated German politics, and Frederick's election proved an effective solution to their power struggle. During his long reign he endeavored to centralize government and authority in Germany but, in the end, reestablished in a new and more orderly form the feudalism which caused Germany to lag behind the monarchical development of France and England.

Contemporary busts of Frederick (there are no portraits) show a smiling face with the tight, stylized curls of hair and beard reminiscent of Roman portraiture. Frederick's uncle, the historian Otto of Freising, described the monarch as well-proportioned:

> He is shorter than very tall men, but taller and more noble than men of medium height. His hair is golden, curling a little above his forehead. . . . His eyes are sharp and piercing, his nose well formed, his beard reddish. . . .

In June of 1149, Frederick married Adela von Vohburg, a slightly older woman whose marriage to him reconciled old family quarrels. She was never crowned as queen, apparently because there was little closeness between them. When Frederick discovered that she had committed adultery, it gave him the excuse to dissolve a marriage which meant nothing to him personally and whose political value was of minor significance after he was elected king. Accordingly, he petitioned the pope to have the marriage annulled; the pope, eager to please the emperor, agreed.

When Frederick chose to remarry in 1156, he selected Beatrix, the daughter of Count Rainald, although she was apparently only ten years old at the time. Her appeal was enhanced by lands in Burgundy which she could claim and whose possession was important to Frederick as part of his grand design for the Empire. Their alliance was both politically useful and personally fulfilling. The first of their four sons was born in 1164.

Life's Work

After his election as King of Germany in 1152, Frederick traveled through his kingdom, showing himself to the people (an act of symbolic importance in medieval Germany). He retained the major advisers of Conrad III so that there was, both in appearance and in fact, a continuity of rule. Frederick was then crowned at Aix-la-Chapelle by the Archbishop of Cologne. His next move was to be crowned Holy Roman Emperor by the pope. Meanwhile, Frederick traveled through his kingdom as an arbitrator of conflicting interests, fulfilling one of his expected roles: maintainer of justice. His fame grew as he was successful in settling a variety of disputes.

The pope, Eugenius III, was eager for Frederick to come to Rome, where one of the traditional functions of the emperor was to protect the pope from social upheaval—in this case, a rebellious urban populace in Rome which wanted to establish a republic. Led by Arnold of Brescia, the common people protested the growing wealth of the Church. Frederick's defense of the pope would mean, as well, open war with King Roger II of Sicily (as a result of earlier commitments made by Conrad III). In 1153, Frederick and the pope signed the Treaty of Constance, which promised mutual assistance. (It was after the signing of this treaty that the pope annulled Frederick's first marriage, leaving the way open for a more politically advantageous union.)

The deaths of Pope Eugenius III in 1153 and King Roger of Sicily in 1154 did not deter Frederick from his purpose, and in 1154 he set out on his journey to Rome. He traveled through the tumultuous city-states of northern Italy and at last reached Rome, where he was met by Pope Adrian IV (the only Englishman ever to be pope), whose reputation among the citizens of Rome had worsened. In spite of the unrest, Adrian crowned Frederick Holy Roman Emperor. The new emperor planned his promised war against Sicily, only to discover that his German princes had done all they intended to in

Italy and were eager to return to Germany. The following year Frederick was back in Augsburg, ready to organize new plans for his empire.

In the early years of his rule, Frederick followed closely the traditional policies laid down by Conrad III (alliance with Greece against Sicily and support and defense of the pope). By 1156, however, Frederick was prepared to change directions. He was assisted by one of the major advisers of his reign, Rainald of Dassel, who served as chancellor for eleven years. (It was Rainald who brought the bones of the Three Wise Men from a rebellious Milan and placed them in his own bishopric in Cologne). A change of political direction was also made easier by a treaty of reconciliation between the pope and the new king of Sicily, William I, thus eliminating the need for a war against Sicily.

Frederick sought to claim for himself a more active role in Germany. Traditionally, the emperor was little more than a protector of justice, protecting old customs but without real authority to enact new laws. Frederick hoped to strengthen and enlarge his political power from a geographical base made up of the areas of Swabia and Alsace (where his family estates were centered), Burgundy (which he could claim through Beatrix, his wife), and Lombardy (the northern Italian area traditionally part of the Holy Roman Empire).

In moving to consolidate his empire, Frederick dealt first with troubles in Bavaria between two of his relatives: Henry the Lion (a Welf) and Henry Jasomirgott (a Babenberg). His division of the duchy established a new constitutional concept of a territorial state with its own ruler, who received more real authority and rights than the traditional rulers had held. Frederick actually began to move away from Germany as a power base and centered his new realm on his family lands. He began a program of constructing new castles and improving roads to connect the cities, many of which were founded under his rule. Frederick also encouraged the rise of an administrative class (*ministeriales*) to act as his agents in the governing of his enlarging territories.

Frederick's major problem in consolidating his empire was the territory of Lombardy, where economic development was different from that in his German states. He raised a large army to cross over into Lombardy, and there he came into conflict with the city of Milan. At first Milan became an imperial city, and Frederick participated in a crown-wearing festival which symbolized his embodiment of divine power as emperor. He issued a series of decrees listing the royal rights which belonged to him and declared that the judges and magistrates held their power from him. Opposition to Frederick, however, developed, eventually leading to riots and attempts on his life. In 1160, he took military action against Milan, and after two years the city succumbed to the emperor's rule.

With the death of Pope Adrian in 1159, the empire became even more unstable. Dissensions within the Church led to the election of two popes:

Alexander III and Victor IV (the latter had the support of Frederick and much of the European aristocracy). Both popes were forced to leave Rome, where the citizens were divided in their support. Meanwhile, Alexander excommunicated Victor and his electors. Both popes were consecrated, however, and both continued to claim the spiritual and temporal power of the Papacy. Frederick endeavored to call a council to resolve the dispute, but Alexander refused to participate, claiming that the pope could not be judged by an emperor.

The council was convened without Alexander III and was attended by the Kings of England and France, as well as the major nobles of Europe. In Alexander's absence, the council selected Victor as the legitimate pope, and Victor responded by legitimately excommunicating Alexander and his supporters. Alexander responded by excommunicating Frederick and, in a barrage of propaganda, claimed that Frederick wanted to establish power over the other lords in Europe. Victor, who found it very difficult to appear independent of Frederick, seemed to give credence to these claims.

The organizational problems of the Church became the governmental problems of Frederick, since Milan had been supportive of Alexander. After the fall of Milan to Frederick's forces, Alexander fled to France. Frederick then began negotiations with Louis IV of France for the return of Alexander to Frederick's control. Frederick and Louis met at yet another council which, stacked in Victor's favor, resulted in Victor's being declared pope. Louis, however, changed his mind and refused to accept this settlement. The death of Victor in 1164 was followed by the election of Paschal III, but the highly political nature of his election led even Frederick to oppose him as a legitimate pope.

Frederick returned to Germany from the troubled area of Lombardy. Meanwhile, Alexander, reconciled with the citizens, planned to reenter Rome. Paschal rushed to reach Rome first but failed to beat Alexander to the Holy City. Frederick raised an army to enter Rome and capture Alexander but arrived too late to seize him. Frederick enthroned Paschal, but the triumph was short-lived. An epidemic struck the city and wiped out much of Frederick's army. The remaining forces returned to Germany, only to find revolt in Lombardy among the hostile cities there (long supporters of Alexander). The disaster in Rome, the death of Rainald from the plague there, and the revolt in Lombardy forced Frederick to reevaluate the plan for centralized territorial control he had devised in 1156. That grand design was abandoned, and Frederick sought a new direction for his rule.

In 1168, Paschal died in Rome and was succeeded by Calixtus III. Frederick initially recognized him as pope and promised support but, by 1169, Frederick was prepared to make overtures to Alexander. His first effort broke down over the problems in Lombardy, where revolt against the emperor continued. In 1175, Frederick cut his losses in Lombardy, and, with the

Treaty of Anagni the following year, Germany at last ended the war with Lombardy and also the schism in the Papacy. Frederick and Alexander met in Venice in 1177 for a great festival of reconciliation.

Politically, Frederick now embarked on another program, this one centering on Germany, where he took advantage of the rising tide of feudalism to support the monarchy. Frederick planned to become a feudal king by extending power over as wide an area as possible. With Germany falling nicely into feudal order, Frederick turned again to his Italian territory. New agreements with the cities of Lombardy left Frederick as imperial lord, but with few actual powers, and the cities were left reasonably free to pursue their own goals. Both Alexander and his successor, Lucius III (who became pope in 1181), relied on the military support of Frederick for their positions. Lucius helped to arrange a marriage between Frederick's son Henry and Constance, aunt of the King of Sicily, which was a major diplomatic triumph and a union of once-hostile forces. Lucius died in 1185 and was succeeded by Urban III (from Milan, thus an enemy of Frederick) and later by Gregory VIII, who once again endeavored to incite the Christian kings of Europe to war against the infidel ruler Saladin, who had conquered Jerusalem in 1187.

Frederick decided that conditions at home were calm enough to enable him to join the Third Crusade as the crowning act of his long reign. Since the chief purpose of the emperor was to protect the Church, and the home of the Church was threatened, it seemed logical that he should go to its defense. At this point, also, the eschatological view of history, dominant in the twelfth century, encouraged the Crusade. Apocalyptic prophecy indicated that the last emperor would go to Jerusalem and lay down his crown and scepter at the Mount of Olives, which would signal the rule of the Antichrist and the Second Coming. Thus, at Pentecost, 1188, Frederick took the cross and departed on the Third Crusade (where he was joined by Philip II of France and Richard I the Lion-Hearted of England).

After careful preparation, Frederick and a disciplined army of knights set forth. The politics of the Byzantine land through which he passed often led to clashes, but Frederick continued. In Armenia, near the city of Seleucia, Frederick stopped to drink at the Saleph River, and there he drowned in 1190. His body was taken to Antioch and buried in the cathedral there. Bereft of its strong central ruler, Germany declined into feudal states, and Pope Innocent III emerged as the strongman within the empire.

Summary

The facts of Frederick's tragic death were soon overshadowed by legends which had a powerful influence in Germany history, even during the Nazi era of the twentieth century. According to one legend, Frederick I Barbarossa never really died but was asleep atop the Kyffhäuser Mountain, and one day he would awaken and restore the glory of the German empire. The legend was popular within a hundred years of Frederick's death and, though initially attached to Frederick III, in its final form centered on Frederick I Barbarossa. The cult of Frederick was very important, as the fragmented German states sought to reestablish a German empire in the late nineteenth century.

Frederick Barbarossa was the first emperor to have a modern vision of monarchy, and his efforts to build a strong monarchy anticipated the stirring of German nationalism in the nineteenth century. Frederick was a man whose ideas were ahead of his time, and, had he been able to unify his territorial states (Swabia, Burgundy, and Lombardy), the history of Western Europe would have taken a different path. He failed because of the divided Papacy, the economic turmoil (which made Lombardy particularly difficult to subdue), and the independence of the German nobles.

In his later years, Frederick accepted the limits of his time and, capitalizing on local conditions in Germany, built a strong feudal state. Unquestionably one of the strongest figures of the twelfth century, Frederick cannot be overlooked in either the history of the Holy Roman Empire or the history of Germany.

Bibliography

Barraclough, Geoffrey. *Medieval Germany, 911-1250*. Oxford: Basil Blackwell, 1967. Useful, especially for constitutional issues raised during the reign of Frederick which had an impact on the development of modern Germany.

____________. *The Origins of Modern Germany*. Oxford: Basil Blackwell, 1966. One of the major scholars of the Middle Ages in general (and Germany in particular) examines the rule of Frederick. There is also an excellent discussion of Frederick's effort to establish his government in the state of northern Italy. One of the best short summaries of the life and impact of Frederick.

Heer, Frederick. *The Holy Roman Empire*. Translated by Janet Sondheimer. New York: Praeger Publishers, 1968. One of many surveys of the Holy Roman Empire which, necessarily, focus on the rule of Frederick. This particular study emphasizes the romantic nature of Frederick's rule, especially as viewed with hindsight by later, nationalist Germans charmed with the legends of their medieval past.

Munz, Peter. *Frederick Barbarossa: A Study in Medieval Politics*. Ithaca, N.Y.: Cornell University Press, 1969. The definitive work on Frederick, this study covers in detail Frederick's reign and his different plans for development of the Empire. A splendid analysis of the legends surrounding Frederick and their origins and impact on German history. It includes an extensive bibliography and genealogical table and an index useful for sorting out the persons who influenced Frederick's reign. Extensive footnotes also assist the reader in finding his way through the twelfth century.

Otto of Freising. *The Deeds of Frederick Barbarossa*. Translated by Charles C. Mierow. New York: Columbia University Press, 1953. The major source for information on the life of Frederick. Written during his lifetime by his uncle, it is politically slanted in favor of Frederick. It includes letters from and to the major figures of the day and provides not only useful information but also a wonderful flavor of the language and thought of the twelfth century.

Stubbs, William. *Germany in the Early Middle Ages, 476-1250*. New York: Howard Fertig, 1969. Includes a solid chapter on the reign of Frederick. Emphasis is on his rule, its chronology, and the other major figures who ruled contemporaneously with Frederick.

Carlanna L. Hendrick

FREDERICK II

Born: December 26, 1194; Iesi, near Ancona
Died: December 13, 1250; Castle Fiorentino, Apulia
Area of Achievement: Government
Contribution: An able administrator, Frederick reorganized the government of Sicily to create a centralized monarchy centuries before its time.

Early Life

Frederick II of Hohenstaufen was born at Iesi, west of Ancona. His father was the Emperor Henry VI, and his mother was Constance of Sicily, the daughter of Roger II, King of Sicily. When Frederick was two years old, his father had him elected King of Germany in order to assure an uncontested succession. When Henry died in 1197, his wife assumed the regency, and the following year at Palermo she had her son crowned King of Sicily. The boy king was reared and educated in Sicily, and at fourteen he was declared to be of age. The following year, he married Constance, the daughter of Alfonso II of Aragon and widow of Emerich, King of Hungary.

During Frederick's youth, Germany was in a state of anarchy, with Philip of Swabia and Otto IV struggling for control. The maturing of Frederick and the death of Philip (1208) caused only a minor shift in the civil war north of the Alps. John of England continued to support Otto, and Philip II of France shifted his support to Frederick. The decisive military encounter was the French victory over Otto at Bouvines in July, 1214.

The following year, Frederick was again crowned the German king, this time at Aachen. Frederick had already begun to make concessions to the Church in Germany, and in 1215, in order to win the full support of Pope Innocent III, he vowed to go on a crusade. Five years later, he had the German nobles elect his young son Henry as German king and then went south to Rome, where Pope Honorius III, Innocent's successor, crowned him Holy Roman Emperor on November 22, 1220. To win the favor of the new pope, Frederick had again made lavish promises. He renewed his commitment to take the Cross, promised to aid the faltering Fifth Crusade, and said that he would fight against heresy. He also renounced the union of Germany and Sicily, a lingering fear of successive popes. Despite all of his promises, Frederick remained in Sicily for the next several years.

Life's Work

Frederick's prolonged absence from Sicily had been marked by rebellion and strife. Frederick first restored his authority and then reorganized the administration of the kingdom. He even founded a university at Naples in 1224. Still, the new pope, Gregory IX, was not impressed. He insisted that the emperor make good his promise to lead a crusade to reinstate Christian control over the Holy Land. To encourage him, the pope arranged, in 1225, for the widowed Frederick to marry Isabella, the daughter of John of Brienne, King of Jerusalem, with the understanding that he would have his father-in-law's title once he had conquered the Holy City. Yet the emperor, who was in no hurry, continued to postpone his departure. When at last, in 1227, Frederick did sail from Brindisi, sickness broke out aboard the ships, and the expedition was halted and again postponed. Gregory was enraged, and he excommunicated the emperor.

The pope's ban was not lifted the following year when Frederick again set sail. Reaching Palestine, he was able to achieve his objectives through negotiating rather than fighting. Jerusalem and the surrounding lands, including Bethlehem and Nazareth, were acquired by the treaty signed on February 18, 1229, and he entered the Holy City and was crowned King of Jerusalem on March 18. Having no desire to remain in Palestine, Frederick returned to Italy in June of the same year to deal with a papal army that had invaded his territories in southern Italy and insurrections which had been inspired by Gregory. These affairs were handled with success, and the ban of excommunication was lifted.

For the next few years, Frederick devoted himself to the political and economic reform of his southern Italian kingdom. He strengthened the central administration at the expense of the old Norman feudal system to create a forerunner of the absolute monarchy. In this, he was several centuries before his time. He also brought about reform in the economic structure of the state. He encouraged trade and agriculture, improved roads and built bridges, held annual fairs, and even minted gold coins, which had all but disappeared in most parts of Europe. As a result of his economic policies, the kingdom of Sicily prospered. Still, Frederick's ever-increasing needs, brought on by his continuous efforts to control northern Italy, led to increased taxation. Meanwhile, the German princes were establishing their near independence from imperial control. He had made major concessions to them over the years in order to gain their loyalty and material support for his crusade and wars in Italy. In addition, his oldest son Henry had also made concessions to the German princes which the emperor felt obliged to accept.

Indeed, young Henry was a problem for his father in the 1230's. As king of Germany, he favored the privileges of the towns over those of the princes. When the latter accompanied the emperor on his crusade, Henry took advantage of the their absence to strengthen his own position. Upon their return, however, he was forced to recognize their virtual independence and to submit to the authority of his father, whom he had defied. The prodigal son went to Italy in 1232 and was forgiven after he had sworn allegiance and obedience. Once back in Germany, however, he again rebelled against the emperor, with limited support of the German nobility. This time he went one step further: He allied himself with his father's most persistent and bitter enemy, the Lombard League. Frederick, with the temporary support of Gregory IX, was able to stabilize his position in Italy by 1235, and with only a token force arriving in Germany. The German princes, who had never been strong supporters of King Henry, flocked to the standard of the emperor. With little fighting, the wayward son was forced to submit once again to his father. The situation this time was very much different from what it had been four years earlier. Not only was this the second time that Henry had rebelled against his father, but he had also committed the unforgivable offense of allying himself with the Lombards. In July, 1235, at the diet held in Worms, Henry was removed from his throne and imprisoned at Apulia, where he remained until his death in 1242.

In August of 1235, Frederick, whose second wife, Isabella, had died in 1228 giving birth to their son Conrad, married Isabella, the daughter of King John of England. In 1237, after a successful campaign against Frederick II, Duke of Austria, which led not only to the subjugation of Austria but also to that of Styria and Carenthia, Frederick secured the election of his second son, Conrad, as German king to replace the deposed Henry. The emperor's bastard son Enzo (whom he had with his Cremonese mistress) was also provided with a kingdom. He was married to Adelasia, the heiress of Sardinia and named king of that island.

The emperor was now at the height of his reign, and he was determined to use all of his power and resources to bring northern Italy under imperial authority. Yet Gregory, who recognized the strong influence of the Church, threw his support to the Lombard League. The struggle continued during the last fifteen years of Frederick's reign, with the fortunes of war and diplomacy swaying back and forth. In September, 1237, the emperor defeated the army of the Cortenuova League, and it appeared as if victory was within his grasp. The failure of the siege of Brescia the following year, however, renewed the spirits of Frederick's enemies, and in 1239, Gregory again excommunicated him. The siege of Rome in 1240 was also a failure, and despite the death of Gregory (August, 1241) and the election of Innocent IV in 1243 (Celestine IV had died within months of his election in 1241), the struggle continued.

The new pope proved to be an even more capable adversary than Gregory. He withdrew from Italy and went to Lyons, on the French border, and held a General Council in June, 1245, at which Frederick was deposed and an anti-emperor, Henry Raspe, Landgrave of Thuringia, was elected. The secular German princes, in particular Duke Otto of Bavaria, the father of King Conrad's wife, tended to side with the emperor; it was in Italy that he faced the greatest defections. Even in southern Italy there were rebellions and defections.

In 1246 and 1247, the imperial forces, strengthened by the support of the very capable Enzo, held their own. Frederick and his son even laid siege to the vital city of Parma in 1247. Then, while the emperor was convalescing from an illness, an army sallied forth from the besieged city and destroyed the imperial army (February, 1248). This defeat was followed in May, 1249, by the defeat and capture of Enzo at La Fossalta by a Bolognese army. With this catastrophe, the hope of victory over the Lombard League came to an end. Frederick, who had never fully regained his health, retired to southern Italy, where he died at the Castle Fiorentino, in Apulia, on December 13, 1250. He was buried in the cathedral of Palermo.

Summary

The reign of Frederick II must be considered a failure. Of his many accomplishments, few survived even his own life span. The Holy Roman Empire would exist primarily on paper and in the minds of those who claimed its title. The German princes had gained virtual independence from the German king and emperor. Northern Italy continued in a state of anarchy for the next three hundred years, with neither kings nor emperors nor popes able to exercise domination except for the briefest periods of time. The kingdom of Sicily, where Frederick had been the most successful in creating a centralized monarchy with an enviable economy, went into decline following the emperor's death. It had been the site of Frederick's finest achievements and the best example of his administrative abilities.

The power and influence of the Church had not been strengthened during Frederick's reign, but neither had they been noticeably weakened. The pontificate of Innocent III is frequently noted as the high point of the medieval Papacy, but Frederick, despite his near-perpetual struggle with successive popes, did not triumph over the Church. In fact, the positions of both the emperor and the Papacy declined in the first half of the twelfth century. It was the secular princes and the cities of Germany which emerged stronger north of the Alps, while in northern Italy, the independent city-states were taking shape. Finally, it should be noted that the death of Frederick II heralded the demise of the house of Hohenstaufen.

Bibliography

Fisher, Herbert. *The Medieval Empire*. 2 vols. New York: AMS Press, 1969. This work on medieval Europe, first published in 1898, is organized topically and does not flow chronologically in a story form. Rather than dividing the Middle Ages into time periods or the reigns of monarchs and popes, the chapters are organized around themes such as imperial finance, the German nobility, culture, the emperors, and the city of Rome. It assumes that the reader is familiar with the chronology of the period.

Kanlorowicz, Ernst. *Frederick the Second, 1194-1250*. Translated by E. O. Lorimer. New York: Richard R. Smith, 1931. Translated from the original German, this 680-page study of Frederick II is the most detailed and thorough account available in the English language. It contains an excellent index and a summary of sources, which takes the form of a brief bibliographical essay.

Mann, Horace K. *The Lives of the Popes in the Middle Ages*. 10 vols. London: Kegan Paul, Trench, Trübner, and Co., 1925. This work, while centering on the popes, has much information on Frederick II. The man and his reign, as well as the institutions of the German monarchy and the Holy Roman Empire, are presented from the point of view of the Papacy. It is very good on Innocent III and young Frederick, as well as on Honorius III, Gregory IX, and the mature emperor.

Setton, Kenneth Meyer, ed. *A History of the Crusades*. Vol. 2, *The Late Crusades, 1189-1311*, edited by Robert Lee Wolff and Henry W. Hazard. Madison: University of Wisconsin Press, 1969. The second volume of this fine six-volume study of the Crusades devotes chapter 12 to the crusade of Frederick II. This chapter, written by Thomas C. Van Cleve, is a thorough account of Frederick's expedition to the Near East; it also deals with the emperor's problems back in Europe to the extent that they influenced the crusade.

Tanner, J. R., C. W. Previté-Orton, and Z. N. Brooke, eds. *The Cambridge Medieval History*. Vol. 6, *Victory of the Papacy*. Cambridge: Cambridge University Press, 1957. The first five chapters are dedicated to central Europe, including Italy, in the first half of the thirteenth century. Chapters 1 and 2 lay the foundation for the reign of Frederick II by dealing with Innocent III and the struggle for control of Germany during Frederick's youth. The next three chapters center on Frederick as King of Germany and the Holy Roman Empire. This work is excellent on the political history and the relations between church and state.

Thompson, James Westfall. *Feudal Germany*. Vol. 1. New York: Frederick Ungar Publishing Co., 1962. In this work, first published in 1928, Thompson treats medieval German history primarily in terms of the relationship of church and state. It is the intrigues and conflicts between Frederick II and Popes Innocent III, Honorius III, and Gregory IX that appeal to the author.

John G. Gallaher

JEAN FROISSART

Born: 1337?; Valenciennes, Hainaut, France
Died: c. 1404; Chimay, Belgium
Area of Achievement: Historiography
Contribution: Froissart was a seminal figure in fourteenth century European historiography. In his *Chronicles*, he offered a vivid panorama of an age in transition that relied for its inspiration on waning codes of chivalry and a growing spirit of Humanism.

Early Life

Jean Froissart, the son of a painter of arms, received a clerical education and entered the service of Margaret of Hainaut sometime between 1350 and her death in 1356. This was the first of many court appointments that enabled him to establish a network of contacts in aristocratic circles, primarily in France and the Low Countries. In 1362, he went to England in order to serve as secretary to Queen Philippa, wife of Edward III. He remained in her entourage as court poet until 1369, during which time he traveled to Scotland with King David II, to France and Spain with Edward, the Black Prince, and to Italy in the bridal party of Lionel, Duke of Clarence, who married Yolanda Visconti of Milan in April, 1368. It was on this trip through Italy, as he visited Ferrara, Bologna, and Rome, that Froissart apparently made the acquaintance of Geoffrey Chaucer, Giovanni Boccaccio, and Petrarch.

Upon his arrival in England, Froissart presented to the court a verse chronicle of the Battle of Poitiers which had been warmly praised by Robert of Namur, Lord of Beaufort and nephew to Queen Philippa. Froissart's early poetry was popular at the court and two works in particular, "L'Éspinette amoureuse" and "Le Joli Buisson de jeunesse," contain allusions to his childhood. In addition to long narrative poetry, he produced short poems with fixed rhyme patterns in the tradition of Guillaume de Machaut, as well as *lais*, *rondeaux*, and *ballades*, before concentrating on what became his principal literary achievement—the four books entitled *Chroniques de France, d'Engleterre, d'Éscoce, de Bretaigne, d'Espaigne, d'Italie, de Flandres et d'Alemaigne* (1373-1410; *The Chronycles of Englande, Fraunce, Spayne . . .*, 1523-1525, better known as *Chronicles*).

Froissart learned the art of chronicle writing from Jean le Bel, canon of Liège, whose example he followed in relying not only upon original documents but also upon eyewitness accounts and interviews. Froissart was essentially interested in passing the traditions of chivalry to succeeding generations. Once his reputation was established, members of the aristocracy sought to provide him with the financial resources and protection necessary to gather research material. As a result, his writing reflects his patrons' system of values. He was ordained sometime after leaving England and, under the patronage of Wenceslas of Luxembourg, Duke of Brabant, he obtained a sinecure as rector of Les Estinnes-au-Mont, where he remained for approximately ten years.

Life's Work

Froissart's *Chronicles* was widely reproduced throughout the fifteenth century, and numerous manuscripts have been preserved. Two of them include paintings made by Froissart himself that show him presenting a copy of the work to aristocratic patrons. Even though he was a priest, Froissart was completely at ease in sophisticated society, and his writing accurately depicts the mannerisms and idiosyncrasies in speech and dress that characterize the period.

In writing *Chronicles*, Froissart was carrying on a French tradition of secular historiography that began with the Crusades and continued into the fifteenth century in the works of Georges Chastellain and Philippe de Commynes. The primary concern of these scholars was to preserve the memorable events of the Hundred Years' War. Froissart classified himself as a historian, not merely a chronicler. The distinction he makes between chronicle and history is based on the amount of information supplied. Chronicles, particularly those following the thirteenth century annalist school established at the monastery of Saint-Denis, present a fairly simplified narrative account, whereas history demands depth and detailed description.

Froissart's *Chronicles* covers significant events in European history from 1326 until 1400. The first volume, completed before 1371, begins with the coronation of Edward III and the accession of Philip of Valois to the crown of France, thus setting the stage for the Hundred Years' War. Book 1 was later revised considerably and its scope was extended to include events up to 1379. Since Froissart annotated book 1 throughout his life, it serves as a valuable indicator of his development as a historian and provides detailed information about his methods of composition.

Book 2, written between 1385 and 1388, recapitulates the events of the last three years of the preceding volume, adding new information, and concludes with the Treaty of Tournai (December, 1385) between Ghent and Philip the Bold, Duke of Burgundy. After the death of Wenceslas in 1384, Froissart became chaplain to Guy de Châtillon, Count of Blois, in whose honor he wrote numerous pastoral poems. In 1388, Froissart visited the court of Gaston Phoebus, Count of Foix, near the Spanish border in Béarn, in order to obtain information concerning wars in Spain and Portugal. This journey, in particular, testifies to the vigorous health that Froissart enjoyed; he had to endure numerous hardships while traveling for several months over difficult terrain. Froissart's curiosity was relentless, and he worked late into the night recording from memory conversations with knights and dignitaries.

Book 3, finished in 1392, relates events that had occurred since 1382, but it gives a fuller account of them. This work ends in 1389 with a three-year truce concluded between France and England, and it anticipates the entry into Paris of Isabella of Bavaria as Queen of France. In his study of the political events in Portugal between 1383 and 1385 that led to the invasion by John of Gaunt, Duke of Lancaster, Froissart made considerable use of Portuguese narrative sources and anecdotal information provided by Gascon knights at Orthez who had served under Edmund Cambridge, Duke of York.

The first fifty chapters of book 4 follow closely upon the material of book 3 as Froissart reexamined the political machinery of France under Charles VI. In 1392, a series of truces between France and England was announced and Froissart took advantage of this opportunity to visit England for three months, under the patronage of William, Count of Ostrevant, cousin to Richard II. Froissart was well received by the English king, but he felt uncomfortable in what he sensed was a highly unstable environment. Book 4 recounts the confusion in England leading to the deposition of Richard, who—despite his tragic ineffectiveness—had maintained an uneasy peace between England and France. *Chronicles* concludes with the death of Richard and the succession of Henry IV, the first of the Lancastrian dynasty, to the English throne. Internal evidence suggests that Froissart composed the account of his journey to England in the months before his death in 1404, while serving as treasurer and canon of the church at Chimay.

Even though Froissart was a historian of chivalry, his *Chronicles* does not constitute a formal history of the aristocracy. In his attempt to demonstrate the relative superiority of the nobility, he used a process of selection; in this way, he was able to isolate significant aspects of gallantry and heroism. Hence he overlooked issues that attracted the attention of other chroniclers: administration of estates, enactment of laws, and tax collection. Nevertheless, Froissart commented openly on French policy during the reign of Charles V, on the relationship between the French monarchy and the vassals of Brittany and Flanders, and on the acute political intrigue found in all governments.

Chronicles was not written as a personal memoir—a form popular with other compilers. Nevertheless, Froissart did include numerous authorial injunctions in his narration. In these usually brief personal entries, he often shared his judgment of the events under discussion, thus creating a bond between chronicler and reader rarely achieved in medieval French prose. In addition, these interventions reveal the techniques of composition that resulted in the independent redactions found in the variant manuscripts of the first two volumes. The mobility evident in these texts is most likely the result of his collaboration with scribes, who may have played a major role in the elaboration of certain episodes. The form of *Chronicles* is derivative of the Arthurian romances, which also include superimposed accounts.

Froissart was an insightful observer of military warfare. One of his intentions was to give a faithful account of the ways in which castles and towns were attacked. He commanded a wide military vocabulary, and his description of siege warfare and pitched battles is graphically detailed in the light of the fact that fourteenth century combat was undergoing a significant change. The religious zeal of the early Crusades and the tradition of feudal loyalty had lost their vitality. Warriors were primarily motivated by personal honor or monetary gain through ransom. One-to-one encounters on horseback no longer had the advantage over the use of well-disciplined soldiers equipped with crossbows, longbows, and knives. Froissart's saga of military exploits naturally stresses individual action, yet his accounts make it clear that in large engagements the victor was usually the side that managed some degree of coordinated tactics. Froissart's astute analysis of tactical warfare and individual heroics lends extraordinary depth to the narrations of the most famous battles of the fourteenth century: Poitiers, Crécy-en-Ponthieu, and Nicopolis.

Summary

Froissart's *Chronicles* benefited greatly from the advent of the printing press. From 1495 to 1520, the work went through at least ten editions. The appearance of Johannes Sleidanus' Latin abridgment in 1537—which was, in turn, translated into English, French, and Dutch—made the work available to Humanist scholars and aristocratic readers across Europe, who considered it prestigious to own a copy. By the middle of the sixteenth century, Froissart's *Chronicles* dominated all narratives of the first half of the Hundred Years' War. The vogue for Froissart reached its peak in 1850, when a statue in his honor was erected in Valenciennes.

Froissart's writing adumbrated the decline of chivalry as the concept of courtesy degenerated into greed and meaningless pageantry. His description of the tournament held at Smithfield in 1390 under the aegis of Richard II implies that courtesy had become a code of etiquette observed by members of the upper class in dealing with one another; it was no longer associated with the protection of the weak by the strong.

Froissart continually reminded his audience that his purpose in compiling the chronicles was to illustrate "les grans merveilles et les biaux faits d'armes" (heroic exploits and military prowess). He accomplished this aim with astonishing regularity despite errors in topology and inconsistencies in dating. Causality is not a significant feature except insofar as the causes of events are personalized. *Chronicles* does not attempt to suggest the operation of historical principles that guide the course of events. Moreover, a certain cohesion is gained from this restriction. This emphasis on human factors, along with Froissart's objectivity, political acumen, variety, and poetic effects, gives *Chronicles* a cosmopolitan flavor that makes the full-blown phenomenon seem less austere and more circumscribed than that produced by clerical chroniclers.

Froissart rarely took sides in the conflicts of knights, although in the evolution of *Chronicles* there are signs of a shift in sympathy from the English to the French and, in book 4, to the Burgundian. He consistently chose to accentuate moderation as an ideal, exemplified by the conduct of Philip the Bold. Even though Edward, the Black Prince, was the hero of the Battle of Poitiers, Froissart criticized the brutality of his treatment of the burghers of Calais and the massacre of civilians at Limoges. In general, Froissart was concerned with deeds and actions, not with biography. Because of his accomplished literary talent, the portraits of the protagonists of *Chronicles* are imbued with a legendary quality.

Froissart often invoked Providence to justify the outcome of events. His philosophical observations reveal a conception of social order based on the controls exerted by a just prince who watches over the commonweal. His accounts of the Jacquerie movement in France in 1358 and the English Peasants' Revolt of 1381 clearly indicate that, in his opinion, urban disintegration was a threat to national stability. Nevertheless, his portrayal of John Ball, the vagrant priest who incited the Peasants' Revolt, conveys a well-balanced appraisal of lower-class misery.

This objectivity is also noted in Froissart's attitude toward the Papal Schism, which he treated as a political issue—the failure of diplomacy on the part of Charles V, who sided with the French cardinals. Froissart's ability to synthesize epic conflicts, like the struggle for hegemony in Western Europe between the Plantagenet and Valois dynasties, gives *Chronicles* its distinctive pedigree. The comparison of the last Crusade, which ended in the defeat of the French at Nicopolis, to the eleventh century French epic *Chanson de Roland* (*Song of Roland*) implies that Froissart understood that the history of Europe was irrevocably determined. The scope and dynamism of Froissart's observations and his effort to re-create a mental and social tableau of fourteenth century life have contributed to the endurance of his reputation as a narrative historian who compares favorably to Herodotus.

Bibliography

Archambault, Paul. *Seven French Chroniclers: Witnesses to History*. Syracuse, N.Y.: Syracuse University Press, 1974. This work contains an instructive essay on Froissart that places him within the context of the French annalist tradition and delineates the trajectory of French chronicle writing from 1200 to 1500, demonstrating that Froissart's emergence coincided with a transitional phase in secular historiography.

Coulton, George Gordon. *The Chroniclers of European Chivalry*. Reprint. Philadelphia: Richard West, 1978. Even though Coulton's view of Froissart as an apologist for a retrograde form of chivalry has been superseded by later critics, this work offers a compelling analysis of Froissart's keen interest in the history of the Low Countries. Coulton points out that Froissart was correct in perceiving Flanders as the focal point of the Anglo-French rivalry.

Dahmus, Joseph. *Seven Medieval Historians*. Chicago: Nelson-Hall Publishers, 1982. The chapter on Froissart includes generous extracts from *Chronicles*. Well researched and fairly comprehensive, this is an important study of the way in which Froissart conceived of history as a conflict of interests among individuals of prominent rank and prestige.

Fowler, Kenneth. *The Age of Plantagenet and Valois: The Struggle for Supremacy, 1328-1498*. New York: G. P. Putnam's Sons, 1967. Fowler attempts to explain the numerous complexities of war neurosis during the fourteenth and fifteenth centuries and includes an informative discussion of the social and artistic life of France, England, and Burgundy. Excellent illustrations and a generous bibliography, but unfortunately without explanatory notes.

Palmer, J. J. N., ed. *Froissart: Historian*. Totowa, N.J.: Rowan and Littlefield, 1981. The ten chapters, two written in French, constitute a unified attempt to exonerate Froissart's reputation from the disparagement inflicted upon it by twentieth century practitioners of the scientific school of criticism. The cumulative effect of this work represents an assessment of the value of *Chronicles* in the light of modern historical scholarship. Maps, tables, detailed notes, and an extensive bibliography.

Shears, Frederick S. *Froissart: Chronicler and Poet*. Folcroft, Pa.: Folcroft Library Editions, 1930. The definitive biography, although perhaps outdated as a result of subsequent scholarship. Shears explores the connection between Froissart's fourteen-thousand-line poetic masterpiece of 1370, *Méliador*, and the literary style of the *Chronicles*. A sympathetic defense of Froissart's proficiency as a historian.

Tuchman, Barbara W. *A Distant Mirror: The Calamitous Fourteenth Century*. New York: Alfred A. Knopf, 1978. This work is a spirited and kaleidoscopic presentation of the life and times of Enguerrand VII de Coucy, son-in-law of Edward III of England. Tuchman contends that Coucy was one of Froissart's patrons; that explains the elevated status accorded to him in *Chronicles*. A brilliantly conceived work with numerous illustrations, extensive notes, and an impressive bibliography.

Robert J. Frail

FUJIWARA MICHINAGA

Born: 966; Kyoto, Japan
Died: January 3, 1028; Kyoto, Japan
Area of Achievement: Government
Contribution: The greatest statesman of the Heian period, Michinaga maintained absolute control of the throne and court for thirty years and brought the Fujiwara family to the height of its power. He epitomizes Japanese leadership during the formative period of Japanese cultural development.

Early Life

Michinaga was born into the powerful Fujiwara family, the fifth son of Fujiwara Kaneie, who served as Great Minister of the Right from 978 to 986 and as regent from 986 until his death in 990. The Fujiwara family had provided the principal support system for the imperial family since 645 and by the end of the eighth century had succeeded to the highest posts and greatest power in the imperial court; beginning with Kaneie, who consolidated the family's power, a Fujiwara would occupy the regency for generations. The regency was important, for it preserved the imperial house and protected the throne. While their power might have been overwhelming, the Fujiwara leaders were sensible enough to recognize that the prestige of their clan derived not only from their own talents but from their blood connection with the reigning house as well. Both factors tended to perpetuate the monarchy, despite its impotence.

Although few details are known about Michinaga's early life, it is not surprising that at the age of fourteen, in 980, Michinaga received the office of Lesser Commander of the Imperial Guards of the Left. This office carried with it Junior Fifth Rank, Lower Grade, which was a relatively high distinction for a man of Michinaga's age. It was natural for him to rise rapidly in rank, and at the age of twenty-one, in 987, he became Acting Middle Counselor and Minister of the Left. Then, in 992, he was named Master of the Empress' Household, with Junior Second Rank. It is clear that nothing was left to chance in his education and training, for he excelled, standing head and shoulders above others at court, particularly in Chinese studies, calligraphy, poetry, archery, and horsemanship.

Michinaga had two older brothers, Fujiwara Michitaka and Fujiwara Michikane, in line ahead of him for higher positions, and other relatives also competed with him for higher posts at court; thus, Michinaga was not expected to rise much further in the hierarchy of the court administration.

Michinaga was a handsome man, distinctive in his words and actions. People of his time commented on his vigor, boldness, and resourcefulness. According to tradition, he stalked his rival, Korechika, beating him in an archery contest and embarrassing him when he was dawdling by the carriage of the Retired Empress Akiko (Michinaga's sister). It is said that Michinaga had his horsemen whip his horses into some tents that Korechika had erected during a court festival.

When Kaneie died in 990, Michitaka succeeded him as regent. He became seriously ill in 995 and, before dying, handed over the regency to his brother, Michikane, who died seven days later. Michinaga then became head of the Fujiwara family and was appointed both Minister of the Right and Examiner of Imperial Documents, an honorary title of great prestige. By 996, Michinaga enjoyed uncontested political dominance.

Life's Work

Michinaga seems to have given Japan a strict and able administration, exercising the powers of regent without assuming the post which his father and brothers held. He felt no need to take the highest rank, although any office in the land would have been his for the asking. He helped to establish a precedent in this regard, for the most powerful rulers in later Japanese history not only allowed sovereignty to remain with the emperor but also were themselves content to occupy relatively modest posts in the hierarchy. Before becoming a monk, Michinaga finally served as regent for two years, from 1016 to 1017, when his grandson became emperor. Entry into the religious life, however, did not mean the end of his political career. By giving up his official posts and having his son, Yorimichi, appointed regent, Michinaga was, in fact, able to devote even more of his energy to the exercise of power during the last ten years of his life.

Although Michinaga was the leading statesman of the Heian period, not much more is known about the man than the emperors he was supposed to serve. There is no extant portrait of Michinaga, and the personal touches in contemporary records are not sufficient to produce any well-rounded picture. This is not because he had a self-effacing nature. Indeed, modesty was not one of his virtues. Michinaga had won the endemic struggle for power within the Fujiwara family—a contest between individuals, not a clash about issues. What concerned a member of the ruling aristocracy was the acquisition of a supreme office for himself and his immediate kin. Having acquired such an office and its many delightful trappings, one was to hold it against all comers. What determined appointments was the support given to the leader who eventually won the power struggle, not administrative ability. Because none of the Fujiwara leaders can be identified with any concrete policy or constructive public service, these statesmen do not emerge as distinct individuals. (This is true even of those who were most prominent during the period, such as Michinaga.) They are usually differentiated in terms of their relative strength of ambition and skill at political intrigue.

Michinaga, however, was a man of remarkable and exceptional gifts who thought and acted with a thoroughness on a generous scale and a focus on the reality of power. Control of three major power groups formed the basis of the political stability that Michinaga maintained to the end of his life. He continued his family's policy of extensive intermarriage with the imperial house. He was generous toward his allies and his rivals, a policy that gained for him widespread support among court officials. He allied himself with the Seiwa Genji branch of the Minamoto family to maintain law and order in the capital region and expand the landholdings and wealth of the Fujiwara throughout the country.

In establishing his position, Michinaga was greatly helped by having among his fourteen children several outstandingly intelligent and attractive daughters, and he used them to forge the strongest possible link with the imperial family. Four of his daughters were married to emperors. His daughter Akiko, at the age of eleven, in 999, was married to the reigning emperor, Ichijo. She soon became the emperor's favorite, and together they had two sons. Although Emperor Sanjō, who was the son of Emperor Reizei, succeeded Ichijo when he died in 1011, Akiko's two children followed him as the Emperors Go-Ichijo (1016-1036) and Go-Suzaku (1036-1045). Such was the pressure upon the emperors to marry Fujiwara women selected for them by Michinaga that Sanjō married Michinaga's second daughter, Go-Ichijo married the third (who was his aunt), and Go-Suzaku married the fourth (his aunt also). Michinaga's last daughter was given to a son of Sanjō, the heir presumptive (who was already married), to cover all possible situations. Clearly, Michinaga was unscrupulous in working for the interests of his own family.

Having a deep understanding of human nature, Michinaga knew how to use friends and win over enemies, and that gave him clout with court officials, who recognized that he had a firm hold on his own temper. Michinaga liked to do things on a large scale and lavished untold sums on building shrines and chapels and on Buddhist services in which thousands of monks took part. The building and dedication of the Hōjō-ji, a Jōdo temple, was a brilliant display of Michinaga's wealth and power. The Heian aristocracy was much addicted to color and pageantry and benefited from Michinaga's efforts to infuse the yearly round of ceremonies with the beauty and elegance that were so important in almost every part of their lives. He also accumulated great wealth by acquiring manorial rights over land commended to him for protection and substantially rewarding those courtiers who were involved in the process.

At the same time, Michinaga could see that Fujiwara private interests were not consistent with a just administration of the affairs of the countryside and that the provincial gentry were growing more conscious of their own strength. Being aware of changes taking place in the country, he foresaw the rise of the military families, and early in his career he made up his mind to cultivate some of the leading warriors, whom he could then trust to support him in case of need. He chose certain members of the Minamoto clan by whose talents he was impressed. It was their presence in the background that enabled him to defeat or intimidate his rivals. Moreover, since the metropolitan police force was incapable of preserving peace, these warriors could be relied upon by Michinaga when he needed them to bring order and security to the capital. For their part, the warriors, working with Michinaga, were able to expand their own tax-free estates while at the same time aiding Michinaga in increasing Fujiwara landholdings throughout the country.

Meanwhile, in the metropolis, where the Fujiwara were dictators of taste and fashion, there flourished a society dedicated to elegant pursuits and happily insulated from the shocks of common life. It was a society devoted to the pursuit of beauty to a degree rarely paralleled in the history of civilization. Michinaga was a patron of architecture, painting, sculpture, music, and literature, and his influence on the development of Japanese culture has been marked.

Summary

The formula for greatness gleaned from Fujiwara Michinaga's life might be summarized thus: Be born to a powerful family and have a handsome and personable appearance, a flair for spectacular actions, talents highly regarded by the society of the day, a certain ruthlessness, and a liberal sprinkling of good fortune. As priest, administrator, poet, and connoisseur of the good life, Michinaga carried the Fujiwara family to its highest point. A patron of arts and letters, Michinaga encouraged the preservation of history, literature, and the Japanese spirit from the distant past to the present. More has been written on him, both fact and fiction, than on any other figure in Japanese history. In an age when provincial war lords' influence was rapidly growing and the Fujiwara power base began to wane, Michinaga was able not only to hold subversive forces in check but also to carry the Fujiwaras to heights of power and glory by sheer political virtuosity.

Bibliography

Morris, Ivan. *The World of the Shining Prince: Court Life in Ancient Japan*. Baltimore: Penguin Books, 1964. Indispensable for understanding the life of the Heian period. Contains much information on the Fujiwara family and Michinaga in particular.

McCullough, Helen Craig, trans. *Okagami, the Great Mirror: Fujiwara Michinaga and His Times*. Princeton, N.J.: Princeton University Press, 1980. Another rendition of the same text.

McCullough, William, and Helen C. McCullough, trans. *A Tale of Flowering Fortunes: Annals of Japanese Aristocratic Life in the Heian Period*. 2 vols. Stanford, Calif.: Stanford University Press, 1980. Marvelous translation of the *Eiga monogatari* (c. 1092; known by other scholars as *Tales of Glory*). Two-thirds of the work written by a lady-in-waiting to the Empress Akiko is a glorification of Fujiwara Michinaga and has constantly been referred to by all scholars working in the field.

Omori, Annie S., and Koichi Doi. *Diaries of Court Ladies of Old Japan*. Boston: Houghton Mifflin Co., 1920. Contains three diaries of this period, one of which, "The Diary of Murasaki Shikibu," has an insight into the character of Michinaga in particular.

Sansom, George. *A History of Japan to 1334*. Stanford, Calif.: Stanford University Press, 1958. The section on the Fujiwara, and Michinaga in particular, is a highly respected source.

Yamagiwa, Joseph K., trans. *The Okagami: A Japanese Historical Tale*. Rutland, Vt.: Charles E. Tuttle Co., 1966. Written in the eleventh century, the work of an unknown hand, it covers Japanese history from 850 to 1025. Appendix 1 is a constructed biography of Michinaga, pieced together from various sections throughout the text. Contains an excellent genealogical chart of the Fujiwara and imperial families.

Edwin L. Neville, Jr.

SAINT FULBERT OF CHARTRES

Born: c. 960; Rome, Italy
Died: April 10, 1028; Chartres, France
Areas of Achievement: Education and church reform
Contribution: Fulbert was founder of the cathedral school at Chartres, whose curriculum was based on the seven liberal arts, thus producing the twelfth century renaissance and Christian humanism.

Early Life

The eleventh century must be characterized as a time of religious zeal and reform. The much-needed reform arose from the era of the "pornographic papacy," as historians have sometimes referred to the tenth century Church. The reform spirit created, in the minds of many, a strong commitment to support traditional theology, monastic conservatism, and the founding of such reforming movements as the Cluniac and later the Cistercian. At the same time, new knowledge from the Arabic world, particularly Spain, and the secular demands of both political and urban revival recommended the use of reason to treat the realities of the world. This viewpoint created a dynamic tension in the eleventh century and introduced several problems that would occupy intellectual life for the next two centuries. No school was more deeply involved in this debate than the one at Chartres, founded by Fulbert.

The eleventh century thus marks the awakening of the medieval mind. The first person in the history of this awakening was Gerbert of Aurillac, who taught at the cathedral school at Reims around 972; he reigned as Pope Sylvester II until his death in 1003. In his acceptance of the dialectical method, his interest in mathematics, and his familiarity with Arabic sources acquired during his stay in Catalonia, Gerbert heralded the new era of intellectual curiosity and dynamic expansion that characterized the High Middle Ages (1000-1300). Equally significant in this creation of the medieval mind was Fulbert of Chartres, one of Gerbert's outstanding students at Reims.

Although it is known that Fulbert was born in Rome about 960, not much information is available about his youth, his family, or his education. It is known, however, that Fulbert studied under Gerbert at Reims sometime between 972 and 990. After his stay at Reims and prior to going to Chartres, Fulbert spent time as a physician. He was practical rather than theoretical in his approach, and his treatment was characterized by his concern for the overall health of the patient rather than a specific ailment. Later, Fulbert would teach medicine, specifically the treatment of diseases, surgery, and pharmacology, all of which he is believed to have learned from Gerbert, who had first learned the practice in Catalonia.

Life's Work

In 990, when he was about twenty-seven, Fulbert appeared in Chartres, where he founded and was the first master of the cathedral school. From this school would emerge many of the great thinkers of the eleventh century. Here too was the birthplace of the twelfth century renaissance and Christian humanism. While there were many schools founded during the eleventh century, none could claim the preeminence of Chartres. After his outstandingly successful career as a teacher, the Church appointed Fulbert to serve as the Bishop of Chartres (1006-1028), a particularly prestigious position, for Chartres was a shrine to the Virgin and a popular pilgrimage center to which many miracles were attributed. Fulbert's temperament suited the assignment, as he was deeply devout and a man of saintly patience. He remained in this office until his death in 1028.

Fulbert's life work clearly began and ended with his teaching in Chartres. It was at Chartres that the humanist movement developed to full flower, epitomized in the thought and writings of another great Bishop of Chartres, John of Salisbury, a man as deeply committed to the liberal arts as Fulbert. Elegance returned to Latin as all available classics were studied, including Arabic translations of Aristotle, the Neoplatonists, and some minor works of Plato. Philosophically, Fulbert was a humanist and a Platonist. He was also a man who maintained order and was practical; he was in tune with the needs of his society and was knowledgeable about the world around him. Fulbert's awareness of contemporary affairs was astute; in particular, he understood the operations of the socioeconomic structure, including the intricacies of feudalism.

In Fulbert's day, the cathedral schools were new institutions, his being one of the first. These schools were therefore not bound by custom and tradition, leaving them free to follow new lines of thought and inquiry developed in the new methodologies. Fulbert instigated the teaching traditions that would be continued by subsequent generations of Chartres teachers. Significant among these traditions was Fulbert's insistence that the proper role of a teacher was to encourage the development of the student's best qualities. He also set the tradition of great loyalty and an affectionate relationship between teacher and student, which gave to medieval education its particular uniqueness, strength, and vitality. R.W. Southern, the renowned Oxford medieval scholar, has called Chartres the greatest of all the cathedral schools. He attributes its excellence to the wise foundation instituted by Fulbert; the curriculum established at Chartres became the model for that century.

The academic program reflected Fulbert's own interests and training: science, medicine, theology, the Scriptures, and especially classical literature. Despite the literary and philosophical emphasis in the curriculum, study still focused on the mysteries of the faith, with the Scriptures and the writings of the church fathers accepted as supreme authority. Remaining faithful to his religious beliefs, Fulbert insisted that when the power of human reason failed to comprehend the divine creation and order of things, it should surrender and cease to look for a reasonable definition. Fulbert's curriculum, however, opened the door to a new confidence in the efficacy of human reason to master all things. Here was the first stirring of modern rationalism. Along with the emphasis on reason, skepticism and pessimism also returned to the Western mind.

The disputed issues focused on whether boundaries must exist between reason and faith and on how much reason could legitimately be applied to Christian thought. No one was more committed to resolving these questions than Fulbert's student Berengar of Tours, who insisted on submitting religious mysteries to the activity of reason, thereby denying traditional authority. His justification for challenging authority was that in reason man most resembled God. Lanfranc of Bec, one of the great conservative minds of the day, rose to refute this position. The turmoil that accompanied the various and controversial medieval interpretations of Aristotle made Chartres the leading school of the twelfth century renaissance. It produced the Thomistic synthesis of reason and faith during the thirteenth century, a synthesis which would ultimately crumble under the weight of its own complexity.

Summary

Above all, Fulbert should be remembered as one of the most influential teachers of the eleventh century, the patriarch of the great masters produced by Chartres. Although he was never officially canonized, Fulbert is recognized as a saint. His feast day is April 10. By all accounts, he was a man of dignity, tolerance, gentle wisdom, and humanity. Though he never wrote anything particularly outstanding, he was notable among the great medieval correspondents. Fortunately, many of his letters have been preserved. They reflect his clear, concise, if not eloquent, style. He wrote in understandable Latin, something refreshing when compared to the laborious, antiquated language of most of his contemporaries.

A gifted teacher, Fulbert spoke to people in a language that they understood. Although he was intrigued by the relationship between words and reality, he started no new school of philosophy. Indeed, Fulbert contributed nothing new to learning but made what he discussed both understandable and familiar to his listeners.

Fulbert's reputation, never tarnished or diminished, was built on the success of his students and their loyalty to him. In his day it was said that Fulbert was the spring from which all the rivers of the medieval mind flowed. This influence lasted for a century after his death, drawing students from all over Europe to his school. In spite of the distinguished reputation of Fulbert and Chartres, however, the school never became a university. Instead, the focus shifted in the twelfth century to Paris, some fifty miles away.

While Chartres is remembered today more for the beauty of its Gothic cathedral and rose windows, which were made famous by Henry Adams' book *Mont-Saint-Michel and Chartres* (1904), in the Middle Ages it was clearly the school and its remarkable teacher and founder, Fulbert, that made it famous.

Bibliography

Copleston, Frederick. *Medieval Philosophy*. New York: Philosophical Library, 1952. A brief, highly readable standard survey of medieval philosophy.

DeWulf, Maurice. *Philosophy and Civilization in the Middle Ages*. Mineola, N.Y.: Dover Publications, 1953. Originally a series of lectures delivered at Princeton University, this collection of essays shows the necessary connection between things of the mind and society in general. DeWulf illustrates the relationship between Fulbert and Chartres within the larger medieval context.

Durant, Will. *Story of Civilization*. Vol. 4, *The Age of Faith*. New York: Simon and Schuster, 1950. While sometimes considered a pedestrian popularization, this lengthy volume is good reading—enjoyable, anecdotal, and accurate—hence, an excellent source for finding little-known facts about Saint Fulbert's life. Contains an extensive index, a standard bibliography, and a detailed table of contents. The many illustrations of Gothic cathedrals are helpful.

Heer, Friedrich. *The Medieval World: Europe, 1100-1350*. Translated by Janet Sondheimer. Cleveland, Ohio: World Publishing Co., 1962. This book is one of the best historical surveys of the High Middle Ages. It is interpretive and provocative in tone, reads well, is topical in arrangement, and covers the standard medieval subjects. For an understanding of Saint Fulbert and the influence of the school at Chartres, the chapters on intellectualism in the universities and the intellectual warfare in Paris are crucial. The pictures are good, and the bibliography contains standard works in English, but most sources are in Latin.

Knowles, David. *The Evolution of Medieval Thought*. Baltimore: Helicon Press, 1962. This English scholar and churchman provides an excellent survey of the philosophical and theological development of the Middle Ages, including Saint Fulbert's influence on his students. This is a synthetic work of notable merit. The bibliographic essay, though brief, contains standard, readily available works on medieval thought.

Leff, Gordon. *Medieval Thought: St. Augustine to Ockham*. Baltimore: Penguin Books, 1958. Leff provides the reader with an easily understood description of the development of the medieval mind. He stresses the influence of Saint Fulbert and his students upon that development. The bibliography is limited.

Marias, Julian. *History of Philosophy*. Mineola, N.Y.: Dover Publications, 1967. A detailed survey which includes some information on Fulbert but is more important for giving the reader an understanding of the major philosophical problems of the age.

Southern, R.W. *The Making of the Middle Ages*. New Haven, Conn.: Yale University Press, 1953. Reflecting years of familiarity with medieval history, Southern produces a brief but enlightening essay illustrating the fluctuating image and influence of Islamic learning on medieval Christian thought. In doing so, he details the contributions made by Saint Fulbert and the school at Chartres.

Waddell, Helen. *The Wandering Scholars*. Garden City, N.Y.: Anchor Books, 1961. Now a classic in medieval studies, this volume was written by one of the outstanding historians who helped to expand modern understanding of the medieval world. Waddell's style is literary, and the bibliography is extensive and useful.

Shirley F. Fredricks

GALEN

Born: 129; in or near Pergamon, the capital of Asia
Died: c. 199; probably Pergamon
Areas of Achievement: Medicine, physiology, and philosophy
Contribution: Although not a first-rate philosopher, Galen was influential in formulating a powerful logical empiricism which took scientific axioms as self-evident rather than hypothetical. His greatest contribution was in medicine, where he made the best presentation of anatomical knowledge in the ancient world; his theories and practices remained dominant during the Middle Ages.

Early Life

Galen was born on an estate in Pergamon, a city situated on the mainland almost opposite the island of Lesbos in Asia Minor. Pergamon lay inland in a fertile valley, and its hilltops were crowned by temples and theaters. Pergamon's library rivaled Alexandria's. Another distinguishing feature was the Asclepieion, or medical temple dedicated to Asclepius, the god of healing. This was a combination religious sanctuary, sanatorium, and place of recreation. Pergamon was one of the great seats of Christianity and held one of the seven churches mentioned by John the Apostle in Revelation (2:12-17). Because of these features, the city became one of the great pilgrimage and entertainment centers in the Roman world, and Galen grew up exposed not only to scholars but also to rhapsodists, musicians, tumblers, actors, and snake-charmers.

Galen's father, Nicon, was an architect and geometer. He was also a prosperous landowner with a farm that cultivated peas, beans, lentils, almonds, figs, olives, and grapes. Nicon himself came from a highly educated family and was able to provide his son with an education partly in the country and partly in the city. Galen (whose name derives from *galenos*, Greek for "calm" or "serene") was closer to his father than to his mother, who scolded the maids and quarreled almost incessantly with her husband. Galen compared her with Socrates' difficult wife, Xanthippe, but was able to keep his distance from her by accompanying his father to lectures in the city. His father provided or supervised Galen's education until the boy reached fourteen, then he directed his son to philosophical studies.

There were four leading philosophical systems at the time—Platonism, Aristotelianism, Stoicism, and Epicureanism—and Galen was not prodded along any single path of knowledge. He had the benefit of a liberal education, although he found confusion in philosophy and had doubts about mathematics. His father wanted a state career for the boy, but after having a dream in which Asclepius directed attention to medicine, Nicon sent Galen, then seventeen, to study under the celebrated anatomist and Sophist Satyros.

Life's Work

When Nicon died, probably in 151, Galen worked with Pelops in Smyrna and with Numisianos in Corinth and Alexandria, where he wrote a treatise in three parts on the movement of the lungs and thorax. He remained in Alexandria for roughly five years, traveling in various parts of Egypt. There were six main medical sects at the time, three ancient (the Hippocratic, Dogmatic, and Empirical) and three "modern" (the Methodist, Pneumatic, and Eclectic). Galen, like any of his colleagues, was free to try combinations of these sects, and he devoted two treatises to the discussion of them.

Upon his return to Pergamon, he was appointed physician to the school of gladiators by the head priest of the Asclepieion. Galen's appointment lasted for more than two years and was a useful experience. Because gladiators often received severe wounds, a physician was obliged to attend to the diet, exercise, and convalescence of these combatants in order to ensure that they were in good health and that they would recover in due course from certain injuries. Galen did not perform much surgery on the gladiators, and his knowledge of anatomy was derived exclusively from dissections on animals—particularly the Barbary ape (for which he was nicknamed the "ape doctor"). Slaves or students would prepare the cadavers of pigs, sheep, oxen, cats, dogs, horses, lions, wolves, birds, and fish by shaving and flaying them, and it is a wonder that Galen and other anatomists were not killed by infection.

Dissection led to insights about the general plan of the body, and Galen showed that this plan was essentially the same from creature to creature. He discovered that arteries contain blood and that a severed artery (even a small one) could drain all the body's blood in one-half hour or less. He showed that the right auricle outlives the rest of the heart and that there is a link between the brain and the larynx.

When a new war between the Pergamonians and the neighboring Galatians began, Galen left for Rome. His life and career coincided with the noble rule of Antoninus Pius and that of his son, Marcus Aurelius. Galen rented a large house, practiced as a physician, attended medical meetings in the Temple of Peace, and continued his interest in philosophy.

He respected the ancients, particularly Aristotle, Plato, and Hippocrates. He argued that all scientific knowledge begins with the senses, or mind, and he was opposed to the Skeptics, who taught their disciples to argue on either side of any point. Galen found it absurd to argue so freely while doubting, as the Skeptics did, the starting points of knowledge. Although somewhat "magical" or irrational in medical practice (he believed in the therapeutic value of excrement and amulets), he was a rationalist in his philosophical method, recognizing a role for syllogistic reasoning and admiring the purposiveness of all nature. He believed, with Aristotle, that nature never makes anything superfluous; he tried in *De usu partium corporis humani* (*On the Usefulness of the Parts of the Body*) to justify the form and function of each organ of the body. He interpreted other philosophers (especially Plato, Aristotle, Theophrastus, Chrysippus, Epicurus), but his many ethical treatises were lost, as was a series of works on lexicographical and stylistic problems.

He held a Platonic view of the soul, recognizing the three parts (nutritive, animal, rational) distinguished in Plato's *Republic* and opposing the Stoic doctrine of a single, indivisible soul. His treatise on the subject ascribes nutrition to the liver and veins, the pneuma or spirit to the lungs and heart, and sensation and muscular movement to the brain and nerves. It is easy to see how physiology and philosophy mixed in Galen's theories, especially in his pneumatic theory which, though derived from Hippocrates and Anaximenes of Miletus, was an interesting revision of those older beliefs. According to Galen, each of the three fundamental members (liver, heart, brain) was dominated by a special pneuma or spirit: the liver by natural or physical spirit—a vapor from blood, which controlled nutrition, growth, and reproduction; the heart by vital spirit, transmitted in the veins and conveying heat and life; the brain by animal or psychical spirit, which regulated the brain, nerves, and feeling. Galen believed that the habits of the soul were influenced by bodily temperament (rather than by climate, as Hippocrates had insisted). Galen's theory of the four humors (based on the four elements earth, air, fire, and water) went back to Empedocles but was a restatement of Hippocrates' theory of four qualities (dry, wet, hot, cold) and of another version of the four humors (blood, yellow bile, black bile, phlegm). This attempted reconciliation of medicine and philosophy was consistent with his claim that the best physician was also a philosopher.

Galen became a friend of the Aristotelian philosopher Eudemos, and when the latter fell ill, Galen was consulted—much to the hostility of the patient's other physicians. A contest of invective, suspicion, and tactlessness broke out between Galen and his rivals. Galen's outspoken and contemptuous criticism of those he considered charlatans put his life in danger; he decided to return to Pergamon.

His recuperation from Rome-weariness was short. He received a letter from the two rulers, Marcus Aurelius and Lucius Verus, ordering him to join the imperial camp in Aquileia (a commercial and military center and one of the great cities of the west), where legions were gathering to march against the Barbarians. These military preparations were disrupted by plague, a form of typhus or smallpox probably brought in from Syria and stubbornly resistant to health measures. The emperors decided to leave the army, but when Verus died in 169, Marcus returned to the field after ordering Galen back to Rome to take medical charge of Marcus' eight-year-old son, Commodus.

As court physician, Galen strengthened his position. He continued in office when Commodus succeeded his father as emperor in 180. Galen remained in Rome until 192, when a fire destroyed the Temple of Peace, as well as many libraries and bookshops. Many of his writings, especially some of his philosophical treatises, which existed only in a few copies, were annihilated.

Under Commodus, the climate for scholars and philosophers became intolerable. The emperor, a superior athlete who regarded himself as a reincarnation of Hercules, placed a premium on hunting and circus games rather than on intellectual pursuits. Galen returned to Pergamon in 192, where he had yet another encounter with the plague. He was saved by letting his own blood. Most of his time was devoted to meditation and writing, and he died about 199.

Summary

Galen's writings were diverse and profuse. Although he did not have students of his own, nor did he found a school, his stature was large in his lifetime and larger after his death. His texts were translated into Syriac and Arabic as Greek culture spread throughout Syria and then into Persia and the Muhammadan world. From the eleventh century onward, Latin translations of Galen made their way into Europe, where the phenomenon of Galenism dominated the medicine of the Middle Ages, despite the plethora of other commentators and forgeries of Galen's texts.

As a medical practitioner and theorist, Galen mixed fact and speculation. Although a brilliant diagnostician, he relied on observations of "critical days," pulse, and urine for his prognoses. He had a deep distaste for surgery, except as a means to repair injuries or suppurations, and confined his operative surgery to nasal polyps, goiters, and tumors of fatty or fibrous tissues. His writing in the field, however, provides information on the use of caustics, unguents for healing wounds, and opium and other drugs for anesthesia. His anatomical knowledge suffered from the unavailability of human cadavers, so his errors were understandable. His physiology was strictly limited, but he was far ahead of his time in developing concepts of digestion, assimilation, blood formation, nerve function, and reproduction.

As a philosopher, he was hardly original, but he was useful for his commentaries on Plato and Hippocrates, and he wrote about logic, ethics, and rational psychology, arguing that "passions" were the result of unbridled energy opposed to reason, and "errors" of the soul were the result of false judgments or opinions. Galen believed that psychological troubles could be related more to the body's predisposition to disease than to disease itself, and so he recommended a daily self-examination as a preventative.

Galen erred in thinking that inadequate medical knowledge could be compensated by general knowledge. Nevertheless, he was versatile, producing works of philology (including two dictionaries) and an autobiography in addition to his more than 100 treatises on medicine. His language was often repetitive and difficult, but he never assumed literary affectations, and he continually revised his work.

Despite the fact that the Renaissance saw the overthrow of many of his theories of anatomy, physiology, and therapy, Galen can be credited for several things: setting a high ideal for the medical profession; insisting on contact with nature as a condition for treating disease; stressing the unity of an organism and the interdependence of its parts; and realizing that a living organism can be understood only in relation to its environment. His fame and theories lasted for nine centuries, before being rivaled by those of the Muslim philosopher-physician Avicenna.

Bibliography

Brock, Arthur John, trans. *Greek Medicine, Being Extracts Illustrative of Medical Writers from Hippocrates to Galen*. London: J. M. Dent and Sons, 1929. A good historical survey by one of the best English translators of Galen. Places Galen in historical context. Includes annotations.

Gilbert, N. W. *Renaissance Concepts of Method*. New York: Columbia University Press, 1960. Contains information on Galen's scientific methodology.

Sarton, George. *Galen of Pergamon*. Lawrence: University of Kansas Press, 1954. Perhaps the most accessible and readable biography of the subject. Contains interesting historical background, but the discussion of philosophy is brief and takes some knowledge for granted.

Temkin, Owsei. *Galenism: Rise and Decline of a Medical Philosophy*. Ithaca, N.Y.: Cornell University Press, 1973. An authoritative overview of the phenomenon that so influenced medieval medicine and philosophy. Also contains a description of the various forgeries of Galen's texts.

Walzer, Richard. *Galen on Jews and Christians*. London: Oxford University Press, 1949. A discussion of Galen's lack of interest in the two major religions and of his belief in the Demiurge and the purposiveness of nature.

Keith Garebian

GENGHIS KHAN
Temüjin

Born: Between 1155 and 1162; Delyun Boldog, near the Gobi Desert
Died: August 18, 1227; Ordos area in northern China
Areas of Achievement: Warfare and government
Contribution: A military genius, Genghis Khan united the clans and tribes of peoples later collectively known as the Mongols, leading them on conquests to the east, south, and west and organizing the Mongol Empire—which under his grandson, Kublai, came to dominate eighty percent of Eurasia.

Early Life

Temüjin, as Genghis Khan was first named, was born in the village of Delyun Boldog on the Odon River in the northeastern borderlands between Mongolia and China on the fringes of the Gobi Desert between 1155 and 1162. Historians cannot agree on the exact year. It is said that there were great "signs" at the time of Temüjin's birth. Stars fell from the sky (possibly a meteor shower), and he was born clutching a blood clot in the shape of a human knuckle. The great-grandson of Khabul Khan, Temüjin was born into the elite Borjigin clan, the son of a Mongol lord, Yesügei, and his captive Merkit wife, Oyelun. According to Mongol custom, at the age of nine Temüjin was betrothed to his first wife, Börte. After the treacherous poisoning death of Yesügei at a banquet hosted by a rival, Temüjin and his family fell on hard times and were periodically held captive by the Merkits. Temüjin often had to survive by hunting, fishing, and even scrounging for rodents in the desert.

Gradually, he rallied around him a group of followers from various clans and tribes, and, using his natural military ability, Temüjin emerged as a bandit-mercenary leader under the protection of Khan Toghril, the Nestorian Christian leader of the Kereits, sometimes referred to in the West as Prester John. As an ally of Toghril and the Chinese in 1194, Temüjin and his band helped to defeat the Tatars. In this campaign, he clearly demonstrated his ability as a military strategist, especially in the use of the cavalry tactics for which his Mongols became so famous and so feared.

Life's Work

After the death of Toghril, Temüjin soon turned on his Kereit allies and subjugated them and then also the Naimans and Merkits. In 1206, he organized these diverse nomadic groups—whose principal occupations had been herding horses and sheep, banditry, mercenary soldiering, and warring with one another—into a militaristic Mongol confederacy based on kinship and personal loyalty. He assumed the title of Genghis Khan and emerged as this new state's divine ruler. He governed with skill, strength, and wisdom, but also relied heavily on popular fear of his awesome power. Quickly, Genghis Khan added to his central Asian domains in the years 1206 to 1209 by conquering the neighboring Oyrats, Kirghiz, and Uighurs.

At the center of this state was the superior Mongol army under the brilliant command of Genghis Khan himself. Eventually, he perfected traditional Mongol cavalry and archery tactics and skillfully combined them with the use of gunpowder and siege technology adopted from the Chinese and Muslims. To keep this army in its numerous campaigns well supplied, a modern, logistic system of support was created. Effective communication between the various military groups and parts of the growing empire was maintained by a pony express-like "postal system." Intelligence was gathered from itinerant merchants, wandering the empire, who came under the personal protection of Genghis Khan. By Börte and other wives, he had four sons: Jochi, Chagatai, Ogatai, and Tolui. They and other relatives became the leading generals and administrators of the increasingly feudal empire.

Genghis Khan established the first Mongol (Uighur-based) written language to unify his people further and promulgated the first Mongol law, a prescriptive law code which was eventually employed from China to Poland. In return for absolute obedience to Genghis Khan and his successors, the law allowed for local political autonomy and religious toleration. Under this code, a system of governance developed in the Mongol Empire similar to the satrapies employed by the ancient Persian Empire of Cyrus the Great. The law also became a basis for the law codes of many of the successor states to the Mongol Empire.

The Mongol Empire rose out of central Asia under its dynamic leader to fill a power vacuum created by the decline of China in the east almost simultaneously with that of the Muslim states to the south and the Byzantine Empire and Kievan Rus in the west. Beginning with Hsi Hsia, from 1209 to 1215, Genghis Khan conquered northern China, finally entering Peking after severely devastating it in 1215. In China, as elsewhere, Genghis Khan readily adapted aspects of the civilization and its human talent to strengthen his position and the Mongol Empire. He conversed extensively with the renowned Taoist monk Chang Chun but remained a shamanist. Genghis Khan also made the Chinese Yeliu Chu his chief astrologer and a principal civil administrator. (Later, in the thirteenth century, Kublai Khan employed the Venetian Marco Polo and Polo's father and uncle as ambassadors and administrators.)

While some historians actually believe that China was always the prime objective of his expansionism, southern China, ruled by the declining Sung Dynasty, seems to have held little appeal for Genghis Khan; after taking Peking, he turned his attention to the West. From 1218 to 1225, he conquered the Persian Khwarizm Empire and thereby gained control of the critical trade routes between China and the Middle East. The caravans which traveled these and the other trade routes of the Mongol Empire were absolutely essential to its economic life and well being. Eventually, Mongol-Turkish domination of these trade routes forced European navigators such as Vasco da Gama and Christopher Columbus to seek alternative ocean routes to the spices, silks, and other riches of Asia.

These southern conquests also for the first time incorporated large numbers of Muslim subjects into the Mongol Empire. In the following decades and centuries most of the Mongols from Transoxiana and westward into Russia were converted to Islam and naturally allied themselves with the emerging Ottoman Empire. In 1223, Genghis Khan sent his brother-in-law and greatest general, Subatai, to attack the Cumans, Byzantines, and Russians and therewith begin the invasion of Europe. (In 1240, the Mongols of the Golden Horde under Batu Khan would take the Russian capital city of Kiev and eventually help to found a new Russian state under the leadership of Moscow.)

Yet, in his absence in the West, the Chinese domains of Genghis Khan went into revolt. He returned east and ruthlessly resubjugated northern China from 1225 to 1227. On his return journey to the Mongol heartland, one month after the death of his son Jochi, Genghis Khan died in the Ordos region in 1227. He was succeeded by his son Ogatai, who died in 1241.

Under Ogatai Khan and his successors, Mongol power and influence swept into Russia, Poland, India, southern China, Indochina, and Korea, culminating in Kublai Khan's failed invasions of Japan from 1274 to 1281. Kublai Khan established the Yüan Dynasty in China, and Mongol dynasties came to power in Persia, India, and elsewhere. The Mongol Empire created by Genghis Khan was never really overthrown. The Mongols generally were culturally inferior to the peoples they conquered and gradually were absorbed by them; they became Chinese, Indian, Muslim, or Russian. Thus, with the weakening of the power and attraction of the Mongol capital, Karakorum, and the heartland and declining leadership, the once-great Mongol Empire of Genghis Khan and Kublai Khan first fragmented into numerous autonomous khanates (for example, Khanate of the Golden Horde) and finally, after several centuries, disappeared. Yet its legacy, and that of Genghis Khan, lives on in its successor states and those descended from them.

Summary

Genghis Khan is one of the most controversial figures in the human past. He was a brutal man in a brutal time and environment. He also was one of the most brilliant military and political leaders in history. The victims of his relentless drive for personal power number in the hundreds of thousands and maybe into the millions, causing many also to judge him as one of the greatest monsters in history. He took a shattered and disparate, primitive people and unified them to form the core of the Mongol Empire, which was, in effect, the personification of his own intellect, ability, and drive. This Eurasian state he created in two short generations became one of the mightiest empires the world has yet known.

Most significant, the Mongol Empire facilitated cultural, political, economic, and technological transfer across Eurasia and thereby helped to revitalize civilization in China, India, the Middle East, and Europe. Genghis Khan once again restated civilization's debt to the barbarians. From horsemanship, the use of gunpowder, communications, military tactics and organization, and government and law to the broadening of the human biological pool, the Mongol input into human history, instigated by Genghis Khan, is long and profound.

Bibliography

Chambers, James. *The Devil's Horsemen: The Mongol Invasion of Europe*. New York: Atheneum Publishers, 1979. The first half of this book concerns itself with Genghis Khan and the rise of the Mongol Empire, providing a somewhat different and very interesting European perspective to the events leading up to the Mongol invasion.

Grousset, Rene. *Conqueror of the World: The Life of Chingis-khan*. New York: Viking Press, 1972. An authoritative and interesting biography. Includes a full examination of the major aspects of his life and times as well as an extensive bibliography. An example of the "Great Man" theory of history.

Hambly, Gavin, ed. *Central Asia*. New York: Delacorte Press, 1969. Contains a straightforward chapter on Genghis Khan and the rise of the Mongol Empire, comparing developments, such as feudalism, in central Asia to similar ones in Europe. Six chapters put Genghis Khan and the Mongols in historical perspective in central Asia.

Howorth, Henry H. *History of the Mongols: From the Ninth to the Nineteenth Century*. Vol. 1. New York: Burt Franklin, 1876. The traditional standard multivolume study from the nineteenth century. One very solid chapter on Genghis Khan.

Kahn, Paul, ed. *The Secret History of the Mongols: An Adaption*. San Francisco: North Point Press, 1984. A superb translation of a basic work on Genghis Khan. Contains an extensive introduction and helpful glossary and appendices. The original was written only a generation after Genghis Khan's death.

Legg, Stuart. *The Heartland*. New York: Capricorn Books, 1971. Very well written. Contains an extensive chapter on Genghis Khan and his accomplishments and another chapter on the Mongol Empire after him, considered in the light of the author's interesting heartland theory.

Martin, Henry Desmond. *The Rise of Chingis Khan and His Conquest of*

North China. New York: Octagon Books, 1977. The first third of this volume deals with the life of Genghis Khan, the rise of his empire, and his preparations for the conquest of northern China. The last two-thirds addresses the actual conquest, which the author believes was Genghis Khan's objective to the point of obsession.

Morgan, David. *The Mongols*. Oxford: Basil Blackwell, 1986. A general study on the Mongols, with two chapters on Genghis Khan and his empire.

Phillips, E. D. *The Mongols*. New York: Praeger Publishers, 1969. Well written and generously illustrated, this work contains a significant chapter on the military and social history behind Genghis Khan.

Prawdin, Michael. *The Mongol Empire: Its Rise and Legacy*. 2d ed. New York: Free Press, 1967. Probably still the best overall history of the Mongol Empire. Almost the whole first half of the book is devoted to a thorough and readable account of Genghis Khan. The opening chapter on his youth is especially good.

Spuler, Bertold. *History of the Mongols: Based on Eastern and Western Accounts of the Thirteenth and Fourteenth Centuries*. Berkeley: University of California Press, 1972. Begins with two major chapters on Genghis Khan and the Mongol Empire. Complete with extensive excerpts from primary source material on him and his people, especially from *The Secret History of the Mongols*.

Vernadsky, George. *The Mongols and Russia*. New Haven, Conn.: Yale University Press, 1953. The opening two chapters consider Genghis Khan and the Mongol Empire as an introduction to the Kievan Rus. The Mongols are considered the pillars of modern Russian (Muscovite) statehood.

Dennis Reinhartz

MAHMUD GHAZAN

Born: November 5, 1271; Abaskun, Iran
Died: May 11, 1304; near Qazvin, northwestern Iran
Areas of Achievement: Government and warfare
Contribution: The greatest of the Mongol Il-Khans of Iran, Mahmud Ghazan was responsible for the conversion of the Il-Khanate to Islam and presided over a remarkable flowering of syncretistic Central Asian and Iranian culture.

Early Life

Mahmud Ghazan, Mongol ruler of Iran from 1295 to 1304, ranks as one of the most important of the medieval rulers of that country. A descendant of Genghis Khan through the latter's grandson, Hülagü, he was the seventh in the line of the Il-Khans. These were the Mongol rulers of a khanate embracing what is today Iran, Iraq, part of Syria, eastern and central Turkey, the region of the Soviet Union south of the Caucasus Mountains, and the greater part of Afghanistan. The word "Il-Khan" meant a subordinate khan, one who acknowledged the overlordship of the Supreme Khan, or Khaqan, in distant Mongolia and China. Ghazan seems, however, to have rejected this overlordship: Unlike his predecessors, he abandoned the practice of including the Khaqan's name and title on his coinage, which consequently came to resemble that of other Middle Eastern rulers. After his conversion to Islam (which was publicly proclaimed on June 19, 1295), his adopted Muslim name of Mahmud was added to his Mongol name on the coinage, and as Mahmud Ghazan his name was thereafter read in the *khutba*, the invocation on behalf of the ruler included in Friday prayers in the principal mosques.

Only the first two Il-Khans, Hülagü (reigned 1256-1265) and Abaqa (reigned 1265-1281), had been outstanding rulers. Hülagü, following the sack of Baghdad and the extinction of the 'Abbasid Caliphate in 1258, had founded the Il-Khanate. It was Abaqa who consolidated his father's achievement. Abaqa's son and Ghazan's father, Arghun (reigned 1284-1291), had been a ruler of fairly modest ability. Like Abaqa, he had sought the cooperation of the hard-pressed crusading states of the Holy Land and of various European rulers in the course of the Mongols' life-and-death struggle with the Mamluk rulers of Egypt, who were also bitter foes of the Crusaders. Although rulers of Christian Europe had hoped that Arghun would become a convert to Christianity, he was by upbringing and inclination a Buddhist, and his eldest son, Ghazan, was also brought up in the Buddhist faith. As Governor of Khorāsān during the reigns of his father and his uncle, Gaykhatu, Ghazan is known to have ordered the construction of Buddhist places of worship in Quchan and elsewhere.

During Arghun's reign, fighting among the Mongol nobles (*noyons*) and military commanders (*amirs*) seriously weakened the authority of the Il-Khan. At Arghun's death, his brother, Gaykhatu, was recognized as his successor; he was formally enthroned on July 23, 1291, at Akhlat, near Lake Van in eastern Turkey. Ghazan was confirmed in the government of Khorāsān. The new Il-Khan's extravagance and licentiousness, however, soon provoked resentment, and he was eventually murdered (March 26, 1295). His cousin Baydu, another grandson of Hülagü, was then enthroned as Il-Khan in April, 1295. Baydu's reign proved exceptionally brief (from April to October, 1295), since Ghazan immediately challenged his accession with the support of a would-be kingmaker, Nawruz. This great Mongol *amir* had been commander-in-chief in Khorāsān at the time when Ghazan was governor there. Nawruz had once led a revolt against Ghazan, but he now threw his formidable weight behind Ghazan's bid for the throne. A longtime Muslim, Nawruz pressed upon Ghazan the political advantages of conversion to Islam, and no doubt the latter readily acknowledged the value of sharing the faith of the majority of his subjects. He may have been sincere in his conversion, but it seems more likely that, to paraphrase the famous quip attributed to Henry IV of France, Tabrīz was worth a *namaz* (formal Muslim prayer).

By the autumn of 1295, Ghazan had gained the upper hand over his rival, who fled toward the north but was easily captured. On October 4, 1295, when Ghazan made his triumphant entry into Tabrīz, henceforth the official capital of the Il-Khanate, Baydu was executed. On the same day, it was proclaimed throughout Tabrīz that Islam was now the official religion of the khanate and that Buddhist temples, Jewish synagogues, and Christian churches were to be destroyed. Court patronage of the minority faiths, hitherto normative, was now withdrawn—in theory, if not always in practice. Yet it is a measure of the shallowness of Ghazan's conversion to Islam that, on departing from Tabrīz to winter across the Aras River, he married a woman who had formerly been a wife of his father and also of his uncle, an act utterly abhorrent to his Muslim subjects and forbidden by the Koran, although customary among the shamanistic Mongol rulers.

Ghazan was ruthless toward all who opposed him. It was not long after his accession that he began to resent the arrogance and ambition of his erstwhile ally Nawruz. A man in Nawruz's position had no lack of enemies, and some past double-dealing with the Mamluk government in Cairo provided grounds for his being denounced to the Il-Khan, who now had a pretext to break with him. Although three of his brothers and his son were executed, Nawruz himself escaped into Khorāsān and sought refuge with the ruler of Herāt, who owed him both his life and his position. Betrayed by his faithless host, however, Nawruz was handed over in 1297 to a rival *amir*, who ordered him to be cut in half and his head sent to Baghdad, where it long adorned one of the city gates. Instrumental in the fall of Nawruz and his family had been the principal prime minister of the Il-Khan, Sadr al-Din Zanjani. Hitherto, this man had shown remarkable powers of survival, for he had been minister to Gaykhatu before coming over to Ghazan. Nevertheless, in 1298 he too was denounced and executed. In their accounts of the inquiries which preceded his downfall, the sources mention for the first time the name of one of his subordinates, the historian Rashid al-Din, a Jewish convert from Hamadān. Al-Din soon became Ghazan's prime minister and trusted adviser, a position which he would continue to occupy under Ghazan's successor, Öljeitü. Meanwhile, the process of Islamicization had been gaining momentum. In November, 1297, Il-Khan and *amirs* together had formally exchanged their broad-brimmed Mongol hats, unsuitable for performing the Muslim prayers, for the traditional Middle Eastern turban.

Life's Work

During the early part of his reign, Ghazan's prime concerns had been internal security and testing the reliability of his *noyons* and *amirs*. From 1299 onward, external relations and campaigning across the frontiers of the Il-Khanate became a major focus. The Il-Khanate was a formidable military power, but it was ringed by foes. To the northeast, there was the rival Chagatai Khanate, ruled by descendants of Genghis Khan's second son, Chagatai. The Amu Darya River served as the *de facto* frontier between these two aggressive neighbors, but raids into each other's territories were frequent. In the northwest, the Il-Khans disputed hegemony of the southern Caucasus region with the Khanate of Kipchak (which the Russians called the Golden Horde), ruled by descendants of Genghis Khan's grandson Batu. The khans of Kipchak had adopted Islam earlier than any of the other Mongol dynasties; they made common cause with the Egyptian Mamluks, with whom they maintained important commercial and cultural contacts, against the Il-Khans of Iran. To the southwest, the region that later became northwestern Iraq and eastern Syria was a zone of perpetual conflict between the Il-Khans and the Egyptian Mamluks, who since the time when the Mongols had first appeared in the Middle East in the 1250's had strenuously repulsed the invaders along a broad north-south front extending from Diyarbakir through Aleppo, Hama, and Homs to Damascus.

Ghazan now had to turn his attention to the danger of encirclement, made more immediate by a 1299 coup in Cairo which brought back as sultan Nasir al-Din Muhammad, a young man who had reigned briefly in the mid-1290's and was to reign again from 1299 to 1340 (with a short break in 1309). In midsummer, 1299, a Mamluk army crossed the Euphrates and penetrated as far as Mardin (now in southeastern Turkey), carrying off vast numbers of captives and leaving a path of devastation behind it. Ghazan retaliated by invading Syria and, bypassing Aleppo and Hama, brought the Mamluks to bay in the vicinity of Homs, where he won a crushing victory over them on December 22, 1299. He then captured Homs and Damascus (although in the case of the latter city, the Mamluks held out in the citadel). In February, 1300, however, Ghazan abruptly withdrew from Damascus, perhaps as a result of rumors of unrest in Iran or of incursions across the Amu Darya frontier, and the Mamluks soon reoccupied all that they had previously forfeited.

In the autumn of 1300, Ghazan embarked upon a second invasion of Syria, again advancing well beyond Aleppo. This time, however, there was to be no direct confrontation between Mongols and Mamluks; excessive rain, flooding, and extremes of cold seem to have kept the two armies apart. In February, 1301, Ghazan recrossed the Euphrates, and later in the year there were diplomatic exchanges between the two governments, although neither side was sincere in its protestations of friendship. A desultory correspondence was also carried on with Pope Boniface VIII, attempting to organize a joint Mongol-Frankish attack upon Syria. Ghazan's letter of April 12, 1302, to the pope still survives in the Vatican archives.

In the autumn of 1302, a third campaign was mounted against the Mamluks. Ghazan advanced into northwestern Iraq, sending an advance force under two trusted commanders, Qutlugh-Shah and Amir Choban, to besiege Aleppo. Although the Il-Khan followed with the main army, he decided to relinquish the conduct of the campaign to his commanders, and he returned over the Euphrates in early April, 1303. Again, there may have been rumors of danger in the east, where his brother Öljeitü was governor of Khorāsān: Civil war was said to be raging in the Mongolian heartlands. Meanwhile, Qutlugh-Shah had moved from Aleppo to the vicinity of Damascus, where Mamluks and Mongols clashed in a bloody two-day battle in which the Mongols were overwhelmingly defeated (April 19-20, 1303). Qutlugh-Shah himself was the first to inform the Il-Khan of the disaster, while Amir Choban brought up the rear with the wounded. An Egyptian source relates that Ghazan was outraged at the news and that following a court of inquiry, Qutlugh-Shah was punished and disgraced. Losses on this scale could not be made good at short notice, but the prestige of the Il-Khanate was at stake. Consequently, preparations began almost immediately for a fourth Syrian campaign. The plan was for the Il-Khan to winter in Baghdad and then advance to the front in the spring of 1304, but by now Ghazan was a sick man, only able to travel by litter and for short distances at a time. He left Tabrīz for Baghdad in September, 1303, but early winter snow on the Zagros Mountains barred his way southward, and he passed the winter somewhere in western Iran. Perhaps sensing that his end was near, when spring came he ordered his entourage to head for Khorāsān. He died near Qazvin on May 11, 1304, having designated his brother Öljeitü as his successor, since he had no sons of his own. His body was then taken to Tabrīz for burial in the magnificent mausoleum which he had built there as his final resting place.

Summary

Mahmud Ghazan contributed decisively to the assimilation of the infidel Mongols into the traditional Islamic culture of the Middle East, although at the time of his death the process was still far from complete. He enjoyed a formidable reputation as a military leader, but his place in Iranian history rests more upon his abilities as an administrator in carrying out far-reaching reforms in taxation and the system of landholding. These aimed at alleviating the suffering of the agricultural population while maximizing the yield of revenue to the government. He also issued stern edicts to protect merchants and encourage trade, enforcing a rough-and-ready justice on bandits and those villagers tempted to plunder passing caravans. Bridges were repaired and roads were kept in good order, weights and measures were standardized, the currency was improved, and customs posts were erected at the frontiers. That these measures were actually enforced is confirmed by the survival of a number of official letters and administrative directives written by his prime minister, Rashid al-Din.

Even before the accession of Ghazan, Tabrīz had become a major international emporium upon which converged trade routes from the Mediterranean, the Russian steppes, China, and India. It is a measure of its commercial importance that both the Venetians and the Genoese maintained consular representatives at the Il-Khan's capital. As part of his official policy of supporting Islam, Ghazan was a munificent builder of mosques, theological colleges, and mausoleums for holy men, but it was his capital which received most of his attention. Adjacent to the west side of Tabrīz he laid out a vast suburb, known as Shenb or Ghazaniya, where his own mausoleum was located, and he enclosed both the suburb and the old city within massive new walls. Nothing now remains of these ambitious buildings. Only the shell of the mosque built by Öljeitü's prime minister, Taj al-Din Ali Shah, at Tabrīz and Öljeitü's magnificent mausoleum at Sultaniyya indicate the scale of later Il-Khanid architecture.

Aside from architecture, the Il-Khans were great patrons of historical writing; under them, Persian historiography experienced a veritable golden age. This was especially true of the reigns of Ghazan and Öljeitü (reigned 1304-1316), during which the great histories of Rashid al-Din, Vassaf, and Mustawfi were written. There is no reason to doubt that this flowering of historical literature owed much to the direct patronage of Ghazan himself, whom contemporaries regarded as an authority on the history and traditions of the Mongols. Although as capable as any of his ancestors of ruthlessness and inhumanity, Ghazan seems to have been, by Mongol standards, a man of some culture. He is said to have known several languages and to have possessed insatiable curiosity concerning a wide range of subjects. There can be no doubt that he had a more benign vision of the responsibility of the ruler toward his subjects than had any of his predecessors.

Bibliography

Bartold, W., and J. A. Boyle. "Ghāzān." In *The Encyclopaedia of Islam*, edited by B. Lewis, C. Pellat, and J. Schacht, vol. 2. 2d ed. Leiden, Netherlands: E. J. Brill, 1965. The best short account of the career of Mahmud Ghazan. Other entries give helpful information regarding numerous aspects of Islamic theology, history, and culture. Illustrations and bibliographies.

Boyle, J. A. "Dynastic and Political History of the Īl-Khāns." In *The Cambridge History of Iran*, vol. 5, edited by J. A. Boyle. Cambridge: Cambridge University Press, 1968. This chapter provides the reader with the most complete account available in English of the Il-Khanid period, including the reign of Ghazan. The volume includes illustrations, maps, and bibliographies.

Lambton, Ann K. S. *Continuity and Change in Medieval Persia*. Albany: State University of New York Press, 1986. This magisterial study of the political and social structure of the Il-Khanid (as well as the Seljuk) period is the most recent and also the best account of conditions in Iran during the lifetime of Mahmud Ghazan.

__________. *Landlord and Peasant in Persia: A Study of Land Tenure and Land Revenue Administration*. New York: Oxford University Press, 1953. Chapter 4 of this classical study of agrarian relations in Iran provides excellent background reading regarding Mahmud Ghazan's administrative reforms. Map and bibliography.

Morgan, David. *The Mongols*. Oxford: Basil Blackwell, 1987. The most recent nonspecialist account of the Mongol Empire, this book is strongly recommended as introductory reading on the period.

Petrushevsky, I. P. "The Socio-economic Condition of Iran Under the Īl-Khāns." In *The Cambridge History of Iran*, vol. 5, edited by J. A. Boyle. Cambridge: Cambridge University Press, 1968. This chapter discusses at length prevailing social conditions as well as the government's economic policies under the Il-Khanid regime.

Wilber, Donald Newton. *The Architecture of Islamic Iran: The Il Khānid Period*. Princeton, N.J.: Princeton University Press, 1955. Still the definitive study of the monuments of the Il-Khanid period (with a useful inventory to which only a few recently identified structures need to be added), this book illuminates Mahmud Ghazan's role as a patron and builder.

Gavin R. G. Hambly

AL-GHAZZALI

Born: 1058; Tus, Khurasan, Iran
Died: December 18, 1111; Tus, Khurasan, Iran
Area of Achievement: Religion
Contribution: Al-Ghazzali is widely regarded as the greatest theologian of Islam; his thought and writing bridged the gap between the Scholastic and the mystical interpretations of religion and formed an ethical and moral structure that has endured.

Early Life

Abu Hamid Muhammad ibn Muhammad al-Tusi al-Ghazzali was one of a number of children born to a prominent family of the Ghazala, specialists distinguished for their knowledge of Muslim canon law (Shari'a). Although little is known of his childhood, his pattern of education strongly suggests that his family intended for him to follow its professional traditions. Much of his education and religious training was at home in Tus, with some time also spent at the important intellectual center of Jurjan. His advanced education was undertaken at the major university city of Nishapur. In 1085, al-Ghazzali visited the influential Nizam al-Mulk, the most important vizier of the early Seljuk period and a major figure himself in the propagation of education and scholarship. In 1091, Nizam appointed al-Ghazzali to a professorship at the university which he had established in Baghdad in 1065.

For several years, al-Ghazzali remained in Baghdad as a popular and successful lecturer, whose classes drew students by the hundreds. Beneath it all, however, al-Ghazzali was a deeply troubled man. His views became increasingly skeptical with respect to theology and deeply critical of the corruption often associated with administration of canon law. He took up a writing campaign against the Isma'ili cult of the Assassins, a political-religious terrorist group of the time whose members, holed up in the mountains of Iran, had been responsible for numerous assassinations of administrative authorities and intellectuals who took issue with the Assassins' eccentric views. Nizam al-Mulk himself was among those who died at their hands.

Around 1095, according to some sources, al-Ghazzali suffered a debilitating nervous illness which forced him to interrupt his career as a scholar and teacher. The illness was only a symptom of the intellectual and spiritual crisis his life had reached. Al-Ghazzali experienced the sort of self-confrontation which inevitably reminds one of the youth of Martin Luther. He had arrived at a crossroads, and his decision was to change direction.

Al-Ghazzali now abandoned his comfortable professorship in Baghdad (taking care to secure it for his younger brother) and embarked upon years of wandering, during most of which he lived a life of poverty and celibacy as a Sufi, a Muslim mystic. After a short stay in Damascus, he went on to Palestine and thence to Mecca, participating in the pilgrimage at the end of 1096. By some accounts, he visited Egypt briefly and even contemplated a journey to the Almoravid court in faraway Morocco.

Life's Work

For more than a decade, al-Ghazzali lived in solitude, meditating and performing mystical rituals. Near the end of this period, he produced his greatest work, *Ihya' 'ulum al-din* (c. 1103; *The Revival of Religious Sciences*, 1964). Around 1106, yielding to the entreaties of the new Seljuk vizier to return to academic life, he took up a professorship in Nishapur. Shortly before his death in 1111, however, he retired once more to a life of meditation at a retreat near Tus, where he gathered a small band of ascetic disciples.

Evaluation of al-Ghazzali's thought and religious doctrine is made difficult by the uncertain authorship of many works attributed to him over the centuries. His influence was such that historians of later generations have tended to identify almost any significant theological treatise of the time with him. Shortly before the end of his life, al-Ghazzali composed a kind of testament of his religious opinions containing much material since inferred to be biographical. The evolution of his thought must be traced using only works indisputably his own.

Al-Ghazzali's earliest writing, late in his Baghdad professorship, sought to expose contradictions between the beliefs of Sunni Islam and the philosophy of Arabic Neoplatonism espoused by the likes of al-Farabi and Avicenna (or Ibn Sina). He first wrote a dispassionate exposition of their beliefs which, ironically, became a welcome guide in lands around the Mediterranean, where Neoplatonism remained popular among Christian and Jewish communities. Al-Ghazzali then produced a severely critical work titled *Tahafut al-falasifa* (*Incoherence of the Philosophers*, 1958), which went so far as to brand certain aspects of Neoplatonism as anti-Muslim.

Al-Ghazzali's most significant work was in the application of logic to Muslim theology, in preference to the intuitive and metaphysical components of Neoplatonic thought. In particular, he made use of the Aristotelian syllogism as a frame of reference and tool for argument. In order to make elements of logic and philosophical argument more available to Muslim clerics and judges, he produced several handbooks.

Throughout his writing, al-Ghazzali calls for careful evaluation and awareness of the sources of religious knowledge. His stand on behalf of logic and his warnings about the seductiveness of emotional and occult movements to those insufficiently grounded in theology partly reflect the atmosphere in northeastern Iran during his life, exemplified by the Assassins, befuddled by hashish and wandering through the countryside in search of victims.

Al-Ghazzali's largest and most important work is *The Revival of Religious Sciences*. For the devout Muslim, it offers a complete guide to spirituality and the pious life. It provides complex prescriptions for life according to the Shari'a and explains how such a life, virtuous and devoid of sin, contributes to human salvation. About half of the work is concerned with what al-Ghazzali regarded as the foundational concepts necessary to devote the mind to the Muslim way.

In the contemporary West, there is a popular tendency to regard al-Ghazzali as a mystic, or at least as sentimentally disposed to mysticism. (It is with respect to this that scholars have raised the most doubts about the authenticity of works attributed to him.) His spiritual torment may have derived in part from mystical experiences. In fact, al-Ghazzali's ideas made it possible for Scholastic Islam and its clerics to coexist with mysticism; here lies his crucial contribution. He argued that the revelations of saintly persons supplement those of the Prophet and give individuals some spiritual independence from the authority and worldliness of the clerics. Al-Ghazzali always insisted, however, that Muhammad and his way must be the final authority in this world. Obedience to the Shari'a was the pathway to piety and salvation.

Whether al-Ghazzali's ideas constitute a reconciliation between Sunni orthodoxy and mysticism is debatable; the great complexity of his writings makes possible many interpretations. On one hand, he is concerned to defend orthodoxy against the doctrine of Isma'ili Shi'ism, which produced the Assassins and other splinter movements in Islam. On the other, al-Ghazzali criticizes the pedantry and corruption of the clerics in administering the Shari'a, as well as their preference for metaphysical explanations rather than careful, logical argument in Muslim apologetics.

The writings of this singular theologian were also essential to the development of later Islamic ideas of ethical government. Al-Ghazzali held the conservative position that a righteous king is one who enforces the Shari'a; one who neglects the Shari'a fails as a ruler. Although he warned that Muslims must obey unjust rulers (without condoning their injustices), his implicit judgment of secular authorities on grounds of their lack of adherence to the Shari'a opened the way for criticism of rulers and thus potential confrontation between religious and secular leadership.

Summary

In the Sunni world and beyond, al-Ghazzali is widely regarded as the greatest and most significant Muslim after Muhammad himself. The title *Hujjat al-Islam* (roof of Islam) is often applied to him. His work introduced a Greek philosophical strain into Islam which has persisted to the present. His impact on Islamic theology has been compared to that of Saint Thomas Aquinas on Christian thought, in that he constructed an essentially Scholastic framework of explanation heavily dependent on Aristotelian reason. Indeed, his writings were so exceptionally popular that some had been translated into Latin by the middle of the twelfth century and so were known to Aquinas.

Many other Christian and Jewish Scholastic theologians were influenced by al-Ghazzali.

Some of al-Ghazzali's critics suggest that the durability of Scholasticism in Islam, in contrast to the disintegration of this mode of thought in much of Christendom at the hands of Protestant theologians, has inhibited the adaptability of Islam to new ideas and conditions. Yet al-Ghazzali gave legitimacy to mystical experience and promoted the devout life based on the Shari'a, both of which strengthened Islam as a personal faith and helped to articulate standards of social and political justice. The interaction between these apparent dichotomies continues to make the writings of al-Ghazzali of vital interest to Muslims and Christians alike.

Bibliography

Alon, Ilai. "Al-Ghazali on Causality." *Journal of the American Oriental Society* 100 (1980): 397-405. Alon takes issue with the widely held view that al-Ghazzali was totally opposed to the notion of causality. A close examination of his writings shows instead a characteristic attempt to compromise between philosophical views and the concept of revelation and timeless being.

Binder, Leonard. "Al-Ghazali's Theory of Islamic Government." *Muslim World* 45 (1955): 229-241. Binder explains that al-Ghazzali argued for a balance of powers and clerical independence for the state. His disposition toward autocracy headed by a kind of philosopher-king reveals probable Hellenistic influence. Al-Ghazzali expressed nostalgia for caliphal power in Islam, which had waned seriously by his time.

Goodman, Lenn E. "Ghazali's Argument from Creation." *International Journal of Middle East Studies* 2 (1971): 67-85, 168-188. Goodman's exposition is an example of how one can attribute too much to an ancient figure. Ideas such as the finite nature of the world derived from creation stories are used to argue that al-Ghazzali was close to intuiting the theory of entropy and other modern cosmological concepts.

Hourani, George F. "The Chronology of Gazali's Writings." *Journal of the American Oriental Society* 79 (1959): 225-233. Provides a framework to study al-Ghazzali's intellectual development by precise dating and sequence of works, supplemented by careful textual study of particular works.

Najm, Sami M. "The Place and Function of Doubt in the Philosophies of Descartes and Al-Ghazali." *Philosophy East and West* 16 (1966): 133-141. Najm shows parallels between the two philosophers with respect to origin of doubt and the use of doubt to discover true knowledge; both concluded that ultimate foundations of knowledge are not subject to proof or demonstration. The possibility of "immediate intuition" is the solution to the problem of doubt.

Padwick, Constance E. "Al-Ghazali and the Arabic Versions of the Gospels." *Muslim World* 29 (1939): 130-140. An example of how Christian apologists have used al-Ghazzali. Padwick argues that he accepted the divine revelation of the Gospels and rejected the idea that they had been tampered with. Mentions numerous cases of collation of al-Ghazzali's references to Christ for use in missionary propaganda in the early twentieth century.

Sharma, Arvind. "The Spiritual Biography of Al-Ghazali." *Studies in Islam* 9 (1972): 65-85. This biographical study of al-Ghazzali is important because it shows how he engaged in a personal rather than a merely theological quest for God and incorporated into his philosophy many tenets of the main intellectual and religious movements of his time.

Watt, W. Montgomery. "The Authenticity of the Works Attributed to al-Ghazali." *Journal of the Royal Asiatic Society of Great Britain and Ireland* (1952): 24-45. Lists of works regarded as authentic, those which are of dubious origin, and those which are definitely to be rejected.

__________. *The Faith and Practice of al-Ghazali*. London: Allen and Unwin, 1953. Contains a translation of al-Ghazzali's spiritual testament, written shortly before his death.

__________. *Muslim Intellectual: A Study of al-Ghazali*. Edinburgh: Edinburgh University Press, 1963. In this study concerned with influences on al-Ghazzali's development, Watt suggests that he turned to mysticism because of the unsatisfactory state of theology and jurisprudence at the time. The author is critical of al-Ghazzali for placing immediate experience above knowledge derived by rational means.

Ronald W. Davis

GIOTTO

Born: c. 1266; Vespignano, near Florence, Italy
Died: January 8, 1337; Florence, Italy
Areas of Achievement: Art and architecture
Contribution: Since his own time, Giotto has been recognized as the first major figure in European painting. He was among the first to concentrate on the individual, an interest later shared by Renaissance artists; his paintings are remarkable for their revelations of human complexity.

Early Life

Giotto, which is perhaps the shortened form of the name Ambrogiotto, was the son of Bondone, a farmer of some distinction. While not much can be authenticated in various legends of Giotto's childhood, there is some warrant for believing that he was a precocious talent picked out at an early age by Cimabue, an important Florentine painter who died sometime around 1302. Evidently, Giotto began to sketch animals as a child without any formal training; he quickly flourished under the apprenticeship of Cimabue. By 1280, Florence was a thriving city of forty-five thousand people, renowned for its bankers, traders, artists, and craftsmen. It is thought that the artist profited from his observations of this earthy and pragmatic city and that his painting reflected a very broad and tolerant sensibility.

Giotto's painting marked such a departure from his predecessors that anecdotes of his self-confidence and originality usually are given some credit. According to one of these stories, he once painted a fly on the nose of a face on which Cimabue was working. The fly was so lifelike that the master tried to brush it off his painting several times before he grasped his student's jest. Giotto was also bold and outspoken: On one occasion he is recorded as having attacked the Franciscans for the fetish they made of their vows of poverty. It is likely that Giotto perfected his technique by traveling with Cimabue and helping him to complete many of his commissioned works.

Life's Work

Many of Giotto's paintings have disappeared, and there is still considerable debate about others that have been attributed to him. Some scholars, for example, identify the decorations in the Upper Church of the Basilica of Saint Francis as Giotto's first major work, but others question whether the painting style is congruent with other, less controversial Giotto frescoes. Perhaps his earliest surviving work is a nineteen-foot crucifix. It has won the admiration of some critics because Christ is depicted somewhat naturalistically, with his flesh sagging, rather than as the tense and trim figure of traditional art. At either end of the cross, the Virgin and Saint John sadly gaze at Christ—another departure from many medieval paintings, which include several allegorical scenes and various kinds of decoration. The emotion that is pictured is graphic yet austerely presented. Although some critics have not been impressed with the work's originality, doubting that it is Giotto's, Ricuccio Pucci, a parishioner of Santa Maria Novella in Florence, left funds in his will to keep a lamp perpetually burning before the crucifix "by the illustrious painter, Giotto."

In about 1304, Giotto began work on a series of thirty-eight frescoes in the Scrovegni Arena Chapel in Padua, painted a cycle of religious scenes that are considered to be some of the greatest works of Italian art, and created a three-part narrative in the Arena Chapel by arranging three horizontal strips of pictures around the walls. The top strip (scenes 1-12) portrays the early life of the Virgin. The second strip (scenes 17-27) depicts the early life of Christ. The final strip reenacts the passion of Christ—those events stemming from Judas' treachery to Pentecost, fifty days after the Resurrection, when the Holy Ghost descended on the disciples in tongues of fire and in the rushing of wind that gave them the power to speak to people of different languages.

The task the artist set for himself was enormous; it was nothing less than a retelling of the entire Christian legend. Not only did he confront the challenge of designing so many different scenes, he also had to find ways of inconspicuously indicating the narrative line and framing scenes so that they had the continuity of a story. The problem was to avoid the static, spectacle-like quality of individual panels, which might easily tire the eye. Somehow the artist had to generate movement between scenes while making them seem complete in themselves. Giotto met this technical challenge the way twentieth century filmmakers would, ensuring that each scene matched the others to form a flawless sequence. He also made sure that each scene flowed from left to right—as a page is read. The central action is in the center of the panel—as in scene 23, *The Baptism of Christ*—but the flanking figures on the left look at and past Christ, whereas the figures on the right look directly at him.

Giotto's deft management of movement in these scenes is complemented by his precise and sensitive handling of the smaller details and individual figures. As one critic points out, the artist never simply paints a symbol; every object bears the mark of careful observation and drawing—as in the tree with its barren branches and the weeping angels that convey the cosmic tragedy of the Crucifixion. The angels in flight who clasp their hands, grip their faces, bow their heads, or raise their faces, evoke the many different postures of suffering, whereas the tree stands alone, to the side, a mute sign of the emptiness that accompanies grief.

The conclusion to Giotto's monumental Christian narrative in the Arena Chapel was *The Last Judgment*, a gigantic fresco on the entrance wall of the chapel. Christ sits, ringed in an oval, surrounded by the Apostles, judging the saved and the damned. Above Christ, angels roll back the heavens to reveal the gates of Paradise. Below Him are the horrors of Hell, full of writhing, bent over, wretched creatures. The fresco abounds with numbers of figures strategically placed to reveal the hierarchy of Creation. The population density and the compositional dynamic are so great that the viewer is overwhelmed with the magnificence of the divine economy. On this one wall, every viewer was expected to find his or her own place in the universe. Perhaps this is one reason that Giotto put himself, as well as Enrico Scrovegni, the donor of the chapel, near the bottom of the fresco among a group of the blessed. Scrovegni is pictured presenting a model of the chapel itself, as though Giotto wanted to emphasize what human hands had wrought. The Arena Chapel is a startling work of religious art, for it invites viewers to admire an artist's conception of the Last Judgment. In a rather modern way, this conceit of the model draws attention to the work of art itself and to the artist.

Giotto went on to create beautiful frescoes in the Peruzzi Chapel and the Bardi Chapel. Among his greatest works are *Saint John the Baptist* and the *Life of Saint Francis*. As in his earlier work, the artist created cycles of scenes that told powerful stories. Nevertheless, he extended his technique by setting his monumental figures against equally monumental buildings, thus creating a deep sense of space absent from his earlier paintings. Although these works are not informed by the principles of perspective that give objects the illusion of three dimensions and measure space in mathematical proportions, the clarity and intricacy of Giotto's compositions come close to achieving the effects of the sophisticated methods perfected shortly after his death. Even when Giotto's paintings are, so to speak, out of perspective—as in the case of *The Raising of Drusiana*, where Saint John the Evangelist's fingers are much too long—the dramatic impact of exaggerating certain parts of the fresco reveal the soundness of Giotto's art. It is the simple, rugged, spiritual power of Saint John's gesturing fingers, not their size, which is important. The saint's sheer physicality makes the story of the raising of Drusiana a palpable experience.

Summary

Late in his career, Giotto turned to architecture, a natural development in an artist given to creating massive frescoes peopled with so many different examples of humanity and architectural forms. Sometime after 1330 he was named chief architect of the cathedral in Florence. He lived as an artist of great influence with many pupils and admirers and was esteemed by such great literary figures as Dante, Petrarch, and Giovanni Boccaccio. Giovanni Villani, a contemporary historian, wrote that Giotto was entombed in the Florentine cathedral "with great honors and at the expense of the commune." This last observation suggests something important about his art: It was communal in the largest sense. A civilization believed that he painted for them and represented to them an encompassing vision of existence with greater imagination than any of his predecessors. The scale on which Giotto worked has never been surpassed. The epic grandeur of his frescoes, the human interest of his smaller scenes, capture the many levels on which life and art can be appreciated.

Bibliography

Battisti, Eugenio. *Giotto: Biographical and Critical Study*. Lausanne, Switzerland: Skira, 1960. Battisti concentrates on the artist in his time, his relationship to sculpture and to his contemporaries, especially Dante and the Franciscans. A section on the biographical records of Giotto's life is organized by key dates. Considerable attention is paid to the Assisi frescoes. Color plates, careful descriptions of individual paintings, a selected bibliography, and an index of names and places make this a valuable study.

Cole, Bruce. *Giotto and Florentine Painting*. New York: Harper and Row, Publishers, 1976. A scholarly monograph with a selected bibliography, an outline of important dates, an index, and fifty-nine illustrations. The first full-scale treatment of Giotto in terms of the Florentine art of his century, with excellent discussions of the painter's materials, style, and technique. Includes informative scholarly notes.

Eimerl, Sarel. *The World of Giotto*. New York: Time, 1967. An excellent overview of the artist's cultural, political, and artistic worlds. Several chapters consider Giotto's fellow artists and other contemporaries. Analyses of individual paintings are clear but rudimentary. Many large black-and-white and color plates give a comprehensive picture of Giotto's career. Bibliography, chronology, and index make this a good introductory study.

Giotto. *The Complete Paintings of Giotto*. Edited by Andrew Martindale and Edi Baccheschi. New York: H. N. Abrams, 1966. A concise introduction to the painter's life and career, including an outline of his critical history. Large sections of Giotto's paintings are produced in handsome color plates. Many small black-and-white plates are accompanied by excellent commentary on their meaning and on the context in which they were created. A catalog of Giotto's works and an annotated bibliography complete this indispensable volume.

Meiss, Millard. *Giotto and Assisi*. New York: New York University Press, 1960. A brief monograph that reads like a transcript of an address given at New York University, this study attempts to outline a solution to the debate over whether Giotto painted the *Legend of Saint Francis*. The issue cannot be completely settled, since certain kinds of evidence are lacking, but the critic makes a spirited case for attributing this important work to Giotto.

Moshe, Barash. *Giotto and the Language of Gesture*. Cambridge: Cambridge

University Press, 1987. Eighty black-and-white illustrations help to support this well-focused study of the "character and history of the gestures depicted in Giotto's paintings." Chapters on how gestures have been interpreted in art and on Giotto's use of the "speaking hand," "covered hands," and the "grasping of the wrist" admirably concentrate on the artist's gift for creating the precise emotional detail—although it is not certain how much Giotto intended by certain gestures that may have been over-interpreted by the critic.

Perkins, F. Mason. *Giotto*. London: George Bell and Sons, 1907. Although superseded in many respects by more recent work, this book is still valuable as a general survey of Giotto's life and work. The writing is very clear and helpful in explaining the development of the artist. Includes thirty-eight illustrations with a bibliography and catalog of the artist's works.

Carl Rollyson
Lisa Paddock

GOTTFRIED VON STRASSBURG

Born: fl. c. 1210; Alsace?
Died: Date unknown; place unknown
Area of Achievement: Literature
Contribution: Gottfried was one of the great writers of the German courtly epic during the High Middle Ages.

Early Life

Little is known of Gottfried von Strassburg's life. It is presumed that he was of middle-class origins, and since he was well educated perhaps he was also a member of the clergy. He may have been born in the Alsace region. He lived around 1200, the zenith of the European Middle Ages and the high point of German courtly culture. It was the era of feudalism, with society composed of the knightly class, the serfs, and the clergy. As the custodians of religious and secular heritage, the priests and monks were the most educated (literate) of the three classes.

During this time, the court of the king and his knight-vassals was the center of worldly culture. It was the age of the courtly love lyric, a well-defined canon of poetry in which the knight proclaimed his love for his lady and pledged to do great deeds in her honor. Through such devotion, the knight was to be lifted to a higher spiritual existence. The great stories of love and adventure, the romance—from the Provençal *romans*—also had their origin in this period of European culture.

Life's Work

As one of the three greatest writers of the courtly epic in Germany (the other two being Wolfram von Eschenbach and Hartmann von Aue), Gottfried was a master of the genre and told his tales with a perfected sense of verse forms and a brilliant command of imagery. He is best known for the epic *Tristan und Isolde* (c. 1210; *Tristan and Isolde*), one of the great romances of the period. Eleven manuscript copies of his text have survived, most of them written in Alsatian dialect. His tale was never completed, and two later writers, Ulrich von Türheim and Heinrich von Freiberg, completed other versions of the Gottfried text. The love story is legendary, that is, a fictionalized account of a historical event the details of which have long been forgotten. The primary source for Gottfried's version was that of the Anglo-Norman poet Thomas von Britanje. There had been an earlier German rendering by Eilhart von Oberge, composed around 1180, which certainly had some influence on Gottfried's tale. The themes of Gottfried's *Tristan and Isolde* are the demoniac and transcendent, or healing, powers of love.

Told in thirty chapters, Gottfried's epic relates the tragic tale of the fated lovers, Tristan and Isolde. Tristan was the child of the model English knight

Rivalin and his love, Blancheflor. Their story foreshadows to a degree the later fate of their son. A knight at the court of King Mark of Cornwall, the young, inexperienced, and somewhat rash Rivalin meets the beautiful and equally youthful Blancheflor. In the typical manner of the courtly romance, they keep their love secret from the world. Their budding relationship is interrupted by the call to battle, and the brash Rivalin suffers a mortal wound. Disguised as a doctor, Blancheflor visits him on the battlefield, and they consummate their love. He is revived from his wounds by her kisses, yet after the two elope, he perishes in a battle. Blancheflor, unaware of her lover's fate, brings a child into the world but dies of grief in the course of premature childbirth when she learns of Rivalin's death. That child is Tristan—whose name, from the French *triste*, suggests sadness. He was conceived in that moment of passion that had revived his father from the brink of death and that would later lead to the loss of his mother. Thus, the story of Tristan's parents ironically establishes the association of love and tragic death that will be the theme of the son's story.

Tristan is reared by Rual and Floraete. He develops into a model student and is skilled in the manly virtues of knighthood. Like his father, he eventually goes to the court of King Mark and impresses all with his skill and learning. King Mark further undertakes Tristan's upbringing and becomes his most trusted friend. On one of his heroic adventures, Tristan visits Ireland and King Morold, who has been demanding large tributes from Mark. He engages in battle with King Morold and kills him. Wounded by the king's poisoned sword, Tristan can be healed only by Morold's sister. Disguised as a minstrel, he visits her and is healed. He then instructs her beautiful daughter, Isolde, in music and the social graces. When he returns to England, Tristan tells King Mark of Isolde's great beauty and the king decides that he must wed her. He sends Tristan back to Ireland to claim Isolde. Tristan is recognized as the one who killed King Morold and is hated by Isolde for murdering her uncle, but after slaying a dragon that has plagued the kingdom Tristan is allowed to take Isolde back as King Mark's bride.

Isolde's mother has brewed a love potion for her daughter and King Mark. On the journey to Cornwall, Isolde's servant, Brangane, confuses the potion with a drink of water she has given to Tristan and Isolde. The two fall madly in love. Tristan breaks his pledge of loyalty to Mark when he consummates his spiritual union with Isolde. The two lovers decide to deceive the king. Yet, discovered by Mark, they are banished from the court. Tristan and Isolde then seek shelter in a secluded grotto that is an enchanted domain of love. They are eventually discovered. Isolde must return to the king, and Tristan voluntarily leaves her so that she will remain safe. He goes to Normandy, where he serves as a knight and eventually marries another, Isolde Weisshand.

Gottfried's version remains incomplete at this point; the conclusion was written by his followers. Tristan is severely wounded in battle and sends for Isolde so that she might heal him with her magic arts. A white sail on the ship is the signal that she is on her way. Tristan's jealous wife, Isolde Weisshand, forces a messenger to lie and report the sighting of a black sail. Tristan dies in despair, and Isolde also perishes from grief upon her arrival. In the end, King Mark has them buried side by side.

Gottfried's epic epitomizes many of the virtues of German knighthood: Tristan's prowess and courage in battle, his proper bearing at court, and his skill and learning all suggest a vision of the ideal knight. Ultimately, he is even loyal to King Mark and fights on his behalf for Isolde. It is a magic love potion that robs him of his will and causes his betrayal of his king. The breaking of the oath of fealty to one's liege lord was a serious offense within the culture of knighthood, but Tristan is clearly at the mercy of powers beyond his control. Gottfried's theme is thus very much about the irrational as it is manifested in human love. Although Gottfried lived during the great era of the courtly love lyric, a highly stylized genre which dealt with the ennobling aspects of a knight's idealized devotion for his chosen lady, his work concentrates on the more secular dimensions of love. Passion (and the irrational) is a kind of demoniac power that disrupts the normal course of society; it causes the individual to ignore its rules and prohibitions. Tristan and Isolde are therefore fated for a tragic end; those who live outside society must finally pay the price.

Yet the theme of passion is not to be interpreted solely in this negative fashion. Tristan and Isolde's love is also a transcendent power; it raises them above the everyday world into what is clearly an exalted realm of harmony and unity, into the oneness and bliss of the love experience (as in the famous episode in the grotto). Thus, love is also a spiritually healing power which abolishes the loneliness and suffering of the individual. It "cures" the ultimate sense of separateness that plagues all human beings. Isolde's healing of Tristan's wounds, for example, suggests this in a symbolic fashion. Gottfried's story of the fated lovers revolves around universal contradictions of the human experience.

Summary

As one of the great authors of the courtly epic during the Middle Ages, Gottfried von Strassburg will surely retain his place not only within German literature but also within world literature. Along with the writings of Wolfram von Eschenbach, which Gottfried abhorred, his work represents the zenith of the courtly epic genre within the German tradition. A master storyteller, his narrative style is flowing, and his verse forms are musical and well constructed. The epic foreshadowing of Tristan and Isolde's fate in the story of Tristan's parents, Rivalin and Blancheflor, suggests a writer who is in full command of the skills of his trade.

In contrast to Wolfram, whose major epic, *Parzival* (c. 1200-1210; English translation, 1894), deals with the spiritual issues of absolute truth and man's proper relationship to God, Gottfried's text treats the earthly and secular themes of beauty, passion, and love. If the Wolfram text revolves around the theme of divine love, then Gottfried's focuses on profane passion. Even when his narrative deals with aspects of physical love, it does so with circumspection and stylistic distance. He depicts these thematic concerns with a degree of elegance and grace that raises his work far above the works of his contemporaries.

Gottfried's *Tristan and Isolde* certainly remains one of the greatest love stories ever told. The intensity of the characters' passion and their tragic fate captures the mysteries and sufferings inherent in the human capacity to love. The power of his story has exerted its influence on subsequent centuries. The nineteenth century German writer Karl Immermann composed a version in 1841 which remained uncompleted, the great composer Richard Wagner wrote an opera based on the legend in 1859, and in 1903 Thomas Mann wrote a novella, *Tristan* (English translation, 1925), which incorporates themes from both Gottfried's and Wagner's versions.

Bibliography

Batts, Michael S. *Gottfried von Strassburg*. New York: Twayne Publishers, 1971. An excellent introduction to Gottfried's life and times with an interpretive focus on his *Tristan and Isolde* and on the legend in general. Contains a bibliography.

Jackson, W. T. H. "The Role of Brangaene in Gottfried's *Tristan*." *The Germanic Review* 27 (1953): 290-296. A brief essay on the pivotal position of Isolde's servant. Contains notes with bibliographical information.

__________. "Tristan the Artist in Gottfried's Poem." *PMLA* 77 (1962): 364-372. This scholarly essay examines the title character and the talents he exhibits at court. Contains notes with bibliographical information.

Loomis, Roger, ed. *Arthurian Literature in the Middle Ages*. Oxford: Clarendon Press, 1959. An important collection of essays on medieval literature with several on Gottfried's epic. Contains a bibliography.

Willson, H. B. "Vicissitudes in Gottfried's *Tristan*." *The Modern Language Review* 52 (1957): 203-213. This essay discusses the narrative structure of Gottfried's text. Contains notes with bibliographical information.

Thomas F. Barry

THE GRACCHI

Tiberius Sempronius Gracchus

Born: 163 B.C.; probably Rome
Died: 133 B.C.; Rome

Gaius Sempronius Gracchus

Born: 153 B.C.; probably Rome
Died: 121 B.C.; Rome
Area of Achievement: Government
Contribution: Although the Gracchi brothers were born into one of the wealthiest and most influential families in Rome, they dedicated their lives to the service of the people. In the waning years of the Roman Republic, when greed and the lust for power consumed the energies of many from the ruling class, the Gracchi tried through a series of reforms to restore the vigor of popular government; many of their ideas were later adopted by rulers such as Julius Caesar and his nephew and heir, Augustus.

Early Lives

Tiberius and Gaius Gracchus were among the twelve children born to Tiberius Sempronius Gracchus and Cornelia, the daughter of Scipio Africanus, the general who defeated the Carthaginian leader Hannibal in the Second Punic War. The elder Gracchus died when Tiberius was twelve and Gaius was barely two, but his widow reared the boys and her other surviving child, a daughter, in the traditions of their ancestors and in the virtues responsible for the greatness of the Republic. She was assisted by Diophanes of Mitylene, a noted master of rhetoric, and Blossius, the famous Stoic philosopher. Ptolemy VI, the King of Egypt, sought to marry Cornelia, but rather than deny her duty to her children, she rejected his suit. Remaining in Rome, she set an example of simplicity and frugality which both amazed and confounded her friends.

A serious youth, Tiberius was quiet, gentle, and always obedient to his elders. To test his courage and further shape his character, he was sent to Africa during the final phase of the Third Punic War to serve under his brother-in-law, Scipio the Younger. At the age of sixteen, Tiberius distinguished himself by being the first to climb the walls of Carthage when the Roman army launched its final assault on the doomed city. Shortly thereafter the war ended, and he returned to Rome, where he was betrothed to and later married Claudia, the daughter of Appius Claudius, a man with tremendous influence and great wealth. In 137, Tiberius was chosen a quaestor, and in the Numantine Wars in Spain which followed his election, he distinguished himself for his bravery and fairness in dealing with the enemies of the Republic. He was elected tribune in 133 at the age of twenty-nine.

Although Gaius Gracchus eventually proved himself to be a more effective politician than his brother, as a young man he had the reputation of being emotional, high-strung, fiery tempered, and extravagant. In his teens he, too, was sent to serve under his brother-in-law, Scipio the Younger, in Spain. When he was twenty, his brother selected him in absentia as one of the commissioners to conduct the redistribution of land under the provisions of the revised agrarian law, but the untimely murder of Tiberius rendered his appointment useless. Gaius returned to Rome, married the daughter of Publius Crassus, and assumed the character of a young man of fashion with very expensive tastes. The senators who were responsible for the death of Tiberius constantly anticipated the revenge of the younger Gracchus.

Goaded by the jibes of his family and friends, Gaius finally sought public office. Chosen a quaestor, he was sent to Sardinia to serve under Aurelius Orestes. Rather than considering his duty an exile, Gaius enjoyed it because at the age of twenty-seven he was not yet ready for a life in public service. Days spent on the march or in camp suited him well. The success of Gaius in Sardinia only deepened the suspicions of his enemies in the senate, and to keep him abroad they extended the term of Orestes and consequently those of his subordinates. This devious manipulation of the civil service infuriated Gaius, who returned to Rome without permission to confront his enemies. Accused of acting contrary to orders, a charge of which he was easily acquitted, Gaius began to consider seriously entering public life. Against the advice of his mother, he offered himself as a candidate for the office of tribune, and in 123 he was elected to that position.

Life's Work

While Tiberius may have been encouraged by his mother and his former tutors to seek a tribuneship, it was the plight of the poor that really moved him to forgo the quiet of private life for the stress and uncertainty of elected office. For decades the number of small family farms had been declining, and Tiberius wanted to reverse this trend. As the Romans conquered their neighbors, thereby laying the foundations of an empire, they increased the slave population by a tremendous percentage since those who resisted the power of the Republic were condemned to perpetual servitude. Many a wealthy Roman had grown even richer by investing first in slaves and then in both public and private land which could be devoted to agriculture. These *latifundia*, great estates worked by slave labor, yielded an enormous profit. Roman farmers were forced to sell their land when they discovered that they could not compete with the cheaper slave-produced foodstuffs which flooded the market. In many instances, they sold their farms to the very men who had driven them to bankruptcy. By the thousands these dispossessed men flocked to Rome with their families hoping to find jobs, but there were none. Tiberius wanted to put this vast army of unemployed farmers back on the land, and his program of agrarian reform was designed to do exactly that.

In 376, the tribunes Licinius and Sextius had passed a law which limited the amount of public land which could be held by one individual to five hundred *iugera*, or 311 acres. This measure was ignored because no mechanism was ever created to enforce it. Tiberius now sought not only to revive it but also to form a three-man commission to see that the letter of the law was fulfilled. On the advice of some of the most respected men in Rome, he sought not to punish those who had violated the law but merely to encourage them to abandon the land they occupied illegally. To make the task easier, compensation in the form of the fair market price of each acre abandoned was offered by the government. The land-rich rejected the reforms of Tiberius and began to offer bribes to anyone they thought could help defeat the measure. Many a senator was counted among those who sold influence in exchange for gold, but an honest man, Marcus Octavius, was persuaded to stop Tiberius. Octavius was the fellow tribune of Tiberius, and he had the obligation to veto any bill proposed by his colleague which in his opinion violated the rights of the Roman people. The founders of the Republic had created this system of checks and balances to ensure honest government, but now this safeguard of liberty was unwittingly corrupted to serve greed. Octavius was convinced that the newly revised law was illegal; thus, he vetoed it. No amount of pleading could make him change his mind. Frustrated at every turn, Tiberius resorted to measures which were ill-advised, if not unlawful.

The mild law was withdrawn and a new measure with no provision for compensation was substituted. Octavius naturally opposed this measure with more energy than he had the previous one, and thus Tiberius appealed to the people to vote Marcus out of office. This was an illegal move, but once aroused, Tiberius would not heed the advice of his family or his associates. When Octavius had been recalled, Tiberius had one of his close supporters elected in his place and the agrarian law was finally passed. The three men quickly appointed to enforce the law were Appius Claudius, Gaius Gracchus, and Publius Crassus. Tiberius had originally reserved one of these places for himself, but he was persuaded to appoint his brother's father-in-law instead.

The method Tiberius used to finance his plan was ingenious. King Attalus III of Pergamum, a state in Asia Minor, had, in his will, left his kingdom and all of his treasure to the Roman people in the hope of sparing his subjects Rome's inevitable conquest. Tiberius now proposed to sell the treasures and use the profits to buy farm tools and livestock for those to receive land under the provisions of the new law. It was a very popular move with the people but not with the senate.

Just as Tiberius began to implement his plan, his term of office expired. Convinced that the success of the new agrarian law depended on him, Tiberius ignored tradition and stood for reelection. The senate responded to his challenge by goading the city mob into a frenzy. In the resulting riot, Tiberius was beaten to death and his body was thrown into the Tiber River. Three hundred of his closest followers were arrested and condemned to death without a trial.

Thus, when Gaius was elected tribune ten years after his brother, the senators who had arranged the murder of Tiberius had reason to fear for their lives. Almost immediately after his election, Gaius proposed legislation to punish Octavius and Popillius, the magistrate who had unjustly sentenced Tiberius' associates to death. Only the intervention of Cornelia saved Octavius, but Popillius fled Rome. Gaius, who craved the adoration of the people and welcomed conflict, revived his brother's agrarian law in the face of certain senatorial opposition. That controversy was only the beginning.

While serving in Sardinia, Gaius had witnessed the privation of the average Roman soldier, who was ill equipped and poorly fed. In quick succession, laws were passed to furnish each soldier with clothing proper to the season and climate at government expense. By law, boys under the age of seventeen were forbidden to enlist in the army. The market price of grain sold to the poor was lowered and the government absorbed the difference. To curtail the control of the senate over the judiciary, he expanded the number of judges and then personally recruited them from the nonsenatorial orders. Roads and public granaries were built, giving jobs to the unemployed. Then, as his first term of office ended, Gaius turned his attention to the founding of colonies as places of settlement for the landless.

When Gaius sought reelection, he met with no open opposition from his enemies in the senate, because he was too popular with the people. Unwisely, Gaius left Rome to supervise personally the laying of the foundations of a new colony on the site of Carthage. In his absence, his opponents began to undermine his policies. Returning to the capital, he found Rome on the verge of anarchy. The issue that led to the downfall of Gaius was his proposal to extend the benefits of Roman citizenship to the Italian allies. This reform would have seriously weakened the power and influence of the senate. Once again he sought the endorsement of the people, but this time he lost at the polls. At last his senatorial enemies had their chance. Gaius was declared an outlaw, and within a day the second of the remarkable Gracchi brothers was dead, the victim of a murder-suicide. Three thousand of his followers were judicially murdered, and an uneasy peace settled over Rome.

Summary

In the middle of the second century before the Christian era, the Roman Republic faced a constitutional crisis which threatened to destroy the fabric of the state. Invincible on the field of battle, Rome suddenly enjoyed unbelievable wealth as the booty from a host of countries flowed into the capital, accompanied by thousands of captives who were reduced to servitude. Condemned to endless labor on the huge farms that dotted the Italian landscape, these slaves drove free Romans from their tiny family farms when they could no longer compete. As they swelled the mob of unemployed in the capital, the Gracchi brothers, Tiberius and Gaius, arose to give them hope. In their respective programs lay the last and best chance for the Republic, and their assassinations were its death knell.

An uneasy quiet descended on Rome after the murder of the Gracchi and their supporters, but within a generation the peace was shattered as two men, Gaius Marius and Lucius Cornelius Sulla, vied for control of the state. Marius was a successful general who modernized the Roman army, transforming it from a force formed of draftees into one filled with long-term volunteers. Most of these recruits were landless peasants who received a tract of land at the end of their service; thus, one of the proposals of the Gracchi was revived and became a permanent part of the Roman system. Marius led the Populares, the party of the Gracchi, while Sulla headed the Optimates, the party composed of the senatorial enemies of Tiberius and Gaius. In the ensuing civil war, thousands of innocent victims from both sides were butchered.

A slave rebellion, countless conspiracies, and another civil war followed in the wake of Sulla's victory. Then the Romans, weary of the bloodshed, turned to Julius Caesar for deliverance. Caesar used a number of the ideas of the Gracchi to win and retain popular support, a practice continued by his imperial successors. The welfare system proposed by Gaius Gracchus thus became a political weapon and then a financial liability during the latter days of the Roman Empire. The distribution of public lands to veterans, however, settled thousands of responsible and loyal citizens on the frontiers of the Empire. Thus, the best that Rome had to offer survived despite the steady decline of the imperial system.

With the rediscovery of classical culture during the Renaissance, the Gracchi once again caught the public's imagination, but it was not until the birth of popular republics in the United States and France that they regained their places in the pantheon of democratic heroes. Their deeds have become legendary and their names are synonymous with reform and the best in the liberal tradition.

Bibliography

Badian, E. *Foreign Clientalae, 264-270 B.C. Oxford*: Clarendon Press, 1958. This scholarly work is extremely valuable because it enables the student to place the Gracchi in the context of Roman history. The bibliography serves as an excellent departure point for further reading.

Bernstein, Alvin H. *Tiberius Sempronius Gracchus, Tradition and Apostasy*. Ithaca, N.Y.: Cornell University Press, 1978. The author has written an excellent, well-balanced biography of the eldest of the Gracchi. Each step in the career of Tiberius is carefully examined and evaluated. The bibliography is comprehensive.

Plutarch. *Plutarch's Lives*. Vol. 10, *Agis and Cleomenes, and Tiberius and Gaius Gracchus, Philopoemen and Titus Flaminus*, 1967. Translated by Bernadotte Perrin. Cambridge, Mass.: Harvard University Press, 1968. Another volume in the Loeb Classical Library, this work contains the Greek original and a very fine English translation. Plutarch supplies his reader with a clear, concise, and moving portrait of the two brothers who might have saved the Roman Republic.

Scullard, H. H. *From the Gracchi to Nero: A History of Rome from 133 B.C. to A.D. 68*. London: Methuen and Co., 1959, 5th ed. 1982. This work chronicles not only the rise and fall of the Gracchi but also the aftermath of their attempts to save the Roman Republic: the tragic decline of Roman liberty from the mid-second century B.C. to the reign of Nero. The author also includes a number of chapters dealing with other aspects of Roman culture.

Stockton, David. *The Gracchi*. Oxford: Clarendon Press, 1979. For those unfamiliar with the actual mechanisms by which the Roman Republic was governed the author provides an excellent foreword. This slim volume provides a detailed treatment of the careers of the Gracchi as well as a series of useful appendices.

Clifton W. Potter, Jr.

GREGORY VII

Born: c. 1020; Sanoa, Tuscany
Died: May 25, 1085; Salerno
Areas of Achievement: Religion and church government
Contribution: As the dominant figure in the medieval Papacy, Gregory VII launched a wave of reform which brought about much of the structure of the modern Roman Catholic church. His clash with Henry IV was merely the first in a series of struggles between the lords spiritual and temporal which characterized the Middle Ages.

Early Life

Little is known of the early life of the man named Hildebrand who became Pope Gregory VII. He was born in Tuscany at Sanoa, probably around 1020, to a family of moderate means. Early biographers, seeking to create or emphasize parallels with the life of Christ, wrote of his early years playing among the wood chips at the feet of his father, a carpenter. Such a picture was greatly exaggerated. Though Hildebrand's father, Bonizo, a Roman citizen, was apparently of humble birth, his mother, Bertha, was well connected. Her brother was abbot of the monastery of Saint Mary, on the Aventine Hill in Rome.

Hildebrand was sent to his uncle and educated at Saint Mary's. He studied Latin rhetoric, mathematics, music, dialectics, and the teachings of the church fathers. He studied also at the Lateran Palace. Not surprisingly, after such an education, he decided to become a monk. He was appalled by the corruption of the Church and turned instead to the ascetic severities of monastic life. He entered the Benedictine Order and traveled in both France and Germany.

Hildebrand returned to Rome as chaplain to Gregory VI, one of three rival claimants to the throne of Saint Peter. When all three were deposed by Emperor Henry III in favor of a German pope, Hildebrand left in exile with Gregory VI. He returned permanently to Rome with Bruno (Pope Leo IX) in 1049. According to tradition, the two traveled to Rome as pilgrims; Bruno refused the papacy until it was offered by the people and clergy of Rome. His subsequent term of service with Pope Leo IX began the long period of Hildebrand's influence in Rome and in the papal administrations of the eleventh century.

Hildebrand was small and slightly built, with a swarthy complexion that was set off by his bright and piercing eyes. Though small in stature, Hildebrand played a giant's role for twenty-five years, during the reigns of Leo IX, Stephen IX, Benedict X, Nicholas II, and Alexander II. Hildebrand traveled to France to promote reform and represented the Papacy in Germany at the court of the queen regent during the minority of King Henry IV. Upon the death of Alexander II in 1073, Hildebrand called for three days of mourning. In the midst of the funeral service, however, the crowd shouted out their desire for Hildebrand to become pope. The cardinals led him to the throne of Saint Peter and there invested him as Pope Gregory VII.

Life's Work

Gregory VII is the dominant figure in eleventh century European religious history. He took a fragmented and corrupt Church and altered it irrevocably, establishing the norm of clerical celibacy and laying the foundation for the doctrine of papal infallibility. (Although the dogma of papal infallibility was not officially adopted by the Roman Catholic church until 1870, many popes before that time had claimed for themselves this supreme apostolic power.) His efforts to enlarge the domain of the Papacy led inevitably toward a prolonged clash with secular powers. Gregory set himself the task of establishing norms in three major areas: clerical celibacy, simony, and lay investiture.

During much of its history, the Catholic church had allowed its priests to marry. From the lowest local priests through the highest bishops, married clergy (or unmarried clergy with recognized concubines) were common in the eleventh century. Only in monasteries was celibacy required. Inspired by the reforms of the Cluny monastic movement in France, Gregory led an attack on married clergy, demanded celibacy, and endeavored (with varying degrees of success) to bar married clergy from the administration of the sacraments. Gregory believed that a married cleric would be not only diverted from single-minded devotion to God but also tempted to lay claim to the office as an inheritance for his children.

The second major reform issue was simony—the purchasing of church office. Since many church positions carried with them considerable territorial possessions and temporal power, they were often in great demand and were awarded on the basis of money paid. Gregory refused to tolerate this practice, condemning those who acquired office in this manner and refusing to allow them to officiate in religious services.

In addition to these two reforms, which concerned practices largely within the church, Gregory attacked the practice of lay investiture—and brought the Church into confrontation with the empire. Traditionally, kings had invested bishops and abbots with their emblems of office (the ring and staff), and the clergy thus invested served in a feudal relationship to the king as well as being responsible to their ecclesiastical superiors. In 1075, Gregory outlawed the practice of lay investiture. This action was truly revolutionary; predictably, it was ignored by the German emperor, Henry IV, who saw investiture as his royal prerogative (a position in which he was supported by the German clergy and nobility). It was also traditional for the king to consent to the election of the pope (though not actually to invest the pope with his official symbols).

In a document called *Dictatus papae*, Gregory listed the basic tenets of his philosophy—for it was more philosophy and politics than theology. Gregory claimed for the Papacy the right to correct abuses and laid down the foundation of papal supremacy by declaring that the clergy were dependent on the pope and that both laity and clergy were subject to the pope in all matters.

While dealing with reforms within the Church, Gregory VII was also active in the secular world, seeking to extend the territorial holdings of the Papacy and to extend his authority in the German and Italian monarchies surrounding him. Inevitably, Gregory came into conflict with Henry IV, despite the fact that Henry had assented to Gregory's elevation to the papacy and the two had initially worked together. When Gregory declared that to disobey the pope was to disobey God's will, Henry became enraged. At the imperial synod at Worms in 1076, Henry deposed Gregory, who responded by excommunicating the emperor and suspending him from governing. It soon became clear to Henry that he had overreacted; he was told by his bishops and princes to seek reconciliation with the pope lest he lose his crown.

Henry determined to go to the pope and seek absolution. Crossing the Alps in midwinter, Henry met the pope at Canossa, where, barefoot and dressed in penitential sackcloth, the emperor received absolution. Although frequently viewed as a triumph of the Church over secular power (indeed, the phrase "go to Canossa" has come to mean "beg forgiveness"), it was in fact a royal victory. It suited Henry's political purposes to seek absolution from the pope, and Henry's presence in Italy created problems for Gregory.

The peace between these two strong men did not last long. Henry soon violated his agreements with the pope, and rebellious German nobles elected Rudolph of Swabia as king. In 1080, Gregory again excommunicated and deposed Henry, offering papal support to Rudolph. Meanwhile, Henry, in full control of the German clergy, declared Gregory deposed and supported the election of Guibert of Ravenna (Clement III) as antipope. Henry conquered Rome, installing Clement III in Saint Peter's; Henry was, in turn, crowned emperor by Clement in 1084. Gregory escaped Rome and fled to Salerno, where he died in 1085. According to one biographer, Gregory's last words were eloquent: "I have loved justice and hated iniquity, therefore I die in exile."

Summary

Gregory VII played a major role in the development of the modern Roman Catholic church. It was his leadership at the Lateran Council of 1059 which established the College of Cardinals and changed the method of papal election. Traditionally, popes had been chosen by the clergy and citizens of Rome, making them subject always to the power of Roman noble families and, later, the German rulers. Though working imperfectly at first, Gregory's effort to establish the College of Cardinals as the vehicle for papal election was one of his most lasting legacies. During the twenty-five-year period after his reign, Gregory's reforming zeal had a particularly strong influence on his successors.

Gregory's rule was the turning point in the medieval Papacy. His insistence upon clerical celibacy turned all the clergy into one great monastic order in an attempt to separate it forever from the conflicting claims of the secular world. His attack upon simony and lay investiture similarly strengthened the Church, setting up barriers to the competitive claims of lay politics. Gregory's overriding achievement was to strengthen the Papacy and extend its influence. He was the first to claim for the pope universal authority. Calling the authority of the pope the authority of Christ, Gregory assumed the power to depose both bishops and emperors: As Christ had given to Saint Peter the power to bind or loose on earth, so the pope could claim such authority in His name. Gregory endeavored to extend papal power over broad areas of Western Europe, seeking to establish papal authority in England, Spain, Corsica, Sardinia, Hungary, Serbia, and Kiev.

For the grandeur of his vision, his efforts to extend power, his zeal for an active life, and even his small stature, Gregory has often been compared to Napoleon. Although Gregory died in exile, deemed a failure by the world, he was triumphant in his effort to move the Church forward, reformed within and extending its power without. He fell as a result of his challenge to the power of the state in the person of Henry IV. It had not been his intention to seek conflict, but his zeal for reform and for expanded papal authority led him into the confrontation.

Gregory possessed a fiery and forceful personality, passionate beliefs, and an inflexible and uncompromising will. Such a man sowing the wind of reform—and in so doing asserting papal authority—could not fail to reap the whirlwind of opposition to his demands on the part of secular rulers. Like Luther in a later era, he could "do no other." In recognition of his formidable character and far-reaching accomplishments, Gregory VII was canonized by Pope Paul V in 1606. His papacy remains one of the rocks on which the Roman Catholic church is built.

Bibliography

Baldwin, Marshall W., ed. *Christianity Through the Thirteenth Century*. New York: Walker and Co., 1970. Useful primarily for an overview of the medieval Church, Baldwin's book does little more than set the stage on which Pope Gregory VII played his role.

Barraclough, Geoffrey. *The Medieval Papacy*. New York: Harcourt, Brace and World, 1968. An excellent and balanced discussion of the Church in the Middle Ages and the role played by Gregory VII. Clearly written, with a straightforward chronological format, this book is particularly helpful to those less familiar with this period of history. Recognizing Gregory's flaws, the author still gives great credit to the character and dominant personality of one of the most significant figures in church history.

Flick, Alexander C. *The Rise of the Mediaeval Church: And Its Influence on the Civilisation of Western Europe from the First to the Thirteenth Century*. New York: Burt Franklin, 1964. An excellent treatment of both the Church and the person of Gregory VII. It is particularly strong in bringing to light the character and passion of Gregory, portraying him as a great church leader and especially as a great politician whose organizing mind left its mark on both church and state. Superior overall analysis of the role played by Gregory.

Kuhner, Hans. *Encyclopedia of the Papacy*. New York: Philosophical Library, 1958. Provides a very brief but accurate picture of Gregory VII. Emphasis is laid on the political aspects of his papacy rather than his role as a reformer. Special attention is given to the quarrels with Henry IV and the Canossa episode.

MacDonald, A. J. *Hildebrand: A Life of Gregory VII*. London: Methuen and Co., 1931. The only readily available full biography of Gregory VII, this book suffers from its age. The style is difficult for a modern reader, and so many minor figures are mentioned that it is often difficult to follow the life of Gregory. It is not a sympathetic portrayal of the reformer pope. MacDonald does provide a detailed analysis of the character and personality of Gregory VII, but blames those traits for much of the conflict which surrounded the rule of Gregory.

Ranke, Leopold von. *History of the Popes*. Vol. 1. New York: Frederick Ungar Publishing Co., 1966. An authoritative historian of the Papacy concentrates largely on the later popes. Therefore, though von Ranke credits Gregory VII with much in the way of reform, the character of the man remains largely hidden.

Carlanna L. Hendrick

GREGORY IX
Ugo of Segni

Born: c. 1170; Anagni, Italy
Died: August 22, 1241; Rome, Italy
Areas of Achievement: Religion, scholarship, and canon law
Contribution: With perseverance, courage, and conviction, under difficult circumstances, Gregory IX defended the Church from every perceived threat, encouraging spiritual life and learning within its structure, particularly in canon law.

Early Life

Little is known of the early life of Gregory IX. He was born Ugo or Ugolino, son of the Count of Segni, at Anagni, probably in 1170. He was descended from equally distinguished noblemen on his mother's side of the family. Ugo was a relative of Innocent III, arguably the most powerful pope of the Middle Ages. Research indicates that he was probably Innocent's grandnephew.

Contemporary biographers describe Ugo as a man of pleasing form, handsome features, and aristocratic bearing. He was also described as possessing a remarkable memory and an active mind. He was an eloquent speaker, and a biblical scholar of distinction who enjoyed discussion of scriptural texts. Said to have been a model of virtue, kind to others, and compassionate to those less fortunate than he, Ugo seems to have been genuinely interested in the spiritual life. Intellectually gifted, he studied at the University of Paris, and probably at Bologna, before being named chaplain to Innocent III. He was elevated to the position of cardinal-deacon of the Church of St. Eustachius in 1198, and became cardinal-bishop of Ostia in 1206.

Throughout his pontificate, Ugo was close to Innocent III, accepting many embassies in his name, and traveling widely to represent papal interests. He was legate to the Germanies when rival claimants to the imperial crown brought on a war. German problems occupied Ugo until 1206. He also represented the pope in northern Italy, in both Tuscany and Lombardy. Innocent's successor, Honorius III, also used Ugo's negotiating skills in those territories to create peaceful cooperation between cities and to facilitate the preaching of a crusade. Wherever assigned, Ugo sought always to preserve ecclesiastical rights against secular encroachment and to foster clerical reform.

During Bishop Ugo's mission to northern Italy, he met Saint Francis of Assisi and was deeply impressed by his piety, simplicity, and zeal. Francis found in the bishop a man to be admired and trusted. Their lasting friendship played a great part in the future of the Franciscan Order.

In 1220, Ugo was in Rome for the coronation of the Holy Roman Emperor Frederick II, and to encourage the new ruler to lead a crusade against the

Turks as he had earlier sworn to do. Ugo returned to Lombardy for a period in 1221; from 1222 until Honorius III's death in 1227, he appears to have been in attendance at the papal court as a principal adviser. On March 19, 1227, after the burial ceremonies for Honorius III, the cardinals met and elected Ugo to the Papacy as Gregory IX. His coronation took place on Easter Sunday, April 11, 1227.

Life's Work

Gregory IX's fourteen-year pontificate was profoundly influenced by the long struggle with Frederick II, which seems to have been its dominant theme. Although this problem is central to any consideration of his papacy, Gregory did accomplish other goals worthy of attention. Gregory had the misfortune of inheriting old problems of church-state relations, as well as a powerful adversary in Frederick, called by his contemporaries "the wonder of the world."

Frederick II inherited from his father, Henry VI, claims to German lands and the imperial title. From his mother, Constance, he held Norman lands in southern Italy and Sicily. Ecclesiastical authorities in Rome perceived these combined realms, which surrounded the Papal States, as constituting a threat to church interests. Frederick's personality and ambition caused further concern. The twelfth and thirteenth centuries saw noteworthy growth in the power of medieval kingship. The Papacy, too, had developed as a medieval monarchy as well as a religious fount. This was to be an era of much dispute on the relative powers of the two jurisdictions. Clashes and challenges were inevitable.

From the moment of Gregory's accession, he urged the emperor and the faithful of Europe to undertake the promised crusade. Reluctantly, Frederick sailed in September of 1227, after keeping the crusading armies waiting for three months. Since disease and disaffection daily diminished the ranks of the fighting men, public opinion became critical of pope and emperor alike. Two days after the embarkation, Frederick returned, pleading ill health. Crusaders who finally arrived in the Holy Land found themselves leaderless and returned—or died in skirmishes resulting from this failed endeavor.

Gregory IX promptly excommunicated the emperor, who ignored the pope's action. Despite his public stance, Gregory privately sought a reconciliation by letter and by sending legates to the emperor. Frederick refused all overtures, and began his long struggle to become the absolute ruler of the territories he claimed, further antagonizing the Papacy by his treatment of clerics within his realm.

In June, 1228, Frederick left Italy for the Holy Land without notifying the pope of his intentions or asking that the excommunication be lifted. He took with him only a small army, since he intended not to fight but to negotiate a treaty with the Saracen authorities. The action brought on a second excommunication. Frederick concluded a treaty with the sultan which returned Jerusalem to Christian hands but failed to provide any defense against the Saracen power. Fearing papal intervention among his vassals, Frederick returned to Italy to assert his independence and regain control of his ancestral lands. From 1228 to 1229, negotiators tried to lessen the tensions between the two parties. In July of 1230, the Treaty of San Germano ushered in an uneasy truce which lasted until 1236. Hostilities were resumed when Frederick invaded Lombardy, arousing on the part of the pope support for the Lombard League against him. The struggle continued through the remaining years of the pontificate, ultimately contributing to the death of Gregory in 1241.

Despite the distraction of this struggle, Gregory was able to accomplish many of his goals. His devotion to learning resulted in a statement of privileges to the masters and students of Paris in 1231 that is regarded as the true charter of the university. The document deals with the government of the school and guarantees its intellectual freedom. In 1210, the Aristotelian texts on natural philosophy had been proscribed by a council and were no longer taught. Gregory wanted the works reconsidered since he found much that was useful in them, in spite of some portions which were regarded as detrimental. He commissioned a distinguished group of masters to examine the books and remove any erroneous or scandalous material so that Aristotle might again be studied.

One of the most significant achievements of Gregory's pontificate was his contribution to the development of canon law. Gregory was himself a shrewd and able lawyer. His experience at the papal court and as a legate had taught him the need of systematizing and unifying the great mass of ecclesiastical law. In the twelfth century, the monk Gratian had collected earlier law, attempting to reconcile its differences and present his own conclusions and synthesis in a volume known as the *Decretum* (c. 1140). Much more still needed to be done, however, as nearly a century of scholarly activity had swelled the collection of materials.

To this end, Gregory appointed the Dominican friar Raymond of Peñafort to compile material including his own decretals (responses of the popes to questions put to them by their bishops on various points of law; scholars known as decretalists researched them and attempted to clarify and organize these responses). The result was a useful compendium which became the basic text at the law school at Bologna. Raymond compiled the materials in five books containing two thousand sections. The work was widely acclaimed and became the basis for the developing body of canon law as well as an influence on other European legal traditions.

Gregory's legal interests also led to the establishment of the Inquisition in 1233. Alarmed by the successful spread of old heresies into Spain and Italy, as well as by the popular mob actions against them, Gregory established a separate tribunal under the direction of the new Dominican Order. The episcopal office, with its inherent inquisitorial powers, had too many other duties to meet the immediate need. The tribunal was firmly grounded in law, although it did not meet modern concepts of justice.

At the end of his pontificate as at the beginning, Frederick II was the pope's nemesis. The emperor had created dissension in Rome, captured a number of leading churchmen, hanged members of the pope's family in northern Italy, and written against him. Finally, he blockaded Rome, forcing the ill and grieving pope to endure the unhealthy summer months there. Gregory IX died on August 22, 1241.

Summary

At Gregory IX's death, he was praised as a good shepherd, a noble and dedicated man. An enlightened figure in many ways for the times, he was torn between his duty as pope and his own desire for peace. He was keenly aware that Innocent III had established precedents for him to follow, but he was uncomfortable with military and political solutions, quickly offering alternatives to his adversaries. It was his misfortune to be pitted against a man of Frederick's ability and ambition.

This pope was far more at ease structuring the rule for the Franciscan Order, presiding over the canonization of Francis, or protecting and assisting orders for religious women. Gregory was the patron of Saint Clare, a friend and disciple of Saint Francis who founded the Order of Poor Clares. He also befriended Agnes, daughter of the King of Bohemia, who wished to enter religious life rather than marry. Placing her under his protection, the pope helped her to enter the Poor Clares.

Gregory's concern for women under monasticism led to concern for all women, and in 1227 he approved the Order of Saint Mary Magdalene, founded as a refuge for repentant prostitutes. These women were permitted to take vows as nuns in the order or to return to the world and marry.

Gregory's interest in spreading the Gospel to Africa and the northern reaches of the Baltic was never realized. Too many problems (including the Mongol invasion of Russia) frustrated these ambitions. Also doomed was his desire for reconciliation with the Eastern church, although some negotiations were opened and some talks took place.

In many ways, Gregory IX was a victim of the clash of state-church rights. The office he inherited had become so embroiled in political affairs that the question of the role of the spiritual in the world had to be addressed. As a lawyer, Gregory believed that his responsibility as the spiritual leader extended to the social consequences of political action. He therefore felt the need to intervene in secular affairs. To that end Gregory IX tirelessly directed his time and energy throughout his pontificate.

Bibliography

Cunningham, Lawrence. *Saint Francis of Assisi*. Boston: Twayne Publishers, 1976. A concise coverage of the saint's life, his problems with the organization and regulation of his order, and the role of Gregory as bishop and pope in assisting and protecting him. Contains several pages of useful bibliography.

Kantorowicz, Ernst. *Frederick the Second, 1194-1250*. New York: Frederick Ungar Publishing Co., 1957. Arguably the best source in English for the complex story of the relationship of the pope and the emperor. The author is an authority on the prevailing political thought of the time and a specialist on the kingship of Frederick.

___________. *The King's Two Bodies: A Study of Medieval Political Theology*. Princeton, N.J.: Princeton University Press, 1957. A volume which has become a classic since its publication. It is a brilliant examination of the development of royal power. Read with the other materials, it provides an understanding of the rival claims and the areas of conflict that developed between secular and spiritual authority.

Mann, Horace K. *The Lives of the Popes in the Middle Ages*. 2d ed. Vol. 13. London: Kegan Paul, Trench, Trübner, 1925. This work remains the basic source in English for detailed accounts of the lives of the medieval popes. Written by an English scholar and priest with impeccable academic credentials, it is based on archival materials, contemporary letters, chronicles, and official documents.

Sabatier, Paul. *Life of St. Francis of Assisi*. Translated by Louise Seymour Houghton. London: Hodder and Stoughton, 1894. The classic life of Saint Francis and still useful. Twice as long as the Cunningham book, it is especially valuable for its treatment of the relationship between pope and saint. Provides invaluable insights into the ideals of Francis which Gregory admired and sought to protect.

Anne R. Vizzier

GREGORY OF NAZIANZUS

Born: 329 or 330; Arianzus, Cappadocia
Died: 389 or 390; Arianzus, Cappadocia
Areas of Achievement: Oratory, literature, and religion
Contribution: A consummate rhetorician, Gregory produced many orations, poems, and letters which provide much information on the religious and social life of Christianity in the second half of the fourth century. As a theologian, Gregory was influential in the formulation of orthodox doctrine regarding the divinity of the Holy Spirit.

Early Life

Gregory was born on the family estate of Arianzus, near Nazianzus, the son of Bishop Gregory the Elder of Nazianzus. His mother, Nonna, a pious woman who had converted her husband to Christianity in 325, was a very formative influence on her son. Young Gregory was educated in the school of rhetoric in Caesarea in Cappadocia, then briefly in the Christian schools of Caesarea in Palestine and of Alexandria, where he became familiar with Christianized Platonism. On his sea journey from Alexandria, his ship encountered a great storm; realizing that he was not yet baptized, Gregory made a solemn vow to spend the rest of his life in the service of the Church if he survived. Finally, he went to the great secular university of Athens, where he spent nine years, becoming an outstanding student of the rhetoricians Prohaeresius and Himerius. There he became an inseparable friend of Basil of Caesarea, whom he commemorated at length in his famous autobiographical poem, *Carmen de vita sua* (c. 382; *On His Life*, 1814).

Life's Work

In 362, Gregory's father ordained him a priest against the young scholar's own will but by popular demand. Gregory subsequently fled to the desert, where he wrote a famous treatise on the priesthood, *Apology for His Flight*, but he soon rejoined his father. He preached his first sermon on Easter Sunday, 362. In this sermon, he likened his father to the patriarch Abraham and himself to Abraham's son Isaac being led forth to sacrifice. Thereafter, he helped to administer his father's diocese. His school friend, Basil, now Bishop of Caesarea, soon appointed him Bishop of Sasima, "a bewitched and miserable little place," according to Gregory, who refused to take possession of the see. After his father's death in 374, Gregory administered the see of Nazianzus for a time. In 375, he retired to a monastery in Seleucia, Isauria, but four years later he was invited to reorganize the dwindling Nicene community in Constantinople, a city rife with Arianism. In 380, Emperor Theodosius the Great formally inducted him into the Church of the Apostles in Constantinople, which he served until the middle of 381. His Forty-second Oration is a speech announcing his resignation from the see of Constantinople, which he characterized as a place "not for priests, but for orators, not for stewards of souls, but for treasurers of money, not for pure offerers of the sacrifice, but for powerful patrons." Though still only in his early fifties, he retired, a prematurely old, sick, and very disillusioned man, to Cappadocia, where he died in 389 or 390.

Gregory's celebrated speeches defending the orthodox teaching on the Trinity against the heretical Eunomians and Macedonians, collected as the *Orationae* (362-381; *Theological Orations*, 1894), earned for him the appellation "the Theologian." These orations represent brilliant defenses of the divinity of the Son and the Holy Spirit. *In laudem Basilii Magni* (381; *On St. Basil the Great*, 1953) is regarded as the finest piece of Greek rhetoric since the time of Demosthenes. Indeed, in Byzantine times Gregory was often called "the Christian Demosthenes." Also surviving are panegyrics on his father, his sister, his brother, and the church fathers Saint Athanasius of Alexandria and Saint Cyprian of Carthage.

Gregory's poetry, though rarely inspired, makes competent use of classical models; it deals didactically with a variety of topics, mainly theological. Some forty of the surviving four hundred poems are dogmatic, dealing with such themes as the Trinity and Divine Providence. Most of the poetry was composed in Gregory's final years of retirement.

Particularly important among his numerous letters, written in a very engaging classical style, are three—addressed to a certain Cledonius—which present a forceful refutation of the popular contemporary heresy of Apollinarianism. In writing to pagans, Gregory quoted authors such as Homer and Demosthenes as freely as he quoted from the Old and New Testaments when writing to Christians.

Summary

Gregory was a man of great sensitivity and spirituality. His was a contemplative nature, very ill-suited to the rough and tumble of ecclesiastical politics in Constantinople at the time of the Second Ecumenical Council of 381. He had great rhetorical skills, and his lasting achievement is the surviving forty-five orations, evidencing a masterful synthesis of classical rhetoric and Christianity. Gregory was particularly adept at countering the logic-chopping of the later Arians, known as Eunomians. He was obviously well trained in Aristotelian and Stoic logic and dialectic. Moreover, his wide knowledge of Scripture also enabled him to outwit his opponents in the deployment and interpretation of scriptural texts. The theological importance of the orations is especially evident in their Trinitarian and christological concerns.

Some of Gregory's autobiographical poems are as deeply spiritual and revealing as the *Confessiones* (397-400; *Confessions*) of Saint Augustine. A careful reading of the poems dealing with his brief tenure in Constantinople can contribute much to an understanding of the ecclesiastical politics of the time, the shallowness and wiliness of some of his fellow bishops at the council, and Gregory's dissatisfaction with the compromise statement on the divinity of the Holy Spirit that emerged in 381.

The original text of his surviving works is contained in volumes 35 to 38 of J.-P. Migne's *Patrologia Graeca* (1842-1853). Gratifying progress is being made by an international committee of scholars in producing new critical texts of his individual works, some of which have been published as part of the series Sources Chrétiennes.

One of Gregory's epitaphs on his father is equally applicable to himself:

> If there was one Moses privileged on the mountain
> to hear the pure voice, there was also the mind of great Gregory,
> whom once God's grace called from afar
> and made a great high-priest.
> Now he dwells near the holy Trinity.

Bibliography

Gregg, Robert C. *Consolation Philosophy: Greek and Christian Paideia in Basil and the Two Gregories*. Cambridge, Mass.: Philadelphia Patristic Foundation, 1975. A useful comparative study of the three great Cappadocians' consolatory letters and discourses, with a consideration of their biblical and Hellenistic background. Letters of consolation and panegyrics are examined in the light of the established rhetorical norms of Greek literature.

Gregory of Nazianzus. *Three Poems*. Translated by Denis M. Meehan, with notes by Thomas P. Halton. Washington, D.C.: Catholic University of America Press, 1986. These poems reveal Gregory's sensitivity and reflect his unrelenting quest for perfection in a world full of intrigue and corruption. A sensitive translation, with a useful introduction, bibliography, and notes. Part of the series The Fathers of the Church.

Gregory of Nazianzus and Saint Ambrose. *Funeral Orations of Saint Gregory Nazianzen and Saint Ambrose*. Translated by Leo P. McCauley and others. Washington, D.C.: Catholic University of America Press, 1968. Particularly useful for the translation of *In laudem Basilii Magni*. Also includes the panegyrics on Gregory's father, brother, and sister.

Kennedy, George A. *Greek Rhetoric Under Christian Emperors*. Princeton, N.J.: Princeton University Press, 1983. Chapter 4, "Christianity and Rhetoric," includes a lengthy and sympathetic study of Gregory, described as "the most important figure in the synthesis of classical rhetoric and Christianity."

Quasten, Johannes. *Patrology*. Vol. 3, *The Golden Age of Greek Patristic Literature*. Westminster, Md.: Newman Press, 1960. Contains a well-documented and sympathetic account of one characterized as "the humanist among the theologians of the fourth century." Part of a four-volume set. Includes copious bibliographies.

Ruether, Rosemary R. *Gregory of Nazianzus, Rhetor and Philosopher*. Oxford: Clarendon Press, 1969. A careful examination of the Hellenistic influences apparent in Gregory's thought. Includes a particularly helpful examination of his early training. Ruether shows that Gregory became a master of numerous rhetorical devices taught in fourth century schools.

Thomas Halton

GREGORY OF NYSSA

Born: c. 335; Caesarea, Cappadocia
Died: c. 394; Constantinople
Areas of Achievement: Religion and theology
Contribution: A profound thinker and theologian, as well as an eloquent preacher, Gregory was one of the brilliant leaders of Christian orthodoxy in the late fourth century. His influence led to the defeat of the Arian heresy and the triumph of the orthodox Nicene position at the Council of Constantinople in 381.

Early Life

One of ten children, Gregory was born in the city of Caesarea, the capital of Cappadocia, to an important and wealthy Christian family which had suffered in the persecutions of the Roman emperor Diocletian. He was the third son and one of the youngest children of Basil the Elder and Emmelia—herself the daughter of a martyr. Gregory was left fatherless at an early age and was reared largely by his older brother, Basil (later called "the Great"), Bishop of Caesarea, and by his sister Macrina. Throughout his life, Gregory looked up to his brother with great affection and respect.

As a young man, Gregory was educated in his native city, attending secular pagan schools. His feeble constitution and natural shyness caused him to concentrate on scholarship rather than physical activities or public life. Thus, his intellectual prowess was enhanced by diligent private study.

While in his youth, Gregory became involved in church activities, but he did so without great conviction. Later in life, he recounted his reluctant, even unwilling, attendance at a ceremony given by his mother in honor of church martyrs. Wearied with his journey and the length of the service—which lasted far into the night—he fell asleep. A terrifying dream soon followed which filled him with a sense of remorse for his neglect of spiritual matters, and he became a lector, or reader of biblical passages in a Christian congregation.

Gregory's youthful years coincided with the last revival of pagan culture, which reached its peak under the emperor Julian the Apostate (reigned 361-363). Gregory was completely won over to the pagan humanistic ideal. Therefore, after a time, Gregory abandoned his church position and devoted himself to secular pursuits. Sometime after the year 360, he accepted a position as a teacher of rhetoric. This desertion from the Christian cause gave his friends and family great pain and brought to him accusations of all kinds.

At about this same time Gregory married a woman named Theosebeia. She is believed to have been the sister of Gregory of Nazianzus, who was a family friend. In a letter written many years later, Gregory of Nazianzus, consoling his friend upon the death of Theosebeia, extolled her as a true priestess, most fair and lustrous. In fact, Gregory's final conversion to the Christian faith undoubtedly resulted in part from the pleadings and remonstrations of both his wife and his friend.

Another contributing factor which led Gregory back to the Church was the increasing distaste he felt for teaching rhetoric. He became discouraged by the results of his efforts to inspire literary tastes among youths who, he complained, were more ready and better suited to enter the army than follow rhetorical studies.

Gregory abandoned his teaching sometime before 370. He then retired to a monastery at Pontus which was presided over by his brother Basil. There he devoted himself to the study of the Scriptures and the works of Christian commentators. He was especially influenced by Origen, as is evident from Gregory's own theological works.

While he was at the monastery, an episode occurred which may reveal a flaw in Gregory's judgment. A rift had arisen between Basil and an aged uncle, also named Gregory, over doctrinal matters. Acting as a self-appointed mediator, the younger Gregory forged some letters which purported to be from his uncle to his brother Basil offering peace. The deception was exposed, and Gregory received a stern but dignified rebuke from his brother.

Life's Work

Around the year 365, Basil had been summoned by Eusebius, Metropolitan of Caesarea, to aid in repelling the assaults of the Arian faction of Christianity on the Nicene orthodox faith. During the next few years, the Arian believers were assisted and encouraged by the emperor Valens. Basil greatly helped orthodox resistance and in 370 was called, by popular voice, to succeed Eusebius upon the latter's death.

To strengthen his position and surround himself with defenders of the orthodox faith in the outposts of his diocese, Basil persuaded Gregory (in spite of his protests) to accept the bishopric of Nyssa, an obscure town of Cappadocia, about ten miles from Caesarea. It was as Bishop of Nyssa that Gregory achieved his greatest fame and realized his greatest accomplishments. When a mutual friend wrote to express his surprise at Basil's choosing such an obscure place for so distinguished a man as Gregory, Basil replied that his brother's merits did indeed make him worthy of governing the entire Church. Basil added, however, that the see should be made famous by its bishop, and not the bishop by his see.

Gregory was consecrated bishop in 372. Nevertheless, as soon as he arrived in Nyssa he faced grave difficulties. Arianism was strong in the city and was supported by the emperor. In addition, one of the emperor's courtiers had wanted the bishopric, and Gregory's appointment made for immediate hostility. A man named Demosthenes had been recently appointed governor of Pontus by the emperor and charged to do all in his power to crush the adherents of the orthodox Nicene faith. After some petty acts of persecution, a synod was summoned in 375 at Ancyra to examine charges made against Gregory, including embezzlement of church property and irregularities surrounding his consecration.

Though Gregory escaped from the band of soldiers sent to arrest him, his Arian enemies continued their persecution. Finally, in 376, another synod was summoned at Nyssa; this time the assembled bishops deposed Gregory. A successor was consecrated and Valens banished Gregory from the city. For many months he was driven from place to place to avoid his enemies. Heartsick over the apparent triumph of Arianism, Gregory nevertheless encouraged his friends to be of good cheer and trust in God. This advice proved to be well-founded. In 378 Valens died and the youthful emperor Gratian restored Gregory to his bishopric.

Soon afterward another event occurred which forever changed Gregory's life; Basil died in 379, and Gregory fell heir to his position of leadership. Basil had been a man of action and an organizer. Gregory was forced to stand on his own, carrying out the work of his brother and bringing it to completion.

From 379 onward, Gregory's activity was limitless. The next two years saw him preach tirelessly against heresies, Arianism especially. Named after Arius, a priest in Alexandria, Egypt, this doctrine denied the true divinity of Jesus Christ by maintaining that the Son of God was not eternal but created by the Father from nothing, that He, therefore, was not God by nature—being a changeable creature—and that His dignity as Son of God was conferred on Him by the Father because of His abiding righteousness. During this time Gregory preached against Eunomius (an Arian bishop); this preaching would lay the foundation for a major theological treatise entitled *Contra Eunomium* (382; against Eunomius).

The spring of 381 marked the pinnacle of Gregory's career. It was then that the emperor Theodosius I convoked the Council of Constantinople. Gregory played a major role in the council. He gave the opening address, influencing many, and witnessed the complete victory of the orthodox Christian doctrines and ideas for which he and Basil had fought. Thus, the work of the Council of Nicaea (in 325) regarding the doctrine of Christ was ratified. The council condemned all varieties of Arianism and added clauses to the Nicene Creed which were supplied by Gregory himself.

After the Council of Constantinople, Gregory became one of the leading personalities of the church in the East. The council gave him jurisdiction, together with two other church leaders, over the regions of Cappadocia and Pontus. He was also sent to Arabia to mediate a dispute between two bishops, though he met with limited success. On his return, he visited the Holy Land, including the city of Jerusalem and the places associated with the life of Christ.

By the end of 381 Gregory was back in Nyssa. The following year, he produced two of his most important theological writings, *Contra Eunomium* and *Adversus Apollinarem* (against Apollinaris), in which he responded to heretical ideas and discussed the doctrines relating to Christ and His nature.

Gregory's influence outside the Church was also at its peak during the years from 381 to 386, and he enjoyed the favor of the imperial court. When Gregory visited the Holy Land, the emperor provided a public chariot for his transportation. Following the success of the Council of Constantinople, Theodosius wanted to hold a council every year; in 383 Gregory was chosen by the emperor to give a major sermon on the divinity of the Son and the Holy Spirit at the convocation. In 385 he was chosen to deliver the funeral eulogies in honor of Empress Flacilla and her daughter Pulcheria, who had died shortly before her mother. At Constantinople, too, Gregory enjoyed the friendship of Olympias, one of the outstanding women of the age.

After 386, Gregory's influence began to decline. His ideas were called into question a number of times, and he had to defend himself against charges that his thinking was tainted with heretical notions. Finally, in Asia Minor, Gregory's prerogatives began to be restricted to his own diocese, and he increasingly came into conflict with the metropolitan, Helladius.

In the year 394, Gregory was invited to attend a synod at Constantinople which was called to decide once and for all the claims of two bishops over the see of Bostra. At the request of Nectarius, who was the presiding official there, Gregory delivered his last recorded sermon. It is very likely that he did not long survive the synod, dying in Constantinople the same year as the meeting.

Summary

Among church fathers and theologians, there is no more honored a name than Gregory of Nyssa. Besides receiving the accolades of his brothers Basil and his friend Gregory of Nazianzus, Gregory of Nyssa was praised by biblical scholar Jerome for the sanctity of his life, his theological learning, and his strenuous defense of the Nicene faith. Gregory came to be regarded as one of the three Cappadocian fathers of the Church, along with Basil the Great and Gregory of Nazianzus.

Though not considered as able an administrator as his brother, Gregory was highly appreciated for his eloquence in writing and speaking. He was chosen to deliver many discourses in the company of other theologians, and his writings show him to be well versed in the work of pagan philosophers as well as in Holy Scripture and the writings of Christian commentators. His works comprise some thirty letters, many sermons and exegetical writings, polemical treatises, including *Contra Eunomium* and *Adversus Apollinarem*, and several ascetic pieces.

Gregory's tireless championing of the Nicene faith and battle against heresies, especially Arianism, are his greatest legacy. Indeed, his efforts seem to have made prophetic the statement of his brother Basil, spoken at the time of Gregory's consecration to the bishopric: Nyssa was ennobled and made famous by its bishop, and not the other way around.

Bibliography

Dunstone, Alan S. *The Atonement in Gregory of Nyssa*. London: Tyndale Press, 1964. This small volume was originally a lecture delivered in Cambridge, England. It provides a succinct discussion of one of the most important themes of Gregory's christological writings and sermons. Its value lies in its concise analysis of Gregory's thinking on a complex theme.

Gregory of Nyssa. Saint. *From Glory to Glory*. Edited by Herbert Musurillo. Crestwood, N.Y.: St. Vladimir's Seminary Press, 1979. This volume comprises an anthology of texts taken from Gregory's mystical and ascetical writings. It also contains a readable, well-organized, and most valuable introduction, which presents a history of Gregory's life and work as well as an analysis of some of his writing. The notes and comments on the texts by the editor are also very enlightening. The selected texts have been translated into modern idiomatic English.

__________. *The Lord's Prayer, the Beatitudes*. Edited and translated by Hilda C. Graef. London: Longmans, Green and Co., 1954. This book is a compilation of various sermons given by Gregory on the subjects of the Lord's Prayer and the Beatitudes. They give the flavor of Gregory's style of preaching. The work contains an adequate introduction, including a sketch of the scholar's life. Gregory's sermons display his imaginative, rhetorical, and devotional talents.

Hardy, Edward Roche, and Cyril Richardson, eds. *The Library of Christian Classics*. Vol. 3, *Christology of the Later Fathers*. Philadelphia: Westminster Press, 1954. This volume devotes almost half of its contents to the writings of Gregory of Nyssa. It provides an excellent biographical sketch of Gregory and a summary of his work. It also contains selections, translated into English, of his more important works. Its greatest value, however, lies in the very thorough bibliography of the works of Gregory, as well as of biographies and articles on his life—a good share of the best ones being written in foreign languages.

Jaeger, Werner, ed. *Two Rediscovered Works of Ancient Christian Literature*. Leiden, Netherlands: E. J. Brill, 1954. A scholarly volume containing critical notes and commentary on two important treatises by Gregory, this book presents the relationships between Greek theologians and Greek philosophy and Gregory's thought. It contains valuable commentary on the cultural context of Gregory's work. The editor is one of the foremost authorities on Gregory.

Schaff, Philip, and Henry Wace, eds. Introduction to *Gregory of Nyssa: Dog-*

matic Treatises. Vol. 5 in *A Select Library of Nicene and Post-Nicene Fathers of the Christian Church*. New York: Christian Literature Co., 1893. This is an important and informative introduction to Gregory's life and work, though the style is somewhat awkward. The selected texts from Gregory's compiled major works are supplemented by scholarly notes and references.

Andrew C. Skinner

GREGORY OF TOURS

Born: November 30, 539; Auvergne
Died: November 17, 594; Tours
Area of Achievement: Historiography
Contribution: Gregory provided historians with their prime source of information on Merovingian Gaul for the years 575-591; he also contributed to the Christian tradition an example of living in accord with the best principles of the Church.

Early Life

Georgius Florentius, who would become Gregory, Bishop of Tours, was born in the capital city of the Arverni (the people of Auvergne). In his *De virtutibus sancti Martini* (c. 593; *The Miracles of Saint Martin*, 1949), he provides the information that he was born on Saint Andrew's Day thirty-four years before his installation in 573 as the nineteenth bishop of Tours—that would be in 539. He was given the name of his father (Georgius) and of his father's father (Florentius), each of whom was of senatorial rank. His mother, Armentaria, was a granddaughter of Saint Tetricus, Bishop of Langres (539-572) and a great-granddaughter of Saint Gregorius, who preceded his son as Bishop of Langres (507-539). Gregory's lineage was clearly that of a noble family consistently influential in the Church.

His father apparently having died when Gregory was a child, he was reared by his uncle, Gallus, Bishop of Clermont-Ferrand (525-551), and, after 551, he resided with the Archdeacon Avitus, who became Bishop of Clermont-Ferrand in the year 573. Gregory had a granduncle who was Bishop of Lyons and a cousin, Eufronius, whom Gregory himself succeeded as Bishop of Tours on August 20, 573.

At the age of twenty-five, he suffered a debilitating illness. He attributed his recovery to Saint Martin; it was at this time also that he was ordained a deacon. He obtained his bishopric nine years later. In the following year, 574, he suffered a deep personal loss: His brother Peter, a deacon, was murdered. Peter had been accused of murdering Silvester, Bishop of Langres, who was one of their relatives. The case had been heard by Nicetius, Bishop of Lyons and a maternal uncle of the accused, and Peter's oath that he was innocent had been accepted by both clergy and diocesan laymen. Within two years, however, Silvester's son attacked Peter in the street, running him through with a spear. Gregory relates the story movingly but objectively in *Historia Francorum* (c. 594; *The History of the Franks*, 1927).

Life's Work

Gregory remained Bishop of Tours from the date of his consecration until his death at age fifty-five. His ability during this time to maintain the tenets and principles of the Church while being privy to the political activities and ambitions of the Merovingian rulers marks him as a person of considerable shrewdness. Considerable too was his industry as a man of letters.

It is best to begin a survey of Gregory's achievements by noting his masterwork, *The History of the Franks*, as it is conventionally called; its actual title is *Historiæ Francorum libri decem* (ten books of histories). In many of the events set down in this history, Gregory was himself a participant. The massive work in ten books opens with the author's profession of his faith and begins its record, as many medieval works of history do, with the Creation and Adam. From the Creation to the year 594, according to Gregory, 6,063 years elapsed (the number of the tally appearing in the manuscript is 5,792, probably a scribal error: Gregory's figures add up to 6,063, as noted). The first book summarizes the Old and New Testaments and moves from the death of Christ through some four centuries to the death of Martin, the patron saint of Tours and Gregory's inspiration. The second book brings the history up through the death in 511 of Clovis, the founder of the dynasty which took its name from Merovech, an early king who died in 456. Clovis had brought most of Gaul into a cohesive monarchy. Books 3 and 4 chronicle the events centering on the sons of Clovis, particularly Lothar I, who continued to unify Gaul under Frankish sovereignty and whose sons, after his death in 561, sustained the wars, conspiracies, and assassinations that determined much of the character of Merovingian history.

There appears at the end of book 3 a report on the harsh winter of 548; book 9 also concludes with a weather report. Books 5, 6, 8, 9, and 10 all include sections on signs and portents, many having to do with the weather. Books 7 and 8 include sections on the miracles of Martin. These and similar preoccupations constitute a rather substantial part of the text.

Books 4 through 10 of *The History of the Franks* deal with happenings in Gregory's own time, from 549 through 593, and the last five books in particular chronicle events coinciding with Gregory's bishopric. These entail the bewildering rivalries and conspiracies of the sons of Lothar I—particularly Kings Charibert, Sigibert, Chilperic, and Guntram—and the ambitions and schemes of Sigibert's wife, Brunhild, and Chilperic's third wife, Fredegund. Plots, violence, bloodshed, murders, and assassinations are recounted matter-of-factly by Gregory and make for very interesting if occasionally disturbing reading.

Characteristic of his history are its amusing sidelights; Gregory has a sense of humor and tosses off many tongue-in-cheek comments. On a larger scale, there is, in the interstices of the narrative, the tale of the Falstaffian Duke Guntram Boso, a thieving, conniving, but irresistible rogue for whom Gregory obviously has unwavering affection. He condemns Boso's excesses but never Boso himself and offers him the protection of sanctuary, which not even royalty can persuade him to lift, and as much help and advice as his ecclesiastical position permits. His description of the killing of Guntram Boso, pierced by so many spears that his body, propped up by them, could not fall to the ground, is an example of the memorable detail of his prose.

Gregory's Latin is anything but classical; nevertheless, it is not as bad as much other medieval Latin. He apologizes for its lack of polish in book 5 and in his preface but insists that his subject is too important to go unrecorded, however imperfect the language of record may be. History has vindicated him.

Gregory's other works were composed more or less concurrently with *The History of the Franks*. *The Miracles of Saint Martin*, mentioned above, comprises four books on the acts of his favorite saint, with periodic entries of devotion, the last datable to July 4, 593. The Latin word *virtus* (manliness, courage, excellence, goodness) is Gregory's word for "miracle." For him, a miracle is evidence of the power of goodness, a power conferred upon those who are worthy of it. *Liber vitae patrum* (sixth century; *Life of the Fathers*, 1949) considers individually twenty-two abbots, bishops, or solitaries worthy of the adjective *sanctus*—or *sancta* in the case of the nun Monegundis, the subject of section 19. *Sanctus* or *sancta* means "blessed" and refers to a person who has in some way produced a miracle. Gregory's writing antedates the formulation of official canonization procedures by about five centuries. Six of his twenty-two subjects were not subsequently canonized officially; to Gregory, however, they were all blessed. The miracles which qualified them as such may be exemplified by those attributed to Gallus. According to his biographer, Gallus put out a fire by walking toward it with a work of Scripture open in his hands, and his bed cured the fever of a man who had napped in it; at his tomb, sufferers were cured of their ailments.

The Miracles of Saint Martin (four books) and *Life of the Fathers* (one book) constitute five of what Gregory called his eight books of miracles. The others are each single volumes—*Liber in gloria martyrum* (glory of the martyrs), *Liber de passione et virtutibus sancti Iuliani martyris* (passion and miracles of Saint Julian, martyr), and *Liber in gloria confessorum* (glory of the confessors).

Gregory is as strong in his ridicule of Greek and Roman myths as he is firm in his belief in Christian miracles. One may dismiss him as naïve on this score, but it would be inadvisable to dismiss him as an unreliable observer because of his acceptance of miracles. This manifestation of his faith marks him as a practical churchman in his own time and in no way intrudes upon the realism with which he describes the actual people, occurrences, and political movements of sixth century France.

Gregory also completed a short work on the miracles of the Apostle Andrew, a translation into Latin of the story of the Seven Sleepers of Ephesus, and a book on astronomy which mentions a comet that preceded (or portended) the assassination of King Sigibert in 575. Two other short works, a commentary on the book of Psalms and a book on Sidonius Apollinaris' masses, are not extant.

These, then, were the three directions taken by the life's work of Gregory of Tours: his effective episcopate, his political dealings with the ruling and feuding principals of Merovingian France, and his historiography and hagiography. There was also a triad in Gregory's personal life. The first important event was his recovery from serious illness—a healing wrought, as he insists, by the intercession of Martin, to whose memory Gregory remained devoted for the last thirty years of his life. The second was his consecration as bishop. The third was the ascension to the papal throne in 590 of the deacon who was to become Gregory the Great. The historian's deep satisfaction in the election of Gregory I is reflected in his beginning the tenth book of *The History of the Franks* with a laudatory biography of the new pope and a transcription of his inaugural address. Gregory of Tours saw his namesake's elevation as a merited natural consequence of belonging to a great family of senatorial rank and ecclesiastical ambience; he had seen his own appointment to a bishopric in the same light. If pride was inherent in this attitude, so was a sense of profound responsibility.

Summary

Gregory's installation as Bishop of Tours was heralded in poetry by his contemporary churchman, Venantius Fortunatus (530-609), an illustrious poet, priest, hagiographer, devotee of Saint Martin, and, after Gregory's death, Bishop of Poitiers. The admiration of Fortunatus for Gregory is evidence of the esteem enjoyed by the nineteenth Bishop of Tours in his lifetime. In all, two dozen poems by Fortunatus, author of the famous sixth century works *Vexilla regis prodeunt* (the royal banners forward go) and *Pange lingua gloriosi praelium certaminis* (sing my tongue the glorious battle) are directed to Gregory. Fortunatus was also a historian, but his contribution to historiography has proved to be insignificant in comparison with Gregory's. His versified life of Martin is superior in its Latinity, but not in its devotion, to Gregory's prose account of the saint's miracles. Fortunatus' poetry, however, displays an artistry that lay well beyond the talents of Gregory. The juxtaposition of Fortunatus and Gregory supplies a reliable perspective from which to view and assess Gregory's importance. He was not a literary master, but he was duly celebrated by one who was patently his inferior as a historian.

Gregory's *The History of the Franks* stands well above all such efforts by his contemporaries. In literary quality, it may be inferior to the history written by the next century's Saint Bede the Venerable, while it is decidedly superior in many respects to the universal history by the preceding century's Paulus Orosius—which Alfred the Great chose to translate into English. For its own century, *The History of the Franks* is without peer. Gregory's divagations on weather, plant life, and bird migrations may not, despite their compelling accuracy, appeal to busy students of history; his inside record of the Merovingian royalty and his objective observations of the political machinations, disasters, and triumphs of the sixth century in Frankish Gaul, however, are not likely ever to lose their value.

Bibliography

Auerbach, Erich. *Mimesis: The Representation of Reality in Western Literature*. Translated by Willard R. Trask. Princeton, N.J.: Princeton University Press, 1953. Chapter 4, "Sicharius and Chramnesindus," presents a segment of *The History of the Franks* and subjects it to an analysis of language and style.

Gregorius, Saint, Bishop of Tours. *The History of the Franks*. Translated by Ormonde Maddock Dalton. 2 vols. Oxford: Oxford University Press, 1927, reprint 1971. The first volume is an extensive introduction; the second is a translation of the work. An indispensable adjunct to the study of the life and writings of Gregory of Tours.

__________. *The History of the Franks*. Translated by Lewis Thorpe. Harmondsworth, England: Penguin Books, 1974. An unpretentious translation of Gregory's history, with an excellent introduction to his life and works. Gregory's Latin does, now and then, elude the translator; for example, *que ad mediam diem pandit egressum*, referring to a gate "which opened to the south," is mistranslated as "which was left open in the daytime." Such lapses are generally negligible. Thorpe's index is exceptionally helpful.

__________. *Life of the Fathers*. Translated and edited by Edward James. Oxford: Oxford University Press, 1985. A scholarly translation of an important hagiographical work by Gregory, with an informative introduction and helpful annotative materials.

Lasko, Peter. *The Kingdom of the Franks: North-West Europe Before Charlemagne*. Edited by David Talbot Rice. New York: McGraw-Hill Book Co., 1971. Part of the Library of Medieval Civilization series, this study is a concise summary of Frankish art, religion, and regal power. Includes 121 illustrations, many in color; an excellent companion to *The History of the Franks*.

Pfister, Christian. "Gaul Under the Merovingian Franks." In *The Cambridge Medieval History*. Vol. 2, *The Rise of the Saracens and the Foundation of the Western Empire*. Cambridge: Cambridge University Press, 1913. An excellent standard work, which, with the introduction by Dalton to *The History of the Franks* (listed above), gives a proper introduction to a detailed study of Gregory. Pfister's material has been condensed by C. W. Previté-Orton in *The Shorter Cambridge Medieval History* (1952; 2 vols.).

Wallace-Hadrill, J. M. *The Barbarian West: 400-1000*. London: Hutchinson

University Library, 1952, rev. ed. 1957. Chapters 4 and 5 concentrate on the Franks. This is a reliable, short introduction to Gregory's milieu and to those which preceded and followed it. Helpful bibliography.

Wormald, P., ed. *Ideal and Reality in Frankish and Anglo-Saxon Society: Studies Presented to J. M. Wallace-Hadrill*. Oxford: Oxford University Press, 1983. This collection of articles includes I. N. Wood's "The Ecclesiastical Politics of Merovingian Clermont," an informative overview of that confluence of the religious and secular environments in which Gregory functioned.

Roy Arthur Swanson

GREGORY THE GREAT

Born: c. 540; Rome, Italy
Died: March 12, 604; Rome, Italy
Areas of Achievement: Religion, government, and monasticism
Contribution: By example and direction, Gregory set the basic patterns for the medieval church of Central and Western Europe in the areas of pastoral administration, interpretation of the Bible, and liturgical usage. He was directly responsible for sending missionaries to England and the consequent organization of the medieval English church. This evangelistic effort was to serve as a model for later missionary activity.

Early Life

Gregory was born in Italy near the city of Rome. Rome, once the center of the political and cultural world of Western civilization, no longer held that position. About two centuries before the birth of Gregory, the capital city of the Roman Empire had been moved eastward to Constantinople. Although Rome at first remained an important city, its role continued to diminish as the years went by. During this time, invaders and migrating peoples made their way into Italy and other sections of the old Roman Empire, cutting the western half away from Constantinople and the eastern portions of the Mediterranean world. As a result, it was difficult for many people—merchants, political leaders, churchmen, and others—to maintain contact and communications with the East. Since the invaders were pagan or Arian Christians (a heretical sect of Christianity), there were unusual tensions in the Church in Gregory's homeland. These factors tended to separate further the leaders of the eastern and western churches, the pope at Rome and the patriarch at Constantinople. This problem was to become a major concern of Gregory later in his life.

The parents of Gregory were old Roman aristocrats. Hence, the young Gregory received the best education available at that time, especially in the traditional areas of grammar and rhetoric. He later studied law, a discipline that prepared him for his later career in civil and ecclesiastical administration. Gregory also was well founded in the teachings of Christianity: Some of his ancestors had served the Church, and his parents and his mother's sisters were well-known for their Christian lives and acts of piety.

Just prior to Gregory's birth, Rome had been restored to rule under Constantinople. In 565, however, the Emperor Justinian, who had inspired the reconquest, died. Many of his recently conquered territories, including Rome, would soon fall away to new waves of foreign conquerors. Rome was captured by the Lombards, a Germanic tribe that had entered Italy in the north. They were heretical Christians, violent and, by Roman standards, uncultured. It is at this juncture that Gregory first appeared on the scene.

Life's Work

Gregory, still a layman, was appointed prefect of the city of Rome shortly after 570. This responsibility was somewhat like that of mayor or city manager of a modern city: He presided over the senate, which was mainly a city council. He also saw to the finances, the public order, defense, and food supplies for Rome.

About 575, his father died. Gregory, believing that he had been called to renounce the cares of the secular world for the monastic life, took his inheritance and founded six monasteries in Sicily and one at the site of the family palace in Rome. To this last one he gave the name St. Andrews, and there he spent his time in study and contemplation. His primary attention was given to the reading and study of the Latin fathers of the church and to the Bible.

In 578, because of his experience and growing reputation, Gregory was named a deacon in the Roman diocese. In the city of Rome, this was an office of honor and responsibility. From 579 to 586, Gregory served as the papal ambassador to Constantinople, where his primary task was to develop and maintain good relations with both emperor and patriarch. This was not a job to be sought after, since there were rivalries and distrust between leaders at Rome and those at Constantinople. Gregory, however, won the respect of many in Constantinople. A group of Eastern monks asked him to present a series of lectures on the Book of Job. These discussions served as the basis for Gregory's most important theological writing, *Moralia in Job* (*Morals on the Book of Job*, 1844-1850; commonly called *Moralia*), a commentary on ethics based on Job.

In 586, Gregory returned to the monastery, serving now as abbot. The position called upon his administrative expertise, as he successfully maintained strict standards of discipline and study for the monks. He continued as an informal adviser to the pope and maintained an awareness of current events. It was during this time that Gregory noticed the English youths on the slave block in the Roman marketplace and vowed to send missionaries to their land to provide the opportunity for their salvation.

During his years at the monastery, Gregory became aware of two other matters which were of great concern to him. The first was the presence in Italy, and the world in general, of heretical expressions of Christianity. To him, Arianism was the most insidious, in that it closely resembled orthodoxy and consequently drew a large following. Other heretical groups, such as Donatists and Pelagians, also concerned Gregory. He pledged to fight for orthodoxy. Second, Gregory saw his homeland suffering under natural disasters, including floods and plague, which he believed constituted God's punishment of a wayward and dissolute people. Gregory and his monks provided physical, emotional, and spiritual relief to the people of Rome.

In 590, the people of Rome turned to Gregory (for there were no cardinals in the Church at this time to carry out papal elections) and asked him to become their bishop. As the Bishop of Rome, Gregory would also be pope. Gregory at first refused, believing that he was not equal to the task. When he finally accepted the call, however, he did so with an extraordinary sense of pastoral responsibility, calling for spiritual renewal and recommitment from the top down.

Gregory's first priority was to defend the city against the attacking Lombards. Deserted by his imperial benefactor in Constantinople, Gregory took matters into his own hands, leading his own army against the Lombards, negotiating with them, even offering his personal resources as tribute in an effort to buy peace. Although there was to be no end to the conflict until after 598, Gregory's method of dealing with the Lombards established a precedent for popes in the years to come.

Because of unsettled political and military conditions, there were many problems with displaced persons in Gregory's Rome. Food supplies were short and medical attention was frequently needed; adequate housing and living conditions were not always available. Gregory responded by calling upon the resources of the Church: Too often, he claimed, the Church had sought to serve its own best interests and had not paid adequate attention to people who were in need. In the same spirit, Gregory was to call upon each member of the clergy to ask himself whether he were fulfilling his duty. According to Gregory, in his influential work *Liber regulae pastoralis* (*Pastoral Care*, 1950), the clergy, like shepherds, must lead the people in God's ways. Gregory called upon the pastor to demonstrate dependence upon God and to be tactful, committed to others, compassionate, pure, meek, sensitive, active, disciplined, merciful, and just. Many generations of clergy have used this model for their own guidance.

Gregory sent Augustine of Canterbury to England in 597, which resulted in the conversion of the Anglo-Saxons to Christianity. Gregory also effectively opposed the spread of heresy, by means of missions to Spain. He was a strong proponent of a united church and successfully asserted his primacy throughout the Western church, regarding the papacy as superior to the patriarchy at Constantinople.

Throughout his papacy, Gregory found himself embroiled in politics: with the kings of the Germanic tribes, Visigoths, Franks, Lombards. Although Gregory's vision and goals were firmly fixed, he frequently had to negotiate, and this usually involved compromise. Gregory stands out as a man of principle and courage throughout his time as pope. In 602, he allowed himself to be misled into supporting the wily tyrant Phocas, Emperor of Byzantium, who had come by his office through the murder of the previous emperor and his family. Phocas, as a result, propagated increasing acts of terror, although he eventually secured peace with the Lombards and thus safety for Italy. Such a peace, coming about despite Gregory's lack of foresight and at the hands of one of the most despised tyrants in history, constitutes the single outstanding flaw in Gregory's otherwise unimpeachable career.

During his years as pope, Gregory found time to write. In addition to the two books already mentioned, he wrote a book of sermons meant to prepare believers for the final judgment; a series of homilies on Ezekiel (593), which explain the text of that book of the Bible in terms that the practicing Christian could apply to his own life; fourteen books of letters, interesting for the light they throw upon Gregory's papacy; and four books of "dialogues," in which Gregory explained the teachings of Saint Augustine.

Gregory also had a deep interest in the liturgy of the Church. He supported the extension of the Roman rite and the search for a uniform style of worship in the Western church. Many of the liturgical changes which he supported came to be incorporated as a part of the medieval liturgical tradition. These changes had to do with liturgical texts, the use of the Alleluia and the Lord's Prayer, and the music of the service. Although Gregory did not actually compose music of the type known as the Gregorian chant, he did express sentiments which led to that form. Gregory did contribute some of the great hymns of the Church; two of them are "Father, We Praise You" and "O Christ, Our King, Creator, Lord." Martin Luther considered the latter to be the best of the hymns.

Gregory stepped down from the papacy early in 604. Within a few weeks, in his mid-sixties, he died.

Summary

Soon after his death, Gregory's contemporaries were calling for his canonization. His writings became well-known and widespread within a short time, and some of them—including *Pastoral Care*, which was translated by King Alfred into Anglo-Saxon—were published in vernacular languages and made available to a relatively large audience. The fact that Gregory's name was early and traditionally associated with the liturgical reforms gave authenticity and authority to them. Although never regarded as a scholar or eminent theologian, Gregory was highly regarded by all the great scholars of the Middle Ages, and he was the most quoted of the Latin fathers. Thomas Aquinas, perhaps the greatest of medieval theologians, cited Gregory more than any other authority; Pope Boniface VIII listed Gregory with the great "doctors" of the Church, placing him in the same category with the best scholars of Western Christendom. As the link between the ancient, classical world and the European Middle Ages, Gregory recast the ideas and teachings of the early church fathers in a new mold, one that shaped not only the medieval Church but European culture and civilization as well.

Bibliography

Anonymous [monk of Whitby]. *The Earliest Life of Gregory the Great*. Edited by Bertram Colgrave. Lawrence: University of Kansas Press, 1968.

Contains a bilingual text with ample notes for understanding a very early biography of Gregory.

Batiffol, Pierre. *Saint Gregory the Great*. London: Burns, Oates and Washbourne, 1929. A brief discussion translated from the French and gives a generally favorable representation of Gregory's life.

Dudden, F. Homes. *Gregory the Great: His Place in History and Thought*. 2 vols. London: Longmans, Green and Co., 1905. This is the most thorough discussion of the subject available—a standard and perhaps a classic. All modern scholarship responds to this work.

Howarth, Henry H. *Saint Gregory the Great*. London: John Murray, 1912. Includes a discussion of the sources. This book was written to supplement the work of Dudden.

Mann, Horace K. *The Lives of the Popes in the Early Middle Ages*. Vol. 1, *The Popes Under the Lombard Rule, St. Gregory I (the Great) to Leo II, 590-795*. Liechtenstein: Kraus, 1964. A reprint edition of a 1902 text, this volume is basically full and accurate, but not as good as the work of Dudden.

Richards, Jeffrey. *Consul of God: The Life and Times of Gregory the Great*. London: Routledge and Kegan Paul, 1980. The best resource for the study of Gregory and his times, endeavoring to provide a balanced interpretation. Contains an extensive bibliography of primary and secondary sources, as well as a fine index.

Thomas O. Kay

GUIDO D'AREZZO

Born: c. 991; possibly Arezzo, Tuscany
Died: 1050; Avellana, Italy
Area of Achievement: Music
Contribution: Guido is generally credited with reestablishing solmization and with perfecting staff notation. His *Micrologus*, a treatise on musical practice, was one of the most widely copied and read books on music in the Middle Ages.

Early Life

Guido d'Arezzo (also known as Guido Aretinus and Guy of Arezzo) was, as his name would indicate, probably born in Arezzo, although at least one source assigns Paris as his birthplace. Nothing is known about his early life and parentage. Music historians have managed, however, to piece together an approximate outline of his career from allusions and references in two letters written by Guido—one to Bishop Theobald of Arezzo, Guido's patron and mentor, and the other to Brother Michael of Pomposa, possibly the coauthor of one of Guido's early musical texts.

Guido was educated at the Benedictine abbey at Pomposa, close to Ferrara on the Adriatic coast. It was probably at this abbey that he began studying music theory and developing his ideas of staff notation; certainly, while he was there he gained acclaim for his ability to train singers to learn new chants in a short time and with a minimum of effort. With his fellow brother Michael, Guido drafted an antiphonary—a collection of liturgical chants—notated according to Guido's new system. Although the antiphonary is now lost, it attracted much favorable attention in monasteries throughout Italy as well as resentment and scorn from Guido's fellow monks at Pomposa, who were wary of any departures from tradition and therefore scorned Guido's innovation.

At some point during his early training, Guido may have spent some time at the monastery of Saint-Maur-des-Fossés near Paris—his familiarity with the music treatise of Odo of Saint-Maur-des-Fossés is evident in his ideas on staff notation, which may have been refined at the French monastery. In his letter to Brother Michael, Guido advocates close study of a work entitled *Enchiridion*, which he attributes to Odo and from which he claims to have learned many of the musical principles underlying his notation system.

Life's Work

Around 1025, Guido moved to Arezzo at the invitation of Bishop Theobald, who appointed him to a teaching post at the cathedral school. Bishop Theobald later commissioned the *Micrologus de disciplina artis musicae* (after 1026; best known as *Micrologus*), which was dedicated to him at its completion. Guido remained under the protection of Bishop Theobald until at least 1036. As a music teacher, he trained singers for the cathedral services, presumably by using the new notation described in the antiphonary.

The *Micrologus*—one of the most influential books of its time—was designed for singers, with the object of improving their skill in using the new notation and in sightsinging both familiar and unfamiliar chants. While much of the work is highly theoretical in both language and content, two chapters are of interest to lay musicians. In one, Guido compares the elements of a melody to the elements in a stanza of poetry: Individual melodic sounds correspond to letters of the alphabet, groups of sounds correspond to syllables, and groups of syllables become analogous to poetic feet. The other chapter, on organum—an early form of polyphony, or music with two or more independent voices—marks an important development in the history of counterpoint. While common practice decreed two voices moving in parallel fourths and fifths, Guido introduced the idea of independent voices that could occasionally move apart or even cross, although the intervals between voices were restricted to consonances (sounds that were restful rather than discordant). As a comprehensive document on music theory and practice, the *Micrologus* was used extensively in both monasteries and universities during the Middle Ages and survives today in about seventy manuscripts dating from the eleventh to the fifteenth century.

Sometime around 1028, Guido traveled to Rome in the company of Dom Peter of Arezzo and Abbot Grunwald, possibly of Badicroce, to the south of Arezzo. The journey was undertaken at the request of Pope John XIX—who may have seen or heard of Guido and Brother Michael's antiphonary and the new system of notation—who wished to have Guido explain his pedagogical system. Before he could accomplish that task, Guido had to leave Rome as a result of ill health, although he did promise to return and resume his explanation of the new notation to the clergy. On the trip home, Guido paused for a visit with the abbot at Pomposa, who, having heard of Guido's visit to Rome, counseled Guido to avoid cities and to settle in a monastery, preferably Pomposa. Guido declined that invitation and about a year later joined the Camaldolese monastery in Avellana, where he eventually became prior.

Not long after his visit to Rome, Guido wrote the *Epistola de ignoto cantu*, (c. 1028), a letter to Brother Michael in which he gave a full description of his theory of solmization, or the method of singing any liturgical melody through the use of the Aretinian scale, involving the six syllables—ut, re, mi, fa, sol, la—which today correspond to the first six tones of the major scale. Although Guido is often credited with inventing solmization, that technique was in fact known to the ancient Greeks; his contribution to music was to establish the practical application of solmization in singing technique. Guido derived the six syllables from a hymn to Saint John—*Ut queant laxis*—in which the six different phrases of the melody begin on six different notes in the ascending order of today's major scale. As with so many of Guido's contributions to music theory, a bit of scholarly controversy surrounds the origin of the hymn. Early historians credited Guido with its authorship, although later scholars identified the text in a manuscript dated around 800. The melody may be Guido's; in fact, he may have composed it as a pedagogical device to use in teaching sightsinging, a valuable skill for clergy and laymen charged with singing during church services. In the letter, Guido informed Brother Michael that the new system had enabled his choirboys to learn new chants rapidly; weeks of training, he wrote, had given way to singing chants on sight.

Two other pieces of writing by Guido are mentioned in some detail in medieval manuscripts. Written after 1030, both were apparently intended as introductory pieces for the lost antiphonary. The *Aliae regulae* (c. 1020-1025), intended as a guide to using the antiphonary, laments the time spent by young singers in learning liturgical chants and committing them to memory and outlines the advantages of a system of line notation—involving four lines and three spaces—based on height of pitch. In this essay, Guido proposes that the lines and spaces composing the system be named after the letters of the pitches they represent. Although he does not specify the number of lines to be thus identified, he does point out that he uses a yellow line for C and a red line for F, with a black line above C and another between C and F. Some manuscripts show a green line for B-flat, with other lines drawn in when necessary, although music historians believe these features to be additions by others and not Guido. The neumes (modern-day musical notes) rest on the lines and in the spaces. Although a number of eleventh and twelfth century manuscripts display the new notation with Guido's colors, thirteenth century manuscripts show that the colored lines were eventually deemed unnecessary. The letter identifications survive today in the C, F, and G clefs. Guido did not invent alphabetical notation; the French were already using an alphabetical system involving the letters from A to P in the late 990's. As with solmization, Guido perfected an awkward system already in use. Guido's system of letter notation uses only the letters A to G in series of capital letters, small letters, and double small letters. The *Regulae rhythmicae in antiphonarii prologum prolate* (c. 1025-1027), also a prologue and written in verse, contains short explanations of several musical concepts—such as intervals and modes and the gamut, or range, of notes available to the singer—described in the *Micrologus*. In addition, Guido expounds further his ideas of a system of notation using colored and lettered lines.

Sigibertus Gemblacensis, a twelfth century theorist, credits Guido with the invention of a pedagogical device called the Guidonian Hand, also known as a hexachord. This device involved labeling each of the nineteen phalanges of the open left hand with nineteen of the notes in the gamut, with the twentieth note in the air above the tip of the middle finger. The Guidonian Hand functioned as an aid in teaching solmization by providing the singer with a visible aid to memorizing intervals. Popular during the Middle Ages, the Guidonian Hand was widely used by singers in learning Gregorian chants. Modern music historians have discounted the notion that Guido invented the Guidonian Hand (although it was named for him); the basic idea of the hand appears in manuscripts dating before Guido's lifetime. More than likely, he popularized and refined an older technique that had been largely ignored by lay musicians and music teachers.

Summary

Although Guido d'Arezzo's enthusiastic admirers through the centuries have credited him with various musical inventions, it seems clear that he was a popularizer rather than an inventor. He himself acknowledged, in the letter to Brother Michael, that he was merely simplifying ideas already in circulation among innovative musicians. Nevertheless, Guido's significant contributions to music are many: He was a renowned teacher in an age when music pedagogy was just becoming a discipline; he saw the practical applications of theoretical concepts and devised ways to teach those applications to singers; and he disseminated his ideas to the world through his writing.

The extent of Guido's influence as a musicologist and teacher is evident in the number of commentaries on his work from the eleventh century to the Renaissance. Written by other music theorists—many of them anonymous—from Italy, England, and Belgium, these commentaries demonstrate the impact of Guido's innovations and reforms on the development of polyphonic liturgical music and on the pedagogical methods used in training singers in monasteries and the great cathedral schools of the Middle Ages. Guido's ideas were disseminated through these commentaries and through copies of his works, which were distributed widely. As late as the sixteenth century, an elaborately illustrated compilation consisting mainly of Guido's *Regulae rhythmicae* and the *Epistola* was circulated as Guido's *Introductorium*.

Bibliography

Babb, Warren, trans. *Hucbald, Guido, and John on Music: Three Medieval Treatises*. New Haven, Conn.: Yale University Press, 1978. Contains a translation of Guido's musical treatise. The introduction, by Claude V. Palisca, provides helpful information on early music theorists. Includes an index of chants and a bibliography.

Brockett, Clyde Waring, Jr. "A Comparison of the Five Monochords of Guido of Arezzo." *Current Musicology* 32 (1981): 29-42. A discussion of the five versions of the monochord (a single-string pitch finder and interval-measuring device) described in the musical treatises of Guido d'Arezzo. The author uses the descriptions as a point of departure for a comparison of the ideas elaborated in Guido's writings. Vocabulary is somewhat technical, although the article is illustrated with diagrams.

Hughes, Dom Anselm, ed. *The New Oxford History of Music*. Vol. 2, *Early Medieval Music up to 1300*. London: Oxford University Press, 1955. Intended for the student of music, although the author points out that he kept the ordinary reader in mind. A discussion of thirteen centuries of European music as it was shaped by contemporary conditions. Some chapters are by noted music historians other than Hughes. Includes illustrations of old manuscripts and notation.

Reese, Gustave. *Music in the Middle Ages*. New York: W. W. Norton and Co., 1940. A style analysis of music up to 1453. This work is densely packed with information, some of it technical although not impossible for the average reader to comprehend. An excellent detailed bibliography is attached at the end of each chapter, as is a list of relevant musical recordings.

Strickling, George F. "Sixth Degree Guido's Scale." *Choral Journal* 10 (July/August, 1969): 16. A one-page generalized summary of Guido d'Arezzo's contributions to music. Credits Guido with placing B-flat on a green line on the musical staff, although many historians agree that the B-flat clef was of anonymous origin.

Edelma Huntley

JOHANN GUTENBERG
Johannes Gensfleisch zur Laden

Born: 1394-1399; Mainz, Germany
Died: Probably February 3, 1468; Mainz, Germany
Areas of Achievement: Invention and technology
Contribution: Gutenberg invented printing with movable metal type.

Early Life

Johann Gutenberg was born in Mainz, an important German city on the Rhine River which was the seat of an archbishop. In the absence of a documented record, his birth date is placed between 1394 and 1399. His family, known as Gensfleisch zur Laden, was of the patrician class, but they were generally called Gutenberg, after their place of residence. Most members of his father's family were skilled metal craftsmen for the archbishop's mint in Mainz. Although there is no firm evidence about Gutenberg's education, he presumably continued his family's association with metalworking by being trained in this craft.

During his youth, Mainz was experiencing political turmoil because of conflicts between patrician and working classes. This civil strife led Gutenberg's father, Friele zum Gutenberg, to go into exile from the city in 1411. After similar disruptions in 1428, during which the Mainz guilds revoked civic privileges from the patricians, Gutenberg, who was probably around thirty years old at that time, settled in Strasbourg, a German city on the Rhine.

Life's Work

Gutenberg's activities during his mature life are of primary interest because of the evidence they contribute to knowledge about the invention of printing with movable type in Western Europe. His life and work can be divided into two chronological periods. During the first period, between 1428 and 1448, when he was living in Strasbourg, he probably began developing the printing process. In the last twenty years of his life, from 1448 to 1468, he returned to Mainz, where he brought his invention of printing with movable metal type to fruition in a Bible (now known as the Gutenberg Bible, the first complete book printed with movable metal type in Europe) and other printed books.

Information about Gutenberg's life in Strasbourg comes mainly from court records of lawsuits in which he was involved. Except for one case in 1436, when he was sued for breach of promise regarding marriage, these records are important because they show that he both practiced metalworking and was developing printing technology. One lawsuit in 1439 provides useful insights into Gutenberg's involvement with printing. The suit arose because, in 1438, Gutenberg had formed a partnership with several Strasbourg citizens to produce mirrors to be sold to pilgrims on a forthcoming pilgrimage to Aachen. Upon learning that the pilgrimage was to take place a year later than they had anticipated, the partners entered into a new contract with Gutenberg so that he would instruct them in other arts that he knew. One clause stipulated that if a partner died, his heirs would receive monetary compensation instead of being taken into the partnership. Soon after the contract was negotiated, one of the partners, Andreas Dritzehn, died, and his two brothers sued to become partners. The court determined that the contract was valid, and Gutenberg won the case.

Testimony of witnesses for this lawsuit has been interpreted as showing that Gutenberg was experimenting with printing using movable metal type. A goldsmith testified that Gutenberg paid him for "materials pertaining to printing." One witness mentioned purchases of metal, a press, and *Formen* (which became the German word for type). Another described how Gutenberg instructed him to dismantle and place on the press an object consisting of four pieces held together with screws which had been reconstructed as a typecasting mold. These combined references indicate that Gutenberg was working out the printing process, but no tangible evidence of his work with printing from this Strasbourg period has survived.

By 1448, Gutenberg had returned to Mainz. One document—a record of an oath made by Johann Fust on November 6, 1455, during a lawsuit that Fust, a Mainz businessman, had brought against Gutenberg—helps to reconstruct Gutenberg's work in Mainz from around 1448 to 1455. The document, known as the Helmasperger Instrument from the name of the notary who drew it up, also has been used to connect this activity with the production of the Gutenberg Bible.

Fust was suing to recover loans that he had made to Gutenberg. The first loan of eight hundred guilders at six percent interest was made in 1450 and the second, also for eight hundred guilders with interest, in 1452. The loans were intended to provide for expenses in making equipment, paying workers' wages, and purchasing paper, parchment, and ink. In the second loan, Fust and Gutenberg became partners for "the work of the books." Testimony also establishes that Gutenberg had several workers and assistants. Peter Schoeffer, who had earlier been a scribe, was a witness for Fust, and soon thereafter Fust and Schoeffer established a flourishing printing business in Mainz. Gutenberg's two witnesses, Berthold Ruppel and Heinrich Kefer, who were his servants or workmen, also later became independent printers. Fust won the suit, since the court decided that Gutenberg should repay the original loan with interest. This document indicates that Gutenberg, using capital loaned to him by Fust, was operating a workshop with assistants for the purpose of producing books, probably by printing.

Bibliographical study of the Gutenberg Bible adds evidence to support the theory that Gutenberg's primary "work of the books" was printing the Gutenberg Bible. Notation in a copy of this Bible at the Bibliothèque Nationale in Paris indicates that Heinrich Cremer, vicar of the church of St. Stephen at Mainz, completed its rubrication and binding in two volumes in August, 1456. Study of paper, ink, and typography of the Gutenberg Bible suggests that it was in production between 1452 and 1454. This analysis also demonstrates that several presses were printing this Bible simultaneously. Thus, evidence from examination of surviving copies of the Gutenberg Bible correlates with information from Fust's lawsuit to show that the Bible was at or near completion at the time of the 1455 suit. Also, the substantial amount of money loaned and the types of expenses for equipment, supplies, and wages for several workmen are consistent with the production scale using several presses. Scholars have thus concluded that soon after Gutenberg returned to Mainz, he was responsible for producing the first complete printed book in Western Europe, the Gutenberg Bible.

A major question about Gutenberg's later life concerns his continued production of printed books after Fust's lawsuit in 1455. Again, documented evidence about this period is meager. He seems to have received some patronage and support from Konrad Humery, a Mainz canonist, who, after Gutenberg's death in early February, 1468, attested that he owned Gutenberg's printing equipment and materials. In addition, in 1465, the Archbishop of Mainz had accorded Gutenberg a civil pension whose privileges included an annual allowance for a suit of clothes, allotments of corn and wine, and exemption from taxes.

Determining Gutenberg's production of printed matter besides the Gutenberg Bible therefore depends on interpretation of these documents, including the financial ramifications of the 1455 lawsuit, and especially bibliographical analysis of early examples of printing. One group of these printed materials is called the "B36" group. The name comes from a Gothic type similar to but somewhat larger and less refined than the type used for the forty-two-line Gutenberg Bible. Works associated with this group include some broadsides, traditional grammar texts by the Roman author Donatus, and a thirty-six-line Bible printed in Bamberg, dated 1458-1459. Another group comes from the press that printed the *Catholicon*, a Latin dictionary put together in a smaller Gothic type by Johannes Balbus in Mainz in 1460. At least two other books and broadsides are connected with this press.

According to some sources, Gutenberg had to give up his printing materials to satisfy repayment to Fust. This financial disaster, combined with the somewhat inferior quality of printing using variants of the thirty-six-line Bible type, suggests that few, if any, other surviving early printed works can be attributed to Gutenberg. Another interpretation holds that the settlement with Fust did not deplete Gutenberg's financial or material resources to which Humery's support added. The comparative irregularities in the B36 type show that it was being developed earlier than the perfected Gutenberg

Bible font, and this evidence suggests that Gutenberg was printing other works concurrently with and subsequently to the Gutenberg Bible using this more experimental type. Technical innovations in the type and setting of the *Catholicon*, along with its colophon extolling the new printing process, make Gutenberg, the inventor of printing, the person most likely to have executed the printing from the *Catholicon* press. Thus, it makes sense that Gutenberg probably printed various items comprising the B36 and *Catholicon* press groups throughout his career based in Mainz.

Summary

While further research in many areas will continue to add greater precision to identifying the corpus of Johann Gutenberg's printed works, his most significant achievement is the invention of printing with movable metal type. From the 1430's to the completion of the Gutenberg Bible around 1455, Gutenberg utilized his metalworking skills to develop a process of casting individual letters that could be arranged repeatedly into any alphabetic text. When combined with paper, his new oil-based typographic ink, and a printing press, Gutenberg's process succeeded in merging several distinct technologies, making possible the production of multiple identical copies of a text. Although the changes that printing brought developed gradually during the succeeding centuries, the use of printing has had major effects on almost every aspect of human endeavor—including communications and literacy, economic patterns of investment, production, and marketing, and a wide range of intellectual ideas.

The Gutenberg Bible is an outstanding symbol of his invention. The copies that are still extant (forty-eight out of an original printing of about 180) demonstrate the high level of technical and aesthetic perfection that this 1,282-page book attained. The regularity of the lines, the justification of the margins, the quality of the ink, and especially the beautiful design of the type show how Gutenberg raised the printing process beyond a technological invention to an art.

Bibliography

Febvre, Lucien, and Henri-Jean Martin. Translated by David Gerard. *The Coming of the Book: The Impact of Printing, 1450-1800*. London: N.L.B., 1976. Discusses Gutenberg's role in the invention of printing in the context of the transition from manuscripts to printed books. Also examines the impact of printing on varied aspects of book production and the book trade in early modern Europe.

Fuhrmann, Otto W. *Gutenberg and the Strasbourg Documents of 1439: An Interpretation*. New York: Press of the Woolly Whale, 1940. Gives a transcription of the original German text of the lawsuit against Gutenberg in Strasbourg in 1439 that is important for reconstructing Gutenberg's early printing efforts. The book provides translations in modern English, German, and French, as well as a discussion of the meaning of the Strasbourg suit.

Goff, Frederick R. *The Permanence of Johann Gutenberg*. Austin: University of Texas at Austin, Humanities Research Center, 1969. Includes an essay on Gutenberg's invention and evidence for what he printed. Also discusses the significance of Gutenberg's invention.

Ing, Janet. "Searching for Gutenberg in the 1980s." *Fine Print* 12 (1986): 212-215. This article summarizes the technical bibliographical studies concerning Gutenberg's printing during the twentieth century. Its focus is on scientific methods of analysis of paper and ink and typographical studies done in the 1970's and 1980's. References are included.

Lehmann-Haupt, Helmut. *Gutenberg and the Master of the Playing Cards*. New Haven: Yale University Press, 1966. This book suggests that Gutenberg may have been involved with developing techniques for printed reproduction of designs for book decoration and illustration necessary to produce, in printed form, the effect of finely illuminated manuscripts.

McMurtrie, Douglas C. *The Gutenberg Documents*. New York: Oxford University Press, 1941. Contains all the known documents associated with Gutenberg in English translation. Includes notes.

Needham, Paul. "Johann Gutenberg and the Catholicon Press." *Papers of the Bibliographical Society of America* 76 (1982): 395-456. Discusses bibliographical problems relating particularly to evidence from paper and typography in works from the *Catholicon* press. Needham's conclusions summarize arguments for Gutenberg's role in printing material in the *Catholicon* press group.

Painter, George D. "Gutenberg and the B36 Group: A Re-Consideration." In *Essays in Honor of Victor Scholderer*, edited by Dennis F. Rhodes. Mainz: Karl Pressler, 1970. This article discusses the examples of printing in the B36 group and argues that Gutenberg printed these pieces.

Scholderer, Victor. *Johann Gutenberg: The Inventor of Printing*. London: Trustees of the British Museum, 1963, rev. ed. 1970. The most complete biography of Gutenberg in English. It covers the various types of evidence for documenting Gutenberg's life and activity as the inventor of printing. Contains bibliographical references and good illustrations.

Karen Gould

GUY DE CHAULIAC

Born: c. 1290; Chauliac, France
Died: July 25, 1368; Avignon, France
Area of Achievement: Medicine
Contribution: Guy wrote the most important treatise on surgery during the later Middle Ages. For more than two centuries, he was considered the leading authority on such diverse medical topics as dissection; surgical procedure; professional ethics; leprosy; plague origins, symptoms, and preventions; anatomical structure; pharmaceutical drugs; dental care; and ophthalmology.

Early Life

Guy de Chauliac (also known as Guigo or Guido de Chaulhaco, Cauliaco, Caillat, or Chaulhac) was born sometime during the last decade of the thirteenth century in the former village of Chauliac, near Auvergne, in the modern department of Lozère. Of agrarian, peasant stock, he exhibited intellectual abilities early in his youth, and was supported in his subsequent academic pursuits by the lords of Mercœur. He first studied medicine in Toulouse and completed his initial medical training in Montpellier under Raymond of Molières. Later, in Bologna, he mastered anatomy under Niccolò Bertruccio, renowned for his pioneering achievements in describing the construction and operation of the brain. Guy perfected his surgical techniques under Alberto of Bologna.

Bologna was vitally important to Guy's career because of its long and distinguished medical history. As early as the middle of the twelfth century, it had a medical faculty which taught Latin translations of Arabic texts, especially those of Avicenna. Of particular significance to Guy's development were the writings of William of Saliceto, a surgeon who produced a treatise in 1275 describing human dissection, Thaddeus of Florence, who encouraged scholar-physicians to make direct translations from the Greek masters, and Mondino dei Liucci, who publicly dissected corpses. Mondino's *Anatomia*, a practical manual of dissection completed in 1316, was the most popular textbook on anatomy before that of Vesalius in the sixteenth century. Finally, Henry of Mondeville, a fellow student of Mondino at Bologna, brought these techniques in the first decade of the fourteenth century to Montpellier. All of these brilliant masters played a major role in Guy's perspective, procedure, and philosophy of medicine.

After his university career, Guy practiced medicine in Paris from 1315 to 1320. Thereafter, he served for an extended period of time in Lyons, where he also was a canon and provost of Saint-Just; he acquired similar posts later at Reims and at Mende. For much of his later life he resided in Avignon, where he was the personal physician to Clement VI, Innocent VI, and

Urban V. He also served these pontiffs as a personal auditor and judge.

It was during these Avignonese years that Guy witnessed some of the most catastrophic events in human history: the Black Death of the 1340's and 1360's, which killed approximately one-third of Europe's population, and the initial bloody episodes of the Hundred Years' War between England and France. In this tragic setting, Guy wrote the most important medical text of the later Middle Ages.

Life's Work

In 1363, Guy finished his masterpiece—the *Chirurgia magna* (great surgery)—and dedicated it to his former colleagues and masters at Montpellier, Bologna, Paris, and Avignon. Systematic and comprehensive, this work contains a synthesis of the best medical ideas of his age, an intensive analysis of earlier literature, especially the treatises of Galen, Aristotle, Rhazes, Albucasis, Avicenna, and Averroës, and a litany of hundreds of his own personal observations.

The *Chirurgia magna* consists of seven major sections (*tractates*), but it is preceded by an introduction (*capitulum singulare*) that provides personal information on Guy's life and advises physicians to acquire a liberal education, maintain a proper diet, keep excellent care of their instruments, and conduct correct surgical procedures. He warned them not to shun patients out of fear as was commonplace during the outbreaks of the Black Death and lambasted the fables perpetrated by some of his predecessors. He cautioned against relying on the occult even though he himself occasionally slips and recommends occult remedies. Guy was concerned with the total education of physicians, their health and physical appearance, their office procedures and equipment, and their ethics and personal deportment. Not since Hippocrates had this facet of the profession been given such intensive emphasis.

In the first section of the *Chirurgia magna*, Guy presents a brief exegesis on anatomy based largely on Galen and Bertruccio. More detailed than the anatomical treatise of Mondino, it stresses the need for all surgeons to be knowledgeable in all facets of this discipline. Some of the format was based on Guy's experience of assisting at dissections and postmortems.

The next section is one of the most popular, durable, and influential in the book. Dealing generally with carbuncles, abscesses, and tumors, Guy recommended operating on cancer in its earliest stages. He described in detail the plague that had recently ravaged Avignon. Based upon personal observation and a brief bout with the disease, he described its Asiatic origins, its causes (unfortunately ascribing them to a number of popular superstitions), its contagious nature, and its prevention. Concerning plague symptoms, Guy lists fever, pains in the side or chest, coughing, shortness of breath, rapid pulse, vomiting of blood, and the appearance of buboes in the groin, under the armpit, or behind the ears. Distinguishing between the bubonic and pneumonic types, he recommended such divergent preventive measures as the avoidance of damp places, the burning of aromatic wood, the abstention from violent exercise and hot baths, and the use of antidotes and drugs.

Section 3 deals with various kinds of wounds, diets for wounded persons, diseases contracted after being wounded, and treatments. Once again, it was unfortunate that he recommended the Galenic method of applying salves and ointments. His contemporary Mondeville had pioneered in the antiseptic treatment of wounds that included cleaning them with wine, stitching their edges, keeping them dry and clean, and permitting nature to heal them. These techniques became standard by the later stages of the Hundred Years' War. Nevertheless, Guy did provide valuable insights in his discussions of the escape of the cerebrospinal fluid, the effect of pressure on respiration, the closing of chest wounds, and the extreme caution needed in treating abdominal wounds.

After describing the numerous types of ulcers in section 4, Guy devotes the entire next section to fractures and dislocations. Although he contributed little original to existing literature, he provided a detailed procedure for treating fractures with splints, pulleys, and weights. His treatments for dislocations of the hands and feet endured for centuries.

In section 6, Guy covers such diverse topics as sciatica, leprosy, localized illnesses, bladder stones, proper eye and dental care, and medical and dental equipment. His work in leprosy was of great importance. He drew attention to the excessive greasiness of a leper's skin and recommended segregation and proper medical treatment. So successful were these methods that by the sixteenth century there was a dramatic reduction in the number of new cases and some of the methods were applied to other diseases. He may have been the first to recommend the use of the catheter to diagnose stones in the bladder. He prescribed a powder made from cuttlebones and other substances for cleaning teeth, the use of ox bone for the replacement of lost teeth, and the fastening of gold wire around loose teeth for strengthening. He even prescribed spectacles as a remedy for poor sight after salves and lotions had failed. The last section catalogs an extremely comprehensive antidotary in which Guy lists about 750 medical substances. In the process, he was one of the first physicians to warn patients about the dangers of excessive or sustained drug use.

Summary

Guy de Chauliac was the most famous and successful surgical writer of the Middle Ages. His *Chirurgia magna* was translated into French, Provençal, Catalan, Italian, English, Dutch, Hebrew, and Irish. Although criticized by some modern writers for his lack of originality, his primary intention was to summarize the knowledge of the most significant medical writers of his own and of preceding ages. Even the longer title of his work—*Inuentarium seu collectorium cyrurgie* (the inventory or collectory of surgery)—testifies to this overall goal. Consequently, he became a founder of didactic surgery—a teacher of surgery as well as a practicing physician-scientist.

Although never a professor of surgery in a prestigious university, Guy had the title of Master of Medicine conferred upon him by the administrative authorities of the University of Montpellier shortly before his death. His surgical work was unparalleled until Ambroise Paré amended it toward the end of the sixteenth century, while his anatomical observations served as the scientific model until 1534 when Vesalius published his great treatise. In the fields of surgery, medicine, and anatomy, Guy served as a standardizer, transmitter, and synthesizer. He was a harbinger of the many significant breakthroughs in these fields that occurred in the scientific revolution.

Bibliography

Campbell, Anna M. *The Black Death and Men of Learning*. New York: Columbia University Press, 1931. A classic study, with excellent coverage of the medical opinions of fourteenth century physicians on the greatest catastrophe in recorded history.

Crombie, A. C. *Augustine to Galileo: The History of Science, A.D. 400-1650*. London: Falcon Press, 1952. Even though Crombie is critical of certain of Guy's anatomical ideas, he extols Guy's position as the leading medical writer in Western Europe prior to the sixteenth century.

Hall, A. R. *The Scientific Revolution: 1500-1800*. 2d ed. Boston: Beacon Press, 1966. This work includes a discussion of the great debt that Ambroise Paré, the most famous sixteenth century French surgeon, owed to Guy's *Chirurgia magna*.

Kibre, Pearl. *Studies in Medieval Science: Alchemy, Astrology, Mathematics, and Medicine*. London: Hambledon Press, 1984. Treatises by Guy and other contemporary medical writers found in the medieval libraries of Western Europe are treated in the last of these republished articles.

Sarton, George. *Introduction to the History of Science: Science and Learning in the Fourteenth Century*. Vol. 3. Baltimore: Williams and Wilkins, 1947-1948. The author comprehensively covers Guy's contributions to medieval anatomy and surgery. A landmark study in the history of science.

Sedgwick, W. T., and H. W. Tyler. *A Short History of Science*. Reprint. New York: Macmillan, 1939. This study describes Guy's debt to his Bolognese medical masters and to Henry of Mondeville, who brought the Italian methods to Montpellier.

Singer, Charles. *A Short History of Anatomy from the Greeks to Harvey*. Reprint. Mineola, N.Y.: Dover Publications, 1957. Guy's position as a standardizer of medieval surgical practices is highlighted in several sections.

Thorndike, Lynn. *A History of Magic and Experimental Science: The Four-*

teenth and Fifteenth Centuries. Vols. 3 and 4. New York: Columbia University Press, 1934. Chapter 30 is devoted to Guy and his contemporary physicians, with a special emphasis on the impact of the Black Death on them and their respective societies.

Wallner, Bjorn, ed. *The Middle English Translation of Guy de Chauliac's Anatomy, with Guy's Essay on the History of Medicine*. Lund, Sweden: CWK Gleerup, 1964. A valuable late fourteenth or early fifteenth century rendering of a portion of Guy's *Chirurgia magna*.

Ronald Edward Zupko

HADRIAN

Born: January 24, 76; Italica, Spain
Died: July 10, 138; Baiae, Bay of Naples
Area of Achievement: Government
Contribution: Hadrian succeeded in bringing a relatively peaceful period to the Roman Empire, in realizing much-needed domestic and civil reforms, and in leaving, through his architectural and artistic gifts, his personal stamp on Rome, Athens, and Jerusalem.

Early Life

Hadrian was born in Italica, Spain, a Roman settlement, of Publius Aelius Hadrianus Afer, a distinguished Roman officer and civil administrator, and Domitia Paulina. Hadrian's parents, however, were not as influential in his development as Hadrian's cousin Trajan, the future Roman emperor who served as his coguardian after his father died when Hadrian was ten years old. Soon after his father's death, Hadrian was sent to Rome to further his education; during his stay in Rome, his study of Greek language, literature, and culture made him so much a Hellenist that he became known as the "Greekling." When he was fifteen, he returned to Italica, where he supposedly entered military service but actually spent his time hunting, a lifelong passion of his. As a result of the jealousy of his brother-in-law Servianus, who complained to Trajan of Hadrian's "dissipation," he was recalled to Rome in 93 and probably never saw Italica again.

In Rome, Hadrian continued his studies, laying the groundwork for a lifelong commitment not only to literature and art but also to music, architecture, astronomy, mathematics, law, and military science. In fact, few rulers have received such appropriate education and been so fortunate in their political connections; he had the support of Trajan and of Trajan's wife, Plotina, who helped to further his advancement. Since Hadrian also began his public career in 93, he added practical experience in public service and in military affairs to his extensive educational background. Through Trajan's influence with Emperor Domitian, Hadrian became a decemvir, a minor magistrate in probate court, as well as a military tribune serving at a Roman outpost on the Danube River.

When Domitian was assassinated in 96, the Roman senate chose Nerva to succeed him. Nerva, in turn, adopted Trajan in 97, and when Nerva died in 98, Trajan became emperor. With his coguardian as emperor, Hadrian rose rapidly within the civil and military ranks, despite Servianus' interference. In 101, he was appointed quaestor and communicated Trajan's messages to the senate; in 107, he became praetor and governor of a province on the Danube; and in 108, he was elected consul and soon began writing Trajan's speeches.

As a provincial governor and as *legatus* of Syria during Trajan's Parthian campaign, Hadrian had military as well as civil responsibilities and he had already demonstrated his military talents during the second Dacian war. Moreover, since Trajan's ambitions had greatly, and precariously, extended Roman rule, Hadrian benefited from firsthand observations of a military conqueror.

On his return from the Parthian campaign in 117, Trajan died; on his deathbed, however, he apparently adopted Hadrian (there is considerable controversy about the "adoption"). The adoption practically guaranteed Hadrian's accession, and after the Syrian troops acclaimed him emperor, the senate quickly confirmed their action. At the age of forty-two, Hadrian became emperor, and his twenty-one-year rule was to be marked by policies and actions almost antithetical to those of his guardian, cousin, and mentor.

Life's Work

Hadrian commanded the largest Roman army at the time of Trajan's death and his ties to the emperor had been close, but his position was far from secure. He had many enemies among the Roman senators, some of whom considered him a provincial upstart opposed to militaristic expansion and enamored of Greek culture. In fact, Hadrian's policy of peace, retrenchment, and reform was diametrically opposed to Trajan's expansionist policy. Domestically, moderation was the order of the day as Hadrian attempted to convert his enemies by exercising restraint even in suppressing rebellious factions; in fact, when his coguardian Attianus became too zealous in his emperor's cause—he had four traitors executed—Hadrian eased him out of power. To gain the support of the Roman populace, Hadrian canceled all debts to the imperial treasury, renounced the emperor's traditional claim to the estates of executed criminals, extended the children's welfare centers, and staged spectacular entertainments for the masses. In addition to these public relations measures, Hadrian accomplished a major overhaul of the administrative system—he created opportunities for the talented as well as the wealthy—and a thorough reform of the army. His domestic achievements culminated in the codification, under Julian's supervision, of Roman statutory law in 121.

Such reforms were necessary, since Hadrian, who never felt at home in Rome, was intent on establishing his rule before leaving to tour the provinces, a task that occupied him, for the most part, from 120 to 131. In fact, Hadrian's travel was consistent with his imperial policy of creating sister relations—with a subsequent loss of prestige for Rome—bound to him as to a patriarch. (He assumed in 128 the title *pater patriae*, "father of the fatherland.") During his extensive travels, Hadrian determined not on expanding the empire but on consolidating it, even reducing where necessary, and establishing *limes*, definite physical boundaries that could be effectively defended.

Accordingly, after visiting Roman outposts on the Rhine River, Hadrian traveled through the Netherlands to England, where rebellious tribes were unwilling to be assimilated. As there was no natural defensive barrier against northern invaders, Hadrian's Wall was constructed. This man-made fortification, parts of which survive today, also served as a seventy-three-mile road which facilitated the defense of the empire. Hadrian then traveled to Spain and Mauretania before he arrived in 124 in Ephesus, in what is now Turkey; there, Hadrian's Temple, one of the Seven Wonders of the ancient world, was constructed. Hadrian's next significant visit was to Bithynia, where he met Antinous, a young man who became his inseparable companion for the next nine years. After a trip to Athens, his intellectual and cultural homeland, Hadrian returned to Rome in 125.

Although he continued his travels, Hadrian's next four years were distinguished primarily by his architectural achievements and the rebuilding, or re-creation, of Rome and Athens. The renowned Roman Pantheon is Hadrian's work, as is his mausoleum, built in imitation of the tomb built for Augustus, the emperor who always served as a model for Hadrian. When he left Rome, he stopped in his beloved Athens, where he constructed bridges, canals, and an elaborate gymnasium.

In the autumn of 129, Hadrian went south, and after literally saving the famous cedars of Lebanon, he made a fateful error involving the Jews in Palestine. An ardent supporter of Hellenism, which was in philosophical conflict with Judaism, and a xenophobe who considered the Jews as foreigners, Hadrian enacted laws against circumcision and also determined to rebuild Jerusalem as a Roman city. Both actions infuriated the Jews, who were almost forced into another rebellion against Rome. After inciting the Jews, Hadrian traveled to Absandria; then, on a trip up the Nile River, he lost his beloved Antinous, who was drowned. It is not certain whether Antinous' death was an accident or suicide—the matter is controversial—but in any case it profoundly affected Hadrian. When he returned to Palestine, Hadrian found the reconstruction of Jerusalem interrupted by a Jewish uprising; although the bloody rebellion was eventually ended in 134, his punitive actions against the Jews, many of whom were sold into slavery, were decidedly uncharacteristic.

The remaining years of Hadrian's life somewhat negated the positive image he had created. Despite his rebuilding of Rome, the Romans never really accepted their provincial ruler who openly preferred Athens. Hadrian's problems were compounded by the onset of debilitating health problems which transformed the athletic emperor into a weak as well as a cruel and vindictive ruler. The man who had used moderation and patience to establish his rule actually began to order some executions, and the troublesome Servianus was finally put to death. The only notable achievement of these troubled years was the villa he had begun to build at Tibur in 126; the villa, itself of immense proportions, was an architectural blend of Roman and Greek styles.

Hadrian's problems even extended to the naming of his successor. Since his wife, Sabina, had failed to produce an heir, Hadrian named Lucius Aelius, who was perhaps his illegitimate son; Lucius, however, died before Hadrian. Hadrian adopted Antoninus Pius, a loyal and capable supporter, and then required that Antoninus in turn adopt the younger Aelius, as well as Marcus Annius Verus (the future philosopher and emperor Marcus Aurelius), Antoninus' nephew. When Hadrian died in 138, it was Antoninus, his successor, who was responsible for persuading a reluctant senate to deify the man whose last few years unfortunately clouded the real accomplishments of the early years of his reign.

Summary

Because he succeeded the militaristic Trajan, who had trained him to be an emperor, Hadrian determined to bring peace to a war-weary Rome, which was already overextended. By consolidating and precisely fixing defendable boundaries, he was able to focus his considerable energies on much-needed civil reforms, among them the law code and the civil service; as a result of his artistic training and architectural expertise, he was able to transform Rome, Athens, and Jerusalem. While he is widely known for the Pantheon and Hadrian's Wall, Hadrian left his architectural stamp on many of the cities he visited in his extensive travels.

Through his rule and his adoption and appointment of Antoninus Pius as his successor, he also was largely responsible for establishing what many historians have regarded as a golden age that lasted through the reigns of Antoninus Pius and his successor, the celebrated philosopher and emperor Marcus Aurelius. (Since he had required Antoninus to adopt his successor, Hadrian was directly involved in Marcus Aurelius' appointment as emperor, even though it occurred after his death.) When an iron age began with the ascension of Commodus, son of Marcus Aurelius, the so-called Antonine dynasty came to an end. Nevertheless, Rome had enjoyed approximately one hundred years of prosperity, greatness, and—with the exception of Trajan's reign—relative peace.

In fact, Hadrian's only significant military campaign, the suppression of the Jewish rebellion late in his reign, also became the indirect cause of an ironic development Hadrian neither intended nor desired: the spread of Christianity throughout the Roman Empire. By banishing the Jews from Jerusalem, the site of both Judaism and Christianity, Hadrian inadvertently caused Christianity to be separated from the Christian Jews who had controlled the early Christian Church. Consequently, as Stewart Perowne has suggested, Hadrian became the "unwitting forerunner of Constantine, and of the triumph of the faith in his own Rome." It seems both ironic and appropriate that Hadrian, the intellectual, artistic Hellenist and advocate of peace, should play such a role in the development of Christianity.

Bibliography

Gray, William Dodge. "A Study of the Life of Hadrian Prior to His Accession." *Smith College Studies in History* 4 (1919): 151-209. Gray provides a scholarly review of Hadrian's pre-accession life and concentrates on his training as Trajan's successor. After examining the evidence, he finds not much proof to support contemporary accounts of a hostile marriage between Hadrian and Sabina, of friction between Hadrian and Trajan, or of a fabricated adoption of Hadrian.

Gregorovius, Ferdinand. *The Emperor Hadrian: A Picture of the Greco-Roman World in His Time*. Translated by Mary E. Robinson with an introduction by Henry Pelham. New York: Macmillan, 1898. Gregorovius' work is particularly helpful in placing Hadrian within the cultural, literary, artistic, and philosophical contexts of his day, but the book, as Pelham indicates, lacks a general thesis to account for Hadrian's individual arts or his apparently contradictory nature. Pelham provides that thesis, although in condensed form.

Henderson, Bernard W. *The Life and Principate of the Emperor Hadrian, A.D. 76-138*. London: Methuen and Co., 1923. The acknowledged standard work in English on Hadrian, Henderson's book is a scholarly and gracefully written biography. Henderson succeeds in rendering Hadrian as a person, not merely a public figure, and his comments on "personalia" provide a glimpse of the man and an objective corrective to those too-lavish apologists for Hadrian.

Ish-Kishor, Sulamith. *Magnificent Hadrian: A Biography of Hadrian, Emperor of Rome*. New York: Minton, Balch and Co., 1935. An extremely sympathetic account of Hadrian's life, this book is also a heavy-handed psychological study designed to outline the "final tragedy of the homosexual temperament" in the relationship between Hadrian and Antinous. Ish-Kishor contrasts Trajan, the life-destroying father figure, with Hadrian, the life-building and life-restoring mother figure.

Perowne, Stewart. *Hadrian*. London: Hodder and Stoughton, 1960. This comparatively short, readable biography is accompanied by a map illustrating Hadrian's travels, a bibliographical essay, appropriate illustrations, and tables outlining the Roman emperors, Hadrian's ancestors, and the problem of succession. Perowne categorizes Hadrian's travels and policies as manifestations of a political philosophy unique in its day.

Thomas L. Erskine

HAFIZ
Shams al-Din Muhammed

Born: c. 1320; Shiraz, Iran
Died: 1389 or 1390; Shiraz, Iran
Area of Achievement: Literature
Contribution: The premier lyric poet in more than a millennium of literary expression in the Persian language, Hafiz represents the culmination of lyrical styles and modes that began some five centuries before him and remains a model for Iranian poets today.

Early Life

Shams al-Din Muhammed of Shiraz, whose nom de plume was to be Hafiz, was born sometime between 1317 and 1326. His merchant father, who had emigrated from Esfahan sometime earlier, apparently died when Hafiz was young. Hafiz received a traditional education in Arabic, Koranic studies, science, and literature. Hafiz's poetry reveals his intimate familiarity with the five centuries of Persian literature that preceded him, as well as his knowledge of Islamic sciences and his special competence in Arabic. His pen name testifies to this last skill, because the word "Hafiz" denotes a person who has memorized the Koran.

Little specific information is available on the private life of the most acclaimed Persian lyric poet in history. Citations in biographical dictionaries, references in chronicles and other historical sources, and possible autobiographical details in his poems are mostly unverifiable. Information is available, however, about the tumultuous political history of Hafiz's native province of Fars and its capital, Shiraz, during his lifetime.

At the time of Hafiz's birth, Mahmud Shah Inju ruled Fars in the name of the Il-Khanid ruler Abu Sa'id. The latter's successor executed Mahmud in 1335. Anarchy ensued, as Mahmud's four sons strove to gain control over their father's kingdom. One of them, Abu Ishaq, took over Shiraz seven years later and ruled, albeit with opposition, until 1352. During this period, Hafiz composed poems in praise of Abu Ishaq and one of his viziers; these poems show that he was a seriously regarded court poet by the time he was thirty years of age.

In 1353 came the capture of Shiraz by the Mozaffarid leader called Mubariz al-Din Muhammad, who had Abu Ishaq summarily beheaded in front of the Achaemenid ruins at Persepolis. Mubariz al-Din, whose family was to control Shiraz until 1393, imposed strict, puritanical Sunni religious observation on the city during his five-year reign, a situation Hafiz bewailed in several poems. In addition, Hafiz's signature on a manuscript dated 1355 implies that he had to seek work as a scribe at that time, either because he was not yet economically established as a poet or because he was out of favor with the Mozaffarid court. In 1358, Mubariz al-Din was deposed, blinded, and succeeded by his son Jalal al-Din Shah Shuja'. Hafiz, whose lot improved when Shah Shuja' ascended the throne, eulogized this royal patron in a number of poems.

Life's Work

It was during the long reign of Shah Shuja', between 1358 and 1384, that Hafiz's fame began to spread throughout the Persian-speaking world, westward to the Arab world and Ottoman Empire, and eastward to Mughal India. Altogether, he composed some five hundred *ghazal* poems and a handful of poems in other traditional Persian verse forms. The fourteenth century was the culminating age of the Persian *ghazal*, and Hafiz was its apogee.

The *ghazal* is a conventional composition of usually between five and thirteen couplets, the first closed and the others open, resulting in a monorhyme pattern such as *aabaca*. Each constituent verse exhibits the same quantitative metrical pattern. The poet's nom de plume generally appears in a *ghazal*'s final couplet.

The basic subject of these poems was idealized love, treated with conventional, stylized imagery in an equally conventional diction. The Hafizian *ghazal*, while displaying amatory, mystical, and panegyrical modes typical of the verse form up to his day, is distinctive in its merging of modes, in Hafiz's creation of an ambivalent lyric world of love in which readers can sense both love of God and passion for a romanticized, this-worldly beloved. An example is the very famous *ghazal* with which Hafiz's *Divan* (c. 1368; English translation, 1891) usually begins:

> O cupbearer, pass around a cup and hand it to me;
> for love appeared at first easy, but difficulties arose.
> In hope of the musk pod the zephyr eventually opens from those tresses,
> what blood spilt in hearts because of musky curls.
> Color the prayer-carpet with wine should the Magian elder so advise;
> for the wayfarer knows the way, and the stages.
> At beloved's abodes what security of pleasure can exist?
> Every second the caravan bells cry out: tie up the loads.
> Dark night, the fear of the waves, and such a terrifying whirlpool—
> how can the lightburdened and shore-bound fathom my state?
> Everything has dragged me from self-interest to infamy;
> how can that secret which inspires gatherings remain secret?
> If you desire the beloved's presence, Hafiz, don't be absent;
> when you meet whom you desire, let the world go, give it up.

A reader's first impression of this poem is of polysemy and multiplicity of patterns of imagery, which is another typical feature of the Hafizian *ghazal*. Once the two levels of the speaker's emotional state as a lover are discerned, however, one begins to sense the poem's integrity. A quasi-temporal and physical setting is implied in the address in the opening couplet of the cup-bearer. The speaker may be in a tavern, seeking consolation in wine for the pains of love. Those who have not given themselves wholeheartedly to love and who have not done the apparently blasphemous bidding of the Zoroastrian priest who is presumed privy to secrets of the heart cannot understand the lover's state. The true lover may lose his reputation. Nevertheless, as the speaker advises at the poem's close, a true lover has to be ready to give up everything.

As for the nature of this love, the seriousness of tone and the religious commitment voiced imply that the speaker is enamored of a romantic beloved but that at the same time he senses the presence of the Creator in the beloved or the potential proximity to God that might be achieved by heeding no calls but love. The translation communicates nothing of the aural force of tight patterns of rhyme, meter, and alliteration of the original Persian or its rhetorical richness in echoing earlier poets and employing conventional figures with touches of novelty. The original is quintessential Hafiz in its thematic ambivalence, powerful imagery, and rich decorativeness.

In 1365, Shah Shuja''s brother Mahmud laid siege to Shiraz along with the Jala'irid Shaykh Uvays. Hafiz may have lived for a year or two in the 1370's in Esfahan or Yazd, but he spent most of his life in Shiraz. In 1384, Zaynu'l-'Abidin succeeded Shah Shuja', and internecine feuds continued within the Mozaffarid family. In 1387, Tamerlane, who had massacred seventy thousand people in Esfahan, reached Shiraz and brought the Mozaffarid dynasty under his control. He named Yahya his local ruler. Soon, however, Yahya's nephew Mansur overthrew his uncle, which brought Tamerlane's wrath down upon Mansur and the whole Mozaffarid family, all of whom Tamerlane proceeded to execute. Hafiz, who had briefly enjoyed the patronage of Yahya and Mansur, died two or three years before Tamerlane's second invasion of Shiraz in 1393.

By the end of his life, Hafiz had become the most respected Middle Eastern lyric poet, a reputation that he retains to the present day. Curiously, however, he never authorized or supervised a collection of his poems. Consequently, the first manuscripts containing all of his *ghazals* were not compiled until a generation after his death, which led to textual problems persisting today with respect to the authenticity of some *ghazals*, of some of their constituent couplets, of the order of couplets within *ghazals*, and of verbal variants. Editorial efforts in Iran since the beginning of World War II have brought the text as close to reliability as is possible.

A further difficulty in the critical appreciation of Hafiz's *ghazals* is that only in the 1960's did serious literary criticism and analysis begin to be applied to Hafiz. Still, Hafiz's popularity has never diminished from his death to the present time.

Summary

It would be difficult to exaggerate the admiration and respect which poetry lovers in the Persian-speaking world feel for Hafiz. Iranians in all walks of life still use verses from Hafiz's *Divan* for prognostication; the Koran is the only other book so used. Hafiz's tomb is Shiraz's most popular monument. Modernist Iranian poets routinely declare their devotion to him and his relevance as inspiration for them. The recitation of Hafizian *ghazals* is a common activity at social gatherings.

Dating back to Sir William Jones's "A Persian Song" (1771), a rendition of the most famous among Hafiz's *ghazals* in the West, more attempts at translating his verses into English have been made than with respect to any other Persian poet. These translations, however, have generally failed to capture Hafiz's spirit and subtlety. Such literary giants as Johann Wolfgang von Goethe and Ralph Waldo Emerson have sensed and rightly lauded Hafiz's poetic genius, but English-speaking readers have yet to experience convincing evidence in the form of appealing translations.

Part of the explanation for the unfortunate fact that a poet so revered and influential in his own culture should remain almost unknown in the English-speaking world six centuries after his death is that Hafiz's voice has had no Edward FitzGerald, as Omar Khayyám's epigrammatic quatrains did, nor a Matthew Arnold, as did Firdusi's epic *Shahnamah* (c. 1010) episode about Sohrab and his father Rostam. In addition, lyric poetry, especially when very culture-specific in form and imagery, seems resistant to translation more than other literary species. The foregoing description of the *ghazal* verse form highlights two almost insurmountable translation problems: transmission of pervasive aural elements and effects from traditional Persian verse to English, and the communication in English of the textual richness and resonances of conventional images, themes, and vocabulary.

As for the nature of Hafiz's special appeal, one Iranian view sees him as a combination of the questioning spirit of Omar Khayyám (1048-1131), the lyricism and skill at versification of Sa'di (c. 1200-c. 1291), and the intensity of feeling and spirit exhibited in the poetry of Jalal al-Din Rumi (1207-1273). From another perspective, Hafiz's special talent is seen as the ability to create a texture of ambivalence in his poetic world, continually forcing the reader to sense both material and spiritual planes of experience. In addition, above and beyond Khayyamic echoes in *carpe diem* invitations and assertions to the effect that scientific inquiry will not fathom the point to life, Hafiz's *ghazals* have a further appeal to Iranian readers in their frequent images of libertines, scandalous models of behavior who answer only to themselves and who disregard what others think or what those in power bid one to do. As this sort of libertine, Hafiz remains inspirational to readers whose own lives do not often allow for such defiant free-spiritedness. Finally, Hafiz's persistent *joie de vivre* and concomitant refusal to be depressed by the difficult times in which he lived give hope to later readers who have found many reasons to despair.

Bibliography

Browne, E. G. "Hafiz of Shiraz." In *A Literary History of Persia*. Vol. 3. Cambridge: Cambridge University Press, 1926, reprint 1969. A review by an eminent Western Persianist of the biographical lore on Hafiz, as well as a commentary on Hafiz translations and attendant problems.

Hafiz. *Hafez, Dance of Life*. Translated by Michael Boylan; illustrated by Hossein Zenderoudi; afterword by Michael C. Hillmann. Washington, D.C.: Mage Publishers, 1988. Twelve plates by a leading Iranian painter giving a Sufi interpretation to twelve poems, which are translated freely by an American poet who emphasizes their earthbound and romantic elements, followed by an afterword which treats reasons for Hafiz's special appeal to Iranians today.

__________. *Poems from the "Divan" of Hafiz*. Translated by Gertrude Lowthian Bell, with a preface by E. Denison Ross. London: William Heinemann, 1928. The most highly regarded English versions of Hafiz, containing forty-three *ghazals* in translation following a lengthy (and sometimes inaccurate) introduction presenting the historical background, the standard biographical lore, and a recapitulation of the extent of Sufi influence on Hafiz.

Hillmann, Michael C. "Classicism, Ornament, Ambivalence, and the Persian Muse." In *Iranian Culture: A Persianist View*. Lanham, Md.: University Press of America, 1988. An attempt to discern enduring Iranian cultural attitudes in an examination of aesthetic aspects and criteria discernible in Hafiz's *ghazals*, among them appreciation of tradition, formality, and ceremony, a penchant for embellishment and the ornamental, and a capacity for ambivalence in attitudes, ideas, beliefs, and standards.

__________. *Unity in the Ghazals of Hafez*. Minneapolis, Minn.: Bibliotheca Islamica, 1976. A formalist analysis of sixteen Hafizian *ghazals* in a response to long-standing charges by Iranian scholars and Orientalists that Hafiz's poems lack unity. Includes an extensive list in notes and bibliography of writings on Hafiz in European languages.

Meisami, Julie Scott. *Medieval Persian Court Poetry*. Princeton, N.J.: Princeton University Press, 1987. A medievalist's attempt to rescue traditional Persian court poetry from the disfavor into which it has fallen, through a demonstration of its similarities with medieval literature in the West. A chapter entitled "*Ghazal*: The Ideals of Love" deals with Sana'i (died 1130?) and Hafiz, who stand at the beginning and end of the period in which *ghazal* writing was at its peak.

Yarshater, Ehsan, comp. and ed. *Persian Poetry*. Albany, N.Y.: State University of New York Press, 1988. The first comprehensive overview of Persian literature since shortly after World War II, with an article on medieval lyric poetry and another on Hafiz.

Michael Craig Hillmann

AL-HALLAJ
al-Husayn ibn Mansur al-Hallaj

Born: c. 858; Beida, Iran
Died: March 26, 922; Baghdad, Iraq
Area of Achievement: Religion
Contribution: By making known his experiences of mystical communion with Allah, al-Hallaj promoted a highly controversial and ultimately influential doctrine of divine grace and knowledge. His imprisonment and martyrdom became one of the most celebrated episodes in the development of Sufi history.

Early Life

In about 858, Husayn ibn Mansur al-Hallaj was born in Beida, a city in southwestern Iran that is situated astride roads between Shiraz and Esfahan. Reputedly among his ancestors was Abu Ayyub, a companion of the Prophet Muhammad, while his paternal grandfather was thought to have been a Zoroastrian. Although evidently his family was partly of Iranian stock, they had become Arabicized; the name Hallaj has been taken as referring to Husayn's father's work as a wool carder. Later the family moved to Wasit, in southern Iraq, probably because of its importance in the textile trade. During an early education which consisted largely of instruction in grammar and religious texts, Husayn developed an extensive knowledge of the Koran. At the age of sixteen, he went on to study under Sahl ibn ʻAbdallah al-Tustari, a noted Sunni scholar whose teachings emphasized introspection and ascetism. After two years, al-Hallaj left for Basra, where he came into contact with other Sufi theologians.

Al-Hallaj's novitiate was spent with ʻAmr ibn ʻUthman al-Makki, a follower of Abu al-Qasim ibn Muhammad al-Junayd, one of the most renowned mystics of that time. Abu Yaʻqub al-Aqtaʻ was also of this group, and at about the age of twenty al-Hallaj married his daughter, Umm al-Husayn. During their life together, at least three sons and one daughter were born to them. Following al-Junayd's advice, he remained in Basra with his father-in-law for a time.

After about six years, al-Hallaj undertook the first of his pilgrimages to Mecca. During this period, he held discussions with other learned men on the nature of personal inspiration, and it would appear that his own views had begun to take form; indeed, some disciples began to gather about him. Al-Aqtaʻ to some extent dissociated himself from such views, and al-Hallaj, with his wife and brother-in-law, moved back to Tustar, near Ahvaz. His public preaching began to attract large audiences. Al-Hallaj's conception of the understanding in relation to the divine nature may have aroused some controversy; for a while, he also cast off the distinctive cloak that was part of

Sufi attire. Evidently it was thought by the authorities that his teachings were subversive of the public order, and at one point he was arrested and underwent flagellation.

Life's Work

At about the age of thirty, al-Hallaj set forth alone on travels which took him to eastern cities on the Iranian Plateau, where his teachings seem to have been well received; on his return journey, however, he encountered some opposition in Esfahan and Qom. Near his home, moreover, unfavorable rumors had begun to spread; some claimed that he had offered to work miracles in public. Indeed, in that region both Sunni and Shi'ite spokesmen regarded his teachings with some suspicion. On his second pilgrimage to Mecca, in about 894, al-Hallaj brought along possibly as many as four hundred followers; afterward, he and his family settled in Baghdad, where they benefited, for the time being, from toleration on the part of local officials.

During the years that followed, al-Hallaj embarked upon the most extensive series of travels of his career; he may have had some missionary intent, as his journeys took him into areas beyond the frontiers of Islamic rule. After a sea voyage, he reached western India, and he traveled as far inland as Kashmir and portions of Turkestan. When al-Hallaj returned to Baghdad, he found that some authorities on legal matters had denounced him to the caliph, but the Shafi'i jurist Abu al-'Abbas Ahmad ibn 'Umar ibn Surayj came to his defense, arguing that the courts could not exercise jurisdiction where matters of mystical inspiration were concerned. The charges were then dropped.

In 902, al-Hallaj undertook his final pilgrimage. It would appear that by this time his ideas and practice had become highly introspective. He claimed that during periods of solitary contemplation he had had encounters with the divine essence, which had embraced and engulfed his own. At the station of Arafat, he prayed that he should be reduced to nothingness, or become despised and outcast, in order that he might approach Allah more closely. On his return journey, in 905, al-Hallaj went on to Medina and Jerusalem. Once back in Baghdad, he commissioned a replica in miniature of the Ka'bah, or sacred shrine, of Mecca; he held that it would serve the devotional purposes of the original.

Some of al-Hallaj's teachings were compiled by his disciples in the *Riwayat*, probably in about 902; this work was based on sayings associated originally with Islamic traditions. A number of his poems and sermons were also collected. It would appear that al-Hallaj's ideas did not follow a prescribed logical schema but rather were prompted by the inward stirrings of inspiration which led him to attempt to communicate to others his experiences of mystical unity. He was most concerned with exploring the personal relationship between Allah and the faithful. Al-Hallaj counseled absolute submission to the will of Allah as the one God whose will was manifested in all creation; this conviction that the divine essence was immanent led him to declare that the nature of Allah could be experienced during states of mystical abstraction. Al-Hallaj's goal was to attain a unity of vision that would bear witness to the oneness of the divine presence; he believed that in transcending sensory perception the votary could reach a condition of spiritual interpenetration with the divine presence. Apparently, al-Hallaj recognized the awkward paradox that could result, for he warned that one who testified about Allah might by so doing upset the essential unity that remained the basis of his monotheistic faith. Still, he believed that the unhappy duality of the worshipper and his God could be overcome when the divine spirit infused the votary. Indeed, some interpretations of al-Hallaj's utterances have suggested that in states of mystic union it is possible for the words of Allah to be conveyed directly by means of his follower. In al-Hallaj's conception, incarnation occurs in the strictest sense on an ideal plane, beyond the realm of the material body; in this elevated realm, the volition and intent of the subject are acted upon by divine grace. At times, al-Hallaj expressed his despondency at the gulf which separates created man from Allah, who by nature is uncreated and ineffable. Yet he taught that love and faith are qualities that allow human beings to approach the essence of Allah, which itself is love.

Much of al-Hallaj's inspiration was of an inward sort, arising from prolonged contemplation and religious study. Although it is clear that his ideas sprang essentially from an Islamic context, parallels with teachings of other traditions have been noted. He may have gained some familiarity with classical philosophy, Neoplatonism, or Christian doctrines at second hand, through the elements of these older traditions that had been incorporated in Muslim learning. Enlarging upon al-Hallaj's declarations of willingness to suffer ignominy and indeed martyrdom for the sake of his convictions, some Western commentators have suggested that in this respect he specifically followed the example of Jesus Christ. It would seem probable that al-Hallaj's views were shaped largely by the Islamic recognition of Christ as one of the prophets whose life and teachings anticipated Islamic theology. At times, too, al-Hallaj seems to echo Christian vocabulary.

Al-Hallaj parted company with other Sufi thinkers in several important ways. Al-Junayd, who had found means of spiritual discipline that were instrumental for entering into mystical states, also insisted upon outward adherence to the more conventional requirements of the faith. His doctrinal beliefs were essentially traditional, and he maintained that pious works were as important as faith in bringing the worshipper closer to Allah. Possibly the most salient difference had to do with their views as to how religious experience could be communicated: Al-Junayd insisted that the votary should keep his mystical experiences private and maintain external propriety, whereas al-Hallaj often was so deeply moved that he would testify before others about the rapture and the sorrows of his own communion with the divine spirit.

Some of al-Hallaj's public utterances had social overtones of sorts; he alarmed those in high places by condemning self-interest and corruption and speaking eloquently of the common good. He was markedly lacking in political acumen. In 908, he became involved in a short-lived attempt to raise Abu al-'Abbas 'Abdallah ibn al-Mu'tazz, a poet and a prince, to the caliphate; when instead al-Muqtadir, an adolescent who was dominated by some rather unscrupulous ministers, came to the throne, al-Hallaj went into hiding, for a while taking refuge in Sus, in the province of Ahvaz. After about three years, he was arrested and returned to Baghdad. Although al-Hallaj had aroused the enmity of certain officials, others were unwilling to take action against him. Finally, in 913, the vizier, 'Ali ibn 'Isa, who was a cousin of one of his followers, put an end to the first trial. To placate the opponents of al-Hallaj, however, the mystic was exposed on the pillory for three days; a placard described him as an agent of the Carmathians, who made up a dissident sect which was widely regarded as a menace to the caliphate. Afterward, al-Hallaj was held in the palace, where he did meet other prisoners and indeed could preach to them.

During this period of confinement, al-Hallaj composed some of his most remarkable works, which were later collected in *Kitab al-tawasin*; the title evidently was suggested by the mysterious characters which begin the twenty-seventh chapter of the Koran. There he rendered tribute in rhyme to Muhammad as he celebrated the light his mission had brought the world. Other passages, however, were provocative and unsettling to his contemporaries. In that work, al-Hallaj made the celebrated statement "Ana al-haqq" (I am the truth), which could be taken to imply personal identification with the deity. Although it seems highly probable that he referred instead to experiences of the divine presence, many Muslims regarded him as attempting to arrogate a place for himself alongside Allah. For Sufi thinkers this expression, while comprehensible to the mystic, was regarded as a dangerous breach of the secrecy which should shroud such experiences. At least as perplexing was al-Hallaj's depiction of Satan as a fallen angel who was unable to grasp the gift of divine grace; indeed, al-Hallaj posed the problem of whether he ever could be brought to the point of accepting redemption. In one disturbing chapter, he contrasted Satan's pride, and that of the biblical Pharaoh, with his own declarations of union with Allah.

Against a background of political intrigue, al-Hallaj's case was reopened in 921; in addition to religious controversies, social unrest may have affected the government's decision to proceed forthwith against the celebrated mystic. Hamid ibn al-'Abbas, a wealthy man who had taken a prominent part in the earlier proceedings against al-Hallaj, had become vizier; Ibn 'Isa continued to oppose his financial ventures. When demonstrations in favor of al-Hallaj were held, they were accompanied by protests against Hamid's fiscal policies.

Marked divisions of public opinion took on political overtones, which Hamid evidently thought would be laid to rest by the formal condemnation of al-Hallaj. With the sanction of Abu 'Umar ibn Yusuf, the rather pliant chief judge, a tribunal was convened; it received the charges against al-Hallaj in a manner which suggested that the outcome had been determined in advance. Although some dissension still was expressed—one jurist who opposed the trial died after being beaten by a guard, while another declined to give judgment—eighty-four members of the court signed the verdict. Al-Hallaj was formally adjudged a *zindiq* (heretic). Many of his statements were held to have been blasphemy. His remarks about the Ka'bah were interpreted in the light of reports that the Carmathians intended to destroy that holy site. Other charges concerned his alleged charlatanism and efforts to perform miracles. Some of the documents that had been produced as evidence against him almost certainly had been forged. After Abu 'Umar pronounced the sentence of death, the caliph temporized for two days and then acquiesced in the wishes of his vizier.

It would appear that for some time al-Hallaj had prepared himself for death. In prison, he had composed some prayers which dwelt alternately upon the end of his life and his hopes for the Resurrection; such sayings later formed the basis for the collection titled *Akhbar al-Hallaj*. His execution became a major public spectacle. Indeed, al-Hallaj's appearance is known mostly from depictions of his martyrdom. Usually, he is pictured as a well-built figure with a black beard and a dark complexion, who seemed to possess a saintly quality. He was flogged with five hundred lashes, his hands and feet were cut off, and he was left hanging on a gibbet overnight. On the morning of March 26, 922, Hamid came by to attend the pronouncement of the death sentence. Al-Hallaj's last words, according to witnesses, were testimony to the oneness of Allah followed by the recitation of lines from the Koran. He was beheaded and his body was burned. Riots broke out throughout the city, as mobs kindled fires to to protest the execution. Reports spread of inexplicable wonders, and some claimed that al-Hallaj's ashes, when they were thrown into the Tigris River, coalesced into words attesting his faith.

Summary

After the execution of al-Hallaj, many of his disciples became dispersed; during the next several years, some of them were put to death, while others fled to outlying regions. Clandestine orders were formed to preserve his teachings. For a while, it was permitted only to cite verses and phrases associated with him, without mentioning him specifically by name. Still, however covertly, his reputation spread across much of the Muslim world. By the twelfth century or so, a revival of interest in al-Hallaj began within some religious circles, and his views came to be regarded with interest by leading writers and thinkers. The poet Farid al-Din 'Attar devoted some moving passages to him, and Jalal al-Din Rumi quoted al-Hallaj. Juridical opinion, even long after his death, remained sharply divided in regard to the justice of his condemnation. Among Sufi orders, those that countenanced certain states of exaltation were most willing to accept the ecstatic elements in al-Hallaj's teachings of love and divine union. Some dervish orders, such as the Bektasi, added rituals symbolic of his martyrdom to their initiation ceremonies.

Later patterns of influence were many and varied. During the nineteenth and twentieth centuries, al-Hallaj's doctrines were received in many parts of Asia and Europe. In the Indian subcontinent, writers such as Mirza Asadullah Khan Ghalib and Sir Muhammad Iqbal cited imagery and ideas found in his writings. Major literary works examining his legacy, including dramas based upon his persecution and trial, have appeared in the Arab countries, while elsewhere in the Middle East his name has been raised in reverence and fascination. Although for some time Western Islamicists showed uncertain reactions to his teachings, modern studies, particularly those of the French scholar Louis Massignon, have contributed to knowledge and understanding of al-Hallaj's part in the development of Islamic mysticism. Moreover, the vitality of al-Hallaj's message of love and spiritual quest, when set beside the tragic fate he suffered, continues to inspire awe and respect wherever his life and doctrines have become known.

Bibliography

Ahlbert, G. "Al-Hallaj." *Moslem World* 15 (1925): 59-62. This short article is of interest largely because it reflects the increased interest in al-Hallaj among Middle East specialists of the early twentieth century.

Jilani, Ghulam. *"Ana al-haqq" Reconsidered*. Lahore, Pakistan: Naqsh-e-awwal Kitab Ghar, 1977. This brief exposition of al-Hallaj's teachings is noteworthy as an indication of the extent to which Sufi doctrines have been important for the Islamic revival of modern times. In commenting on the *Kitab al-tawasin*, the author suggests that mystical ideas should have a continuing place in Muslim thought.

Mason, Herbert. "Hallaj: A Martyr for the Truth." *Boston University Journal* 21, no. 3 (1973): 7-19. The dramatic confrontations that occurred during al-Hallaj's trial and execution are recaptured in this brief retelling of major events associated with his life.

Massignon, Louis. *The Passion of al-Hallaj: Mystic and Martyr of Islam*. Translated by Herbert Mason. 4 vols. Princeton, N.J.: Princeton University Press, 1982. A work of towering erudition, this study represents a thoroughgoing and sympathetic treatment of its subject's life and times; it also supplies a running evaluation of the sources that concern al-Hallaj's career and teachings. It provides a well-informed account of al-Hallaj's mission, based upon indefatigable research and the painstaking quest to distinguish historical knowledge from legend and tradition. Includes a lengthy exposition of al-Hallaj's doctrinal beliefs, as well as an examination of his influence upon subsequent philosophers and theologians. An outstanding achievement in modern Islamic studies.

O'Leary, DeLacy Evans. "Al-Hallaj." *Philosophy East and West* 1 (April, 1951): 56-62. In this brief and sympathetic evaluation of al-Hallaj's teachings, the author attempts to make them comprehensible by referring to Western intellectual sources.

Schimmel, Annemarie. "Mystic Impact of Hallaj." In *Iqbal: Poet-Philosopher of Pakistan*, edited by Hafeez Malik. New York: Columbia University Press, 1971. As an example of the extraordinary effects of al-Hallaj's ideas throughout the Muslim world, the author shows how Sir Muhammad Iqbal, one of the most significant and searching thinkers of modern Islam, became interested in Louis Massignon's early studies of the great mystic and eventually began to compare himself with al-Hallaj in his own works.

__________. *Mystical Dimensions of Islam*. Chapel Hill: University of North Carolina Press, 1975. As a much broader study of Islamic mysticism, this work discusses the essential contexts of al-Hallaj's ideas and their later effects, along with many other topics. The life and views of the great martyr are considered in one section. In general, this study is useful in suggesting the richness and diversity of the mystical tradition.

Singh, Darshan. "Attitudes of al-Junayd and al-Hallaj Towards the *Sunna* and *Ahwal* and *Maqamat*." *Islamic Culture* 58 (1984): 217-226. Contrasting views of two great mystics on questions of Islamic piety are set forth in this brief study; the author takes note of differences between outwardly respectable and more expressive professions of faith, suggesting that both were important in broadening interpretations of Muslim theology.

Thompson, O. H. "Al Hallaj, Saint and Martyr." *Moslem World* 19 (1929): 383-402. Material for this article was derived largely from Massignon's writings, though the author, in some remarks favorable to his subject, attempts to supply a Christian interpretation to al-Hallaj's willingness to die for his beliefs.

J. R. Broadus

HAMMURABI

Born: c. 1810 B.C.; Babylon
Died: 1750 B.C.; Babylon
Areas of Achievement: Government and law
Contribution: Building upon an Amorite sheikhdom of four generations of ancestors, this long-reigning representative of the dynasty matured gradually in power until he was able to stretch his control over the entire length of the Euphrates and Tigris river valleys. The literary creativity of the age brought into being the Old Babylonian dialect, most fully exemplified in the codification of law remembered under Hammurabi's name.

Early Life

The founder of Babylon and the creator of the first Babylonian dynasty was a nineteenth century B.C. Amorite chieftain named Sumu-abum. His ancestral predecessors are known by name back into the twenty-first century B.C., when Shulgi, King of the Third Dynasty of Ur in southern Sumer, first began to encounter the movements of Amorite-speaking Semitic peoples down the Euphrates. A famine began to devastate the economy of the Sumerian city-states, weakening their defenses so that old centers such as Larsa and Isin passed directly into the newcomers' hands.

Another family within the same tribal grouping as Sumu-abum replaced his control, and with that shift came into being the dynasty which Hammurabi recalled in his inscriptions. He was son of Sin-muballit, grandson of Apil Sin, great-grandson of Sabium, and great-great-grandson of the dynastic founder, Sumu-la-el. The rapidity of succession brought Hammurabi to the throne as quite a young man.

The initial years of Hammurabi's life were lived in the shadow of greater or longer-established chieftains of comparable ancestry. The region to the east along the Diyala River was centered on Ibal-pi-El II at Eshnunna. The region to the south was centered on Rim-Sin at Larsa. Rim-Sin's reign was long, but there are only a few inscriptions, mainly concerned with that piety of building for the gods which was one of the principal ways of proving one's greatness as a ruler in those times. Rim-Sin's thirtieth year, during which he captured Isin, was the year when Hammurabi assumed the throne at Babylon.

During Hammurabi's father's reign, Babylon was in the particular shadow of Shamshi-Adad I, who had gained control of the capital of Assyria and had spread his influence not only up the Tigris but also across the steppes and tributaries to the Euphrates itself, placing his own son on the throne at the great trading center of Mari. Much of what is known about this earlier period comes from the vast archival records found in excavations at Mari since 1929.

Life's Work

Hammurabi, upon ascending the throne in 1792, found himself hemmed in on all sides by formidable powers. The political situation is well described in a letter from a Mari diplomat or spy to his king: "No one king is strong by himself. Ten to fifteen go after Hammurapi man of Babylon, similarly after Rim-Sin man of Larsa, similarly after Ibal-pi-el man of Eshnunna, similarly after Amut-pi-el man of Qatanum. Twenty go after Yarim-Lim man of Yamhad."

Thus, the whole country was split among petty chiefs joined together in leagues with some stronger figure nominally as head. Rather than a clear-cut struggle between well-defined, uniformly large states, it was a situation requiring a constant shuffling of alliances among aggregations of minor rulers under some stronger chief as head. These combinations changed often. Economic issues played a major role in the formation of alliances.

From the variety of year-names of the various chiefs, it is possible to reconstruct an overall picture of the way Hammurabi was hemmed in at the time of his accession. The sheikhdom of Larsa, by conquering Isin in the south, covered almost all the territory that had once been Sumer.

At Mari, the situation had undergone change. In the middle of the nineteenth century, in the days of Sabium, great-grandfather of Hammurabi, Mari had been ruled by Iaggid-Lim. When Iaggid-Lim broke a treaty made with Ila-kabkabu, father of Shamshi-Adad I of Ashur, there was retaliation. The occasion was used effectively by Shamshi-Adad to take over rule in Mari, where he placed his son, Iasmah-Adad, on the throne. Mari was retained as long as Shamshi-Adad was alive, but in the days of his successor at Ashur, Ishme-Dagan, the old line at Mari was reinstated under Zimri-Lim. These latter two, neither as strong as his predecessor, were the ones with whom Hammurabi had to deal. From the time of Zimri-Lim, the district of Terqa, just to the north of Mari, was entirely denuded of trees, so that the lucrative timber trade came to an end and the area received an ecological blow from which it never recovered.

When Hammurabi took over, Babylon was a small principality. In his second year, Hammurabi established "righteousness in the land." He remitted debts and other obligations, allowing land to revert to original owners. In undertaking such measures, he was following the tradition of his royal ancestors.

In 1787, Hammurabi captured Uruk and Isin, indicating that he and his allies were strong enough to challenge Rim-Sin in the latter's territory. It would appear, however, that the success was ephemeral: The cities were taken back. In 1783, Hammurabi destroyed Malgum on the Tigris, south of the Diyala. In 1782, he took Rapiqum on the Euphrates; it was close to a major caravan crossing and thus provided for him access to the west.

Mention of this achievement is the last reference to military accomplishments during this period in Hammurabi's official inscriptions, which thereafter focus on pious deeds of rebuilding walls and refurbishing temples. Their index illustrates, if not the extent of the Babylonian sheikhdom, at least the increasing strength of its economic base. From Mari, letters give account of Hammurabi's diplomatic relations; messengers went back and forth between Mari and Hammurabi's court.

In the inscriptions for 1763, the chronicle of Hammurabi's military conquests is taken up once more, beginning with his defeat of Elamite troops at the boundaries of Mahashi, Subartu, Eshnunna, Gutium, and Malgum—all to his east. He successfully opposed a concerted attack of northern and eastern principalities surrounding him, though there is no reference to his annexation of territory. Hammurabi was intent upon restoring the foundations of old "Sumer and Akkad."

These victories allowed Hammurabi to turn undivided attention to the south. In 1762, he fought successfully against the very old Rim-Sin of Larsa, who was brought alive in a cage to Babylon. With this termination of the independent dynasty of Larsa, all southern Mesopotamia passed into Hammurabi's hands.

In 1761, a core of the old coalition of enemies was against Hammurabi again. He defeated the armies of Subartu, Eshnunna, and Gutium and conquered all the territory along the Tigris as far north as the border of Assyria. In 1760, he fought with Mari on the Euphrates and Malgum, south of Eshnunna. In 1758, he destroyed the walls of both Mari and Malgum. A change in relations with Mari occurred once more. Hammurabi had previously sent troops to assist Zimri-Lim, and the latter had been instrumental in his taking over Eshnunna. Now native rule at Mari ended. In 1755, the "great waters destroyed" Eshnunna; it is not clear whether the reference is to a natural disaster or to Hammurabi's damming up and diverting a river. In any case, the inscriptions make no further mention of Eshnunna until the time of Hammurabi's son.

In 1754, Hammurabi conquered all of his enemies as far as the land of Subartu, east beyond the Tigris. With this success, he was established as the dominant figure in all Mesopotamia. No further references to warfare are made in the chronicle of his reign. To this final period belongs the monumental edition of his law code, upon which he is portrayed standing humbly before Shamash, the sun god and overseer of justice. Its prologue identifies his control over twenty-six cities, from each of whose deities, whose temples he adorned, he received powers to make justice in the land.

By intensive restructuring of the whole geographical area under his control, Hammurabi had inadvertently set in motion the forces which during the next century and a half were to terminate the dynasty and its Amorite leadership—a decline culminating in the Hittite's sacking of Babylon in 1595. The prosperity of Babylon depended upon remuneration from its conquered territories for massive construction of buildings and waterworks organized by Hammurabi with the help of appointed officials. Once a system of governors and palace dependents was created, however, this bureaucracy established itself in hereditary positions, so that the territories fed local rather than royal interests.

Already before Hammurabi's death, his son Samsuiluna reported in a letter to an official, Etil-pi-Marduk, that his father was ill and that he had to assume charge of what was by then no longer a mere sheikhdom but instead a real kingdom. Hammurabi was succeeded by Samsuiluna and his grandson Abi-eshu. There remained three further generations, Ammi-ditana, Ammi-zaduga, and Samsu-ditana, before Hammurabi's achievement was terminated by Kassite invaders, dividing the realm again into petty sheikhdoms warring on relatively equal terms.

Summary

Coming at the middle of the First Dynasty of Babylon, Hammurabi created out of a small principality not merely an imperial kingdom but a distinctive city whose name is not to be forgotten: Old "Sumer and Akkad" became thereafter Babylonia. From the many preserved Old Babylonian letters, especially those to or by Hammurabi, it is possible to understand the administrative structure of his power and that of Babylon. These letters document the lines of communication existing within the capital itself and out to the official governors appointed to administer annexed cities and territories. Two large collections are illustrative: those related to Sin-idinnam, Hammurabi's governor of Larsa after the defeat of Rim-Sin, and those related to Shamash-hazir, a lesser official, also at Larsa, who managed for the king the landholdings and the landholders.

Extensive economic records from the various cities, especially Sippar, provide details of royal involvement. At Sippar, Hammurabi's sister Iltani engaged in business transactions on behalf of the gods Lord Shamash and Lady Aja for more than fifty years, at least until 1755. She lived in that unique Old Babylonian institution, the *gaga* (cloister), as one of the many *naditu*-women, among whom she ranked the highest. *Naditu*-women were dedicated to a god, often from youth; they were usually unmarried and were always forbidden to have children, but they frequently played significant economic roles.

The period was one of great literary creativity. Epic poetry, some of it based on Sumerian-derived sources, addressed central issues and problems of human existence. Two epics of the period, for example, took up issues of life and death in their glorification of the heroes Gilgamesh and Atra-hasis. Another remembered the ancient Etana. During this time, the chief god Marduk replaced older creator gods, just as Babylon had replaced the older Sumerian city-states.

Aside from the monumental copy of Hammurabi's code, clay tablet examples demonstrate that its text was regularly copied in both Babylonia and Assyria until the era of the Seleucid state at Uruk (third century B.C.). The great stela itself was carried off as a prize to Susa by the twelfth century B.C. Elamite king Shutruk-nakhunte I. There it remained until January, 1902, when its rediscovery changed Hammurabi from simply another ruler among many into a world-famous lawgiver with a status comparable to that of the biblical Moses or the Byzantine Justinian I.

The last great king of Assyria, the seventh century B.C. Ashurbanipal, sought texts of Hammurabi's era for his library at Nineveh. While no building attributable to Hammurabi has been excavated beneath the rubble of Babylon, it is known that its last king, Nabonidus (sixth century B.C.) knew of his work and remembered him.

Bibliography

Driver, G. R., and John C. Miles. *The Babylonian Laws*. 2 vols. Oxford: Clarendon Press, 1952-1955. Volume 1 provides a detailed commentary upon all Babylonian law, with special focus upon the Code of Hammurabi. Volume 2 contains the transliterated texts with full translation, philological notes, and glossary.

Finkelstein, J. J. "The Genealogy of the Hammurabi Dynasty." *Journal of Cuneiform Studies* 20 (1966): 95-118. The discovery of a new text within the large collection of the British Museum allowed the connection of Assyrian and Babylonian royal ancestries within a common Amorite genealogy.

Leemans, W. F. *The Old Babylonian Merchant: His Business and His Social Position*. Leiden, Netherlands: E. J. Brill, 1950. Beginning from provisions in Hammurabi's code, and on the basis of texts coming from various archives, especially those of Larsa and Sippar, the nature, role, and function of the merchant class are described as independent but bound by the law of the king.

Munn-Rankin, J. M. "Diplomacy in Western Asia in the Early Second Millennium B.C." *Iraq* 18 (1956): 68-110. This major essay, working from the Mari archive, puts in perspective the historical situation and the interaction among major figures during Hammurabi's reign.

Pallis, S. A. *The Antiquity of Iraq: A Handbook of Assyriology*. Copenhagen, Denmark: Ejnar Munksgaard, 1956. This volume is a vast storehouse of information including a history of Babylon, a description of the city, an account of its rediscovery in the nineteenth century, and the subsequent excavations. Chapter 8 explains the chronological shift in dating Hammurabi, made possible by the discovery of the Mari archive and the correlation with Shamshi-Adad of Assyria. Chapter 10 provides a picture of Hammurabi and his age, with extensive discussion of the code.

Yoffee, Norman. *The Economic Role of the Crown in the Old Babylonian Period*. Malibu, Calif.: Undena Publications, 1977. This study is significant for its close analysis of economic texts from various urban archives, shedding light on the operations of Hammurabi's palace economy and the administration of conquered realms. Extensive bibliography.

Clyde Curry Smith

HANNIBAL

Born: 247 B.C.; probably Carthage, North Africa
Died: 182 B.C.; Libyssa, Bithynia, Asia Minor
Area of Achievement: Warfare
Contribution: During the Second Punic War, Hannibal led an army of mercenaries across the Alps into Italy, where, for fifteen years, he exhibited superior generalship, defeating the Romans in one battle after another.

Early Life

Hannibal was born in 247 B.C., probably in Carthage, of an aristocratic family which claimed descent from Dido, the legendary foundress of the city. Of his mother nothing is known, but his father, Hamilcar Barca, was for nearly twenty years the supreme military commander of the Carthaginian forces. Assuming this position in the year of Hannibal's birth, Hamilcar guided his country through the last difficult years of the First Punic War and then began the construction of a new empire in Spain. After his death, in 229 B.C., Hamilcar's son-in-law, Hasdrubal, extended Carthaginian dominion northward to the Ebro River and founded New Carthage.

Little is known of Hannibal during these years. Livy, the principal source of information, notes that when Hannibal was nine years of age, he accompanied his father to Spain. Prior to their departure, Hamilcar invoked the blessings of the gods with a sacrifice at which Hannibal was compelled to swear that he would never be a friend to Rome. Such was the hostile atmosphere in which the youth was reared. Although little is known about the years of Hannibal's apprenticeship under his father and later under Hasdrubal, there can be little doubt that Hannibal would benefit immeasurably from the rigors of frontier life. When Hasdrubal was assassinated in 221, Hannibal, age twenty-six, was ready to assume command. That he had already distinguished himself as a warrior and a leader is indicated by the alacrity with which the army proclaimed him commander.

Life's Work

Hannibal was the epitome of a warrior. According to silver coins supposedly bearing his likeness, he had curly hair, a straight nose, a sloping forehead, a strong neck, and a look of determination in his eyes. A man with a mission, in his mid-twenties Hannibal was ready to carry his father's dream to completion. All that was needed was an excuse. The opportunity presented itself in 219, when Rome violated a treaty with Carthage by intervening in the political affairs of the Spanish state of Saguntum. Hannibal dismissed a Roman commission sent to investigate the matter and then laid siege to the city, which fell eight months later. Rome's failure to aid its client state probably encouraged Hannibal to extend Carthaginian dominion northward to the Pyrenees. When Carthage refused to surrender Hannibal, Rome declared war.

The Roman strategy was to end the war quickly. One army was dispatched under the leadership of the consul Publius Cornelius Scipio to confront Hannibal in Spain, while the other consul, Tiberius Sempronius Longus, was to attack Carthage. In this matter, however, the Romans greatly underestimated the military genius and determination of Hannibal. In the spring of 218, Hannibal gathered his army of Numidians and Spaniards—variously estimated at forty thousand to sixty thousand men—and, in one of the most celebrated marches in history, crossed the Pyrenees, the Rhone River, and finally the snow-laden Alps to reach the Po River valley. It was a perilous five-month journey fraught with dangers of all sorts—hostile tribes, bad weather, impenetrable geographical barriers, and a scarcity of provisions. Thousands of Hannibal's soldiers and many of the elephants perished along the way. By journey's end, Hannibal's forces had been reduced to about twenty thousand infantry and six thousand cavalry, too few to undertake the conquest of Roman Italy. The success of the venture would depend on Hannibal's ability to lure many of Rome's disaffected allies to his side.

In the meantime, after hearing of Hannibal's departure from Spain, the two consuls rushed northward to meet the threat. Scipio, in a move of future importance, sent his army on to Spain to prevent reinforcements from joining Hannibal. In December, the two consuls joined forces to stop Hannibal's advance, but the Romans fell into an ambush in the frigid waters of the Trebia River. Approximately two-thirds of the Roman force was lost. Although Rome managed to conceal the defeat from its citizens, it was necessary to abandon the Po River valley to the Punic forces. Hannibal, to curry favor with the natives, released his Italian prisoners.

Hannibal wintered in northern Italy. During that time, his army grew with the addition of Celtic recruits to about fifty thousand in number. In the spring of 217, Hannibal moved southward into the peninsula. The Romans sent the consul Gaius Flaminius with orders to hold Hannibal at the Apennines. Hannibal, wily as ever, slipped around the Roman commander by sloshing through the marshes of the Arno River into Etruria. Along the way, Hannibal contracted malaria and lost the sight of one eye. Flaminius regained his composure and eventually caught up with Hannibal's forces, only to suffer a crushing defeat at Lake Trasimene. Flaminius and virtually all of his soldiers perished in the battle.

A second major defeat was more than Rome could endure. In desperation, Rome resurrected an old emergency procedure and appointed a dictator, Quintus Fabius Maximus, to handle the crisis. Nicknamed the "delayer," Fabius refused to meet Hannibal in open battle, preferring hit-and-run tactics. He also used a scorched-earth policy to prevent Hannibal from living off the land. While the strategy worked and restored Roman morale, public opinion favored more aggressive action. In 216, Rome felt strong enough to send the consuls Lucius Aemilius Paulus and Gaius Terentius Varro with an army of about sixty thousand men to engage Hannibal in open battle at Cannae in northern Apulia. Although numerically superior, the Romans fell prey once again to Hannibal's genius. While the Romans drove hard through the middle of the Carthaginian line, they were gradually encircled and destroyed. Only a fraction of the Roman force managed to escape. Hannibal's double-envelopment maneuver has since been copied many times by other generals.

The news of defeat threw Rome into chaos. Hannibal, contrary to the advice of his generals, refused to march on the panic-stricken city. The reasons for his cautious behavior are not clear, though he probably understood that Rome was strongly fortified, and he may have continued to hope that Rome's allies would now defect. The major rebellion for which he had hoped never occurred. There were, however, encouraging signs. Much of southern Italy, including Capua, second only to Rome in importance, went over to Hannibal's side. He also gained the support of Macedonia's King Philip V, who hoped to involve Rome in a war in the east.

Hannibal was supreme for the moment, but he had not broken the indomitable Roman spirit. There were also some encouraging signs for Rome. Many of Rome's allies, especially in central Italy, had remained faithful. Property qualifications for military service were lowered and new armies were raised which returned to Fabius' successful tactics of the past. Furthermore, the decision to remain in Spain, coupled with Rome's continued mastery of the sea, made it difficult for Hannibal to receive reinforcements. While Hannibal moved his diminished, bedraggled army from one encampment to another without benefit of open battle, the Romans began to reconquer the lost cities and provinces. In 211, both Capua and Syracuse were retaken. Compounding Hannibal's problems was the fact that the alliance with Philip V had proved ineffectual.

In the meantime, Rome had gained the advantage in Spain through the efforts of the brilliant young general Publius Cornelius Scipio. In 209, New Carthage, the major city of Hannibal's Iberian empire, was captured by Scipio's forces, along with vast quantities of supplies. He could not prevent Hasdrubal, Hannibal's brother, from crossing the Pyrenees in an attempt to reach Hannibal in Italy, but the relief expedition was intercepted and defeated at the Metaurus River in 207. Nevertheless, Hannibal and his diminished army remained a threat. In 211, he appeared before the walls of Rome, though he took no action, while he defeated and killed the consuls Gnaeus Fulvius and Marcus Claudius Marcellus in other battles. It was becoming increasingly obvious, however, that Hannibal could not win the war.

In 205, Scipio returned triumphantly from Spain to assume the consulship.

Under his leadership, Rome was ready to take the offensive. In the following year, Scipio invaded Africa and after a brief campaign forced Carthage to capitulate. Hannibal and his army were recalled from Italy, ostensibly as a part of the peace agreement. Once he and his fifteen thousand veterans were on African soil, however, the Carthaginians broke off the negotiations and renewed the war. In 202, Scipio and Hannibal met at Zama in a titanic battle. Using tactics he had learned from Hannibal, Scipio was victorious.

Following Zama, a harsh treaty, termed a "Carthaginian Peace" ever since, was imposed on the defeated Carthage. Hannibal remained in the city for five years and worked hard to build a more unified and democratic state. His enemies would give him no rest, however, and in 196, he fled first to Syria and then to Bithynia, where he served briefly as commander of the army in a war with the Romans. In 182, Hannibal committed suicide rather than surrender to his enemies.

Summary

The Second Punic War was, in large part, the biography of Hannibal of Carthage. Perhaps no other man in history has so thoroughly dominated a conflict. The historian Polybius observed that Hannibal was the architect of all things, good and bad, which came to the Romans and Carthaginians. His feats, although recorded by reliable ancient historians, are almost legendary. After inheriting his father's struggle with Rome, he crossed the Alps into Italy, where for fifteen years he moved about the countryside at will. He never lost a major battle, scoring decisive victories at the Trebia River, Lake Trasimene, and Cannae. Hannibal's impact was so great that the Romans were driven at times to desperate measures—the appointment of dictators, human sacrifice to appease the gods, and what today is known as guerrilla warfare.

Roman historians, through whose eyes the conflict must be viewed, were not niggardly in their praise. Livy recounts with amazement the fact that Hannibal was able to hold his army of various nationalities and beliefs together for so long a time in hostile territory. That he succeeded was the result in large part of his courage, an element of recklessness, and an excellent rapport with his men. Yet, Livy continues, he was capable of great cruelty and had little respect for either gods or men. According to Polybius, on the other hand, while Hannibal might have been guilty of these things, he was forced by circumstances and the influence of friends to behave in this paradoxical manner.

Hannibal was, in the eyes of both his contemporaries and modern scholars, the perfect general. Yet, like Pyrrhus before him, he was fighting an unwinnable war. Rome had the advantages of terrain, command of the sea, and inexhaustible reserves of men. In the end, he lost, and Rome, from which much of Western civilization is derived, remained in the ascendant for the next six centuries. Nevertheless, Hannibal remains one of the most fascinating figures in the annals of military history.

Bibliography

Baker, George P. *Hannibal*. New York: Barnes and Noble Books, 1930, 2d ed. 1967. A good introductory work for the student. The author uses primary materials to good advantage, but the style more closely resembles a historical novel.

Bradford, Ernle. *Hannibal: The General from Carthage*. New York: McGraw-Hill Book Co., 1981. One of the most recent studies, derived in large part from the accounts of Livy and Polybius. Provides excellent descriptions of the major battles at the Trebia River, Lake Trasimene, and Cannae. The author attempts to put Hannibal's career in better perspective through the use of modern examples.

Cary, M., and H. H. Scullard. *A History of Rome*. New York: St. Martin's Press, 1935, 3d ed. 1976. For many years one of the standard texts for Roman history. Provides a very good overview of Hannibal's career. Excellent maps illustrate the disposition of troops at Lake Trasimene, Cannae, and Zama.

De Beer, Gavin. *Hannibal: Challenging Rome's Supremacy*. New York: Viking Press, 1969. A well-written and copiously illustrated biography. The author puts much emphasis on geography, especially on the march from Spain over the Alps into Italy. Excellent for the beginning student.

Livy. *The War with Hannibal*. Translated by Aubrey de Sélincourt. Baltimore: Penguin Books, 1965. Written by a patriotic Roman historian who greatly admired Hannibal's military genius. Along with Polybius' work, it is the best source of information on the Punic Wars. Useful for the more knowledgeable reader. The Penguin edition has been taken from Livy's overall history of Rome.

Polybius. *The Histories of Polybius*. Translated by Evelyn S. Shuckburgh. 2 vols. Bloomington: Indiana University Press, 1962. A history of Rome from the onset of the First Punic War in 264 B.C. to the destruction of Carthage in 146 B.C. One of the best sources of information about Hannibal. Like Livy's account, recommended for the more advanced student.

Sinnigen, William G., and Arthur E. A. Boak. *A History of Rome to A.D. 565*. 6th ed. New York: Macmillan, 1977. One of the better surveys of Roman history. Includes a valuable chapter on the conflict with Carthage in which the chief events of Hannibal's career are mentioned. Useful for scholars and students alike.

Starr, Chester G. *The Ancient Romans*. New York: Oxford University Press, 1971. A well-illustrated topical history. One-fourth of the book is devoted to the Punic Wars, with particular attention to Hannibal. An excellent introduction to the subject.

Toynbee, Arnold. *Hannibal's Legacy*. 2 vols. New York: Oxford University Press, 1965. An expanded version of lectures delivered in 1913-1914 at Oxford. The beginning student will find it ponderous, but it is a valuable study which goes far beyond Hannibal.

Larry W. Usilton

HANNO

Born: c. 520-510 B.C.; place unknown
Died: Date unknown; place unknown
Area of Achievement: Exploration
Contribution: Hanno successfully founded the first trading colonies along the western African coast and then pushed on to explore the coast at least as far as modern Sierra Leone. His account of his journey provided the only reasonably accurate account of Africa until the time of Prince Henry the Navigator.

Early Life

Hanno belongs to that lamentably large class of ancients whose names have survived the centuries for a single history-shaping deed, but about whom little else is known. Apart from scattered, confused references to his voyage in a few ancient authors, the main source of information on the man Hanno is the text known as the *Periplus* (*The Voyage of Hanno*, 1797; best known as *Periplus*). Consisting of just under 650 words of Greek, it purports to be a translation of the public inscription Hanno erected in the temple of Kronos at Carthage to commemorate his voyage.

The introduction to the *Periplus* calls Hanno a king. The Carthaginian constitution had no kings but placed supreme power in two *suffetes*. In any case, Hanno was surely of the ruling nobility of Carthage. The dating of Hanno's life depends on the dating of his voyage. Pliny the Elder asserts twice that the voyage was undertaken when the power of Carthage was at its peak; modern scholars have suggested a date just prior to 480 B.C. Before this time, Carthage enjoyed a period of prosperity and expansion in the western Mediterranean. Just at the time the Persians were losing their war with the Greeks at Thermopylae and Salamis, however, so too the Carthaginians, led by Hamilcar, fell decisively to Gelon of Syracuse at the Battle of Himera. Subsequently, it took several decades for Carthage to regain its former strength and influence. This fact, together with philological evidence dating the Greek text to the fifth century, makes it seem best to place Hanno's exploits prior to the Carthaginian defeat at Himera.

There are two men named Hanno known from this period, one the father and the other the son of the Hamilcar who died at Himera. The birth dates given above result from adding the probable age of a magistrate and state-sponsored explorer (between thirty and forty) to the upper limit of the date of the voyage (480). With this date, evidence seems to lean toward the younger Hanno, but there is ample room for doubt.

One can easily understand what may have inspired Hanno's career. As a member of the ruling class, he viewed at first hand the cosmopolitan activity of a trading town such as Carthage. A young man could have been readily lured by the possibility of travel and exploration as he walked along the busy docks and through the hectic markets of Carthage, which traded with Etruria, Phoenicia, and countless Greek city-states and African nations. It can be assumed that Hanno received the best Punic education of his day. His inscription, translated though it is, remains the longest bit of Punic literature available to modern scholars.

Life's Work

The *Periplus* begins by stating that the Carthaginians instructed Hanno to sail "beyond the Pillars of Heracles" (Gibraltar) to found Lybyophoenician cities. Modern scholars suggest plausibly that these cities were to serve as bases for trade with inner Africa, perhaps in precious metals.

The narrative claims that he left with thirty thousand colonists and sixty fifty-oared ships. Since such ships were small fighting craft, they must have served as a convoy for the colonists in transports. Two days beyond Gibraltar, Hanno founded his first city; five others followed in rapid succession. He then pushed along the western coast of Africa, stopping at Lixus River (now Wad Dra) to recruit interpreters before sailing along the coast of the Sahara Desert. He thereupon came to an island which he named Kerne and upon which he founded his seventh colony.

From here, his colonizing done, Hanno became an explorer. The *Periplus* tells of two excursions south from Kerne. On the first, Hanno encountered wild, skin-clad savages who pelted his crew with rocks; he discovered a river, filled with crocodiles and hippopotamuses, which he called the Chretes. On the second, apparently longer exploration, he eventually came to forests from which his crew heard the sounds of pipes, cymbals, and shouting. Terrified, they fled until they came to a burning country, filled with fragrant odors and from which burning streams flowed to the sea. In the midst of it stood a towering, blazing mountain which Hanno called the Chariot of the Gods, from whose summit fire shot up almost to the stars. Three days later, he reached an island inhabited by small, hairy "wild men" who threw rocks at the Carthaginians. The nimble males escaped, but Hanno's crew managed to capture three scratching, biting females, who were promptly skinned. According to Pliny the Elder, two of these skins were on display in the temple of Juno at Carthage until its destruction by the Romans in 146 B.C. Hanno's interpreters informed him that these creatures were called "gorillae." Following the account of this incident, the *Periplus* notes rather abruptly that Hanno ran out of supplies and returned home.

There is no persuasive reason to believe that the *Periplus* is either a forgery or a literary exercise. It is exactly what it purports to be—a public version, probably abridged, of an actual voyage. Its few sentences, however, have caused rivers of ink (and no small amount of vitriol) to flow, all in an attempt to determine where Hanno went. Nineteenth century investigators tended to shorten the voyage too much, even claiming that Hanno never got beyond the Atlantic border of Morocco. A confused Pliny the Elder went to the other extreme, stating that Hanno sailed from Cádiz to the borders of Arabia. Somewhere in between lies the truth.

The solution to this problem hinges on the identification of several key places mentioned in the text, and one must first be aware of its limitations. It is at best a translation of an abridgment, and in spots the text is in question. There are no consistent indications of distance from one point to another; where measurements are given, they are in days. How many hours a day were spent in sailing? Were the exploreres under sail or oars? Were they against or with the wind and currents?

Despite all these problems, a consensus seems to exist among many scholars on some matters. It is generally accepted that Hanno's first six colonies dotted the northwest Atlantic coast of Africa, all fairly close to the Pillars. The location of the seventh colony, Kerne, reached in two days after the Lixus River, is as difficult as it is crucial. When "two" is emended to "nine," as it often is, it suggests a small island named Herne, lying opposite the Río de Oro off Western Sahara. Another candidate for Kerne is the Island of Arguin, farther still to the south.

One site of Hanno's first exploration is accepted without question. The river full of crocodiles and hippopotamuses can only be the Senegal. It is the first river he could have reached with the requisite wildlife, and Pliny the Elder elsewhere remarks that the name of this river was the Bambotum, a name plausibly explained as a corruption of *behemoth*, the Semitic word for hippopotamus.

In recounting his adventures farther south, Hanno's reports seem to take on a less believable tone. Nevertheless, his descriptions of aromatic, blazing lands, of the mountain called the Chariot of the Gods, and of the wild, hairy gorillas, once scorned as fictions, can be explained in such a way as to make them plausible.

An early report from the explorer Mungo Park, for example, made clear that the fires Hanno saw sweeping the plains were the natives' annual burning of the fields to increase their fertility. Hanno's description of the "fiery streams" rushing to the sea and of the Chariot of the Gods with its fire reaching to the stars has prompted many, ancient and modern, to suppose a volcano is meant. Rather far to the south lies Mount Cameroon, a volcanic peak towering 13,353 feet over the plain and quite visible from the coast. The time given in the text for this leg of the trip, however, is clearly insufficient for Hanno to have reached this latitude. Other scholars, therefore, choose to see the Chariot of the Gods in the much closer Mount Kakulima in Guinea (on some maps called Souzos or Sagres). At 3,300 feet, it is much less spectacular, but ablaze it could perhaps resemble a volcano. There are sound arguments for and against either site, and the choice is significant in determining the southern extent of the voyage. It is safest to say that Hanno reached at least as far as Sierra Leone.

Finally, there are the much-debated gorillas. One of the few things agreed upon concerning this segment of the *Periplus* is that these are surely not gorillas in the modern sense of the word, for these animals are not found in this part of Africa. Most scholars believe that Hanno saw either chimpanzees or baboons, while a few hold to the earlier belief that they were pygmies or dwarfs. "Gorilla" in its modern sense was first used by Thomas Savage, an American missionary who happened to see some gorilla skulls and in 1847 announced to the world a new creature, locally called a *pongo*. Since this word was already in use scientifically, he recalled Hanno's hairy creatures and bestowed the name gorilla upon his new find. Any attempt to claim that Hanno saw real gorillas—and thus to extend his voyage as far south as Gabon—is undoubtedly incorrect.

Summary

Hanno's work itself seems not to have been widely acclaimed in antiquity, and his reputation could not have been helped by the fact that he was a Carthaginian. The authors who cited him were often confused, and several seem incredulous. Educated guesses about Hanno's dates and true identity are all that is possible. Yet much the same is true of Homer, and his influence is undenied. Hanno must be judged by his work.

Hanno was not the first to attempt a voyage down the western coast of Africa. Herodotus says that Pharaoh Necho II (early sixth century) engaged Phoenicians to circumnavigate Africa from east to west and that they did so in a three-year voyage. Most scholars treat the story with caution, and its lack of any precise geographical details does make it suspect. Herodotus also notes that in the fifth century King Xerxes I of Persia commuted the sentence of death by impalement of a certain Sataspes with the provision that he attempt to circumnavigate Africa from west to east. Sataspes returned a failure and, perhaps to appease the king, told a tale of dwarfish races he had seen. The ploy did not work, and Sataspes was promptly impaled. A third sailor, a Greek from Massalia named Euthymenes, claimed to have sailed south along Africa until he saw a river filled with crocodiles (the Senegal?). His date, however, is merest conjecture. These tales demonstrate at the least that the idea of such a voyage was in circulation before Hanno attempted it. Also, the fact that his charge was to establish settlements along the coast indicates that the Carthaginians knew at least the closer, northwestern shore of Africa.

These facts, however, do not detract from Hanno's accomplishments. His is the earliest believable and documented voyage of this scope. Moreover, later authors suggest that the colonies, including southern Kerne, continued to engage in trade up to the destruction of Carthage by Rome in 146. Furthermore, there are no records of any further voyages of this length along the African coast until the Middle Ages, when ships routinely turned back at the "impassable" Cape Bojador. It was not until the expeditions of Prince Henry the Navigator that ships went farther, and then it took them forty years to get as far as Hanno had done.

Thus, in one summer, Hanno traveled farther than anyone was to do for some two thousand years. Moreover, his written record of his voyages, flawed as it may be, remained the sole source for the geography of western Africa during all the intervening years. Few explorers since have had such an influence.

Bibliography

Bunbury, Edward Herbert. *A History of Ancient Geography Among the Greeks and Romans, from the Earliest Ages till the Fall of the Roman Empire*. London: J. Murray, 1879. 2d ed. New York: Dover Publications, 1959. Features a reasonable discussion of the *Periplus*, with a fine map. Identifies Herne as Kerne, Kakulima with the Chariot of the Gods, and chimpanzees as the gorillas.

Carpenter, Rhys. *Beyond the Pillars of Heracles*. New York: Delacorte Press, 1966. Includes a translation of the *Periplus* and a lucid discussion of the practical problems of sailing times. Carpenter emends the text to produce a new identification of Herne with Saint-Louis at the mouth of the Senegal. Excellent source.

Cary, Max, and E. H. Warmington. *The Ancient Explorers*. London: Methuen and Co., 1929. Rev. ed. Baltimore: Pelican Books, 1963. Provides treatments of Euthymenes, Hanno, Necho, and Sataspes. A map of northwest Africa, with major landfalls marked, is of great use. Balanced interpretation of the evidence for Hanno's itinerary.

Hyde, Walter Woodburn. *Ancient Greek Mariners*. New York: Oxford University Press, 1947. Includes an extended discussion of the gorilla question. Good summary of Hanno's text. The maps, however, are of low quality.

Kaeppel, Carl. *Off the Beaten Track in Classics*. Melbourne, Australia: Melbourne University Press, 1936. This essay, entirely devoted to Hanno, is a fine example of the passionate writing the *Periplus* has evoked. Excellent discussion of all questionable locations and of the results of the voyage.

Thomson, J. O. *History of Ancient Geography*. Cambridge: Cambridge University Press, 1948. Good sections on Hanno and his predecessors. Excellent bicolored map shows various theories as to locations of Hanno's landfalls.

Kenneth F. Kitchell, Jr.

HARSHA

Born: c. 590; probably Thanesar, India
Died: c. 647; possibly Kanauj, India
Areas of Achievement: Government, warfare, religion, and theater
Contribution: One of the last great rulers of the classical age of Hindu India, Harsha defended Buddhism in its homeland, established relations with the Chinese Empire, and distinguished himself in classical Sanskrit theater.

Early Life

Much of the information recorded about Harsha's youth comes from the account of Baña, a contemporary Sanskrit poet. Harsha was the second son of Prabhakaravardhana, the raja of Thanesar (probably a small, independent state in the Punjab). The death of his father ultimately led Harsha, however reluctantly, to rule for more than forty years over a great north Indian empire. Yet the path to the throne was neither easy nor obvious.

After their mother, Yasomati, committed suttee—self-sacrifice on her husband's funeral pyre—both Harsha and his elder brother, Rajyavardhana, declined the succession. Thus matters remained, until their sister, Rajyasri, who had married Grahavarman, the Maukhari king of Kanauj, was imprisoned after the death of her husband by Devaqupta, King of Malava (in west-central India). Rajyavardhana, abandoning his ascetic life, defeated Devaqupta; unfortunately, the young king was assassinated by Devaqupta's ally, Sasanka, King of Gauda (modern Bengal). On learning of her brother's death, Rajyasri—who had been freed by a sympathetic noble—wandered into the Vindhya Mountains, while Rajyavardhana's army fell into disarray. Harsha, who had been left in charge of the government by his brother, rallied the royal forces; formed an alliance with another of Sasanka's enemies, Bhaskaravarman, King of Kamarupa; and found his sister, who was about to mount a funeral pyre in the mountains.

Vowing vengeance against Sasanka, his brother's murderer, the sixteen-year-old Harsha began a war of universal conquest. Although his objective would not be achieved, he nevertheless managed to transform a desperate situation. According to tradition, his initial hesitance about ascending the throne was overcome by encouragement from the statue of Avalokitesvara Bodhisattva (the merciful, earthly manifestation of the eternal Buddha). Although apocryphal, this story of the statue certainly indicates the spiritual dimension of Harsha's personality.

Life's Work

The rich details provided by Baña in *Sri Harshacharita* (seventh century; *The Harshacharita of Banabhatta*, 1892) break off abruptly with Harsha's reunion with his sister. Aside from royal seals and inscriptions, the account of a contemporary Buddhist pilgrim, Hsüan-tsang, is the only record of the remainder of Harsha's lengthy reign. Unfortunately, Hsüan-tsang only met the king around 643 and left India in 644, three years before Harsha's death. Thus much about Harsha's reign remains unknown.

Harsha, who was always on the move, amassed a huge standing army; his forces easily exceeded those of Chandragupta Maurya in the fourth century B.C., even if figures of sixty thousand elephants, 100,000 cavalry, and perhaps one million infantry are discounted as hyperbole. Although he apparently campaigned vigorously even in the early years of his reign, by about 620 he was deeply involved in warfare, battling the forces of King Pulesin II of the Chalukya dynasty of the northern Deccan and after 636 annexing much of Bengal, Bihar, and Orissa. These facts somewhat modify contemporary claims of thirty years of peace under his rule. Historical opinion is divided as to the extent of his conquests and the range of his empire. He suffered defeat at the hands of the Chalukya, which may or may not have established the sacred Narmada River as his southern boundary. He never apparently defeated his avowed enemy Sasanka (who cut down the Bodhi tree at Gaya), only making his eastern acquisitions sometime after the latter's death in about 637. Apparently, Harsha also had little success against the states of western India. Lata, Malava, and Gurjara were buffer states protected by Pulakesin, and powerful Sindh fought him off, although Dharasena IV of Valabhi became his son-in-law.

Harsha's political power, based in Kanauj (a minor village today with few traces left of his era), embraced the populous, traditional heartland of the Gangetic plain. His prestige and influence extended throughout northern India but was counterbalanced by the Chalukya of the Deccan plateau region. His empire was not a centralized one under his direct control as has sometimes been asserted.

The state was highly organized, yet few details about it are known. In a traditional society based on bureaucratic villages, tours of inspection through the provinces and districts were the means of control. Taxes were light and 50 percent of the budget went to religion and the arts. (At quinquennial assemblies, the treasury surpluses of the past five years were distributed to religious sects and the solitary poor.) An infrastructure to protect travelers, the poor, and the sick, including rest houses, stupas, and monasteries, was in place. The judicial system (inherited from the Gupta, a north Indian dynasty which ruled from the early fourth to the mid-sixth century) was based on social morality and filial duty; its deterrents included imprisonments, mutilations, banishments, and fines. The economy, based on textiles and metals, was prosperous, as was shown by the fact that the assembly's distributed wealth was always replenished in the following ten days.

Although a Hindu (probably a Shaivite), Harsha seems to have been committed early to Buddhism, most likely its Mahayana form, although it was not uncommon for rulers to follow a tolerant and eclectic religious policy. His brother Rajyavardhana had been a Buddhist and his sister Rajyasri became a Buddhist nun. In 643 Harsha demanded the presence of the illustrious Chinese Buddhist Hsüan-tsang, who had studied at Nalanda University in his realm, bringing him from the court of his ally, Bhaskaravarman of Kamarupa, by threat of force. In the last years of his reign, Harsha sought to model himself after Aśoka the Great as the chief patron of his religion—at a time when Buddhism was losing its position to Hinduism. At the sixth quinquennial assembly at Prayaqa in 643, he favored Buddhism in his distribution of the wealth. He also convoked a grand religious assembly at Kanauj—attended by twenty kings—marked by twenty-one days of festival centered on a one-hundred-foot tower holding a life-size statue of the Buddha. During this festival, Harsha arranged a theological disputation, with Hsüan-tsang as the Buddhist champion. The tensions arising from this advocacy led to two frustrated murder conspiracies: Hinayanist Buddhists conspired against Hsüan-tsang, and on the last day of the festival Brahmanas, using a diversionary fire, attacked Harsha with a knife.

Harsha opened diplomatic relations with the Chinese Empire in 641. This action led to a series of Chinese embassies: in 641, under Liang-hoai-king; in 643, under Li-y-piao; and, stimulated by Hsüan-tsang's return to China, in 647, under Wang-hiuen-tse, which arrived after Harsha's death. Apparently attacked by Harsha's usurping minister, Arjuna, Wang's embassy, with Nepalese, Tibetan, and Kamarupa help, captured Arjuna and brought him to China. Wang returned to India in 657 and 664, and the Chinese connection lasted until 787. As for Hsüan-tsang, given gold and an elephant by Harsha, the pilgrim returned to China with 520 cases of Indian religious documents and founded the Buddhist Ideation Only School, which later strongly influenced Japanese Buddhism.

In addition to these achievements, Harsha was a leading Sanskrit playwright in the mold of Kālidāsa, writing *Ratnāvāli* (seventh century; *Retnavali: Or, The Necklace*, 1827) and *Priyadarśikā* (seventh century; English translation, 1923), which contains the new device of a play-within-a-play. His last work, the *Nágánanda* (seventh century; *Nágánanda: Or, The Joy of the Snake-World*, 1872), contains Buddhist themes of the bodhisattva and self-sacrifice in a Hindu framework (perhaps Harsha played Garuda, the redeemed mythical bird). Although his authorship has been disputed, Harsha clearly was a patron of learning and the arts in a period marked by the breakdown of the classical Gupta achievement.

Summary

Though the uniqueness of his role in Indian history has been seriously challenged, including the true extent of his empire, his military record, and his depiction as the last great Buddhist-Hindu ruler before Islam, the fact remains that Harsha constructed a dominant, celebrated political entity out of a petty state amid the disintegration of the Gupta world, holding it together for more than forty years, although it fragmented upon his death. Indeed, one of the chronological eras of Indian history is fixed upon his reign. Harsha's advocacy of Buddhism in a Hindu frame fired Hsüan-tsang to carry its message to the Far East, even as that religion was about to lose force in its homeland. Harsha was essentially a philosopher-king inspired by *dharma* in his character and in his rule of an enlightened welfare state. He was a lion of activity, who ignored food and sleep and found the day too short. The power of his personality is shown by the grim humor of his reply to Bhaskaravarman, who had offered to send his head in place of Hsüan-tsang to Harsha's court, "Send head per bearer," and by his defense of Hsüan-tsang's life at Kanauj, when he threatened to cut out the tongues of the pilgrim's enemies.

Bibliography

Baña. *The Harsa-carita*. Translated by E. B. Cowell and F. W. Thomas. London: Royal Asiatic Society, 1897. Baña, a Brahman and Harsha's court poet, covers Harsha's life until he gained the throne in 612. Written in a masterly, highly ornate style, his work is the first Sanskrit biography.

Devahuti, Deva. *Harsha: A Political Study*. Oxford: Clarendon Press, 1970. An updated assessment, written from the Indian perspective, of Harsha's role in Indian history. Using the greater documentation and information at his disposal, Devahuti balances the more extreme views of R. C. Majumdar and R. K. Mookerji (below). Includes genealogical tables and twelve plates.

Hsüan-tsang. *Si-yu-ki: Buddhist Records of the Western World*. Translated by Samuel Beal. 2 vols. Boston: J. R. Osgood and Co., 1885. The Chinese Buddhist pilgrim Hsüan-tsang covers his friend's reign historically, although with a pronounced religious bias. This panegyric was written after Hsüan-tsang's return to China in 645. Another translation may be found in Thomas Watter's *On Yuan Chwang's Travels in India, 629-645 A.D.* (1904-1905).

Majumdar, R. C., ed. *The History and Culture of the Indian People*. Vol. 3, *The Classical Age*. Bombay: Bharatiya Vidya Bhavan, 1954. A very influential revisionist Indian historian, Majumdar challenges the traditional view of Harsha put forward by Mookerji and Devahuti. Chapter 9 contains a highly detailed, balanced evaluation of all the extant evidence of Harsha's reign. Provides an index, notes, and a bibliography.

Mookerji, R. K. *Harsha*. Oxford: H. Milford, 1926. Part of the Rulers of India series, Mookerji's seminal study was one of the first to promote Harsha's importance in classical India. This biography gathers together all the then-known information about this myth-shrouded figure. Includes indexes and notes.

Panikkar, K. M. *Sri Harsha of Kanauj: A Monograph on the History of India in the First Half of the Seventh Century* A.D. Bombay: D. B. Taraporevaja Sons and Co., 1922. One of the pioneer studies in Indian history, this work builds up Harsha as a king of enormous influence and power, setting him against the background of his era. Includes indexes and notes.

Smith, Vincent A. *The Early History of India from 600* B.C. *to the Muhammadan Conquest, Including the Invasion of Alexander the Great*. Oxford: Clarendon Press, 1904, 4th ed. 1924. This study, written by the editor of *The Oxford History of India* (1920), helped to bring Harsha to public attention. Written from the viewpoint of a British Indian civil servant, this work provides a more moderate view than that of Panikkar. Includes an index, notes, illustrations, and maps.

Tripathi, R. S. *History of Kanauj to the Moslem Conquest*. Delhi: Motilal Banarsidass, 1937. This important University of London thesis, often cited by scholars of classical Indian history, provides original research on Harsha's capital and the heart of his domain. Approaches the subject as regional history rather than as biographical study.

Ralph Smiley

HARTMANN VON AUE

Born: c. 1160-1165; Swabia
Died: c. 1210-1220; Swabia
Area of Achievement: Literature
Contribution: Through its language, style, and literary form, Hartmann's work provided a model for the composition of courtly epic verse and stands at the beginning of the Hohenstaufen renaissance in German literature.

Early Life

As is often the case with medieval literary figures, what is known about the life of Hartmann von Aue is mainly conjecture. What knowledge there is does not come from official documents of the time but rather from personal comments which he makes in his own works and an analysis of his language. There are also several brief references to him in the work of his contemporaries and a coat of arms found in manuscript illustrations. Thus, even his place of birth is questioned by some scholars. Because of the peculiarities of his language, which point to the Alemmanic dialect area in southwestern Germany, it is generally believed that Hartmann was born in Swabia.

Hartmann was probably a ministerial or landless nobleman in service to a patron. A miniature dating from the fourteenth century shows him on horseback with the armor and dress of a knight. His work includes a lament of the loss of his liege lord and a vow to go on a crusade, either in 1189 under Frederick I Barbarossa or in 1197 under Henry VI. Hartmann was an educated man, possibly receiving his formal education at the monastery school at Reichenau, a conclusion drawn from his introductory words to *Der arme Heinrich* (c. 1195; English translation, 1931), where he describes himself as an educated knight (*Ritter*) and a vassal in service at Aue.

The exact order in which Hartmann's work was written is open to debate by scholars, although there seems to be more general agreement as to the order of the works than as to their dates of composition. Among his early works is a long, didactic poem on love, sometimes referred to as *Das Büchlein* (little book) but more often called *Die Klage* (c. 1185; the lament) in recent scholarship. His other major early work is an adaptation of a work by Chrétien de Troyes, *Erec* (c. 1180-1185; English translation, 1982). Both *Die Klage* and *Erec*—as well as some of Hartmann's earlier lyric poetry (*Lieder*), or courtly love songs—were written in the period between 1180 and 1190.

Die Klage shows Hartmann's ability to manipulate the forms of the tradition of courtly love. His poem (1,914 verses long) presents an argument between the heart and the body in which the ideals of service to the beloved and self-denial are extolled. The basis for these ideas comes from twelfth century songs of the Provençal troubadours, although Hartmann's own clear style and didactic tone reveal two characteristics appearing in his mature works as well.

His Arthurian romance *Erec* demonstrates his talent in the genre where he is considered strongest and where he is certainly best known, the courtly epic. His source was the earliest Arthurian romance of the same name by Chrétien, and, although the basic plot is not changed, the purpose behind the story is altered to stress the concept of moderation, or *mâze*, in a knight's life. Erec realizes through his experiences that neither complete devotion to his lady nor total dedication to brave deeds can produce an ideal knight. Instead, he must attain a proper balance between the two.

Both *Die Klage* and *Erec* lay the groundwork for Hartmann von Aue's later compositions, showing a gradual mastery of literary form and establishing themes that form the basis of subsequent works. In fact, Hartmann returned to the Arthurian romance for *Iwein* (c. 1200-1203; *Iwein: The Knight with the Lion*, 1979), his last courtly epic.

Life's Work

With *Erec*, Hartmann composed the first German Arthurian romance and set the focus of his later epics, the question of moral conduct and ideal character. This work also stands at the beginning of several generations of German poets who drew on the same Arthurian legends and the ideals of chivalry. In Hartmann's work there are two parallel threads: the profane literature of his love lyrics and Arthurian romances and the religious themes of his crusade poetry, *Gregorius* (c. 1187-1195; English translation, 1955, 1966) and *Der arme Heinrich*. These two strands reflect opposing currents of his times but are by no means totally separate within his own work.

Hartmann's love lyrics, or *Minne*, which follow the medieval courtly tradition, are most often classified among his earliest compositions. In general, they have been regarded with less esteem than his later crusading poems, which have often been singled out for special attention. In addition, some of the themes and elements introduced in the lyric poetry have parallels in his narrative works. From traditional devotional songs to a noble lady, he progressed to the praise of love for women of a humbler station, for example; then in *Der arme Heinrich*, the unselfish girl who saves her noble lord is the daughter of a peasant, and her immense value is in her willingness to sacrifice herself for him. The themes of estrangement, or alienation from a loved one, reappear in the romances *Erec* and *Iwein*.

One event frequently mentioned in discussing Hartmann's life is the death of his master, which seems to have moved him deeply and to which he refers in a poem showing great devotion. After this event, he may have gone on a crusade (1197), although this is by no means certain, and the crusade may have been an earlier one. Some critics have also suggested that this death marked a turning away from profane love songs to his crusading poems showing a new way of life in the service of Christ (*Gottesminne*). The unhappiness of the lover who admires a lady who withholds her notice is now transformed into the happiness of a more dangerous but also more rewarding love. The religious sanction of the Crusades transforms the enterprise into a loving service of God. The conclusion that such a change was brought about by the shock of his master's death has been disputed by other critics, who remind the reader that medieval poetry was often an expression of societal ideals and feelings and cannot be so directly related to an individual's personal experience as modern verse is. Hartmann's poetry, including courtly love songs, songs renouncing this love, and crusade songs, places him in the tradition of Reinmar von Hagenau and Walther von der Vogelweide and can be considered to accompany the full span of his narrative work.

In his Arthurian romances, Hartmann was concerned with questions of moral conduct, even though the story was essentially profane or secular. Following *Erec*, however, he wrote two narratives specifically concerned with humility before the power of God, *Gregorius* and *Der arme Heinrich*. Hartmann's source for *Gregorius* was an older version of a French poem, appearing in two versions in the twelfth century. Yet he added his own style and language as well as a strong religious-didactic element. The legend tells of a noble sinner who repents of his sin of unknowing incest and inflicts a penance on himself so strict that he is purified. As a sign of his purification, he is chosen as Pope, and both he and his mother are forgiven. The clear lesson is that sinful man can obtain salvation, no matter how grievous his sin, through repentance and atonement.

His following narrative, *Der arme Heinrich*, tells of a nobleman suffering from leprosy who learns humility through the unselfish example of a peasant's daughter. Although this premise offered Hartmann the opportunity to describe the horrible ravages of the disease in gruesome detail, he chose to concentrate instead on its tragic effect on Heinrich's life as he is abandoned to his fate and, most intently, on the young girl who demonstrates the pure spirit of self-sacrifice when she agrees to offer her blood to cleanse him. When Heinrich finds the humility to refuse her sacrifice, he is miraculously cured. In this work, Hartmann blends a religious legend with realistic and historic elements of medieval life. Instead of using a noble to illustrate the highest virtues, he presents a peasant as his ideal figure.

Hartmann's most popular work in his own time was his second Arthurian romance, *Iwein*, which is referred to in other medieval works and of which some twenty-eight manuscripts exist. The main theme, as with *Erec*, deals with the chivalric code of the knights, complete with the elements of love, generosity, refinement, and *mâze*. The poet uses the external symbols of the Church in all of his courtly epics, but the role of God is not confined to his two versions of religious legends. His introduction to *Iwein* clearly states that true kindness (or goodness) receives God's favor and men's honor (or esteem). Thus, the currents of religious and secular rewards are combined for individuals with this important quality. Just as surely, pride or haughtiness (*superbia*) without regard for compassion is punished. Heinrich's sin in *Der arme Heinrich* was not so very different, nor was Gregorius' first error, as he abandoned the religious life for which he was destined to pursue adventure as a knight. Hartmann's work shows clearly how important moral and social commitments were for him; both religious and secular currents shaped his work.

Summary

The appearance of four particularly gifted poets paved the way for the development of a body of high-quality literature in the German language rather than in Latin as had been the norm before the period of the High Middle Ages. This new literature reached a level of refinement above previous attempts in the vernacular. Among the best-known poets of the period are Walther von der Vogelweide in the area of lyric poetry and Gottfried von Strassburg and Wolfram von Eschenbach along with Hartmann von Aue in the area of the courtly epic. Hartmann's lasting fame rests mainly on his Arthurian romances. His polished verses found favor at the courts and stand as a model for future developments in narrative literature in German. Furthermore, in the amount and versatility of his work, he is exceptional for his times.

Hartmann's very strong sense of moral rectitude and his concern for the correct knightly behavior of the code of chivalry permeate his work and are in harmony with the medieval period. His great individual contribution is a clarity of style, reflecting, according to some critics, the practice of the *ornatus facilis* of medieval rhetoric, which is characterized by figures of repetition while avoiding forced imagery and artificiality. Gottfried von Strassburg praised Hartmann's refined language, eloquence, and clearness by using the image of crystalline words to emphasize what he considered to be his contemporary's greatest literary quality. Contrasting with that of earlier German narratives, Hartmann's polished language and style exerted strong influence on the medieval poets Wolfram von Eschenbach, Walther von der Vogelweide, and Reinmar von Hagenau. Later medieval poets were also familiar with Hartmann's work, which continued to influence courtly novels and heroic narrative well beyond his lifetime. For his contributions, Hartmann is certainly to be counted among the master poets of medieval German literature.

Bibliography

Bell, Clair Hayden. *Peasant Life in Old German Epics: Meier Helmbrecht and "Der arme Heinrich."* New York: Columbia University Press, 1931. Contains an English translation of *Der arme Heinrich*, with explanatory endnotes as well as a bibliography. The introduction discusses points of comparison between *Gregorius* and an epic poem by Wernher der Gärtner, *Meier Helmbrecht* (c. 1250; partially translated as *Meier Helmbrecht, a German Farmer of the Thirteenth Century*, 1894). Includes general information about Hartmann and his work and discussion of the role of the peasant in medieval times.

Hartmann von Aue. *Hartmann Von Aue: "Gregorius, the Good Sinner."* Translated by Sheema Zeben Buehne. New York: Frederick Ungar Publishing Co., 1966. This volume includes short introductory remarks about the work and the translation but is most valuable for the complete text of *Gregorius*, with original language on one side and English translation on the other, and helpful explanatory notes.

Jackson, W. T. H. *The Literature of the Middle Ages*. New York: Columbia University Press, 1960. A major study of the literature of the Middle Ages, including information on the development of the literature and its various forms. In the discussion of the romance, Hartmann is considered in the context of his times. He is compared with his contemporaries, and *Erec* and *Iwein* are analyzed specifically. Includes a chronology of the important works of the period and an extensive bibliography arranged by topic.

Loomis, Roger Shermann. *Arthurian Literature in the Middle Ages: A Collaborative History*. Oxford: Clarendon Press, 1959. An important survey of literature dealing with the Arthurian legend, with articles by specialists in each field. An individual chapter, "Hartmann von Aue and His Successors," focuses on the development of the German Arthurian romance. Related chapters discuss Chrétien de Troyes, the source for Hartmann's romances, and Hartmann's contemporaries Wolfram von Eschenbach and Gottfried von Strassburg. Footnotes supply bibliographical information for each topic.

Resler, Michael. Introduction to *Hartmann von Aue: "Erec."* Philadelphia: University of Pennsylvania Press, 1987. An extensive introduction including general historical and cultural background, specific information on the life of Hartmann, a discussion of Arthurian romance, and a full consideration of the sources, structure, and thematic issues of this work. This volume also contains a translation of *Erec* plus explanatory endnotes. Includes helpful selected bibliography, although the majority of the references are to sources in German.

Richey, M. F. *Essays on Mediaeval German Poetry*. New York: Barnes and Noble Books, 1969. With an explanation of *Minne*, individual chapters on various medieval German poets (including the study of a poem by Hartmann), and a short selection of German sources, this volume provides a good orientation to the literary form but no extensive information on Hartmann. The article by Leslie Seiffert is especially helpful.

Sayce, Olive. *The Poets of the Minnesang*. Oxford: Clarendon Press, 1967. A representative survey of lyric poetry written in Germany, Austria, and Switzerland from 1150 to 1400. Good material on the origins and conventions of the *Minne*. With specific reference to Hartmann, including a representative sample of his poems in their original form without English translation.

Seiffert, Leslie. "Hartmann von Aue and His Lyric Poetry." *Oxford German Studies* 3 (1968): 1-29. Very informative article supplementing the more general references by Richey and Sayce. Considers the place of Hartmann in medieval lyric poetry and shows the role such poetry played in his life and literary production. Discusses briefly the research and current opinion on his lyric poetry and examines themes, motifs, and a pattern of moods within the work. Detailed interpretations of poems included.

Thomas, J. W. Introduction to *Hartmann von Aue: "Erec."* Lincoln: University of Nebraska Press, 1982. Includes information on Hartmann's life and works, as well as the theme, plot structure, motifs, and style of the translated work. Explanatory notes at the end provide bibliographical information on each of these topics. A readable translation of the text follows.

____________. Introduction to *Hartmann von Aue: "Iwein."* Lincoln: University of Nebraska Press, 1979. An informative introduction with an overview of Hartmann's works and discussions of the theme of *Iwein*, structure and motifs, and the narrative style. Notes include important bibliographical references as well as helpful information. The translation included in this volume is very readable.

Tobin, Frank J. *"Gregorius" and "Der arme Heinrich": Hartmann's Dualistic and Gradualistic Views of Reality*. Bern, Switzerland: Verlag Herbert Lang, 1973. A scholarly treatment of the two works, with important insights into the view of the world implicit in these texts. Includes extensive discussion of the content and themes of the two works, as well as an orientation to the terms "dualism" and "gradualism" as applied to the analysis. The bibliography includes both German and English references.

Zeydel, Edwin H., and B. Q. Morgan, eds. *"Gregorius": A Medieval Oedipus Legend by Hartmann von Aue*. Chapel Hill: University of North Carolina Press, 1955. Introduction and explanatory endnotes accompany this translation of *Gregorius* into rhyming couplets. Contains commentary on the verse form and the Gregorius legend, along with related legends in literature, particularly the Oedipus legend. Also includes information about the life of Hartmann and the surviving manuscripts of this work.

Susan L. Piepke

HARUN AL-RASHID

Born: February, 766; al-Rayy, northern Iran
Died: March 24, 809; probably Khorasan Province, Iran
Areas of Achievement: Government and warfare
Contribution: Harun al-Rashid counts among the most famous holders of the office of caliph in the 'Abbasid Dynasty in Baghdad (eighth to thirteenth century). His most notable accomplishments were quelling revolts, establishing peace, and promoting industry and trade.

Early Life

The man who was to become the fifth Islamic caliph in the line of the 'Abbasid family was born in 766 in al-Rayy in north-central Iran. He was the third son of Caliph al-Mahdi and the second child of al-Mahdi's wife al-Khayzuran, a former slave of the fourth 'Abbasid caliph. Had it not been for the influence of al-Khayzuran and others close to the seat of power in Baghdad, Harun might never have ascended the throne. His older brother al-Hadi, who was the initial successor to al-Mahdi, reigned only a year (785-786) following the death of their father. Al-Hadi's death was said to have been the result of a court conspiracy, and Harun's claim to succession at the very young age of twenty required the concentrated action of supporters who could intervene on his behalf. His chief supporter was one Yahya ibn Khalid al-Barmaki, who had been the prince's secretarial aide and instructor during his early youth. Ibn Khalid's loyalty to the claimant probably stemmed from the circumstances of Harun's earliest appointments to key positions appropriate to an 'Abbasid prince. During a period of renewed warfare between the Arab caliphate and the Byzantine Greek Empire (first in 779-780 and again in 781-782), Harun had been named commander of two expeditions, one of which penetrated as far as the shores of the Bosporus opposite the Byzantine capital at Constantinople. Despite the fact that the real commanders of these military campaigns were accomplished soldiers and officials, the prince received several honorific governorships for his service in the field. These included posts in Ifriqiyah (modern Tunisia), Egypt, Syria, Armenia, and Azerbaijan Province in Iran. On each occasion, the real man in control seems to have been Ibn Khalid, Harun's Barmakid adviser.

The fruit of Harun's close dependence on his former tutor was to be seen in Ibn Khalid's intervention, with the assistance of the prince's mother, al-Khayzuran, to secure Harun's selection as second heir to the throne. This became very critical when intrigues broke out over al-Mahdi's apparent last-minute decision to bypass al-Hadi in favor of Ibn Khalid's protégé. As soon as Harun succeeded to the throne following al-Hadi's murder, he recognized Ibn Khalid and his two sons as his official viziers, or primary ministers. This ascendancy of a small group of caliphal advisers lasted until the Barmakids themselves fell victim to court intrigues nearly two decades later (in 803).

This pattern in Harun al-Rashid's early life might seem to suggest that, as caliph, it would be his nature to bend to the will of others. His accomplishments as ruler of the 'Abbasid Empire until 809, however, left a very different legacy.

Life's Work

Apparently, Harun al-Rashid's early experiences as prince-commander of the caliphal armies sent against the Byzantine emperor left a strong mark. Throughout his reign, he placed great emphasis on defending the Islamic-Christian border. He would even create a special military province, called Awasim, in the zone separating the two empires. Particular care went into the strengthening of the fortifications of Tarsus, which would serve as a military deployment zone. The state of the caliph's military preparedness was tested at the very outset of his reign, when Constantine VI, son of the Byzantine Empress Irene, came of age and denounced his mother's generally peaceful relations with the Caliph of Baghdad. Border fighting surged between 795 and 797. In the latter year, the empress overthrew her young successor, blinded him, and restored general terms of peace with Caliph Harun.

Conditions deteriorated dramatically later in Harun's reign when Irene was overthrown by Nicephorus, a rebellious Byzantine aristocrat, in 802. Nicephorus broke relations with Baghdad and attacked in 804, only to be vigorously repulsed by an army led by Caliph Harun. This force advanced well into Asia Minor and menaced the city of Constantinople itself. Harun laid down new terms of peace in 806, including a humiliating clause requiring the Byzantine emperor to pay annual tribute to Baghdad. A few years earlier, Arab naval forces temporarily recaptured the island of Cyprus, which had returned to Christian hands shortly after the earliest years of Arab Muslim campaigns against Constantinople in the mid-seventh century.

Perhaps the reason that Harun's victories against the Christian Byzantines were not carried further at this time is to be found in the many signs of internal division that had appeared within the Islamic Empire. These divisions had both a geographic and a religio-cultural schismatic side to them. On the one hand, there is no doubt that, by the time of Harun's reign, the central caliphate showed signs of being unable to control its most distant provinces. Both along the southern coasts of the Mediterranean (the Maghrib, or western provinces of modern Morocco, Algeria, and Tunisia) and in the east (primarily the Province of Khorasan, in eastern Iran, but also in the core provinces of Arabia and Iraq), revolts and independence movements troubled Harun's reign on many occasions. These weakened his capacity to impose not only political but also important economic bonds of caliphal control.

In addition, one must take into consideration the fact that Islamic schismatic movements—most under the banner of the Alids, Shi'a followers of the imamate descending from the Prophet's son-in-law Ali—had weakened the cultural and religious authority of the Baghdad caliphate. Harun al-Rashid's methods of dealing with Alid threats were sometimes preemptive, bordering on outright persecution. Members of families descending from Ali were warned against establishing themselves in distant retreats and teaching Alid doctrines that might be turned against the caliph. Some, including Yahya ibn Abdullah, brother of the defeated Alid pretender Muhammad al-Nafs al-Zakiyya, were brought to Baghdad under a promise of security, only to be imprisoned for life. Such treacherous policies undoubtedly alienated many others whose loyalty to the Islamic realm, irrespective of questions of religious doctrines, was wearing thin by the time of Harun's death in 809.

The circumstances surrounding Harun al-Rashid's succession bear witness to growing divisions that were weakening the political ascendancy of the 'Abbasid caliphate. Several years prior to his death, at a time when his ruling strength seemed to be at its zenith, Harun revealed what came to be known as the Covenant of the Ka'aba. This document designated his firstborn son, Muhammad al-Amin, as Harun's successor to the caliphate. Al-Amin's younger brothers, Abdullah al-Ma'mun (Harun's son by a Persian slave) and al-Kasim (later al-Mu'tasim), were assigned full powers as governors of the eastern (Iranian) provinces and Mesopotamia (Iraq), respectively. Harun's intention was that, while al-Amin would assume the office and functions of caliph, his other heirs would have a nearly equal share in the responsibilities of imperial rule. Al-Amin's almost immediate redefinition of the extent of al-Kasim's authority in Iraq and his attempts to exclude al-Ma'mun from his assumed eventual right to succeed to the caliphate, however, deteriorated into a situation of civil war by 810. Although al-Ma'mun succeeded in overcoming the forces of Harun's first chosen successor, he managed this only with the aid of Iranian forces under the command of one Tahir ibn-al-Husayn, victor in an important battle at Rayy. Later, Tahir proceeded to Baghdad, where, in 813, his forces killed Caliph al-Amin and proclaimed the succession of Harun's second son, al-Ma'mun. The fact that the new caliph remained behind for some time in the capital of the Province of Khorasan before assuming the responsibilities of his office in Baghdad itself is significant. It underlined the determination of his Iranian "protectors" to make certain that no caliph after Harun al-Rashid would assume that the eastern provinces could be ruled from Baghdad. Thus, Harun al-Rashid's mistake in trying to arrange his own succession cost the institution of the caliphate a high price. This price involved the emergence, in a few years' time, of the first autonomous dynasty of non-Arab governors over Iran. Its founder was Tahir ibn al-Husayn himself. Its main cities, especially Nishapur and Samarkand, would soon attract as many eminent representatives of medieval Islamic civilization and culture as had Harun al-Rashid's capital city of Baghdad.

Summary

Too frequently the name Harun al-Rashid has been associated with a romantic, if not even mythological, vision of the Islamic world in the time of the Baghdad caliphs. This tendency to glorify and romanticize has not been limited to accounts of his reign in the Western world. The themes of the famous anthology of *The Arabian Nights' Entertainments* (c. 1450) are products of the literary and cultural imagination of the Islamic world in which he lived; inevitably, therefore, they contributed to subsequent romantic images in European accounts.

On a political level, the temptation has been strong to compare Harun al-Rashid to his equally famous Catholic contemporary, the Emperor Charlemagne. Traditional but undocumented accounts tell of diplomatic contacts between the two and even of exchanges to support mutual recognition of respective imperial spheres—at the expense of their shared rival on the throne of the Byzantine Empire at Constantinople. Probably more important than such comparisons, however, is the challenge to study indices of economic exchanges, which, at the height of the caliphs' ascendancy over all Islamic provinces east and west, had come to represent an interregional network which was capable of deciding the future material fate of the Byzantine Empire. Hence, Harun's dealings with the Byzantines and, even more, his dealings with distant eastern zones (the Red Sea, the Persian Gulf, and the eastern provinces of Iran bordering on Turkistan) that tied the Islamic Empire to sources of trade in the Far East had to do with much more than mere political ascendancy. These contacts would determine which of the two empires, Islamic or Greek Byzantine, would hold sway over world trade.

In such a geopolitical framework, the relatively recent phenomenon of a restored "Roman" Empire in the West must have been considered of very peripheral importance. An objective approach to Harun al-Rashid's reign, therefore, would study interlinking political, economic, social, and cultural factors that either helped the caliphs of his era to retain the greatness of Baghdad as a world capital or presaged its decline. The caliphs' religious policy, as well as attitudes toward provincial autonomy from Baghdad's direct control, were factors that had, by the time of Harun's reign, become issues reflecting future dilemmas, and the eventual decline, of the 'Abbasid Caliphate.

Bibliography

Bishai, Wilson B. *Islamic History of the Middle East*. Boston: Allyn and Bacon, 1968. This survey of Islamic history is less detailed than Carl Brockelmann's 1939 synthesis of Middle Eastern developments from the rise of Muhammad into the twentieth century (see listing below). It tends, however, to be somewhat freer in interpretative analysis than are more traditional histories; this makes the work more readable, if less precisely documented. A full section is devoted to the career of Harun al-Rashid, based mainly on al-Tabari's *Ta'rikh al-rusul wa al-muluk*.

Brockelmann, Carl. *History of the Islamic Peoples*. New York: Capricorn Books, 1960. This history, originally published in German in 1939, is well-known for its detailed, if dry, accounts of the main dynasties of Islamic civilization, including the 'Abbasid period of Harun al-Rashid. Includes a synopsis of cultural history for each period covered. The synopsis included in his treatment of the reign of Harun is among the most developed and useful case studies in the book.

Gabrieli, Francesco. *The Arabs: A Compact History*. New York: Hawthorn Books, 1963. This book, first published in Italian in 1957, is less detailed than Bishai's and Brockelmann's works. Gabrieli's coverage of the reign of Harun al-Rashid nevertheless covers several subjects that merit more attention than many more complete political histories offer. These include tax policies and attitudes of the caliph toward "loyal" critics among Sunni jurisprudents responsible for the elaboration of Islamic law.

Glubb, John Bagot. *Haroon al Rasheed and the Great 'Abbasids*. London: Hodder and Stoughton, 1976. This monograph was written by the well-known "Glubb Pasha," British commanding officer of the Arab Legion in Jordan until his retirement in 1956. It is not the product of detailed academic research, but remains very readable, especially for its picturesque accounts of the social and cultural milieu of Baghdad during the reign of Harun al-Rashid. Although it is sparsely footnoted, there is a useful general bibliography of works in European languages and Arabic.

Sourdel, Dominique. "The Abbasid Caliphate." In *The Cambridge History of Islam*. Vol. 1, edited by Peter M. Holt, Ann K. Lambton, and Bernard Lewis. Cambridge: Cambridge University Press, 1970. A brief but scholarly account of the Baghdad caliphate. Because of the importance of Harun's reign, the main aspects of military and religious history, including the key question of civil war following Harun's death, are covered. An extensive bibliography and a glossary, although not the work of Sourdel, are important supplements to the coverage of the caliphate in Harun's generation.

Byron D. Cannon

AL-HASAN AL-BASRI

Born: 642; Medina, Arabia
Died: 728; Basra, Iraq
Area of Achievement: Religion
Contribution: Al-Hasan was the most famous of Muslim teachers and preachers of the generation that followed the age of the Prophet Muhammad and his Companions. His views on religion and politics in the early stages of the Islamic Empire, as well as his code of conduct, made him the model of the pious Muslim in the formative age of Islam.

Early Life

Abu Sa'id ibn Abi al-Hasan Yasar al-Basri was born in Medina in 642, ten years after the death of the Prophet Muhammad. His father, Yasar, of non-Arab origin, had been taken prisoner when the Muslims conquered Maysan in Iraq. He was brought to Medina, where he was manumitted by his owner, and married Hasan's mother, Khayra, also a slave. Some medieval Arab historians assert that al-Hasan's parents were manumitted only after his birth.

Al-Hasan's childhood is surrounded by the mist of legend. The tradition that was formed around him after his death placed his childhood in the sacred circle of the Prophet Muhammad himself. It is said that as an infant he was at times suckled by one of the wives of the Prophet, Umm Salama, who owned his mother. One source has it that by drinking from a pitcher that had been used by the Prophet, the boy imbibed divine wisdom.

He grew up in Wadi al-Qura, near Medina, where he was exposed to the pure Arabic tongue of the Bedouins. The child accompanied his mother while she served in the house of Umm Salama. Thus he was exposed, at a very early age, to the circle of the Prophet's house and to some of the Companions (*sahaba*) of the Prophet who were still living. At fourteen, al-Hasan had already memorized the Koran and was adept in writing and arithmetic.

Al-Hasan grew up to be tall and handsome, with a fair complexion and blue eyes. His appearance was slightly marred by a small deformation of his nose, the result of a riding accident. His family moved to Basra, Iraq, in 657. At age twenty-two, al-Hasan participated in the campaigns of Arab conquests in the East. He saw action in northeastern Persia and in Afghanistan, assisting at the storming of Kabul. At age thirty, he became a secretary to the governor of Khorāsān Province.

Life's Work

Al-Hasan returned from the East at age thirty-two to reside in Basra until the end of his life. Basra was a bustling city situated between Arabia and the newly conquered territories to the east. The Arabs who were flocking to

Basra shared the city with an increasing number of *mawalis* (non-Arab Muslims who were clients of Arabian tribes), whose influence in the economic, political, and religious life of the Islamic Empire was increasing steadily.

Being one of the *mawalis* did not hinder al-Hasan from becoming the most celebrated teacher of his age. Most of the religious scholars of that age, in fact, were of this class. He was one of many learned men who established a circle of followers and students. He met with his disciples at the mosque, or occasionally at his residence, lecturing on and discussing theological and ethical subjects. At this early stage of Islamic history, these circles were the closest thing to a collegiate institution of learning.

Al-Hasan's fame spread to other areas of the expanding Islamic Empire. He was well-known and respected by the governors of the province of Iraq as well as at the seat of the caliphate in Damascus. He was a contemporary of ten caliphs, some of whom sought his advice on matters of policy, dogma, and ethics. A letter by al-Hasan to the Umayyad caliph 'Abd al-Malik (reigned 685-705) has been preserved; it responds to an inquiry by the caliph as to al-Hasan's opinions on the subject of free will.

To draw a fully accurate picture of al-Hasan's lifework may prove an impossible task, despite the fact that most Arabic medieval chroniclers, historians, and theologians make reference to him. He emerges from these writings as a man for all seasons, a teacher of universal appeal. Almost all Islamic sects and schools of thought that came after his time regarded him as a champion or patron. It is impossible to separate totally the legend from the historical man.

The rebellion which led to the assassination of the third caliph, 'Uthman (reigned 644-656)—which al-Hasan witnessed in Medina as a boy of fourteen—along with the wars of conquest in Asia, was instrumental in forming al-Hasan's lifelong philosophy of peaceful living and religious piety. He spoke eloquently against both insurrection and the divisive political and religious argumentation that was rampant at that time. It was this attitude that kept him from arousing the ire of the governors and caliphs of his time, although he did occasionally criticize their incessant pursuit of wealth and power; indeed, he pointed out their misdeeds with clarity and audacity.

Al-Hasan's teaching career was not the only reason for his legendary status among his contemporaries and later generations. His powerful Arabic prose style and rhetoric, resplendent with vivid images and striking antitheses, were praised and imitated by later writers and preachers. There is a wealth of pronouncements and clever sayings in flawless Arabic attributed to him by medieval Arab authors.

Al-Hasan's life-style was another important factor in the making of the legend. Islamic mystics (Sufis) honor him as their first master. He preached the renunciation of this world and its goods in order to seek the rewards of the afterlife, a principle that he applied to his own conduct. His fear of God and constant awareness of the coming Day of Judgment made him a sober man who rarely smiled. Al-Hasan ruled himself and his household by the principle of *zuhd*, voluntary poverty. For example, he refused a grant of uncultivated state land; when he received a gift or donation, he would distribute most of it to the poor, keeping only enough to meet his immediate needs. He refused to give his daughter in marriage to a rich man, for he judged that such a wealthy individual either must have amassed his money by dishonest means or must be selfish and miserly.

Al-Hasan flourished during that critical period of Islamic history that followed the murder of the caliph ʻUthman. It was a time of divisiveness in the political and religious life of the Islamic realm. The party of Ali (Shiʻa) was emerging as a strong movement of opposition to the newly established Umayyad dynasty in Damascus; it was also presenting a challenge to the doctrinal unity of Islam. Disputes over succession and the governance of the new empire were causing political and religious schisms. A variety of schools of Koranic interpretation emerged in support of various political parties. Numerous Arab tribal conflicts, inherited from pre-Islamic time, were also reemerging. The generation of *sahaba*, or Companions of the Prophet, who were regarded as authorities on the interpretation of the Koran, was dying out. A group of *tabiʻun* (followers, a following generation) was taking over the task of interpretation and judgment. Al-Hasan al-Basri was the earliest and most prominent member of this group.

In this atmosphere of heterodoxy, dissension, and revolutions in Islam, religious scholars often championed and promoted one party or the other. Al-Hasan managed to steer a course above narrow partisanship. He did not refrain from criticizing those in power, yet he managed to avoid undermining their authority. There were times when he went into hiding after speaking openly and forcefully against the governor of Iraq, al-Hajjaj, who was known for his strictness and cruelty. Nevertheless, the two men occasionally exchanged visits and counsel.

Al-Hasan was able to survive and flourish in this age of conflict because of his categorical opposition to revolt against established authority. He taught that people should try to reform their own lives before taking upon themselves the reformation of the state. Thus the Umayyads, who had their hands full with revolts in Iraq and farther east and who sometimes used excessive force in putting down these revolts, tolerated and even appreciated al-Hasan, despite his criticisms of them.

The Umayyad caliph ʻUmar II (reigned 717-720), who was a devout and pious man, had a good rapport with al-Hasan al-Basri. They exchanged many letters, and the caliph sought al-Hasan's advice on matters of policy. ʻUmar's reforms reflected some of al-Hasan's teachings, and the caliph's simple lifestyle reflected the model of piety set by al-Hasan.

It was during this period of time that al-Hasan was appointed a judge. He resigned after a short tenure, possibly because of his old age. Shortly after the death of 'Umar II, and at the height of the Islamic Empire's territorial expansion, al-Hasan died. The Muslims' trend toward power and wealth—and toward political and religious dissension—would continue unabated.

Al-Hasan al-Basri did not leave any written legacy. Tradition has it that on his deathbed he ordered his books and all of his writings burned so that, as he put it, there would be nothing in them that might incriminate him on Judgment Day.

Summary

Most of the Islamic schools of thought and mystic orders that flourished in the following centuries claimed al-Hasan as a founder or a member. The Sufi mystics, for example, claimed him as their first master. Opposing parties of later generations often quoted him in support of their causes. As a result, the figure of al-Hasan al-Basri came to assume mythic proportions. During his long and distinguished career, he was obsessed mostly with two things: his personal salvation and pious conduct, and the unity and propagation of Islam. Without his writings, and in the absence of any impartial contemporary accounts of his life, al-Hasan must remain a figure of legend as much as of history.

Bibliography

Brockelmann, Carl. *History of the Islamic Peoples*. Translated by Joel Carmichael and Moshe Perlmann. New York: Capricorn Books, 1960. This volume is still the classic work on Islamic history and civilization. Places al-Hasan al-Basri within the political, cultural, and religious context of his time. Bibliography.

Obermann, Julian. "Political Theory in Early Islam." *Journal of the American Oriental Society* 55 (1935): 138-162. Obermann addresses the question of the authenticity of the letter to Caliph 'Abd al-Malik, attributed to al-Hasan. The author rules that it was al-Hasan's own work.

Ritter, H. "Hasan al-Basri." In *The Encyclopaedia of Islam*. Leiden, Netherlands: E. J. Brill, 1971. This is a concise and useful sketch of his life and work. It contains a bibliography of the most prominent sources on al-Hasan in medieval Arabic writings. It also includes a short list of works in French and German in which al-Hasan is mentioned.

Schimmel, Annemarie. *Mystical Dimensions of Islam*. Chapel Hill: University of North Carolina Press, 1975. One of the best treatments of its subject. Schimmel's discussion is aimed primarily at scholars, yet her book is eminently readable. Includes a bibliography.

Smith, Margaret. *The Way of the Mystics: The Early Christian Mystics and the Rise of the Sufis*. London: Sheldon Press, 1976. Discusses al-Hasan within the context of the mystical tradition, drawing parallels between early Christianity and Sufism. A scholarly work, yet accessible to the general reader. Bibliography.

Hassan S. Haddad

HATSHEPSUT

Born: Mid- to late sixteenth century B.C.; probably near Thebes, Egypt
Died: c. 1482 B.C.; place unknown
Area of Achievement: Government
Contribution: Governing in her own right, Hatshepsut gave to Egypt two decades of peace and prosperity and beautified Thebes with temples and monuments.

Early Life

Hatshepsut, or Hatshopsitu, was the daughter of Thutmose I and his consort (the Egyptian title was "great royal wife") Ahmose. Nothing is known of Hatshepsut's date of birth and early life. Although Thutmose I was the third king of the powerful Eighteenth Dynasty, he was probably not of royal blood on his mother's side; the princess Ahmose, however, was of the highest rank. During the period in Egyptian history known as the Empire or New Kingdom (from the Eighteenth to the Twentieth Dynasty; c. 1570-1075 B.C.), royal women began to play a more active role in political affairs. Among her titles, the pharaoh's chief wife was called the "divine consort of Amon" (Amon was one of the principal Theban deities). Being the wife of a god increased her status, and her offspring were given a certain precedence over the children of minor wives or concubines.

In addition to Princess Hatshepsut, at least two sons were born to Thutmose I and Ahmose, but both of the boys died young. The male line had to be continued through a third son, born to a minor wife, who was married to his half sister, Hatshepsut. Thutmose II's claim to the throne was strengthened by this marriage; he succeeded his father around 1512.

A daughter, Neferure, was born of this union but apparently no son was born. The ancient records are fragmentary and at times obscure, but there is evidence that Thutmose II was not very healthy and thus his reign was short, ending around 1504. Once more there was no male of pure royal blood to become pharaoh; thus, the title passed to a son of Thutmose II by a concubine named Isis. This boy, also named Thutmose, was at the time of his father's death between the ages of six and ten, and dedicated to the service of the god Amon at the temple at Karnak. Since he was underage, the logical choice as regent was his aunt Hatshepsut, now the queen mother.

Life's Work

Hatshepsut soon proved to be a woman of great ability and large ambitions. The regency was not enough for her; she wanted the glory of being called pharaoh as well as the responsibility for Egypt and the young king. To accomplish this desire, however, seemed impossible. There had never been a female pharaoh—only a man could assume that title, take a "Horus name," and become king of Upper and Lower Egypt.

For a time Hatshepsut looked for possible allies, finding them among the various court officials, the most notable being the architect and bureaucrat Senmut (or Senenmut), and among the priests of Amon. By 1503 her moment had come. Accompanied by young Thutmose, she went to Luxor to participate in one of the great feasts honoring Amon; during the ceremonies, she had herself crowned. There was no question of deposing Thutmose III, but he was in effect forced to accept a coregency in which he played a lesser part.

To justify this unique coronation, Hatshepsut asserted that she had been crowned already with the sanction of her father the pharaoh. To support this claim an account was given of her miraculous birth, which was later inscribed at her temple at Dayr el-Bahrī on the west bank of the Nile. According to this account, Amon himself, assuming the guise of Thutmose, had fathered Hatshepsut. With the approval of both a divine and a human parent, none could oppose the new pharaoh's will, while Thutmose remained a child and the army and the priests supported her.

Hatshepsut did not merely assume the masculine titles and authority of a pharaoh; she ordered that statues be made showing her as a man. In the stylized portraiture of Egyptian royalty, the king is usually shown bare-chested and wearing a short, stiff kilt, a striped wig-cover concealing the hair, and a ceremonial beard. The number of statues commissioned by Hatshepsut is not known, but in spite of later efforts by Thutmose III to blot out the memory of his hated relative, several examples exist, showing Hatshepsut kneeling, sitting, or standing, looking as aloof and masculine as her predecessors.

Neferure, the daughter of Hatshepsut and Thutmose II, was married to Thutmose III. This marriage served the dual purpose of strengthening the succession and binding the king closer to his aunt, now his mother-in-law. Hatshepsut then focused her attention on domestic prosperity and foreign trade, activities more to her personal inclination than conquest. Throughout Egypt an extensive building program was begun. At Karnak four large obelisks and a shrine to Amon were built. Another temple was constructed at Beni-Hasan in Middle Egypt. Several tombs were cut for her, including one in the Valley of the Kings. Her inscriptions claim that she was the first pharaoh to repair damages caused by the Hyksos, Asian invaders who had conquered Egypt in the eighteenth through mid-sixteenth centuries with the aid of new technologies, such as war chariots pulled by horses. The usurpation of these foreign kings was an unpleasant and recent memory to the proud, self-sufficient Egyptians; Hatshepsut's restorations probably increased her popularity.

The crowning architectural triumph of her reign was her beautiful funerary temple at Dayr el-Bahrī. Built by Senmut, her chief architect and adviser, it was constructed on three levels against the cliffs; the temple, a harmonious progression of ramps, courts, and porticoes, was decorated in the interior with scenes of the major events of the queen's reign.

Probably the most interesting of the achievements so portrayed was the expedition sent to the kingdom of Punt, located at the southern end of the Red Sea. As the story is told, in the seventh or eighth year of her reign, Hatshepsut was instructed by Amon to send forth five ships laden with goods to exchange for incense and living myrrh trees as well as such exotic imports as apes, leopard skins, greyhounds, ivory, ebony, and gold. Pictured in detail are the natives' round huts, built on stilts, and the arrival of the Prince and Princess of Punt to greet the Egyptians. The portrait of the princess is unusual, because it is one of the rare examples in Egyptian art in which a fat and deformed person is depicted.

In addition to the voyage to Punt, Hatshepsut reopened the long-unused mines of Sinai, which produced blue and green stones. Tribute was received from Asian and Libyan tribes, and she participated in a brief military expedition to Nubia. Despite the latter endeavors, Hatshepsut's primary concern was peace, not imperialistic expansion. In this regard, her actions were in sharp contrast to those of her rival and successor Thutmose III, who was very much the warrior-king.

It would not be sufficient, however, to explain Hatshepsut's less aggressive policies on the basis of her sex. Traditionally, the Egyptians had been isolationists. Convinced that their land had been blessed by the gods with almost everything necessary, the Egyptians had throughout much of their earlier history treated their neighbors as foreign barbarians, unworthy of serious consideration. Hatshepsut and her advisers seem to have chosen this conservative course.

As Hatshepsut's reign continued, unpleasant changes began to occur. Her favorite, Senmut, died around 1487. In addition to the numerous offices and titles related to agriculture, public works, and the priesthood, he had also been named a guardian and tutor to Neferure. No less than six statues show Senmut with the royal child in his arms. At the end of his life, he may have fallen from favor by presuming to include images of himself in his mistress' temple. Most were discovered and mutilated, presumably during Hatshepsut's lifetime and with her approval since her names remained undisturbed.

Princess Neferure died young, perhaps even before Senmut's death, leaving Hatshepsut to face the growing power of Thutmose III. The king had reached adulthood: He was now the leader of the army and demanded a more important role in the coregency. His presence at major festivals became more obvious, although Hatshepsut's name continued to be linked with his until 1482.

It is not known exactly where or when Hatshepsut died or whether she might have been deposed and murdered. That her relations with her nephew and son-in-law were strained is evident from the revenge Thutmose exacted after her death: Her temples and tombs were broken into and her statues destroyed. Her cartouches, carved oval or oblong figures which encased the royal name, were erased, and in many cases her name was replaced by that of her husband or even of her father. She was eliminated from the list of kings. Thutmose III ruled in her stead and did his best to see that she was forgotten both by gods and by men.

Summary

The nature and scope of Hatshepsut's achievements are still subject to debate. Traditional historians have emphasized the irregularity of her succession, the usurpation of Thutmose III's authority, and her disinterest in military success. Revisionist studies are more generous in assessing this unique woman, praising her for her promotion of peaceful trade and her extensive building program at home.

Her influence throughout Egypt, though brief and limited only to her reign, must have been profound. The considerable number of temples, tombs, and monuments constructed at her command would have provided work for many of her subjects, just as surely as the wars of her father and nephew provided employment in another capacity. Art, devotion to the gods, and propaganda were inextricably mingled in the architectural endeavors of every pharaoh. Hatshepsut's devotion to the gods, especially the Theban deity Amon, and her evident need to justify her succession and her achievements enriched her nation with some of its finest examples of New Kingdom art.

Controversial in her own lifetime and still something of a mysterious figure, Hatshepsut continues to inspire conflicting views about herself and the nature of Egyptian kingship. She was a bold figure who chose to change the role assigned to royal women, yet at the same time, she seems to have been a traditionalist leading a faction that wanted Egypt to remain self-sufficient and essentially peaceful. Perhaps that was yet another reason that she and Thutmose III were so much at odds. His vision of Egypt as a conquering empire would be that of the future. She was looking back to the past.

Bibliography

Aldred, Cyril. *The Development of Ancient Egyptian Art from 3200 to 1315 B.C.* London: A. Tiranti, 1952. Reprint. London: Academy Editions, 1973. The title indicates the focus of the work. There are more than fifteen plates depicting Hatshepsut, other members of her family, and her adviser Senmut. Detailed explanations accompany each picture, and there is also an index and a bibliography.

Edgerton, William F. *The Thutmosid Succession*. Chicago: University of Chicago Press, 1933. This brief work contains a considerable amount of technical information on hieroglyphs and disputes among Egyptologists, although it presumes some knowledge on the part of the reader of the period from Thutmose I to the death of Hatshepsut.

Gardiner, Sir Alan. *Egypt of the Pharaohs*. Oxford: Oxford University Press, 1961. Although a lengthy study, Gardiner's work is pleasantly written, with balanced views of both Hatshepsut and her successor, Thutmose III. Provides a good background for the less knowledgeable reader. Includes an index, a bibliography, and a comprehensive chronological list of kings. Illustrated.

Hayes, William C. "Egypt: Internal Affairs from Thuthmosis I to the Death of Amenophis III." In *Cambridge Ancient History*. Vol. 2, *History of the Middle East and the Aegean Region, c. 1800-1380 B.C.* 3d ed. Cambridge: Cambridge University Press, 1973. Much information about Hatshepsut is given, although Hayes indicates a definite preference for Thutmose III.

Maspero, Gaston. *History of Egypt, Chaldea, Syria, Babylonia, and Assyria*. 13 vols. London: Grolier Society, 1903-1906. Maspero's work, though dated in some respects, is a mine of information. Many drawings that illustrate the text, taken from on-site photographs, are beautifully detailed; they cover everything from temples and bas-reliefs to statues, weapons, and the mummies of Thutmose I and Thutmose II. The material devoted to Hatshepsut is in volume 4, and the account of her reign is generally favorable.

Nims, Charles F. *Thebes of the Pharaohs: Pattern for Every City*. New York: Stein and Day, 1965. The city of Thebes was extremely important to Hatshepsut and her family as both a political and a religious center. This book is helpful because it places the queen in her environment.

Wenig, Steffen. *The Woman in Egyptian Art*. New York: McGraw-Hill Book Co., 1969. This book is extremely well illustrated with both color and black-and-white photographs as well as drawings. The period covered is from c. 4000 B.C. to c. A.D. 300. Contains a chronology and an extensive bibliography and is written for the general reader.

Wilson, John A. *The Burden of Egypt*. Chicago: University of Chicago Press, 1951. This extensive study is both detailed and well written; it deals with the importance of geography to Egypt. Includes maps, a bibliography, illustrations, and a chronology of rulers. Wilson's analysis of political theories and discussion of possible motivations of the pharaohs is very useful in understanding the conflict between Hatshepsut and Thutmose III.

Dorothy T. Potter

HENRY II THE SAINT

Born: May 6, 973; Abbach, Bavaria
Died: July 13, 1024; near Göttingen (in modern West Germany)
Area of Achievement: Government
Contribution: Using patience, common sense, and a realistic approach to the intrigues and problems of eleventh century Germany and Italy, Henry restored the monarchy north of the Alps and supported and encouraged Church reforms.

Early Life

The son of Duke Henry II of Bavaria and Gisela, the daughter of Conrad, King of Burgundy, Henry could claim direct descent through his father's line from Henry the Fowler. In addition, his grandfather was the younger brother of the emperor Otto the Great. When Duke Henry I was imprisoned by Otto III for leading a rebellion against the emperor, young Henry was placed in the care of Abraham, Bishop of Freising, and then sent to Hildesheim, where he was reared and educated. Because it was believed that he would enter the Church, his education was that of a cleric and scholar, not of a soldier and king.

When his father was freed and restored to his duchy, however, the boy returned to Bavaria, where his education and training were put into the hands of Wolfgang of Ratisbon. The death of his father in 995 made him Duke of Bavaria at the age of twenty-two. Shortly thereafter, he married Kunigunde, the daughter of Siegfried, Count of Luxemburg. As Duke of Bavaria, Henry remained loyal to Otto III, accompanying him on two Italian campaigns, until the emperor's death in 1002.

Otto died without an heir, thus ending the direct male line of Otto the Great and opening the way for a struggle to determine the new King of Germany and Holy Roman Emperor. The former was decided by heredity or by election; the latter required the cooperation of the Pope. Several of the great German dukes wished to succeed Otto as King of Germany, notably the Duke of Carinthia, grandson of Otto the Great. Others who sought the kingship were Henry of Bavaria, who was descended from the direct, male, imperial line, and Eckhard, Margrave of Meissen, who was the choice of the Saxon princes. When Eckhard was killed in April, 1002, and Otto pledged his support to Henry, however, the matter was settled. Henry was elected King of Germany and crowned on June 7, 1002, at Mayence.

The new German king was a well-educated, pious, and sensitive young man. Although not brilliant, he possessed the admirable qualities of common sense and good judgment, which served him well throughout his life. His physical appearance seems to have been quite ordinary, as there is little written on the subject. Allegations that he was lame are legends, not facts. His health was generally poor, however, and should be considered when assessing the limited success of his reign.

Life's Work

Henry's coronation at Mayence was not universally recognized by the German nobility. He had little more than the support of the Bavarians and Franconians. Following his coronation, Dietrich, Duke of Upper Lorraine, pledged his support, but Lower Lorraine, Saxony, and Swabia refused to accept Henry. He first secured recognition from the Saxon nobility by agreeing to respect their local laws and customs. Then he turned his attention to Lower Lorraine and through diplomacy won over its support. Only Swabia remained; when the local duke found himself isolated, he negotiated and finally submitted. Germany was at last, if only temporarily, united, but Henry's troubles had only begun. As the emperor's heir apparent, he also aspired to the vacant imperial throne. Otto III, however, had left a weakened and disunited empire: Poland, Bohemia, and Lombardy were all in varying stages of rebellion.

The most serious challenge came from the east. Bolesław Chrobry, the son of Mieszko, had been installed Duke of Poland in 992 upon the death of his father. He united the various tribes of the Oder and Vistula and won major concessions from Otto III. With the death of the emperor in 1002, Bolesław sought total independence from German vassalage. At the head of a strong army, he conquered the lands west of the Elbe and when Henry refused to recognize his conquests, took advantage of the turbulent conditions in Bohemia to add that duchy to his expanded holdings. Henry was unable to deal with this eastern threat, because internal problems required his full attention. He first put an end to disloyalty in Lorraine and then turned to face a more serious rebellion, supported by the Duke of Poland, that included his own brother, Bruno. The fighting, bitter at times, lasted into 1004, but the king prevailed; once again peace and order were restored within the kingdom.

Henry was now ready to address the problems of the empire. While the Polish/Bohemian situation may have been the most serious, it would also be the most difficult to resolve. A favorable solution in Italy, on the other hand, seemed more attainable. Thus Henry gathered his army and crossed the Alps. The campaign itself was successful, but it did not solve the German monarch's fundamental problem of lasting control. Marching by way of Trent and Verona, picking up support along the way, he reached Pavia in May, 1004. There he was elected King of the Lombards on May 14 and crowned the following day in the Basilica of Saint Michael. His rival, Ardoin, Marquess of Ivrea, who had himself been crowned King of the Lombards two years earlier in the same church, fled to the west as his support faded. Henry's triumph seemed complete, although it was marred when fighting broke out between the Germans and Italians in Pavia. The city was partially destroyed, with substantial loss of life. Unfortunately, Henry was not able to remain in Italy to consolidate his newly won position. Bohemia and Bolesław required his immediate attention. In June, Henry marched back across the Alps leaving behind a dubiously loyal Lombardy.

Upon his return to Germany, Henry reorganized his army and prepared for a Bohemian campaign. Crossing the Erzgebirge without opposition, he was joined by Jaromir, the deposed Duke of Bohemia. The Bohemians, who had no love for the Duke of Poland, posed no obstacle. Bolesław, fully aware of the approaching danger and without local support, withdrew to the north. Henry entered Prague amid rejoicing and restored Jaromir. The Duke of Bohemia, realizing that his position depended on German assistance, remained faithful to Henry and supported him in his Polish wars. Bolesław's setback, however, in no way eliminated Henry's eastern problems: Although a temporary peace was made while Bolesław turned his attention to Kiev, Henry was forced to make repeated campaigns in order to secure his eastern frontier. Finally, a more lasting peace was signed at Bautzen in 1018, although it represented no German victory, merely recognizing the status quo. Bolesław kept the lands east of the Elbe and was virtually independent of any German control, even proclaiming himself King of Poland before Henry's death. Bohemia, however, remained loyal, and at last Henry had true peace on his eastern border.

In the west, Henry also had problems. The great nobles of Lorraine defied him at every opportunity, and he was forced to make several campaigns across the Rhine in order to maintain even nominal control. Burgundy was also defiant. King Rudolf III was a weak monarch who struggled constantly (and usually unsuccessfully) with his nobles. In 1016, he sought Henry's support. The German king, who claimed to be the rightful heir to the throne of Burgundy when his uncle should die, was very willing to intervene. Rudolf acknowledged Henry's right of succession, and in 1018, having secured his eastern border, Henry undertook an expedition into Burgundy. The affair was not a success. The Burgundian nobility remained lawless, and Henry's claim remained doubtful; it became a moot issue when he died before Rudolf.

Italy provided yet another source of frustration. In the ten years that passed following his first expedition south of the Alps, Henry's authority and influence had waned, and civil war was the normal state of affairs. The pro-German faction, primarily the bishops and abbots, rallied about Bishop Leo of Vercelli. Ardoin, the deposed Lombard king, led the defiant faction, which was largely secular. Henry not only needed to restore his rule in Lombardy but also wished to be crowned Holy Roman Emperor. This additional title would add strength to his position in both Germany and Italy. Therefore, he marched south accompanied by Queen Kunigund in late fall of 1013.

By Christmas, he was in Pavia, and in January, 1014, he moved on to Ravenna. At a synod he convened in Ravenna, Henry put the affairs of northern Italy in order; Ardoin's support melted away. He reached Rome on February 14 and was crowned that same day by Pope Benedict VIII. Unfortunately, within a week of the coronation fighting broke out between his German entourage and the Romans. Withdrawing from the city, Henry returned to Lombardy and in June recrossed the Alps. Henry's second Italian expedition was at least a partial success: New life was given to the empire and relations were established between the Pope and the new emperor. Yet northern Italy remained unsettled. With the emperor's departure, civil war again broke out, and even after the abdication and later death of Ardoin, the Lombards resisted Henry's authority.

He made one last expedition to Italy in 1021-1022. The principal purpose of the journey was a campaign against the Byzantine province in the south, where some Lombard princes had allied themselves with the Byzantine forces. At Verona in early December, Henry's formidable German army was joined by his Italian supporters; in January, 1022, they marched south. Sickness became rampant in his army, however, and he turned back, having made only a minor impact on southern Italy. Back in Lombardy, he turned his attention to church reform and was more successful than he had been with political affairs. In the autumn, he returned to Germany, where he died on July 13, 1024, and was buried in Bamberg.

Summary

Henry II's life was a continual struggle to revive the political institutions of the German kingdom and Holy Roman Empire following their decline. He was able to achieve a considerable degree of success in Germany but was less successful in Italy. His greatest triumphs were the improvement of church-state relations and religious reform. Henry strengthened the position of the Church in both Germany and Italy, following an aggressive policy of granting lands and titles to the bishops and abbots as a means of reducing the power and influence of the secular nobility, over whom he had less influence and control. Having the right to nominate, Henry installed loyal bishops upon whom he could depend to remain faithful in his unceasing wars with his vassals. He also strongly supported reform within the Church, particularly the Cluniac movement. At the synod of Pavia, August, 1022, with the support of Pope Benedict, he was able to secure the denunciation of clerical marriage in both Germany and Italy.

Bibliography

Bryce, James. *The Holy Roman Empire*. Rev. ed. New York: Macmillan, 1922. This work provides a good general introduction to the medieval German Empire, although it does not deal with Henry in detail.

Fisher, Herbert. *The Medieval Empire*. 2 vols. Reprint. New York: AMS Press, 1969. Although Fisher wrote these two volumes at the turn of the century, they continue to hold up well under modern scrutiny. His approach is topical rather than chronological, thus the reign of Henry is found in several chapters in both volumes.

Gwatkin, H. M., J. P. Whitney, J. R. Tanner, and C. W. Previté-Orton, eds. *The Cambridge Medieval History*. Vol. 3, *Germany and the Western Empire*. Cambridge: Cambridge University Press, 1957. Chapter 10 of this volume, entitled "The Emperor Henry II," provides one of the most comprehensive accounts of the life and times of Henry II. It is primarily a political history of his reign, although other chapters cover related individuals and events which are not central to his life. There is an extensive bibliography and index.

Henderson, Ernest F. *A History of Germany in the Middle Ages*. Reprint. New York: Haskell House Publishers, 1968. Chapter 11 of Henderson's straightforward political narrative is devoted to the reigns of Henry II and Conrad II. A good starting point for a study of the last male descendant of Otto the Great.

Mann, Horace K. *The Lives of the Popes in the Early Middle Ages*. Vols. 4-5, *The Popes in the Days of Anarchy: Formosa to Damascus II, 891-1048*. London: Kegan Paul, Trench, Trübner and Co., 1925. This work provides a good account of the reign of Henry II from the point of view of the Papacy, as well as portraying the Church in both Germany and Italy. Although concentrating on Pope Benedict VIII and his relationship with the emperor, because of the involvement of the clergy in secular affairs, the study also considers political intrigues and warfare.

Thompson, James Westfall. *Feudal Germany*. Chicago: University of Chicago Press, 1928. 2d ed. New York: Frederick Ungar Publishing Co., 1962. Thompson treats medieval German history primarily in terms of the relationship between church and state and tends to emphasize the conflict between Henry II and Benedict VIII.

John G. Gallaher

HENRY IV

Born: November 11, 1050; Goslar, Saxony
Died: August 7, 1106; Liège
Areas of Achievement: Politics and government
Contribution: Henry's struggles with the German nobility and the Papacy had a decisive impact on the future constitutional and political development of Germany. Although his tenacious defense of the rights and prerogatives of the monarchy was largely unsuccessful, it still marked him as one of the greatest of the German kings.

Early Life

Henry IV was born on November 11, 1050, the son and heir of Henry III and his wife, Agnes of Poitou. Henry was well educated for the period: He could read and write, knew Latin, and had an interest in music and architecture. His childhood was very tumultuous and would have an inordinate influence on his personality and his later decisions.

In 1056 his father died. The German nobles accepted the five-year-old Henry as king only because his father had earlier forced them three times to swear allegiance to him. Control of the monarchy quickly fell to Henry's mother, a weak, retiring woman thoroughly unsuited to the rough world of German politics. She did her best, but under her regency the interests of the monarchy were not advanced, royal lands were alienated to various princes, and the political situation in Germany began to unravel.

These problems became very clear when in April, 1062, Archbishop Anno of Cologne enticed the twelve-year-old Henry onto a gaily decorated boat on the Rhine River at Kaiserwerth and kidnapped him. Henry tried to escape by jumping over the side and he was rescued only with great difficulty. The conspirators' motivation was simply to satisfy their own selfish desires while allowing Henry only a semblance of power. Probably relieved to be done with the responsibility of being regent, Agnes made no objection, nor did any other significant group in Germany, to the kidnapping; instead she fulfilled her long-held desire to enter a convent.

By 1066, when he was able to assume power for himself at the age of sixteen, Henry was a tall, attractive man, who despite frequent illnesses had an imposing physical presence. Lacking the piety of his father, Henry reacted against the restraints of his childhood by living a dissolute life. His experiences with the German princes during the regency had not only taught him trickery, deceit, and cunning, but had also filled him with an intense pride in the dignity of the monarchy and a burning desire to preserve and defend its rights. The protection of the monarchy would remain the constant goal of his reign; in 1066, Henry was ready to begin the arduous task of restoring the power and prestige of the Crown.

Life's Work

Because of the erosion of royal authority during the regency, Henry's first priority was to create a firm economic foundation for the monarchy, enabling it to act independently of the desires of the German nobility. That required the reinstitution of royal properties in Saxony, making it the center of royal power. Such a program was certain to be opposed by the Saxon nobles, who would see it as a threat to the gains they had made during the regency, and by the free Saxon peasants, who correctly perceived any increase in the monarchy's power as leading to servitude. Led by Otto von Nordheim and Magnus Billung, these groups rebelled in 1070. Although the Saxons had some success against Henry, the issue was never in serious doubt and on June 9, 1075, the imperial army decisively defeated a Saxon army of nobles and peasants at Langensalza on the river Unstrutt. Broken and crushed, Saxony appeared completely subjugated and Henry was poised to govern it directly through royal officials, *ministeriales*, with Goslar as his capital. Had this success proved lasting, there is little doubt that Henry would have completed the political program of the Ottonian and Salian kings: the creation of a German "state" like that of Norman England. At the very moment of his greatest victory, however, Henry was suddenly faced with an even more perilous enemy in the person of Pope Gregory VII.

Gregory, formerly the Cluniac monk Hildebrand, was elected pope in 1073 while Henry was preoccupied with Saxony. At first, relations between the two were quite friendly. Gregory followed ancient custom by informing the German king of his election and requesting Henry's confirmation, which was granted. Had Henry understood the true aims and beliefs of Gregory, however, this approval would not have been forthcoming.

Within this short, pale, and plebeian fifty-year-old Pope burned a revolutionary vision of the Church and its place in society. Essentially, Gregory saw himself called by God to free the Church from the chains of secular authority. He envisioned a Church, under the absolute control of the Papacy, having ultimate primacy over all society. All authority, secular and clerical, would serve the will of the Pope. Indeed, Gregory attacked the German king and the German church precisely because it was the most organized and disciplined in Europe. It had been reformed by Henry II and Henry III and therefore was attached to the Crown and not to the Papacy. Thus, if absolute papal control of the Church and society were to become a reality in Europe, first the secular control of the German church had to be destroyed. His contemporaries were very aware that Gregory's program was revolutionary, breaking with ancient custom and tradition.

Gregory carefully planned his move against Henry, choosing to strike just as the Saxon revolt was coming to its climax. At the Lenten Synod of 1075, Gregory, as part of a sweeping reform program against simoniac German clergy, forbade Henry to perform any lay investitures or suffer severe penalties—a mortal challenge to the monarchy's ability to rule. The German kings had long used prelates as the chief officials of the kingdom and to deny them the power to appoint and to invest the bishops and the abbots of the imperial abbeys was to shred the Crown's capacity to govern.

Henry ignored the Pope's decree and once the Saxons were reduced, he turned his attention to Milan, where he appointed an archbishop in direct opposition to Gregory, who had supported another candidate. The Pope retaliated with his famous letter of December 8, 1075, in which he called Henry to penance and threatened him with the loss of his throne. He also ordered his messengers to berate Henry personally for his moral faults, making it clear that if the king did not submit, excommunication and deposition would follow.

Gregory had miscalculated. By taking such an extreme position, one that imperiled civil order in Germany, he drove the German bishops and Henry together; on January 24, 1076, they met at Worms. There Henry and his bishops approved a letter castigating the Pope. It began "Hildebrand, no longer pope but false monk" and concluded by stating "We Henry, king by the grace of God, with all our bishops say to you: come down, come down!" This letter reached Gregory in February, 1076, but now it was Henry who had overreached. The Pope immediately excommunicated and deposed the king and absolved all of his subjects of their fealty to him. Within months Henry found himself isolated, deserted by his former allies, and facing an increasingly more powerful opposition. In October, the German nobility met at Tribur to decide how to treat the excommunicated monarch. Henry had to agree to remove the excommunication within a year or the nobles would no longer consider him king. They apparently believed that Henry would be unable to fulfill this requirement, for they also invited Gregory to meet with them as a mediator at Augsburg on February 2, 1077. Henry realized that if the Augsburg meeting took place the monarchy was doomed.

At this juncture Henry performed a brilliant political maneuver. Secretly crossing the Alps, for all the major passes were blocked by nobles hostile to the monarchy, he appeared before Gregory at Cannossa on January 25, 1077; for three days Henry stood in the cold and snow wearing only sackcloth as penance. Gregory was reluctant to grant absolution, but he was a priest and a priest could not refuse forgiveness to a sincere penitent, as Henry well knew. As a result of this dramatic action Henry was absolved and restored to his throne.

The German princes were furious with Gregory. The meeting at Augsburg had only been a week away, but now with the excommunication removed, they had no legitimate reason for rebellion. Nevertheless, they elected Rudolf of Swabia as antiking and Germany was plunged into three years of civil war. Henry knew that Rudolf was not a serious threat as long as Gregory did not recognize Rudolf as the rightful king. Gregory remained neutral for three years and then, possibly fearful that Henry was reconsolidating his power, excommunicated him again at the Lenten Synod of 1080 and declared Rudolf the legitimate king. Rudolf, however, was killed in battle the following October; this time, the German clergy and nobility stood by Henry, for they realized that Gregory posed as much a threat to their privileges as to the king's. With this support Henry held a council at Mainz that deposed Gregory and established an antipope. It was now Gregory who was isolated, and in 1081, Henry invaded Italy. Gregory took refuge in the Castel Sant' Angelo in Rome and, though faced with certain defeat, he refused to compromise. He was finally rescued by his Norman allies, with whom he retreated to southern Italy. Broken by this extraordinary conflict, Gregory died at Salerno on May 25, 1085.

It appeared that Henry had achieved his goals. Gregory had been driven into exile and Henry's position in Germany never seemed stronger. In 1087, his eldest son, Conrad, was crowned the next king, and in 1089, after his wife Bertha's death, Henry married Adelheid, the daughter of a Russian prince. Yet within a few years, Henry's world began to collapse around him. In 1088 Bishop Otto of Ostia was elected Pope Urban II. Because of his political genius, Urban was a much more potent adversary than was his predecessor; he successfully exploited conditions in Germany to advance the papal program. Urban was aided by Henry's family problems.

In 1093 the papal party persuaded the impressionable Conrad to desert his father and be crowned King of the Lombards. Simultaneously, Henry's young wife, Adelheid, after being imprisoned for adultery, escaped and spread incredible tales about Henry's moral corruption. The forces that Henry had opposed since 1066 once again arrayed themselves against him; from 1090 to 1096 he was trapped in a castle near Verona. In 1096, however, Henry was able to return to Germany and at Mainz he held a diet that deposed Conrad (who died in 1101) and crowned his brother, Henry, heir. Henry also tried to make peace with Urban, but the Pope refused these overtures and renewed Henry's excommunication. At this moment young Henry betrayed his father. Henry IV, who by now was understandably suspicious of his family, was nevertheless tricked by his son into leaving his armed escort and accompanying him to the castle at Böckelheim. There Henry became his son's prisoner and was forced to confess his sins and to renounce his rights to the throne. Henry V had staged a successful coup; before he could mount a counterstroke, Henry IV died at Liège on August 7, 1106.

Summary

Henry IV's reign was a turning point in German history. His political goal had been to continue the policy initiated by Conrad II of consolidating royal power at the expense of the German nobility and clergy. Henry's vision was for a feudal monarchy whose every aspect would be inspired and controlled by the king. He was well aware of the strong opposition he would face in attempting to achieve this ambitious plan, but Henry was never dismayed by adversity and he did have some success. A royal capital was created, royal lands were extended, and for a period of time the nobility was held in check. Henry's development of a bureaucratic government employing civil servants called *ministeriales* anticipated similar reforms accomplished under the Capetians in France and the Plantagenets in England.

The Investiture Conflict halted the evolution toward a strong, centralized monarchy, however, and started a steady dissolution of the Crown's authority. With the monarchy preoccupied with its fight with the Papacy, developing noble families, such as the Zahringer of Swabia, were able to consolidate their own position. By the time of Henry's death in 1106, the German nobility was already in the ascendancy and Germany had started down the long, tortuous path of feudalism just as the other monarchies in France and England were beginning to create new types of royal government and to extend their authority into increasingly broader areas of society.

It is not difficult to see the heroic character of Henry IV. He struggled mightily and with extraordinary courage to preserve and to expand royal power. In his mind's eye, Henry had grasped the vague outline of the future course of government better than had any of his contemporaries. It if is true, as James Westfall Thompson states, that "a man is to be judged not by what he achieves, but by what he labors to accomplish," then Henry IV was the greatest German monarch of the Middle Ages.

Bibliography

Barraclough, G. *The Origins of Modern Germany*. 4th ed. Oxford: Basil, Blackwell and Mott, 1962. This is a very impressive survey of Germany from 800 to 1939. Constitutional issues and the development of a central government are stressed. The period of 1025-1075 is seen as a time of royal consolidation, while the era from 1075, when the Investiture Conflict breaks out, to 1152 is perceived as a period of decline for the German monarchy.

Fuhrmann, Horst. *Germany in the High Middle Ages, 1050-1200*. Cambridge: Cambridge University Press, 1986. This work provides an outstanding summary of Henry IV's reign and places it within the context of the history of medieval Germany. The discussion of the Investiture Contest and the Saxon rebellion is concise yet detailed. The bibliography is the best of any of the works cited here and details only those studies done in English.

Hampe, Karl. *Germany Under the Salian and Hohenstaufen Emperors*. Translated by Ralph Bennett. Totowa, N.J.: Rowman and Littlefield, 1973. Originally published in 1909, this book is still regarded as one of the most readable and reliable accounts of eleventh and twelfth century Germany. Hampe sees Henry IV's policies as reactionary with their object of restoring ancient rights of the monarchy. There are some excellent insights regarding Henry's motives and character. Highly recommended.

Joachimsen, Paul. "The Investiture Contest and the German Constitution." In *Studies in Medieval History: Medieval Germany, 911-1250*. Vol. 2, *Essays by German Historians*. Edited by G. Barraclough. 4th ed. London: Basil, Blackwell and Mott, 1967. Considered by some to be a classic in the field, this article succinctly discusses the constitutional issues of the Investiture Contest and maintains that the historical significance of Henry IV's reign is the fact that he took issue with the Papacy's view that the German monarchy was solely an electoral monarchy with no regard given to the rights of blood or heredity.

Thompson, James Westfall. *Feudal Germany*. Chicago: University of Chicago Press, 1928. This book was criticized when first published for not including the latest scholarship. It maintains that the root of Henry's struggle with the Papacy was economic. Rome wanted to gain complete control of the Church in Germany and Henry IV could not allow this to happen. There is a very detailed description of the Saxon rebellion and some fine descriptions of Henry.

Ronald F. Smith

HENRY THE LION

Born: 1129; place unknown
Died: August 6, 1195; Brunswick, Saxony
Area of Achievement: Government
Contribution: Henry was the most important of the twelfth century German nobles who resisted the authority of the Holy Roman Emperor. He was also a leader in the movement to extend German colonization into Slavic territory.

Early Life

Even kings considered themselves clients of Henry the Lion, Duke of Saxony and Bavaria. He was a very capable and determined person, but these traits alone would not have made him one of the most important people of the age. The timing of his birth and the political conditions in Germany allowed him to attain a degree of power and influence seldom reached in the twelfth century by anyone without royal status. Between 1076, when Pope Gregory VII attempted to depose Emperor Henry IV, and Henry the Lion's birth, the German nobility gained so much independence from the throne that the result was nearly anarchy. This situation had arisen because the emperors were distracted by the conflict with the papacy and because they had lost their struggle to make succession to the imperial throne hereditary. The conflict with the various popes required concentration on Italy rather than Germany, and the principle of election to the throne meant that feuds, granting of favors in return for electoral support, and uncertainty about the future created political instability. Enjoying freedom from imperial control, aggressive knights carved out domains for themselves and began to give themselves territorial designations based on the names of their castles: thus Lothar of Supplinburg, grandfather of Henry the Lion.

Lothar was one of the new men, so new that his family is unknown except for the name of his father. Yet he was able to become Duke of Saxony and, finally, Emperor Lothar III. He had no sons, but he married his daughter, Gertrude, to Henry the Proud, a member of the Bavarian Welf family. Despite all of his efforts to have Henry the Proud recognized as his successor, when Lothar died in 1137 Henry was not elected. Throughout Lothar's reign, a feud had continued between the Welf and Hohenstaufen families. The Hohenstaufen party not only prevented Henry the Proud's election but also deprived him of his title as Duke of Saxony. The Saxons, however, remained loyal to him and war broke out between his forces and those of Albert the Bear, the newly appointed Duke of Saxony. Henry the Proud appeared to be winning when he suddenly died in 1139, leaving his ten-year-old son, Henry the Lion, to carry on the struggle.

Contrary to expectation, the Welf cause did not collapse with the death of

Henry the Proud. The Saxon nobles and the Welf family continued the fight until a negotiated settlement in 1142 recognized Henry the Lion as Duke of Saxony. As part of the settlement, Gertrude, Henry the Lion's mother, married the newly named Duke of Bavaria. She died in childbirth the next year, leaving Henry alone at the age of fourteen. Albert the Bear lost his title but remained a problem for the Welfs. He was given a small territory on the Saxon border and remained Henry's archenemy for the rest of his life.

Life's Work

In addition to his struggle to maintain and increase his influence and holdings at the expense of his fellow nobles and the emperor, Henry expanded his domain and consequently that of German culture, into previously Slavic regions. These activities made him second in power only to the emperor within Germany and a prominent figure in international affairs. He displayed the ruthless methods he would use throughout his life from the very beginning of his tenure as Duke of Saxony at the age of thirteen. One of his first acts was to claim the lands of one of his vassals who died childless. In the course of the ensuing dispute, he imprisoned the Archbishop of Bremen, who was the deceased's brother, and other church officials. He released them only after the emperor intervened. These high-handed methods were to be the primary cause of the revolt by his vassals that led to his deposition in 1180.

Henry's campaign against the Slavs was similarly characterized by ruthless determination. As early as 1147, Henry had been involved in the Crusade against the heathen Slavs that had been authorized by the Pope in lieu of warring in the Holy Land. The Crusade of 1147 had few results because of the quarreling among the Crusaders, but Albert the Bear and Henry the Lion—as well as other Saxon nobles—continued the attempt to establish colonies beyond their eastern borders. Albert cooperated with the Church, although he would not allow church officials to impose heavier tithes on the converted Slavs than on the German colonists. He also prevented the Crusade of 1157 from being conducted in his territory. Henry, on the other hand, was less interested in Christianizing the Slavs than in obtaining tribute from them. He crossed the Elbe River in 1160 and subdued the area around Mecklenburg, which he managed to hold for seven years. Even after he was forced to return most of it to a Slav prince, the acquisition and exploitation of Slavic lands remained a constant feature of his policy. By the time of his deposition in 1180, the area between the Elbe and the Baltic Sea to the Danish border had been colonized by Germans and was under Saxon control.

Henry was also interested in extending his power by encouraging trade and commerce. One of his most successful enterprises was the development and promotion of the city of Lübeck into an important commercial center on the Baltic coast. The city was founded in 1143, and Henry had gained control of it with his usual ruthless tactics by 1160. Thereafter, he favored it in every way he could and in return received considerable revenue from its markets. In a similar way, he raised the city of Munich to commercial importance by building a bridge for the transport of salt from Salzburg. Bishop Otto of Freising complained that Henry had, in effect, stolen the tolls from the salt trade by diverting traffic to Munich from the bishop's territory, but the complaint produced no results.

These high-handed methods and efforts to increase his power finally brought Henry to grief. He took every opportunity to weaken the Saxon nobility, who bitterly resented him. The practice that aroused the most fury was the seizure of the lands of vassals who died without adult male heirs. He added insult to injury by attempting to make the counts into his direct administrative subordinates. By the standards of a later age, this movement toward centralization and the attempt to gain control of independent, frequently feuding, and continually troublesome nobles may seem laudable, but in the twelfth century the view was that nobles should be free to govern their lands as they pleased as long as they met their feudal obligations. That was the position of Henry's vassals, who protested vigorously to his overlord, Emperor Frederick I Barbarossa.

Henry probably could not have withstood the conspiracies against him by the Saxon nobles as long as he did without the support of the emperor. Frederick, who had been elected emperor in 1152, was a staunch friend to Henry as well as being his first cousin. Frederick's mother, Judith, was Henry the Proud's sister. This kinship did not, however, make Frederick a Welf partisan, for he had equal ties of kinship to the Hohenstaufen family. It seems that the two men were genuinely fond of each other. At any rate, they supported each other. Frederick allowed Henry to do as he pleased in Saxony, and Henry participated in Frederick's military campaigns in Italy. It was after the Italian campaign of 1155, in which Henry had performed particularly valuable service, that Frederick made him Duke of Bavaria as well as Saxony and thus returned the old Welf territories to the family that had traditionally possessed them. By the time his arch rival, Albert the Bear, died in 1170, Henry had been able to quell the rebellions against him so successfully and had become so powerful that a period of relative peace ensued. He felt secure enough to leave his lands in the care of his wife and go on a crusade to Jerusalem in 1172, but he returned after only a short stay.

Relations between Henry and Frederick became less cordial after 1174. Henry apparently refused to take part in the Italian campaign of that year even though his troops were desperately needed. The two men are reported to have met for the last time in 1176, when Frederick is supposed to have gone so far as to beg for Henry's help in Italy. Henry is said to have demanded the important castle and fief of Goslar in return for military aid. Frederick refused, and the two parted on bad terms. The negotiations at this meeting, if it actually occurred, are matters of speculation. No contemporary record of it exists.

Whatever the immediate circumstances of the quarrel between Henry and Frederick, it was the result of the policies both men had pursued. Frederick was attempting to assert his authority in Germany and Italy just as Henry was trying to consolidate his in Saxony. While Henry wanted to subordinate his own vassals, he also wanted to maintain his freedom from imperial control. The demand for Goslar, regardless of whether it occurred, is symbolic of this struggle for power.

Part of the struggle involved Henry's dealings with foreign princes. A civil war in Denmark enabled him to make the King of Denmark practically a vassal in return for his support. The king paid tribute to Henry and remained under his control from 1157 until 1171, when he tried to break away. The attempt failed, and Denmark remained a Saxon client until Henry's fall. Frederick was less concerned with Henry's Danish venture than with his friendship toward foreign enemies of imperial policy. He was particularly disturbed by Henry's relations with some of the Italian nobles Frederick was trying to subdue. Henry also visited the Byzantine emperor, who was unfriendly to Frederick. Another of Frederick's enemies, Henry II of England, was a potential problem, as Henry the Lion had married his daughter, Matilda, in 1168.

The final break with the emperor came in 1178. A bishop who had been dispossessed of some of his lands by Henry appealed to Frederick for justice. Naturally, the Saxon nobility supported the bishop. Frederick, who had dismissed many such complaints against Henry on previous occasions, took this opportunity to call his overly powerful vassal to account. Henry ignored three different summonses to appear at the imperial court during 1179 and was outlawed in January, 1180. Bernard of Anhalt, a son of Albert the Bear, became Duke of Saxony, and Saxony became a much smaller territory as many of its fiefs went back to the Church or to other magnates. Frederick was careful not to create such a powerful threat to imperial authority as Henry had.

Henry attempted to fight back but without success. His former vassals proved undependable, and his appeals to foreign courts for aid went unheeded. Finally, in 1182, he went into exile at the court of his father-in-law, Henry II of England. He and his family were well treated in England. His son, Otto, became a favorite of Richard I, who became King of England in 1189. Richard and Otto were first cousins and similar in appearance as well as tastes. Richard made him Earl of York in 1190, when he was only eight years old, tried to obtain the Scottish throne for him, and was his primary supporter when he was elected Holy Roman Emperor Otto IV.

The differences between Frederick and Henry were reconciled, and Henry returned to Germany in 1194. He established a court at Brunswick, where he patronized the troubadours who were to make him the hero of many ballads. He also saw to the building of the church where he and his wife are buried. His interest in history led him to collect a number of chronicles and to oversee the writing of an informational book that he titled *Lucidarius*. Despite the Latin title, it is written in the vernacular German of the period. He had only one year to enjoy these activities, as he died in 1195.

Summary

Henry the Lion was in many ways a product of his time, but his personal attributes qualified him for his time very well. He was probably the most powerful and archetypical of the nobles who prevented the Holy Roman Emperor from establishing a unified government in Germany. There were many other reasons for the failure of Germany to develop a central government after the French or English model, but the ability of the great nobles to maintain their own authority at the expense of central government was one of the key factors.

He was also one of the most important figures in the expansion of Germany to the east. The territory he wrested from the Slavs may have fallen from his personal control, but those areas settled by German colonists were to remain permanently Germanized.

It is interesting to speculate about the results if Henry had succeeded in establishing a centralized, independent Saxony. Bavaria and Saxony, as they then existed, constituted about one third of modern Germany. Such a state in Central Europe would have had profound consequences. He failed, however, and remains interesting only as a prime example of the powerful subjects whose defeat was such an important feature of nation building by medieval European kings. The difference in this case is that there was no building of a German state.

Bibliography

Barraclough, Geoffrey. *The Origins of Modern Germany*. Reprint. New York: W. W. Norton and Co., 1984. Although published originally in 1947, this book remains the standard work in English on medieval Germany. Barraclough takes the position that Henry resented giving up Goslar to Frederick in 1168 and was determined to regain it but that Henry lost all chance of success when Frederick made peace with the Church in 1177. The author also believes that Frederick pursued a policy of keeping the nobles weak after Henry's fall.

____________, ed. *Medieval Germany, 911-1250: Essays by German Historians*. 2 vols. Oxford: Basil Blackwell, 1961. The issue of most interest to modern historians is the interpretation of the constitutional struggle between Frederick and Henry, and some of the articles in this work deal with this topic.

Hampe, Karl. *Germany Under the Salian and Hohenstaufen Emperors*. London: Rowman and Littlefield, 1973. A classic work. With an introduction by Ralph Bennet which comments on the latest German and English works in this field and gives the latest interpretations of the constitutional struggle between Frederick and Henry.

Munz, Peter. *Frederick Barbarossa: A Study in Medieval Politics*. Ithaca, N.Y.: Cornell University Press, 1969. Munz believes that assigning motives of modern state building to twelfth century is anachronistic and that Frederick did not want to centralize his authority. He argues that Frederick's real aim was to keep the German nobles embroiled with one another so he would be free to go on crusades.

Otto of Freising. *The Deeds of Frederick Barbarossa*. New York: W. W. Norton and Co., 1953, rev. ed. 1966. There is little about Henry in this work, but it is worth looking at because Otto was a contemporary of Henry and was involved in a quarrel with him. It is also worthwhile in that it deals extensively with Frederick, who is of obvious importance to Henry's story.

Thompson, James Westfall. *Feudal Germany*. Chicago: University of Chicago Press, 1928. Dated, but probably one of the more readily available works. Thompson champions Henry as a forward-looking ruler who was trying to build a modern, centralized state and who was patriotically trying to prevent abortive, wasteful military campaigns in Italy. He further argues that one of Frederick's greatest wrongs was the destruction of Saxony.

Philip Dwight Jones

PRINCE HENRY THE NAVIGATOR

Born: March 4, 1394; Porto, Portugal
Died: November 13, 1460; Sagres, Portugal
Areas of Achievement: Exploration and warfare
Contribution: Although Prince Henry considered crusading against the North African Muslims to be his primary task, it was his African explorations that later put Portugal at the forefront of the European age of discovery.

Early Life

On February 14, 1387, King John I of Portugal married Philippa, the eldest daughter of Prince John of Gaunt of England. The union proved quite fertile, and the queen gave birth to a succession of children: Duarte in 1391, Pedro in 1392, and her best-known child, Henry (or Enrique) on March 4, Ash Wednesday, 1394. These children were followed by a daughter, Isabel, and two more sons, John and Fernando. Little is known about Prince Henry's youth, although it appears that he grew up in close association with his two elder brothers. They received the usual upbringing of noble youths, learning horsemanship, hunting, and the skills and values associated with late medieval chivalry.

Chivalric values were new to late fourteenth century Portugal, with its isolated location on Western Europe's periphery. It appears that these values arrived with the chaste Queen Philippa from England, and King John I quite readily adopted chivalric ideals for his court and family. Chivalry imposed restraint and sophistication on the rough and ready crusading spirit that had long been indigenous to the Iberian peninsula. These twin value systems of chivalry and crusade against infidels would be the predominant influences on Prince Henry's actions through his entire life.

In 1411, King John I made peace with Castile and declared that he would celebrate the occasion with a joust during which his three oldest sons would be knighted. His sons objected, however, and asked that they be given a chance to earn their knighthood in actual combat according to the best chivalric practices. Since Portugal had just reached a peace treaty with neighboring Castile, the warlike energies of John I's sons needed to be directed farther afield. The Moorish city of Ceuta, located strategically opposite Gibraltar, became their objective. It would be the first major Portuguese move against Islamic territory since about 1250. The expedition was quite large, consisting of 240 ships, thirty thousand sailors, and twenty thousand soldiers, and took two years to prepare. Sailing from the Tagus River on July 23, 1415, the expedition landed at Ceuta on August 21 and immediately assaulted the city. An easy and overwhelming victory resulted for the Crusaders. John's three sons all fought bravely and earned their knighthoods.

Furthermore, Pedro obtained the additional reward of the dukedom of Coimbra, while Henry received the dukedom of Viseu. Returning to Portugal, the young Prince Henry took up frontier guard duty at Viseu for the next several years.

Life's Work

The capture of Ceuta proved quickly to be an expensive disappointment for the Portuguese. Its thriving caravan trade was soon diverted to other coastal cities, while the surrounding Muslim states maintained an attitude of implacable hostility. One party of Portuguese had opposed the expedition to Ceuta from the beginning, and after the conquest they advocated immediate evacuation. Another party, which included Prince Henry, called for the retention of Ceuta and further expansion against the Muslim powers. Their ultimate goal was the winning of North Africa for Christendom. To achieve their objective, Prince Henry advanced a policy of attacking the Muslims head-on in the region of Ceuta, while at the same time trying to approach them from behind by a flanking movement down the west coast of Africa.

In 1416, King John I appointed Prince Henry as governor of Ceuta, although the young man continued to reside at Viseu. A Muslim threat against Ceuta in 1418 prompted Portugal to organize a relief expedition under Henry's command. By this time, the character of the young prince was formed, and he was at the height of his physical powers. According to his chronicler, Gomes Eannes de Zurara, Prince Henry was tall and dark, with a large build and thick, shaggy black hair. His face wore a grave expression that aroused a sense of fear in those around him. Unlike many profligate noblemen of the late Middle Ages, he ascetically shunned both wine and women. In fact, he never married and was reputed to have died a virgin. Instead, Prince Henry directed his abundant energies into crusading and exploring.

Crusading and exploration were expensive enterprises, and throughout his life Prince Henry, who enjoyed living in a princely style, was chronically short of money. He drew revenues from his dukedom of Viseu, to which were added the governorship of Algarve in 1419 and the headship of the Military Order of Christ in 1420. Still, these were not enough, and Henry continually had to seek further sources of revenue. It is this constant quest for money that explains his role in the settlement of Madeira and the Azores Islands and in the Castilian-Portuguese rivalry over the Canary Islands.

It is possible that Europeans discovered the Madeiras as early as 1339, but it is definite that they knew about the islands by 1417, when a strong Castilian expedition visited Porto Santo. Portugal reacted by quickly occupying the islands during 1419 and 1420 with settlers from Prince Henry's province of Algarve. In 1433, King Duarte granted the islands to Henry as a fief, and he drew income from their production of dye-stuffs and grain. The same situation applied to the Azores, which the Portuguese Diogo de Senill discovered in 1427. Domestic animals were dropped off on the islands during the early 1430's in preparation for human settlement. It was not until 1439 that the regent Dom Pedro gave his brother Prince Henry a charter to settle the islands; colonization was begun in the early 1440's. Once again, the production of dye-stuffs and grain provided the profits which helped to fuel Prince Henry's explorations and crusades.

Meanwhile, the exploration of the African coast was delayed by the navigational and psychological barrier of Cape Bojador. This barren promontory extended twenty-five miles out into the Atlantic, where great waves crashed and adverse winds and currents made sailing treacherous. Beyond lay the "Green Sea of Darkness" from which no one ever returned. Between 1424 and 1434, Prince Henry sent out fifteen expeditions with orders to round it. Finally, in 1434, a squire of Prince Henry's household, Gil Eannes, sailed past the dreaded cape on his second attempt. His success removed a formidable psychological barrier to exploration, although the cape still remained a serious navigational menace. The conquest of Cape Bojador was probably Prince Henry's most important contribution to European exploration.

After the passage of Cape Bojador, exploration of the African coast made greater progress. In 1436, the explorer Afonso Gonzalves Baldia reached the bay that he mistakenly called the Rio de Ouro. After that, however, exploration stopped temporarily while Prince Henry concentrated on his true love, a crusade against the Muslims in what became the disastrous Tangier expedition of 1437. From 1438 to 1441, the tumultuous early years of the minority of Afonso V intervened to occupy Portuguese energies, until Henry's brother Pedro defeated the Queen-Mother Lenora for the regency.

A return of stability brought a resumption of exploration. In 1441, Antao Gonzalves brought back the first black slaves from Africa, beginning a profitable but inhumane trade, while Nuno Tristano discovered Cape Blanc. The next year, 1442, saw the first African gold brought back to Portugal, an achievement which allowed them to bypass the Muslim caravan trade. At that point, Prince Henry obtained a royal monopoly of all trading south of Cape Bojador and proceeded for a fee to issue trading licenses to eager merchants.

By 1446, trading expeditions far outnumbered voyages of further discovery. Still, exploration also progressed rapidly with the encouragement of both Prince Henry and his brother Dom Pedro, whose role in early Portuguese exploration has been unfairly ignored. With their encouragement, Dinis Dias discovered Cape Verde in 1444, while Alvaro Fernandes reached the Gambia River the following year. After Pedro fell into disgrace in 1448, however, and was killed at the Battle of Alfarrobeira on May 20, 1449, much of the drive for new discoveries appears to have ended. It revived somewhat during 1454, when the Venetian merchant Alvise da Cadamosto joined the service of Prince Henry. He reached Portuguese Guinea in 1455 and proceeded even farther south the following year, accidentally discovering the Cape Verde Islands and the Bissagos Islands. Cadamosto's primary interest was trading, and it was between 1455 and 1461 that Prince Henry established the fortress-trading post on Arguim Island, near Cape Blanc.

Meanwhile, back in Portugal, the siren call of a crusade against the Muslims tempted the aging Prince Henry once again. During 1456 and 1457, Portugal prepared for a papal crusade against the Ottoman Turks in response to their capture of Constantinople in 1453. When the general crusade failed to materialize, the Portuguese simply redirected their efforts against the Muslims of North Africa. Their fleet, including King Afonso and Prince Henry, sailed on October 17, 1458, and arrived off the Muslim city of Alcacer-Seguer on October 22, capturing it two days later. It was to be Prince Henry's last crusade.

Exploration of the African coast also slowed during Henry's last years, although a brisk trade continued. Pedro de Sintra may have reached Sierra Leone in 1460, but as the farthest point of Portuguese discovery achieved in Prince Henry's lifetime, it was not a particularly impressive addition to the achievements of Cadamosto in 1456. Back in Portugal, the old Prince Henry fell ill at his residence of Sagres and died on November 13, 1460.

Summary

Prince Henry the Navigator is one of the romantic historical figures of whom stories are told to all schoolchildren in the Western world. Modern society finds this Henry attractive, since he was supposedly a lone giant pushing back the darkness of geographic ignorance. It is claimed that he was a navigational innovator, the founder of a school and an observatory for geographic studies at Sagres, and a systematic promoter of exploration, with a view to reaching India by sea. In fact, he was none of these things. Recent scholarship finds no evidence for any technical innovations, any school, or any systematic plan of exploration, especially anything including India as its ultimate goal. Present-day Portuguese do not even recognize him as "the Navigator"; that title was bestowed on him by his English biographer Richard Henry Major in 1868.

The fact is that Prince Henry was a man of the late Middle Ages; chivalric and crusading values motivated him to attack the Muslims and to explore Africa. In addition, as his chronicler Zurara pointed out, his actions befitted the stars under which he was born. Prince Henry's horoscope showed that he "should toil at high and mighty conquests, especially in seeking out things that were hidden from other men and secret." People in medieval times took these predictions seriously, and it was as a medieval Crusader that Prince Henry uncovered places that were hidden and secret and inadvertently helped to open up the great age of discovery in the late fifteenth and sixteenth centuries.

Bibliography

Beazley, Charles Raymond. *Prince Henry the Navigator: The Hero of Portugal and of Modern Discovery, 1394-1400 A.D.* New York: G. P. Putnam's Sons, 1894. Reprint. New York: Burt Franklin, 1968. Beazley follows Major (see below) in viewing Prince Henry as a man of science living before his true time and as a great precursor of the age of exploration. Almost half the book deals with geographical, scientific, and political developments leading up to the time of Prince Henry.

Diffie, Bailey W., and George D. Winius. *Foundations of the Portuguese Empire, 1415-1580*. Minneapolis: University of Minnesota Press, 1977. Although part of a general history of the Portuguese Empire, the first quarter of the volume provides information and interpretation of Prince Henry's career. It is a well-written study and solidly based on primary and secondary sources. Prince Henry clearly appears as a medieval Crusader.

Major, Richard Henry. *The Life of Prince Henry of Portugal Surnamed the Navigator and Its Results*. London: A. Asher and Co., 1868. Reprint. London: Frank Cass, 1967. Major is responsible for Prince Henry being popularly known throughout the English-speaking world as "the Navigator." This biography remains useful, even though it is quite dated in its attribution to Henry of a scientific spirit and of the sole motivating force behind Portuguese exploration.

Sanceau, Elaine. *Henry the Navigator: The Story of a Great Prince and His Times*. New York: W. W. Norton and Co., 1947. As the author of several biographies of great figures from the age of Portuguese expansion, Sanceau possesses considerable skill in artfully blending documentary evidence into an exciting narrative. Unfortunately, she follows the romantic school of interpretation regarding Prince Henry. Her biography should be preferred, however, to the more recent one by John Ure.

Ure, John. *Prince Henry the Navigator*. London: Constable, 1977. Written by an English diplomat who served in Portugal, this full-scale biography does a good job of emphasizing Henry's medieval crusading mentality. It unfortunately also continues to view him as possessing a modern spirit of inquiry and so is largely a mild updating of the earlier romantic interpretations of Prince Henry as the indispensable man of the age of discovery.

Zurara, Gomes Eannes de. *The Chronicle of the Discovery and Conquest of Guinea*. 2 vols. Edited and translated by Charles Raymond Beazley and Edgar Prestage. London: Hakluyt Society, 1896-1899. These contemporary chronicles are the most extensive source for an account of the early Portuguese discoveries and are the only source for some incidents. Unfortunately, they end with the year 1448. The values of chivalry and crusading definitely influenced Zurara, a member of the Order of Christ and the official historian of Prince Henry's career.

Ronald H. Fritze

HERACLITUS OF EPHESUS

Born: fl. 505-500 B.C.; Ephesus, Greece
Died: Date unknown; place unknown
Area of Achievement: Philosophy
Contribution: Heraclitus formulated one of the earliest and most comprehensive theories of the nature of the world, the cosmos, and the soul. His theory that the soul pervaded all parts of the universe and its inhabitants stood in contrast to the ideas of his more mechanistic contemporaries.

Early Life

According to Diogenes Laërtius, Heraclitus was born in the city of Ephesus to an important family that had an ancient and respected reputation. Through his family he inherited public office but resigned in favor of his brother. When his friend Hermodorus was expelled from Ephesus, Heraclitus protested publicly and subsequently withdrew from public life. Heraclitus was a man of great personal integrity, whose main purpose in life was to find the truth and proclaim it for the benefit of humankind, irrespective of the consequences. He attacked the sacred festival of the Bacchanalia, condemned the worship of images of the gods, and spoke unkind words about Pythagoras, Xenophanes, Hecataeus, and Hesiod. His arrogance was legendary. Heraclitus insisted that he was the sole bearer of the truth. He thought that the multitude of common men were too weak of wit to understand the truth, claiming that his work was meant for the few who were intelligent.

To complicate the difficulty presented by this posture, his writings (those that survived) present special problems. Aristotle and Theophrastus observed that his statements were sometimes ambiguous, incomplete, and contradictory. It is no wonder that his contemporaries named him "The Riddler," "The Obscure One," and "The Dark One." Heraclitus was well aware of their criticism, but he was dedicated to his own high purposes.

Life's Work

Heraclitus' book was entitled *Peri physeos* (c. 500 B.C.; *On Nature*). He dedicated the work to Artemis and left a scroll of it in her temple, an act that was not unusual in that culture. Heraclitus would not qualify as a scientist; his talent was more that of the mystic. He had the ability to see further into the nature of things than others did. He was the first to unify the natural and the spiritual worlds, while others saw only the discrete components of nature. Anaximander and Heraclitus were both impressed with the ceaseless change of the temporal world and formulated theories about the primal matter of the universe. Anaximander's primal matter was colorless and tasteless, and otherwise had no characteristics. For Heraclitus, however, that which underlay the world of form and matter was not substance, it was process.

Heraclitus saw the world as a place where change, at every level and every phase of existence, was the most important phenomenon. The basic element of change, and at the heart of the process, was fire. The processes governing the world involved the four elements: fire, water, air, and earth. According to Heraclitus, fire was the element from which the others devolved, and it was always in motion. It was fire in the form of body heat that kept animal forms in motion; it was also able to transform and consume the other basic elements. In essence, air was hot and wet, water was cold and wet, earth was cold and dry, and fire was hot and dry. Under certain circumstances, each of the four elements could be transformed into another (enough water could quench fire; a hot enough fire could reduce earth to ash, or water to steam). All the possible transformations were happening at any given time somewhere in the universe, such as in the cooking of a meal, the thawing of the winter ice, the volcanism of Mount Etna—and even in phenomena known to Heraclitus, such as the atmospheric disturbances of the sunspot cycle or the explosion of a supernova.

Heraclitus described two fundamental directions of this change. In the downward path, some of the fire thickens and becomes the ocean, while part of the ocean dies and becomes land. On the upward path, moist exhalations from the ocean and the land rise and become clouds; they then ignite (perhaps in the form of lightning) and return to fire (presumably the fiery ether, which was thought to dwell in the heights of the sky). If the fiery clouds from which the lightning comes are extinguished, however, then there is a whirlwind (a waterspout, perhaps), and once again the fire returns to the sea and the cycle is complete. All this change and transformation was not, however, simply random motion. There was a cosmic master plan, the Logos. Nothing in the English language translates Logos perfectly. As it stands in the beginning of the Gospel of John, it is usually translated as the Word, which is clearly inadequate in context and requires a definition. In Heraclitus' time, Logos could mean reputation or high worth. This meaning devolved from another definition of Logos: narrative or story.

The flexibility of the word has been a source of considerable debate. The three most important meanings of the word are: (1) general rule or general principle; (2) the carrying out of a general principle; and (3) that which belongs distinctly to the realm of humanness, the faculty of reasoning. First and foremost, the Logos is the universal law, or plan, or process, that animates the whole cosmos. The Logos is the cosmos; it inhabits the cosmos. It is also what makes the difference between the sleeping human and the awakened human. It is, in humans, the wisdom to perceive that the Logos (on the highest level of abstraction) is immanent in the cosmos, that it is the universe's governing principle. That is the fountainhead of true knowledge in Heraclitus' system. All humans have the Logos in common. What they specifically have in common is the realization or perception that they are a part of the whole, which is the Logos. Without that realization they are fundamentally asleep. Within the slumbering human, the Logos lies dormant. Even if a human is technically awake, however, he can still be subject to error if he follows his own private "truth," that is, his own inclinations, and prefers his subjectivity more than he values the Logos. The self-dependence that one would call individuality could then be considered a violation of the Logos.

Though the physical senses are not attuned to the perception of the Logos, they are important in the process that leads to wisdom. For example, the ability to see is a prerequisite that may eventually lead to the perception that there is a plan to the universe. The senses are the mediators between that which is human and that which is cosmic. They are the windows which, during waking hours, connect the human with the portion of the Logos that can be perceived. During sleeping hours those channels are closed and the direct participation in the cosmos ceases. Respiration then becomes a channel by which the direct access can be maintained; the act of breathing maintains minimal contact. The Logos can be considered the soul of the universe. Each awakened human has a portion of higher enlightenment: the soul. Logos, Soul, and Cosmic Fire are eventually different aspects of the same abstraction—the everlasting truth that directs the universe and its conscious constituents. According to Heraclitus, the enlightened soul is hot and dry, like fire, which is why it tends upward, in the direction of the fiery ether. Soul and ether are the same material.

Soul is linked to Logos, but its roots are in the human body which it inhabits. Soul is possibly the healing principle in the body: Heraclitus likened the soul to a spider which, when its web is torn, goes to the site of the injury. Soul is born from moisture and dies when it absorbs too much water. Drunkenness was to Heraclitus a truly bad habit: A moist soul had diminished faculties as its body was also diminished, in that its intellect was stunted and its physical strength lessened.

Though the body was subject to decomposition, some souls seem to have been exempted from physical death (becoming water). Certain situations, among them dying in battle, tune the soul to such a heightened state (with the soul unusually motivated and not weakened by illness and old age) that it merged directly with the world fire. After death, there seems to be no survival of personal identity, though it is likely that the soul-stuff is merged with the Logos and that the Logos is the source of souls that exist in the physical world. Evidently, soul material follows a cycling process of its own. Heraclitus saw that the world was a unity of many parts, but the unity was not immediately manifest. The oneness of the world was the result of an infinite multiplicity. Heraclitus thought that the key to understanding this multiplicity was to look upon the world in terms of the abstract concept of Harmony.

Pythagoras had previously used musical harmony in explaining the attunement and orderliness that he saw in the universe. Heraclitus, however, used the concept of Harmony in a different way. He believed that Harmony existed only where and when there was opposition. A single note struck on a lyre has no harmony of itself. Any two notes struck together, however, form a tension or a contrast between the two sounds, creating a continuum of possible notes between the two notes that have been struck. In terms of a continuum of hot and cold temperatures, not only do the extremes exist, but so also does the continuum exist, bounded by the extremes. At every point between the extremes of hot and cold there is an identifiable point which has a specific temperature that is a function of both extremes.

Similarly, every virtue has a corresponding vice. Neither extreme on this scale is especially significant in human behavior: Few people, if any, represent extremes of either virtue or vice; most live in the continuum between. Ethical considerations motivate good individuals to tend toward the good in a choice between good and evil, and the measure of a person's soul is where one stands on the continuum defined by good and evil. Heraclitus' most controversial statement on the subject was that the opposites that define the continuum are identical. Hate and love, therefore, would have to be one and the same. The absence of either defining term destroys the continuum, and without the continuum the two extremes cannot relate to each other. They define a world in which the people are passionate haters and ardent lovers, with no real people in between. The Harmony that Heraclitus discerned was dependent on the tension between two opposites. The cosmos was, for him, a carefully and beautifully balanced entity, poised between a great multiplicity of contrasting interests, engaged in continual strife. The sum total of all these contrasting interests, however, was the Harmony that no one saw except the truly enlightened souls. Only the Logos, which was One, and which created and tuned the Harmony, was exempt from the balancing of opposites.

Perhaps the best-known of Heraclitus' observations is that everything in the universe is incessantly moving and changing. He considered all matter to be in a state of constant transformation from one form to a different form and, at the same time, from one set of physical qualities to another. Not only did he believe that the Logos bestowed life on all its parts, but he also believed that the forms of matter were intrinsically alive and that the flux was a function of the life within the matter. All life was caught up in the constant change: Everything was involved in processes of decomposition and in the reconstitution of new forms from the products of decay.

As the Greeks viewed the world, they saw only the portions of the movement that were available within the limits of their senses. Though they were not aware of the whole spectrum of movement, they were intelligent enough to extrapolate from what they could perceive. A continuous stream of water wearing away a stone was to them a good reminder of the fact that many processes of change were not perceptible in their time scale.

Heraclitus summed it up poetically in his famous analogy: "You cannot step twice into the same river, for fresh waters are flowing on." From one second to the next, the flux of things changes the world; though the river is the same river, the flux of things has moved its waters downstream, and new water from upstream has replaced the old. According to Diogenes Laërtius and others, "The cosmos is born out of fire and again resolved into fire in alternate periods for ever." One line of interpretation is that the world is periodically destroyed by a universal conflagration. More plausible, however, is the assumption that this is a restatement of Heraclitus' doctrine that fire is the one primal element from which all others derive and into which all elements are eventually transmuted by the workings of the eternal flux. In support of this argument is a phrase from the remaining fragments of Heraclitus' work: "From all things one, and from one all things." In Heraclitus' cosmology, however, there was the concept of a Great Year that occurred every 10,800 years, at which time the sun, moon, and other heavenly bodies returned to a hypothetical starting place. These bodies, though they were not exempt from the principle of constant flux, were permanent in their forms and in their heavenly paths. Beyond the measured paths of their orbits was the fiery ether of the unmoving Logos.

Summary

Heraclitus was quite unlike his contemporaries, both in terms of his personality and in the nature and scope of his thoughts. Whereas the works of his contemporaries were more in the line of primitive scientific inquiry, the endeavors of Heraclitus were more closely akin to poesy and perhaps prophecy. His aim was not to discover the material world but to seek out the governing principles within and behind the physical forms. In this respect, he was the most mystical of the Greeks.

Though the body of Heraclitus' work is faulted by time, by problems of interpretation, and by obscurity of the text (some of which was solely Heraclitus' fault), it is clear that he believed he had provided a definitive view of the processes that govern the cosmos and the workings of the human soul. His ideas were novel and daring in their time. At the center of his cosmos is the concept of constant change, which masks the concept of unity: All things are in balance, yet all things are in motion and transition, with fire playing the central role, and the Logos disposing and directing the parts. The Logos also governs human actions, reaching into the deeper parts of the personality, with the Oversoul touching the soul material within, fire outside calling to the fire within to awake, to look, to learn, to become, and to unite.

Bibliography

Burnet, John. *Early Greek Philosophy*. London: A. and C. Black, 1892, 4th ed. 1952. Chapter 3 is devoted to Heraclitus and is probably the best of the nineteenth century English works that discuss Heraclitus. It has considerable insight and is readable without being dated.

Fairbanks, Arthur. *The First Philosophers of Greece*. London: K. Paul, Trench, Trübner, and Co., 1898. This volume has a good section on Heraclitus, including the Greek text of the fragments as well as an English translation. The discussion is short and basic and covers most of the important points.

Guthrie, W. K. C. *A History of Greek Philosophy*. Vol. 1, *The Earlier Presocratics and the Pythagoreans*. Cambridge: Cambridge University Press, 1962. This volume is one of the best works on Heraclitus' contemporaries and contains an excellent extended discussion of Heraclitus.

Heidegger, Martin, and Eugen Fink. *Heraclitus Seminar, 1966-67*. University: University of Alabama Press, 1979. This work is an extended dialogue between two important scholars, with Fink supplying more of the conversation. The subject is (in general) the relation of the one to the many in the works of Heraclitus.

Kahn, Charles H. *The Art and Thought of Heraclitus: An Edition of the Fragments with Translation and Commentary*. Cambridge: Cambridge University Press, 1979. This volume is a fine and useful scholarly tool, although not comprehensive. It includes the Greek text of the fragments and an English translation, as well as a short but very provocative appendix that discusses the possibility of a link between Heraclitus and the Orient.

Kirk, G. S. *Heraclitus, the Cosmic Fragments*. Cambridge: Cambridge University Press, 1954. A deep and thorough analysis of some of the Heraclitian fragments, this volume focuses on the "Cosmic" fragments—those that are relevant to the world as a whole, the Logos, the doctrine of opposites, and the action of fire.

Kirk, G. S., and J. E. Raven. *The Pre-Socratic Philosophers: A Critical History with a Selection of Texts*. Cambridge: Cambridge University Press, 1957, reprint 1983. One of the chapters provides a very good short analysis of Heraclitus. The book itself is one of the very best on Greek thought and the individual Greek philosophers.

Mourelatos, Alexander. *The Pre-Socratics: A Collection of Critical Essays*. Garden City, N.Y.: Anchor Books, 1974. A collection of critical essays covering the major contemporaries of Heraclitus. Included in the book are four fine essays on Heraclitus.

Sallis, John, and Kenneth Maly, eds. *Heraclitean Fragments: A Companion Volume to the Heidegger/Fink Seminar on Heraclitus*. University: University of Alabama Press, 1980. This is a companion volume to a seminar that addressed Heraclitean topics. It pursues further some aspects of the Heidegger-Fink dialogue, but it also discusses a number of other topics related to Heraclitus.

Schofield, Malcolm, and Martha Craven Nussbaum, eds. *Language and Logos: Studies in Ancient Greek Philosophy Presented to G. E. L. Owen*. Cambridge: Cambridge University Press, 1982. This collection of articles includes two rather good ones on Heraclitus.

West, M. L. *Early Greek Philosophy and the Orient*. Oxford: Clarendon Press, 1971. Book examines the possibility between Greek thought and the ideas of the Middle East. About half of the text is relevant to Heraclitus.

Wheelwright, Philip. *Heraclitus*. Princeton, N.J.: Princeton University Press, 1959. An excellent and well-written volume, the text reads very well because footnotes and matter not relevant to main points are relegated to an appendix. Includes a very good bibliography.

Richard Badessa

HERACLIUS

Born: c. 575; possibly Cappadocia
Died: Probably February 11, 641; Constantinople
Areas of Achievement: Government and conquest
Contribution: Seizing the East Roman (Byzantine) Imperial throne amid seemingly fatal crises, Heraclius turned back the onslaughts of the Persians and Avars, only to see his work largely undone by the Arab conquests. Nevertheless, he and his successors initiated institutional reorganization that would save and revitalize the empire.

Early Life

Heraclius came from a wealthy and distinguished Cappadocian family in central Asia Minor, possibly (though not incontrovertibly) of Armenian descent. His father, an able general of the same name, was rewarded for his services by his old friend the emperor Maurice (c. 539-602) with the office of exarch, or viceroy, of North Africa. When his father took up residence in its capital, Carthage, about 600, the younger Heraclius was about twenty-five years old. No information survives about the son's life until then.

In 602, the emperor Maurice was dethroned and cruelly murdered by a crude, half-barbarian usurper named Phocas. His regime became a reign of terror against the nobility in the capital, Constantinople, while the previously strong military efforts against the empire's enemies were totally neglected. The elder Heraclius was apparently planning some action of his own against the murderer of his old friend and benefactor when he was invited in 608 by exasperated leaders in Constantinople to assist them in removing the tyrant. Too old to lead the action in person, the exarch organized a long-range strategy of rebellion to be led by his kinsmen. Under his nephew, Nicetas, son of the exarch's brother, and his chief-of-staff, Gregory, a force was able to win control of the strategic province of Egypt by late 609 or early 610.

The second phase of the project was a naval expedition led by the exarch's son, the younger Heraclius, then about thirty-four or thirty-five years old. He reached Constantinople by the end of September, 610, and his arrival prompted a rising there which brought down Phocas. With the usurper roughly dispatched, there was apparently some uncertainty about the choice of his successor, and his dissident son-in-law, the general Priscus, may have hoped to claim it. Yet the senate and the populace declared Heraclius their rescuer. Thus, on October 5, 610, Heraclius was crowned emperor and, at the same time, was married to his first wife, Eudoxia.

Life's Work

Heraclius assumed rule of a state that soon seemed headed for destruction from paired foreign threats. In the Balkans, the Turkic Avars and their Slavic subject peoples were breaking through the borders and mounting a drive toward Constantinople itself. Meanwhile, Khosrow II (590-628), the Persian king, had invaded the imperial territory supposedly to avenge his former ally Maurice, but his aggression soon became a campaign to restore the great empire of Achaemenid days. Imperial forces were unable to hold back a series of Persian thrusts which captured Antioch, Damascus, and Jerusalem, the latter with terrible slaughter and calculated violation of the supreme Christian shrines. Egypt was invaded and overrun by 620, and attacks were launched at Asia Minor, with talk of the new Xerxes crossing soon to Europe.

Against these threats, Heraclius seems to have done little in his first ten years of reign. Although physically strong, brave, and intelligent, Heraclius displayed fluctuations between boldness and indecisiveness; patterns of emotional imbalance in his family suggest that he may have been a manic-depressive type himself. He also faced acute problems, both personal and political, in his early years in power. Following the death of his father, the old exarch, came the death in 612 of his epileptic wife, Eudoxia, after she had given birth to two children. In his grief, he was persuaded by his mother to marry, about eighteen months later, his own niece, Martina, twenty-three years his junior. This intelligent and devoted, if ambitious, woman made him a good wife, but the marriage provoked Church indignation and popular hostility, while the fact that most of their eventual ten children were born defective was taken as proof of divine retribution for their incest.

Heraclius also had to assert his right to lead. Priscus, resentful perhaps because he missed his chance at the throne, was openly rude and unreliable; only by a carefully planned ruse was Heraclius able, in late 612, to strip him of command and imprison him. Beyond this, Heraclius had to deal with the veritable collapse of the empire's once-fine military system and the rapid dwindling of resources and revenue. Heraclius was by no means inactive, but he may well have had his moments of despair. According to one source, around 619 he considered leaving Constantinople to make Carthage his base for a military countereffort. According to this report, panic in the capital prompted the patriarch Sergius I to exact an oath from Heraclius that he would never abandon Constantinople. The story reflects the fact that Sergius made an understanding with the emperor by which vast quantities of the Church's wealth were made available as its contribution to the vindication of both empire and Christian faith. With these resources, Heraclius seems to have begun building a new military force, one emphasizing cavalry. He is said to have retired to study strategy and military lore intensively, and it is possible that the *Strategikon*, or military manual, traditionally attributed to the emperor Maurice, might have been written, or at least rewritten, by Heraclius during this period of military buildup.

Heraclius also broke a tradition of more than two centuries, that the emperor left military campaigning to his generals, by insisting that he would lead his troops in person. After a solemn departure ceremony on April 4, 622, Heraclius crossed to Asia Minor, outmaneuvered the Persian forces for some months, and then won a handsome victory in February, 623, temporarily relieving the threat to that area. Back in Constantinople, he was obliged to negotiate anew with the restless Avars, from whom he had already purchased a truce at the cost of heavy tribute; at one point, he barely escaped capture by them in a treacherous ambush. With no response to his overtures for peace with the Persians, Heraclius renewed his offensive in early 624, determined to carry the war into the Persians' land. Invading by way of Armenia and causing the Persian king to flee, Heraclius stormed and desecrated the Zoroastrian shrine city, in retaliation for the profanation of Jerusalem. Heraclius spent the following year cultivating allies among the peoples of the Caucasia and trying to take control of Armenian territories.

In 626, as his operations returned to Asia Minor, Heraclius faced a new crisis. The Persians had menaced Constantinople only passingly before, but now they entered into an agreement with the Avars, encouraging and supporting them in a direct attack on the capital. The Avars seemed genuinely determined to take the city, while the Persians hoped that the attack would force Heraclius to come to its rescue, thereby abandoning his campaign against them. The emperor, however, gambled that the city could hold out without him, relying on its magnificent fortifications, its able commanders, and the leadership of Sergius. His risk proved worth taking: After a ferocious siege, from late June to early August, the Avars admitted failure and withdrew, their power in the Balkans crumbling. Heraclius, who had continued his operations meanwhile in Asia Minor, was able now to redouble his efforts with enhanced prestige.

Much of 627 was spent in further building of his forces and arranging an alliance with the powerful Khazars of the Caucasia. At the end of the year, he resumed his invasion of Persian territory, and on December 12, 627, he confronted the Persian army before the ruins of ancient Nineveh. The outcome was a crushing defeat for the Persians, whose army was broken, but the emperor failed to follow up on his victory immediately, resuming his pursuit of the fleeing Persian king only after some weeks. Taking one royal capital, Dastagird, the vacillating Heraclius decided not to attack another. Yet obstinate to the end, Khosrow was dethroned by a rebellion and murdered in late February, 628, his place taken by his son. The new king sued for peace, and Heraclius gladly negotiated a reestablishment of original boundaries and restoration of holy relics. Making a triumphal procession to Constantinople, Heraclius entered it amid wild rejoicing in September, 628. During the next two years, Heraclius supervised the recovery of the liberated territories and at some point ceremonially restored the Holy Cross to Jerusalem as a symbol of Christian victory.

Aging and worn out, Heraclius devoted the ensuing years to securing the reestablishment of imperial government in the recovered territories, to pursuing religious pacification, and to arranging provisions of succession among members of his growing family. Yet he was not allowed to rest on his laurels: Barely was his heroic war of recovery ended when he was faced with the unexpected onslaught of the Arab conquests. Newly unified under the banner of the prophet Muhammad and taking advantage of the mutual exhaustion of Persia and the empire, the Arabs launched initial raids that soon turned into programs of conquest. Imperial forces resisting them were twice defeated in 634 and again the following year, when the Arabs were able to take Damascus. Heraclius attempted to coordinate a defensive program in person and gathered a final, large army. Yet its ambush and destruction on the banks of the Yarmuk River in August, 636, removed all hope of successful resistance. Heraclius abandoned Syria in despair while the cities of the region fell in rapid succession to the conquerors: Jerusalem capitulating in 638, and the imperial capital of Caesarea in 640. By that time, with Syria-Palestine overrun, the Arabs had begun their invasion of Egypt.

Meanwhile, broken and ailing, Heraclius halted his progress to Constantinople at the Bosporos Thracius, refusing for many months to cross into his capital. A congenital hydrophobia, reinforced by a prophecy of his death by water, held him back until, in early 638, under threats of conspiracies and succession problems, a crossing was arranged: A vast pontoon bridge was built across the channel, with trees and shrubbery planted on either side to hide the water from view as he moved across. Back in his capital, Heraclius attempted to resolve the long-standing religious disputes, hoping to mollify the dissident Monophysites, whose unrest in Syria-Palestine and Egypt is thought to have undermined the defense of those areas. Later in 638, he issued his doctrinal decree on this matter, the *Ekthesis*, and thereafter attempted to negotiate its acceptance among various branches of the Church. Heraclius' health continued to decay, and he at last died on February 11, 641.

Summary

Heraclius' sometimes inconsistent character, together with the disasters of his last years, has compromised the brilliance of his real achievements. It is true that, after saving the empire heroically from one nearly fatal crisis, he died unable to protect it from another. Yet he was fighting external forces beyond his control. Also foredoomed was his effort to resolve the Monophysite dissent: By introducing the compromise doctrine of Monothelitism in his *Ekthesis*, he only complicated further an already unsolvable situation. Nevertheless, if he left a set of grim legacies behind him, he also left the dynasty he founded, including several emperors of dedication and talent, who were to cope with these legacies through the rest of the sixth century.

He also left at least the beginnings of a governmental transformation that would help make possible the successful struggle of his heirs. Much controversy has surrounded the development of the so-called Theme System, which is dated generally to the sixth century. Under this system, Asia Minor was divided into a set of military districts, garrisoned by native troops supported by the revenues of small agricultural freeholds. This military pattern soon took over the local civil functions and was eventually applied to other parts of the empire's territories, becoming in time the basis for the surviving empire's military, administrative, agrarian, and fiscal organization. It has been traditional to credit Heraclius with initiating these organizational reforms—whether as a part of his preparations for war with the Persians or after his victory over them (and even in imitation of their institutions)—but historians are by no means agreed on how clear or complete such credit should be. To Heraclius' age is attributed also the final abandonment of older Roman administrative forms and Latin titles and their replacement with a more fully Hellenized chancery.

While controversy about him and his achievements will remain, there is no doubt of Heraclius' genuine role as a savior of his state and of his age as a turning point in the transformation of the late Roman into the Byzantine Empire. In the later medieval West, he would be remembered as a prototype of the "crusader" sovereign, triumphant over unbelievers in the cause of the Christian faith.

Bibliography

Bury, J. B. *A History of the Later Roman Empire from Arcadius to Irene, 395 A.D. to 800 A.D.* 2 vols. London: Macmillan, 1889. In 1923, Bury published another two-volume study to replace this one, but it extends only to 565, leaving volume 2 of this older set still a useful, if somewhat outdated, treatment. Several chapters deal with the life and age of Heraclius.

Maurice. *Maurice's Strategikon: Handbook of Byzantine Military Strategy*. Translated by George T. Dennis. Philadelphia: University of Pennsylvania Press, 1984. This important military manual is still ascribed to Heraclius' most significant predecessor, but its contents reflect the kind of organization with which Heraclius achieved his victories. The excellent translation has a useful introduction.

Ostrogorsky, George. *History of the Byzantine State*. Rev. ed. New Brunswick, N.J.: Rutgers University Press, 1969. Although slightly out of date on bibliography and interpretation, this work is still the most comprehensive one-volume study of the history and institutions of the empire from the early fourth through the mid-fifteenth century. Ostrogorsky's arguments on the Theme System are no longer fully acceptable, but his treatment of the age of Heraclius and his successors still puts the system in excellent perspective.

Stratos, Andreas N. *Byzantium in the Seventh Century*. Vol. 1, *602-634*, and Vol. 2, *634-641*. Amsterdam: Adolf M. Hakkert, 1968, 1972. These are the opening volumes (of six in the original Greek version, five in the English translation) of a massive work, the most complete on the entire seventh century. In the absence of any conventional biography of Heraclius, these two volumes are a viable substitute. Stratos discusses in detail the confused, fragmentary, and problematical sources from this difficult epoch. The most comprehensive, exhaustive, and up-to-date study available.

Theophanes. *The Chronicle of Theophanes: An English Translation of anni mundi 6095-6305 (A.D. 602-813)*. Translated by Harry Turtledove. Philadelphia: University of Pennsylvania Press, 1982. There is no English translation of the most important contemporary source for Heraclius' life and reign, the historical epic by poet George of Pisidi, but the appropriate sections of the monkish chronicle by the early ninth century Theophanes, for all of its faults or limitations, is still one of the most important surviving texts on the Heraclian age. The sole English translation (and it is only a partial one), with excellent introduction and notes clarifying some of the problems involved with using this source.

John W. Barker

HERO OF ALEXANDRIA

Born: fl. A.D. 62; Alexandria
Died: Date unknown; Alexandria
Areas of Achievement: Mathematics and science
Contribution: Hero wrote about mechanical devices and is the most important ancient authority on them. Some of these were his own inventions, including a rudimentary steam engine and windmill. He also investigated mathematics, where his most noted contribution was a method for approximating square roots.

Early Life

Virtually nothing is known about the personal life of Hero (also known as Heron) of Alexandria, other than the fact that an eclipse of the moon visible from Alexandria and mentioned in one of his books occurred in A.D. 62. Under the Roman Empire, Alexandria flourished somewhat less than it had under the Ptolemies, but the famous museum was still a center of research and learning where scientists and philosophers were active. Technology also continued to make amazing strides, so that Hero found an atmosphere conducive to his own theories and inventions. His writings show that he was an educated man, familiar with Greek, Latin, Egyptian, and even Mesopotamian sources, and reveal a wide-ranging mind unusual for his time. There is no indication that he worked for either a Roman patron or the Roman government.

Life's Work

Hero's greatest renown results from the fact that many of his writings on mechanics and mathematics are extant. The mechanical works include the two-volume *Pneumatica* (*The Pneumatics of Hero of Alexandria*, 1851), on devices operated by compressed air, steam, and water; *Peri automatopoietikes* (*Automata*, 1971), on contrivances to produce miraculous appearances in temples; the three-volume *Mechanica*, surviving in Arabic, on weight-moving machines; *Dioptra* (partial English translation, 1963), on instruments for sighting and other purposes; *Catoptrica* (surviving in Latin), on mirrors; and two artillery manuals, *Belopoeïca* (English translation, 1971) and *Cheiroballistra* (English translation, 1971), on different types of catapults. Missing are other works on weight-lifting machines (*Baroulkos*, which might be a name for part of *Mechanica*), water clocks, astrolabes, balances, and the construction of vaults.

Of his mathematical treatises, there exist the three-volume *Metrica*, on the measurement and division of surfaces and bodies, and *Definitiones*, on geometrical terms. There are other works, more or less heavily edited by later redactors, such as *Geometrica*, *Stereometrica*, and *Peri metron* (also known as *On Measures*), all treatises on measurement, as well as *Geodaesia* and *Geoponica* or *Liber geeponicus*, on the measurement of land. A commentary on Euclid is represented by extensive quotations in the Arabic work of an-Nairīzī.

The contents of Hero's mechanical works reveal the state of technological knowledge during the early Roman Empire, reflecting the heritage of the Hellenistic period and Ptolemaic Alexandria in particular. Later writers referred to him as "the mechanic" (*ho mechanikos*). In most cases, he gives the best or most complete description extant of ancient machines. In *Mechanica*, he gives attention to the simple machines—lever, pulley, wheel and axle, inclined plane, screw, and wedge—but he goes on to present others, there and in his other books, that are more complex.

Devices described by Hero include a machine for cutting screw threads on a wooden cylinder; a syringe; an apparatus for throwing water on a fire by hydraulic pressure, which is produced by a two-cylinder force pump (designed by the earlier Alexandrian mechanic, Ctesibius); and the odometer, for measuring distances by a wheeled vehicle. Of value to scholars, there was a pantograph for enlarging drawings and an automatic wick-trimmer for lamps. Hero provides a careful account of the diopter, a sighting instrument used in surveying and astronomy which contains sophisticated gears.

The automata mentioned by Hero are of fascinating variety, including singing birds, drinking animals, hissing serpents, dancing bacchants, and gods such as Dionysus and Hercules performing various actions. Some of these were activated by lighting a fire on an altar or pouring libations into a container, and their effect on worshippers when seen in temples can be imagined. Hero also described coin-operated machines to dispense holy water, a sacred wand that whistled when dipped into water, and a device powered by heated air that would open temple doors without any visible human effort. In order to invent such a device, Hero had to recognize that a vessel containing air was not empty but contained a substance which could exert force, a fact that he clearly explained in *The Pneumatics*. His demonstration depends on the observation that water will not enter a vessel filled with air unless the air is allowed to escape. He also was aware that air is compressible, which he said was the result of its being made up of particles separated by space.

The nonproductive character of some of the inventions just mentioned has led some modern critics to call Hero's technology impractical, but he also described demonstrably useful machines. Cranes, which could be used to lower actors portraying gods into theaters (the famous *deus ex machina*), also were available to help in heavy construction. There were other weight-lifting machines utilizing gears. Cogs and gears were highly developed even before Hero's day, as archaeological evidence such as the Antikythera Machine, a calendrical, mechanical analogue computer retrieved from the Aegean seafloor, demonstrates. Hero also describes a twin screw press. He knew the use of compound pulleys, winches, and cogwheels interacting with screws. Not merely theoretical, his catapults were effective in war, particularly in siege operations. There was also the *gastraphetes* or "belly shooter," a kind of crossbow.

Hero's most famous invention was a prototype steam engine called the aeolipile. A hollow sphere, free-spinning, was mounted on a pipe and bracket on the lid of a boiling vessel. Steam from the vessel came up through the pipe and escaped through open, bent pipes on the sphere's surface, causing the sphere to rotate. Less often remarked but also significant is his windmill, used to work the water pump of a musical organ. Both of these show that Hero recommended harnessing sources of power which were not actually exploited until centuries later. In the form in which he presented them, to be sure, these engines were extremely inefficient, and the industrial processes of the first century might not have allowed improvement to the point where they could have been widely used.

In mathematics, Hero emphasized pragmatic applications rather than pure theory. For example, he showed methods of approximating the values of square and cube roots. In his writings on geometry, he followed Euclid closely, making only minor original comments or improvements. The first book of *Peri metron* deals with the mensuration of plane and solid figures, and the second explains the way to calculate the volumes of various solids. The third explains problems of the division of plane and solid figures.

Summary

Hero of Alexandria looms large in the history of ancient technology because a considerable portion of his writings on mechanics still exists, and little else on the subject survives from the Greek and Roman world. He preserved much information that came to him from earlier writers whose works have been lost, and his own contribution has been downgraded by some modern scholars because it is unclear how much he owes to previous writers, including Archimedes, Strato of Lampsacus, Philon of Byzantium, and especially Ctesibius of Alexandria. This tendency is probably unfair, however, since his work reflects a systematic mind and tireless research. Moreover, some of his ideas, such as the harnessing of steam and wind power, were clearly ahead of their time.

Although he was interested in the principles of mechanics, Hero was not primarily a theoretician. His mechanics and his mathematics are presented in a way that would have made them useful to the practical engineer of his day. For example, in *Stereometrica*, he shows how to calculate the number of spectators a theater would hold and the number of wine jars that could be stacked in the hold of a ship of a certain size. Both are approximations intended for utilitarian needs.

Hero's writings were prized by later authors. Both Pappus of Alexandria (fourth century A.D.) and Proclus (fifth century) quoted from his works. Some of his works were translated and preserved by learned Arabs, and an-Nairīzī commented extensively on Hero's critique of Euclid. Four of Hero's shorter books on mechanics were published in Paris in 1693. Interest in Hero accelerated with the Industrial Revolution, and he has received much attention in histories of mechanics and mathematics which have appeared in the twentieth century.

Bibliography

Drachmann, Aage Gerhardt. *The Mechanical Technology of Greek and Roman Antiquity: A Study of the Literary Sources*. Madison: University of Wisconsin Press, 1963. Contains translations of Hero's mechanical writings, with useful running commentary. Also including sections from Vitruvius and Oreibasios, this book gives a clear idea of the written evidence for ancient mechanical technology.

Heath, Thomas. *A History of Greek Mathematics*. 2 vols. Oxford: Clarendon Press, 1921. Volume 2 includes an excellent, detailed chapter on Hero's mathematical achievements. Heath's comments about Hero's dates have now been superseded by good evidence that he lived in the mid-first century A.D.

Landels, John G. *Engineering in the Ancient World*. Berkeley: University of California Press, 1978. Hero is discussed in the context of the development of technology, and Landels provides a useful brief treatment of Hero and his major writings in the final chapter.

Marsden, E. W. *Greek and Roman Artillery: Technical Treatises*. Oxford: Clarendon Press, 1971. This book includes the texts and translation of Hero's two works on war machines, *Belopoïeca* and *Cheiroballistra*, with illuminating diagrams and helpful notes and commentary.

Singer, Charles Joseph, ed. *A History of Technology*. Vol. 3, *From the Renaissance to the Industrial Revolution, c. 1500-c. 1750*. Oxford: Clarendon Press, 1954-1978. Despite its title, volume 3 contains an informative section on Hero's diopter.

J. Donald Hughes

HEROD THE GREAT

Born: 73 B.C.; probably Idumaea, Palestine
Died: Spring, 4 B.C.; Jericho
Area of Achievement: Government
Contribution: As a loyal king of Judaea under Roman administration, Herod brought peace, prosperity, and a cultural flowering to the land he ruled. Nevertheless, negative aspects of his reign—including harsh dealings with family members and the inability to placate his Jewish subjects—have tended to overshadow these positive achievements.

Early Life

Herod was born into a prominent family of Idumaeans, an Arab people whose capital was Hebron, a city south of Jerusalem. During the time of Herod's grandfather, Antipater, Idumaea had been conquered by Jewish armies and its citizens were forced to convert to Judaism. It is not clear, at that time or in subsequent periods, exactly how deeply the beliefs and practices of Judaism were ingrained into the lives of Idumaeans such as Herod's family.

At the time of the Idumaean conquest, the Jews of the Holy Land were politically independent and ruled over by a royal family known as the Hasmonaeans. They were descendants of Judas Maccabees and his brothers, who had led a successful revolt (beginning in 168 or 167 B.C.) against their Syrian overlords and for the continuance of the monotheistic faith of Israel. When the Idumaeans came under Jewish domination later in that century, Herod's grandfather served members of the Hasmonaean dynasty with some distinction. Herod's father, also named Antipater, in turn was also closely allied to some of the Hasmonaeans. By the time of Herod's birth, a rift had developed in the Jewish royal family, with two brothers, Aristobulus and Hyrcanus, vying for the throne and the religiously significant position of high priest. Herod's father supported the elder of the brothers, Hyrcanus, but the matter was still in doubt when the rival claimants both appealed for support to the Roman general Pompey the Great, then in Damascus, Syria. That was in 63, when Herod himself was about ten years old.

Antipater's maneuvers were decisive in winning Pompey's support for Hyrcanus, whose personality seemed as weak and passive as Antipater's was aggressive and active. During the years that Herod was growing up, his father continued to show support for Hyrcanus. In fact, Antipater's actions were aimed as much at bringing his own family to the favorable notice of powerful Romans. These twin concerns—family and Rome—continued to be prominent in the subsequent career of Antipater's most famous son, Herod.

In the early 40's, Julius Caesar became a force in the Near East, and Antipater provided him with significant military support. For this, he was rewarded by Caesar, who confirmed his growing prestige while not totally displacing the Hasmonaean Hyrcanus. Antipater was able to name Herod as governor of the area of Galilee and to place other of his children (he had four sons and a daughter) in positions of power. Shortly after Caesar's death, Antipater was assassinated, a murder that Herod himself avenged. In the decade that followed, the confusion in Rome was mirrored in the provinces, and local leaders such as Herod had to be resourceful to retain power—and their lives. Herod succeeded admirably.

Hyrcanus' brother had been killed, but one of his nephews joined with the Parthians (an eastern rival to the Romans) to wrest the throne from Hyrcanus. The resultant civil war forced Herod to flee. This turned out to be but a temporary setback, however, for Herod ultimately reached Rome and gained the friendship and backing of the two most powerful individuals of the day, Marc Antony and Octavian (later Augustus). In response to their urging, the senate of Rome declared that henceforth Herod was to be King of Judaea. That was in the year 40, when Herod was in his early thirties.

Life's Work

On the basis of his family background and earlier achievements, it would appear that Herod was an ideal choice to occupy the kingship of Judaea—at least from the Roman point of view. He and his family had shown themselves to be loyal subjects and deft leaders. Herod, it seemed, could give the Romans what they wanted most: steady payment of taxes and other levies, military support against common enemies, internal peace and stability within the lands he ruled. Moreover, Herod possessed physical characteristics that the Romans appreciated. He was tall, athletic, and able to enjoy and appreciate manly activities such as hunting and riding. Dressed in proper Roman garb, he looked and acted at home in the courts of the powerful Romans whom he had to please.

There is every reason to think that his Roman benefactors were very pleased indeed with Herod's initial actions. In 40, he became a king in name, but not in fact, for his capital, Jerusalem, was still in the hands of his rivals. Within three years, that is, by 37, he had regained control of his capital and the land that was now his kingdom. At this point, Herod probably looked forward to a long and relatively serene reign. Longevity he got (approximately thirty-three years); serenity was to prove far more elusive.

From the beginning, there were substantial numbers of Jewish subjects who doubted the depth of Herod's commitment to Judaism. His Idumaean ancestry led to the taunt that he was but a half Jew. His commitment to Rome, with its polytheism and philosophical pluralism, was—in the opinion of many in Jerusalem—incompatible with the relatively austere monotheistic faith of Israel. Criticisms of Herod in this regard preceded his assumption of the kingship, and they undoubtedly increased as he consolidated power. A more pressing challenge, however, soon presented itself.

Herod was a king, and there was no mistaking it. Yet the Jews still had their own royal dynasty in the surviving members of the Hasmonaean family. Hyrcanus, while essentially powerless, was still a potential rival. Herod sought to neutralize this threat, even turn it to his advantage, by marrying Hyrcanus' granddaughter, Mariamne. Now, he may have thought, people would at last tire of bringing up details of his past, for the children he and Mariamne would produce would be royal from both the Jewish and the Roman perspective. If such were his thoughts, he erred grievously. Hyrcanus was too old to pose a threat, but Mariamne's mother, Alexandra, and eventually Mariamne herself were not. Then, too, there was Mariamne's brother Aristobulus, whom Herod was forced to appoint as high priest. One by one, these Hasmonaeans were to be eliminated by Herod, for faults real and imagined. His murder of Mariamne in 29 was especially unsettling for Herod and may have pushed him to—and over—the brink of mental disorder and instability. In his anti-Hasmonaean actions, Herod was generally supported by members of his Idumaean family and in particular by his sister, Salome.

The Romans were not overly concerned about Herod's domestic problems at this time. Herod had grown very close to Antony, who was the virtual ruler of the eastern portion of the Empire that included the lands Herod governed. When Antony did intervene, it was usually at the insistence of his queen, Cleopatra VII, who, according to one account, coveted the person of Herod as much as she did his lands. The civil war of the late 30's that pitted Antony against Octavian found Herod continuing to provide vital assistance to his benefactor, Antony. It is a credit to Herod's extraordinary abilities as diplomat and as briber that Octavian allowed him to retain his position after Antony's resounding defeat.

The fifteen-year period from 28 to 13 B.C. was the high point of Herod's reign. The most visible sign of this prosperity was the ambitious building program that Herod undertook. Throughout his kingdom and beyond, he constructed temples, amphitheaters, and even an entire city (Caesarea, on the Mediterranean coast) to honor the Romans and the civilization they represented. Part of that civilization was the worship of many gods through sacrificial offerings, athletic and dramatic competitions, and a wide array of other public functions. Herod actively promoted such activities, partly because he knew that they were important to his Roman overlords and partly—it is fair to say—because he himself enjoyed them. The Romans and their gods had been good to him, and he was only giving them their due.

Herod was not without gratitude toward the God of Israel, whose people he ruled and whose favor he also solicited. Herod's rebuilding of the Temple of Jerusalem, a vast complex that stood at the very center of the Judaism of his day, was the most tangible expression of his concerns in this regard. Moreover, he sometimes was able to accommodate his own ambitions to the religious sensitivities of his subjects. For example, he generally refrained from setting up images—which would be seen as infringements of the Ten Commandments—in locations where they would attract attention. Nevertheless, most Judaean Jews were not as "broad-minded" as their monarch, nor did they regularly join in the praise Herod received when he aided Jewish communities outside Judaea.

During the last ten years of his life, domestic difficulties came to overshadow and almost cancel out all else. Herod had married ten times and produced numerous offspring. As he grew older, several of his sons grew bolder in their efforts to guarantee that they would succeed him. Some of them may even have plotted to hasten the day of their father's death. The most prominent players in this deadly game were Mariamne's sons, Alexander and Aristobulus, and Antipater, the son of Herod's first wife. Mariamne's sons, as the last heirs of the Hasmonaean dynasty, were especially dangerous. They may well have been guilty of treasonous activities against the man who had killed their mother, uncle, grandmother, and great-grandfather. In this case, Augustus was unable to effect a final reconciliation between father and sons. Their execution occurred in 7 or 6 B.C. Herod was almost seventy years old, in very poor health, and in need of an heir.

For most of the period until his death, that heir was Antipater. Unwilling to wait gracefully, he persisted in meddling in his father's plans to arrange the marriages of other offspring. More important, he grew impatient, and that impatience cost him his life and the throne just prior to Herod's own gruesome death in the early spring of 4 B.C. Herod managed to identify three of his sons whom he judged to be worthy of portions of his kingdom. When Augustus, who was a prime financial beneficiary of Herod's will, confirmed these choices, Herod's legacy was, in one sense, complete and secure. In another sense, there is much about Herod's legacy that is puzzling, even troubling.

Summary

It is difficult for contemporary scholars to take the measure of Herod as a man and as a ruler. This difficulty is almost as old as Herod himself. Nearly everything that is known of Herod is contained in the works of the Jewish historian Flavius Josephus, who wrote almost a century after Herod's death. Josephus used both pro- and anti-Herod sources and was not without biases of his own. Moreover, Josephus described Herod's reign in two separate writings, *Peri tou Ioudaikou polemou* (A.D. 75-79; *Jewish War*) and *Ioudaikē archaiologia* (c. A.D. 93; *The Antiquities of the Jews*), and the accounts are often contradictory. The problem described here is not unique to Herod. It recurs, for example, in the study of Alexander the Great, Julius Caesar, and other leaders of antiquity.

In the case of Herod, it does seem possible to affirm certain definite things. His loyalty to Rome and the values it espoused is beyond question. His ability to conceive and carry out large-scale building projects cannot be doubted. His success in organizing his kingdom to produce vast revenues for Rome, himself, and his supporters was an impressive, if not always welcome, accomplishment. All of this was compatible, in Herod's view, with a devotion to the Jewish religion and to the Jewish people. Herod undoubtedly believed that loyal support for Rome was the only hope for Jewish survival. Rebellion could only lead to disaster—a judgment that the Jewish revolts of the following centuries revealed as all too true.

Balanced against Herod's achievements was, first of all, a cruelty so monstrous that it led the author of the Gospel of Matthew to write that Herod had ordered the slaughter of innocent children (see Matthew, chapter 2). Many historians do not believe that such an event ever occurred. Nevertheless, a man who would slaughter close members of his own family was certainly capable of the actions Matthew attributed to him. It was actions of this sort that led Augustus to say, in a play on words in Latin, that he would have preferred to be Herod's pig than his son—or, one might add, his wife, his mother-in-law, or brother-in-law. Even in an admittedly violent age, it must be acknowledged, Herod's cruelty, perhaps the result of some mental disorder, stands out.

Herod's view of Judaism and Jewish survival was not without value. Still, it is hard to see what sort of Judaism Herod actually had in mind. His active support for polytheistic institutions would, it seems likely, have ultimately led to a dilution of Judaism's insistence on monotheism. A Jewish people may then have survived, but without the distinctive features of their ancestral religion.

Sometime in antiquity, the epithet "the Great" was first applied to Herod. Initially, it may have served to designate him as an older son of Antipater or to distinguish him from several other individuals named Herod who followed him. At some point, it came to describe certain elements of his personality and career. In that context, it is appropriate. In an overall evaluation of Herod, however, "great" is not the word most likely to come to mind for most observers of this complex and somehow fascinating man.

Bibliography

Brandon, S. G. F. "Herod the Great: Judaea's Most Able but Most Hated King." *History Today* 12 (1962): 234-242. A brief, accessible account that presents a good overview of Herod's achievements and of the wide variety of judgments to which he has been subjected.

Grant, Michael. *Herod the Great*. London: Weidenfeld and Nicolson, 1971. A straightforward account of the reign of Herod. Grant takes care to place Herod in the larger political and cultural context of first century B.C. Rome. Viewed from this perspective, Herod, while far from a saint, is not quite the total sinner that he is made out to be in many other modern accounts. Beautifully illustrated.

Hoehner, Harold W. *Herod Antipas*. Cambridge: Cambridge University Press, 1972. Originally a doctoral dissertation, this work is a detailed account of the reign of one of Herod's heirs. It is particularly valuable because of its extensive bibliography that fully covers the reign of Herod and his successors.

Josephus, Flavius. *Josephus*. Vol. 2, *The Jewish War*, translated by H. St. James Thackeray, and vols. 7 and 8, *The Jewish Antiquities*, translated by Ralph Marcus. Cambridge, Mass.: Harvard University Press, 1927-1963. As described above, these are the primary ancient sources for the personal and public life of Herod. In this Loeb Classical Library edition, the original Greek text of Josephus is printed along with an authoritative English translation and notes. This is the essential starting point for all research on Herod.

Perowne, Stewart. *The Life and Times of Herod the Great*. London: Hodder and Stoughton, 1956. A balanced and sober account. Well-illustrated. Like Grant, Perowne makes the point that Herod was largely a product of his own time and must, to a degree at least, be judged by the standards of that period. Perowne continued his narrative in a second volume entitled *The Later Herods* (London: Hodder and Stoughton, 1958).

Sandmel, Samuel. *Herod: Profile of a Tyrant*. Philadelphia: J. B. Lippincott Co., 1967. A clear and well-written account of the life and times of Herod. Sandmel attempts to re-create Herod's mental state at key moments, such as when he had Mariamne killed. The author's overall assessment of Herod is succinctly captured in the subtitle of his book.

Zeitlin, Solomon. "Herod: A Malevolent Maniac." *Jewish Quarterly Review* 54 (1963): 1-27. The title of this article leaves no doubt as to the author's overall assessment of Herod. Zeitlin is not concerned here with a retelling of Herod's entire career. Rather, he focuses on key issues such as the reliability of Josephus, details of Mariamne's execution, and Herod's relations with the Hasmonaeans Hyrcanus and Alexandra (Mariamne's mother). Zeitlin provides a fuller account in relevant sections of his *Rise and Fall of the Judaean State: A Political, Social, and Religious History of the Second Commonwealth* (Philadelphia: Jewish Publication Society of America, 1962).

Leonard J. Greenspoon

HERODOTUS

Born: c. 484 B.C.; Halicarnassus, Asia Minor
Died: c. 424 B.C.; probably Thurii, Italy
Area of Achievement: Historiography
Contribution: For having written the first work of history, Herodotus is commonly called "the father of history."

Early Life

Herodotus was born about 484 into a notable family of Halicarnassus, near the modern city of Bodrum, Turkey. He received the education available to well-born Greek men of his day. An intellectual and creative ferment was sweeping the Greek world, and Miletus, a major center of this enlightenment, was only about forty miles from Halicarnassus. Such philosopher-scientists as Anaximander and Thales and the geographer Hecataeus influenced Herodotus. He read Hesiod, Sappho, Sophocles, Aeschylus, and Pindar, and also learned from the Sophists. The writings of Homer, in particular, shaped his worldview. If the intellectual atmosphere of the Greek world encouraged Herodotus to study the affairs of humans, it was probably Homer's masterpiece on the Trojan War that caused Herodotus to recognize that the Persian invasion of Greece, which had occurred when he was a child, was the great drama of his own age.

His early surroundings also educated Herodotus. The rich diversity of cultures in Asia Minor provided the foundation for the remarkable cosmopolitan scope and tone of his writing. Travel further shaped his mind. According to tradition, he went into a brief exile to Samos after taking part in Halicarnassian political upheavals and later left his home city permanently.

His travels took him to Athens, where intellectual and artistic life was flourishing in the age of Pericles. Around 443, Herodotus joined a Greek colony at Thurii, in Italy. From there, he probably continued the travels that provided the foundation for his history. He later said that he had interviewed people from forty Greek states and thirty foreign nations. He visited Egypt, Cyrene in North Africa, Babylon, and areas of the present-day southern Soviet Union. No physical descriptions of Herodotus exist, but his travels in the ancient world testify to his physical vigor and strength and to his insatiable curiosity.

Life's Work

As Homer had preserved the stories of the Trojan War by rendering them into poetry, Herodotus came to realize that during his childhood another historic confrontation had occurred between the East and the West. The Persian War embodied all the drama and tragedy of human life, and its effects reverberated through his lifetime. He captured this human drama in one of the world's first great prose works and pioneered a new form of intellectual endeavor, history.

Herodotus states his intentions in the first sentence of *Historiai Herodotou* (c. 425; *The History*, 1709):

> I, Herodotus of Halicarnassus, am here setting forth my history, that time may not draw the color from what man has brought into being, nor those great and wonderful deeds, manifested by both Greeks and barbarians, fail of their report, and, together with all this, the reason why they fought one another.

He intended to transmit to future generations the record of men and women's deeds in this dramatic era, and in so doing explore the tragedy of human existence. In Herodotus' worldview, people were subject to a cosmic order working by rules that they did not understand, an order in which fate or destiny destroyed those who aspired to excessive achievements. He would show that rationalism, a growing force in his age, could not protect against the contingencies of existence. Nevertheless, though humans could not change the cosmic order, Herodotus could combat the ravages of time by preserving the memory of their deeds. Herodotus was interested in people and in all of their diverse ways of living and acting. He used his history to contrast East and West, detailing the diversity of the peoples of the known world but finding common humanity beneath the differences.

Herodotus wrote a narrative history of his world, from the age of myth to his own time. He did not have available to him the kinds of written records on which modern historians rely, but based his history on oral accounts. He placed most trust in his own experience and others' eyewitness accounts, but used hearsay when he deemed it proper to do so. Regarding the latter, he wrote: "I must tell what is said, but I am not at all bound to believe it, and this comment of mine holds about my whole *History*." He sometimes recorded stories that he found dubious because he realized that just as time changed the fortunes of all people, it changed truth also. At times, he recorded material that seemed significant despite its questionable validity, because its meaning might become clear in the future. He was aware that there was a mythical element in much that people told him, but he realized as well that human myths carry a truth that makes them as important as other interpretations of reality.

Herodotus, the father of history, more than almost any of his offspring, was a master storyteller, able to hold the interest of his audience today as easily as he did thousands of years ago. He begins his story with Croesus, the last king of Lydia, who, after having begun the Asiatic incursion against the Greeks, trapped himself in the web of fate by believing himself the most blessed of humankind. Cyrus conquered Croesus and began constructing the huge and powerful Persian Empire. Through the nine books of *The History*,

Herodotus follows Cyrus, Cambyses, Darius I, and finally Xerxes I, as these Persian rulers extended their power over the known world of Asia and Africa. Eventually, they turned to Europe and the Greeks.

As Herodotus follows Persian expansion, he begins his renowned "digressions" on the Lydians, Egyptians, Assyrians, Scythians, Libyans, Greeks, and others. In these digressions, which make up the bulk of *The History*, he describes the geography and economies of the various lands, the religious practices of the people, the roles of women, and the customs of everyday life. Human creations fascinated him, and he carefully described the pyramids, the walls surrounding Babylon, canal systems, and famous temples.

The so-called digressions are a carefully wrought expression of Herodotus' larger purposes in writing *The History*. A religious man, he wanted to show that all people, Greeks and Asians alike, were living in a cosmos that destroyed the excessive aspirations of even the best and greatest. Herodotus also intended to use the story of the Persian War as a backdrop to his study of the range of possibilities expressed by humans in their social, political, and spiritual lives. He seldom condemned any custom he described, but gloried in the spectacle of life and in human achievements. The digressions, then, are part of his examination of the human condition. He knew that any custom, no matter how strange, had validity and meaning for the people who observed it: "As for the stories told by the Egyptians, let whoever finds them credible use them." The Persian ruler Cambyses revealed his madness, Herodotus believed, when he stabbed the Egyptian sacred bull. If he had not been mad,

> he would never have set about the mockery of what other men hold sacred and customary. For if there were a proposition put before mankind, according to which each should, after examination, choose the best customs in the world, each nation would certainly think its own customs the best. Indeed, it is natural for no one but a madman to make a mockery of such things.

Herodotus adds, "I think Pindar is right when he says, 'Custom is king of all.'"

Whether from the shadows of the pyramids or from the walls of Babylon, Herodotus' gaze always returned to the developing conflict of Greece with the steadily expanding Persian Empire. He gives attention to Darius' first probe into Europe, blocked by the Greeks at the Battle of Marathon in 490. Darius then laid careful plans to conduct a full-scale invasion, but died before he could make another foray into the Greek world. In 480, his successor, Xerxes, invaded with a huge force. The Greeks fought heroically at Thermopylae, and in such battles as Salamis and Plataea, Athens, Sparta, and other Greek city-states defeated the Persians. It is here that Herodotus' history comes to a close.

Most historians believe that *The History* was published in stages between

430 and 424, although a minority of historians believe it contains references to events as late as 421. Most scholars place Herodotus' death at about 424, in Thurii.

Summary

Herodotus has attracted extravagant admiration. He has been commonly called the father of history, and some see him as an equally great geographer, anthropologist, and folklorist. He had his detractors also, one of whom called him "the father of lies." He was too cosmopolitan to fit well with the surge of Greek patriotism of later years; some critics saw him as a detractor of the gods because he spoke so casually of religious practices that differed from the Greeks', but others, in more rational ages, regarded him as too superstitious. As the centuries passed, his admiration for the East and his breadth of sympathy for different cultures placed him out of step with the parochial West.

Herodotus always, however, had his admirers, who usually regarded him as a charming, if credulous, storyteller. His work was first translated into English in 1584, but scholars neglected him until the nineteenth century, when archaeology began to verify much of his account. Even then, his work was seen as a loose collection of moral tales of great men.

His achievement became clearer as twentieth century historians traced the evolution of historical writing and more fully understood the intellectual breakthrough Herodotus had made in separating history from other intellectual endeavors. He established the methods that historians still use: gathering evidence, weighing its credibility, selecting from it, and writing a prose narrative. He assumed a role of neutrality, of objectivity, and, while expressing personal opinions, he never dropped his stance of universal sympathy. He tried to find the rational causes and effects of events; yet he was skeptical enough to understand that rationalism could not explain everything, perhaps not even the most important things, in human life. In recent years, admiration for him has grown as scholars have used literary analysis to show how tightly integrated were the famous Herodotean anecdotes and digressions into his larger purposes. His book is a literary masterpiece and one of the greatest works of history produced in the Western world.

Bibliography

De Selincourt, Aubrey. *The World of Herodotus*. San Francisco: North Point Press, 1982. This work retraces Herodotus' literary journey based on twentieth century knowledge of his world. De Selincourt translated *The History* for the Penguin Classics series.

Evans, J. A. *Herodotus*. Boston: Twayne Publishers, 1982. A recent biography that covers the known facts of Herodotus' life and clearly explains the various scholarly controversies surrounding him.

Flory, Stewart. *The Archaic Smile of Herodotus*. Detroit: Wayne State University Press, 1987. An analysis of literary motifs in *The History*, showing the tightness of its structure and the larger purposes Herodotus had in mind, beyond chronicling the Persian War.

Herodotus. *The History*. Translated by David Grene. Chicago: University of Chicago Press, 1987. This translation by a noted classicist includes a commentary which provides an excellent introduction to Herodotus. Illustrated with helpful maps.

How, Walter W., and Joseph Wells, eds. *A Commentary on Herodotus*. 2 vols. Oxford: Clarendon Press, 1928. This is the standard commentary on Herodotus and provides almost a line-by-line analysis.

Hunter, Virginia. *Past and Process in Herodotus and Thucydides*. Princeton, N.J.: Princeton University Press, 1982. An analysis of the first two historians, finding great similarities in their worldviews.

Myres, John L. *Herodotus: Father of History*. New York: Oxford University Press, 1953. Reprint. Chicago: Henry Regnery Co., 1971. Myres reveals the tight and deliberate construction of *The History*.

William E. Pemberton

HEROPHILUS

Born: c. 335 B.C.; Chalcedon, Bithynia
Died: c. 280 B.C.; probably Alexandria, Egypt
Areas of Achievement: Medicine and physiology
Contribution: The first systematic dissector, and possibly vivisector, of the human body, the Greek physician Herophilus made numerous anatomical discoveries and significantly enriched anatomical nomenclature. His knowledge of human anatomy was superior to that of his precursors, and he laid the foundation for subsequent Western anatomy. Herophilus' analysis of the pulse and his dream theory also exercised a strong influence on medicine and psychology in later centuries.

Early Life

The sparse ancient evidence suggests that Herophilus left his native city of Chalcedon for an apprenticeship with the distinguished physician Praxagoras of Cos before settling in the recently founded North African city of Alexandria. An Athenian sojourn is implied by the report of Hyginus, a second century Roman mythographer, that a young Athenian woman, in guileful reaction against the exclusion of women from the medical profession, disguised herself as a man and completed an apprenticeship with Herophilus. As a consequence of her popularity with female patients, who alone knew that she was a woman, Herophilus' pupil was brought before an Athenian jury on charges of seducing and corrupting her women patients. In court she raised her tunic and revealed her gender. After she received assertive support from women, Hyginus relates, "the Athenians amended the law so that free-born women could learn the art of medicine." No independent evidence corroborates Hyginus' account—which formally belongs to the genre of invention fables—but it is worth noting that Herophilus' contributions to gynecology and obstetrics are richly attested.

Life's Work

The first scientist to violate the entrenched Greek taboo against cutting open a human corpse, Herophilus made spectacular discoveries in human anatomy. From classical antiquity until the early Renaissance, anatomical accounts were mainly based on comparative anatomy—Aristotle and Galen, in particular, dissected numerous animals—and on chance observations of the wounded or injured. While Herophilus continued this practice of dissecting animals, he and his contemporary Erasistratus apparently were the only pre-Renaissance scientists to perform systematic dissections on humans. Furthermore, if the controversial but unequivocal evidence of several later authors is trustworthy, Herophilus also performed vivisectory experiments on convicted criminals. Herophilus was able to break the spell of the taboo because of an exceptional constellation of circumstances in Alexandria. The combination of ambitious, autocratic patrons of science (the Ptolemies), bold scientists such as Euclid and Archimedes, a new city on foreign soil in which traditional Greek values initially were not accepted as intrinsically superior, and a cosmopolitan intelligentsia committed to literary, technological, and scientific frontiersmanship made it possible for Herophilus to overcome tenacious inhibitions against opening the human body. The native Egyptian practice of mummification, sanctioned by centuries of stable religious belief, might have been invoked as a precedent, although embalming was in fact very different from scientific dissection. The Egyptian embalmers, for example, scraped and drained the brain piecemeal through the nostrils of the corpse, mangling it beyond anatomic recognition, whereas Herophilus dissected the brain meticulously enough to distinguish some of its ventricles and to identify several of its smaller parts with unprecedented accuracy.

One of Herophilus' more noteworthy discoveries was the nerves. He distinguished between sensory and "voluntary" (motor) nerves, described the paths of at least seven pairs of cranial nerves, and recognized unique features of the optic nerve. He also was the first to observe and name the calamus scriptorius, a cavity in the floor of the fourth cerebral ventricle. His careful dissection of the eye yielded the discovery not only of the optic nerve but also of several coats of the eye (probably the sclera, cornea, iris, retina, and chorioid coat), an achievement all the more remarkable in the absence of the microscope.

Like his other works, Herophilus' main anatomical work, *Anatomika* (*On Anatomy*), survives only in fragments and secondhand reports. From its second book, ancient sources have preserved the first classic description of the human liver: The shape, size, position, and texture of the liver as well as its connections with other parts are described with admirable accuracy. The pancreas and small intestine, or duodenum (a Latin version of the name Herophilus first gave it), are among the other parts in the abdominal cavity which he explored. The third book of *On Anatomy* appears to have been devoted to the reproductive organs. In the male, Herophilus distinguished between various parts of the spermatic duct system, meticulously identifying anatomical features previously unknown. As for the female, Herophilus seems to have abandoned the traditional theory of a bicameral human uterus, and, using the male analogy, to have discovered the ovaries (which he calls female twins or testicles), the Fallopian tubes (although he did not determine their true course and function), and several other features of female reproductive anatomy. In the fourth book, Herophilus dealt with the anatomy of the blood vessels. Accepting Praxagoras' distinction between veins and arteries, he provided further anatomical precision and offered some basic observations on the heart valves, the chambers of the heart, and a variety of vessels and vascular structures. The torcular Herophili, a confluence of several great venous cavities or sinuses in the skull, was first identified by Herophilus and still bears his name.

In his physiopathology, Herophilus appears to have accepted the traditional theory of a balance or imbalance between humors (or moistures) in the body as the cause of health and disease, respectively, but he insisted that all causal explanation is provisional or hypothetical. One must start from appearances, or observation, he said, and then proceed on a hypothetical basis to what is not visible, including cause. The command center of the body is located in the fourth cerebral ventricle or in the cerebellum (which is indeed the center responsible for muscular coordination and maintenance of the equilibrium of the body). From the brain and spinal marrow, nerves—sensory and motor—proceed like offshoots. Neural transmission, at least in the case of the optic nerves, apparently takes place through pneuma, a warm, moist, airlike substance flowing through the nerves and ultimately derived from external air by respiration.

Among the involuntary motions in the human body (that is, ones for which the motor nerves are not responsible), Herophilus gave novel, detailed accounts of two: respiration, which he attributed to a natural tendency of the lungs to dilate and contract through a four-part cycle, and the pulse, which he attributed to a faculty that flows to the arteries from the heart through the arterial coats, causing the arteries to dilate and contract. His treatise *Peri sphygmōn* (*On Pulses*) is the first work devoted to the subject, and it became the foundation of all ancient and of much subsequent pulse lore.

Central to Herophilus' vascular physiology is the theory that the arteries transport a mixture of blood and pneuma (similar to the modern view that the arteries carry blood and oxygen), whereas the veins contain only blood. Here he parted ways with his teacher Praxagoras and his contemporary Erasistratus, both of whom believed the arteries contain only pneuma. The arteries, Herophilus believed, pulsate in such intricate, differentiated patterns that the pulse is a major diagnostic tool. Deploying sustained analogies between musical-metrical theory and pulse rhythm, Herophilus described nature's music in the arteries as successively assuming pyrrhic, trochaic, spondaic, and iambic rhythmic relations between diastole and systole as one passes through four stages of life—from infancy (pyrrhic) through childhood and adulthood to old age (iambic). Deviations from these rhythms indicate disorders.

Herophilus had such faith in the diagnostic value of the pulse that he constructed a portable water clock, or clepsydra, to measure the frequency (rate?) of his patients' pulses. The device could be calibrated to fit the age of each patient. One example of its clinical application suggests that it also functioned as a protothermometer: "By as much as the movements of the pulse exceeded the number that is natural for filling up the clepsydra, by that much Herophilus declared the pulse too frequent, i.e., that the patient had either more or less of a fever" (quoted from the second century Marcellinus). Herophilus' pulse theory represents an unusual attempt within ancient medicine to introduce measurement and quantification into nonpharmacological contexts. Besides rhythm and frequency, he used size, strength, and perhaps speed and volume to distinguish one pulse from another.

Reproductive physiology and pathology represent other strengths of Herophilus. He accepted, in general, Aristotle's view that male seed is formed from the blood and, according to Saint Augustine's acquaintance Vindician, Herophilus characteristically tried to defend it by arguments based on dissection. He wrote the first known treatise devoted only to obstetrics, *Maiōtikon* (*Midwifery*; also known as *On Delivery*), in which he tried to demystify the uterus, arguing that it is constituted of the same material elements as the rest of the body and is regulated by the same faculties. There is no disease peculiar to women, he asserts, though he concedes that certain "affections" are experienced only by women: menstruation, conception, parturition, and lactation. The causes of difficult childbirth, embryological questions (such as, is the fetus a living being, since it possesses involuntary but not voluntary motions?), and the normal duration of pregnancy are among the other subjects apparently explored by Herophilus. The church father Tertullian implied that the Alexandrian performed abortions and charged him with having possessed an instrument known as a "fetus-slayer" (*embryo-sphaktes*).

In his treatise *Pros tas koinas doxas* (*Against Common Opinions*), Herophilus also dealt with gynecological and obstetrical issues, attacking the common opinion that menstruation is good for every woman's health and for childbearing, and, characteristically, adopting a more discriminating view: Menstruation is helpful to some women, harmful to others, depending on individual circumstances. For all of his emphasis on the hypothetical nature of causal explanations, Herophilus tried to determine the causes of many individual disorders, including fevers, heart diseases, and pneumonia. He also described the symptoms of several physical and mental disorders and developed a semiotic system known as a "triple-timed inference from signs," which used a combination of the patients' past signs or symptoms, the present signs, and the "future signs" (inferences from what has happened to other similarly afflicted patients) for diagnostic, prognostic, and therapeutic purposes.

In *Die Traumdeutung* (1900; *The Interpretation of Dreams*, 1915), Sigmund Freud recognized Herophilus' importance in another area: dream theory. Dreams, Herophilus believed, belong to one of three classes by origin: "godsent" dreams occur inevitably or by necessity; "natural" dreams arise when the soul forms for itself an image of what is to its advantage; and "compound" or "mixed" dreams arise when one sees what one desires. Freud acknowledged Herophilus' emphasis on the fulfillment of sexual and other wishes in dreams as an important anticipation of his own theory. With modifications, Herophilus' tripartite classification of dreams reappears in several pagan and Christian authors, thus representing another influential part of his legacy.

Summary

The frequent modern lag between scientific discovery and clinical application, between theory and therapy, also characterized Herophilus' work. Despite his brilliant discoveries in anatomy and physiology, he was a traditionalist in practice. In his works *Diaitētikon* (*Regimen*) and *Therapeutika* (*Therapeutics*), Herophilus prescribed a preventive regimen, bloodletting, various simple and compound drugs (with at least some innovative ingredients), and a limited amount of surgical intervention (with a felicitous emphasis on checking hemorrhages). He perhaps also prompted the influential Alexandrian tradition of exegesis of Hippocratic texts, to which several of Herophilus' adherents made major contributions by taking a keen, critical interest in Hippocratic works. One of Herophilus' pupils, Philinus of Cos, broke with him and became a leader of the powerful Empiricist school of medicine, but many others continued proclaiming themselves his followers. As the old taboos against human dissection reasserted themselves after Herophilus' death, the Herophileans abandoned this central part of the founder's legacy. Yet the rich history of his school, both in Alexandria and in Laodicea-on-Lycus (Turkey), can be traced for at least three centuries after Herophilus' death. Through Galen's detailed acclaim of Herophilus' dissections and of his pulse theory, the Alexandrian's fame survived the polemics of those Christians and pagans who believed that what had been concealed by God or Nature should not be revealed by humans.

Bibliography

Fraser, P. M. *Ptolemaic Alexandria*. 3 vols. Oxford: Clarendon Press, 1972. An excellent comprehensive treatment of Alexandria at the time of Herophilus. Chapter 7 offers a good introduction to Herophilus and other Alexandrian physicians.

Lloyd, G. E. R. *Greek Science After Aristotle*. London: Chatto and Windus, 1973. Chapter 6 offers a very useful general introduction to Hellenistic biology and medicine, with a valuable assessment of Herophilus' place in the history of science.

____________. *Science, Folklore, and Ideology*. Cambridge: Cambridge University Press, 1983. Excellent observations throughout, especially on Herophilus' contributions to reproductive theory and the standardization of anatomical terminology.

Longrigg, James. "Superlative Achievement and Comparative Neglect: Alexandrian Medical Science and Modern Historical Research." *History of Science* 19 (1981): 155-200. A solid overview of the scientific views of Herophilus and Erasistratus by a classicist and historian of medicine.

Potter, Paul. "Herophilus of Chalcedon: An Assessment of His Place in the History of Anatomy." *Bulletin of the History of Medicine* 50 (1976): 45-60. A physician and historian of medicine subjects Herophilus' anatomical descriptions to thoughtful, informed scrutiny.

Solmsen, Friedrich. "Greek Philosophy and the Discovery of the Nerves." *Museum Helveticum* 18 (1961): 150-197. A pioneering, now classic, analysis of Herophilus' and Erasistratus' contributions to the discovery of the nerves.

von Staden, Heinrich. "Hairesis and Heresy." In *Jewish and Christian Self-Definition*. Vol. 3, *Self-Definition in the Graeco-Roman World*, edited by Ben F. Meyer and E. P. Sanders. Philadelphia: Fortress Press, 1983. This analysis of group self-definitions includes detailed observations on the dynamic, changing character of Herophilus' school after his death.

____________. *Herophilus: The Art of Medicine in Early Alexandria*. Cambridge: Cambridge University Press, 1988. The first comprehensive collection, translation, and evaluation of the ancient evidence concerning Herophilus. Part 1 includes extensive essays on his anatomy, physiopathology, therapeutics, and theory of method; part 2 traces his followers from 250 B.C. to A.D. 50.

Heinrich von Staden